Pharmakon

Pharmakon

Plato, Drug Culture, and Identity in Ancient Athens

Michael A. Rinella

LEXINGTON BOOKS
A division of
ROWMAN & LITTLEFIELD PUBLISHERS, INC.
Lanham • Boulder • New York • Toronto • Plymouth, UK

Published by Lexington Books
A wholly owned subsidary of The Rowman & Littlefield Publishing Group, Inc.
4501 Forbes Boulevard, Suite 200, Lanham, Maryland 20706
http://www.lexingtonbooks.com

Estover Road, Plymouth PL6 7PY, United Kingdom

British Library Cataloguing in Publication Information Available

The hardback edition of this book was previously catalogued by the Library of Congress
as follows:

Library of Congress Cataloging-in-Publication Data

Rinella, Michael A. (Michael Anthony)
  Pharmakon : Plato, drug culture, and identity in ancient Athens / Michael A.
Rinella.
     p. cm.
  Includes bibliographical references and index.
  1. Plato. 2. Drug abuse—Greece. 3. Plato. Symposium. 4. Greece—
Civilization—To 146 B.C. I. Title.

B395.R56 2010
184--dc22   2010006940

ISBN: 978-0-7391-4686-6 (cloth : alk. paper)
ISBN: 978-0-7391-4687-3 (pbk. : alk. paper)

☉™ The paper used in this publication meets the minimum requirements of American
National Standard for Information Sciences—Permanence of Paper for Printed Library
Materials, ANSI/NISO Z39.48-1992.

Printed in the United States of America

To my mother and father, for always believing in me.

Contents

Acknowledgements

I would like to thank Anthony Preus for his extensive comments on the original draft of the manuscript. His careful reading, both stimulating and challenging, has improved almost every page. I would like to also express my gratitude to my editor Jana Wilson at Lexington Books and for the comments of manuscript reviewer Carl A. P. Ruck. Finally, my thanks go to Sarah "Skye" Miles at Columbia College, South Carolina for proofreading the final indices.

Early versions of sections of the following chapters have been previously published. Chapter 6: "Supplementing the Ecstatic: Plato, the Eleusinian Mysteries, and the *Phaedrus*," *Polis—The Journal of the Society of Greek Political Thought* 17, nos. 1 & 2 (2000): 61–78. Chapter 10: "Revisiting the Pharmacy: Plato, Derrida, and the Morality of Political Deceit," *Polis—The Journal of the Society of Greek Political Thought* 24, no. 1 (2007): 134–53. In addition I would like to thank the members of the panel "Intoxication, Moderation and Envy in Plato's Dialogues" at the 2009 meeting of the Midwest Political Science Association for their comments on a version of chapter 3 titled "Plato's Reformulation of the *Symposion*."

Introduction

The *Pharmakon*, Ecstasy, and Identity

In an interview shortly before his death in 1984 the French philosopher Michel Foucault described the possibility of creating, in contrast to the history of *ideas* that has preoccupied much of Western philosophy, a history of *thought* based on the study of "what one could call the element of problems, or more exactly, problemizations."[1] At the center of such a history would be an investigation of how certain human behaviors became the subject of a sustained critical reflection, a *general form* of problemization to which diverse solutions were then proposed. Over time a *domain of action* previously accepted as given evolved into something deemed worthy of sustained critical commentary, often in association with particular social, economic, or political processes. A history of thought would not only try to see how these *diverse solutions* to a problem were constructed, but also to "see how these different solutions result from a specific form of problemization."[2] Over time new solutions might be formulated, arising from difficulties contemporary to their time and place, "modifying only several of the postulates or principles on which one bases the response that one gives" but *not* the general form of problemization itself.[3]

The Use of Pleasure, the second volume of Foucault's history of sexuality, mentions in passing that the connections between ancient Greek sexual ethics and what he calls *alimentary ethics*—the use of food and intoxicants like wine—only gradually became disengaged or uncoupled, believing it would be interesting to trace "the evolution of their respective importance" and the "gradual differentiation of their specific structure."[4] This work will trace the history of thought with regard to what may be considered *drug ethics* more generally and *the ethics of drug intoxication* in particular, with a focus on ancient Greece (ca. 750–146 BCE), particularly the Classical Period (ca. 500 to 336 BCE) and especially the dialogues of the Athenian philosopher Plato (427–347 BCE). Plato merits this level of attention due to both the "extraordinary modernity of some of [his] thought"[5] as well as the enormous impact of his writing on much of the subsequent history of Western thought, an influence that extends to include how the "drug problem" has been viewed and the solutions that have at various times been proposed to solve difficulties seen as arising from that problem.[6]

Plato, Foucault believed, was among those in ancient Greece who occasionally saw the victory of self-control over pleasure as "characterized by the complete extirpation or expulsion of desire. But much more often, it was identified by the setting up of a solid and stable rule of the self over the self: the intensity of the desires did not disappear, but the moderate subject controlled it" in an act of self-domination.[7] Foucault did not deny that "a complex ethical discourse surrounded all [the] appetites."[8] At the same time he excuses himself from examining these alimentary ethics because he believed that "in the reflection of the Greeks of the Classical Period, it does seem that the moral problemization of food, drink, and sexual activity were carried out in the same manner."[9] And it is true: Plato's proposed solutions to deal with the problem of *aphrodisia*, the sexual pleasures, have similarities and parallels with his attitudes toward the problems of food (*edodai*) and drink (*potoi*, including drinks that bring the pleasures of *methe*, intoxication). All three "brought forces into play that were natural, but that always tended to be excessive; and they all raised the same question: how could one, how must one 'make use' (*chresthai*) of this dynamics of pleasures, desires, and acts? A question of right use."[10]

The question would seem to be begged: what forces, excessive how? I would agree with philosopher Martha Nussbaum when she writes that Foucault's "assimilation of sex to eating and drinking can mislead us," but for very different reasons. Nussbaum accepts without question Foucault's preoccupation with the *aphrodisia*, writing that "the ethical questions" posed by sex, because they "involve not only one's own self-mastery, but the well-being, happiness, and ethical goodness of another," are "far more complicated than the ethical questions posed by food and drink," her reason being "the glutton does no harm to food, nor the drunkard to wine."[11] However true that may be, the question begged remains begged. The issue, as I shall argue, is not just ethical but also deeply psychological. The three appetites are not Plato's real concern *per se.* They are not the cause and as such the *source* of the difficulty in need of being moderated. There is a common quality behind or beneath each of them, an indication of which lurks within Foucault's regular use of terms describing the psychology of these desires and their pleasures as *strong, imperative, violent* and *intense*. The concern with controlling appetites such as lust, gluttony, and intoxication that appears in ancient thought in general and the Platonic dialogues in particular are indications of a growing difficulty with *something else*. The continuing preoccupation with ancient sexuality at the expense of the alimentary appetites leads, I believe, to an obscuration of the general form of problemization that was occurring in ancient Greece. Sexuality and *aphrodisia* were but one locus of a number of suspect behaviors that a growing set of solutions was being proposed to deal with. That something else may be identified as psychological states of ecstasy, and their threat to identity.

The Problem of Ecstasy

Ecstasy may be thought of as a softening, diminishment, blurring or loss of the psychological boundaries or barriers that in a "normal" context define, sustain and preserve a singular, self-contained subjective identity. In this sense ecstasy may be said to involve an alteration of human cognitive capacity, the act or process of knowing, including both awareness and judgment.[12] As a form of human experience the ecstatic is commonly described as being intensely pleasurable, but it is more than simply a type of pleasure. Ecstasy can be, alternately or simultaneously, a sense of wonder, sublimity, terror, hilarity, uncanniness and still other conditionalities. Part of its essence is precisely this nondefinability along any seemingly consistent set of descriptive parameters.

Although often misunderstood or misrepresented in contemporary discourse as a relinquishing of *all* reasoning capacity, ecstasy is not, in the strictest sense, reducible to such a loss. It is rather a temporary reduction, of variable intensity and duration, of the reasoning mind's ability to patrol and defend the borders of identity from intrusions of otherness. Ecstasy "sensitizes us to the contingency of identity and the in-dependence of the Other. It is a recognition that one's state, however personal or collective, is never an authentic or stable condition but a product of strange, contradictory and ever-changing forces. From this perspective, *ekstasis* liquidates the 'positivist' boundaries of meaning, brings forth 'the experience of an extra dimension, an expansion of the human condition' that entices the *logos* of the Other."[13]

Intoxication is one manifestation of ecstasy and is the primary focus of this book.[14] There are of course a myriad of other forms ecstasy may take, many of which have been viewed as being in some way suspect and a difficulty to be grappled with at one time or another, including ancient Greece, such as the frenzy inspired by particular forms of dance, many forms of music, the rapture of the lover for the beloved, the enthusiasm of a crowd "carried away" by a speaker's rhetoric, and so on.[15] Contrary to Karl Popper's claim in *The Open Society and its Enemies* that Plato represents a deep-seated longing to arrest or even reverse what Popper calls "the breakdown of Greek tribalism," something he equates with a kind of collective group identity that fails to distinguish individual from individual, or individual from nature, this work shall argue that Plato's dialogues in fact root out and cast the cold water of rational reflection on all claims of knowledge based on forms of psychological ecstasy.[16] Popper misunderstands Plato, conflating the Platonic yearning for amiable *homonoia* in the politics of the *polis* with a proto-totalitarian anti-rational retreat or return to forms of tribal ecstasy. Quite the contrary: the valuation of identitarian thinking in Plato's idealistic philosophy is virtually if not entirely absolute.

Methodology

Foucault's excavation of ancient Greek sexual ethics in *The Use of Pleasure* consists of a sophisticated yet relatively straightforward analysis of a number of prescriptive documents, most of them philosophical and medical. Very little effort is made on his part to engage the secondary literature written by specialists in Hellenistic and Roman philosophy and medicine or, more importantly, situate those texts in any sort of unfolding historical context.[17] And certainly that lack of context has come under fire, for example in classicist James Davidson's *Courtesans and Fishcakes*.[18] In fairness to Foucault this was never his intention. He "does not intend to work as an historian. He produces genealogy: 'Genealogy means that I begin my analysis from a question posed in the present.'"[19] Moving "back and forth between original texts and general reading principles," Foucault draws out "transversal sections" in Hellenistic and Roman philosophy, fashioning an "ethical reading in terms of practices of the self."[20]

While I see myself as on a certain level engaging in a similar "ethical reading" I have also endeavored to develop, in the manner of historian G. E. R. Lloyd in his many examinations of ancient science and medicine, what I call the *dense background* behind Greek social institutions where alcohol and drug use took place, such as the *symposion*. Lloyd has argued, and I agree, that while students of ancient Greece cannot be ethnographers in the strict sense, since the society in question no longer exists, this should not serve as an excuse from "emulating, as far as our materials permit, the kind of dense . . . account that considers the data concerning a belief system against the whole background of the geographical, economic, technological, social and political situation of the society under investigation."[21] A similar approach, applied to ancient Greek magic, is utilized by classicist Matthew W. Dickie. Ancient Greece must be understood in its own terms; "by paying careful attention" we can "recreate" some of that world as it understood itself and while we cannot completely free ourselves from our own cultural presuppositions that does not mean the effort "is by definition impossible," only that "it is a difficult enterprise."[22]

I am similarly indebted to the work of Patrick E. McGovern whose pioneering research in the field of molecular archaeology has helped to revolutionize our understanding of ancient oenology. Until recently just about anyone in the humanities, such as classicist Carl A. P. Ruck, or in the social sciences, such as a political scientist like myself, bold enough to argue that ancient wine included many drugs, and not simply alcohol, was met with a sort of indifferent hostility, and that was from the few within our disciplines who even took the time to notice.[23] Since the early 1980s our ability to detect ancient organic compounds such as lipids, resins, dyes, perfume ingredients, and drugs has advanced at an ever accelerating rate thanks to a host of new, highly sensitive, analytic tools.[24] McGovern's work is not "merely" innovative archaeology however and traverses the physical sciences, archaeology and the humanities. As he notes, whole new chapters are being opened "in human and environmental history, including ethnicity and genetic development, diet, disease, cuisine, and materials process-ing."[25] And, it goes without saying, pharmacology. A complete account of the practices of ancient peoples, including the ancient Greeks, incorporates but *no longer solely relies upon* the "complicated skein" of mythology and other "liter-ary evidence."[26] To arrive at "the kernel of historical reality" requires a heuristic "delving into the available archeological resources" as well as "linguistic, bo-tanical, and other scientific data."[27]

The Use of Pleasure fails to recognize ecstasy as the general form of prob-lemization in ancient thought because, I would argue, in the case of ancient Greece Foucault does not generate any sustained discussion of the social, eco-nomic or political processes he believed accompanied the initial problemization of a domain of behavior. Yet he was certainly capable of generating this sort of discussion as he did with great rhetorical effect in, for example, his discussion of the birth of modern penology in *Discipline and Punish*. In this earlier work Fou-cault argued that delinquency, i.e. controlled illegality, was "an agent for the illegality of dominant groups," representing a "diversion of illegality for the illicit circuits of profit and power of the dominant class." This delinquent milieu existed "in complicity with a self-interested Puritanism" and included, in addi-tion to prostitution, "arms trafficking, the illegal sale of alcohol in prohibition countries, [and] more recently drug trafficking."[28]

Nor was Foucault uninterested in the subject of drug intoxication. As early as 1967 he defended the use of drugs "as a means of entering into 'a state of "nonreason"' in which the experience of madness is outside the distinction be-tween the normal and the pathological."[29] In interviews given during the 1970s and early 1980s he was frequently critical of that era's crusade against recrea-tional drugs. For example in 1971, in the French magazine *Actuel*, Foucault is quoted as saying: "the campaign against drugs is a pretext for the reinforcement of social repression; not only through police raids, but also through the indirect exaltation of the normal, rational, conscientious, and well-adjusted individual."[30] And by 1982 he was even raising the possibility of writing "a study of the cul-ture of drugs or drugs as culture in the West from the beginning of the nine-teenth century. No doubt it started much earlier, but it would come up to the present, it's so closely tied to the artistic life in the West."[31] Of course Nietzsche had raised virtually the same possibility exactly a century earlier in section 86 of *The Gay Science*: "Who will ever relate the whole history of narcotica? . . . It is almost the history of 'culture,' our so-called higher culture."[32]

Clearly, then, the subject of drugs was of great interest to Foucault. "The figure of the addict walks silently through the corridors of his hospitals, asy-lums, and prisons. Drugs are implicit in all of his works, bound up with his stud-ies of medicine, psychiatry, and the penal code, his studies of the shifting defini-tions and treatments of sickness, insanity, and crime. And if all his stories deal with the uses and deployments of the body, drugs are the point at which they all converge."[33] If not for his premature death I suspect that had he pursued the sub-ject of drugs and Western culture Foucault would have taken an approach simi-lar to the one I employ here, beginning not with the nineteenth century but much earlier, with the Greeks, for the "exaltation" he wrote of did not spring autochthonously from, to give just one example, the literature of the mental hygiene movement that contributed to the theory of addiction that underlies so much of today's disease model of recreational drug use.[34] The process as I shall argue is already underway even as myth gives way to enlightenment, in the temptations of Odysseus in the *Odyssey*, and rapidly accelerates in the philosophy of Plato, which means the exaltation of the normal, rational, conscientious, and well-adjusted individual is almost as old as Western civilization itself.[35]

My discussion of the problem of ecstasy, the difficulties with intoxication, and the solutions proposed in the ancient Greek context does not proceed in a neat, step-by-step progression. The complexity and density of the issues being explored, and the nature of the source materials themselves, does not permit a single, sufficient presentation. The mosaic of everyday life, the overwhelming "medley of sights, smells and noises that would have assailed us, had we walked through the *agora*" has only made its way to us in a skewed and sanitized form; only "stray scraps of information" occasionally "betray something of the reality."[36] Genealogy, as Foucault noted, "operates on a field of tangled and confused parchments, on documents that have been scratched over and recopied many times."[37] The source materials for this work, coming from ancient documents as diverse as literature, philosophy, medicine, botany, pharmacology, religion, magic and law, certainly fit this description. A topic or topics in a chapter may appear to be discussed to the point of exhaustion, only to reappear in additional chapters where, usually in a different context, further dimensions are investigated. In this sense my approach bears some similarity to that of political theorist William E. Connolly in *The Augustinian Imperative*.[38]

An important assumption of this work is that Plato's dialogues have more than a mere historical significance. On the one hand the thoughts that the dialogues express and the difficulties they address are heavily bound up in the time and circumstances Plato lived and wrote in, and need to be examined as such. The internecine struggles between pro-democratic and anti-democratic segments of the Athenian aristocracy in the late fifth and early fourth centuries, for example, form the foundation of many of Plato's observations including—even especially—his views on intoxication. At the same time two things would seem equally apparent. First, Plato also addresses himself to posterity, to an audience that will come to his words *after* he has passed from the scene and is no longer able to defend and elaborate upon them himself. He harbors the hope, for example in the *Republic* (499c–d), that if his thoughts are too untimely, later generations in a time and place "far outside" his "range of vision" will see their wisdom and adopt them. Second, we cannot ignore the possible existence of larger cultural developments that each Platonic text may have partially contributed to, whatever else *he* may have intended.

One such development, I argue, involved (a) the difficulties revolving around the subject of intoxication, especially as they were related to, or were rooted in, (b) the broader problemization of loss of identity due to psychological states of ecstasy. To speak of intoxication in ancient Greece we must, naturally and of necessity, examine the word for drug, *pharmakon* (plural *pharmaka*). This word is commonly translated as "remedy" or "poison" but was in fact a signifier for many other things that do not easily fit that binary, and that invoke in one way or another the perception-altering powers of *intoxication*, such as "perfume," "pigment," "magical charm, philter, or talisman," and "recreational drug." While previous articles and books have discussed the place of the word *pharmakon* in one or two Platonic dialogues, or one or two meanings of the word, few if any have discussed the importance of the term in all its multifaceted meanings within the full Platonic corpus. Just as importantly few if any works have situated Plato's deployment of this term in the rich detail of the ancient Greek historical context, where doctors, midwives, magicians, painters, rhetoricians and still others all laid claim to their powers being derived from, connected with, or likened to a *pharmakon*.

The sources that have survived make it difficult to easily capture the many occupations that, as part of the goods and services they had to offer in ancient Greece, would have utilized some form of *pharmakon*, even in Classical Athens. Quite simply, there are "large areas of human existence" that these documents "ignore or that were in some sense invisible to them."[39] Plato clearly is an example of this tendency. He does not appear entirely unaware of either (a) or (b) but at the same time their presence in his dialogues continually advances and retreats, at one moment occupying center stage and speaking directly to the reader, at another standing off to one side, visible yet mute, at still another quietly skulking deep in the recesses of the background scenery, invisible until that scenery is peeled back and their presence revealed. Their importance continually oscillates, not only between different dialogues but frequently within a single dialogue and even within a single passage. While more direct than either mythopoetic thought or the contemplation of most of his contemporaries, Plato's cognizance of these issues is still only partial. The ambiguities present in the ancient Greek, in the meaning of *pharmakon* most of all, possess a *limited* autonomy, manipulating Plato even as he is manipulating those ambiguities for his own purposes. Thus while I believe recovering historical context and authorial intention is important, it is all the same insufficient because we can at the same time—thanks to the methods used in this work—identify the supra-intentional thematic developments of a partially autonomous text.

Part One

How did the ancient world view drug and alcohol intoxication? Was intoxicated behavior truly a *problem*? How so? To whom? Why? The entire matter is without doubt multisided, multilayered, and complicated. We are, first of all, constrained by the surviving documentary record, which is almost entirely limited to the viewpoint of men whose class status provided them with sufficient leisure to record their thoughts in writing. The perspectives of women and non-leisured classes we are almost always left to infer using other sources and methods. I also do not claim to be providing an exhaustive answer to any of these questions. I merely hope to (a) establish the outlines of the *ordinary* perspective on each of these questions, (b) demonstrate the *extraordinary* response to that perspective in the thought of Plato and a few of his contemporaries and (c) reveal to what extent they felt *politics* ought (or ought not) to be concerned with the matter of intoxication, and, if it should be concerned, *how* politics ought to respond.

In chapter 1 I begin by briefly exploring the technology of wine making in the ancient world, starting with the known origins of wine and continuing up to wine production as it existed in the Classical Period of Greece. I then examine the pharmacology of that wine. Ancient wines, I shall demonstrate, were infused with a wide variety of alcohol-soluble substances, many of which had their own intoxicating effects. The ancient Greek practice of diluting wine with water, as for example within the ancient *symposion*, on many occasions may have had less to do with moderation on the part of ancient drinkers and more to do with the dangers posed by drinking beverages so potent that consumption of even small quantities in an unmixed state could lead to dire health consequences, including permanent brain damage and even death. Even in the question of drinking wine the analyst quickly finds himself or herself immersed in questions of a wide variety of *drugs*, their uses, their effects on the body, and ancient difficulties with them.

For the remainder of the first chapter I discuss the ethics of wine intoxication in the specific context of the *symposion* of the Greek city-states, primarily Athens. The decision to pursue this line of argument was necessitated in part by the sources that have managed to survive on the one hand, and on the other because it is the drinking ethics of the *symposion* that Plato addresses most directly, and in the most detail. Understanding the Greek drinking *symposion* is crucial to understanding Plato, yet the subject rarely received the treatment it deserved until the 1970s, beginning with the writings of L. E. Rossi, Massimo Vetta, and Enzio Pellizer, and then the works of, for example, Francios Lissarrague and Oswyn Murray. In contrast to this work, these authors for the most part treat Plato as one ancient source among many permitting us to fashion as detailed a reconstruction of the *symposion* as a social institution as the gulf of time can permit. What they largely do not consider is how intoxication within the *symposion* may have been intertwined with such matters as Plato's depiction of Socrates, his defense of the philosophic life, his program for reforming moral education, and his vision of the ideal *polis*.

In chapter 2 I begin by examining what may be called the ordinary ethics of intoxication in ancient Greece, especially that of the *symposion*. One reason I do so is to demonstrate what many writers seem to suspect, or tend to assert without further explanation: the "literary" versions of symposia given to us by Plato and Xenophon may not be wholly representative of what occurred in a typical fifth- or fourth-century aristocratic *symposion*. The *symposion* was a private setting that aspired to a nominally regulated intoxication and a group exploration of ecstasy, but on many occasions this merely ethical superstructure collapsed, the celebrants spilling out and confronting the larger community in what was known as the *komos*, a public procession of wildly drunken aristocratic revelers who flouted their contempt for prevailing norms, insulting and frequently assaulting those of lesser social standing. The intoxicated *komos* was a primary source of the crime known as *hubris*, behavior that was believed to lead to animosity and conflict between social classes, i.e. *stasis*.

In chapter 3 I examine the institution of the *symposion* as it appears in a number of Plato's dialogues. When read carefully, I argue, the portrait of sympotic practice is, virtually without exception, thoroughly dismissive and negative. I then proceed to a detailed juxtaposition of the character of Socrates with a number of other characters in the Platonic dialogue named the *Symposium*, where I believe Plato utilized the figure of Socrates as an idealized model of what sympotic behavior ought to look like. After examining the *Symposium* I turn to Plato's final dialogue, the *Laws*, frequently regarded as a last-minute reversal of his views on the institution of the *symposion* and the value of wine drinking, a concession to the needs and frailty of human beings and the limitations of reason as a basis of knowledge. Looking at the first and second books of the dialogue closely, and in the context of the preceding discussions, I conclude that in the *Laws* Plato seals off the experience of intoxication as emphatically as ever, and as far as the ancient Greek context would allow.

Part Two

In the *Birth of Tragedy* Nietzsche repeatedly emphasizes that the ecstatic is in essence a *natural* psychological state. It is "an overwhelming sense of unity that goes back to the very heart of nature" (section 7). This natural state was "unaffected by knowledge," entirely pre-cognitive, more authentic, and more truthful than the mendacious "lie of culture masquerading as the sole reality" (section 8) and when the "rigid law of individuation," with its demands for self-knowledge and moderation, imposed itself upon "the true magic of nature itself," the product was "a monstrous crime against nature" (section 9).[40] Ancient morality, I shall argue, viewed states of ecstasy, on the whole, as an essential and natural human condition. In other words, for most ancient Greeks ecstasy was no problem.

Plato in contrast regarded most of these same experiences as forming the core of what he termed the unnecessary pleasures, and any desire for said pleasures must be removed from a political regime in the name of preempting the emergence of *stasis* both within the individual soul and the *polis* as a whole. Ecstasy, far from being in any way rational or healthy, or a legitimate source of knowledge or path to wisdom was, as Plato describes it, an epithymetic compulsion, a disease condition that imprisoned and deranged human beings in an amoral bestial existence they would be helpless to either effectively manage or escape from. One such development—and a central theme of this book—was the difficulties revolving around the cultural presence of the drug, the *pharmakon*.

In chapter 4 I begin to examine more fully the importance of drugs, drug use, and drug intoxication in ancient Greek life. I begin with arguably the most important pedagogical source of education for the literate Greek, Homer's epic poetry, particularly the *Odyssey*. One finds in the *Odyssey*, especially the temptations of Odysseus, a persistent unease with, and growing cordoning off of, the powers of *pharmaka*. From there I examine two ancient Greek religions where the use of drugs is either largely confirmed or very strongly suspected: the cult of Dionysus and the Eleusinian Mysteries. As classicist Georg Luck has observed, the "idea that drugs played a role in the great religions of antiquity as they do in tribal societies in Africa and South America is still abhorrent to many scholars," and that especially extends to the study of ancient Greece.[41] Evidence from the field of cultural anthropology, more specifically ethnobotony and ethnopharmacology, is drawn upon to demonstrate the knowledge and use of often powerful intoxicating drugs in Greek religious life. In the course of my analysis Dionysus emerges as the god not only of wine but of all intoxicating drugs. Furthermore, like many examples of religions revelation in the ancient world, there is evidence that the sublime vision of the Eleusinian Mysteries (where Dionysus was also present in the guise of Triptolemus), called the *epopteia*, was also drug-induced, brought about through the drinking of a potion called the *kykeon*.

The death of Socrates in 399 BCE at the hands of the Athenian democracy exerted enormous influence on the development of Plato's arguments, and because of this has rippled through the history of political philosophy as a whole. Plato began his philosophic career with the *Apology*, a work that purports to be Socrates' defense at his trial for what the Greeks called *asebeia*. While perhaps Plato's most accurate depiction of the views of the "historical" Socrates, the argument within the *Apology* is still, first and foremost, Plato's defense of Socrates and the life of the philosopher against numerous influential detractors. In chapter 5 I will argue that Plato's ongoing polemic against those who felt that the practice of philosophy was impious lasted well beyond the *Apology* and was always more than a refutation of charges that philosophy promoted atheism. In this chapter I present evidence that in the final quarter of the fifth century Socrates was viewed as a profaner of the Eleusinian Mysteries. Philosophy was moreover perceived as an illicit form of ecstasy, influencing the *demos* in the manner of the spells and *pharmaka* of black magic, a form of impiety encompassed within the crime known as *asebeia*. To demonstrate this three separate arguments are needed. First, I consider what a number of ancient sources have to say about Socrates' accusers, both who they were and their possible motivations for bringing charges against him. Second, and more importantly, I then examine in detail the scandals of 415 BCE, where members of Athens' aristocracy, many of whom circulated in the same social circles as Socrates, were implicated in two acts of impiety: the mutilation of the city's Herms and profanations of the Eleusinian Mysteries. Finally I will discuss the evidence in favor of viewing Socrates as having a public image, before and at the time of his trial, as a practitioner of black magic, a *goes* or *pharmakeus*, using several of Aristophanes' comedies.

Many of Plato's early and middle dialogues may be read as more or less thinly disguised continuations of the same project as the *Apology*. In chapter 6 I turn to the place of the *pharmakon* in the *Phaedrus*, the dialogue that in a certain sense rehabilitates Socrates of having profaned the Eleusinian Mysteries. In Platonic philosophy Socrates, safely distanced from his oligarchic associates implicated in the politically disastrous scandals of 415 BCE, introduces a rationalized ecstasy to supplant the many non-rational forms available during Plato's lifetime, especially the Eleusinian Mysteries. The Eleusinian Mysteries, I argue in this chapter and in agreement with Carl A. P. Ruck and others, revolved around the use of a *pharmakon*, one found in the potion initiates drank called the *kykeon*.[42] With Plato a very different sort of ecstasy begins to emerge, one that was internally derived and based on contemplation of the Forms, accessed not via some *pharmakon* but solely through the exercise of reason. In these initial moments, with the charge of impiety an ever present danger, philosophy strategically aligned itself with, and appropriated from, the language of religious ecstasy, including and most significantly the *epopteia* of the Eleusinian Mysteries.

Part Three

Regimen (*diaita*) figures heavily in the set of solutions that Plato advances to deal with the problem of ecstasy (the difficulties of intoxication being one subset of this larger problem). Regimen clearly has a bodily component, what I call somatic regimen. It also has a mental or psychological component, what I call noetic regimen. Finally it has a spoken or verbal component, what I call discursive regimen. In the first three chapters of Part Three I will demonstrate that Plato recognized a need for philosophy to investigate and address the importance of each type of regimen. For example, in the *Republic*, inappropriate imitations are prohibited because they "become established as habits and nature, in body and sounds and in thought" (395c–d). If a person is allowed to imitate "slavish" and "shameful" behavior, the same passage continues, they get "a taste for the being from its imitation," i.e. they slip across the borders of identity, into the ecstatic wilderness of the Other. Through either malformation or malfunction regimen constitutes the basis of ecstasy's poisonous threat, but at the same time regimen as administered by the philosopher is the basis of the neutralization of that threat. Plato constructs the foundations of a new social order or what may be termed a *moral economy* that, I shall argue, will provide for ecstasy's permanent (dis)solution.[43]

How prominent a place do medicine (including food preparation, diet, and physical training), magic, and (political) rhetoric occupy in Plato's dialogues? To the modern observer these occupations would not appear to have all that much in common with each other, but within the context of the ancient Greek interpretive framework, including and especially Plato's, they most certainly did. One of the elements uniting them—the most important common denominator I would argue—is the power of the *pharmakon*, no longer understood simply as "drug" as it largely was in Part One and Part Two but in a broader sense now encompassing all the variability the word possessed in the Greek. A *pharmakon* could be a remedy used in medicine or an ointment applied as part of bodily training, but it could also be the basis of a spell, charm, or talisman used in sorcery or divination, and it could be an analogue to the power of the spoken word and its ability to place an audience under the influence of the speaker. What is more, in the ancient worldview understanding of these activities was deeply interwoven.

In chapter 7 I look at (a) the state of medical theory and practice up to and including Plato's lifetime, particularly its methods for diagnosing disease; (b) the place of drug treatment within ancient Greek medicine; (c) Plato's relationship to these developments, the degree to which he accepted the aetiology of his contemporaries or modified it for his own purposes; and finally (d) his concern to go beyond contemporary medical diagnosis and treatment of somatic ill health in favor of what he calls the disease of the soul. Early Greek medicine, like healing practices in other parts of the world, has shamanic roots and shamans the world over "use plants in order to travel to another reality."[44] Along with philosopher John P. Anton I would agree that "there is a deep relationship between the art of medicine, the moral quest, philosophical ethics and the art of statesmanship" in Plato's writings.[45] Plato often appeals to Greek medical practice, in part because it was generally if not universally held in high repute.[46] The degree of this "borrowing from the field of medicine," Anton points out, is "quite conspicuous."[47]

Classicist Walter Jaeger long ago noted it is "really astonishing to read the medical texts and discover how much they prefigure the method of Socrates' as described by Plato."[48] More recently classicist Trevor J. Saunders has matter-of-factly observed that the use of "medical language is pervasive" in Plato's writings.[49] Plato's discussion of "both medicine and public justice," medical historian Fridolf Kudlien writes, occurs "in the closest connection," usually suggesting "that chronic internal diseases are in some way immoral," and for that reason "of the greatest political and social importance."[50] While a necessary part of *polis* life, strictly somatic medicine and gymnastic training are incapable of producing psychic health on their own due to their inability to diagnose or remedy immoral behavior. They merely treat the diseased soul *ex post facto* and even then only to address the physical symptoms of that illness, not the true causes. Somatic health, for Plato, is predicated upon noetic and discursive health, the latter two forms of health belonging to the field of ethics, not medicine. Before real healing of the body can take place a *moral physician*—the philosopher— must bring purification to the soul.

In chapter 8 I turn to philosophy's role in the production of noetic health. Socrates' manner of conversation is often depicted by Plato as having an impact on the thought of those exposed to it similar to a kind of nefarious magic, even a kind of drugging. Ancient Greek magic, like philosophy, was concerned with the power to control human thought, and the art of magic was practiced on a scale ranging from the individual sorcerer (known as a *goes*, *pharmakeus* and other names) to entire communities. I begin the chapter by (a) discussing the development of a concept of magic among the ancient Greeks. Classical scholarship has for the most part traditionally accepted without criticism "the nineteenth century notion that magic is either 'bad' religion or 'bad' science—that 'magic' represents a 'primitive' worldview that has not evolved."[51] The use of "Judeo-Christian and modern scientific models for, respectively, religion and science to identify phenomena that do not conform as [being merely] magical" tells us little about ancient magical practices.[52] It is a "modern day prejudice" that ought not to be allowed to "obscure the importance in ancient societies of therapies based on ritual and religion."[53]

I then proceed by (b) discussing the sorts of men and women whose activities would fall under the heading of magic as well as (c) the prevalence of *pharmaka* in much of their practices. As Georg Luck notes, drugs were used in magic "probably more regularly and consistently" than in religion, because magic was a business transaction "between the practitioner and the client" with the latter expecting results "here and now."[54] Next, (d) the problematic nature of sorcery, including the record of instances of legal prosecution, is examined. I then proceed to argue that (e) the practice of magic is referred to with too great a frequency in Plato's dialogues to simply pass over it as a rationalist's condemnation of superstitious beliefs and (f) it is quite clear, both in Plato's dialogues and other ancient texts, that the presence of the *pharmakon* in ancient times was as pervasive in magic as it often was in religion. Finally, I show (g) how Plato attempts to distance the practice of philosophy from magic, but at the same time the powers of the spell and the charm are incorporated into a two-tier system of ethical pedagogy intended to produce an orderly noetic regimen within each individual.

In chapter 9 I turn from medicine and magic to forms of speech (*logos*), such as those found in tragedy, comedy, and especially a *techne* whose emergence was roughly contemporary with that of philosophy: training in public rhetoric as taught by the Sophist school of educators. The practice of sophistic instruction and the use of rhetoric in politics, the courts, and elsewhere were dangerous threats to any claim made by philosophy to be the superior means of instilling healthy thought and speech on a mass level. I examine Plato's response to this tradition, starting with the literary figure of Gorgias as presented in Plato's *Gorgias* and the surviving fragments of the historical Gorgias. In both cases *logos* is seen as a *pharmakon* with a magical power to sway an audience in virtually any direction. Rhetoric appears as the apex of the sort of false technical arts (*technai*) that unduly influence noetic and discursive formation, a form of pandering that is more concerned with overcoming emotional stability, rather than instilling any sort of sound-minded virtue. Polus and Callicles emerge as two case studies of the disordered, contradictory, and amoral noetic patterns that students form from prolonged exposure to an art like that taught by Gorgias.

Rhetoric is not entirely worthless but like medicine it was for Plato an art based on a haphazard acquisition of empirical knack, lacking any truly scientific or theoretical underpinning. Rhetoric is the guardian of what he calls the *unwritten law*, ideally a set of linguistic valuations of right and wrong that shape thought and behavior and act as the foundation of any written legislation. Discursive regimen, as we see in Plato's final dialogue, the *Laws*, is important (a) in and of itself and (b) because it serves as the foundation of noetic and somatic moderation and order. This rhetoric is in rare circumstances similar to a free physician explaining "almost like a philosopher" both diagnosis and treatment to a free patient. Usually, however, it more closely resembles the speech of a slave's physician, a one-way conversation more closely resembling a "tyrannical prescription" that demands mute obedience. Language must be continually overseen, shaped, molded, and controlled from the beginning of life. Once a useful discursive regimen is established the members of the *polis* must forever speak with a single voice on ethical matters just as their law code, once set in place and modified for a period of ten years, becomes forever unchangeable. The problem of the ceaseless ebb and flow of identity is solved by Plato by freezing it in one moment of historical time.

Ultimately Plato attempts to lead philosophy beyond any kind of magic, charm, or *pharmakon*, except it would appear the sort of *pharmakon* that a philosopher might possess. In chapter 10, building on philosopher Jacques Derrida's study of the *pharmakon* in the *Phaedrus*, I argue that Plato continues to refine the relationship between *logos* and *pharmakon*, for example the description of the philosopher in the *Theatetus* as a midwife, singing charms and administering simple *pharmaka*. The deep ambiguity of the *logos-pharmakon* dynamic was something that Plato attempted "to master, to dominate by inserting [that dynamic] into simple, clear-cut oppositions: good and evil, inside and outside, true and false, essence and appearance."[55] The word-prescription of the moral physician becomes the supplement that both adds to and replaces all other *pharmaka*. For non-philosophers moderation is only possible through the administration of a *pharmakon* reserved to philosophers. That *pharmakon*, while embracing many of the ambiguities present in the Greek, is as philosopher Carl Page has observed, knowledge of an *art of lying*, albeit in a *well-born* fashion to a *demos* having no more say in the matter than a slave might when conversing with a slave's physician.[56] Solving the problem of ecstasy, when we come full circle, becomes the art of administering the nobly deceitful *pharmakon* of philosophy.

Between Exegesis and Eisegesis

The line between exegesis and eisegesis is thin and easily crossed. When it comes to classical scholarship, political philosophy and issues pertaining to the ancients, ecstasy, drugs, and intoxication errors arising out of presentism—

"retrojecting distinctive characteristics of the modern world into an interpretation of the past"[57]—occur on an all too regular basis. Sometimes this is done accidentally and unconsciously, arising from an incomplete understanding of the texts and other evidence, sometimes it is done deliberately and consciously, arising out of prejudicial and selective misreading of the texts and the deliberate marginalizing, dismissal and outright exclusion of other evidence. In these errors it is easy to see reflected the fears and hostilities the general issue of drugs and intoxication have evoked in contemporary market economies, and indeed has evoked in the West since the beginning of the Industrial Revolution.[58]

At the same time, to write about drugs outside the narrow boundaries of the "treat-the-addict" and "incarcerate-the-criminal" paradigms is potentially dangerous, i.e. if the author does not reflexively condemn the recreational consumption of these substances he himself must be a practicing member of the subculture in question.[59] Such accusations are naturally facile and, as in so many cases in the past, meant to silence debate and allow sterile rhetoric to maintain its hegemonic authority. There is, however, the possibility that even a broadminded treatment of the subject of intoxication in antiquity might succumb to presentism. I am not a Hellenist but I have taken care to familiarize myself with the Greek, and to have the Greek double-checked by classicists, insofar as it pertains to the themes of ecstasy, drugs, intoxication and other matters under consideration here. One can disagree with the interpretation of particular details and certainly the source materials are on a number of occasions pushed to their limit. I am confident all the same that *Pharmakon* advances a theoretically informed and evidentially supported argument about the form and content of ancient works and about the external evidence for their meaning that is new and worthy of consideration.[60]

Notes

1. Paul Rabinow, *The Foucault Reader* (New York: Pantheon Books, 1984), 388. The interview, titled "Polemics, Politics, and Problemizations," was conducted in May. Foucault died on June 25.

2. Rabinow, *The Foucault Reader*, 389.

3. Rabinow, *The Foucault Reader*, 389.

4. Michel Foucault, *The Use of Pleasure—The History of Sexuality, Vol. 2* (New York: Vintage Books, 1986), 51.

5. Giovanni Reale "According to Plato, The Evils of the Body Cannot be Cured without also Curing the Evils of the Soul," in *Person, Society, and Value: Towards a Personalist Concept of Health,* ed. Paulina Taboada, Kateryna F. Cuddeback, and Patricia Donohue-White (Dordrect, Netherlands: Kluwer Academic Publishing, 2002), 27.

6. The influence of Plato's thought on, and the confluences of Plato's thought with, contemporary drug issues and the solutions offered to solve them are discussed briefly in the afterword, below.

7. Foucault, *The Use of Pleasure*, 69. The appearance of this "care of the self" or *epimeleia heautou* in Greek culture, which Foucault calls the "Socratic/Platonic Mo-

ment," is discussed in the context of a reading of the *Alcibiades I*. See Michel Foucault, *The Hermeneutics of the Subject—Lectures at the College de France, 1981–1982* (New York: Picador, 2005), 30–79.

8. Martha C. Nussbaum, "Eros and Ethical Norms: Philosophers Respond to a Social Dilemma," in *The Sleep of Reason: Erotic Experience and Sexual Ethics in Ancient Greece*, ed. Martha C. Nussbaum and Juha Sihvola (Chicago: University of Chicago Press, 2002), 57.

9. Foucault, *The Use of Pleasure*, 51.

10. Foucault, *The Use of Pleasure*, 51–52. A discussion of the ethics of food in ancient Greece may be found in David Coveny, *Food, Morals, and Meaning: The Pleasures and Anxiety of Eating* (New York: Routledge, 2000), 30–55. See also Peter Garnsey, *Food and Society in Classical Antiquity* (Cambridge: Cambridge University Press, 1999).

11. Nussbaum, "Eros and Ethical Norms," 58. The assertion might appear a little odd to anyone familiar with obesity statistics and the health costs of obesity, or drug arrests and the costs of incarcerating recreational drug users.

12. David Allison, "Nietzsche's Dionysian High: Morphin' with Endorphins," in *High Culture: Reflections on Addiction and Modernity*, ed. Anna Alexander and Mark S. Roberts (Albany, NY: State University of New York Press, 2003) 45–46. See also Zvi Lothane, "Schreber's Ecstasies, or Who Ever Listened to Daniel Paul?" in *High Culture: Reflections on Addiction and Modernity* (Albany, NY: State University of New York Press, 2003), 254.

13. Costas M. Constantinou, *States of Political Discourse: Words, Regimes, Seditions*, (New York: Routledge, 2004), 10.

14. Nietzsche describes *rausch* or *intoxication* as indispensible for "any sort of aesthetic activity or perception to exist" and gives several examples in section 8 of "Expeditions of an Untimely Man" in *Twilight of the Idols*; the context however makes clear that he is talking about psychological states of *ecstasy*. See Friedrich Nietzsche, *The Twilight of the Idols and The Anti-Christ: Or how to Philosophize with a Hammer* (New York: Penguin, 2003), 82–83. *Rausch* is in fact translated by some writers as "ecstasy." Others use "inebriation" or "rapture" but these do not truly fit Nietzsche's use or the ancient Greek psychology he was attempting to investigate.

15. On the subject of dance and psychological displacement in ancient Greece, including Plato, see Stephen H. Lonsdale, *Dance and Ritual Play in Greek Religion* (Baltimore, MD: Johns Hopkins University Press, 1993). On the subject of music and psychological displacement in ancient Greece, including Plato, see Gilbert Rouget, *Music and Trance—A Theory of the Relationship between Music and Trance* (Chicago: University of Chicago Press, 1985), 187–226.

16. Karl R. Popper, *The Open Society and its Enemies, Volume I: The Spell of Plato* (Princeton, NJ: Princeton University Press, 1966), 169–201, especially 171–75, 182–83, 188–89, 195–97, and 199.

17. Nussbaum makes both these points while reviewing *The Use of Pleasure* shortly after its publication. See Martha C. Nussbaum, "Review of Michel Foucault's *The Use of Pleasure. The History of Sexuality* Volume 2 ['Affections of the Greeks'], *New York Times*, November 10, 1985, 13–14. Similar criticisms of Foucault may be found in Giulia Sissa, *Sex and Sexuality in the Ancient World* (New Haven, CT: Yale University Press, 2008). Gros points out that in the early 1980s scholarly secondary literature on ancient sexuality was "still slight" and Foucault cannot be taken to task because he "did not refer to a critical literature that did not yet exist: he was, rather, a pioneer in these studies." See Foucault, *The Hermeneutics of the Self*, 519–20.

18. James Davidson, *Courtesans and Fishcakes: The Consuming Passions of Classical Athens* (New York: Harper Perennial, 1999).

19. Foucault, *The Hermeneutics of the Self,* 521.

20. See the long discussion provided by Gros in Foucault, *The Hermeneutics of the Self,* 507–21. It is important to point out, as Gros does, that "Foucault does not abandon politics to dedicate himself to ethics, but *complicates* the study of governmentalities through the exploration of the care of the self."

21. G. E. R. Lloyd, *Demystifying Mentalities* (Cambridge: Cambridge University Press, 1990), 30. Lloyd's approach is further developed and extended by Robert Hahn, *Anaximander and the Architects—The Contributions of Egyptian and Greek Architectural Technologies to the Origins of Greek Philosophy* (Albany, NY: State University of New York Press, 2001), Couprie et al., *Anaximander in Context: New Studies on the Origins of Greek Philosophy* (Albany, NY: State University of New York Press, 2003) and Gerrard Naddaf, *The Greek Concept of Nature* (Albany, NY: State University of New York Press, 2005).

22. Matthew W. Dickie, *Magic and Magicians in the Greco-Roman World* (New York: Routledge, 2001), 19. In terms reminiscent of Lloyd, Dickie continues on the same page "There is no overwhelming reason, accordingly, to abandon the attempt to see the world through the eyes of the members of the society studied, even though our own preconceptions and prejudices may from time to time affect our judgment and understanding. That is to say, the emic approach to the study of culture should not be abandoned in favor of the etic."

23. R. Gordon Wasson, et al., *The Road to Eleusis: Unveiling the Secrets of the Mysteries* (Los Angeles: William Daly Rare Books, 1998), 11–12. In this twentieth anniversary edition co-author Carl A. P. Ruck indicated the book received only two reviews, neither particularly welcoming, at the time of its initial publication in 1978. The summary dismissal of the book in classicist Walter Burkert's *Ancient Mystery Cults,* published a decade later, ended the matter, at least as far as mainstream classical studies was concerned.

24. Patrick E. McGovern, *Ancient Wine: The Search for the Origins of Viniculture* (Princeton, NJ: Princeton University Press, 2003), 48–49. "In the last 20 years. . . . [a] range of highly sensitive analytic tools—gas and liquid chromatographs, mass spectrometers, nuclear magnetic resonance instruments, DNA sequencers—has become standard laboratory equipment. Refinements in other techniques, such as infrared spectrometry, have also occurred. The upshot is that the modern archaeological scientist now has tools that can measure milli-, even microgram, quantities of ancient organics."

25. McGovern, *Ancient Wine,* 49.

26. McGovern, *Ancient Wine,* 241–42.

27. McGovern, *Ancient Wine,* 242, 244, and 301. A similar method is advocated by Garnsey, *Food and Society in Classical Antiquity,* 1–11.

28. Michel Foucault, *Discipline and Punish: The Birth of the Prison* (New York: Vintage Books, 1979), 279–80. There appear to be echoes of Althusser's structuralism in passages such as this. See Louis Althusser, *Lenin and Philosophy and Other Essays* (New York: Monthly Review Press, 2001) especially his essay on the state "Ideology and Ideological State Apparatuses: Notes Towards an Investigation." Foucault's arguments also recall those made by the Italian Marxist theorist Antonio Gramsci regarding American Prohibition in passages of "Americanism and Fordism," one of the essays in Antonio Gramsci, *Selections from the Prison Notebooks* (New York: International Publishers, 1971).

29. Quoted in Brian Taylor, *Responding to Men in Crisis: Masculinities, Distress and the Postmodern Political Landscape* (New York: Routledge, 2006), 229 n. 37. See also David M. Halperin, *Saint Foucault: Towards a Gay Hagiography* (New York: Oxford University Press, 1995), 94. Halperin writes, "It was to intensify experiences of pleasure 'at the limit of the subject' that Foucault advocated the use of what he called '*good* drugs.'"

30. Quoted in William E. Connolly "Beyond Good and Evil—The Ethical Sensibility of Michel Foucault," *Political Theory* 21, no. 3. Connolly does not mention the source of the quotation. See Michele Barrett, *The Politics of Truth: From Marx to Foucault* (Palo Alto, CA: Stanford University Press, 1991), 148 and Jeremy Moss, *The Later Foucault: Politics and Philosophy,* (Thousand Oaks, CA: Sage Publications, 1998), 109 who both identify the quote as originating in the *Actuel* interview.

31. Quoted in Sadie Plant, "Writing on Drugs," in *Culture and Power: Challenging Discourses,* ed. Maria Jose Coperias Aguilar (Valencia, Spain: Servei de Publicacions, 2000), 5. Plant writes on the same page "A book on drugs would have made the perfect compliment to [Foucault's] existing portfolio of research on madness, disease, crime and sexuality, and it is easy to imagine the enthusiasm with which he would have embarked on this research. The tangled and evasive history of drugs . . . would have allowed him to explore many of his favorite philosophical and historical issues. One can only imagine that Foucault would have been looking for some evidence or possibility of a counter-discourse on drugs." I will address the possibility of just such a counter-discourse in the afterword.

32. Friedrich Nietzsche, *The Gay Science* (New York: Vintage Books, 1974), 142. The quote is reproduced, fittingly enough, on the opening page of Alexander and Roberts, *High Culture*, 1.

33. Plant, "Writing on Drugs," 6. See also Jon Simons, *Foucault and the Political* (New York: Routledge, 1995), 95–96.

34. A collection of essays that takes the nineteenth century problemization of drug use as its starting point is Janet Farrell Brodie and Marc Redfield, eds., *High Anxieties—Cultural Studies in Addiction* (Berkeley, CA: University of California Press, 2002).

35. A point first raised by Adorno and Horkheimer in *Dialectic of Enlightenment* albeit in a speculative manner without any detail, documentation, or historical context. All the same the importance of their arguments for a discussion of the drug problem in modernity has been recognized, for example, in Jacques Derrida, "The Rhetoric of Drugs," in *High Culture: Reflections on Addiction and Modernity* ed. Anna Alexander and Mark S. Roberts (Albany, NY: State University of New York Press, 2003), 31.

36. Dickie, *Magic and Magicians in the Greco-Roman World*, 76–77.

37. Rabinow, *The Foucault Reader*, 76.

38. William E. Connolly, *The Augustinian Imperative: A Reflection on the Politics of Modernity* (London: Sage, 1993).

39. Dickie, *Magic and Magicians in the Greco-Roman World*, 76.

40. Friedrich Nietzsche, *The Birth of Tragedy out of the Spirit of Music* (New York: Penguin, 1993), 39, 41. Nietzsche's continually evolving notion of the ecstatic is discussed in Robert Luysterm, "Nietzsche/Dionysus: Ecstasy, Heroism and the Monstrous," *Journal of Nietzsche Studies* 21, No. 1 (Spring 2001): 1–26.

41. Georg Luck, *Arcana Mundi—Magic and the Occult in the Greek and Roman Worlds. A Collection of Ancient Texts* (Baltimore, MD: The Johns Hopkins University Press, 2006), 479.

42. Wasson, et al., *The Road to Eleusis* remains in most ways the definitive text.

43. On "moral economy" see Connolly, *The Augustinian Imperative*, 132. A similar concept is expressed in Barrett, *The Politics of Truth*, 148.

44. Luck, *Arcana Mundi*, 481.

45. John P. Anton, "Dialectic and Health in Plato's *Gorgias*: Presuppositions and Implications," *Ancient Philosophy* 1, No. 1 (1980): 51.

46. D. S. Hutchinson, "Doctrines of the Mean and the Debate Concerning Skills in Fourth Century Medicine, Rhetoric and Ethics," *Apeiron* 21, No. 2 (1988): 18.

47. Anton, "Dialectic and Health in Plato's *Gorgias*," 49.

48. Werner W. Jaeger, *Paideia: The Ideals of Greek Culture* (New York: Oxford University Press, 1965), 389 n. 3.

49. Trevor J. Saunders, *Plato's Penal Code—Tradition, Controversy, and Reform in Greek Penology* (Oxford: Clarendon Press, 1991), 164.

50. Fridolf Kudlien, "Early Greek Primative Medicine," *Clio Medica* 3 (1968): 318.

51. C. R. Phillips, "*Nullum Crimen sine Lege*: Socioreligious Sanctions on Magic," in *Magika Hiera—Ancient Greek Magic and Religion*, ed. Christopher A. Faraone and Dirk Obbink (New York: Oxford University Press, 1991), 260.

52. C. R. Phillips, "*Nullum Crimen sine Lege*," 262.

53. Walter Burkert, *The Orientalizing Revolution: Near Eastern Influences on Greek Culture in the Early Archaic Age* (Cambridge, MA: Cambridge University Press, 1992), 41. It is ironic that Burkert would write this, given his distinctly modern aversion to serious discussion of the use of drugs in ancient societies.

54. Luck, *Arcana Mundi*, 479.

55. Jacques Derrida, *Dissemination* (Chicago: University of Chicago Press, 1981), 103.

56. Carl Page, "The Truth about Lies in Plato's *Republic*," *Ancient Philosophy* 11, No. 1 (1991): 1–33. A more in-depth discussion may be found in Randall Baldwin Clark, *The Law Most Beautiful and Best—Medical Argument and Magical Rhetoric in Plato's Laws* (Lanham, MD: Lexington Books, 2003).

57. Robert Sallares, *The Ecology of the Ancient Greek World* (Ithaca, NY: Cornell University Press, 1991), 13–14.

58. See my discussion of the future of drugs and intoxication in a post-industrial setting in the afterword, below.

59. A point raised, among other places, in both Plant, "Writing on Drugs," 3 and in David Boothroyd, *Culture on Drugs: Narco-cultural Studies of High Modernity* (Manchester, UK: Manchester University Press, 2007).

60. John G. Gunnell, *Political Philosophy and Time* (Middletown, CT: Wesleyan University Press, 1987), xi–xiv. Gunnell discusses the rarity of this approach within the field of political theory.

Part One

Plato and the Politics of Intoxication

Chapter One

Wine and the *Symposion*

It is vitally important to establish the composition of alcoholic beverages in the ancient world and the settings where they were consumed before discussing such subjects as the ethics of wine drinking and intoxication in Classical Greece and Plato's response to those ethics. This is so for three reasons. First, there is abundant evidence that wine was but one mind-altering drug among several available in Classical Greece.[1] Second, these drugs were added to wine with such regularity in the ancient world that it becomes difficult, bordering on impossible, to speak of wine intoxication as something separate and distinct from drug intoxication more generally. Third, wine consumption could be imbued with both recreational and religious meaning, and could be experienced in both public and private settings, and furthermore these four aspects were far more extensively intertwined than is the case for contemporary readers.[2]

Ancient Wine—Production

The wild grapes found on the Eurasian grapevine *Vitis vinifera sylvestris* are not particularly suited for making wine.[3] Even so it has been hypothesized that wine may have been produced in the Paleolithic/Old Stone Age period using, for example, "baskets, leather bags, or wooden containers," but the chances of archaeology "ever finding a preserved container with intact ancient organics or microorganisms that can be identified as exclusively due to wine" are remote.[4] On a technological level the intentional human production of fermented beverages such as wine requires knowledge of fire, pottery, and organized agriculture.[5] These have existed since the Neolithic/New Stone Age period in the Near East.[6] The origins of wine made from the grapes of the domesticated grapevine *Vitis vinifera vinifera* continue to be pushed backward in time by emerging disci-

3

plines such as molecular archaeology, a field that has taken advantage of ever-accelerating advances in a number of technologies.[7]

Archeological, chemical, and DNA analysis of wine-related artifacts and grape remains found in the Neolithic village of Hajji Firuz (ca. 5,400–5,000 BCE) located in the Zagros Mountains of northwestern Iran, for example, predate the next oldest evidence by two millennia.[8] Neolithic sites in the Taurus Mountains of what is now eastern Turkey may be hundreds of years older. The generally accepted scenario is that grape domestication and wine production began in these transcaucasian highlands and then fanned out to Lower Mesopotamia and Egypt (ca. 3,500–3,000 BCE), and then Crete (ca. 2,200 BCE).[9] The origins of both viniculture and wine production in mainland Greece similarly continue to be pushed backwards. There is on the one hand evidence that viniculture may have made its way to Greece "from western Anatolia or the Balkans, whether by land through Macedonia or by sea," yet on the other the sophistication and sheer magnitude of wine production in Minoan Crete, and similar *pithoi* found at "Aghios Kosmas in Attica, about 20 kilometers south of Athens near the coast," points at the very least to "a shared technology and sophisticated winemaking in Crete and on the mainland."[10]

In ancient Greece fermenting wine was stored underground in vessels known as *pithoi*, storage vats that could be as large as ten feet high with a mouth three feet across.[11] Fermentation took place over a six-month period with the vats being opened during the festival of the "opening of the vats" or *pithoigia*, roughly our month of February. Prior to sale the wine would be transferred to skins or containers called *amphoreus*, better known according to the Latin *amphorae*. Along with the export of commodities such as olive oil and pottery the export of wine had become, by the Classical Period, a cornerstone of the ancient Greek economy.[12] By the fifth century BCE Greek wine was being transported from vineyards on "the islands and coasts of the Aegean" to "Sicily, south and central Italy, Gaul, the Iberians of Spain, the Illyrians and Thracians on the Adriatic coast, the Danube and the Balkans, the Scythians of southern Russia, Asia minor, Cyprus and the Syrian coast, and Egypt."[13]

Fermentation cannot yield a wine more potent than about 14 percent alcohol, since above this level "natural fermentation . . . is limited . . . by the pickling effect of the alcohol itself upon the growing yeast which produces it as a by-product of the fungal activity upon the sugars of the juice."[14] Most wine in ancient Greece would not, however, have had an alcohol content exceeding eight percent.[15] One finds many references to the wine/water ratios used during the *symposion*'s mixing ceremony in *The Sophists at Dinner* (*The Deipnosophists*) by Athenaeus (ca. 170–ca. 230 CE).[16] Typical ratios were: 1:1; 1:2; 2:3; 2:5; etc. with 1:3 seemingly the most frequent (10.425–26). A drinker at a *symposion*, in other words, would have been lucky if he managed to imbibe a wine with more than a four percent alcohol content.

Water as an additive to wine simply blunts the beverage's "sensory, medicinal, and psychoactive effects."[17] A long history of scholarship, going back to the nineteenth century and extending right up to the present, has viewed this copious addition of water to wine as simply an indication the ancient Greeks were an essentially *temperate* people.[18] This literature has argued "it would not have been easy to get drunk on such a mixture."[19] Even recent studies have described the alcohol drunk in the *symposion* as a weak concoction "roughly equal in alcoholic strength to modern beer."[20] Others have attempted to explain the custom of blending water with wine as being "certainly due to its high alcohol content, which in turn was due to a late harvest, after the leaves have fallen."[21] Similarly, it has been argued that the drug most commonly associated with the god Dionysus, wine, "is not sufficient to induce true *bakcheia* (frenzy)."[22] These positions, taken by writers who are otherwise well-versed in the customs and practices of the *symposion*, betray a fundamental misunderstanding of ancient oenology. Regrettable within their own disciplines, these misunderstandings have unfortunately also filtered into our study of Greek philosophers such as Plato.[23]

Ancient Wine—Pharmacology

There are many possible explanations as to why ancient peoples would have modified their alcohol, particularly wine, during both manufacture and consumption. It is difficult to determine the intentional from the merely accidental; for example it is doubtful ancient winemakers made a distinction between "those substances which were meant to ferment and those simply added to, or macerated in, a fermented beverage for flavor."[24] Diluting wine with water would have made the wine more palatable in situations where quenching thirst rather than intoxication was the primary consideration. There would also have been occasions where there would have been a desire for (a) the addition of attractive tastes; (b) the addition of attractive odors; (c) modifying wines with more or less accidental impurities (an overabundance of methyl alcohol or other aldehydes in addition to ethyl alcohol); and (d) adding additional substances known to the ancient Greeks to have psychoactive properties. The concern here is chiefly with (d) although (a), (b) and (c) are also important.

On at least some occasions ancient wines were diluted with water because it was necessary to make them *safe* to consume. The texts continually refer to the physiological dangers of unmixed wine, especially when drunk habitually and in large quantities. These wines were capable of damaging eyesight, for example Dionysius the Younger whom Plato tried to provide an education in philosophy (Athenaeus 10.435d–e), and causing blindness (Aristotle, *Nicomachean Ethics* 1114a). This may have been a result of ancient wines having dangerous levels of aldehydes.[25] Methanol can occur with ethanol and breaks down into formic acid and formaldehyde within the body, which causes damage to the nervous system, especially the optic nerve.[26] Drinking of undiluted wine was believed to cause permanent brain damage and even death (Herodotus, *History* 6.75–84, Pseudo-Aristotle *Problems* 3.23 and 3.26, Athenaeus 10.436–37).[27] Small amounts of

wine were used to commit suicide or as a means to hasten death by several philosophers (Hermippus frg. 44, Diogenes Laertius *Lives*, 2.120; 4.44; 4.61; 4.65;
7.184; 10.15–6). Distillation technology cannot be reliably dated prior to twelfth
century Italy.[28] How, then, could ancient wine have been so dangerous to consume?

The answer to this question is relatively straightforward: ancient wines were
not at all like our modern mass-produced vintages. Like other ancient winemakers the Greeks were faced with several distinctly non-modern problems.
One such problem was that the *pithoi* used to ferment and store wine were po-
rous.[29] To combat oxygen leaking in they were smeared both within and without
with pitch or resin, such as that of the Aleppo pine (*Pinus halepenis*).[30] Any
such wine produced in this manner would have smelled and tasted strongly of
these substances.[31] To counteract this Greek wine was suffused with various
herbs, spices, and unguents in the process of manufacture, and/or further modified by adding additional substances during the *symposion*'s mixing ceremony.[32]
Another indication of this practice may be found in a wine's strength being
called its *anthos* or "flower" (Xenophon, *Hellenica* 6.2.6), and to be "deficient
in flower" meant a wine was lacking in inebriating qualities (Aristophanes,
Frogs 1150).[33]

A second major issue faced by all ancient winemakers was spoilage. Lacking methods to stop the fermentation process such as cork stoppers, wood barrels, or impermeable glass bottles, Greek wine had to be consumed in three or
four years, otherwise acidity would render the wine undrinkable, turning it into
vinegar.[34] Pliny the Elder (ca. 23–79 CE) discusses this "wine disease" at length
in book 14 of his *Natural History* (*Historia naturalis*). At higher elevations in
the Near East the wild grapevine "actually grows on and is supported by" the
terebinth tree (*Pistacia atlantica*), a source of resin.[35] Resins such as terebinth,
pine, and cedar impede the reproduction of "bacteria that convert ethanol into to
acetic acid or vinegar."[36] Resins were already in use as a medicinal before they
began to be mixed with wine, either accidentally or intentionally.[37] Resinated
wine is very old, nearly as old as the production of wine itself: large scale production may date as far back as the Neolithic period.[38] In modern Greece resin is
still added to wine to produce retsina, one of a handful of reminders of a time
when a wide variety of substances could have been found in any given mixing
bowl (*krater*).[39]

In addition to tree resins the Greeks added a number of other substances to
improve the taste of wine, including chalk, lime prepared from marble or shells,
and sea water.[40] These would have had the effect of "binding up the acids and
accentuating the sugar," producing a sweet tasting wine that in the ancient world
was regarded as "the ultimate indulgence."[41] Indeed a wine in antiquity was valued according to both its strength and sweetness and the two were mutually intertwined, with the term *glykys* meaning "sweet" as in "sugary" and the term
hedus meaning "sweet" as in "delightful."[42] Honey was the supreme sweetener
but it was expensive.[43] Wine is described as *melieides*, meaning "honey-sweet,"

and *meliphron*, meaning "honey-hearted," throughout Homer's epic poems the *Iliad* and *Odyssey*.[44]

Finally, to improve the smell and taste of the wine on the one hand, and to increase its intoxicating properties on the other, the ancients added plant matter, aromatic herbs and spices. A surviving fragment written by the pre-Socratic philosopher Xenophanes (ca. 570–480 BCE) reads: "Now clean is the floor, and clean the hands of all and the vessels: one person places on our heads the woven garlands, another offers sweet-scented myrrh in a flask. The mixing bowl stands full of delight (*euphrosyne*); more wine is ready, and claims it will never give out, sweet in its jars, flower-scented" (Athenaeus 11.462d). Among the many fragrant substances added to wine, Dioscorides (ca. 40–ca. 90 CE) tells us in his treatise on medical botany *On Medical Materials* (*De materia medica*), were oil of crocus (*krokos* 1.64), oil of marjoram (*amarakon* 1.68), myrrh (*smyrna* 1.77), and frankincense (*libanotes*)(1.82). Taken internally myrrh is an analgesic.[45] Frankincense "probably contains tetrahydrocannabinol, like hashish, and can act in the same way."[46] Other additives included cinnamon, "pepper, wormwood (*Artemisia absinthum*), capers, saffron, and many other herbs and spices."[47] Pliny the Elder writes of a plant from Bactria (current Turkestan) and the shores of Borysthene (the Dnepr) called *gelotophyllis* ("grass which gives a drunken melee mad laughter")—most likely hemp (*Cannabis sativa*)—that when mixed with wine and myrrh produced intense mental excitement and laughter lacking in moderation (*Natural History* 24.164).

Besides the archeological evidence, including both molecular analysis of pottery residue and vases whose exterior art depicts herbs and plants being mixed into wine, the literary evidence for this practice is profuse. In Homer's *Odyssey* (4.220–26) Helen adds a drug to the wine, a substance many commentators identify as opium.[48] Mixed with wine it causes one to forget the ills of the world, even the death of a loved one, "when it's mixed in the wine bowl."[49] Another wine additive based on opium was *mekonion*, made by boiling the poppy's leaves and capsules, "and which was less potent than opium."[50] Aristotle (384–322 BCE) in his *Sense and Sensabilia*—during a discussion of the sense of smell, specifically odors that are pleasant as their primary attribute such as flowers (whereas the pleasant smell of foods is secondary, being meant to stimulate the appetite)—quotes approvingly from Strattis' ridicule of Euripides: "'Use not perfumery to flavor soup'" and goes on to say that "those who nowadays introduce such flavors into beverages deforce our sense of pleasure by habituating us to them" (443b–444a).

Theophrastus (ca. 370–287 BCE) in his botanical work *History of Plants* (*Historia plantarum*) indicates that the root of oleander (*Nerium oleander*), *onotheras* in the Greek, when administered in wine, "makes a man's temper more gentle and cheerful (*praoteron kai hilaroteron*)" (9.19.1).[51] The plant, he continues, "has a leaf like the almond, but smaller, and the flower is red like the rose. It is a large bush; the root is red and large, and exudes a fragrance like wine; it loves mountainous places."[52] The overall context of his description of oleander is a discussion of plants that have "powers as drugs" (*pharmakodeis . . . du-*

nameis).[53] Pliny the Elder cites cyclamen (25.67) as well as oleander (21.45) being added to wine, in both cases the purpose being to increase the wine's inebriating properties. According to the *Natural History* oleander root added to wine was soporific, while the sap produced madness (21.45). While Theophrastus expressed his concern, describing the belief "that both effects should be caused by one and the same nature" as "absurd" (*History of Plants* 9.18.4), ancient pharmacology frequently held to the belief that "opposing effects could be produced by the same or similar substances."[54]

Wine-like Drugs

Intoxicating plants were frequently described as having the power of wine, *dynamis oinodes*. The immediate context of Theophrastus' discussion of plants added to wine is "drugs that affect the mind" (*pharmaka pros de ten psychen*), including those substances that cause "mental derangement" (*ekstatikas*).[55] Mandrake (*Mandragora officinarum*), deadly nightshade (*Atropa belladonna*) and henbane (*Hyoscyamus niger*) were all understood as having wine-like effects in the ancient world. Each contains the tropane alkaloid scopolamine, a substance that produces "intoxication followed by narcosis in which hallucinations occur during the transition state between consciousness and sleep."[56] In the *Republic* Plato exhibits an awareness of mandrake's intoxicating powers while describing the danger of "the noble ship owner" being overpowered with mandrake, wine or other drugs by a mutinous crew only interested in "drinking and feasting" (488c). Xenophon's Socrates compares *Mandragora* and wine as having a similar effect on the mind (*Symposium* 2.24). Theophrastus compares the appearance and effect of the round bluish black berries of nightshade with wine (*History of Plants* 6.2.9). Dioscorides compares henbane's "frenzies" with the inebriation of drunkenness (*On Medical Matters* 4.68 and 6.15). Pliny the Elder describes henbane's effects as being "like wine" (*Natural History* 25.35–37).

There is then an abundance of evidence compelling us to resist viewing ancient wines, including those found in Classical Greece, as being similar to wine manufactured using contemporary methods.[57] The knowledge of all these substances points to ancient wines being more akin to chemically complex tinctures—and almost certainly more intoxicating.[58] Two surviving fragments of Aristotle's *On Drunkenness* give further credence to this complexity. Rhodian cups, Aristotle writes, are used at drinking parties because of their pleasant taste, and their tendency to arrest intoxication to such an extent that even erotic desires are cast out (Athenaeus 11.464c–d). The drink was made by adding "myrrh, aromatic rush, anise, saffron, costmary, cardamom and cinnamon" to boiling water, and later adding this to the wine (whether before sale or during the mixing ceremony of the *symposion* is not clear). While few recipes as complete as Aristotle's Rhodian cups have survived, it is fair to suppose that many such concoctions would have resulted in a more rather than less intense intoxication. Aristotle was said to have been aware of a certain Samagorean wine of which only three half-pints, mixed with water, were capable of making forty men drunk (Athenaeus 10.429f).

During a discussion of the drinking cup (*kylix*), Athenaeus mentions Polemon's *On Morychus*, which describes a Syracusian custom of taking a cup aboard a ship when it puts out to sea.[59] When the temple of Athena was lost from sight the cup, *sans* wine but otherwise filled with "flowers, honeycomb, frankincense in lumps, and some other spices, would be dropped into the sea" (11.462b–c). The phrase "the wine-dark sea" was a metaphor used extensively from Homer onward, and points to the Syracusian practice having connotations of an actual wine mixing ritual, where any of those substances (or indeed more than one of them) might be added to the wine before consumption. Greek culture drew "multiple analogies . . . among wine, the sea, navigation, and the *symposion*."[60] For example Xenarchos says "I'm starting to nod off; that cup I drank to Zeus the Savior has completely wrecked me, the sailor, and sent me to the bottom, as you can see" (Athenaeus 15.693b, and cf. Plato's *Symposium* 176b).

"tripping" [handwritten annotation in margin]

Other Fermented Intoxicants

The ancient world had virtually no understanding of the fermentation process, which consists of yeast converting sugar into ethyl alcohol and carbon dioxide. Xenophon describes large numbers of Greek soldiers who had eaten honey looted from a district full of beehives as behaving foolishly and unable to stand up; "those who had eaten a little bit seemed as if they were extremely drunk, while those who had eaten a lot seemed as if they were crazy or even dying" (*Anabasis* 4.8.20–1). At the same time the ancients were quite talented at producing intoxicating drinks from not only fruits and honey (fructose and glucose), but also from sugar cane (sucrose), milk (lactose), and cereals (maltose). Fermented fruit juices, such as that made from the fruit and sap of the date palm, appear to have been an early popular alcoholic beverage in the ancient Near East. Dates were combined with honey during the fermentation process to produce a date-wine with a high alcohol content, perhaps the strongest alcohol-based intoxicant of pre-classical antiquity.[61] Xenophon refers to date-wine as "a pleasant drink causing headaches" (*Anabasis* 2.5.14).

Along with wine, mead and beer were the most popular alcoholic beverages of the ancient world.[62] Mead made from honey is arguably the ancestor of all fermented intoxicants, predating both wine and beer.[63] In contrast to wine, mead requires neither fire nor pottery to produce.[64] Many variations of mead were apparently available for consumption in ancient Greece, including but not limited to *hydromel* (honey and water), *metheglin* (honey, water, and spices), and *oinomeli* or *mulsum* (wine mixed with honey and water). In Plato's *Symposium* Diotima recounts how Poros became drunk with nectar in the Garden of Zeus, "for wine was not yet known" (203b).[65]

Many different varieties of beer were produced in the ancient Near East, being mentioned in "early Sumerian and Akkadian texts, and from the Protoliterate period of Mesopotamia (ca. 3,200 [BCE])."[66] Beer was known to the ancient Greeks under several names, including *pinion* and *bryton*. It was identified as "a drink of Thracians, Paeonians, and Phrygians . . . in the seventh century [BCE] while in the fifth century [BCE] it was further also known as a drink of Egyptians."[67] The first opponent of beer appears to have been the playwright Aeschylus (ca. 525–456 BCE). His "attack on beer . . . became, it seems, common in later dramatists also writing plays performed yearly at the great festival of the god Dionysus, and perhaps due to his influence."[68] Some beers were despised by the Greeks as only fit for barbarians, as for example in Sophocles' *Triptolemus* (Athenaeus 10.447b). Others, such as the sweet and spicy beer of Egypt were praised by Diodorus Siculus for having "a smell and sweetness . . . not much inferior to wine" (*Library of World History* 1.3). In one Greek tradition the god Dionysus emigrated from Mesopotamia to Thrace due to the popularity of beer among the inhabitants, who are denigrated as "froth blowers."[69] While it is true that "later Greek writers and gourmands dismissed beer as a barbarian drink" we should not summarily dismiss "evidence for its production there."[70]

Wine and Intoxication

The original Greek word signifying "to be drunk" was *methyein*. This term was derived from *methy* (intoxicating drink), whose origins suggest connotations of honey/mead and other intoxicants in a wide spectrum of ancient Indo-European-Finno-Ugric languages.[71] *Methe* is usually translated as "intoxication." In contrast *oinion* (to intoxicate with wine), from *oinos* (wine), arrived on the scene later and was at first less common. Eventually *oinos* itself would become a generic term for any intoxicant, regardless of the drug (*pharmakon*) being referred to. It has been suggested that *oinos* may have been "derived from a very ancient Indo-European word, ultimately related to the Latin word for 'grape vine' (*vitis*) and the Greek *itys*, 'circular rim,' as of a wheel supported by spokes."[72] A circular rim in the fashion of a wheel supported by spokes is "a common ideogram for the mushroom cap viewed from its gilled underside."[73] It is possible, then, that *oinos* referred originally to some intoxicant other than wine, perhaps one more aptly described with the metaphor of *itys*.[74]

Experiencing Alcohol: The *Symposion*

If one were to draw up a short list of the definitive elements of ancient Greek culture and society one would have to include the *symposion*. Like any organic social institution the *symposion* was in a state of continual evolution, with characteristics of older and newer forms existing side by side and even intermingling. The written descriptions that we possess of the *symposion* are drawn from the symposia of tyrants and the aristocracy, so inevitably they reflect an elite social perspective. There is reason to believe that by the fifth century BCE Greece's mercantile, artisan, and peasant hoplite classes held their own symposia, but as these social groups lacked the leisure time necessary for writing, we know little of their practices.[75] The documentary record that has survived, moreover, for the most part dates from the fourth century BCE onwards, with Athenaeus' *Deipnosophists*, written centuries later in the third century CE, being the single largest source of quotations.[76] The discussion here, unless noted otherwise, will pertain to the symposia of the Athenian elite during Socrates' and Plato's lifetime.

The aristocratic *symposion* was a festive "psychological and cultural microverse" cordoned off from public life.[77] On the surface the aim of the *symposion* was the celebration of certain specific occasions, most especially those marking exceptional moments in the lives of either one or more of those present, or the symposiasts as a group. But beneath this surface the *symposion* was also the primary setting "for the transmission of cultural ideals and the forging of political and interpersonal relationships."[78] Spatially a typical *symposion* would take place in a small room, the *andron* or "men's room."[79] Couches on raised platforms, usually seven to fifteen in number, would be arranged in a circle, against the walls, to ensure that nothing occurred behind the participants. Organized in this manner the entire *symposion* was fashioned so as to create converging lines of sight and establish the communicative reciprocity among the guests.[80] The *andron* would not contain more than between fourteen and thirty adult male guests.[81] If the number of celebrants was very large the number of rooms, rather than the number of individuals within the same room, would be increased.

Qualitatively the event was a male gathering, having origins in the "feast of merit" practiced by the Homeric warrior elite.[82] This earlier incarnation of the *symposion* took place in the *megaron*, or banqueting hall.[83] The feast of merit was a ritualized display of generosity: a leading warrior (*basileus*) would use his agricultural surplus to entertain other elite male companions (*hetairoi*), producing ties of loyalty and serving "in general to enhance the status of the *basileus* within the community," while at the same time providing him with a "band of *hetairoi* obligated to follow him in military and naval exploits, from petty cattle raiding and piracy to accepting his leadership in more formal warfare."[84] Formal warfare, such as the Trojan War, was in contrast to private ventures a public affair that ordinary men participated in. It was expected of the warrior elite to subsidize public feasting in such circumstances, for possession of surplus wine and food was a major determinant of status within the community.[85] Changes in military equipment, tactics, and organization, such as the emergence of the hoplite army organized by the *polis*, wherein the aristocrats tended to be generals or members of the cavalry, eroded the more strictly martial purposes found in the pre-classical *symposion*.[86]

The *symposion* of the Classical Period of ancient Greek history became a refuge, a retreat from the world, including the world of politics, where aristocratic influence was on the wane.[87] Increasingly its aim became the pleasure/delight (*euphrosyne*) of the participants.[88] Influences from the Near East began to appear, one of the more important being the custom of reclining on a *kline* or banquet couch.[89] Only men normally reclined in this fashion; women and youth, if present at all, would typically sit nearby (Xenophon *Symposium* 1.8). Wives and other "respectable" women never or almost never attended symposia (Plato *Symposium* 176e).[90] Female participants consisted of musicians, dancers and acrobats, *hetairai* (courtesans) and slaves. Or in other words "the only women who participated [in the *symposion*] were those with no reputation to lose."[91] The intoxication of *hetairai* was "according to Athenaeus, a commonplace of the comic tradition (10.587b)."[92] On many painted vases prostitutes and courtesans are visible joining in the pleasures of the *krater*.[93] This is not to imply that other Greek women, even elite women, were forbidden to drink wine, as at least some Roman women apparently were.[94] Greek women regularly drank wine for recreational, ritual and medicinal purposes.[95] The drunken old woman with an unquenchable thirst for wine was a commonplace of Old, Middle and New Comedy and there is reason to believe "the figure of the drunken sorceress was a standard one" in comedy as well.[96] The Athenian Stranger in Plato's *Laws* (637c), in response to Megillus' negative comment about the Dionysia celebrated in Athens—where women and slaves were allowed to celebrate with citizen men—seems to imply that among other vices Spartan women would get drunk. In any event, according to Athenaeus, the fondness of women for wine was common knowledge (10.440e).[97]

Temporally the *symposion*, when the recreational drinking took place, was the second half of the *deipnon*, a dinner party.[98] A meal generally without wine would first be eaten. After the meal it was customary to make offerings, accompanied by prayer, of unmixed wine to the Good Spirit (*Agathos Daimon*), followed by three offerings of wine to Olympian Zeus and Hera, the heroes, and Zeus the Savior (Aristophanes *Wasps* 525 and 1217, and cf. Plato *Philebus* 66d and *Symposium* 176a). According to Theophrastus in a surviving fragment of his *On Drunkenness*, this unmixed wine was drunk "only in small quantity" as a lawful acknowledgement of the powers being invoked, "as a reminder, through a mere taste, of the strength of the god's gift" (Athenaeus 15.693d). Wine was a substance that could only be consumed cautiously, being "a *pharmakon* [drug] which sends men mad if they do not control its consumption as regards strength and quality."[99] Only after this offering of unmixed wine would the recreational drinking commence.

A female *aulos* player was normally expected at a well-to-do *symposion*.[100] As skilled labor they were expensive to hire.[101] The usual drinking and entertainment would typically commence when the *auletris* began to play. In Aristophanes' *Wasps* the music of the *aulos* is identified as the instigator of the party-songs Bdelycleon expects Philocleon to be prepared for at the *symposion* they are attending (1219–1222).[102] In Xenophon's *Symposium* the evening's entertainment consists of "a fine [*auletris*], a dancing girl—one of those skilled in acrobatic tricks—and a very handsome boy, who was expert at playing the cither and at dancing" (2.1). As the evening's drinking intensified there would appear to have been many occasions when the sexual satisfaction of the male participants became a priority.[103] A female *auletris* was, it appears, customarily the subject of mock auctions "most certainly not for [their] musical services."[104] Practices of this sort were commonplace for other female entertainers as well.[105]

The *symposion*'s rules were intended to establish "a setting of shared pleasure," pleasures arranged with the psychic and physical satisfaction of the participants in mind.[106] Drinking, music, dance, and the erotic, all mixed with conversation. At the center of the *symposion* was the mixing bowl, a large *krater*. The *krater* was the starting point for the distribution of wine.[107] As a container holding mixed wine the *krater* was a symbol of civilization, whereas the goatskin, for example, held pure wine. This is mirrored in the drinking vessels: the *skyphos* was for mixed wine, the Scythian drinking horn, the *rhyton*, for pure wine.[108] Water from the *hydria* or water jug would typically be placed into the *krater* with a ladle called the *kyanthos*, and the prepared libation served in a bowl-like drinking cup (*kylix, kantharos,* or *kotyle*). Symposiasts would generally pass the cup around, from left to right. *Kraters* would be emptied one after another in this fashion. Light foods, called *tragemata* (things to chew with wine), would be served as a compliment to the recreational drinking.[109]

Numerous drinking games would be played at symposia. Several were based on balance, using for example an inflated greased wine-skin (*askos*), the player trying to stay upright (*orthos*). This game of the wine-skin, or *askoliasmos*, generated a kind of displacement, only it was the container itself, rather than the wine, that disoriented and dizzied the drinker.[110] The Greek word for headache/dizziness, *karos*, appears to be related to the Akkadian *karu* (to be dizzy) and the Aramaic *karah* (to be ill), hence "one can imagine that the term came to the Greeks from the eastern banqueting fashions."[111] According to the Greek historian Philochoros (fl. third century BCE), Dionysus taught Amphictyon, ruler of Athens, the fineries of mixing wine; the king "erected an alter to Dionysus the upstanding (*orthos*)" in honor of this art that allowed "men . . . to stay upright while drinking" (Athenaeus 2.38c–d). On many vases one finds, in the depiction of the *komos*, "a series of juggling tricks played with items of drinking equipment," a virtuosity that is one of the *komos*' defining elements, since wine, dancing and music frequently merged, often in a context that expressed aristocratic contempt for democratic authority.[112]

Other games involved aim and judgment, such as the oft-depicted game known as *kottabos*, wherein contestants flicked wine at various kinds of targets. Before letting the wine fly a declaration was made, frequently to a lover, and if the target lost its equilibrium it indicated both "the uncertainty that takes hold of a lover in the presence of the beloved" and a divinatory indication of "amorous success."[113] Wine, both when drunk and when played with, had the power to reveal *truth*. Riddles, word games, and jokes would also be told in the course of the *symposion* (e.g. see Athenaeus 10.457c–f, and Plato *Republic* 479b–480a). Evidently winners might receive "kisses which were loathsome to men of independent feelings, while the penalty imposed upon those who are beaten is to drink unmixed wine, which they do more gladly than they would the cup of health" (Athenaeus 10.475d). One of the drinking songs of the *symposion*, the *skolion*, in which the singers strove to outdo each other, was frequently political or moral in nature (Aristophanes *Wasps* 1220–28, Plato *Gorgias* 451e).[114] Guests would lampoon each other as well (Aristophanes *Wasps* 1299–1321, Plato *Symposium* 215a–b).

Drinking Ethics

Within the *symposion* the social norms that governed ordinary public life could, for a time, be ignored or disobeyed. Despite the outrageous behavior of some symposiasts, however, this should not be understood as an indication of a complete absence of restraint or a condition where anything and everything was permitted. The sympotic celebration usually occurred within the structure of a "series of ritual acts regulated by a very precise set of norms."[115] It was a social ritual in the broadest sense, comprising a "series of acts that [were] strictly codified and ordered prior to their accomplishment."[116] Within this unwritten codification any written laws of the *polis* that may have existed were secondary to what may be termed an *ethical-aesthetic sensibility* that each gathering consensually imposed upon itself, and might vary significantly depending on the particular locality and the individual gathering.[117] This sensibility had four defining elements.

First, the *symposion* was a medium for the orchestration of a regulated intoxication, an "elaborate *ars bibendi* [art of drinking]."[118] An ad hoc "ruler" or "king" would act as a moderator of the drinking. Plato refers to this individual as *archon* in both the *Symposium* (213e) and *Laws* (640d), although *basileus*, *symposiarchos*, and other terms were also used in the Classical Period. The *symposiarchos*, as overseer of the festivities, would define the rules for the mixing of the drinks, the number of *kraters* to be drunk, and other rules for drinking, striving for a successful balance between the dull rationality of the sober man, the extreme of complete abstinence (*nephein*) on the one hand, and wild Dionysiac irrationality or harmful drunkenness (*methyesthai, paroinein, kraipalan*) on the other.[119]

The Greeks proudly defined themselves by this at least nominally regulated intoxication, contrasting it to the behavior of various barbarian races, as the lyric poet Anacreon (570–488 BCE) apparently did: "Let's not fall into drunken disorder with our wine, like the Scythians, but let us drink in moderation listening to the lovely hymns" (Athenaeus 10.427a–b). One can see the same sentiment expressed in Plato's *Laws* (637d–e), where the Athenian visitor compares the extreme policy of complete abstention from drunkenness practiced by the Spartans, and smugly lauded by Megillus, to such belligerent races as the Persians, Carthaginians, Celts (of Gaul), Iberians, and especially the Scythians and Thracians who "drink wine completely undiluted, women as well as men, and pour it over their cloaks, believing that they're engaging in a fine and happy practice."[120] Xenophon in his *Anabasis* speaks of the Armenians' strange drinking habits, which include "slurping (*rhophounta*) like an ox" (4.5.32). People such as these were regarded as being incapable of making appropriate use of wine, traditionally the last of the drugs Dionysus gave as a gift to man (Aristophanes *Archanians* 77–79). The same difficulty existed among many Greeks as well. In Plato's *Minos*, in contrast to the lawgiver Minos who was a confidant of Zeus and who instituted laws "not to drink together to the point of drunkenness," there are others who take confidant to mean "drinking companion and playfellow of Zeus" (319e–320b). They say nothing, Socrates says, for among the "many human beings both Greek and barbarian" only the Cretans and the Lacedaemonians (who learned from the Cretans) "refrain from drinking parties and from the play that takes place where there is wine" and drunkenness (320a).

Second, the *symposion* may be seen as a space within which ancient Greek society provided for the controlled disruption of identity, a careful invocation of ecstasy. The drinking of wine and the ritual around it allowed for "experience at another level," a brief sojourn "outside normal boundaries."[121] Symposia granted the "extraordinary but necessary experience of the Other" in a society where the exclusion of women, slaves, and foreigners from citizenship formed the basis of the entire political structure.[122] Reflecting on this exclusion, the natural philosopher Thales (ca. 640–546 BCE) was reputed to have given three reasons for being grateful to the gods: "First, because by birth I am human and not a beast; second, because I am a man and not a woman; and finally because I am a Greek and not a foreigner" (Diogenes Laertius, *Lives* 1.33).

One finds a number of ancient Greek drinking containers in the shape of a human head (or two heads joined back to back). These vessels depict "only women, male and female blacks, Asians, and satyrs."[123] The Greek male is never found, as though these vases were "meant to define the opposite of the Greek drinker and to hold up to him all the things that he was not."[124] Mixing bowls also depict male symposiasts dressed in the garb of the Other: as women, barbarians like the Scythians, and most especially as satyrs, the half-man, half-animal creatures who comprised Dionysus's male retinue. In sum the experience of wine in the regulated atmosphere of the *symposion* allowed for "an interference in the axiological articulation of the social microcosm concerned," an intentional provocation of the negative forces, dysphoric and/or aggressive, that intoxication is capable of generating and which constitute an ever present danger.[125]

Third, within the social setting of the *symposion* there can be found an elaborate system of communication, what has been called a *logos sympotikos*. The *symposion* was "a deliberate, controlled, collective exploration of the universe of the passions, not without anxieties about elements of contravention which can reveal themselves once passions have been unleashed by drunkenness."[126] This anxiety stemmed from the understanding that unlike the god Dionysus, who could drink any amount of unmixed wine, human beings could "only approach this drug by controlling . . . the proper use of wine within the framework of a regulated conviviality."[127] That framework was almost entirely ethical and discursive in nature.[128]

Poetry of virtually any form might be read in the course of the *symposion* including: "light verse, love poems, and admonitory or political verse," improvised by the talented, prepared beforehand by the less gifted.[129] Songs would be sung, either solo or choral (Plato *Symposium* 180e). The result was a verbal confrontation of the symposiasts, a contest, and an exhibition of their individual abilities, exposed to the scrutiny of the group. Beneath the pursuit of the group's collective pleasure and gratification (*euphrosyne*) each participant risked the "self-representation . . . constructed as part of their participation in social life," exposing this delicate mask to each others scrutiny.[130] In this agonistic interplay both positive and negative models of ethical and aesthetic behavior were established: sympotic discourse was often "*determinative* and *normative*."[131]

Fourth, a favorite topic of discussion at the *symposion* was the subject of *eros* and the pleasures of love. Contemporary philosophical discussion seems practically addicted to this particular aspect of the *symposion*, perhaps influenced by the sanitizing tendencies of Plato's and Xenophon's works. In these discussions one reads a relatively straightforward investigation that takes as its starting point that the subject of a work like Plato's *Symposium* is *eros*, a term conveying sexual desire, affection broadly speaking, or a powerful preference of some sort.[132] It is not my intention to dispute such a reading. The discussion of *eros* was certainly an important element of the *symposion*, one that functioned as a release for "a complex series of emotional pressures," and could find expression in a variety of forms, from the sort of elevated discourse found in Plato's *Symposium* to light-hearted banter between enthusiasts of hetero and homosexual love, to "the most unregulated orgiastic . . . practices."[133] In contrast to the conventional approach, my own is that the first three features of the *symposion* deserve equally close scrutiny. Plato does not have much to say about the pleasures of the food that could be found at the *symposion* and, in all truth, says little about that institution's tangible sexual practices.[134] The praise or admonishment of these pleasures were manifestly important to many ancient writers, as any reader of Athenaeus could attest. Concerning the ecstatic pleasures of intoxication within the *symposion*, however, Plato says considerably more.

Notes

1. In addition to alcohol this work will discuss and present evidence for the existence of several other mind-altering drugs in Classical Greece. These include opium (*Papaver somniferum*), wormwood (*Artemsia absinthium*), ergot (*Claviceps purpurea*), frankincense or oblibanum (*Boswell carteri*), hemp (*Cannabis sativa*), henbane (*Hyoscyamus niger*), belladonna (*Atropa belladonna*), mandrake (*Mandragora officinarum*), myrrh (*Commiphora myrrha*), and certain psychotropic mushrooms.

2. The Anthesteria, a festival of the new wine, may be characterized as a religious-public intoxication. The City Dionysia, where wine drinking and sacrifices took place

prior to theatrical performances, may be thought of as primarily recreational-public, although the high priest of Dionysus was seated in the front row during performances. The intoxication of the *symposion* was recreational-private, while the ritual libations poured to commence the drinking at the *symposion* were religious-private.

3. The wild grape is dioecious; the male flowers rarely produce fruit. The fruit that is produced has many seeds, a tough skin, is high in acid and low in the sugar that is essential to the fermentation process.

4. Patrick E. McGovern, *Ancient Wine: The Search for the Origins of Viniculture* (Princeton, NJ: Princeton University Press, 2003), 8–11. Even if wine was known during this period, McGovern writes, "Paleolithic humans would have had little control over the fermentation process."

5. R. J. Forbes, *Studies in Ancient Technology, Vol. 3* (Leiden, Netherlands: E. J. Brill, 1965), 61 and McGovern, *Ancient Wine*, 65–68. Humans may have learned how to control fire as much as 1.7 million years ago. Cereal agriculture, something that made possible year-round food reserves, dates back to at least 9,500 BCE. Pottery has been in use since about 6,000 BCE.

6. See McGovern, *Ancient Wine*, 64–84.

7. McGovern, *Ancient Wine*, 48–49, 300–301. See also my Introduction, above.

8. McGovern, *Ancient Wine*, 64–68, 72–73.

9. McGovern, *Ancient Wine*, 14.

10. McGovern, *Ancient Wine*, 247–59.

11. When the destruction of war led to homelessness these oversized *pithoi* were used as a form of emergency housing. Aristophanes' *Knights* (795) refers to these "vat-sleepers" or *pithaknai*.

12. Tim Unwin, *Wine and the Vine* (New York: Routledge, 1996), 94–133. Plato mentions "Sarambus the [wine] dealer" in the *Gorgias* (518b).

13. Forbes, *Studies Vol. 3*, 112. Forbes goes on to say that "Greek colonization and the introduction of Greek wine" were practically identical. See also Plato, *Laws* 637d–e.

14. Carl A. P. Ruck, "The Wild and the Cultivated: Wine in Euripides' *Bacchae*," in R. Gordon Wasson, Stella Kramrisch, Carl A. P. Ruck, and Jonathan Ott, *Persephone's Quest: Entheogens and the Origin of Religion*, (New Haven, CT: Yale University Press, 1986), 197. Cf. Herbert G. Baker, *Plants and Civilization* (Belmont, CA: Wadsworth Publishing, 1970), 120, and R. Gordon Wasson, Albert Hofmann and Carl A. P. Ruck, *The Road to Eleusis* (Los Angeles: William Dailey Rare Books, 1998), 99.

15. Arthur P. McKinlay, "Attic Temperance," *Quarterly Journal of Studies on Alcohol*, 12, no. 1 (1951): 84.

16. Unless otherwise noted quotes from Athenaeus' *The Deipnosophists* (hereafter simply Athenaeus) are from Charles Burton Gulick, trans., *Athenaeus—The Deipnosophists* [7 Volumes] (New York: Cambridge University Press, 1951).

17. McGovern, *Ancient Wine*, 308–309.

18. See for example Benjamin Parsons, *Anti-Bacchus* (London: John Snow, 1840), 74–93. Unlike many twentieth-century scholars Parsons recognizes that ancient wines were frequently drugged. Contemporary Christian texts emphasize, like Parsons, the creation and drinking of a non-alcoholic beverage based on grapes boiled down to a thick syrup, to which water could later be added, confusing it with wine more generally, arguing in essence that in contrast to we "decadent moderns" the ancients were fundamentally grape-juice drinking teetotalers. See for example Robert Stein, "Wine-Drinking in New Testament Times," *Christianity Today*, June 20, 1975, 9–11.

19. McKinlay, "Attic Temperance," 84.

20. Oswyn Murray, *Early Greece,* 2nd Edition (Cambridge, MA: Harvard University Press, 1993), 208.

21. François Lissarrague, *The Aesthetics of the Greek Banquet* (Princeton, NJ: Princeton University Press, 1990), 6.

22. Walter Burkert, *Ancient Mystery Cults* (Cambridge, MA: Harvard University Press, 1987), 112.

23. See for example Elizabeth Belfiore, "Wine and Catharsis of the Emotions in Plato's *Laws*," *Classical Quarterly* 36, no. 2 (1986): 430. While almost reluctantly agreeing that "the Greeks got, if anything, even more drunk than do modern imbibers," Belfiore resists conceding that the wine the Greeks drank contained anything more potent than alcohol. She mischaracterizes the "intriguing but controversial" arguments made by Carl A. P. Ruck in *The Road to Eleusis* as *only* arguing that "Greek wine was mixed with hallucinogens as well as water." In truth Ruck's position has always been that "Greek wines . . . *in some cases* were actually more hallucinogens than alcoholic beverages." Ruck, "The Wild and the Cultivated," 197, emphasis mine. Belfiore refers her reader to the work of Walter Burkert. Burkert does not even concede that the Greeks got more drunk than modern imbibers, still less that they possessed any drug other than wine, and misunderstands or grotesquely misrepresents (depending on one's level of generosity) the arguments made by Ruck in *The Road to Eleusis.*

24. Max Nelson, *A Barbarian's Beverage: A History of Beer in Ancient Europe,* (New York: Routledge, 2005), 2.

25. Regarding the oxidation of ethanol to acetaldehyde by direct chemical reaction with air, see H. L. Wildenradt and V. L. Singleton, "The Production of Aldehydes as a Result of Oxidation of Polyphenolic Compounds and its Relation to Wine Aging," *American Journal of Enology and Viticulture* 25, no. 2 (1974) and Andrew L. Waterhouse and V. Felipe Laurie, "Oxidation of Wine Phenolics: A Critical Evaluation and Hypothesis," *American Journal of Enology and Viticulture* 57, no. 3 (2006).

26. A mere four ounces of methanol is usually fatal. Initial symptoms include headache, dizziness, nausea, confusion and drowsiness, and progress to a second stage that includes blurred or complete loss of vision, and may progress to death by respiratory failure.

27. See Agnes Carr Vaughan, *Madness in Greek Thought and Custom* (Baltimore, MD: J. H. Furst Company, 1919), 51. Vaughn notes that "when madness was caused by drinking certain wines, the *Lapis Topazontes* hung about the neck was believed to be of curative value." A healing talisman, like a medicinal remedy, could be called a *pharmakon.* See chapter 8, below.

28. See Forbes, *Studies Vol. 3,* 141 and Fernand Braudel, *Civilization and Capitalism, 15th–18th Century, Vol. 1* (New York: Harper and Row, 1981), 241–42. The introduction of distillation in Western and Southern Europe is discussed in the afterword, below.

29. Forbes, *Studies Vol. 3,* 77, and McGovern, *Ancient Wine,* 309.

30. A pine native to the Mediterranean whose range extends from Morocco to the Levant.

31. Carl A. P. Ruck, "On the Sacred Name of Iamos and Ion," *The Classical Journal* 71, no. 3 (1976): 241.

32. The practice was widespread in the ancient world. Forbes, *Studies Vol. 3,* 73, mentions Mesopotamia and Palestine. McGovern, *Ancient Wine,* 95–209 includes both these locations as well several others, such as Egypt and several Near East cultures.

33. Today, we still speak of a wine's "bouquet," an echo and perhaps a surviving trace vestige of these ancient practices.

34. Forbes, *Studies Vol. 3*, 80. The traditional view is that wood barrels were not used until the third century CE by the Romans, who borrowed the practice from the Gauls. McGovern, *Ancient Wine*, 262–63 suspects that, given how sophisticated ancient shipbuilding technology was, including "a knowledge of toasting oak staves to bend them" the "tradition of ageing wine in oak barrels might have a much earlier pedigree." This however remains simply speculation. The cork stopper was not incorporated into the manufacture of wine until well into the seventeenth century.

35. McGovern, *Ancient Wine*, 71–72.

36. McGovern, *Ancient Wine*, 309. The Greek for turpentine, *terebinthine*, derives from the terebinth tree. See Robert K. Barnhart, *The Barnhart Concise Dictionary of Etymology* (New York: Harper Collins, 1995).

37. McGovern, *Ancient Wine*, 69–72.

38. The evidence from the Neolithic village of Hajji Firuz located in what is now northwestern Iran is strong, while Minoan *pithoi* dating to 2,200 BCE "represent the earliest chemical evidence for resinated wine from ancient Greece." See McGovern, *Ancient Wine*, 250.

39. See McGovern, *Ancient Wine*, 311–312. The sangria of southern Spain would be another example.

40. Forbes, *Studies Vol. 3*, 117–18, and McGovern, *Ancient Wine*, 309–310.

41. McGovern, *Ancient Wine*, 309.

42. Harold Tarrant, "Wine in Ancient Greece—Some Platonist Ponderings," in *Wine and Philosophy*, ed. Fritz Allhoff (Malden, MA: Blackwell Publishing, 2008), 15.

43. McGovern, *Ancient Wine*, 310.

44. All references from the *Iliad* and *Odyssey* in this chapter are from the translations by Robert Fagles, and refer to the line numbers of his translation, not the line numbers of the original Greek text. Robert Fagles, trans., *Homer—The Iliad* (New York: Penguin Press, 1990) and Robert Fagles, trans., *Homer—The Odyssey* (New York: Penguin, 1996). Wine is referred to as *melieides* in the *Iliad* at 4.401, 6.307, 8.586, 10.670, 12.371, and 18.634, and in the *Odyssey* at 3.46, 9.208, 14.78, and 16.52. Wine is referred to as *meliphron* in the *Iliad* at 8.586, 8.634, and 24.336, and in the *Odyssey* at 7.216, 10.394, 13.61, and 15.163. Additional references to wine in Homer's epic poetry are mentioned in chapter 2, below.

45. McGovern, *Ancient Wine*, 71 and 133.

46. Georg Luck, *Arcana Mundi—Magic and the Occult in the Greek and Roman Worlds*, (Baltimore, MD: The Johns Hopkins University Press, 2006), 485.

47. McGovern, *Ancient Wine*, 309. Absinthe, a highly alcoholic liqueur containing wormwood, anise and other botanicals, is reemerging as a legal product after a century of widespread prohibition.

48. P. G. Kritikos and S. P. Papadaki, "The History of the Poppy and of Opium and their Expansion in Antiquity in the Eastern Mediterranean Area," *Bulletin on Narcotics* 19, no. 3 (1967), 8–9, and John Scarborough, "The Opium Poppy in Hellenistic and Roman Medicine," in *Drugs and Narcotics in History*, ed. Roy Porter and Mikulas Teich (New York: Cambridge University Press, 1995), 4 for example. On the Greek word for "drug," *pharmakon*, see chapter 4, below.

49. Helen's *pharmakon* as well as several other drugs found in the *Odyssey* are discussed in chapter 4, below.

50. Kritikos and Papadaki, "The History of the Poppy," 22.

51. Christopher A. Faraone, *Ancient Greek Love Magic* (Cambridge, MA: Harvard University Press, 1999), 126.

52. Additional references to oleander in ancient sources may be found in Wilhelmina Mary Feemster Jashemski and Frederick G. Meyer, *The Natural History of Pompeii* (New York: Cambridge University Press, 2002), 133.

53. Oleander contains several potent toxins including oleandrin and nerioside, which are very similar to foxglove. The sap can cause skin irritations, severe eye inflammation and irritation, and allergy reactions characterized by dermatitis. In addition to gastrointestinal and cardiac effects the plant can also affect the central nervous system, with symptoms including drowsiness, tremors, shaking of the muscles, seizures, collapse, and even coma that can lead to death.

54. Randall B. Clark, *The Law Most Beautiful and Best: Medical Argument and Magical Rhetoric in Plato's* Laws (Lanham, MD: Lexington Books, 2003), 45 n. 16.

55. Anthony Preus, "Drugs and Psychic States in Theophrastus' *History of Plants* 9.8–20," in *Theophrastean Studies*, ed. William W. Fortenbaugh and Robert W. Sharples (New Brunswick, NJ and Oxford, UK: Transaction Books, 1988), 87. See my discussion of *ekstasis* in chapter 2, below.

56. Richard Evans Schultes and Albert Hofmann, *Plants of the Gods—Their Sacred, Healing and Hallucinogenic Powers* (Rochester, VT: Healing Arts Press, 1992), 86, and see also 49, 87–90. Additional discussions may be found in John Scarborough, "The Pharmacology of Sacred Plants, Herbs, and Roots," in *Magika Hiera—Ancient Greek Magic and Religion*, ed. Christopher A. Faraone and Dirk Obbink (New York and Oxford: Oxford University Press, 1991), 158, and Richard Rudgley, *The Alchemy of Culture—Intoxicants in Society* (London: British Museum Press, 1993), 93–95.

57. As Nelson points out the alcohol consumed by ancient Europeans was quite different than ours. Lacking our rigid categories of what constituted "wine" or "beer" or "mead," they thought nothing of blending together "various fruits, or fruits and honey, fruits and cereals, honey and cereals, or even fruits, honey, and cereals. Furthermore, numerous types of plants, spices, and other substances (including narcotic drugs) could be added to the beverage before or after fermentation." Nelson, *A Barbarian's Beverage*, 2. McGovern calls this blending of wine, barley beer, and mead "grog" and discusses the creation of such mixtures by the Greeks. See McGovern, *Ancient Wine*, 239–78. He takes no firm position on Greek wines containing the "other substances" Nelson mentions, often implying the likelihood of "narcotic substances" having been mixed into wine but then gingerly sidestepping the matter.

58. McGovern, *Ancient Wine*, 308–312.

59. Desiderius Erasmus (1466–1536 CE), a Christian theologian and classical scholar, writes "Zenodotus tells us that in Sicily Morychus was a nickname for Bacchus." Quoted in Roger Aubrey Baskerville Mynors, *Collected Works of Erasmus (Volume 34) Adages IIviiI to IIIiiiI00* (Toronto: University of Toronto Press, 1992), 89.

60. Lissarrague, *The Aesthetics of the Greek Banquet*, 107–22, and cf. M. Davies, "Sailing, Rowing and Sporting in One's Cup on the Wine Dark Sea," in *Athens Comes of Age: From Solon to Salamis*, ed. William A. P. Childs (Princeton, NJ: Princeton University Press, 1978), 72–92.

61. Forbes, *Studies Vol. 3*, 63.

62. Nelson, *A Barbarian's Beverage*, 1.

63. Maguelonne Toussaint-Samat, *History of Food* (Boston: Blackwell Publishing, 1994), 34–38 and Eva Crane, *The World History of Beekeeping and Honey Hunting* (New York: Routledge, 1999), 513–14.

64. A detailed recipe for preparing mead may be found in *On Agriculture (De Re Rustica)* by the Roman writer Columella (ca. 4–70 CE).

65. On Poros see Arlene W. Saxonhouse, *Fear of Diversity: The Birth of Political Science in Ancient Greek Thought* (Chicago: University of Chicago Press, 1995), 174–75 as well as Kevin Corrigan and Elena Glazov-Corrigan, *Plato's Dialectic at Play: Argument, Structure and Myth in the* Symposium (University Park, PA: Penn State Press, 2004), 121–22.

66. Rudgley, *The Alchemy of Culture*, 31. A more detailed discussion of beer's origins may be found in Nelson, *A Barbarian's Beverage*, 9–24.

67. Nelson, *A Barbarian's Beverage*, 25.

68. Nelson, *A Barbarian's Beverage*, 32.

69. Forbes, *Studies Vol. 3*, 73. See also R. J. Forbes, "Food and Drink," in *A History of Technology, Volume 2—The Mediterranean Civilizations to the Middle Ages c. 700 BC—c. AD 1500*, ed. Charles Singer, E. J. Holmyard, A. R. Hall and Trevor I. Williams (New York: Oxford University Press, 1956), 128–29, and McGovern, *Ancient Wine*, 149.

70. McGovern, *Ancient Wine*, 296.

71. Carl Kerényi, *Dionysus—Archetypal Image of Indestructible Life* (Princeton, NJ: Pantheon Books, 1976), 35–36, and Rudgley, *The Alchemy of Culture*, 39.

72. Ruck, "The Wild and the Cultivated," 208.

73. Carl A. P. Ruck, *Sacred Mushrooms of the Goddess and the Secrets of Eleusis,* (Berkeley, CA: Ronin Publishing, 2006): 165.

74. See my discussion of the cult of Dionysus in chapter 4, below.

75. Oswyn Murray, *Early Greece,* 1st Edition (Palo Alto, CA: Stanford University Press, 1983), 265; Pellizer 1990: 181.

76. Using Athenaeus to bring to life aspects of the symposion in the Classical Greece must of course be done with some caution. Peter Garnsey, *Food and Society in Classical Antiquity,* (New York: Cambridge University Press, 1999), 74 wryly observes that if Athenaeus were our only source for Plato's *Republic* "we would possess only a minor part of an intriguing exchange [372a] between Glaucon and Socrates, in the course of which Socrates presents two dietary regimes for his new citizens, one frugal ... one luxurious."

77. Ezio Pellizer, "Outlines of a Morphology of Sympotic Entertainment," in *Sympotica—A Symposium on the* Symposion, ed. Oswyn Murray (Oxford: Clarendon Press, 1990), 177.

78. Joseph M. Bryant, *Moral Codes and Social Structure in Ancient Greece: A Sociology of Greek Ethics from Homer to the Epicureans and Stoic* (Albany, NY: State University of New York Press, 1996), 83.

79. Oswyn Murray, *Early Greece,* 2nd Edition (Cambridge, MA: Harvard University Press, 1993), 208, see also O. Murray, *Early Greece* [1st Edition], 264, and Von Blackenhagen 1992: 54–55).

80. Lissarrague, *The Aesthetics of the Greek Banquet,* 14, and cf. O. Murray, *Early Greece, 2nd Edition,* 208.

81. Oswyn Murray, "Forms of Sociability," in *The Greeks,* ed. Jean-Pierre Vernant (Chicago: University of Chicago Press, 1995), 224.

82. O. Murray, *Early Greece,* 2nd Edition, 207, and cf. O. Murray "Forms of Sociability," 221, Bryant, *Moral Codes and Social Structure in Ancient Greece,* 83, and Garnsey, *Food in Classical Antiquity,* 130.

83. O. Murray, "Forms of Sociability," 221.

84. O. Murray, *Early Greece,* 1st Edition, 259–60. See for example *Odyssey* 9.5–10 and 14.228–290.

85. O. Murray, "Forms of Sociability," 222.

86. O. Murray, *Early Greece,* 1st Edition, 263.

87. Barry S. Strauss, *Athens after the Peloponnesian War: Class, Faction and Policy 403–386 BC* (Ithaca, NY: Cornell University Press, 1986), 11–12.

88. O. Murray, "Forms of Sociability," 229.

89. O. Murray, *Early Greece*, 1st Edition, 263, Walter Burkert, *The Orientalizing Revolution—Near Eastern Influences on Greek Culture in the Early Archaic Age* (Cambridge, MA: Harvard University Press, 1992), 79. O. Murray, "Forms of Sociability," 224 writes that "Reclining as part of an established set of social customs is first attested by the prophet Amos in Samaria in the eighth century (Amos 6.3–7), and it may well have been a custom adopted by the Greeks from contact with Phoenician culture."

90. Women remained in the spaces within the home specifically designated for them, such as the *gynaeceum.* O. Murray, "Forms of Sociability," 230 writes that citizen women "were never present at Greek symposia; there is no evidence that they even attended wedding feasts and funeral feasts, two areas with which women are traditionally closely connected." Women may have had their own forms of feasting and commensality, but virtually no evidence survives to indicate what it may have consisted of or looked like.

91. Bryant, *Moral Codes and Social Structure in Ancient Greece*, 109.

92. Laura McClure, *Courtesans at Table: Gender and Greek Literary Culture in Athenaeus* (New York: Routledge, 2003), 73. Athenaeus even indicates the nickname of one courtesan was Paroinos, a word than McClure translates as "drunken" although most other sources translate this word along the lines of "fond of sitting beside wine" and the same word can also mean "quarrelsome" and "violent" leaving the meaning of the nickname ambiguous.

93. Matthew W. Dickie, *Magic and Magicians in the Greco-Roman World* (New York: Routledge, 2001), 90.

94. During the time of the Greek historian Polybius (ca. 203–120 BCE). See Dickie, *Magic and Magicians in the Greco-Roman World*, 184–87 who in addition to Polybius mentions Fabius Pictor, Cato the Elder, Cicero, and others. Denied wine, Roman women were reported to have drunk a raisin-based alcohol called *passum.* See for example Athenaeus 10.440e. The attitude of the Romans toward female intoxication is discussed in Arthur P. McKinlay, "The Roman Attitude Towards Women Drinking," in *Drinking and Intoxication: Selected Readings in Social Attitudes and Controls*, ed. R. G. McCarthy (Glencoe, IL: The Free Press, 1959), 58–61 and E. M. Jellinek, Carole D. Yawney, and Robert E. Popham, "Drinkers and Alcoholics in Ancient Rome," *Journal of Studies on Alcohol* 37, no. 11 (1976): 1729–30.

95. Lisa Marie Elliot, *Gendering the Production and Consumption of Wine and Olive Oil in Ancient Greece* (M.A. thesis, Miami University, 2006), 29–37.

96. Dickie, *Magic and Magicians in the Greco-Roman World*, 89–91. The significance of these depictions lies not in their accuracy but rather their appeal to the expectations of their audience; drunkenness is an expected behavior of aging *hetairai.*

97. Dickie, *Magic and Magicians in the Greco-Roman World*, 185 writes that the epithets given to old women in the *Greek Anthology* (6.291, 7.353, 7.455, 7.456, 7.457, 11.409) reflect their fondness for wine.

98. Garnsey, *Food and Society in Classical Antiquity*, 129. See also O. Murray, "Forms of Sociability," 224–25.

99. Lissarrague, *The Aesthetics of the Greek Banquet*, 202.

100. Different instruments went by the name *aulos* (plural *auloi*), including a single piped instrument called the *monaulos*, and a single piped instrument held horizontally, as the modern flute, called the *plagiaulos*, both of which were reedless, but the most common variety was a double-reeded instrument like an oboe. The word "*aulos*" (meaning

"tube" or "duct") is often translated as "flute" though this is technically accurate only when referring to the *plagiaulos* when in fact what is meant is the double-reeded instrument. I have retained the Greek in most instances to avoid any confusion. Greater detail on the *aulos* may be found in Sheramy D. Bundrick, *Music and Image in Classical Athens* (New York: Cambridge University Press, 2005), 34.

101. Chester G. Starr, "An Evening with the Flute Girls," *La Parola del Passato* 33, no. 183 (1978): 406–7. The music of the *aulos* is discussed in greater detail in chapter 3, below.

102. One of the most popular games at symposia consisted of one guest singing a line or two from a song, while holding a myrtle-branch. He would then pass the branch to another reveler, who would then have the choice of continuing the song faithfully, ad-libbing new lyrics, or singing the lines from yet another song with a related theme. See Alan H. Sommerstein, *The Comedies of Aristophanes, Vol. 4* (Warminster, Wilts, England: Aris and Phillips, 1983), 228, and Lissarrague, *The Aesthetics of the Greek Banquet*, 129.

103. Starr, "An Evening with the Flute Girls," 408, O. Murray, *Early Greece, 2nd Edition*, 210, 214.

104. Pellizer, "Outlines of a Morphology of Sympotic Entertainment," 181. See also T. B. L. Webster, *Athenian Culture and Society* (Berkeley and Los Angeles: University of California Press, 1973), 53–54, Sheramy Bundrick, *Music and Image in Classical Athens*, 39 (figure 24) and cf. Athenaeus 13.607d–e.

105. See McClure, *Courtesans at the Table*, 21–22.

106. Lissarrague, *The Aesthetics of the Greek Banquet*, 19.

107. Once mixed the wine would be cooled in a vessel known as the *psykter*. See O. Murray, "Forms of Sociability," 225.

108. François Lissarrague, "Around the Krater: An Aspect of Banquet Imagery," in *Sympotica—A Symposium on the* Symposion, ed. Oswyn Murray (Oxford: Clarendon Press, 1990), 202, and Lissarrague, *Aesthetics of the Greek Banquet*, 90–91.

109. Kathy K. Kaufman, *Cooking in Ancient Civilizations* (Westport, CT: Greenwood Press, 2006), 79. These included "fruits, often dried, and sweet pastries as well as savory items, such as fresh beans, tiny birds, nuts, and cheeses." See also Elizabeth Craik, "Diet, *Diaita* and Dietetics," in *The Greek World*, ed. Anton Powell (London: Routledge, 1995), 391, who discusses Plato's use of *tragemata* in *Republic* 372c–d.

110. Lissarrague, *The Aesthetics of the Greek Banquet*, 72.

111. Walter Burkert, *The Orientalizing Revolution—Near Eastern Influences on Greek Culture in the Early Archaic Age* (Cambridge, MA: Harvard University Press, 1992), 79.

112. See chapter 2, below.

113. Lissarrague, *The Aesthetics of the Greek Banquet*, 80–85.

114. See O. Murray, *Early Greece*, 2nd Edition, 210, 274, 280 and Webster, *Athenian Culture and Society*, 166.

115. Pellizer, "Outline of a Morphology of Sympotic Entertainment," 178.

116. Lissarrague, *The Aesthetics of the Greek Banquet*, 25.

117. The term "ethical-aesthetic sensibility" is borrowed from William E. Connolly, *The Augustinian Imperative: A Reflection on the Politics of Morality* (London: Sage, 1993), 138–45.

118. Pellizer, "Outline of a Morphology of Sympotic Entertainment," 178.

119. Pellizer, "Outline of a Morphology of Sympotic Entertainment," 178 and Lissarrague, *The Aesthetics of the Greek Banquet*, 8.

120. On this passage see Forbes, *Studies Vol. 3*, 112.

121. Lissarrague, *The Aesthetics of the Greek Banquet*, 10–11.

122. Lissarrague, *The Aesthetics of the Greek Banquet*, 11. On the exclusion of women see Nancy H. Demand, *Birth, Death, and Motherhood in Classical Greece* (Baltimore, MD: The Johns Hopkins University Press, 1994).

123. Lissarrague, *The Aesthetics of the Greek Banquet*, 57–58.

124. Lissarrague, *The Aesthetics of the Greek Banquet*, 58.

125. Pellizer, "Outline of a Morphology of Sympotic Entertainment," 179.

126. Pellizer, "Outline of a Morphology of Sympotic Entertainment," 179.

127. Jean-Louis Durand, Francoise Frontisis-Ducroux and Francois Lissarrague, "Wine: Human and Divine," in *A City of Images—Iconography and Society in Ancient Greece* ed. Claude Bérard, Christiane Bron, Jean-Louis Durand, Francoise Frontisi-Ducroux, François Lissarrgue, Alain Schnapp, and Jean-Paul Vernant (Princeton, NJ: Princeton University Press, 1989), 121.

128. Michel Foucault, "On the Genealogy of Ethics: An Overview of Work in Progress," in *The Foucault Reader* ed. Paul Rabinow (New York: Pantheon Books, 1984) discusses this.

129. Daniel B. Levine, "Symposium and *Polis*," in *Theognis of Megara—Poetry and the Polis*, cd. Thomas J. Figueira and Gregory Nagy, (Baltimore, MD: Johns Hopkins University Press, 1985), 176. See also Bruno Gentili, *Poetry and Its Public in Ancient Greece* (Baltimore, MD: Johns Hopkins University Press, 1988), 89–103.

130. Pellizer, "Outline of a Morphology of Sympotic Entertainment," 183.

131. Pellizer, "Outline of a Morphology of Sympotic Entertainment," 180, emphasis Pellizer's. This helps to explain Plato's deep concern with drinking ethics, from his detailed juxtapositioning of the intoxication of Alcibiades with the sobriety of Socrates in the *Symposium*, to his thorough interweaving of his discussion of drinking parties with a system of education and the importance of ethical foundations in the *Laws*.

132. See for example K. J. Dover, "Aristophanes' Speech in Plato's *Symposium*," in K. J. Dover, *The Greeks and their Legacy: Collected Papers Volume II: Prose Literature, History, Society, Transmission, Influence* (Oxford: Blackwell Publishing, 1988), 112–13, Peter H. Von Blanckenhagen, "Stage and Actors in Plato's *Symposium*," *Greek, Roman and Byzantine Studies* 33, no. 1 (1992): 64–65, and Robin A. Waterfield, *Plato—Symposium* (New York: Oxford University Press, 1994), xi.

133. Pellizer, "Outline of a Morphology of Sympotic Entertainment," 182.

134. Plato was certainly concerned with dietary ethics, but he more often than not situates those ethics as part of an overall concern with luxury (*truphe*) and does not appear to single out the food of the *symposion* as worthy of sustained commentary; Isocrates, Xenophon, and writers in the Hellenistic period are of a similar mind. It is worth noting Plato does mention the *tragemata* of symposia at *Republic* 372c. One of the more famous works on the subject of food and luxury was *Life of Luxury* by the poet Archestratus (fl. 330 BCE) of which sixty-one fragments are preserved in Athenaeus. See Garnsey, *Food and Society in Classical Antiquity*, 72–77.

Chapter Two

The *Symposion* and the Question of *Stasis*

In Plato's *Symposium* the character Pausanias says at one point during his speech on love that it is generally true of "any activity that, simply of itself, it is neither good nor bad. Take what we're doing now, for example, that is to say drinking, or singing, or talking. None of these is good or bad in itself, but each becomes so depending on the way it is done. Well and rightly done, it is good; wrongly done, it is bad" (180e–181a). His perspective is not idiosyncratic and encapsulates quite well how ancient Greece, to the very limited extent it did so, problematized the difficulties encountered with behaviors arising out of intoxication.[1] They are not so much a matter for religious morality to censure through fear, or a legal apparatus to regulate through codification and punitive sanction, nor are they a disease condition to be subjected to a medico-therapeutic intervention, but an *ethics of right use.*[2]

Intoxication: Good and Bad

References to "honey-sweet" and "honey-hearted" wine, as we saw in chapter 1, occur frequently in Homer's *Iliad* and *Odyssey.*[3] The expression of a "difficulty" with intoxication in these works, however, is largely embryonic.[4] Most of these depictions of wine and wine-drinking are examples of the prestige elite individuals sought to gain through giving gifts of wine and hosting "special wine-drinking ceremonies."[5] There are however exceptions. In the *Iliad* Hector meets his mother Hecuba in the palace of Troy after battle and, seeing how weary he is, she offers to refresh him with "honeyed, mellow wine" telling him that when "a man's exhausted, wine will build his strength" (6.307–311). Hector rejects her suggestion saying "Don't offer me mellow wine, mother, not now—you'd sap my limbs, I'd lose my nerve for war. And I'd be ashamed to pour a glistening cup [of wine] to Zeus [as a libation before drinking] with unwashed hands. I'm splattered with blood and filth—how could I pray to the lord of storm and lightning?" (6.313–317). The consumption of wine, especially excessive consumption, had by the Greek Dark Ages (ca. 1,100–800 BCE) been connotatively linked to gender.[6] Drinking wine to the point of intoxication feminized the warrior. Homer values as *agathos* (good) men who are brave and skilled at the art of war, while the goodness of women resides in their skills in household management and motherhood. Men are *kakos* (bad) when they are fearful or cowardly. Intoxication brought about illogical thought and uncontrolled emotions, qualities that were associated with women.[7]

In the *Odyssey* the deleterious effects of wine on thought and speech are somewhat more clearly articulated. As the suitors feast and drink into the night, Odysseus, disguised as a beggar, volunteers to keep the fires burning so that the maids may cheer the queen in her room. The women laugh at him in wonder, the beautiful Melantho asking "Wine's got your wits?—Or do you always play the fool and babble nonsense?" (18.375–76). Antinous later rebukes the still-disguised Odysseus when the latter, attending the suitors' banquet as a guest, suggests that he be given the chance to string the bow that will win the hand of Queen Penelope, saying that the wine must be overpowering him, as it does all who drink immoderately (21.327–29). Antinous then compares what he sees as the outrageous banquet behavior of Odysseus to that of the Centaur Eurytion. Invited to the wedding of Peirithoos, Eurytion became drunk on wine and brought destructive violence upon himself and his Centaur kin; drink destroyed the Centaur's mind and made him wild with outrageous desire for the bride. Antinous cites this wine-induced Centauromachy as an example of the evil a man brings "on himself by drowning in his cups" (21.330–342).[8]

In the collection of writings gathered around the name of the poet Theognis of Megara (fl. ca. 550–490 BCE), the *Elegies*, wine is an object of both praise and blame, hate and love, good and bad (873–76).[9] While virtually every aspect of the historical Theognis is uncertain, the author of the work "displays the attitudes of the typical sixth century aristocrat" and all his poems are written in "the elegiac metre, which was normally accompanied by the flute," and the purpose of several of the poems was to use them as "drinking songs" at symposia.[10] In these poems the poet, much like the character of Pausanias in Plato's *Symposium*, continually recommends a middle course, for example:

> To drink too much is bad, but if you would
> Drink wisely, you'd find wine not bad, but good (509–510)

The reason for the poet's caution: wine makes the mind, the *noos*, evaporate whenever it is drunk beyond moderation (497–498). Drunk in an immoderate fashion wine is a drug that can put even the wise (*sophos*) man to shame (499–502). Overpowered by a head heavy with wine one is no longer in control of one's good judgment, one's *gnome* (503–508). Despite these difficulties Theognis continually extols the pleasures of "drinking well" and "singing to the notes of the flute" while attending the *symposion* (533–534).[11] The alternative to drinking wine, abstinence, is summarily rejected: attempts to persuade the poet "not to drink" will be no more effective than persuasion to "get too drunk" (837–40).

We find on one drinking cup that has survived the phrase *Khaire kai piei eu*, "Be of good cheer and drink well," the Greek adverb *eu* simultaneously encompassing the sense of "have an enjoyable drink," and "drink with reservation."[12] The Greek has a distinctly moral connotation, one aimed at a *regulated* intoxication.[13] Any notion of the typical symposiast drinking with reservation, however, must be viewed against the apparent popularity of drinking wine neat, indicated by such phrases as "make it Scythian," a reference to one of a number of non-Greek peoples who drank their wine undiluted with water. The word for stronger, *akratesteron,* means "unmixed [wine]" (Athenaeus 10.427c–d). Theopompus of Chios (378–ca. 320 BCE) describes the eating and drinking practices of the Ardiaeans as so *akratesteron* that the Celts were able to trick them with bread filled with a drug that powerfully upset their stomachs (*Fragments of the Greek Historians* 115 F 40).

A *symposion*'s opening libation consisted of unmixed wine, and this alone appears to have been capable of producing a deep intoxication (Athenaeus 15.693b). There are many indications that drinking unmixed wine or only minimally mixed wine was a popular practice. In Meander's *Tinker's Holiday* we read: "That's the custom nowadays, as you know: they bawled 'Unmixed wine!' 'The big cup!'" (Athenaeus 11.502e). The practice of mixing water with wine was by no means universally popular. Diphilus says "Make it stronger; everything watery has an evil soul" (Athenaeus 10.423f) and in a fragment of a comedy by Pherecrates, the *Corianno*, a character vociferously complains that with a ratio of two parts water to four of wine, the servant who has prepared the drinks ought be serving them to frogs (Athenaeus 10.430d–e).

There are, however, several traces of a concern, of a growing difficulty, not with the sympotic drinking *per se*, but with disorder arising out of the intoxication occurring within the *symposion*. Anacreon (570–488 BCE) warns against drinking to excess since it leads to a *symposion* filled with uproar and shouting in the manner of the barbarous Scythians (fr. 356b). Xenophanes (570–480 BCE) writes that there is no "outrage in drinking as much as you can hold" but at the same time we should "praise that man of men who when he has drunk [heavily] brings worthy things to light"—he does not speak of "the fictions of earlier men or of violent civil discord; in such things there is nothing useful" (fr. 1).[14] Theognis questions the worth of winning a drinking contest, the reason being a bad man can often best a good one (971–972). Lines 467–496 of Theognis are traditionally attributed to Evenos of Paros, a poet and rhetorician who apparently was a contemporary of Socrates.[15] The poet warns that the man who exceeds the bounds of judicious drinking is "no longer master of his own tongue or his mind" and talks recklessly, saying things that embarrass his sober friends and feeling no shame himself.[16] Critias (ca. 460–403 BCE), Plato's uncle, who like his nephew appears to have been influenced by Theognis on matters pertaining to wine, describes intoxication as a "dark mist" settling upon the eyes, the melting of memory "into oblivion" and the complete loss of reason (Athenaeus 10.432e).[17]

"Why do drunkards tremble, especially if they drink unmixed wine?" is one of the many questions concerning intoxication raised in the Pseudo-Aristotelian *Problems*, where one also finds indications that wine consumption could lead to health problems, including double vision (3.30.875b); and if drunk in large enough quantities, the death of the consumer (3.2.871a, 3.5.871b). Side by side with these physical matters one finds concern that wine could lead to troublesome disorder (3.27.875a). Theophrastus, in his *On Dizziness* (11–12), includes "alcoholic drinks . . . and administerings of drugs" as the sorts of things that "weigh upon and separate the rotations in the head."[18] An Athenian physician named Mnesitheus (fl. 350 BCE) was, if we are to believe Athenaeus, concerned enough with intoxication to compose a letter titled *On Hard Drinking*, evidently concluding that while the practice of drinking unmixed wine was on occasion medicinally beneficial, owing to the purgative effect, the general "result of people drinking unmixed wine at social gatherings is considerable injury done to body and mind" (11.483f–484a). He also praises wine mixed with drugs as being medicinally useful. Mixing wine and water in equal parts, Mnesitheus believed, led to madness while drinking unmixed wine led to bodily collapse (Athenaeus 2.36a–b).

Further indications of the health effects resulting from the drinking of unmixed wine may be found in Nicander's *Alexipharmaka* where the effects of aconite (*Aconitum napellus*) are described as producing a "grievous weight" in the head, followed by throbbing in the temples and double vision "like a man at night overcome with unmixed wine" (12–30).[19] Frankincense (*libanotes*) and wine, Dioscorides writes, has medicinal value, but only if drunk by those really in need of a cure; otherwise it brought madness and, in large enough quantities, death (*On Medical Materials* 1.82). The practice must have been common enough among the healthy for Dioscorides to have considered it worthy of inserting a precautionary remark. Among the Western Locrians, or Ozoli, it was said that "if anyone drank unmixed wine without a physician's prescription to effect a cure, the penalty was death under the code instituted by Zaleucus" (Athenaeus 10.429a). Establishing a code was one thing, enforcing it quite another. Clearly, however, wine was understood as being capable of producing permanent noetic degradation, and the ancients were casting about for effective answers to the difficulties it generated.

The New Testament contains the Greek word *paroinos*, a term that means, roughly, "at, or beside, wine" or in other words a person who sits beside the drinking cup, the *kylix,* for an extended period of time.[20] Plato uses the word *philoinos* (wine-lover, ever ready for a drink) with negative connotations in the *Republic* (475a). We find in late antiquity words including *philopotes* (a lover of drinking bouts), and *kothonist* (habituated to the cup).[21] Even so, on close examination one finds that the ancient Greeks almost never considered the matter one of saying yes or no to wine or any other *pharmakon*, as would be the case in subsequent recastings of the ethics of intoxication. The main concerns of the Archaic and Classical Greek periods center around (a) who might or might not be allowed to drink wine, (b) when they ought to be allowed to drink it, (c) how much should be drunk, (d) in what fashion should drinking occur, (e) to what purpose, and so on.

Intoxication: A Gendered Experience

These concerns applied to drinking by women as much as they did drinking by men.[22] The challenge that wine presented the male head of the household (*oikos*) was evidently one of "keeping it away from those members of his household likely to use it against his interests, including women and slaves whom he needed to perform regular tasks in an efficient fashion."[23] The intoxication of women, to judge by Greek comedy at least, was the concern of every adult male with wine at his disposal. Young women in comedy "are consistently portrayed as flighty, weak, manipulative, and unable to control their passions."[24] In the "honor/shame orientation" present in ancient Greece even "the slightest hint of impropriety" by a woman might lead to a legal attack by rivals or enemies of that particular *oikos*.[25] In his *Oeconomicus* Xenophon's Ischomachus comments with approval that his wife had been taught to control her appetites before her marriage (7.6), and had spent the first fifteen years of her life "under careful supervision so that she might see and hear and speak as little as possible" (7.5).[26] Certainly this control would have extended to wine as well as food.[27] In the Demosthenic speech *Against Neaera*, as part of their charge that Stephanus "lived with Neaera as his wife contrary to the law since she was a noncitizen" the case brought by his accusers consists primarily of evidence meant to slur her "behavior and reputation; for example, her presence at dinner parties with men was repeatedly put forward as evidence she was a prostitute."[28]

The figure of the old woman in Greek comedy—or at least old women of humble birth—was regularly one of an avid thirst for unmixed wine, heavy drinking, and lechery.[29] These depictions may have been a reflection of "the greater freedom allowed old women in contrast to the strict controls imposed on young unmarried women or married women of child-bearing age."[30] But on the other hand well-born women are not depicted thus, leaving the impression that the criterion was not so much age as it was the place a woman occupied in society.[31] Prostitutes and courtesans—most of whom it is fairly safe to assume would still have been very young or at least young enough to still be capable of bearing children—are "regularly depicted drinking on Attic vases."[32] Playwrights cater to their audience's expectations, and in works such as Aristophanes *Lysistrata* (463–66), *Thesmophoriazusae* (347–48, 730–37), and *Wealth* (435–36), Pherecrates' *Corianno*, and Epicrates' *Antilais*, aging courtesans are depicted as heavy drinkers.[33]

We might go so far as to say that the consumption of wine "in the Classical and Hellenistic periods became increasingly gendered, or regulated based primarily on the consumer's sex."[34] The question of women and intoxication in antiquity is certainly significant. My discussion in the remainder of this chapter will however be confined to the thoughts of men concerning the use of wine and the presence of intoxication within the *symposion*, which as we saw in chapter 1 was an explicitly male space. It is this drinking and its accompanying intoxicated disruption of identity, not the drinking of wine by women, which was viewed as having consequences for the politics of the *polis* as a whole, rather than particular *oikoi*.

Intoxication and Politics: The *Komos*

Komos is the root of the verb *komazein*, to stage a feast, and the noun *komastes*, a reveler. At the end of the *symposion* the participants would often leave the privacy of the *andron* and display their intoxication to the wider community.[35] In a strictly literal sense *komos* denotes a procession of inebriated revelers, the "movement of a group with dancing, music and wine."[36] The literal meaning glosses over the frequent political overtones present in the *komos*, which often resembled a drunken public riot intended to demonstrate "the power and lawlessness of the drinking group."[37] Theognis exhorts those attending a banquet to stick by men who are good (*agathoi*), for they will teach what is genuine and noble; to associate with the wicked, eating and drinking with them, will in contrast cause a person to "lose what mind [*noos*]" he now has (27–38). When proper order, the *kosmos*, what is above (*kathuperthen*), is supplanted by what is below (*hupenerthe*), by the earthy and riotous drunken revel, the *komos*, "then it is time for us to stop drinking and go home" (841–844, and cf. 475–480).

In one legal document, *Against Konon* (Oration 54), the Athenian statesman and orator Demosthenes (384–322 BCE) points out that Konon, his son, and his friends were thoroughly drunk when they assaulted Ariston, his client.[38] They were regular drinking companions, with a tendency to commit violent assault and stage obscene mock-initiation rites when intoxicated.[39] This amounted to *hubris* against the citizens of less refined social standing. Demosthenes contends that "there are many people in the city, sons of gentlemen, who in jest like young men have given themselves nicknames such as *Ithyphalloi* [the Erections] and *Autolekythoi* [the Wankers], and who often come to blows over *hetairai*." Demosthenes simultaneously evokes the jury's pity and outrage, pointing out the sufferings, both physical and emotional, of the victim, while also counseling them "it is in their own interests to check the anti-social careers, the random, drunken thuggery, of Konon and his wealthy co-symposiasts."[40] The speech begins from what appears to have been a general acceptance of hubristic behavior at the symposia of young men (*epheboi*) before proceeding to the question of the permissible limits of that behavior, while apparently anticipating the re-

[handwritten marginal note: Kosmos disrupted by Komos]

sponse of the defense will be founded upon "the naturalness of young men engaging in such drunken escapades."[41] Similar legal cases are discussed in Aeschines' *Against Timarchus* (96), and Lysias' *Against Alcibiades* (1.25) and *For Mantitheus* (11).

A comedic depiction of this sympotic violence may be found in Aristophanes' *Wasps* where the old man Philocleon outstrips the younger men in drunkenness and disorderly conduct, behaving outrageously at a *symposion* he and his son attend, beating his slave Xanthais while crying out "*pai, pai*" and then assaulting everyone he meets on his way home (1291–1325). The word *pai* was used to address both slaves and young boys. Neither were viewed as possessing much *time* (honor, standing, etc.) and both it appears were frequently beaten.[42] Completely drunk, with a stolen flute-girl in tow, Philocleon is pursued by outraged citizens claiming damages for assault.[43] Catching up to Philocleon one accuser says "Old man, I summon you on a charge of wanton outrage [*hubris*]" (1418). His son Bdelycleon expresses a level of alarm in keeping with the seriousness of the charge, and offers to pay any amount necessary to keep the matter out of court. The amusing element lies in the reversal of roles; it must have been far more common for fathers to have to answer to charges of *hubris*, or some other offense, made against their drunken sons, or rather than answering the charges kicking the son and his drinking companions out of the house, a practice Plato appears to allude to in the *Republic* (569a).

Earlier in the *Wasps* Philocleon tells his son, as a typical father might, that drinking "was a bad thing" and that "door-breaking, striking and stoning" came from wine, forcing one to pay reparations "while the hangover's on you" (1253–55). Apparently the perpetrator of such misdeeds would try to avoid a court date with a profuse apology or "some witty story" he had learned at a *symposion*, so as to "turn the whole thing into a laughing matter" and thereby get the offended party to leave without pressing charges (1256–61). This is exactly what the intoxicated Philocleon tries to do in order to mollify the man who has accused him of *hubris*, but in the comedy his responses only manage to fan the flames of the accuser's outrage to an even greater extent. Abandoning his attempt to make peace with the man Philocleon ends up striking him again, this time in front of the witness he has brought along.

Besides violence minor acts of sacrilege were also a staple of the *komos*, including "urinating on wayside shrines or stealing and eating the gods' share of sacrificial meat."[44] In the legal records one finds for example a drinking group named *Triballoi* being accused of such offenses as "defecating at the shrines of Hecate," and stealing and eating both "the portions of victims which had been used for purifications and laid out at shrines of Hecate," as well as the "pig's testicles from assembly sacrifices."[45] This last offense may have been particularly reprehensible. According to a scholium on Aeschines' *Speech against Timarchus*, every Athenian assembly (*ekklesia*) was preceded by a two-part ritual, with a pig slaughtered "to purify the space and chase away the 'unclean daemons that often obstruct the thoughts of people'" followed by the burning of fragrant incenses "to attract benevolent spirits, to make sure that, through their presence (*parousia*), the Athenians would reach good decisions."[46] These drunken affronts to public *time* "would seem a natural and normal type, characteristic of the upper class, and hence was especially what the laws [against *hubris*] were designed to stop."[47] In a passage from the sixth century we find the poet Theognis admonishing "Boy, do not indulge in a *komos*, but obey your elder. It is not proper for a young man to indulge in a *komos*" (1351–52). In Classical Athens there evidently were some drinking regulations including fines for insulting language toward, and violent behaviors against, fellow guests but these appear ineffectual given the instances of repeat offenders, and oftentimes the master of the feast would apparently overlook such transgressions.[48]

Intoxication as *Hubris*

Unlike literary works whose setting was the *symposion*, such as those written by Plato and Xenophon, the many pictures of sympotic behavior we find on the vases and cups of the Classical Period generally lack any exemplary purpose, any deep philosophical or moral message. Theirs is merely a reflective function as for example their depiction of drunken behavior.[49] This is not to imply greater objectivity on the part of vase painters. What the painter chooses to depict mirrors the "social imagination, that is to say the code, the system of values, through which a society sees itself in a particular moment in history."[50] What is significant about these painted vases is that in stark contrast to the sedate celebrations we find in the symposia depicted by writers such as Plato or Xenophon, one finds symposiasts—typically young men—reeling, staggering, vomiting, staging the *komos*, and even in the middle of rowdy brawls where all the traditional instruments of the *symposion* are violently misused.[51]

What exactly was the offense known as *hubris*?[52] The definition of the term remains disputed.[53] Two things, however, are largely agreed on. First, *hubris* was a concept fundamental to the social and political life of both Archaic and Classical Athens.[54] The moral lesson of Hesiod's *Works and Days* may be found in line 213 when the poet writes "Observe justice, *dike*, do not allow immoderation, *hubris*, to grow."[55] The poems of Athenian statesman and lawmaker Solon (ca. 640–561 BCE) identify the cause of social unrest in *hubris* and *koros* (insolence). Different social classes were believed to have differing amounts of honor (*geras*) and *time*. *Time* was the value, honor, and respect an individual enjoyed, or believed he ought to enjoy. To be deprived of *time* subjected a man to *atimia*, a partial or complete deprivation of his rights as a citizen.[56] Honor and its potential loss through dishonor were, in ancient Greece, "closely related to social and political status with their attendant rights and duties" while *hubris* "in Solon's poetry, as well as in the later legal texts, designates behavior intended to have an effect on the social fabric, by depriving those of whatever class of their due *time*."[57] In the Classical Period laws against *hubris* were seen as a cornerstone of the democratic legal system. It is significant, then, that the intoxicated profanations of the Eleusinian Mysteries in 415 BCE, with their far-reaching legal and political consequences, took place at aristocratic symposia, and were described by Thucydides in his *History* as having occurred in a spirit of *hubris* (6.28.1).[58]

Second, the recreational intoxication of the *symposion* lies at the heart of the problem of *hubris*.[59] Solon implies that there is not only disorder within the private confines of the *symposion*—the same chaos spills out into the public realm. *Hubris*, typified by the drunken violence that expressed itself in the *komos*, the riotous public procession that typically brought the aristocratic *symposion* to conclusion, was "part of a pattern of behavior intended to assert the supremacy of an aristocracy over its rivals," a "deliberate dishonoring of those who are not members of the group in order to reduce their *time* in the community."[60] The typical persons who were accused of being *hubristai* (those who commit *hubris*), Aristotle tells us, were young and rich, thinking "that they thereby show their superiority" (*Rhetoric* 1378b). In the *Constitution of Naxos* Aristotle mentions a *komos* by drunken youths as precipitating a civil war (Athenaeus 8.248).

Solon complains that the wealthy

> are willing to destroy the *polis* with their mindlessness, and the mind [*noos*] of
> the leaders of the *demos* is without *dike*. They will soon suffer many pains as a
> result of their great *hubris*. For they do not know how to withstand *koros*, nor
> how to put in order [*kosmein*] their present *euphrosune* [the delights of the sym-
> *posion*] in the quietude of the banquet [*dais*]" (fragment 4.9–10).[61]

Despite these concerns Solon's strongest legislative action appears to have been the introduction of several regulations requiring wine to be sold in a prediluted condition, the intention being to control access to unmixed wine and thereby promote moderation (Athenaeus 10.431d–e). Given that we find the mixing bowl present on so many occasions it is safe to conclude "Solon's plan came to naught."[62]

Solon also reputedly made drunkenness by a magistrate an act punishable by death (Diogenes Laertius, *Lives* 1.57). This is not surprising since magistrates often acted as overseers at public functions, many of which might include a great deal of wine drinking. According to Athenaeus public banquets were attended by three state-appointed wine inspectors, derogatorily referred to as "Eyes" (*Ophthalmoi*), whose purpose was to supply lamps and wicks and see that no individual guest drank an unequal share of the wine (10.425a–b). These magistrates appear to have been widely reviled, as can be gleaned from a fragment of *The Thousand Islandtowns* by Eupolis (ca. 446–411 BCE), who says "Men whom you wouldn't have chosen to be your wine inspectors in the old days, we now have for leaders of the army" (Athenaeus 10.425a–b). Even the *Ophthalmoi* cannot really be viewed as guardians of temperance: part of their duty was to tell those who refused to drink "to depart in accordance with that celebrated law 'drink or begone.'"[63] Solon's unsuccessful attempt to restrict the sale of unmixed wine and the prosecutions concerning drunken *hubris* may be viewed as indirect measures, operating at the fringes of the drinking party, rather than a redefinition of any of the four essential features of the *symposion* outlined in chapter 1. It would remain for Plato to begin to fashion such an advocacy.

External *Stasis*

Stasis is usually understood as a word meaning "civil strife" or "political revolution." By Plato's lifetime the original meaning of *stasis* as "standing" and thus "a way or place of standing," a posture or position, had come to mean political strife, mostly likely after being used to refer to a position in politics taken by a political faction.[64] While this is the most common interpretation and at least partially captures the meaning of *stasis*, it appears to fall short of how the ancient Greeks themselves understood the term.[65] The Greek understanding, it should be emphasized, was deeply rooted in the medical view of *stasis* understood as a disease, a *nosos*,[66] in the sense of a "halt" or "arrest" of normal functioning.[67] Through *stasis* the unity of the community, viewed in the sense of political friendship or *homonoia*—literally "together-mindedness"—was fractured.[68] The citizen turned away "from institutions perceived to be dysfunctional or unresponsive" and sought justice through the expression of the "discordant passions of anger and hatred."[69] Regardless of who was addressing *stasis*—the poets, the historians, the medical literature, or philosophy—in each case it is agreed that (a) *stasis* is a disease, a plague, and worst of all evil, (b) *stasis* has no redeeming value, as for example might be found in concepts such as "political faction" or "sedition" or "revolution"[70] and (c) *stasis* constitutes a public threat or menace to the well-being of the *polis*.

Even before appearing in the works of Greek medicine and philosophy the subject of *stasis* was a frequent theme of Greek poetry, even where the word itself does not appear. Examples include Aristophanes' *Knights*, Sophocles' *Ajax*, *Oedipus Colonnus*, and *Antigone*, and Euripides' *Orestes*.[71] Other works are more explicit. Theognis in the *Elegies* prays to Apollo (773–82) to protect the city from "the mindless lack of unity" i.e. the *stasis* that weakens the Greek people. In Aeschylus' *Eumenides* (976–83) the chorus says "I pray that *stasis*, greedy for evil, may never clamor in this city, and may the dust not drink the black blood of its people, and through passion cause ruinous murder for vengeance to the destruction of the state."[72] For the pre-Socratic philosopher Democritus (ca. 460–ca. 370 BCE) the starting point of *stasis* was envy.[73]

The historian Thucydides, like his predecessors, identified *stasis* as a defective form of politics "that had accompanying psychological consequences."[74] The general traits of *stasis* included (a) *stasis* as a deviant process, the product of the noetic decline of individuals; (b) *stasis* being preceded by the inversion of the values that previously constituted acceptable public behavior and speech (*logos*); (c) the dissolution of the traditional familial and community bonds of friendship (*philia*) and piety (*eusebia*), and the limitations on action these imposed; (d) the breakdown of law and the abandonment of restraint in both what

[margin note: → similar to political implications of psychedelics in the 60s though reversed]

constituted acceptable means in politics and the exchange of distinct, limited ends, in favor of far more open-ended goals with unspecified spoils of victory, and finally (e) the legitimating and unleashing of uncontrollable passion, particularly wrath (*ogre*) that, like a wildfire, was capable of consuming everything in its path.[75]

In contrast to previous reflections on *stasis*, which lacked systematic presentation, even in the case of Thucydides, Plato created a theoretical underpinning for these traits.[76] In addition to the *polis*, *stasis* may arise in many complex entities characterized by multiple and interdependent parts, whether it is the human body, friendships, a ship's crew, or an army camp (*Republic*, 351c). He reworked the idea of *stasis* as disease to argue that what *stasis* consisted of was the ability to disrupt the right working, or *ergon*, of such entities. In the *Republic* (351d) Socrates puts to Thrasymachus the proposition that factions (*staseis*), like hatreds and quarrels, "are the outcome of injustice," while justice "brings oneness of mind (*homonoia*) and love (*philia*)." Injustice causes individuals to "hate and be at strife (*stasiazein*) with one another" and prevents them effectively acting as a whole and in common (351d–e, and cf. *Laws* 694b).[77] Plato's view of *stasis* and disease sees them as effects and outcomes, rather than causes. The *cause* of *stasis* is an unnatural order within the organism. The statesman must look to prevent the changes that disturb the order, the right working, on which health depends.

The older view such as that held by Solon (quoted above) saw justice, *dike*, as passive quietude, as *hesuchia*, with its opposite being disturbance, *tarache*. Injustice was the result of *hubris*, meddling, *polupragmosune*. The *Republic* too indicates that to "do one's own business and to not be a busy body is justice" (433a). Plato places rational self-possession, *sophrosyne*, in opposition to *hubris*, and it would appear within the *Republic*, at the very least, justice and moderation function in ways that make them virtually indistinct. Although it is translated in a variety of ways the literal meaning of the noun *sophrosyne* is "to keep the mind safe."[78] Plato saw the essence of justice not in *heuchia* but instead in *homonia*, and this common-minded community was produced by expert knowledge, *episteme*. In Plato *homonia* becomes defined in terms of *epimeleia heautou*, a "taking care of the self."[79] The dialogues construct a new *paideia*, a new system of educative enculturation that rejects the mythopoetic predecessors of philosophy and their reliance on ecstatic psychological states within the performer, audience, or both.

Internal *Stasis*

The social condition of *stasis* as the ancient Greeks understood it contained the idea of a noetic unraveling of the minds of individuals. Intertwined with the danger of *stasis* is another problem, what Plato's *Republic* calls *stasiazonta*, or "stasis within" (352a, 444b, and 554d). Whereas justice is characterized by

bonds of *homonoia*, literally "together-mindedness," *stasiazonta* is characterized
by the absence of those bonds, *dichonoia* or "apart-mindedness." The unbinding
and destruction of the harmonious unity of an organism was known as *lusis*.[80]
Plato as well as others incorporated *lusis* into the political realm, where it came
to mean the end product of injustice.[81] One aspect of this poisonous danger of
noetic unraveling, unbinding, unbonding, etc., of *dichonoia*, is the danger of
ecstasy.[82]

The term *ekstasis* is most literally translated as a flight of the soul from the
body, deriving from *ek* (out of, away from, beyond) and *stasis* (here understood
as a position, where one stood).[83] An earlier word used to connote a similar condition appears to have been *existanai*, "to derange," from *ex* (out) and *histanai*
(to cause to stand motionless). Most importantly *ekstasis*, for the ancient world
in general and ancient Greece in particular, did not consist of possessing a
knowledge that allowed for "controlling or mastering the Other," but was rather
"a cosmological knowledge, a means of knowing the Other in order to know
oneself anew."[84] It is easy to confuse or conflate descriptions of *ekstasis* with
enthousiasmos (rapturous enthusiasm) and similar words.[85] The two terms *ekstasis* and *enthousiasmos*, for example, refer to kindred states, often indistinguishable, but "*enthousiasmos* was from the first mainly a theological conception,
while *ekstasis*, on the other hand, comes form the domain of medical terminology."[86]

Plato, who was certainly no stranger to medical terminology, exhibits a very
keen awareness of ecstatic psychological states even if he is not consistent with
the words he chooses to describe them, lacking a single precise term to describe
stasiazonta in such a manner that it is clearly distinguished from *stasis*.[87] The
Greek word for ecstasy, *ekstasis,* does not appear in any of his dialogues.[88] In
the *Ion* Plato speaks of both *entheoi* (inspired, as by the gods) and *enthousiazontes* (gripped by enthusiasm), closely related terms that suggest "the notion of 'a
god within.'"[89] In the *Philebus* he describes the intense pleasures as being overwhelming, frenzied, and "unbalanced to the point of insanity" (45d–e, 47a–b).
The general classical term for madness or insanity, *mania*, occurs thirty times in
Plato, while *paranoia* is used to denote mental derangement several times, most
notably at *Laws* 929d–e in the discussion of how a son ought to proceed if he
believes his father has become mentally unstable.[90] "All the Platonic *manias* are
characterized by *ekstasis*, an alienation of the mind as it is thrown out of its
normal state, whether by organic madness, by 'daemonic' possession, by love,
by awestruck wonder (the 'ecstasy of admiration') or by the higher forms of
rapture."[91]

While it is true the word *ekstasis* does not appear in Plato, it appears in the
writings of both Aristotle and Theophrastus. In a curious passage from his *Parts
of Animals* Aristotle describes bulls as mentally deranged, *ekstatikoi*, because
they are among those animals having "thick and abundant fibers in their blood,"
making them "of a more earthly temperament, and liable to bursts of passion."[92]
There is a remote possibility this may be a faded remembrance of a plant either
associated with bulls, such as the coprophilic *Stropharia cubensis* mushroom, or

that bulls were known to eat, much as Siberian reindeer are known to become intoxicated eating the *Amanita muscaria* mushroom.[93] Aristotle even indicates in his *History of Animals* that, just as human beings do, animals seek out herbal remedies (611b–612b).[94] *Ekstasis* appears in the Pseudo-Aristotelian *Problems* (30.1). Heracles betrayed his melancholy "by his *ekstasis* [frenzy] towards his children." While it is generally agreed that Aristotle did not write the *Problems* he was known to have authored a similar book on similar topics (possibly even with the same title), elements of which may have been incorporated into the *Problems*, a work that was probably written by a member of the Peripatetic School. Book 30, which refers to *ekstasis*, is vouched for as Aristotelian by both Plutarch and Cicero.[95]

Theophrastus' *History of Plants* describes the misuse of mind-altering drugs by a sculptor named Pandeios: "Of those [roots] that are sweet there are some that cause mental derangement [*ekstatikai*], as the plant like the 'golden thistle' [*Skolymus hispanicus*] which grows near Tegea: of this Pandeios the sculptor ate, and went mad [*exeste*] while he was working in the temple" (9.13.4).[96] The immediate context of Theophrastus' discussion of plants added to wine in his *History of Plants* are drugs that affect the mind (*pharmaka pros de ten psychen*), including those substances that cause mental derangement (*ekstatikas*).[97] Given that Aristotle was Plato's student and later his colleague, and Theophrastus was a student and later a colleague of Aristotle, it does not seem impossible that a medical term like *ekstasis* could have appeared during a conversation or lecture at the Academy attended by Plato during his final years.[98] That a person chooses not to use a word when expressing himself in writing does not prove beyond doubt that the term was not a part of their spoken or known vocabulary.

Be that as it may, the problem of the psychological condition of ecstasy is at the core of Plato's thought even if the word *ekstasis* does not appear in his writings. Drinking, drugs, and intoxication were a primary manifestation of that condition. Plato's teaching of the soul taking flight and leaving the body after death in the *Phaedo* "became closely linked with similar doctrines in the *Phaedrus* about good and bad madness."[99] Aristotle disagreed with Plato on many issues, but not "where melancholy madness was concerned" and when he "explained these frenzies and inspired madness" he did so "by analogy with men drunk with wine."[100] Aristotle points out in *Problems* 30 that "persons sometimes take on 'melancholic moods' when they drink large quantities of wine, or become 'merciful' or 'savage' or 'silent' or 'affectionate,' even to kiss on the mouth 'someone whom no one would ever kiss if he were sober'" (953a–b).[101] The analogy was a "classical commonplace; it became a Stoic one, then a Christian one. Plato, Aristotle, Seneca, Gregory of Nyssa, Erasmus or Montaigne pass just as easily . . . from questions of drink to questions of ecstasy and melancholy madness."[102]

Intoxication as Internal Tyranny

When Plato's guardian class is forbidden the experience of intoxication (*methe*) in the *Republic* (398e), the prohibition is not something unique to that particular dialogue, nor is it a trivial or marginal part of the *Republic*'s discussion of the just regime. Plato continually discusses the unnecessary pleasures in a manner alluding to the feasting, drinking, and sex that so often occurred within the Greek *symposion*. The oligarchic city, divided into competing poor and rich, is mirrored in a man like his own city, never "free from *stasis* within himself . . . in some sense twofold" rather than a single, simple, unity. It is only out of fear, not reasoned self-persuasion arising out of the right sort of moral education, that the oligarchic man forcibly holds down his "bad desires," his "worse desires," these desires "that are akin to the drone," with some more decent part of himself (554d). The typical citizen of the democratic city in contrast lives capriciously, each day "gratifying the desire that occurs to him, at one time drinking and listening to the flute [at symposia], at another downing water and reducing; now practicing gymnastic, and again idling and neglecting everything; and sometimes spending his time as though he were occupied with philosophy" (561c–d).[103] The offspring of democratic leaders are consumed by desire for "feasts, revels, parties, prostitutes," and live lives "overflowing with incense, myrrh, crowns, wines and all the pleasures" democratic cities are known to be rife with. Clearly this is all happening in a *sympotic* world.[104] Plato repeatedly uses the image of intoxication (*methe*) to describe the strongest desires unleashed by the part of the soul fixated on satisfying the appetites of the body, the *epithymetikon*.[105] He uses *methe* in this manner not only in the *Republic* (398e and 403e) but also in the *Critias* (121a), *Phaedo* (79c), *Phaedrus* (238b and 256b–c) and *Laws* (639b, 839a).

The youth of the democratic city, exposed to the many and subtle pleasures found, for example, at the *symposion*, become "too soft to resist pleasures and pains, and too idle" and so enamored of change and spending they fail to act when the poor form alliances with powers outside the *polis* in order to overthrow it (555d–556b). The tyrant is the epitome of desire unleashed, willing to do anything to maintain his unchecked power and voracious—distinctly sympotic—lifestyle. Should the populace, realizing its mistake, attempt to remove him from power "like a father driving a son along with his troublesome drinking fellows out of the house," they will discover just "what sort of beast they have begotten, welcomed and made great" (*Republic* 569a–b). This passage must draw its inspiration from behavior that was common enough, at least in aristocratic households, to have been recognizable by Plato's readers.

The psychological portrait of the tyrant in Plato's *Republic* is that of a creature of wild internal *stasis*, an unrestrained *symposiarch*, such as when Socrates asks "doesn't a drunken man have something of a tyrannic turn of mind," and isn't it a fact that "a man becomes tyrannic in the precise sense when, either by nature or by his practices or both, he has become drunken, erotic, and melancholic?" (573c, and cf. 568e and *Timaeus* 86e–87b). One is reminded here of the heavily intoxicated, unmistakably Dionysian Alcibiades intruding upon Agathon's celebration in Plato's *Symposium*, demanding in the manner of an over-indulging and unrestrained *komastes* to be made master of the banquet and given the power to dictate the course of the drinking.[106]

Stasis, Ekstasis, Being, and Time

The life of the tyrant is most like being "bound in . . . a prison" which, far from being the most free and happy is the most "perfectly wretched" (579b, 579d). Like the city he rules over, the tyrant's soul is comprised of all the better elements enslaved to "the most depraved and maddest"; his spirit is "necessarily . . . poverty ridden and insatiable"; emotionally he is always "full of fear," surrounded by nothing but enemies, constantly "complaining, sighing, lamenting and suffering" (577d–578a, 579b). Such is the "harvest . . . of a man who has a bad regime in himself" (579c). To expect a man "not having control over himself" to adequately rule over others is like expecting "a body which is sick and without control over itself" to be able to spend its time publicly "contesting and fighting other bodies" (579c–d).

The Athenian aristocracy had suffered a loss of power in the half century before the death of Socrates in 399 BCE. It is "characteristic of ruling elites (and particularly those whose grip on power has been loosened) to regard the political realm not as an area for the adjudication of legitimate conflicts, but as a state or condition of health-disease, order-anarchy."[107] Plato's language depicts the rise of *stasis* as a sickness or disease, a disorderly lack of internal self-control, with the soul of the tyrant as the imprisonment or enslavement of the soul's better elements, particularly reason and wisdom. As a member of the Athenian social elite, one whose reflection was so strongly centered on the notion of *sophrosyne*, *stasis* and what would soon become known as *ekstasis*—including the ecstasy of intoxication—were two sides of the same problem; both are forms of anarchy, *ad captandum vulgus*.[108] In the *Republic*, for example, he says that on the one hand the philosopher, by keeping company with the "divine and orderly . . . becomes orderly and divine, to the extent that it is possible for a human being" (500c–d), while the blame for the many being "harshly disposed towards philosophy" rests with outsiders who have, in the fashion of the *komos*, "burst in like drunken revelers, abusing one another and indulging a taste for quarreling" or in other words "doing what is least seemly in philosophy" (500b).

The nature of the difficulty with intoxication runs something like this, although no single author in the Classical Greek world including Plato appears to state it quite so systematically: recreational intoxication occurring within the *symposion* can be problematic because it gives rise to the *komos*; the *komos*, wherein the mind or *noos* is placed in a condition of discordant mental derangement or *ekstasis*, in turn frequently leads to acts of *hubris*; acts of *hubris* are in turn predominantly committed by the aristocracy and aimed at members of lower social classes and/or individuals with lesser *time*, generating enmity and class friction, and ultimately disrupting the healthy autonomic functioning of the *polis*, a condition known as *stasis*. It is *stasis* that, like a disease, destroys *dike* and it was within this context that writers such as Plato appear to have problematized intoxication.

With Plato political corruption becomes noetic corruption. His remedy lies in what has been termed "'therapeutic' philosophy."[109] For Plato *therapeia* for the *psyche* was analogous to what the *Republic* (518e) calls bodily "habits and exercises" and what ancient Greek medicine characterized as regimen, *diaita*.[110] The problems of the *komos, hubris,* and *stasis* are not solely, or even primarily, cured through the fusion of philosophy with political power, a strategy the *Republic* appears to advocate only to ultimately reject most notably at the end of Book IX (592a–b, and cf. *Laws* 709e–712b). The *Republic*'s true aim is to lay "a pattern . . . down for the man who wants to found a city within himself" (592b), something that is not all that different from the program of the *Alcibiades*.[111] The well-founded *internal* regime is the best bulwark against the *nosos* of what Plato calls *stasiazonta*. A key aspect of this "pattern," as we will discover below, is the formulation of a new and substantially different set of ethics governing the use of drugs, in two senses. First, with regard to the recreational intoxication of the *symposion* in particular, and second, with regard to all the meanings of the word for drug, *pharmakon*, more generally.

Notes

1. Cf. Aristotle, *Nicomachean Ethics* 1154a. What makes a man bad is not experiencing bodily pleasures but rather pursuing them to excess. "Everyone," he writes, "enjoys tasty food and wine and sex in some degree, but not everyone to the right degree."

2. Michel Foucault, *The Use of Pleasure—The History of Sexuality, Vol. 2* (New York: Vintage Books, 1986), 52. See Harold Tarrant, "Wine in Ancient Greece—Some Platonist Ponderings," in *Wine and Philosophy: A Symposium on Thinking and Drinking*, ed. Fritz Allhoff (Malden, MA: Blackwell Publishing, 2008), 18–21, for a parallel, though somewhat different, view about Greek drinking ethics. Tarrant's interpretation of the details of these ethics is, however, needlessly speculative.

3. Tim Unwin, *Wine and the Vine* (New York: Routledge, 1996), 86. A few of the many additional references to wine in the *Iliad* include 1.559–62, 11.754–58, and 23.249–53, in the *Odyssey* include 2.376–79, 4.698–701, 9.385–89 (discussed further in chapter 4, below), and 13.56–62. All line number references from the *Iliad* and *Odyssey* in this chapter are from the translations by Robert Fagles, and refer to his translation, not the line numbers of the original Greek text. Robert Fagles, trans., *Homer—The Iliad* (New York: Penguin Press, 1990) and Robert Fagles, trans., *Homer—The Odyssey* (New York: Penguin, 1996).

4. Arthur P. McKinlay, "New Light on the Question of Homeric Temperance," *Quarterly Journal of Studies on Alcohol* 14, no. 1 (1953): 78–93 makes this point with

regards to epic poetry and alcohol. I do the same for epic poetry and intoxicating drugs more generally in chapter 4, below.

5. Patrick E. McGovern, *Ancient Wine: The Search for the Origins of Viniculture* (Princeton, NJ: Princeton University Press, 2003), 258. As McGovern observes, in Greece "this phenomenon is best exemplified by the classical Greek *symposion,* but its roots can be traced back to Middle Minoan times and Mycenaean palace life."

6. Lisa Marie Elliot, *Gendering the Production and Consumption of Wine and Olive Oil in Ancient Greece* (M.A. thesis, Miami University, 2006), 25.

7. Hesiod views women much more dimly than Homer, criticizing them as idle and scheming in addition to other defects.

8. Quoted in Martin Heidegger, *Sojourns—The Journey to Greece* (Albany, NY: State University of New York Press, 2005), 68 n. 12.

9. Unless otherwise indicated, quotes of Theognis in this chapter are from Dorthea Wender, trans. *Hesiod: Theogny, Works and Days* (New York: Penguin Books, 1973).

10. See Wender, *Hesiod,* 89–95. Each of these is significant for understanding Plato and the *symposion*: Plato's views are also aristocratic; he however expresses serious difficulties with music—that of the flute in particular—and he also expresses difficulty with the drinking songs sung at the *symposion.* See chapter 3, below.

11. The translation of this quote and the one in the sentence to follow are taken from Thomas Figueira and Gregory Nagy, *Theognis of Megara—Poetry and the Polis* (Baltimore, MD: The Johns Hopkins University Press, 1985).

12. François Lissarrgue, *The Aesthetics of the Greek Banquet—Images of Wine and Ritual* (Princeton, NJ: Princeton University Press, 1990), 63–4.

13. Lissarrgue, *The Aesthetics of the Greek Banquet,* 65. In modern advertising wine users are urged to "enjoy responsibly" in a manner that recalls ancient ethics, but under the weight of addiction theory, enjoyment and intoxication have become far more dichotomous, i.e. "right" enjoyment of a legal recreational drug such as wine is defined in terms of a *lack* of intoxication, and responsibility is often defined in terms of refusing recreational drugs altogether. John J. Rumbarger, *Profits, Power, and Prohibition: American Alcohol Reform and the Industrializing of America, 1800–1930* (Albany, NY: State University of New York Press, 1989) is instructive, in the case of alcohol. Late nineteenth century prohibition activists utilized a discourse that viewed any form of intoxication as a threat, couching that threat in terms that were founded on traditional Judeo-Christian concepts of sin while simultaneously blending that discourse with ethnic prejudices and newly emerging concepts of industrial efficiency.

14. Translation by Andrew M. Miller, *Greek Lyric: An Anthology in Translation* (Indianapolis, IN: Hackett Publishing, 1996), 107–8.

15. Evenos is said to be an acquaintance of Socrates in Plato's *Phaedo* 61c.

16. This quote from Theognis is from the translation by Miller, *Greek Lyric,* 88.

17. Critias was known to have composed tragedies, elegies, and prose works, but his name survives largely because he was a leading member of the Thirty Tyrants, a pro-Spartan oligarchy that was installed after Athens was defeated by Sparta in the Peloponnesian War. His lost work *Constitution of Sparta* praised moderation in drinking and argued against "intoxicating the body with unmeasured drinking." See Matthew Dillon and Lynda Garland, *Ancient Greece: Social and Historical Documents from Archaic Times to the Death of Socrates, Second Edition* (New York: Routledge, 2000), 189.

18. William W. Fortenbaugh, Robert W. Sharples, and Michael G. Sollenberger, eds., *Theophrastus of Eresus. On Sweat, On Dizziness and On Fatigue* (Leiden, Netherlands: Brill, 2003), 195. See also 199, 230–31.

19. Nicander continues the passage on aconite by saying that just as "the Silens, the nurses of the horned Dionysus, crushed the wild grapes, and having for the first time fortified their spirits with the foaming drink, were confused in their sight and on reeling feet rushed madly about the hill of Nysa, even so is the sight of these men [who drink aconite] darkened beneath the weight of an evil doom" (30–35).

20. 1 Timothy 3:3; Titus 1:7. The word also could mean "quarrelsome" or "violent." As discussed in chapter 1, above, *paroinein* was one of the Greek terms for violently irrational or harmful drunkenness.

21. *Kothonist* is often mistranslated as "addicted to the cup" as if the ancients understood such behavior in pejorative terms approximating the modern meaning of the term addiction. This is but a single example of the presentism that continues to plague studies of drug use in the ancient world.

22. Elliot, *Gendering the Production and Consumption of Wine and Olive Oil in Ancient Greece*, 29 for example writes that women's consumption of wine differed from that of men "in the location in which it was consumed. Why women were restricted from consuming wine in certain environments, such as a symposium, is probably less a question about concern for health and more a statement about social roles."

23. Harold Tarrant, "Wine in Ancient Greece—Some Platonist Ponderings," in *Wine and Philosophy: A Symposium on Thinking and Drinking*, ed. Fritz Allhoff (Malden, MA: Blackwell Publishing, 2008), 17.

24. Nancy Demand, *Birth, Death, and Motherhood in Classical Greece* (Baltimore, MD: The Johns Hopkins University Press, 1994), 27.

25. Demand, *Birth, Death, and Motherhood in Classical Greece*, 147.

26. Sarah B. Pomeroy, trans., *Xenophon—Oeconomicus—A Social and Historical Commentary* (New York: Oxford University Press, 1994). Women's self-control or restraint (one of the several meanings of *sophrosyne*) was largely defined by their *silence*: "for instance at *Ajax* 586 'Ask me no questions./Possess yourself in patience [*sophrosyne*]', *Herakleidai* 476–77 and *Andromache* 465." See Barbara E. Goff, *The Noose of Words—Readings of Desire, Violence and Language in Euripides'* Hippolytos (New York: Cambridge University Press, 1990), 39.

27. Demand, *Birth, Death, and Motherhood in Classical Greece*, 8–9 places these passages in the context of "evidence that growing girls were fed less than boys" but the context is clearly broader and is meant to encompass all the appetites and this control is cited as being equally desirable for men as well as women.

28. Demand, *Birth, Death, and Motherhood in Classical Greece*, 148–49. The women whose presence at the *symposion* was considered unproblematic are discussed in chapter 1, above.

29. Jeffrey Henderson, "Older Women in Attic Old Comedy," *Transactions of the American Philological Association* 117 (1987): 119–20. Dickie adds loquacity to the other characteristics. See Matthew W. Dickie, *Magic and Magicians in the Greco-Roman World* (New York: Routledge, 2001), 185.

30. Dickie, *Magic and Magicians in the Greco-Roman World*, 89. Additional details regarding the rights of the older woman may be found in Demand, *Birth, Death, and Motherhood in Classical Greece*, 27–29.

31. This extends to the view of women and intoxication in ancient Rome. "Had the Romans [such as Cicero and Polybius] who condemn drinking in women had in mind women of every class and condition, they would not have justified their condemnation by appealing to the power that wine has to incite the female sex to adultery. What concerns them are the morals of respectable Roman women." Dickie, *Magic and Magicians in the Greco-Roman World*, 186–87.

32. Dickie, *Magic and Magicians in the Greco-Roman World*, 90.

33. On this theme see Dickie, *Magic and Magicians in the Greco-Roman World*, 89–91.

34. Elliot, *Gendering the Production and Consumption of Wine and Olive Oil in Ancient Greece*, 31.

35. Oswyn Murray, "Forms of Sociality," in *The Greeks*, ed. Jean-Pierre Vernant (Chicago: University of Chicago Press, 1995): 232.

36. Lissarrgue, *The Aesthetics of the Greek Banquet*, 29–31.

37. Oswyn Murray, "The Affair of the Mysteries: Democracy and Drinking Group," in *Sympotica—A Symposium on the* Symposion, ed. Oswyn Murray (Oxford: Clarendon Press, 1990), 150.

38. Murray, "The Affair of the Mysteries," 157 describes the case as "our most revealing source for the less reputable side of sympotic behavior."

39. The plaintiff in the case against Konon also suggests, in a language that Murray describes as "curiously religious," that "these groups practice unspeakable forms of sexual initiation." See Murray, "The Affair of the Mysteries," 157. I return to the matter of mock-initiation rites held during the *symposion* in chapter 5, below.

40. Oswyn Murray, "The Solonian Law on *Hubris*," in *Nomos—Essays in Athenian Law, Politics, and Society*, ed. Paul Cartledge, Paul Millett and Stephen Todd (Cambridge: Cambridge University Press, 1990), 131–32.

41. Murray, "The Solonian Law on *Hubris*," 139–40.

42. Alan H. Sommerstein, trans., *The Comedies of Aristophanes. Volume 4—Wasps* (Warminster, Wilts, UK: Aris and Philips, 1983), 235. On the issue of slaves and *hubris* see Nick Fisher, "*Hybris*, Status, and Slavery," in *The Greek World*, ed. Anton Powell (London: Routledge, 1995).

43. A. M. Bowie, *Aristophanes—Myth, Ritual, and Comedy* (New York: Cambridge University Press, 1993), 96 writes that this loss of identity is "surely the antithesis of the adult Philocleon, serving in courts and phalanx, with his violence checked (nominally, at least) by convention and law, and enjoying the pleasures of family life due to an old man."

44. Murray, "Forms of Sociality," 240.

45. Murray, "The Affair of the Mysteries," 157.

46. Georg Luck, *Arcana Mundi—Magic and the Occult in the Greek and Roman Worlds. A Collection of Ancient Texts*, 2nd Edition (Baltimore, MD: The Johns Hopkins University Press, 2006): 482.

47. Nick Fisher, "The Law of *Hubris* in Athens," *Nomos—Essays in Athenian Law, Politics, and Society*, ed. Paul Cartledge, Paul Millett and Stephen Todd (Cambridge: Cambridge University Press, 1990), 128–29.

48. Mckinlay, "New Light on the Question of Homeric Temperance," 70.

49. Lissarrague, *The Aesthetics of the Greek Banquet*, 28.

50. François Lissarrague, "Around the Krater: An Aspect of Banquet Imagery," in *Sympotica—A Symposium on the* Symposion, ed. Oswyn Murray (Oxford: Clarendon Press, 1990), 196.

51. Jean-Louis Durand, Francoise Frontisi-Ducroux, and François Lissarrague, "Wine: Human and Divine," in *A City of Images—Iconography and Society in Ancient Greece*, ed. Claude Bérard (Princeton, NJ: Princeton University Press, 1989), 125–26; Lissarrague, *The Aesthetics of the Greek Banquet*, 28–31, 96; Ezio Pellizer, "Outline of a Morphology of Sympotic Entertainment," in *Sympotica—A Symposium on the* Symposion, ed. Oswyn Murray (Oxford: Clarendon Press, 1990), 181–82. See also François Lissarrague, *The Greek Vases—The Athenians and their Images* (New York: Riverside

Book Company, 2001) and David Walsh, *Distorted Ideals in Greek Vase Painting: The World of Mythological Burlesque* (New York: Cambridge University Press, 2009).

52. Also spelled *hybris* by some writers.

53. Fisher, "*Hybris*, Status, and Slavery," 45–46 and cf. M. Gagarin, "The Athenian Law against Hybris," in *Arktouros: Hellenic Studies Presented to Bernard M. W. Knox,* ed. Glen W. Bowersock (Berlin and New York: Walter de Gruyter, 1979).

54. Murray, "The Solonian Law of *Hubris*," 141, and Fisher, "Hybris, Status, and Slavery," 46.

55. Quoted in Jean-Pierre Vernant, *Myth and Thought Among the Greeks* (London: Routledge and Kegan Paul, 1983), 3.

56. See the glossary in Paul Cartledge, Paul Millett, and Stephen Todd, eds. *Nomos: Essays in Athenian Law, Politics and Society* (New York: Cambridge University Press, 1990), 218–19 and 239.

57. Murray, "The Solonian Law of *Hubris*," 142.

58. See chapter 5, below.

59. Nick Fisher, "Drink, *Hybris*, and the Promotion of Harmony in Sparta," in *Classical Sparta—Techniques Behind Her Success*, ed. Anton Powell (Norman, OK: University of Oklahoma Press, 1988), 29 writes that "*hybris* was a common danger of the *symposion* which got out of control, and was a major element in Solon's poetic analysis of the problems in Athens, perhaps producing from him a law to restrain it." He does not appear to be aware of the legislation Athenaeus attributes to Solon. Instead he conjectures that Solon's legislation consisted of "double penalties for drunken assaults," referring to a lawmaker named Pittacus, ruler of Mytilene, in the early sixth century. Although he does not cite a primary source, the Pittacus he mentions is almost certainly the one discussed by Aristotle. Aristotle, however, merely says that Pittacus implemented a law "that if drunken men commit an offense they should pay a larger fine than sober men," so as to set an example for others (*Politics* 1274b). Saunders interprets this difficult passage correctly. See Trevor J. Saunders, *Plato's Penal Code—Tradition, Controversy and Reform in Greek Penology* (Oxford: Clarendon Press, 1991), 111.

60. Murray, "The Solonian Law of *Hubris*," 144, and cf. Fisher, "Hybris, Status, and Slavery," 46.

61. Hundreds of years later Athenaeus voices concern with his contemporaries in Alexandria, writing of individuals who "shout, bawl, and objurgate the wine-pourer, the waiter and the chef; the slaves are in tears, being buffeted by knuckles right and left. To say nothing of the guests, who dine in complete embarrassment" (10.420e). The drinking party allowed to go on for days on end gives rise to derision among the guests, then abuse and counter-abuse, followed by "blows . . . and drunken brawling" (10.421a–b).

62. Arthur P. McKinlay, "Attic Temperance," *Quarterly Journal of Studies on Alcohol* 11, no. 1 (1951): 84. Peter Garnsey, *Food and Society in Classical Antiquity* (Cambridge: Cambridge University Press, 1999), 83 writes "Greco-Roman societies . . . were relatively free from taboos and restrictive regulations regarding food."

63. William L. Brown, *An Address on Inebriety amongst the Ancients and How they "Cured" It* (London: Aberdeen University Press, 1898): 15. Francoise Frontisi-Ducroux, "In the Mirror of the Mask," in *A City of Images—Iconography and Society in Ancient Greece*, ed. Claude Bérard (Princeton, NJ: Princeton University Press, 1989), 154, 156, while correct in noting the importance the Greeks placed on a measure of order at the *symposion*, insinuates the Ophthalmoi contributed to this order by monitoring the drinking and the drinkers. This would appear to be a misunderstanding of their basic function.

64. Andrew Lintott, *Violence, Civil Strife and Revolution in the Classical City—750–330 B.C.* (Baltimore, MD: The Johns Hopkins University Press, 1982), 34. The ar-

gument being that *stasis* arose from *histasthai*, usually translated as "to stand or be standing."

65. Kostas Kalimtzis, *Aristotle on Political Enmity and Disease—An Inquiry into Stasis* (Albany, NY: State University of New York Press, 2000), xiv, 18–19. Kalimtzis indicates that at their worst, contemporary definitions approach tautology, "in which *stasis*, a state of conflict, is said to be caused by a standing of conflicting parties."

66. Kalimtzis, *Aristotle on Political Enmity and Disease*, 8 writes that the *nosos-stasis* pairing appears and reappears in the works of "Aeschylus, Euripides, Plato, Aristotle, Demosthenes, Isocrates, Lysias, and others. The concept of *stasis* as a *nosos* will serve Aristotle as an unstated first principle, which he will not refer to in any special way because it was so commonplace in his culture."

67. Kalimtzis, *Aristotle on Political Enmity and Disease*, 18. Oddly, this "connotation of bringing or coming to standstill, or stopping" is virtually absent from the literature on *stasis*, even though it is "one of the meanings of [*istemi*] and its passive intransitive form, [*istamai*], from which the noun *stasis* is derived."

68. See the discussion by Kalimtzis in *Aristotle on Political Enmity and Disease*, 196–97 n. 16, and cf. 197 n. 21.

69. Kalimtzis, *Aristotle on Political Enmity and Disease*, xv. On the emphasis given to controlling anger and rage in antiquity see William V. Harris, *Restraining Rage: The Ideology of Anger Control in Classical Antiquity* (Cambridge, MA: Harvard University Press, 2001) and Susanna Braund and Glenn W. Most, *Ancient Anger: Perspectives from Homer to Galen* (New York: Cambridge University Press, 2003).

70. An unbroken tradition from Plato to Hobbes viewed *stasis* negatively; modernity on the other hand reconstructed the concept into a positive value. On this reconstruction see Paul A. Rahe, *Republics Ancient and Modern: Classical Republicanism and the American Revolution* (Chapel Hill, NC: University of North Carolina Press, 1992).

71. Kalimtzis, *Aristotle on Political Enmity and Disease*, 2.

72. Quoted in Herbert W. Smyth, trans., *Aeschylus—Agamemnon, Libation-Bearers, Eumenides, Fragments* (Cambridge, MA: Harvard University Press, 1960). The grammatical relation of the words in this passage is difficult to convey. The imagery being conjured here runs along the lines that *stasis* is like a ravenous carnivore, who greedily seizes upon vengeance against the *polis*, producing calamity where the reprisal for bloodshed is yet more blood.

73. Kalimtzis, *Aristotle on Political Enmity and Disease*, 191 n. 3.

74. Kalimtzis, *Aristotle on Political Enmity and Disease*, 9.

75. Kalimtzis, *Aristotle on Political Enmity and Disease*, 8–13.

76. This discussion of Plato and *stasis* relies heavily on Kalimtzis, *Aristotle on Political Enmity and Disease*, 15–31 and Costas M. Constantinou, *States of Political Discourse: Words, Regimes, Seditions* (New York: Routledge, 2004), 1–14.

77. Kalimtzis, *Aristotle on Political Enmity and Disease*, 23–24.

78. Froma I. Zeitlin, "Figuring Fidelity in Homer's *Odyssey*," in *The Distaff Side: Representing the Female in Homer's* Odyssey, ed. Beth Cohen (New York: Oxford University Press, 1995), 151 n. 57.

79. Kalimtzis, *Aristotle on Political Enmity and Disease*, 26. See also Foucault, *The Hermeneutics of the Subject*, 31–79 who discusses this at length.

80. Kalimtzis, *Aristotle on Political Enmity and Disease*, 196 n. 13.

81. Kalimtzis, *Aristotle on Political Enmity and Disease*, 23.

82. See my Introduction, above.

83. E. R. Dodds, *Pagan and Christian in an Age of Anxiety* (Cambridge, MA: Cambridge University Press, 1965), 70–71 writes that "*ekstasis* and its cognates have in fact a

very wide range of application. In classical Greek they are used to describe any departure from the normal condition, any abrupt change of mind or mood, and out of this usage various more specialized senses developed."

84. Constantinou, *States of Political Discourse*, 10.

85. Rohde, for example, writes that *ekstasis* "is a 'brief madness,' just as madness is a prolonged *ekstasis*. But the *ekstasis*, the temporary *alienatio mentis* of the Dionysiac cult was not thought of as a vain purposeless wandering in a region of pure delusion, but as a *heiromania*, a sacred madness in which the soul, leaving the body, winged its way to union with the god. It is now with and in the god, in the condition of *enthousiasmos*; those who are possessed . . . *entheoi* live and have their being in the god." Erwin Rohde, *Psyche—The Cult of Souls and the Belief in Immortality among the Greeks* (New York and London: Routledge and Kegan Paul, 1925), 259.

86. Samual Angus, *Mystery Religions and Christianity* (New Hyde Park, NY: University Books, 1975), 101, 104.

87. Plato's extensive use of medical terminology is discussed in chapter 7, below.

88. Gilbert Rouget, *Music and Trance—A Theory of the Relations between Music and Possession* (Chicago: The University of Chicago Press, 1985), 7. See also Leonard Brandwood, *Word Index to Plato* (Leeds, UK: W. S. Maney and Son, 1976).

89. Alan Bloom, "Ion," in *The Roots of Political Philosophy—Ten Forgotten Socratic Dialogues*, ed. Thomas L. Pangle (Ithaca, NY: Cornell University Press, 1987), 361.

90. Gerald C. Moss, "Mental Disorders in Antiquity," in *Diseases in Antiquity—A Survey of the Diseases, Injuries and Surgery of Early Populations*, ed. Don Brothwell and A. T. Sandison (Springfield, IL: Charles C. Thomas, 1967), 714 n. 30.

91. Theodore W. Brown, "Descartes, Dualism, and Psychosomatic Medicine," in *The Anatomy of Madness: Essays in the History of Psychiatry. Volume 1: People and Ideas*, ed. W. F. Bynum, Roy Porter, and Michael Shepard (New York: Routledge, 1985), 29–30.

92. Anthony J. Preus, "Drugs and Psychic States in Theophrastus' *Historia plantarum* 9.8–20," in *Theophrastean Studies*, ed. William W. Fortenbaugh and Robert W. Sharples (New Brunswick and Oxford: Transaction Books, 1988), 97 n. 29.

93. The bull figures prominently in the worship of Dionysus, something that would be another reason to associate them with intoxicating mushrooms and ecstasy. See chapter 4, below.

94. Preus "Drugs and Psychic States in Theophrastus' *Historia plantarum* 9.8–20," 83. Aristotle's *On Divination in Sleep* (464a) also mentions *ekstatikoi*.

95. W. S. Hett, *Aristotle—Problems (Vols. 1 and 2)* (Cambridge, MA: Harvard University Press, 1961), vii.

96. Quoted in Randall B. Clark, *The Law Most Beautiful and Best: Medical Argument and Magical Rhetoric in Plato's* Laws (Lanham, MD: Lexington Books, 2003), 30.

97. Preus "Drugs and Psychic States in Theophrastus' *Historia plantarum* 9.8–20," 87.

98. Angus, *Mystery Religions and Christianity*, 104 states that *ekstasis* "was not applied till long after Plato's day to the rapturous state of a soul delivered from earthly conditions" but this does not appear tenable to me, given its appearance and usage in both Aristotle and Theophrastus.

99. M. A. Screech, *Montaigne and Melancholy: The Wisdom of the* Essays (Lanham, MD: Rowman & Littlefield, 2000), 30. On the *Phaedrus* and ecstasy see chapter 6, below.

100. Screech, *Montaigne and Melancholy*, 31.

101. Jeffrey Walker, "Pathos and *Katharsis* in 'Aristotelian' Rhetoric: Some Implications," in *Rereading Aristotle's Rhetoric*, ed. Alan G. Gross and Arthur E. Walzer (Carbondale, IL: Southern Illinois University Press, 2000), 78.

102. Screech, *Montaigne and Melancholy,* 31–2. Worth consulting is Montaigne's own essay "On Drunkenness" in M. A. Screech, trans., *Michel de Montaigne. The Essays: A Selection* (New York: Penguin, 1993), 132–42. The topic of this short essay is as much ecstasy as it is wine intoxication.

103. The "life of the many" is likened to that of cattle "always looking down and with their heads bent to earth," feeding and "fattening themselves, and copulating," when they are not killing each other for more of the same (586a–b, and cf. 430e–431e, 442c–d, 493a–b, 496c–d). It is a position maintained right up until the very end in the *Laws*, where "excessive freedom and liberty" for "the multitude" is drawn out in a similar manner. As Joseph M. Bryant, "Enlightenment Psychology and Political Reaction in Plato's Social Philosophy: An Ideological Contradiction?" *History of Political Thought* 11, no. 3 (1990): 391 points out, "surely all this bears the impress of a reactionary class ideology rather than any philosophical insight."

104. Manuela Tecusan, "*Logos Sympotikos*: Patterns of the Irrational and Philosophical Drinking—Plato Outside the *Symposium*," in *Sympotika—A Symposium on the Symposion*, ed. Oswyn Murray (Oxford: Clarendon Press, 1990), 239. At the same time Plato's text appears to repeat passages from Euripides' *Bacchae* such as: "Dionysus, son of Zeus, delights in banquets"; "Dionysus will not compel women to control their lusts"; "the air is thick with Syrian myrrh"; "so [let] us wear the ivy-wreath and join the dancing"; "wine [is] his gift that charms all grief away . . . [and] soothes the sore regret. . . . Men have to but take their fill [of it] and the sufferings of an unhappy race are banished . . . this is our only cure for the weariness of life."

105. On the *epithymetikon* see chapter 7, below.

106. See chapter 3, below, for further discussion of Alcibiades.

107. Bryant, "Enlightenment Psychology and Political Reaction in Plato's Social Philosophy: An Ideological Contradiction?" 391.

108. Bryant, "Enlightenment Psychology and Political Reaction in Plato's Social Philosophy: An Ideological Contradiction?" 393, n. 49 argues, and I agree, "the decisive elements in Plato's 'exclusionary politics' are not internally derived from his core philosophical principles—least of all from his 'enlightenment psychology'—but constitute ideological residue reflective of the sociopolitical struggles of classical Polis society," i.e. between *demos* and aristocratic *kaloikagathoi*. Yet while he is well aware that this ideological residue might "bear the impress of various social and existential factors" he does not consider how ecstatic religion and drinking within the *symposion*, with their emphasis on the disruption of the participant's identity, might have impinged on Plato's assessment of desire, pleasure, and human character in the democratic regime.

109. J. Peter Euben, *The Tragedy of Political Theory: The Road Not Taken* (Princeton, NJ: Princeton University Press, 1990), 240. See also, for example, Clark, *The Law Most Beautiful and Best*.

110. The importance of *diaita* in ancient Greek medicine is discussed in chapter 7, below.

111. Foucault, for example, mentions that "the approach taken by the *Alcibiades* is in some way the same [as the *Republic*] but turned around; that is to say, in trying to find out what it is to govern well and the nature of good harmony and just government in the city, the interlocutors of the *Alcibiades* inquire about the nature of the soul and look for the *analogon* and model of the city in the individual soul." See Foucault, *The Hermeneutics of the Self*, 54.

Chapter Three

Plato's Reformulation of the *Symposion*

At the very beginning of the *Republic* the elderly Cephalus testifies to the tranquility and freedom he now enjoys very late in life, contrasting it to most of his associates who continue to lament and reminiscence about the sex, "drinking bouts and feasts" they all enjoyed in their youth (329a).[1] To be free of the desire for these pleasures, he assures Socrates, is "to be rid of very many mad masters" (329d).[2] The lamentations of these unnamed companions of Cephalus are almost certainly a reflection of traditional sympotic ethics such as those found in the writings of the poet Theognis who advocates giving "our hearts to banqueting" and, while it is still possible, to "find pleasure in delightful things" because "glorious youth goes by as fast as thought" (983–988). The poet recommends drinking to forget both poverty and enemies, mourning "lovely Youth, which goes from men"—each of us should "weep that painful Age is coming fast" (1129–1132). The analogue between *symposion* and *polis* is evident in the writing of Theognis, who makes the poet the paradigm model of moderate behavior.[3] Plato fashions a model of moderate behavior as well, only with the paradigmatic philosopher, i.e. Socrates.[4] Plato's ethics of intoxication are however remarkably different than that of predecessors such as Theognis. Plato's Socrates regularly opposes or acts in ways contrary to ordinary sympotic ethics.[5]

The *Symposion* in Plato's Dialogues

Many of Plato's dialogues contain references or allusions to sympotic practice or are themselves pervaded by a sympotic atmosphere.[6] In the *Apology* Socrates claims that in contrast to others he did not care for such things as money-making, the management of a household, generalships, public oratory, "and the other offices and conspiracies and the factions that come to be in the city," the latter being another reference to the political cliques (*hetaireiai*) formed through sympotic associations (36b–c).[7] In the *Crito* Socrates likens the kind of life he would lead were he to escape prison and avoid his death sentence to the life of a slave or a vile banqueter in the Thessalian revelries (53e).[8] To flee from the laws of Athens is to move closer to the intoxicated mindlessness of a sympotic lifestyle, a choice Socrates clearly rejects. In the *Phaedo*, as the moment to drink the poison (*pharmakon*) draws near, Socrates rejects the same Crito's offer to give himself up one last time to the pleasures of food, drink, and sex as other condemned men evidently did prior to the execution of their sentence. Earlier in the same dialogue, as he is describing the sort of wicked soul that is compelled to wander graveyards as a shadowy phantom, Socrates names the cultivators of gluttony, lechery, and drunkenness as the sorts of souls likely to be reincarnated as an ass in their next life (81e, and cf. Aristophanes' *Wasps* 1310). When he is at last handed the *pharmakon* that will shortly put an end to his life, the Socrates of the *Phaedo* asks (117b) whether he may pour some of the liquid out as a libation, presumably to the gods, as would be done at a typical *symposion* to commence the drinking (e.g. see Plato *Symposium* 176a and Xenophon *Symposium* 2.1).[9] The request is refused.

The *Theatetus* also finds the philosopher contrasted to the man of worldly affairs in a manner that is distinctly opposed to the traditional aristocratic-sympotic lifestyle. The philosopher, Socrates explains, remains relatively ignorant of such matters as the way to the marketplace (*agora*), where the law-courts (*dikasterion*), council chamber (*bouleuterion*), and other places of public assembly are, nor does he become involved in the "scrambling of political cliques (*hetaireiai*) for office; social functions, dinners, parties with flute girls—such things never enter his head even in a dream" (173d). While other men indulge in such diversions as "drinking parties and the other things that go along with these," the *Phaedrus* informs us that the really knowledgeable man finds his amusement in a more sedate pastime consisting of writing down his thoughts (276d). Unwilling to fall in with the men of politics who like savage "wild beasts" are bent on perpetrating injustice, or join "the madness of the many," the rare human being who keeps company with philosophy, we are told in the *Republic*, "keeps quiet and minds his own business—as a man in a storm, when dust and rain are blown about by the wind" (496c–d). He retreats into an isolated private life, content if he can manage to live his own life free and pure of "injustice and unholy deeds" (496d–e).

The *Protagoras* exhibits "a cautious wavering between a friendly *synousia* [word feast] and a more sophisticated *symposion*."[10] For example, as the conversation between Socrates and Protagoras is about to get underway it is suggested that the benches and couches be rearranged in a circle; some of the discussants appear to sit while others recline in a sympotic manner (317d). Socrates expresses displeasure with both the form (long speeches) and the content (Simonides' lyric poetry) of the conversation and threatens to leave the group (335b). In doing this he would be attacking two central elements of the classical *symposion*. Simonides (ca. 556–468 BCE) was reputed to have placed first in fifty-six dithyrambic competitions.[11] Of the poetry sung at symposia, much of which was frequently political in character, that of Alkaios, Stesichorus, Anakeon and Simonides were the most popular.[12]

Socrates complains that poetry, either its recitation or the critical discussion of it, belongs to "the wine parties of second rate and commonplace people" (347c). This appears to be another indication that, by the Classical Period at least, drinking symposia occurred outside the circle of the "sons of the old families of Athens."[13] At any rate, poetry accompanied by music was a defining feature of the *symposion*. The *aulos* "was the instrument . . . of elegiac poetry in particular," while stringed instruments such as the *barbiton* were the instruments of lyric poetry.[14] Men of "worth and culture," Socrates argues in the *Protagoras*, can find enjoyment without such "frivolous nonsense" as girls "piping or dancing or harping" (347d). He then describes a different sympotic program based on reciprocal speeches, consisting of "sober discussion" that tests the mettle of each participant, something he says remains possible "even if the drinking is really heavy" (347d–e).[15]

When neither Socrates nor Protagoras is willing to compromise by altering his manner of speaking, Hippias responds by advocating, much like a speaker in a democratic assembly, the appointment of an "arbitrator, referee or president" to moderate the discussion, something that in itself is also distinctly sympotic, and prevent either man from becoming offensive to the other (337a–338b). Hippias' proposal wins "general consent and a round of applause" from the group and would appear to reinforce the collaborative atmosphere at this moment. Socrates, however, refuses to abide by the group's wishes, escaping their decision with some clever rhetoric (it would be offensive to Protagoras to try to appoint anyone his overseer; he is surely the wisest), and comes up with an alternative more to his own liking: since Protagoras' answers are too long and he will not shorten them, he may ask the questions and Socrates will demonstrate how a respondent *should* answer (338c–e).

In the *Philebus* Socrates calls upon Dionysus and Hephaestus to guide the discussion of the good life as one of "mixed" pleasures (61b). Dionysus is "invoked in his function as wine-blender, Hephaestus as the maker of metal alloys (or perhaps as wine-server to the gods)."[16] The joining of the act of mixing with prayer again recalls sympotic practice, as does the later reference to Zeus the Deliverer (66d). Reflecting a growing pessimism over the capacity of most people to live their lives guided by reason alone, the *Philebus* adopts a position that it is appropriate to human nature to create a mixture of *hedone* and *phronesis*, the work of two wine-pourers, who blend the sweet honey of desire with the harsh water of wisdom (61b–c).

The mix, however, isn't quite that simple. Pure reason is mixed in, as are less pure types (62c–d). Ultimately *all* types of reason are allowed into the Good Life (62c–d). As for the pleasures, all *necessary* pleasures are allowed into the mixture (62e–63a). The unnecessary pleasures, the sympotic or drone-like pleasures mentioned in the *Republic*, are not part of the Good Life.[17] See table 1 at the end of this chapter. These pleasures endlessly create "trouble" for a person, owing to their "frenzied irrationality," something that disturbs the soul; they prevent the formation of intellect and reason for the most part, and if such capacities do come into being they "spoil a man utterly by making him lazy and hence forgetful" (63c–d). It would be illogical, Socrates says, to create a mixture of pleasure and intellect that includes those pleasures that "accompany self-indulgence and other forms of vice" (63e–64a).

Where the effort at mixture fails, leading to a lack of moderation and proportion, the mix fails, ruining both the components and itself, leaving only an "unmixed confusion" (64d–e). The point of Plato's discussion is clear enough: "one drop of wine in a glass of water is disproportionate; the mixture 'does away with its components' in that the wine can no longer be said to exist, 'and with itself' in that it cannot be said to be a real mixture."[18] The passage could be read as saying the exact opposite: if too little water, in other words reason as intellect, is added to the honey/wine, i.e. the pleasures, what remains would still be unmixed wine and, were the context a *symposion*, this invites the disordered confusion of the *komos*. Plato regularly uses the word for intoxication, *methe,* to describe the influential pull that desires can exert upon the soul (*Phaedo* 79c, *Republic* 403e, *Phaedrus* 238b and 256b, and *Laws* 639b and 839a). Desires compel most individuals like a mad, frenzied, savage master.[19] They are an *epithymetic compulsion* that must be subjected to philosophy's reordering intervention.[20]

Intoxication in Plato's *Symposium*

The *Symposium* is another vivid, and arguably the most sustained, indicator of Plato's hostile attitudes towards a number of sympotic motifs, including what appear to be prevailing Greek drinking ethics.[21] The dialogue, believed to have been written between 385–370 BCE, critiques the specific ethics structuring the drinking party and the pedagogical function that structure served in the formation of ethical discourse generally. Plato, in other words, is no friend of that defining feature of the *symposion*, the *logos sympotikos*, discussed above in chapter 1. On the one hand the dialogue is an important commentary on the perception of others that Socrates was a man of *hubris*.[22] On the other the dialogue is also at the same time a commentary on one of the most guilty profaners of the Eleusinian Mysteries, Alcibiades, and the man who accused Socrates of the same, Aristophanes. It is a dialogue that seeks to revise the reader's understanding of the relationship between "Socrates, Alcibiades, philosophy, *eros* and Eleusis . . . against the background of the profanations of the summer of 415."[23] Put another way, the *Symposium* should be understood as yet another *apology* of Socrates.[24]

The story of the *Symposium* is narrated by a follower of Socrates named Apollodorus, who is recalling what he was told by yet another follower named Aristodemus. It was a good thing, the poet Theognis wrote, to "be invited to a banquet and sit by a good [*esthlos*] man who knows all sorts of wisdom [*sophie*] (563–64). This is precisely what will happen within the dialogue, with Aristodemus being fortunate enough to sit next to Socrates. When he first meets Socrates at the beginning of the *Symposium*, Aristodemus notices that not only is Socrates clean and his hair brushed, he is wearing shoes (174a). Socrates apparently owns a pair of shoes, even if he rarely wears them (*Phaedrus* 229a), and he has decent standards of personal hygiene, at least in contrast to the unwashed and shoeless Socrates of Aristophanes' *Clouds* and *Birds*. It is not clear how unusual Socrates' lack of bathing might have been.[25] At the end of the dialogue Socrates goes to the Lyceum, a public bath and gymnasium, for a wash (223d).

Socrates tells Aristodemus that he avoided the first night of Agathon's celebration altogether, offering the seemingly weak excuse that he "couldn't face the crowd" (174a). Although Aristodemus has no formal invitation to Agathon's celebration, Socrates lags behind, "absorbed in his own thoughts," letting his associate suffer the mild embarrassment of arriving uninvited (174d–e). The uninvited guest, the buffoon or *akletos*, was a standard device of sympotic literature.[26] Socrates doesn't appear until the banquet meal is half completed (175c). He finishes eating with the others, and we are very briefly told that offerings are poured, hymns sung, and "all the usual things" that go on at symposia (176a). By "usual things" Plato means the end of the *deipnon* and the commencement of the *symposion*, with its recreational drinking and other entertainment such as the *skolion* or drinking song (cf. *Gorgias* 451e).[27] The offerings of wine marked an important moment in the ritual order of a typical sympotic celebration. Plato however skips over this religious aspect of the *symposion* with scarcely a word.[28]

At this point, Aristodemus recalls, "our thoughts turned to drinking." Another guest, Pausanias, makes a somewhat curious suggestion. He asks how the drinking can be made "as painless as possible" because he is still feeling "rather frail" after the previous day's intoxication. Aristophanes too begs off "another evening of hard drinking," since he was among those who "sank without trace" during the first night's festivities (176b). This is a clear indication the drinking had been quite heavy. Eryximachus, a physician, speaking for himself, Aristodemus, and Phaedrus, says it would be fortunate indeed for them, being inexperienced drinkers, "if you hard drinkers are prepared to take an evening off" (176c). Since Socrates is neutral on the subject, at least according to Eryximachus, everyone agrees to drink whatever they are comfortable with, instead of treating the situation as a *compulsory* command to become drunk (176e).

Within the ethical-aesthetic structure of the typical fifth- or fourth-century *symposion*, there must have frequently been a group expectation of drinking well past the point of light inebriation, albeit in an often ritualized manner more or less casually guided by a leader referred to, as we saw above in chapter 1, as a *symposiarch, archon,* etc. Xenophon, writing of conditions in Sparta in his *Constitution of Sparta* (5.5), lauds the Spartan common meal, the *syssitia*, as something that gave little opportunity for insolence, drunken uproar, immodest acts, and unseemly talk, the inference being that in other cities, like Athens, such behavior was the norm at private banquets. Lycurgus, Xenophon writes, did away with compulsory drinking, a practice he believed was ruinous of both body and mind (5.4). In contrast the imperative *pithi* (drink!) appears to have been common at Athenian symposia (e.g. Athenaeus 10.445f–446c). In the Athenian *symposion* one found such customs as *examystizein*, or drinking an entire cup "in one breath," something that was done even with unmixed wine (11.783d); using music to speed the tempo of the drinking (11.783e); requiring those who failed to answer a riddle correctly to drink (10.448e); proposing toasts and declarations of love and then passing the cup from left to right for everyone to drink (10.432d–e). Acts of overindulgence are further confirmed by vases and drinking cups that, for example, depict acts of vomiting, sometimes from the bottom of the drinking vessels themselves.[29]

Shortly after the guests within Plato's *Symposium* have agreed to drink as they like, not as others might wish, Eryximachus then suggests (176e)—from all appearances successfully—that they send the female *auletris* away, again surely not the usual sort of behavior one would expect at an Athenian *symposion* circa 416 BCE. While atypical, his suggestion is, however, in keeping with nearly identical hostility expressed by Socrates in several other Platonic dialogues. The philosopher, it is said in the *Theatetus*, wouldn't even dream of going to a party with flute girls (173d). In the *Protagoras* Socrates complains that only uneducated men "put up the price of female musicians," and find entertainment in their "piping or dancing or harping" (374c–d). The *aulos* is called an unnecessary "extraneous voice" that a mannered *symposion* can do without (374d). In the *Republic* certain Ionian and Lydian harmonic modes that would have often been found at symposia are rejected as effeminate (398e), the *aulos* being the example *par excellence* of the "drunkenness, softness, and idleness," such music fosters (398e, 399d, and cf. 573d).[30]

Plato's hostility to heavy drinking and the music of the *aulos* in the *symposion* is not a product of reticence or merely a personal eccentricity: because of their role in launching the *komos* there were important ethical and political ramifications.[31] The *aulos* "arouses dance and inspires trance" and can "also be the instrument of delirium, madness and the cries of possession."[32] The *aulos* possessed the capacity of creating "an opening to alterity," a "sudden eruption of otherness."[33] On one drinking cup (*kylix*) we can plainly observe a young man holding both a lyre and a *krater*; he is walking forward, head thrown back in a recognizably ecstatic fashion, with the open-mouthed deportment of a singer. Issuing from his lips is a string of letters which read "I go making the *komos* to the sound of the flute."[34] Ecstatic *methe* and the enjoyment of the *aulos* within the *symposion* were, for the philosopher at any rate, largely one and the same.[35]

In a manner that recalls the behavior of Socrates in the *Protagoras* (347d, 348a), Eryximachus in the *Symposium* suggests that a better sort of *symposion* ought to "stick to conversation" (176e). He then introduces the topic that the dialogue is conventionally said to revolve around, a series of speeches in praise of the god Eros. The eulogistic speech competition was frequently enjoyed at symposia. Yet Plato's Socrates denigrates the activity as "a question of hyperbole and rhetoric, regardless of truth and falsehood," and instead of giving his own speech to compete with the others begs their indulgence, asking (rhetorically it would seem) "Do you want to hear *the truth* about Eros? And may I use whatever language and forms of speech come naturally?" (198d–199b, emphasis mine). Plato is extremely careful to indicate that while Socrates may have been an occasional, if reluctant, participant at aristocratic symposia he was not a willing party either overtly or, as in this case, covertly, to most of its traditional practices. All notions of a "word feast" aside, philosophy and the discourse of the *symposion*, the *logos sympotikos*, border on the mutually exclusive.[36]

Eryximachus' speech has traditionally been denigrated by scholars as being of little more than "historical interest" and the subject of "unkind parody" on Plato's part.[37] The physician is, however, a key figure in many of Plato's works, including the *Symposium*.[38] The traditional assessment of Eryximachus as a peripheral figure might be accepted if *eros* was the only subject to be found in Plato's *Symposium* but, tradition notwithstanding, it is *eros* that ought to be viewed as the peripheral matter. In all truth the *Symposium*'s speeches, both their praise for a deity long inert, and the relations between an older "lover" (*erastes*) and younger, passive "beloved" (*eromeonus* or *baidika*), are the matters with little or nothing more than historical interest. Plato cannot tell us what *he* intended when he wrote the *Symposium*, but a complex panoply of concerns are visibly arranged beneath or behind the putative theme of *eros*, subjects an intelligent fourth-century reader would have been capable of recognizing.

The physician of the *Symposium* is not a caricature but a historically accurate depiction of a man of medicine in the Classical Period of ancient Greece, one that is both realistic and whose depiction is not without sympathy.[39] Socrates singles out the speech of Eryximachus for special praise (194a). Alcibiades speaks well of both Eryximachus and his father (Acumenus, also a well-known physician) and avers to his authority (214b–c). In both the *Protagoras* (315c) and *Phaedrus* (268a–b) Eryximachus is spoken of in a respectful manner and while speaking to Phaedrus in the latter dialogue Socrates refers to Acumenus as "our common friend" (227a). Yet while the importance of Eryximachus has been recognized, the role of the physician in the *Symposium* is confined to his place within "the framework of the dialogue" or, to put it differently, his literary function.[40] Eryximachus introduces the topic; along with Phaedrus, his lover, he is the person to whom the speeches would have been formally addressed; he and Phaedrus keep the conversation moving when it begins to stray; he manages to convince the party-crashing Alcibiades to give a speech like everyone else (214a–c) rather than simply lead the symposiasts into the depths of intoxication they had previously agreed upon to avoid. Toward the very end of the dialogue (223b) when yet another "crowd of people on their way home from a party" intrudes upon the conversation, bringing the noise, disorder, and finally the sort of heavy drinking that was normally found within the *symposion*, Eryximachus, Phaedrus and some of the original discussants choose to go home.

There is much more to the importance of Eryximachus than the way he functions in supporting the dialogue's architecture. The physician speaks with "a degree of systematic exposition and intellectual rigor . . . that is incompatible with sheer parody."[41] The doctrines of harmony in Eryximachus' speech "are a condensed but accurate expression of current medical theory," and appear to derive from the Hippocratic work *On Regimen*.[42] This background can be discerned through such positions as (a) the "doctrine of opposites in harmony," (b) "the interdependence of human and cosmic systems," and (c) "the analysis of crafts as productive of harmonious structure."[43] As Diotima will do later on in the dialogue, more explicitly and often utilizing the language of the Eleusinian Mysteries (207a, 208e–209a, 210d), Eryximachus essentially proposes *to* Socrates a portrait *of* Socrates.[44] While Diotima's portrait is metaphysical and concerned with philosophical themes, Eryximachus' is ethical and concerned with practical matters. As befits the setting of the dialogue, a *symposion*, the matter most at hand in the physician's discourse is *methe* (intoxication).

What the traditional physician proposes to all those present at Agathon's *symposion*, including Socrates, is an ethics of drinking that parallels Socrates' own behavior in the dialogue. Observing that the after-effects of the previous night's drinking still hang over both the host and several of his guests, Eryximachus puts forth the suggestion he be allowed to tell "*the truth* about getting drunk," taking pains to stress his desire not to cause excessive offense and carefully indicating his opinions are based on his personal experience as a practitioner of his healing art (176c–d, emphasis mine). He stresses that he neither drinks to a state of *methe* himself, nor would he advise anyone else to, all the more so if their minds are still clouded by previous excesses. The physician's final verdict is unequivocal: there is "no doubt that *getting drunk is bad for you*" (176d, emphasis mine). When he leaves Agathon's *symposion* there is no reason to believe he has through his own behavior violated this judgment. One is reminded of Euboulus' stricture that after the wine of the third *krater* is consumed "those who are deemed judicious go home."

The Aristophanes of the *Symposium* is said to have only two interests in life: Dionysus and Aphrodite (177e). We find in the Pseudo-Aristotelian *Problems* that "wine makes men inclined to love [*aphrodisiastikous*], and Dionysus and Aphrodite are rightly associated with each other [because of this]" (30.1). The poet was rumored to have composed while drunk (Atheneaus 10.429a) and was purported to have said "Wine, Aphrodite's milk, is a pleasant drink" (10.444d).[45] His *Knights* has many sympotic themes, pays tribute to the "inventive powers" of wine and indicates that when men drink wine they "grow rich, do business, win lawsuits, prosper, and help their friends" (85–9).[46] His *Acharnians* "treats the peaceful *polis* as though it were a banquet."[47] The play's main character, Dikaiopolis or "Just City," celebrates a peace treaty with a variety of foods (975). Peace, a central theme of the play, is presented as a *deipnon*, a feast (987–1002). Late in the play (1198–1234) Dikaiopolis brags he has poured out a wineskin full of unmixed wine and drained it in one breath. His deed is proclaimed noble and he is given a huge wineskin as a prize. Supported by prostitutes he is led offstage, while behind him the chorus sing "in praise of wisdom mixed with wine" (1232–34).

When his turn to speak in Plato's *Symposium* occurs, Aristophanes finds he cannot, because he has the hiccups "from eating too much, or for some other reason" (185c).[48] Whatever the reason for the comic poet's hiccups, their severity is evident, as only the "sneezing cure" Eryximachus prescribes manages to put an end to them. Aristophanes seems to suggest (189a) that what he calls the "well-ordered" part of his body, his *logistikon* we might say, demanded this treatment as a result of, perhaps, his previous excess. Eryximachus finds him unable to concentrate satisfactorily, and threatens to censor him if he continues to fool around (189b–c). Aristophanes' speech on the origins of the two sexes, it has been suggested, has the air of ignorant folklore.[49] At one point, when Zeus is contemplating whether or not to weaken humanity by halving the original sexes, he tells the other gods that if mankind remains unable to behave while walking upright on two legs he will "cut them in half again and they can go hopping along on one leg" (190d). This may be an oblique reference to Aristophanes' depiction of Socrates as a practitioner of black magic in the company of the one-legged Sciapodes in the *Birds*.[50] Shortly thereafter the host Agathon does indeed jest "*Pharmattein boulei me, o Socrates*," indicating that the philosopher is using "a little black magic" (with perhaps connotations of drugging) to unnerve him before he gives his speech (194a).[51]

As Socrates concludes his own lecture on Eros, and before Aristophanes can voice some difference or disagreement he wishes to express, there is a violent banging on the door, "followed by the notes of the flute and the sound of festive brawling in the street" (212c). In the courtyard are several people, including a thoroughly intoxicated Alcibiades, apparently on their way home from another *symposion* in what may be seen as a typical *komos*. Along with Aristophanes, who may have eaten too much, Alcibiades embodies the ordinary ethics of the fourth century, in this case its drinking ethics. With his head adorned with ribbons, ivy and violets (212e), he is Dionysus and democratic Athens personified.[52] Alcibiades is described as roaring like a bull (*boontos*, 212d), appropriate enough seeing as Dionysus could be known as Brimios, the "thunderer" or "roarer." The dramatic setting of the *Symposium*, we might recall, was the celebration of Agathon's victory at the Lenaia, a festival of Dionysus Lenaias, for the Maenads of Dionysus.[53]

Alcibiades is the unmistakable antithesis to Eryximachus' verbal prescriptions about drinking and Socrates' actual behavior. His intoxication is repeatedly emphasized: "very drunk" (212d); "it's grossly unfair to ask me, drunk, to compete with you sober" (214c); "when you're as drunk as I am" (215a); "I'm drunk" (217e). Moreover, he is supported by the very sort of flute girl Eryximachus has previously convinced the group to send away (212d). Seeing that everyone is still "pretty sober," a condition he finds unacceptable, he demands—again in keeping with sympotic custom—that everyone *must* drink, and tries to appoint himself overseer (*archon*) of the entire proceedings (213e, and cf. *Laws* 671b where this exact behavior is explicitly criticized). While Plato uses *archon* at 213e, the overall context reminds one of the term *komarchos*, the "master of the revels," and Alcibiades has the unmistakable temperament of a *komastes*, a reveler, one who enjoys the drunken disorder of the *komos*.[54]

Alcibiades utters the Greek equivalent of the Latin *in vino veritas*, saying "truth comes from wine (as the saying goes), whether or not I take children into account" (217e).[55] He embodies the unquenchable democratic thirst for freedom, and is one of the *Republic*'s "bad winebearers" whose leadership gets a city "more drunk than it should" (562c–d). Alcibiades was said to have introduced Athens to the disreputable practice of drinking in the daytime.[56] Daylight drinking was considered emblematic of the hubristic excess found in Athens during the city's glory. Horace (ca. 18 BCE), in his *Art of Poetry*, wrote that the Athenians began to "appease their genius on festal days by drinking without restraint and in the daytime" (209–10). A fragment of the lyric poet Alcaeus (fl. seventh–sixth century BCE) preserved in Atheneaus (10.430c–d) expresses an impatience that may have been common:

> Let us drink. Why wait for the lighting of the lamps?
> Night is but the briefest moment away.
> Boy, take down the large painted cups from the shelf;
> For the son of Semele and Zeus [i.e. Dionysus] gave us wine to forget our
> cares.
> Pour it out, mixing one and two, full to the brim;
> and let us being to empty them—urgently.

Socrates is, quite clearly, the diametric opposite of Alcibiades, both ethically and behaviorally. Alcibiades refers to him as "a model of restraint" who merely appears to be like other men, when in truth he has an "astonishing contempt" for all the pleasures that normally concern men in human society (216d–e). Alcibiades, in a manner that is obvious even to himself, pursues these pleasures with reckless enthusiasm (216b). Socrates, in contrast, goes without food longer than anyone (220a) and his ability to rebuff even the most brazen sexual advances, as divulged by a shameless and still desiring Alcibiades, is absolute. Before making this confession he hints that he is revealing something reserved for those already initiated into "this wild passion for philosophy," begs their forgiveness, and warns "the servants, and anyone else who's easily shocked, or doesn't know what I'm talking about [i.e. anyone who has not been initiated], they'll just have to put something over their ears" (218b). What he is about to tell, like the secrets of the Eleusinian Mysteries he will sacrilegiously reveal a few months later, cannot be divulged outside the circle of initiates.[57] The story is unspeakable, *arrheta*.[58]

After Alcibiades drains a large container—one said to hold eight *kotylai*, roughly two quarts—of unmixed wine, it is refilled and passed straight to Socrates, who also empties it. Alcibiades attests that "it doesn't matter how much you give him to drink, he'll drink it and be none the worse for wear" (214a). Socrates, he goes on to say, never chooses to drink, but when compelled to by the insistence of others, such as in the present circumstances, he can drink any man under the table. Most astounding of all, Socrates, although he can drink as much as or more than anyone, *never* becomes intoxicated. Alcibiades makes it clear: "no man has ever seen Socrates drunk" (220a).[59] This is a portrait of an ascetic, and an impossible one at that, in the sense that *his drinking behavior is such that no human being would be capable of emulating it.* "One can see the interruption of the flute girl [by Eryximachus] and of Alcibiades, drunk, ready for pleasure, hungry to tell his story of thwarted desire for Socrates' body, as Plato's own argument for sobriety and hatred of the body, except as a temporary vehicle of the soul."[60]

Intoxication in Plato's *Laws*

The subject of intoxication occupies the better part of the first two books of Plato's final dialogue, the *Laws*. Despite the importance suggested by its sheer length, the argument has been largely "scorned and neglected" by scholars, who for many years viewed the dialogue as a whole as one of senescence if not senility,[61] with the little analysis that has emerged being characterized by extensive "puzzlement and inaccuracy."[62] Little wonder. The conversation with the Cretan Kleinias and the Spartan Megillus begins acrimoniously, with the Stranger from Athens, after gaining permission to criticize Dorian laws, suggesting "the law should inure its subjects to pleasure as well as pain," otherwise the result will be "lack of restraint with regard to pleasure" such as found in Cretan sexual practices (636c).[63] After some initial resistance he secures their permission to "speak at greater length about the whole subject of intoxication" (637d).

The Athenian Stranger sweeps aside the "sober necessity" of "ancestral law" advocated at the start of the dialogue by Kleinias and Megillus with "talk of getting drunk and bedding boys," certainly not the sort of subject matter one would expect from "three august old men traveling to Crete's holiest sanctuary."[64] The Stranger has more serious objectives in mind, however, involving "the opposition between virtuous and improper drinking. Correctly used . . . wine should inspire courage rather than merely fueling pleasure."[65] This playful, even perverse "discussion of illicit pleasures" serves to distract Kleinias and Megillus long enough to demonstrate the shortsightedness of their "failure to allow their subjects the enjoyment, among many other pleasures, of the communal drinking of wine."[66]

Plato's *Laws*—so a certain line of argument goes—indicates a willingness to allow drinking parties, so long as they are *rightly regulated*. In sum "the Stranger takes some base Dorian practice and reforms it in accordance with the idealism of Socratic philosophy, thereby demonstrating to the dialogue's philosophical on-lookers that even [the recreational intoxication of the Athenian *symposion*], if rightly reordered, can nourish the highest virtues of the human soul."[67] But is this true? To establish his authority in an admittedly controversial matter the mysterious and nameless "Athenian Stranger" claims to have an ex-

ceptionally sound knowledge of sympotic custom, based in part on direct experience (639d), hints he has examined the sympotic customs of thousands of
different cities (638e), and at any rate the number is "a great many"—so many
in fact that he feels confident enough to say he has "investigated pretty nearly all
of them" (639d). His dissatisfaction with actual and real symposia is evident.
With the exception of "a few insignificant details" he makes the claim that *all*
symposia, everywhere, have been mismanaged (639e).

The Athenian is in agreement with the Spartan Megillus, who in his defense
of laws in his homeland aiming at the complete elimination of drunken *hubris*
(636e–637b) reminds everyone of the riotous intoxication he observed at the
festival of Dionysus in both Athens and the Spartan colony of Tarentum, where
on both occasions he "saw the entire city drunk." The ways of Sparta are in his
opinion "the finest to be found among human kind," and this sort of intoxicated
"insolence and mindlessness" just doesn't exist among his people.[68] Later in the
dialogue Plato writes (775b) that drinking to the point of *methe* is "nowhere
seemly except at the feasts of the God, the Giver of wine," a passage that has
been interpreted as evidence that "during the Dionysian festival the Athenians
customarily drank wine before the theatrical performances."[69] Both passages hint
at the extent to which intoxication was not only tolerated by, but actually inte-
grated within, the everyday functioning of, at the very least, the Athenian *polis*.

What follows in the first two books of the *Laws* is for the most part a pleading for the *potential* educative value of the *symposion*. The drinking party the
Athenian goes on to describe is a fictional construct the author clearly believes
cannot be found anywhere on earth. It is fully in keeping with his general en-
dorsement of "any fiction for the sake of the good effect on the young" (663d–
e).[70] There "should always be someone in control" of the drinking party (640a),
utilizing "the proper surveillance" (641b).[71] This overseer "must lay down laws"
for the banquet (671c). He himself should remain "sober and sagacious" and be
older than the other celebrants, so that no "grave disaster"—like the *komos*, presumably—occurs (640d). Without the authority of this "unperturbed and sober"
officer the "battle with intoxication [*methe*] is more hazardous than a battle
against an enemy in the field without unperturbed commanders" (671d). Plato's
overseer resembles an idealized, inverted image of the state-appointed wine inspectors, the *Ophthalmoi*, who attended public banquets. While the *Ophthalmoi*
might expel a person for failing to drink, Plato's *archon* expels anyone who
drinks to excess and becomes disorderly.

Moving past an initial stage of convivial intoxication there will be, inevitably, increasing noise and disorder as "the drinking goes further and further"
(671a). In the heat of this linguistic confusion the soul of the drinker becomes
soft and malleable, like heated iron, and psychologically his mind is like a
child's (671b–c, and cf. 645e "the mental condition . . . of remote infancy").
Pleasures and pains at this stage of the drinking party become intensified, while
"perceptions, memories, beliefs [and] knowledge . . . desert a man altogether"
(645d–e). The drinker becomes "swollen with the conceit of his own wisdom to
the pitch of complete license of speech and action" (649a–b). Within this second

stage of the *symposion* each soul becomes tyrannical, and each person thinks at that moment they are competent to give orders not only to themselves but all around them (671b, and cf. 645e "self-command is at its lowest").

The danger that the *symposion*, that miniature *polis*, will break apart in discordant enmity and threaten to spread infectiously to the larger body politic, is now at its greatest. The intoxicated are at this moment puppets, pulled by the leaden strings of desire (644d–645c). It is at this moment, as *methe* takes over and identity blurs and verges on the precipice of erasure, that the *archon* steps in. His task is to ensure that the symposiasts will remain "guided by laws in all their intercourse" (671e). He moulds and adjudicates their discourse so as to control any who have become "confident and bold and unduly shameless, and unwilling to submit to the proper limits of silence and speech, of drinking and music, making him consent to do in all ways the opposite" (671c–d). They must "listen to the directions" given to them by the sober *archon*, and obey without question (671e–672a). What is perhaps most remarkable is that the Plato of the *Laws* does not intend this sort of discursive control for merely those attending private drinking parties, but for everyone in the community, "at all times and throughout the entirety of their lives" (664a).[72]

The Athenian appears to anticipate there would be considerable difficulties in establishing what is, for him, largely a test of character, stating that if the state cannot make "an orderly use" of drinking within the *symposion*, taking the matter seriously (as he has) and using it with the aim of instilling habits of moderation, and instead allows "anyone whatsoever to drink whatever he likes, with anyone he likes," then a total prohibition of *methe* is justified: "I would not vote for the use of drunkenness *at any time* by this city or this man. Indeed I would go beyond the Cretan and the Lacedaimonian usage, and advocate the Carthaginian law which forbids anyone to taste of this drink while out on campaign and requires that only water be drunk for all at that time" (674a, emphasis mine). Excluded outright from participation in wine drinking are those under eighteen years of age (666a); slaves, both male and female; magistrates in office; steersman and juryman on duty; any councilor intending to take part in an important discussion; men and women intending to procreate; everyone during the day, save those needing wine for the purposes of training or health; and "a great many other situations" that the Athenian does not explicitly spell out but which any sensible, law-respecting person would be capable of recognizing (674b–c and 775c–d).[73]

The institution of "regulated drinking" in the *Laws* is as utopian a construct as anything found in the ideal state of the *Republic*, or the sanitized account of the *symposion* in the *Symposium*. There simply isn't evidence, in the discussion of drinking and the *symposion* in the *Laws*, of a last minute reversal of Plato's valuation of either the *symposion* or the pleasures of *methe*.[74] His hostility towards both, as we have just seen, extends through his entire *oeuvre*. It is possible to situate Plato in a tradition "mostly from the more or less committedly Laconising sections of Athenian society," one that saw intoxication, particularly that arising in the aristocratic *symposion*, as a threatening loss of identity and a primary source of *hubris*; this tradition looked longingly at the success of the Spartan *syssitia* "in avoiding social tensions, disruptions, and *stasis*."[75] Plato's hostility to the popular valorization of wine seems on the whole consistent with these other writers.

Yet at the same time Plato's arguments go considerably beyond his contemporaries. He does not accept the idea of a simple substitution of Spartan institutions for Athenian ones, as he is as critical of the former as he is of the latter.[76] Instead he utilizes *methe* as part of his effort to reorder the Athenian *symposion* into a counterfactual vehicle whose aim, as we shall see in Part Three, is the creation of a *moral economy*, including a regimen for a reflexively reproduced normative discourse, that provides the foundation for the orderly rule of both unwritten ethics and legislatively written laws that remain more or less unchanged over time.[77] Plato subsumes the language, ritual, and ecstatic experience of intoxication (*methe*) found in the *symposion* within his plans for a new system of enculturation (*paideia*), in much the same way that he subsumes the language, ritual and ecstatic experience of the Eleusinian Mysteries.[78]

Driving the argument home with his elderly companions, the Stranger declares at the end of Book II they should not "simply blame any more the gift of Dionysus, as if it were evil and unacceptable in a city" (672a). Wine is a divinely granted *pharmakon*. "As a man approaches forty," Plato writes, "he is to share in the enjoyment of the common meals, invoking the presence of the other gods, and especially Dionysus, at this mystery-rite and play of older men, which he has bestowed on human beings as a drug [*pharmakon*] that heals the austerity of old age" (666b). Wine is not something bestowed on humanity "out of revenge" in order to "drive us mad," Plato writes, it is instead "a medicine [*pharmakon*]" with opposite intention, namely "to put awe in the soul and health as well as strength in the body" (672d). The viewpoint on intoxication in the *Laws* is, then, not as far from the *Symposium* as might be thought. The experience of ecstasy is rationalized and wine becomes a kind of remedy for mental rigidity.

We might ask ourselves as we conclude this discussion of the politics of intoxication whether the saying of the poet Theognis (510) that if someone "drinks expertly, it is not an evil (*kakon*) thing but a good (*agathon*) thing" remains true for the philosopher, for Plato, or are there the beginnings of Greek tradition being replaced by a new valuation? The first two books of Plato's *Laws* are hardly eccentric or the product of a declining mind. Both Aristotle and Theophrastus were also apparently concerned enough about *methe* to write works titled *On Drunkenness*. Unfortunately, other than a few fragments, neither work has survived. The fourth head of Plato's Academy, Polemo (314–270 BCE), was reputed to have drunk nothing but water after the age of thirty (Athenaeus 2.44e). What should we make of all this? Has nothing of importance happened here? The impossible asceticism of the Platonic Socrates in the *Symposium* has given way to true asceticism in the space of a century. There is already, in Plato's dialogues, "the birth and development of a certain number of ascetic themes" that will be carried through antiquity and directly borrowed by early Christian ethics.[79]

The *Laws* cannot quite conceive of a set of prohibitory regulations to restrict popular access to society's many *pharmaka* and hence emphatically deny all *methe* to the citizens of the *polis*—believing it impossible to enforce, even were it to be legislated—other than perhaps restricting the number of vineyards and hence the supply of wine in circulation (675c). It is all the same clear that outside of his counterfactual construct, the stranger from Athens, if for different reasons and with different goals in mind, has as little and perhaps even less tolerance for intoxication than either of his two compatriots.[80] In Plato's philosophy the experience of *methe* is rendered almost unrecognizable, dismissed even while it is, however cautiously, praised. The Platonic world is "a world where one is only apparently intoxicated, in which reason acts the drunkard and sings a Dionysian tune while none the less remaining 'pure' reason."[81] Wherever *methe* conflicts with the goals of philosophic *paideia* there can be little doubt that the former will be sacrificed at the slightest indication that it threatens to hinder the smooth functioning of the latter.

Notes

1. Plato's dialogue on the nature of the just launches itself when Cephalus says that the cause of his peaceful condition is not simply the result of his advanced age. What he enjoys is the result of something else, a quality that resides in "the character of human beings [*anthropos*]" (329d). Old age will turn out to be as hard to endure as the mad passions of youth for those who are not "orderly and content with themselves" (329d).

2. While Manuela Tecusan, "*Logos Sympotikos*: Patterns of the Irrational in Philosophical Drinking—Plato Outside the *Symposium*," in *Sympotika—A Symposium on the Symposion*, ed. Oswyn Murray (Oxford: Clarendon Press, 1990) recognizes that Cephalus is referring to the *symposion*, she passes over what I believe is the other significant element of his speech: that the pleasures one might find within the *symposion* are accompanied by desires that compel like a mad, frenzied, savage master. It is this *epithymetic compulsion* that is the subject of Plato's reordering intervention.

3. Daniel B. Levine, "Symposium and *Polis*," in *Theognis of Megara—Poetry and the Polis*, ed. Thomas J. Figueira and Gregory Nagy (Baltimore, MD: The Johns Hopkins University Press, 1985), 180, referring to Theognis 475–78. Wender's translation, however, indicates this particular part of the *Theognida* is widely believed to have been written by Euenos, a sophist contemporary of Plato. See Dorthea Wender, *Hesiod: Theogny, Works and Days. Theognis: Elegies* (New York: Penguin Books, 1973), 161.

4. Theognis is mentioned during the discussion of wine-drinking in what is usually regarded as Plato's last work, the *Laws* (630a).

5. Tecusan, "*Logos Sympotikos*," 239.

6. Tecusan, "*Logos Sympotikos*," 239.

7. See George Miller Calhoun, *Athenian Clubs in Politics and Litigation* (Austin, TX: The University of Texas Bulletin, 1913), 1–9, 23–25, 35–38.

8. Thessaly was a wealthy region of northeastern Greece, situated between Doris to the south and Macedon to the north. According to Thucydides' *History* it was governed by a few noble families (4.73.3), and among other aspects of its wealth it was known for exporting horses to Athens and other portions of Greece.

9. Making such a request at just this moment shows a deeply ironic, near impious contempt for traditional drinking ritual and those who practice it.

10. Tecusan, *"Logos Sympotikos,"* 242.

11. Alan H. Sommerstein, *The Comedies of Aristophanes. Vol. 2—Clouds* (Warminster, Wilts, England: Aris and Phillips, 1983), 241.

12. T. B. L. Webster, *Athenian Culture and Society* (Berkeley and Los Angeles: University of California Press, 1973), 166.

13. Arthur P. McKinlay, "Attic Temperance," *Quarterly Journal of Studies on Alcohol* 12, no. 1 (1951): 73.

14. Oswyn Murray, "Forms of Sociality," in *The Greeks*, ed. Jean-Pierre Vernant (Chicago: University of Chicago Press, 1995), 225–26.

15. This is another sign of the wavering Tecusan points to in *"Logos Sympotikos."*

16. Robin A. Waterfield, trans., *Plato—Philebus* (New York: Penguin Books, 1988), 139 n. 1.

17. The figure of the drone in Plato's *Republic* is discussed in chapter 2, above.

18. Robin A. Waterfield, trans., *Plato—Symposium* (New York: Oxford University Press, 1994), 145 n. 1.

19. As was just pointed out at the beginning of the chapter, Cephalus, in the *Republic* (329a–d), testifies to the tranquility and freedom he now enjoys in extreme old age, as opposed to the desires of youth, which he likens to a mad master.

20. The parallels with our contemporary "rhetoric of drugs" will be drawn out in the afterword, below.

21. Harold Tarrant, "Wine in Ancient Greece—Some Platonist Ponderings," in *Wine and Philosophy: A Symposium on Thinking and Drinking*, ed. Fritz Allhoff (Malden, MA: Blackwell Publishing, 2008), 22–5 would have us believe the opposite. It is commendable to claim the dialogue is an important statement about ancient drinking ethics; surprisingly few have done so. Yet Tarrant makes no real distinction between ancient and modern wine, provides no historical context to the dialogue, wrongly attributes the views of Eryximachus on wine to Socrates at one point, and would have the reader believe that because the Socrates of the *Charmides* admits to feeling strong sexual desire the Socrates of the *Symposium* might admit to feeling the same way about wine. The *Symposium* is no more a "celebration of wine" than any of the other dialogues Plato wrote.

22. William S. Cobb, trans. *The Symposium and Phaedrus: Plato's Erotic Dialogues* (Albany, NY: State University of New York Press, 1993), 180 n. 14. Specifically 175e, 215b, 219c, 221e, and 222a.

23. Michael L. Morgan, *Platonic Piety: Philosophy and Ritual in Fourth Century Athens* (New Haven, CT: Yale University Press, 1990), 81. The scandal of 415 BCE is discussed in detail in chapter 5, below. Phaedrus and Eryximachus, who both appear in the *Symposium*, would be sent into exile as a result of the scandal. See also Peter H. Von Blackenhagen, "Stage and Actors in Plato's Symposium," *Greek, Roman, and Byzantine Studies* 33, no. 1 (1992): 58. Von Blackenhagen argues that Agathon's *symposion* is a reunion of many of the participants who had gathered together in a sympotic atmosphere roughly fifteen years before in Plato's *Protagoras*.

24. I shall argue the *Phaedrus* is as well. See chapter 6, below.

25. In his translation notes to *Symposium* 174a, Waterfield, *Plato—Symposium*, 74 writes "an Athenian might have his body oiled and then all the sweat and dirt scrapped off with a strigil, and once in a while he might take a full bath; but bathing only became a common occurrence in the Western world in the last hundred years or so." There is reason to doubt this however. M. L. Werner, *Life in Greece in Ancient Times* (Barcelona: Liber, 1977), 60–1 indicates that while baths were unusual in Homeric times it gradually

became customary in Athens and elsewhere "for people to take baths every day, in mid-afternoon," with some people bathing twice or even three times a day. Archeological evidence indicates that many private households had their own baths.

26. Oswyn Murray, "Forms of Sociality," 229.

27. Regarding *Gorgias* 451e and the *skolion*, see Albin Lesky, *A History of Greek Literature* (Indianapolis, IN: Hackett Publishing, 1996), 173. On drinking songs generally see chapter 1, above.

28. The reason, most likely, is that Plato would have expected anyone reading the dialogue to know the details of sympotic custom; there would no need for him to describe the well-known. There is also the possibility that he would have been sensitive to any appearance of impiety.

29. See Werner, *Life in Greece in Ancient Times*, 72. See also Jean-Louis Durand, Francoise Frontisi-Ducroux and François Lissarrague, "Wine: Human and Divine," in *A City of Images—Iconography and Society in Ancient Greece*, ed. Claude Bérard (Princeton, NJ: Princeton University Press, 1989), 126, and François Lissarrague, *The Aesthetics of the Greek Banquet: Images of Wine and Ritual* (Princeton, NJ: Princeton University Press, 1990), 21–2.

30. One is reminded again of Aristophanes' *Wasps* (1335–81) where a drunk and disorderly Philocleon arrives home with a nude *auletris* he has stolen from the *symposion* he has just attended; she escapes when the man is confronted by his mortified son.

31. Aristotle, in the *Politics* (1341a), condemns the *aulos* as an impediment to education, writing that it was "not a moral instrument but one that excites the emotions," and ought to be limited to "circumstances where the spectacle offers more potential for *kartharsis* than for learning." Quoted in Sheramy D. Bundrick, *Music and Image in Classical Athens* (New York: Cambridge University Press, 2005), 35.

32. Francoise Frontisi-Ducroux, "In the Mirror of the Mask," in *A City of Images—Iconography and Society in Ancient Greece*, ed. Claude Bérard (Princeton, NJ: Princeton University Press, 1989), 159.

33. Frontisi-Ducroux, "In the Mirror of the Mask," 163.

34. François Lissarrague, "Around the Krater: An Aspect of Banquet Imagery," in *Sympotica—A Symposium on the Symposion*, ed. Oswyn Murray (Oxford: Clarendon Press, 1990), 198–99. See also Lissarrague, *The Aesthetics of the Greek Banquet*, 131–32, 139, where the god Dionysus himself is depicted in a similar posture.

35. Bundrick, *Music and Image in Classical Athens*, 39–41 points out that many vases depict more sedate use of the *aulos*. The views of Plato and Aristotle, he argues, were most likely outliers not shared by many of their contemporaries. "In short, fifth-century Athenian imagery does not suggest a wholesale rejection of the *aulos*, or even a consistent picture of immorality and immoderation. Like so many things in Greek culture—including wine, for example, the *aulos* was evidently considered best in moderation and in appropriate settings."

36. The opposition of philosophic discourse and rhetorical discourse in Plato is discussed in chapter 9, below.

37. K. J. Dover, "Aristophanes' Speech in Plato's *Symposium*," in *The Greeks and their Legacy: Collected Papers Volume II: Prose Literature, History, Society, Transmission, Influence* (New York: Basil Blackwell, 1988), 113 n. 44.

38. Here I am in agreement with Ludwig Edelstein, who views Eryximachus as "a prominent figure" and even the most important in the *Symposium* other than Socrates. See Ludwig Edelstein, *Ancient Medicine: Selected Papers of Ludwig Edelstein* (Baltimore, MD: The Johns Hopkins University Press, 1967), 162–64. Plato's overall respect for

physicians, and his casting of the philosopher as a moral physician, is discussed throughout Part Three, below.

39. Edelstein, *Ancient Medicine*, 159 and 162. Edelstein demonstrates quite well that
the *Symposium*'s physician is not overly pedantic, showy, or conceited, nor any more
dogmatic about his speech than any of the other guests who give a speech on *eros*.

40. Edelstein, *Ancient Medicine*, 162 and 164. This perspective continues to receive
play. See Von Blackenhagen, "Stage and Actors in Plato's *Symposium*," 56–8.

41. David Konstan (with Elizabeth Young-Bruehl), "Eryximachus' Speech in the
Symposium," *Apeiron* 16 (1982), 45 n. 1.

42. Konstan, "Eryximachus' Speech in the *Symposium*," 42–4. See also my discussion of Greek medicine in chapter 7, below.

43. Konstan, "Eryximachus' Speech in the *Symposium*," 42–3. While pointing out
the medical theory that underpins Eryximachus' views, Konstan and Young-Bruehl deliberately avoid situating his speech "in the wider meaning of the *Symposium* as a
whole." It would seem, however, that once we have established his importance in the
dialogue this is precisely what must be done.

44. Cf. Jacques Derrida, *Dissemination* (Chicago: University of Chicago Press,
1981), 117, who concurs.

45. On the tradition of comics composing while drunk see the excellent discussion in
John Wilkins, *The Boastful Chef—The Discourse of Food in Ancient Comedy* (New
York: Oxford University Press, 2000), 202–256.

46. A. M. Bowie, "Thinking with Drinking: Wine and the Symposium in Aristophanes," *Journal of Hellenic Studies* 117 (1997): 1–21 examines the sympotic themes
found in the *Knights*.

47. Levine, "Symposium and *Polis*," 195.

48. The hiccups are discussed in Steven Lowenstam, "Aristophanes' Hiccups,"
Greek, Roman, and Byzantine Studies 27, no. 1 (1986): 43–56.

49. Dover, "Aristophanes' Speech in Plato's *Symposium*," 107.

50. See chapter 5, below.

51. Drugs were clearly a large part of ancient Greek magic. See chapter 8, below.

52. Martha C. Nussbaum, *The Fragility of Goodness—Luck and Ethics in Greek
Tragedy and Philosophy* (New York: Cambridge University Press, 1986), 193–95, Kevin
Corrigan and Elena Glazov-Corrigan, *Plato's Dialectic at Play: Argument, Structure, and
Myth in the Symposium* (University Park, PA: Penn State Press, 2004), 164, and Water-
field, *Plato—Symposium*, 90–3.

53. Sir Arthur Pickard-Cambridge, *The Dramatic Festivals of Athens*, Second Edition (Oxford: Clarendon Press, 1968), 30, Erika Simon, *Festivals of Attika: An Archeological Commentary* (Madison, WI: The University of Wisconsin Press, 1983), 100–1,
Michael Morgan, *Platonic Piety: Philosophy and Ritual in Fourth Century Athens* (New
Haven, CT and London: Yale University Press, 1990), 94.

54. Lissarrgue, *The Aesthetics of the Greek Banquet*, 31–32.

55. The proverb in Greek was "Truth comes from wine and children" but the words
for children and slaves, *paides*, were identical, so it is unclear which of the two he may be
referring to. Given the proverb and his heavily intoxicated condition it is more likely the
former.

56. McKinlay, "Attic Temperance," 67.

57. On the profanation scandal see chapter 5, below. On the evidence suggesting use
of drugs in the Eleusinian Mysteries see chapter 4 and chapter 6, below.

58. "It is explicit in Aristotle, Proclus, and Plutarch that the mysteries were experienced, not explained. In fact, they were considered *arrheta*, unspeakable, not just because

it was illegal to disclose what transpired in the sanctuary, but because the transcendent nature of the experience defied attempts to communicate it in language." See David Fideler, *Alexandria 2: The Journal of Western Cosmological Traditions* (Grand Rapids, MI: Phanes Press, 1993), 77. See also Silvia Montiglio, *Silence in the Land of Logos* (Princeton, NJ: Princeton University Press, 2000), 37 who observes the "ancient sources . . . label the mysteries both as *aporrheta* (forbidden), and as *arrheta* (unspeakable)."

59. This portrait may have had some basis in historical fact. In Aristophanes' *Clouds* (412–19) Socrates and his followers appear to abstain from wine as part of their intellectual training; in Xenophon's *Memorabilia* (2.6.1) he warns against expecting to find good friends among those enslaved to the drinking cup; in Plutarch's *Rules for the Preservation of Health* (6) he advises against habit-inducing drinks, and in the same author's *On Talkativeness* (22) the advice is to resist those drinks that tempt even when one is not thirsty. The Socrates of Xenophon's *Symposium* (2.24–26) does not appear to wholly disapprove of wine, however, so no final conclusions may be drawn about the attitude of historical Socrates towards intoxication.

60. Page DuBois, *Sappho is Burning* (Chicago: University of Chicago Press, 1995), 95.

61. Elizabeth Belfiore, "Wine and Catharsis of the Emotions in Plato's *Laws*," *Classical Quarterly* 36, no. 2 (1986), 241. Leo Strauss, *The Argument and Action of Plato's* Laws (Chicago: University of Chicago Press, 1975) does little more than recapitulate Plato's argument.

62. Nick Fisher, "Drink, *Hybris*, and the Promotion of Harmony in Sparta," in *Classical Sparta—Techniques Behind Her Success*, ed. Anton Powell (New York: Routledge, 1988), 27–29. Fisher indicates this problem may be found even among such distinguished interpreters of Plato as Guthrie, Morrow, and Saunders. These writers downplay Plato's discussion in the first two books of the *Laws* as tedious and downright odd (Guthrie), best seen as tongue-in-cheek, and hence not truly in earnest (Saunders), and fail to deal with the topic in a sustained and critical manner, misreading the Athenian's comrades as endorsing some form of prohibition (Guthrie and Morrow). An important exception is Randall B. Clark, *The Law Most Beautiful and Best: Medical Argument and Magical Rhetoric in Plato's* Laws (Lanham, MD: Lexington Books, 2003), although Clark's focus is not so much on intoxication as the magical and medical discourses that permeate the *Laws*. Clark also does not discuss the Greek *symposion* in the detail presented here, nor discuss the theme of intoxication throughout the dialogues. He also does not discuss intoxication as a political problem, yet it certainly appears that there were difficulties being expressed on just that subject in ancient Greece, and Plato was a significant contributor to that discussion.

63. Clark, *The Law Most Beautiful and Best*, 109.

64. Clark, *The Law Most Beautiful and Best*, 140.

65. John W. I. Lee, *A Greek Army on the March: Soldiers and Survival in Xenophon's* Anabasis (Cambridge, MA: Cambridge University Press, 2008), 228–29.

66. Clark, *The Law Most Beautiful and Best*, 140. Clark humorously observes that the Stranger from Athens "could scarcely have done better had he begun the pilgrimage with a goatskin full of Odysseus's strong Ismarian wine hidden under his cloak."

67. Clark, *The Law Most Beautiful and Best*, 140.

68. The *political* ramifications of this, in the ancient Greek context, would have been considerable. See chapter 2, above.

69. W. B. Stanford, *Greek Tragedy and the Emotions—An Introductory Study* (London: Routledge and Kegan Paul, 1983), 12–13.

70. I discuss the art of political lying as its own *pharmakon* in chapter 10, below.

71. Compare this need for close surveillance and control of appetitive behavior with Xenophon's *Oeconomicus* (7.5–7.6).

72. See chapter 9, below.

73. In the *Republic* the guardian class is expressly forbidden the experience of *methe* at 398e.

74. Belfiore argues that "a serious and important psychological study" may be found in these books, and points to their containing "considerable philosophical importance." See Belfiore, "Wine and the Catharsis of the Emotions in Plato's *Laws*," 421. In sum "a radically different psychological theory, with important aesthetic implications, appears in the discussion of wine drinking." I am not convinced of the difference, at least where the intoxicated disruption of identity is concerned. Tecusan similarly writes that in the first two books of the *Laws* "people are called to truth and virtue mainly by irrational means" and that wine "in certain circumstances can make them love *paideia*, become masters of themselves, or obey the rules." See Tecusan, "*Logos Sympotikos*," 250. I see little evidence of a profound difference or turn in Plato's attitude toward *methe* in the discussion of wine in the *Laws*. The "circumstances" are a fictional construct, and within this construct the use of wine is so heavily controlled precisely because Plato sees intoxication as impeding *paideia*, overthrowing self-mastery, and undermining obedience to society's rules.

75. Fisher "Drink, *Hybris*, and the Promotion of Harmony in Sparta," 30. An example of this pro-Spartan leaning in matters pertaining to drink would be Plato's own uncle, Critias, who praises Spartan wine-drinking as "evenly disposed" and one that avoids "drinking healths in wine-cups beyond measure" because it both "delights yet causes pain for all time." See Matthew Dillon and Lynda Garland, *Ancient Greece: Social and Historical Documents from Archaic Times to the Death of Socrates, Second Edition* (New York: Routledge, 2000), 189.

76. See, for example, *Republic* 547d–548c.

77. See chapter 9, below.

78. See my discussion of the *Phaedrus* in chapter 6, below.

79. Paul Rabinow, ed., *The Foucault Reader* (New York: Pantheon Books, 1984), 361.

80. Plato pushes the argument against *methe* as far as his interpretive framework will allow. It is tempting to speculate what Plato might have written had he access to, for example, a Judeo-Christian or other monotheistic concept of "sin" or a modern medical concept such as "addiction." Thus informed the *Laws* would have been quite comfortable defending prohibitionist laws concerning intoxication against any and all detractors. On the other hand it is doubtful Plato would have appreciated *The Symposium: A Treatise on Chastity* by the early Christian St. Methodius of Olympus (died ca. 311 CE), a work that "despite the great wealth of Platonic quotation and allusion," leaves one with "the definite impression that even where Methodius has not positively misunderstood Plato and failed to comprehend the complexities of his system, he was not really interested in his doctrine." Quoted in Herbert Musurillo, trans. *St. Methodius—The Symposium: A Treatise on Chastity* (New York: Paulist Press, 1958), 17.

81. Gilles Deleuze and Paul Patton, *Difference and Repetition* (New York and London: Continuum International Publishing Group, 1994), 332.

Table 1

JUST AND INTENSE PLEASURES
IN THE *PHILEBUS*

JUST PLEASURES	INTENSE PLEASURES
1. Are temperate (44d–e)	1. Are "intemperate, unrestrained" (45b) and "exceed all bounds" (45e)
2. Are healthy (45a–b)	2. Are sick, degenerate and "forms of illness" (45b–46a)
3. Are true (40c)	3. Are illusory, false, and "apparent but not real" (44a, 51a)
4. Are orderly (52c)	4. Are "unbalanced to the point of insanity," possessed, ecstatic, and frenzied (45d–e, 47a–b)
5. Are unmixed, pure (52b)	5. Are mixed, adulterated (46b–47a)

EXAMPLES OF JUST PLEASURES	EXAMPLES OF INTENSE PLEASURES
1. Smells (51e) Cf. *Republic* (584c) *Timaeus* (66e–67a)	1. Itching (46a) and tickling (46d) Cf. *Gorgias* (494c)
2. Color (51b) Cf. *Gorgias* (474d)	2. Crying (48a) Cf. *Symposium* (215d–216c)
3. Pure tones (51d) Cf. *Gorgias* (474d)	3. Laughter (48a) Cf. *Gorgias* (473e) *Republic* (388e–389a) *Laws* (672b, 815c–d)
4. Geometric symmetry (51c) Cf. *Timaeus* (88c–d)	4. Dancing Cf. *Ion* (533e–534a) *Laws* (672b, 815c–d)
5. Learning (51e–52b) Cf. *Republic* (441a–b)	5. Alcohol intoxication Cf. *Symposium* (212c-223b) *Laws* 645d–646a.

Part Two

The *Pharmakon* and the Defense of Socrates

Chapter Four

Drugs, Epic Poetry, and Religion

The etymology of the ancient Greek word *pharmakon* has not been definitively established. There is some notion that, early on, *pharmakon* meant "that which pertains to an attack of demonic possession or is used as a curative against such an attack."[1] This would certainly be in keeping with ancient medical practice, prior to the development of Hippocratic medicine, being characterized by theurgy "in its widest sense of supernatural or divine agencies in both diseases and their treatment."[2] The squill plant (*Urginea maritime*) reflected this duality, being both an effective medicinal remedy and a potent means to drive out evil.[3] On the one hand, when taken internally, squill "has a digitalis-like action on the heart, and in small amounts is employed occasionally as an expectorant."[4] On the other, external contact with the leaves "can cause serious topical irritation."[5] Both Theognis and his contemporary Hipponax (fl. 540–537 BCE) demonstrate an association between plants such as squill and the "religious practice of expelling a scapegoat (*pharmakos*) to cleanse the community of impurities or pollution."[6] The *pharmakos* would be struck (*pharma*) with squill, the leaves sometimes wrapped around other marginal plants such as the twigs of the fig tree, and expelled from the city to rid it of plague or pestilence.[7]

In Plato's *Laws* the Cretan Kleinias claims he is related to Epimenides, a famous itinerant wonder-worker who purified Athens and was well known for both his mastery of spoken incantations and his fondness for a certain strain of squill.[8] Nicander of Colophon (fl. 130 BCE), in his *Alexipharmaka*, hints that wrapping squill leaves around subtle branches of the fig-tree made an effective punishment for children.[9] Tzetzes (ca. 1110–1180 CE), a late Byzantine poet and grammarian, "labels his account as one of *katharma* (ritual cleansing); but squill as an acrid cultivator and widely known herbal remedy for coughs, asthma, and *alexipharmakon* [antidote] when 'hung in front of entrances [to houses]' is closely intertwined with the concept of *pharmakos*, an obvious analogue of *pharmakon*, first noted as 'poison' or 'beneficial drug' or 'spell' in the Homeric epics."[10] Indeed, the poems of Homer utilize eight different adjectives to divide the effects of *pharmaka*.[11] When the ancient Greeks spoke of *pharmatto*, "to work on by means of a drug," the context might be religious, medicinal, magical, rhetorical, social-recreational, or some combination.[12] A *pharmakon* might be, alternately and simultaneously, a sacrament, remedy, poison, talisman, pigment, cosmetic, perfume, or intoxicant.[13] The essence of the *pharmakon* is its very lack of a stable essence.[14]

Drug Use in Epic Poetry

While there is some evidence suggesting a carryover of Mycenaean drug practices into Homeric times, it is only in Homer's *Iliad* and *Odyssey* that one finds a clear articulation of "drug" among the ancient Greeks, represented in its broadest meaning by the word *pharmakon*.[15] Both the *Iliad* and the *Odyssey* are examples of an oral story-telling tradition that stretches back through the "Dark Age" of Greece (ca. tenth to ninth centuries BCE) to the Mycenaean Age (ca. fifteenth to eleventh centuries BCE). They are "composite works, containing materials 'sedimented' from several distinct historical periods—a feature common to traditions of oral composition."[16] It is highly significant that as early as the epic poetry of Homer there are abundant signs of an increasing unease with drug use, requiring "a circle of discourse and depiction" be drawn around a pleasure seen as too threatening to be allowed to speak for itself, for it posed the danger of relinquishing "social control to the point of ecstasy, of 'standing outside of ourselves.'"[17] In the *Odyssey* what was surely a millennia-old form of human behavior—intoxication through drugs—begins to become an object of a conscious, if hazy, reflection; the "veiled lines about *pharmaka* [drugs]" in epic poetry are indicative of "an on-going inquiry into such matters, albeit rather muffled."[18] The conclusion of that inquiry is clear enough: where the newly self-conscious and differentiated psyche and the *pharmakon* are concerned there can be no peaceful coexistence. To the extent that drug use may be described any longer, it may only be done in the manner of a "wistful stylization of what can no longer be celebrated."[19]

The *Odyssey* is about a homecoming (*nostos*), a return home.[20] Twenty years pass between Odysseus' departure from Ithaca and his return: ten years fighting the Trojan War, seven stranded with Calypso, and three on his return voyage (an entire year of which is spent with Circe).[21] The hero of the tale is "a transitional man, composite of warrior hero on the one hand and more primitive and elemental trickster on the other," the beginnings of a "more sophisticated type of protagonist for whom self-consciousness is the most significant attribute."[22] What is most remarkable about the hero's return voyage are the identity-effacing temptations he faces, and the prevalence of drugs throughout the journey.[23] The psychic danger in each encounter, the threat of "removing the self from its logical course," remains consistently the same however.[24] The mind (*noos*) and homecoming (*nostos*) are etymologically related, and "Odysseus, in enacting the latter, also embodies the former."[25]

The social status of a mature male, his reputation (*kleos*)—which in the value system of the ancient Greeks far outweighed any inner consciousness of right and wrong—was largely defined through his success or failure in command of a household. Put another way, the home or estate (*oikos*), as the center of the adult male's life, was the major determinant of his identity within Homeric society.[26] Odysseus is remarkable for the extent to which he never loses ✶ sight of his ultimate goal of returning home or, as might just as easily be said, preserving his identity.[27] It is no mere nostalgia then that moves him as Calypso continually tries "to spellbind his heart with suave, seductive words" so as to "wipe all thought of Ithaca from his mind" (1.67–68). His desperation to return to the *oikos* and reestablish an identity cast adrift is so intense that, denied its possibility, he is said to long for death (1.69–71). This desperation extends to the household he has left behind. Without its rightful master all within the *oikos* is disordered. The suitors are a nuisance, the servants do not serve properly, Penelope cannot be a true wife,[28] and Telemarchos cannot be a true son.[29]

Calypso is in some sense a magical creature but her attempt to entice Odysseus into forgetting his homeland remains gentle and loving, since she desires a husband and not a slave. Only after Hermes' visit, when it becomes clear that Odysseus will soon depart, does her language take on a more threatening tone (5.223–36). In her conversation with Hermes (5.129–133), Calypso complains that goddesses are denied the love of mortal men, even when they take them as husbands. As an example she mentions Demeter's love of Iasion. When Demeter "gave way to her passion and made love with Iasion" in a field, Calypso tells Hermes, Zeus learned of the act and "blasted the man to death with flashing bolts" (5.138–42). Odysseus later relates to Queen Arete that the promise of immortality that the "dangerous nymph" tried to sway him with never managed to win the heart within his breast (7.291–97). While Homer does not elaborate, Iasion may be translated as "the man of the drug" leaving the impulse that Demeter yielded to—and Calypso would have herself and Odysseus yield to—more ambiguous than is generally supposed.[30]

There are several instances of drugs being put into wine in the *Odyssey*, such as the drugs of Ephyra that the suitors fear Telemarchos may be seeking, so as to poison their wine (2.364–66). In a famous scene (4.243–69), one that may be "the earliest reference to compound *pharmaka* in the Greek world,"[31] Helen mixes one of the "cunning" drugs she learned from Thon's wife Polydamna in Egypt into the wine of Odysseus' household to raise their spirits and improve the quality of their conversation.[32] Three different adjectives are used to describe this drug: it is grief-removing (*nepenthes*), anger-removing (*akholon*) and induces forgetfulness (*kakon epilethon hapanton*).[33] The *pharmakon* added to the wine causes one to forget the ills of the world, even the death of a loved one, when it's placed in the "mixing bowl" with the wine.[34] The identity of Helen's *pharmakon* continues to be debated.[35] There is enough evidence at hand to identify it as opium (*Papaver somniferum*), a substance that is soluble in both water and wine and which was well known in the ancient world in a wide variety of ingestible forms.[36] Ironically, the opium poppy emanated from Asia Minor, so Homer "would be speaking of a 'local' plant, even though the drug allegedly came from Egypt."[37]

The Lotus-Eaters are said to live in a "lush-green land" (23.355). In addition to fruit and flowers, they eat a plant called the lotus. The lotus itself surely embodies some sort of naturally occurring *pharmakon*. While the pharmaceutical powers of the lotus are left unspecified by the poet, to taste of its sweetness is to let memory of home fade from the mind—which in the ancient Greek world would have been tantamount to saying it dissolved identity. The seductive temptation of the Lotus-Eaters and their drug harkens back to a "primitive state without work and struggle in the 'fertile land' . . . a stage more ancient than agriculture, cattle-rearing and even hunting, older, in fact, than all production."[38] The Mycenaean Linear B tablets suggest the foundations of ancient Greece's economy underwent a radical transformation in the centuries between the fall of the Mycenaean world and the eighth century BCE. A heavily labor-intensive economy based on the raising of grain replaced a comparatively more relaxed way of living—quite probably represented by the Lotus-Eaters—with "enormous social and psychological repercussions."[39] Indeed, Odysseus sends his scouts out with the purpose of determining whether or not the strangers are "men like us" who "live on bread" (9.100–102).[40]

Odysseus occupies a position diametrically opposed to the Lotus-Eaters. The eating of flowers and naturally occurring drugs such as the Lotus are indicative of "a state [of being] in which the reproduction of life is independent of conscious self-preservation," thus it constitutes a threat of "oblivion and surrender of the will" which is impermissible for the adherents of "the rationale of self-preservation" Odysseus himself personifies.[41] There is no textual evidence that Odysseus himself is tempted by the plant,[42] but the danger it poses to the weaker minds of his crew is manifest. The scouts eat the lotus and not only fail to return, they don't even bother to send a message back explaining their situation. It is said that any crewmen who set to "grazing on lotus" saw their desire to return home permanently dissolved (10.106–110). The lure is so great that Odysseus must forcibly drag the weeping men back to the ship, lash them beneath the rowing benches, and command their more steady shipmates to make a hasty departure. The Odysseus of the *Odyssey* is the embodiment of identity-preserving reason, and as such he can only perceive the pleasures of the Lotus-Eaters as "lingering in the shade of the image of bliss," the mere "illusion of happiness, a dull vegetation, as meager as an animal's bare existence, and at best the absence of the awareness of misfortune."[43]

The Cyclops of the *Odyssey* are described as being lawless and outrageous. They live in isolated family units without legal institutions and, lacking agriculture, they simply trust that the gods will provide them with wheat and barley and "full-bodied wine from clustered grapes" (9.118–28). Polyphemus, the Cyclops encountered by Odysseus and a party of his men, is described as a "grim loner" whose mind is firmly fixed on "lawless ways" (9.210). This refers not simply to a disregard for "the laws of civilization, but also that his mind itself, his thinking, is lawless, unsystematic, and rhapsodical," rendering him incapable of performing any "straightforward mental task" such as deciphering "the sophistic double meaning in Odysseus's false name."[44] Odysseus carries with him a goatskin of the "ruddy, irresistible wine" given to him as a gift from "Maron, son of Euanthes," and a priest of Apollo (9.218–26). This wine is unmixed, wonderfully fragrant, truly a "drink fit for the gods" (9.228). It is also fantastically strong, magically irresistible once one has smelled its honey sweet aroma in the mixing bowl (9.231–35).[45] The most common ratio of wine to water during the mixing ceremony of the *symposion* was one to three. Maron's wine, we learn, requires *twenty* parts water to be consumed civilly. If not simply exaggeration, what is being elaborated here is a wine "quite outstandingly intoxicating."[46] The need for such severe dilution was not necessitated by the wine but, as we saw in chapter 1, by substances such as botanical drugs added to it. Finding himself trapped in the cave of Polyphemus, Odysseus offers the Cyclops his black wine to drink. Being barbarians the Cyclops do not bother with dilution, drinking their wine unmixed. The libation has the desired effect: Polyphemus is incapacitated and then blinded, paving the way for Odysseus' escape.[47]

Of all the Odyssean stories, the encounter with Circe was perhaps the most popular with Attic vase-painters.[48] Whether or not one agrees to label her a sorceress, Circe's powers are explicitly *pharmaceutical.*[49] Like Calypso she is described as a dangerous divine being, a "terrible goddess with a human voice" (*deine theos audeessa*) and like the episode with Helen there are drugs presented in the context of "god-delivered and god-derived powers and knowledge."[50] Odysseus' comrades, approaching her home, find it surrounded by tame mountain lions and wolves who the goddess had given "magic drugs" and "bewitched" (10.231–32). Inviting the men inside she serves them a "potion" (*kykeon*) consisting of "cheese, barley and pale honey mulled in Pramnian wine" (10.257–58). Into this wine she stirs "wicked drugs" (*pharmaka lugra*) and soon thereafter the men take on the outward appearance of pigs; only "the men's minds [*nous*] stayed steadfast as before" (10.261–65). While their minds remain human it would seem their individual identities are lost during the transformation, because the intent of Circe's potion is explicitly described as being "to wipe from their memories any thought of home" (10.260). Circe is described in some translations as performing her mischief with a magic wand (in the manner of a contemporary stage magician) but what she holds, a *rhabdos*, could simply mean "stick" in Greek. Circe's powers clearly lie with her *pharmaka lugra*, not some sort of magic wand.[51] She simply uses the latter to herd the transformed crew members into animal pens. On one Attic cup Circe can be seen mixing her potion with this same "wand."[52]

Odysseus' reaction to the loss of his men is to prepare for battle, but Hermes appears to chastise him for being ignorant of his surroundings. Force will not work in such a situation, only an effective/good drug (*pharmakon esthlon*) to counteract Circe's bad/evil one (*pharmakon kakon*). Hermes gives Odysseus the *moly*, a plant black at the root with a milky flower, telling him that if he takes "this good drug to the house of Circe" (*tode pharmakon esthlon echon es domata Kirkes*) he will be safe.[53] There is some textual confusion in the encounter between Odysseus and Hermes. Hermes appears to hand over the antidote to Odysseus at 10.318, yet the *moly* does not appear until 10.335 and thereafter.[54] Hermes indicates he must show/explain/reveal the whole "nature" or *phusis* of the plant, *kai moi phusin autou edeixe* (10.337). This ought to include details regarding both its external appearance and the pharmacology of its internal properties but "Homer only explicitly refers to the external properties."[55] While his men were overcome by drugged wine, Hermes appears to warn Odysseus that Circe will give him a potion (*kykeon*) and drugged food (10.321). When Odysseus finally reaches "the great house of Circe, who knows many drugs (*polypharmakos*)"[56] and meets her face to face there is no mention of the *moly* or anything else being put into either the cup or food she sets before him, to counteract her drug or drugs.

Like the account of the Cyclops there is evidence of a number of oral traditions being imperfectly adapted when set down in writing. "We are clearly dealing with a long tradition of 'witch' tales centering on Circe, and Homer is trying to adapt them to the particular circumstances of the *Odyssey*. In particular he is trying to cut out the excessively magical."[57] It may not be correct to view what Circe practices as "magic:" There is nothing in the Greek to suggest that Circe's actions are invested by the author of the *Odyssey* "with the same significance that the actions of magicians are invested with at a later date."[58] She is less a "sorceress" and more a *rhizotomos*, a cutter of roots.[59] All the same there *is* a tradition, and Homer *is* adapting it; it would be more aptly said that Homer was trying to cut out the excessively *pharmaceutical*.[60] The power of Circe's drugs is absolute, and can admit of no middle ground; "one either succumbs" to their powers, "and forgets one's *nostos*, or one escapes."[61] Circe's response is telling: no man has drunk her drugged potion without losing himself to her, never; resisting this *pharmakon* once it passes the lips and is swallowed is simply impossible (10.362–64). And yet that is what the epic hero, having taken his own antidrug, has done.[62] Her astonishment just about sums up the *Odyssey*'s didactic purpose in a single line (10.365): "You have a mind [*noos*] in *you* no magic can enchant!"[63]

To understand Plato's hostility to the ethics and aesthetics of the drinking *symposion*, including the pleasures of *methe*, it is important to remember that by the fourth century BCE the "vitality of Homeric symbolism had been played out, and its ties with the transcendent had been replaced by its adaptation as a tool of *political education*; Homer not only was a source of educational material but had become virtually institutionalized in Greek society."[64] An example of this pedagogical importance may be found in Xenophon's *Symposium*. At Socrates' request each speaker recounts what he considers the most valuable knowledge in his possession. Niceratus says that his father, in order to make him a good person, chose "as a means to this end [to compel] me to memorize all of Homer; and so now I can repeat the whole *Iliad* and *Odyssey* by heart" (3.5).

When he speaks of the "old quarrel" between philosophy and poetry in the *Republic* (607b), Plato both situates himself in a polemical battle with Homer begun by Hesiod, while indicating philosophy's formulation of the truth is superior.[65] Plato's objections do not arise out of the difficulty with *pharmaka* and intoxication expressed in Homer's poetry but rather the *conspicuousness* of Homer's treatment. In the *Republic* (389e–390b), for example, he objects to lines like "heavy with wine, with eyes of a dog and heart of a deer" that appear in the *Iliad* (1.225), as well as similar fare in the *Odyssey* (9.8–10), as not being "fit for the young to hear, so far as moderation is concerned."[66] Homer's budding awareness of the dangers drug use posed to subjective identity blossoms, more fully and more systematically articulated, in the dialogues of Plato.

Dionysus—God of all Drugs

The Greek god Dionysus remains mired in paradox and controversy. Male but fundamentally androgynous, oftentimes dying but essentially immortal, his cult was ancient and viewed as violent and dangerous, simultaneously wild, strange, and comprehensible only to initiates. No other god of the ancient Greeks has produced such a wide spectrum of "different and often contradictory interpretations."[67] The four major provinces traditionally associated with Dionysus—wine, ritual madness, the mask and the theater, and the promise of a happy life after death—have been a rich source of discussion and disputation. The debate has only intensified since Nietzsche, who argued in works such as *Twilight of the Idols* that "it is only in the Dionysian mysteries, in the psychology of the Dionysian state, that the *fundamental fact* of the Hellenistic instinct expresses itself— it's 'will to life.'"[68] Dionysus was known by a multitude of names.[69] It is the afterlife that most closely links Dionysus with the Eleusinian Mysteries.[70] In the persona of Triptolemus Dionysus was often represented as "traveling throughout the world on a serpent chariot spreading the gospel of the cultivation of grain."[71] The importance of Triptolemus' mission rose and fell with Athens's imperial fortunes.[72]

From uncertain beginnings—perhaps Asia Minor—Dionysus was thought to have been introduced into Attica from both the north, via Thrace, and the west/south, via the Aegean islands and especially Minoan Crete, a civilization that originated around 6,000 BCE and had flourished since approximately 3,000 BCE.[73] Linear B evidence indicates the god was the subject of worship among the Greeks as early as 1,500 BCE.[74] The name Dionysus can be said to mean, roughly, the Zeus (Dios) of Nysa, and he was called the Divine Bridegroom.[75] Nysa was the common name for locations where maenadic celebrations took place.[76] Etymologically Nysa appears related to *nystazo* (to nod and doze in sleep), a reaction that was attributed to a plant known as the *narkissos*, and *nysos* (a Thracian word for bride) and *nysso* (to sting). In botanic lore Dionysus' own plant, the *kissos* or ivy (reputed to have its own mind-altering properties) was called *nysa*.[77] Many of the words associated with Dionysiac cult practice were assimilated into Greek from earlier Mediterranean dialects including *ampelos* (vine), *oenos* (wine), *botrys* (grape cluster), *thyrsos* (sacred branch or wand) and words ending in *inthos* and *issos*.[78] The herbs stored in the *thyrsos* were placed in the fennel reed (*Ferula communis*) at the top of thyrsos; this area of the wand was called the *narthex*, "literally the *narko-thex* or 'narcotic storage.'"[79]

Even as late as the Homeric epics Dionysus was not particularly well-regarded, being "something quite alien, an insult to all municipal order."[80] He is but rarely mentioned in the *Iliad* and the *Odyssey*, possibly indicating "that while viticulture and wine were common in Greece during the eighth century [BCE] the cult of Dionysus was not yet widespread."[81] His rise in prominence in the centuries thereafter occurred in a period of social upheaval characterized by class struggles, during which "the social and political rise of the lower classes was accompanied also by the penetration of their religious conceptions into higher intellectual life, thus smoothing the way for decisive changes. This revolution was heralded by the mounting esteem in which the cult of Dionysus now came to be held."[82] In the sixth century and frequently for political reasons the worship of Dionysus came into favor with tyrants such as Periander of Corinth (627–585 BCE), and Peisistratus of Athens (ca. 607–528 BCE) "who were representative of the social stratum newly coming to power."[83] Peisistratus incorporated the worship of Dionysus into the civic calendar,[84] and established the greatest of the drama festivals, the Great Dionysia.[85]

Paralleling the rise of Dionysus were "the ancient local mysteries, including Eleusis, which were favored by much the same political forces."[86] The shift away from what has been termed the traditional "Delphic theology" that saw the gods of Olympus as essentially distant and powerful and mortals as frail and endangered was further accelerated by the costly Peloponnesian War.[87] During the war, as the traditional ruling aristocracy was being penetrated by "a new class of nonlanded artisans and merchants," the traditional cosmology went into decline, invaded "in part by deified human beings" and "more prominently by imported divinities, and ultimately the worshippers themselves."[88] The Eleusinian Mysteries grew in importance and popularity during this time, a part of a more widespread and not wholly successful effort to "institutionalize ecstasy."[89]

The new piety, in contrast to the old, emphasized "practices in which the individual strove for a new, disengaged status or achieved such a status by means of divine possession."[90] By either their own action, or by accessing the divine, men and women became, for an instant in time, godlike, and this acted as a promise of a more permanent divinity at a later time. Greek rites and the cults associated with them are not dissimilar to "shamanic" religions that may be found in contemporary Africa and elsewhere.[91] Central to shamanistic practices and beliefs is the notion of the ecstatic vision or trance, a state "simultaneously terrifying, hilarious, awe-inspiring, familiar and bizarre."[92] The use of drugs is common in shamanic religions.[93] The ancient Greeks were aware of both religious and social use of drugs by their neighbors, the Scythians.[94] Herodotus (ca. 484–425 BCE) describes their use of hemp smoke during their funeral practices as "giving off a vapor unsurpassed by any vapor-bath one could find in Greece. The Scythians enjoy it so much they howl with joy [*agamenoi oruontai*]" (*Histories* 5.72–5).[95] Plato denigrates the recreational drinking practices of the Scythians in the *Laws* (637e).[96]

A common theme in Greek mythology was the reconciliation of old and new orders, both the iconography of the deities and their rites of worship retaining, albeit in altered form, "very ancient, pre-Indo-European aspects."[97] The association of Dionysus with the vine and wine came only later, gradually superseding a variety of plants "reputed to be intoxicating or poisonous."[98] He was a god "of all intoxication" with wine merely "one of the many drugs at his disposal."[99] In Minoan-Mycenaean practice Dionysus was a subordinate figure to his mother, the goddess of the Earth, Gaia.[100] For the Greeks he was the son of Zeus and Semele, uniquely "twice born," in one tradition being brought to term inside Zeus' thigh after his mother was consumed by a blast of lightning. Semele, though supposedly mortal, was accorded her own cult as a goddess and was equated by Apollodorus with Ge, the Thracian form of Gaia, which at least suggests that Semele herself may have been an earth goddess.[101]

The lightning bolt or *keraunion*, associated with the Indo-European Zeus, "can be traced as a symbol of enlightenment in Asiatic shamanism."[102] In the Vedic hymns Agni, the god of mystic illumination identified with the mushroom god Soma, was said to have been created when "the Father God Indra threw a lightning bolt at the Earth."[103] The double birth of Dionysus is paralleled in one of the oldest Vedic metaphysical treatises, where one finds the gods taking Soma/Agni and putting him in the right thigh of the Indra.[104] The ancient Greeks had knowledge of Indian deities, referring to Siva as the "Indian Dionysus." Siva, too, was no stranger to drugs. The *Vedas* record that Siva brought the hemp plant down from the Himalayas, and was so fond of eating it he was called the Lord of Bhang.[105] While the parallels between Zeus/Dionysus and Indra/Agni are evident, the points of correspondence between Dionysus and Siva are equally as numerous: "wine, ecstasy, the bull, the mountains, nocturnal rites with drums and dancing, frenzied women, fertility, the imposition of an alien cult upon established orthodoxy and, finally, the coincidence of opposites."[106]

The association of lightning/thunder with mushrooms was widespread in antiquity. Theophrastus (*History of Plants* 1.6.5) associates *keraunion* with the name of a particular mushroom. In Thrace "*keraunion* was called *oiton*: this word is a dialectical variant of *hydnon* and the mushroom presumably the same."[107] Plutarch (*Moralia* 8.4.2) inquired into the popular belief that thunder caused the *hydnon* to grow, finding no sure answer. Atheneaus, quoting Theophrastus, writes that mushrooms "grow when autumn rains come with severe thunderstorms; the more thundering there is, the more they grow, the presumption being this is the more important cause" (2.62). In the Orphic tradition the Titans "opposed the evolution of Dionysus into the assimilated son of Zeus and feasted atavistically on his flesh, cooked in perversion of the culinary arts."[108] Because they shredded, cooked and ate the infant Dionysus, the Titans themselves were punished with a lethal bolt of lightning. Zeus then resurrected both

In the left margin, handwritten: "mushrooms as "food of gods" *"

Dionysus and the Titans, the latter as the present day race of men.[109] Mankind, in other words, arises as a race of punished mushroom eaters. Among the Greeks mushrooms were apparently called "food of the gods" (*broma theon*), while the neoplatonic philosopher Porphyry (ca. 233–309 CE) called them "nurslings of the gods" (*theotrophos*).[110]

In the oldest known dithyrambic fragment, written by Arkhilokhos (ca. 680–ca. 645 BCE), one finds the rarely used word συγκεραυνωθείς (*synkeraunōtheis*). While the passage in the fragment refers prominently to "music and wine in the context of dithyrambic performance," *synkeraunōtheis* is not an apt metaphor for the effects of wine since the *syn-* prefix "conveys the completion of the act, altogether, completely," and in this case the act, κεραυνόω (*keraunoō*), is "to strike with thunderbolts."[111] The word conveys "devastating natural violence rather than inebriate poetic exultation" and means something akin to being "utterly blasted with lightning"—the conclusion being that its origin is religious rather than simply poetic. Individuals who had been struck by lightning and happened to be fortunate enough to have survived were held in special religious reverence by the Greeks. The ramifications are compelling. Lightning strikes Semele, i.e. the earth, and brings forth the child of Zeus, the nursling Dionysus. The worship of Dionysus, at least in its earliest cult stages, may well have been a mushroom cult and, prior to his later gifts such as wine, an initiate became one with Dionysus through a form of intoxication far removed from alcohol inebriation.[112]

Dionysus was frequently associated with bulls and was thought to have the power to transform himself into a bull, the taurine symbolism being another sign that the provenance of his intoxicant predates viticulture.[113] In Euripides' *Bacchae* the Chorus of Asian women announce the deity's arrival from the "far off lands of Asia," describing how "Zeus bore the bull-horned god" from a secret womb and placed on his head "wreaths of writhing snakes," and finally extolling his abundant generosity to mankind, an earth that "flows with milk, flows with wine, flows with the nectar of bees."[114] As just mentioned in chapter 3, one of the names associated with Dionysus was Brimios, "the thunderer" or "roarer." *Mykema*, "the roaring of a bull or thunder," resembles *mykes*, "mushroom"— both date from the syllabary of the Mycenaean period, where the initial sounds of both words would have been written with the pictogram of a bull's head, and *mykema* "seems to have been a metaphor for the imagined cry of the fruiting bodies of the mushroom as they burst forth from the earth or are harvested."[115] Mycenae, or Mykenai, may well derive from *mykes*, suggesting the possibility the *mykes* figured in Mycenaean religion. Snakes appear with a number of Minoan goddesses.[116] Nicander in his *Alexipharmaka* describes mushrooms as an "evil ferment of the soil" that are said to derive their powers by absorbing the venom of a snake coiled below in its lair (521–25).[117] Pliny the Elder wrote that mushrooms could only be safely harvested during the period of serpent hibernation (*Natural History* 22.95).

According to Apollonius Rhodius (fl. 3rd century BCE), Dionysus was fed honey by his nurses as an infant at Nysa (4.1134–36). Honey and its intoxicant

mead were assimilated into Greece from Minoan culture. Bees, like the maenadic women gathering flowers in the wild, go from flower to flower, collecting
their (in)toxicants, believed to be "related to the venom of serpents, but its beneficial antithesis, instead of a poison."[118] In the Minoan-Mycenaean myth of
Glaukos, son of King Minos and the moon goddess Pasiphae, as recorded by
Pseudo-Apollodorus (*Library* 3.3.1–3.3.2), one finds "all the motifs of a barely
remembered mushroom cult" including "themes of death and rebirth, cattle, serpents with herbal knowledge, and a blue-gray child who is preserved in
honey."[119] Glaukos may be translated as meaning "greenish blue" (i.e. sea-
green) or "blue-gray."[120] The flesh of *Stropharia cubensis* stains a similar color
when bruised or broken, an enzymatic reaction indicative of psilocybin. Honey
was commonly used as a preservative in antiquity.[121]

Eleusis and "the Pharmacological Question"

The Eleusinian Mysteries were Minoan in origin and, like the cult of Dionysus,
remain an object of considerable discussion and dispute.[122] It has been argued by
some that the secrets of Eleusis are permanently lost.[123] Still others have argued
that while we may discern and discuss particular facets of those secrets it is simply impossible to come away with any certainties regarding them.[124] Even if we
could understand those secrets, it has been claimed, the chasm between "pure
observation and the experience of those involved in the real proceedings remains
unbridgeable."[125] It is not my intention here to provide an exhaustive summary
of the experience of initiation into the Greater Mysteries. One could devote an
entire book to them, and still not exhaust the topic.[126] My sole concern in the
present discussion is the possibility of the presence and use of one or more
pharmaka at Eleusis.

The village of Eleusis was located several miles northwest of Athens. The
name is a reference to the underworld but in a positive sense, being translated as
"the place of happy arrival."[127] Eleusis was annexed and made a part of Attica
by Solon in the early part of the sixth century; until that time it had been an object of contention between Athens and Megara.[128] In comparison to the Greater
Mysteries little is known of the Lesser Mysteries, whose rites took place at Agri,
a village southeast of Athens,[129] except that they preceded the Greater Mysteries
by half a year and were clearly a prerequisite for participation in the rites at
Eleusis.[130] The emphasis of the Greater Mysteries "was redemption from death
by the incorporation of the underworld's putrefaction into a larger scheme where
it would function as a source of fertility," whereas the Lesser Mysteries "occurred in the wild . . . and involved the preliminary to reintegration, the Dionysian theme of Persephone's illegal abduction while gathering intoxicating uncul-
tivated flowers."[131]

The Greater Mysteries comprised, simultaneously, a harvest festival involving the cultivated grains raised on the nearby Rarian plain, the marking of yet

another descent by Persephone into the underworld, her separation and subsequent reunion with her mother the grain goddess Demeter, and a tribute to Dionysus. The involvement of Dionysus with the goddesses of the Greater Mysteries, at first disputed but now widely accepted, is complex and multifaceted. In the guise of Iakchos, Dionysus was a mediator between the two goddesses.[132] Through Dionysus, who was the god of *ekstasis* and *enthousiasmos*, the initiates could identify themselves with Demeter and her quest to be reunified with Persephone. A statue of Iakchos led the song-filled procession from Athens to Eleusis, the festive spirit of which may be gleaned from Aristophanes' *Frogs* (324–335).

Demeter's name is derived from *deai* (barley) and *meter* (mother). As Mother Barley or Mother Grain she was associated with all cultivated vegetation, and was often depicted holding or crowned with poppies, slit in a manner which yields raw opium, or with poppies in her hands, a practice which dates from the Minoans.[133] Persephone, her daughter, as described in the *Homeric Hymn to Demeter* (ca. 650–550 BCE), was abducted while frolicking and picking flowers with the daughters of Ocean at a place called Nysa. Lured by the astonishingly fragrant scent of a hundred-headed plant called the *narkissos*, the maiden "was charmed" and then seized by Hades (3–21).[134] Abductions of this sort, usually linked to plants with mind-altering properties, permeate Greek mythology and literature.[135] Plato refers to one such abduction in the *Phaedrus* (229c). Oreithyia ("she who rages in the mountains" or "mountain ecstatic female") was blown off a cliff while playing with Pharmakeia ("the use of drugs").[136]

The longevity of the Eleusinian Mysteries, the most significant spiritual experience of the ancient world, lay "in the fact that they possessed no dogma but, rather, involved certain sacred acts that engendered religious feelings and into which each successive age could project the symbolism it desired."[137] The requirements for becoming an initiate were relatively modest: the candidate had to be able to speak Greek, could not be guilty of the crime of murder, and was required to supply a piglet that would be ritually bathed in the sea and later on sacrificed.[138] At the center of the initiation experience were nine days of fasting, *aischrologia* (ritualized mock verbal abuse), and drinking of the *kykeon* within the initiation hall, the *telesterion*.[139] Archeological excavations at Eleusis indicate that the layout of the *telesterion* was incompatible with it being a theatre where stagecraft was performed.[140] Within the *telesterion* the *dromena* (things performed) were accompanied by the *deiknymena* (showing of holy objects), such as those kept in the *kiste* (covered baskets), and the *logomena* (secret spoken words) rhythmically sung or chanted by the participants, during which a gong, the *echeion*, was struck, preparing the initiates for the great revelation, the *epopteia*.[141]

Drinking the *kykeon* of Eleusis was said to be followed by the experience of an ecstatic, rapturous vision: the *epopteia*. Thereafter one was forever an *epoptes* (one who had seen).[142] Owing to their sublime nature, only highly generalized and veiled references to, or descriptions of, the *epopteia* were permissible, anything else being considered a serious profanity. Candidates for initiation were required to take an oath of silence, most importantly agreeing "not to reveal the mystical secrets about to be imparted to any save the initiated."[143] Being found guilty of revealing the secrets could result in a death sentence, helping to explain why the tragic poet Aeschylus would, according to Plato (*Republic* 563c), "say whatever just came to [his] lips" in his defense and plead, according to Aristotle (*Nicomachean Ethics* 1111a), that he "did not know it was a secret." What the initiates at Eleusis saw during the *epopteia* were not actors, nor stagecraft, but an apparition (*phasma*) or apparitions (*phasmata*), specifically the spirit of Persephone returning from Hades, with her new-born son.[144]

Was the *Kykeon* a *Pharmakon*?

The question of drug use and the Eleusinian Mysteries is an old one. It was raised, for example, in the second half of the nineteenth century by Nietzsche. In *The Birth of Tragedy*, written in 1871 and published in 1872, he included "the influence of narcotic potions, of which all primitive peoples and races speak in hymns" as one possible source of Dionysian ecstasy.[145] In the same work the lines "the hope of the *epopts* was the rebirth of Dionysus, which we can now interpret, with some foreboding, as the end of individuation" without question refer to Eleusis. In the preface he added to the 1886 edition Nietzsche describes "visions and hallucinations, which took hold of entire communities, entire cult assemblies," the latter being almost certainly a reference to the visionary *epopteia* experienced by initiates assembled at Eleusis.[146] Nietzsche would lament that nearly everything pertaining to the question "what is Dionysiac" remained to be discovered and unearthed.[147] After languishing for more than a half century the pharmacological question reappeared in the second half of the twentieth century, the growing sophistication of the answers being matched, perhaps, only by the vehemence with which others would attempt to refute them.[148]

Was the sacred potion drunk by initiates at Eleusis merely a "barley soup" consumed to break a ritual fast?[149] Or did it contain something psychoactive? It is generally agreed, based on texts such as the *Homeric Hymn to Demeter* (198–211), that a beverage of barley, water, and mint was drunk just prior to the culmination of one's initiation into the Greater Mysteries: the *kykeon*, a word that means "mixture" or "potion."[150] There was a long literary tradition associating such potions with religious ritual and drugs.[151] In the *Iliad* (11.754–58) Nestor's mistress Hecamede mixes a *kykeon* consisting of Pramnian wine, grated goat's cheese, and white barley meal.[152] In Plato's *Ion* (538b–d) Socrates implies that Hecamede's potion was prepared "specifically for its medicinal/pharmacological properties."[153] The *pharmakon* present in Hecamede's *kykeon* is unclear, but whether it was analgesic or psychotropic "the pharmacological properties" exceed "what can be attributed to a high alcoholic content."[154] The noun *kykeon* appears three times in Homer.[155] In the *Odyssey* (10.351) Circe is described as preparing for Odysseus a potion (*kykeon*) in a cup of gold and placing into it a drug (*pharmakon*) with evil intent in her heart. The potion Circe prepares for Odysseus' shipmates (10.256–60) consists of cheese, barley and pale honey mulled in Pramnian wine into which she mixes a wicked drug or drugs.

In Plato's *Republic* Pramnian wine is criticized as nothing more than a refreshment (405e–406a) and, concerning the reference to "gentle drugs" being sprinkled on Menelaus' wound by practitioners of temple medicine in the *Iliad* (4.251), Plato emphasizes (408a–b) the inadequacy of believing these drugs or a potion such as "a drink mixed with barely, cheese and wine" can cure men without an accompanying prescription of a "healthy and orderly" regimen of living.[156] *Kykeon* appears 22 times in the Hippocratic corpus, the nature of the *pharmaka* added to the mixture varying with the therapeutic function it was intended to serve.[157] Finally, in Aristophanes' *Peace* (712) the indigestion of Trygaeus is said to be curable if he follows the advice of Hermes and drinks a *kykeon* flavored with mint.

Hipponax, of Epheusus, was a Greek iambic poet expelled from his home in 540 BCE by the tyrant Athenagoras. He went to Clazomenae where he lived in poverty the rest of his life. The surviving fragments of his poetry, which are highly satiric in nature, frequently mention the speaker's poverty. In fragment 48 the speaker tells whomever he is addressing that if he isn't supplied with barley for his *kykeon*, he will commit suicide. The fragment calls this drink a *pharmakon* against the wretched poverty of the speaker. The speaker may simply be using *pharmakon* as a metaphor for "relief" or at most using the word in a "nutritive-medicinal" sense (the traditional interpretation), but elements of the fragment point towards the drug having a "ritualistic-sacramental" purpose; the *kykeon* of Hipponax fragment 48 is analogous to the *kykeon* of the *Homeric Hymn to Demeter*, and hence to the *kykeon* of Eleusis.[158] Clearly, then, there are many precedents for associating the Eleusinian *kykeon* with a potion or drink containing drugs.

Although various drugs have been nominated as the source of the Eleusinian *epopteia*, including alcohol,[159] mushrooms,[160] and opium,[161] the most likely explanation for the *phasmata* experienced at Eleusis is the grain itself that was present in the *kykeon*.[162] Up until the twentieth century "there was no such thing as a field of wheat or of barley."[163] Multiple weeds and infections grew and were harvested with the main cereal crop. Through a combination of evidence drawn from textual, archeological, and ethnobotanical sources, the source of the "hallucinatory reality" seen at Eleusis has been most persuasively identified as *Claviceps purpurea*, more commonly known as ergot.[164] Ergot refers to the purple-black sclerotia that may be found on many plants, several of which were present in ancient Greece, such as barley, wheat, or darnel (*Lolium temulentum*).

There is textual evidence that the ancient Greeks had some degree of awareness of ergot, which they called *erysibe*.[165] The *Etymologicum Gudianum* (210.25) gives the Eleusinian goddess Demeter the epithet Erysibe, "as though her gift of grain could exist only through the aversion of the darker persona that was her own and its antithesis."[166] Ergot represented some aspect of Apollo's supplanted avatar, the secret offering enclosed in the sheaf of wheat from the mythical Hyperboreans; in Strabo (ca. 63/64 BCE–24 CE) the god bears the epithet Erysibios (*Geography* 13.1.64), "literally the metaphor of the fungus as the reddening corruption or 'rust' (*erysibe*) upon the grain."[167] The Hippocratic works *Diseases of Women* and *Sterile Women* both mention a substance called *melanthion* (black flower). This substance, obtained from wheat and used for gynecological and obstetrical purposes, "cannot refer to an ordinary plant, but is more likely . . . the well known fungal parasite ergot, found on various grass-crops and cereals."[168]

Darnel, known to the Greeks as *aira*, was also called *thyaros* (the plant of frenzy), which appears to indicate "an awareness of the psychotropic properties of ergot itself."[169] Greek farmers also utilized a sieve-like implement called the *airapinon* to separate the *aira* from their cultivated grain. Meaning "*aira* drinker," *airapinon* was apparently a folk metaphor for a person intoxicated by *aira*.[170] Aristotle's *On Sleep* (456b), in a list of plants called *hupnotika* (which produces a heaviness of the head), mentions the poppy, mandragora, wine and darnel. Darnel's psychotropic effects are described or alluded to in several ancient sources, including Theophrastus (*History of Plants* 8.8.3), Plautus (*Miles Gloriosus* 315–23), Ovid (*Fasti* 1.691) and Pliny the Elder (*Natural History* 18.44). Plato, in what is widely agreed to be an allusion to the *epopteia* of the Eleusinian Mysteries in the *Phaedrus* (251a–c), practically gives a textbook description of darnel intoxication.[171]

The ceremonial vessels used at Eleusis to prepare the *kykeon*, called *kerna* and *kernoi*, were themselves referred to as mixing bowels, "*krateres* of the Mystery."[172] As we saw above in chapter 1, the function of the *krater* in the aristocratic *symposion* was the ceremonial preparation of wine, during which time a variety of drugs might be added. Wine was forbidden at Eleusis but *krater* would have been the natural term to use "to describe the utensil for mixing *other* drinks also, especially *if the drink like wine was an inebriant*."[173] In the *Republic* (363c–d), Plato's accusation, which refers to the reputed founder of the Eleusinian mysteries, Musaeus' son (Eumolpus), as teaching "the finest wage of virtue is an eternal intoxication," essentially an afterlife that is just one perpetual *symposion*, might be read as a further indication that the Eleusinian *kykeon*, the most famous mixture of all, also contained some sort of *pharmakon*, and that an initiate experienced the *epopteia* in a state of intoxication.[174] Nietzsche, it turns out, may have been right all along.

Notes

1. Jacques Derrida, *Dissemination* (Chicago: University of Chicago Press, 1981), 132 n. 59.

2. John Scarborough, "The Pharmacology of Sacred Plants, Herbs, and Roots," in *Magika Hiera—Ancient Greek Magic and Religion*, ed. Christopher A. Faraone and Dirk

Obbink (New York and Oxford: Oxford University Press, 1991), 142. See also my discussion of ancient Greek medicine in chapter 7, below.

3. Jerry Stannard, "Squill in Ancient and Medieval Materia Medica, with Special Reference to its Deployment for Dropsy," *Bulletin of the New York Academy of Medicine* 50 (1974): 684–713. The medicinal uses of squill are, in addition to the gynecological works of the Hippocratic School, discussed in Dioscorides' *On Medical Materials* (2.167) and Pliny's *Natural History* (19.30.93–95 and 20.39.97).

4. See Scarborough, "The Pharmacology of Sacred Plants, Herbs, and Roots," 170 n. 132. Randall B. Clark, *The Law Most Beautiful and Best: Medical Argument and Magical Rhetoric in Plato's* Laws (Lanham, MD: Lexington Books, 2003), 115 n. 12 indicates "American physicians effectively abandoned the use of squill in the 1950s and 1960s, often for digitoxin and digoxin, preparations that contain digitalis, a cardiac glycoside similar to the one found in squill."

5. Clark, *The Law Most Beautiful and Best*, 110.

6. Scarborough "The Pharmacology of Sacred Plants, Herbs, and Roots," 146. See also Clark, *The Law Most Beautiful and Best*, 110–11.

7. Jan N. Bremmer, "Scapegoat Rituals in Ancient Greece," *Harvard Studies in Classical Philology* 87 (1983): 308–313. Bremmer's contention that these plants were purely symbolic ignores, as Scarborough points out in "The Pharmacology of Sacred Plants, Herbs, and Roots," 169 n. 100, "the plentiful evidence of squills and their use in medicine and herbal remedies."

8. On the wandering wonder-worker see Matthew W. Dickie, *Magic and Magicians in the Greco-Roman World* (New York: Routledge, 2003), 74–75, and my discussion of ancient Greek magic in chapter 8, below. On Epimenides and squill see Clark, *The Law Most Beautiful and Best*, 115 n. 11, citing Strabo *Geography* (10.479) and Theophrastus *History of Plants* (7.12).

9. Clark, *The Law Most Beautiful and Best*, 110 and 115 n. 16. Nicander is discussed in greater detail in chapter 7, below.

10. Scarborough, "The Pharmacology of Sacred Plants, Herbs, and Roots," 147. Tzetzes' most important work, the *Book of Histories*, like Athenaeus' *The Deipnosophists*, is valuable chiefly because it preserves the thought of literally hundreds of other works that are now lost but were accessible to the author.

11. Scarborough, "The Pharmacology of Sacred Plants, Herbs, and Roots," 139–40.

12. The religious use of *pharmaka* will be discussed primarily in this chapter. Social-recreational drug use, in addition to the discussion in chapter 1, will be discussed in chapter 5. Medicine and *pharmaka* use will be examined in chapter 7, magic and *pharmaka* in chapter 8, and rhetoric and *pharmaka* in chapter 9, below.

13. Interpreting *pharmakon* within a "remedy/poison" bifurcation is terribly simplistic yet this is what most of the literature, misreading Derrida's "Plato's Pharmacy," does. See my discussion of the multivariate meanings of the term in chapter 10, below.

14. Derrida, *Dissemination*, 125–26 for example points out that the *pharmakon* "is aneidetic, firstly because it is not monoeidetic (in the sense in which [Plato's] *Phaedo* speaks of the *eidos* as something simple, noncomposite: *monoeides*). But neither it is a composite . . . partaking of several simple essences. It is rather the prior medium in which differentiation in general is produced . . . analogous to the one that will, subsequent to and according to the decision of philosophy, be reserved for transcendental imagination." See also chapter 10, below.

15. Scarborough, "The Pharmacology of Sacred Plants, Herbs, and Roots," 139. I will leave to one side such questions as whether or not historical personages named "Homer" and "Hesiod" were the genuine authors of the works attributed to them, when

they wrote their works, and whether or not they were contemporaries. For our purposes the importance of the works traditionally assigned to these two names lies in their being situated at the beginning of a transformation from oral to literature culture that occurred in Greece between about 750 and 350 BCE.

16. Joseph M. Bryant, *Moral Codes and Social Structure in Ancient Greece: A Sociology of Greek Ethics from Homer to the Epicureans and Stoics* (Albany, NY: State University of New York Press, 1996), 15.

17. David Lenson, *On Drugs* (Minneapolis, MN: University of Minnesota Press, 1995), 7–8. On the Greek notion of *ekstasis* see chapter 2, above.

18. Scarborough, "The Pharmacology of Sacred Plants, Herbs, and Roots," 139.

19. Theodor Adorno and Max Horkheimer, *Dialectic of Enlightenment—Philosophical Fragments*, trans. John Cumming (Palo Alto, CA: Stanford University Press, 1972), 43. Unless otherwise noted quotes from this work are from the translation by John Cumming.

20. Unless otherwise noted all quotes from Homer's *Iliad* and *Odyssey* in the main text of this chapter are from the translations by Robert Fagles and line numbers refer to his translation, not the line numbers of the original Greek text. Robert Fagles, trans., *Homer—The Iliad* (New York: Penguin Press, 1990) and Robert Fagles, trans., *Homer—The Odyssey* (New York: Penguin, 1996).

21. On Ithaca, see Robert Brittlestone (with James Diggle and John Underhill), *Odysseus Unbound: The Search for Homer's Ithaca* (New York: Cambridge University Press, 2005).

22. James Hogan, "The Temptation of Odysseus," *Proceedings of the American Philological Association* 106 (1976): 204.

23. Not all of the temptations that Odysseus faces involve a drug, of course. The Sirens, for example, have no intoxicant other than their song. But the power of their song is distinctly intoxicating. Pierre Vidal-Naquet, *The Black Hunter—Forms of Thought and Forms of Society in the Greek World* (Baltimore, MD: Johns Hopkins University Press, 1986), 23 argues that the "Sirens are a fiercer version of the Lotus-Eaters. To surrender to their seduction means never to return home (12.41–45) but, like the Lotus-Eaters, they may be foiled."

24. Adorno and Horkheimer, *Dialectic of Enlightenment*, 47.

25. Edward McCrorie, trans. *The Odyssey* (Baltimore, MD: The Johns Hopkins University Press, 2004), 387.

26. P. V. Jones, *Homer's Odyssey—A Companion to the Translation of Richard Lattimore* (Carbondale, IL: Southern Illinois University Press, 1988), 7–8, 82, and cf. Trevor J. Saunders, *Plato's Penal Code—Tradition, Controversy, and Reform in Greek Penology* (Oxford: Clarendon Press, 1991), 10–11.

27. Julian Jaynes, *The Origin of Consciousness in the Breakdown of the Bicameral Mind* (Boston: Houghton Mifflin, 1976), 273, 276–77 assesses the *Odyssey* as "a story of identity, of a voyage to the self," with Odysseus as "the hero of the new mentality" of firm noetic self-mastery.

28. Froma I. Zeitlin, "Figuring Fidelity in Homer's *Odyssey*," in *The Distaff Side: Representing the Female in Homer's Odyssey*, ed. Beth Cohen (New York: Oxford University Press, 1995), 151 n. 57 writes "fidelity is figured by Penelope's immobility in the house and her continuous weeping. . . . Fidelity is less an affair of the heart than of the mind (*noos*), and infidelity is as much equated with changing that *noos* or failing to remember it as it is to engage in conscious and active deception. Thus Penelope's epithet, *echephron* (keeping good sense) not only attests to her intelligence and perspicacity but

also includes a capacity to maintain steadfast in that *noos*, keeping her husband always in mind."

29. His son Telemachus also suffers from an acute identity crisis, feeling aggrieved and helpless (1.114–17), wishing he had a different father (1.215–20) or at least one who died gloriously in battle (1.234–243), lamenting that the constant pressure of the suitors is wasting away his substance and will soon break him into pieces altogether (1.245–251). Athena has to intervene (1.207–12, 1.296–7, 1.298–305, and 1.320–21) to instill "determination and courage" in the young man's dejected spirit, "and she does so by likening him to Odysseus . . . urging him to abandon childhood . . . and reminding him of the example of Orestes." See Jones, *Homer's* Odyssey, 3.

30. Carl A. P. Ruck, "Mushrooms and Philosophers," in *Persephone's Quest: Entheogens and the Origins of Religion*, ed. R. Gordon Wasson (New Haven, CT: Yale University Press, 1986), 172, and Carl A. P. Ruck, "On the Sacred Names of Iamos and Ion: Ethnobotanical References in the Hero's Parentage," *The Classical Journal* 71, no. 3 (1976): 235–52 both point out that the "*ia*" root that may be found in *iatros* (healer or doctor) and *iasthai* (to heal) can be found in names such as Iason (Jason), Iamos, and Iasion. See also Carl A. P. Ruck, *Sacred Mushrooms of the Goddess and the Secrets of Eleusis* (Berkeley, CA: Ronin Publishing, 2006). In one version of this myth Demeter sleeps with Iasion in a thrice-plowed field and gives birth to Ploutos (e.g. Hesiod, *Theogny* 976–78).

31. Scarborough, "The Pharmacology of Sacred Plants, Herbs, and Roots," 165 n. 29.

32. The *Odyssey* describes Egypt as a place where numerous different *pharmaka* may be found, many of them good, many of them baneful (*polla men esthla, memigmena polla de lugra*). Homer associates Polydamna with "the race of Paeon (healer)," indicating perhaps on at least one level, though certainly not all, Helen's *pharmakon* may be considered medicinal. The fame of Egypt's healing remedies is mentioned in Aristophanes *Peace* (1253) and, according to James Longrigg, *Greek Rational Medicine: Philosophy and Medicine from Alcmaeon to the Alexandrians* (New York: Routledge, 1991), 10 drugs "carrying the label 'Egyptian' appear in several Hippocratic drug prescriptions."

33. Simon Goldhill, "Reading Differences: The *Odyssey* and Juxtaposition," in *Homer: Critical Assessments. Volume 4—Homer's Art* , ed. Irene J. F. de Jong (New York: Routledge, 1999), 418.

34. Lattimore's translation of this *pharmakon* as a "medicine of heartsease" tends to obliterate the ambiguity of the drug's powers—not to mention the recreational wine it is mixed with. See Richard Lattimore, trans., *The Odyssey of Homer* (New York: Harper and Row, 1967).

35. The opposition argument runs along the lines put forward by Jones, *Homer's* Odyssey, 38 that opium would have caused the conversation to collapse into a "drug-induced stupor," something that need hardly have happened with the essentially natural and unrefined forms of opium consumed in the ancient world, which were nothing like the smoking opium of the nineteenth century or contemporary opium derivatives like morphine and heroin.

36. P. G. Kritikos and S. P. Papadaki, "The History of the Poppy and of Opium and their Expansion in Antiquity in the Eastern Mediterranean Area," *Bulletin on Narcotics* 19, no. 4 (1967): 8–9, and Richard Scarborough, "The Opium Poppy in Hellenistic and Roman Medicine," in *Drugs and Narcotics in History* (New York: Cambridge University Press, 1995), 4. Among the methods for taking opium internally in antiquity: placing it on hot clay tiles or plates and inhaling the vapors; mixing the juice with some liquid, like

wine, or placing it in confections; simply rolling the raw sap between the fingers into a small pellet and swallowing; by means of anal suppositories.

37. Scarborough, "The Pharmacology of Sacred Plants, Herbs, and Roots," 140.

38. Adorno and Horkheimer, *Dialectic of Enlightenment*, 62–63.

39. Linda A. Sussman, "Workers and Drones: Labor, Idleness and Gender Definition in Hesiod's Beehive," *Arethusa* 11, No. 1 & 2 (1978): 31. See also Graeme Barker, *The Agricultural Revolution in Prehistory—Why did Foragers become Farmers?* (Oxford: Oxford University Press, 2006).

40. Hesiod in his *Works and Days* (146–7) records that early man "did not eat *sistos* (grain)" and when Herodotus in his *History* (4.17) indicates "they grow and eat grain," it indicates, as Craik points out, "an advanced stage of human development." See Elizabeth Craik, "Diet, *Diaita* and Dietetics," in *The Greek World*, ed. Anton Powell (New York: Cambridge University Press, 1995), 390.

41. Adorno and Horkheimer, *The Dialectic of Enlightenment*, 63.

42. Hogan, "The Temptation of Odysseus," 188–89, 200.

43. Adorno and Horkheimer, *The Dialectic of Enlightenment*, 63. In this portion of *Dialectic of Enlightenment* Adorno and Horkheimer appear to borrow almost verbatim from Kant's discussion of opium intoxication in *The Metaphysics of Morals*, specifically the article titled "On Stupefying Oneself by Excessive Use of Food and Drink." See Mary Gregor, trans., *Immanuel Kant—The Metaphysics of Morals* (Cambridge: Cambridge University Press, 1996), 180–81.

44. Adorno and Horkheimer, *Dialectic of Enlightenment—Philosophical Fragments*, trans. Edmund Jephcott (Palo Alto, CA: Stanford University Press, 2002), 51.

45. Jones, *Homer's Odyssey*, 84 recognizes that describing the wine in this sort of detail reveals its importance, but draws the wrong conclusion. He writes "Maron is a name formed from Maroneia, the Thracian town where this famous vintage was made. 'Euanthes' means 'with lovely flowers'—referring to the vineyards?" The flowers have nothing to do with the vineyards. As we saw in chapter 1, above, they have been added to the wine, giving it its strong aroma and incredible potency.

46. Jones, *Homer's Odyssey*, 84.

47. There is some confusion in the text, for Polyphemus is referred to as a milk drinker (9.280–281), something that implies he is inexperienced with alcohol and thus would be more vulnerable to Odysseus' drugged wine, but twice—once by Polyphemus himself—the Cyclops are said to be producers of "wine of strength" (9.124 and 9.401). At 9.334 Polyphemus drinks "milk unmixed with water" while eating two of Odysseus' men. This is probably evidence of contradictions that were present in the oral traditions, leading to errors when they were set to writing. In at least one of these traditions the barbarian Polyphemus must have been drinking "wine unmixed with water" with his dinner of human flesh, so that only an extraordinarily drugged wine would be capable of rendering him unconscious. Peter Garnsey, *Food and Society in Classical Antiquity* (Cambridge: Cambridge University Press, 1999), 65 indicates that writers of every period of antiquity exploited "a dichotomy between civilized, sedentary farmers who lived off the land and domesticated plants, and uncivilized, pastoral nomads who are 'eaters of meat and drinkers of milk.' The tradition goes as far back as Homer."

48. H. A. Shapiro, *Myth into Art—Poet and Painter in Classical Greece* (New York: Routledge, 1994), 56.

49. Dickie, *Magic and Magicians in the Greco-Roman World*, 23 writes that while Circe was commonly assumed to be a sorceress in later traditions, "there is nothing in the Greek text to suggest that its author possesses the concept of magic and that he thought of

Circe as a sorceress." She is, in this reading, merely a particularly "frightening and sinister" cutter of roots, a *rhizotomos*. See my discussion of root-cutters in chapter 7, below.

50. Line 10.136 in the original Greek, reading *deine theos audeessa* as "the terrible goddess with a human voice" with Vidal-Naquet, *The Black Hunter*, 19. On the link between Circe and Helen see Scarborough, "The Pharmacology of Sacred Plants, Herbs, and Roots," 140. On the link between Circe and Calypso see Vidal-Naquet, *The Black Hunter*, 19 who writes "Circe causes us to wonder whether we are dealing with a woman or a goddess: but finally, just as with Calypso the humanity is merely in outward form, in the voice."

51. Lucian of Samosata (fl. second century CE), in his satirical *Verae Historiae* (*True History* or *True Story*), complains that in the past "poets, historians and philosophers wrote much about what is miraculous or mythical" taking as their guide "Homer's Odysseus, who tells Alkinoos and his court about . . . the transformation of his comrades which was achieved with drugs" (1.2–4).

52. Shapiro, *Myth into Art*, 57. In addition to being labeled as a sorceress, the Circe legend underwent a gradual deterioration. See my discussion in chapter 8, below.

53. This is my own translation, based on the one in Vidal-Naquet, *The Black Hunter*, 33 n. 49. Another way of translating *pharmakon esthlon* in this context would be "effective drug."

54. The botanical identity of *moly* has been much debated, using evidence drawn primarily from later Greek sources, but as Scarborough, "The Pharmacology of Sacred Plants, Herbs, and Roots," 141 points out, "early Greek was marvelously fluid in its descriptions of thought, intelligence, and consciousness," hence it is a futile exercise to chase down the exact identities of plants mentioned in the *Iliad* and the *Odyssey* unless there is—as in the case of the opium poppy—"particular evidence (internal or external) supporting special nomenclature." Daniel Perrine, "Mixing the *Kykeon*—Part 2," *Eleusis: Journal of Psychoactive Plants and Compounds* 4 (2000): 17 writes that *moly* "is probably related to the Sanskrit *mulam*, a root."

55. Gregory Naddaf, *The Greek Concept of Nature* (Albany, NY: State University of New York Press, 2005), 14, referring to lines 10.287–92 of the original Greek. Naddaf indicates that this "is the one and only occurrence of the word *phusis* in the Homeric corpus. Indeed, it is the first occurrence of the term prior to its use by a pre-Socratic philosopher. . . . In order to be able to ward off magic, Odysseus needs more than simple possession of the *moly* plant when he confronts Circe. To make use of the plant's magical power, it is likely Odysseus must understand why the gods created it, an understanding that requires that he comprehend its *phusis*—that is, the whole process of the growth of the moly plant from beginning to end."

56. Here reading the Greek term *polypharmakos* at 10.276 in the original Greek as "knowing many drugs" as does Matthew Dillon, *Girls and Women in Classical Greek Religion* (New York: Routledge, 2002), 169. Fagles' translation of the term as "skilled in spells," while technically accurate, effaces the presence of drugs—drugs that are clearly present throughout the initial encounters with Circe. Lattimore's translation, which has "skilled in medicine," is even more inadequate. Circe is not a physician of any sort.

57. Jones, *Homer's Odyssey*, 95.

58. Dickie, *Magic and Magicians in the Greco-Roman World*, 23, and cf. 84 for Circe's association with drug-using magic, e.g. Aristophanes *Wealth* (303–10).

59. See chapter 7, below.

60. Thomas D. Seymour, *Life in the Homeric Age* (New York: Biblo and Tannen, 1963), 625 appears to agree, writing "Of Circe's drugs themselves, served in a posset, naturally the poet gives no details."

61. Hogan, "The Temptation of Odysseus," 200 and cf. Goldhill, "Reading Differences: The *Odyssey* and Juxtaposition," 418 who writes forgetting "a homecoming (rather than forgetting evils) is the threat of Circe's attractions for Odysseus, even though he has taken the counter-drug of Hermes' [*moly*]."

62. Robert Graves, *Difficult Questions, Easy Answers* (London: Cassell & Company, 1971), 111 speculated that the *moly* had oxygenated Odysseus' blood, making it resistant to intoxication.

63. This is my own reading of the text *soi de tis en stethessin akeletos noos estin* at 10.329 in the original Greek.

64. John G. Gunnell, *Political Philosophy and Time* (Middletown, CT: Wesleyan University Press, 1987), 129, emphasis mine.

65. Penelope Murray, "Poetic Inspiration in Early Greece," *The Journal of Hellenic Studies* 101 (1981): 91 points out that the "conventional . . . interpretation is that Hesiod [contrasts] the true content of his own poetry with the plausible fiction of Homeric Epic."

66. The translation of this passage from the *Iliad* is from Bloom's translation of the *Republic* and the line references are to the original Greek. Arthur P. McKinlay, "Attic Temperance," *Quarterly Journal of Studies on Alcohol* 12, no. 1 (1951): 61–102 argues that the *Iliad* and *Odyssey* contain several scenes that strongly suggest the Homeric Greeks were copious drinkers who enjoyed wine for hours at a time, citing lines 1.225 and 8.228–34 of the *Iliad* and 1.227, 1.339–40, 2.57–58, 3.138–9, 9.44–45, 11.61, 18.240, and 21.293–304 of the *Odyssey*. He says nothing of the other *pharmaka* besides wine that Homer mentions.

67. Albert Heinrichs, "Loss of Self, Suffering, Violence: The Modern View of Dionysus from Nietzsche to Girard," *Harvard Studies in Classical Philology* 88 (1984): 240.

68. Friedrich Nietzsche, *Twilight of the Idols and The Anti-Christ*, trans. R. J. Hollingdale (New York: Penguin Books, 2003), 120.

69. Including "Dionysus (the Phrygian term), Zagreus (of Orphic Tradition), Bacchus (a name the Romans later adopted, often identifying him with their god, Liber), Iaccus (the god of the Eleusinian Mysteries), Bromius (the thunderer), Lenaëus (of the wine-press), Lyaëus (he who frees), and Dendrites (of the trees)." See David Allison, *Reading the New Nietzsche* (Lanham, MD: Rowman and Littlefield, 2001), 21.

70. Albert Heinrichs, "Changing Dionysiac Identities," in *Jewish and Christian Self-Definition III: Self-Definition in the Greco-Roman World*, ed. B. F. Meyer and E. P. Sanders (London: SCM Press, 1982), 160, and Michael Morgan, *Platonic Piety: Philosophy and Ritual in Fourth Century Athens* (New Haven, CT: Yale University Press, 1990), 97.

71. R. Gordon Wasson, Albert Hofmann, and Carl A. P. Ruck, *The Road to Eleusis: Unveiling the Secrets of the Mysteries* [Twentieth Anniversary Edition] (Los Angeles: William Dailey Rare Books, 1998), 54–55.

72. Susan B. Matheson, "The Mission of Triptolemus and the Politics of Athens," *Greek Roman, and Byzantine Studies* 35, no. 4 (1994).

73. Carl Kerényi, *Dionysus—Archetypal Image of Indestructible Life* (Princeton, NJ: Pantheon Books, 1976): xxvi.

74. T. B. L. Webster, *Athenian Culture and Society* (Berkeley and Los Angeles: University of California Press, 1973), 80.

75. Ruck, *Sacred Mushrooms of the Goddess and the Secrets of Eleusis*, 85 indicates "he was synonymous, as Heracleitus informs us [fr. 15], with Hades, the lord of death and the nuptial abductor of the goddess Persephone."

76. Wasson et al., *The Road to Eleusis*, 98.

77. Wasson et al., *The Road to Eleusis*, 98. On ivy specifically see Ruck, *Sacred Mushrooms of the Goddess and the Secrets of Eleusis*, 89–92.

78. Carl A. P. Ruck, "The Wild and the Cultivated: Wine in Euripides Bacchae," in *Persephone's Quest: Entheogens and the Origins of Religion*, ed. R. Gordon Wasson (New Haven, CT: Yale University Press, 1986), 181–3. In addition to the *thyrsos* the maenads of Dionysus were depicted wielding gigantic pestles, a further indication of the many *pharmaka* associated with the god.

79. Ruck, *Sacred Mushrooms of the Goddess and the Secrets of Eleusis*, 86.

80. Werner W. Jaeger, *The Theology of the Early Greek Philosophers* (Oxford: Clarendon Press, 1947), 57, and cf. Walter F. Otto, *Dionysus—Myth and Cult* (Bloomington, IN: Indiana University Press, 1965), 57.

81. Tim Unwin, *Wine and the Vine* (New York: Routledge, 1991), 86. The references to Dionysus in the *Iliad* occur at 6.132–40 and 14.325, while in the *Odyssey* they occur at 11.325 and 24.74.

82. Jaeger, *The Theology of the Early Greek Philosophers*, 57.

83. Jaeger, *The Theology of the Early Greek Philosophers*, 57–8, and cf. Bryant, *Moral Codes and Social Structure in Ancient Greece*, 125.

84. Ruck, "The Wild and the Cultivated," 194.

85. Tadeusz Zielinski, *The Religion of Ancient Greece: An Outline* (Freeport, NY: Libraries Press, 1970), 47–49.

86. Jaeger, *The Theology of the Early Greek Philosophers*, 58, and cf. Morgan, *Platonic Piety*, 8 and 15.

87. Morgan, *Platonic Piety*, 18–20.

88. Morgan, *Platonic Piety*, 19.

89. Morgan, *Platonic Piety*, 21.

90. Morgan, *Platonic Piety*, 20.

91. Examples of plants used religiously include, for example, Iboga (*Tabernanthe iboga*), containing the indole alkaloid ibogaine, used by the Bwiti cults of West Africa. Dozens of other cases have been documented. See Richard Evans Schultes, "Hallucinogens of Plant Origin," *Science* 163 (1969): 245–54, Andrew Weil, *The Natural Mind: A New Way of Looking at Drugs and the Higher Consciousness* (Boston: Houghton Mifflin, 1972), Daniel Efron, Bo Holmstedt and Nathan S. Kline, eds., *Ethno-Pharmacologic Search for Psychoactive Drugs* (New York: Raven Press, 1979), Richard Evans Schultes and Albert Hofmann, *Plants of the Gods—Their Sacred, Healing and Hallucinogenic Powers* (Rochester, VT: Healing Arts Press, 1992), Terrence McKenna, *Food of the Gods: The Search for the Original Tree of Knowledge* (New York: Bantam Books, 1992) and Robert M. Torrance, *The Spiritual Quest—Transcendence in Myth, Religion, and Science* (Berkeley: University of California Press, 1994).

92. McKenna, *Food of the Gods*, 59. Put very simply the shaman combines the role of doctor, priest, and sorcerer. He would act as mediator between human and spirit realms, seeking communion with the latter. As Torrance, *The Spiritual Quest*, 155 points out, this communion was meant to "restore the harmony shattered for the individual by illness or death, and for the people by loss of primordial unity with kindred spirits in the heavens and fellow creatures on the earth."

93. Morgan's *Platonic Piety* relies on sources that regard the use of "narcotics" as a late, "decadent" phase of shamanism, for example the works such as I. M. Lewis, *Ecstatic Religion—A Study of Shamanism and Spirit Possession* (New York: Routledge, 1971), and especially Mircea Eliade, *Shamanism: Archaic Techniques of Ecstasy* (Princeton, NJ: Princeton University Press, 1964). In contrast to these works I agree with those who argue the opposite position, namely that the use of various drugs, in particular hallu-

cinogens, is characteristic of shamanism when it is alive and authentic, and it is the elaborate rituals, ordeals, and reliance on pathological personalities that is more reflective of shamanism in decline. This viewpoint is found in numerous works such as Schultes and Hofmann, *Plants of the Gods*, 1992, McKenna, *Food of the Gods*, 1992, and Torrance, *The Spiritual Quest*, 1994. I also agree with Richard Rudgley, *The Alchemy of Culture—Intoxicants in Society* (London: British Museum Press, 1993), 38 who summarizes Eliade's positions as being less the product of "scholarly impartiality" and more the product of "his bourgeois aversion to intoxication in relation to religious life."

94. The Scythians, according to Torrance, *The Spiritual Quest*, 152 were a "migratory Indo-Iranian or possibly Altaic people" whose territory, at its greatest, stretched "from near the Black Sea to the borders of China, penetrating westward into the Balkans and Prussia and southward, for a brief time, into Palestine and almost to Egypt."

95. François Hartog, *The Mirror of Herodotus—The Representation of the Other in the Writing of History* (Berkeley: University of California Press, 1988), 150 describes the howling and joy as suggesting "a context of shamanism." K. Meuli, "Scythica," *Hermes* 70 (1935): 122 and K. Meuli, *Gesammelte Schriften* (Basel: Schwabe, 1975), 821–22 believed the ceremony revealed a shamanistic religion based on ecstasy. Torrance, *The Spiritual Quest*, 152 reaches the same conclusion as Harthog and Meuli writing that the entire passage has affinities "with Central Asian, Siberian and American shamanisms observed over two thousand years later."

96. Given that the Athenian Stranger in the *Laws* appears well versed in Scythian drinking customs, Plato may also have been aware of the drugs used in Scythian funeral practices and the evidently inferior Grecian vapor baths mentioned by Herodotus.

97. Ruck, "The Wild and the Cultivated," 192, and cf. Graves, *Difficult Questions, Easy Answers*, 66–7, Mary Settgast, *Plato—Prehistorian. 10,000 to 5,000 B. C. in Myth and Archeology* (Cambridge, MA: Rotenberg Press, 1986), 162–97, and McKenna, *Food of the Gods*, 82–87, 122–28.

98. Ruck, "The Wild and the Cultivated," 185, and see also 186–87, 191.

99. R. P. Winnington-Ingram, *Euripides and Dionysus—An Interpretation of the Bacchae* (Amsterdam: Adolf M. Hakkert, 1969), 49. See also Charles Segal, *Dionysiac Poetics and Euripides' Bacchae* (Princeton, NJ: Princeton University Press, 1997), 318.

100. Comparisons of the Minoan-Mycenaean Dionysus and the Dionysus of Classical Greece may be found in Martin P. Nilsson, *A History of Greek Religion* (Oxford: Oxford University Press, 1949), 9–75, Kerényi, *Dionysus—Archetypal Image of Indestructible Life*, 5–125, 273–388, and Arthur Evans, *The God of Ecstasy—Sex Roles and the Madness of Dionysus* (New York: St. Martin's Press, 1988), 39–61, 101–5.

101. Charles Segal, "The Menace of Dionysus: Sex Roles and Reversals in Euripides' *Bacchae*," *Arethusa* 11, no. 1 & 2 (1978): 191, and McKenna, *Food of the Gods*, 129–30. More detailed discussions of Semele's possible divinity may be found in Evans, *The God of Ecstasy—Sex Roles and the Madness of Dionysus*, 62–63 and Graves, *Difficult Questions, Easy Answers*, 96–97.

102. Ruck, "The Wild and the Cultivated," 189.

103. Graves, *Difficult Questions, Easy Answers*, 96.

104. Graves, *Difficult Questions, Easy Answers*, 110, and Ruck, "The Wild and the Cultivated," 201.

105. Martin Booth, *Cannabis: A History* (New York: St. Martin's Pres, 2003), 24. Worth consulting is Jean H. Langenheim, *Plant Resins: Chemistry, Evolution, Ecology, and Ethnobotany* (Portland, OR: Timber Press, 2003), 291. By the tenth century CE *bhang* (a hemp preparation consumed as a drink, or as a candy called *majun*) had attained a popular reputation as *indracanna*, "food of the gods," in India.

106. Wendy Doniger O'Flaherty, "Dionysus and Siva: Parallel Patterns in Two Pairs of Myths," *History of Religions* 20, no. 1 (1980): 81.

107. Wasson, *Persephone's Quest*, 84.

108. Ruck, "The Wild and the Cultivated," 193, and cf. Cara L. Sailor, *The Function of Mythology and Religion in Greek Society* (M. A. thesis, East Tennessee University, 2007), 56–57. The Titans were sent by Hera, who gave the heart to Zeus to consume. Dionysus had the epithet Zagreus, meaning "torn to pieces."

109. Daniel Mendelsohn, "ΣΥΓΚΕΡΑΥΝΟΩ: Dithyrambic Language and Dionysiac Cult," *The Classical Journal* 87, no. 2 (1992): 119–23.

110. Spanish documents from the sixteenth century CE condemn the Aztecs for their use of "food of the gods" or "flesh of the gods" (*teonanacatl*), a species of mushroom that was employed in magic, religion, and medicine. See Schultes, "Hallucinogens of Plant Origin," 246–47, Efron et al., *Ethno-Pharmacologic Search for Psychoactive Drugs*, 59, and Schultes and Hofmann, *Plants of the Gods*, 144–46. Graves, *Difficult Questions, Easy Answers*, 96–99 draws attention to the similarity between the Indian god Agni, the Greek Dionysus, and the Central American Tlaloc, all of whom were apparently associated with mushrooms.

111. Mendelsohn, "ΣΥΓΚΕΡΑΥΝΟΩ: Dithyrambic Language and Dionysiac Cult," 109–110.

112. Joseph Wohlberg, "Haoma-Soma in the World of Ancient Greece," *Journal of Psychoactive Drugs* 22, no. 3 (1990): 333–42.

113. Among the Indo-Ayrans the bull was the commonest metaphor for Soma. It is now widely though not universally accepted that the god Soma of the Sanskrit *Rg Veda* (ca. 2,000 BCE), from which an inebriating drug was extracted for a sacred potion, was a mushroom. See R. Gordon Wasson, *Soma: Divine Mushroom of Immortality* (New York: Harcourt, Brace, and Jovanovich, 1971), Ruck, "The Wild and the Cultivated," 187–88, and R. M. Rosen, "Hipponax fr. 48 Dg. and the Eleusinian *Kykeon*," *American Journal of Philology* 108 (1987): 422–23.

114. Philip Vellacott, trans., *The Bacchae and other Plays* (New York: Penguin Books, 1973), 193–96.

115. Wasson et al., *The Road to Eleusis*, 128–31, and cf. Carl A. P. Ruck, "Duality and the Madness of Herakles," *Arethusa* 9, no. 1 (1976): 244, Ruck, "The Wild and the Cultivated," 190 and Ruck, *Sacred Mushrooms of the Goddess and the Secrets of Eleusis*, 87–89.

116. Ruck, "The Wild and the Cultivated," 199 writes that in Minoan religion snakes, like birds of prey and magical plants, are "representative of the possessing chthonic spirit in shamanic rites of sacred marriage."

117. In his other known work, *Theriaca*, Nicander describes over a dozen snakes and the effects of their poisons. See chapter 7, below, for a more detailed discussion of the *Alexipharmaka*.

118. Ruck, "The Wild and the Cultivated," 187. A gold signet ring from a tomb near Knossos depicts women with the heads of insects dancing amidst flowers. Their dance, Ruck writes, depicts them experiencing "the mystical apotheosis of a deity."

119. McKenna, *Food of the Gods*, 128. Pasiphae, described as possessing witchcraft-like powers of drug administration (*pharmakeia*), was said to be a sister of Circe and Aeetes, for example in Cicero's *The Nature of the Gods* (*De natura deorum*) (3.19).

120. Oscar E. Nybakken, *Greek and Latin in Scientific Terminology* (Ames, IA: Blackwell Publishing, 1959), 165.

121. The body of Alexander the Great, for example, was reportedly immersed in honey after his death.

122. Anne Mary Farrell, *Plato's Use of Eleusinian Mystery Motifs* (Ph. D. Thesis, University of Texas at Austin, 1999), 4–10. Of the many authors that address the question of drugs and Eleusis, Farrell mentions only Kerényi by name, whereas my discussion will emphasize this aspect of the debate.

123. George Mylonas, *Eleusis and the Eleusinian Mysteries* (Princeton, NJ: Princeton University Press, 1961), 281, 285.

124. Claude Bérard, "Festivals and Mysteries," in *A City of Images—Iconography and Society in Ancient Greece*, ed. by Claude Bérard (Princeton, NJ: Princeton University Press, 1989), 117. In his otherwise pioneering and excellent study of ancient wine Patrick McGovern, *Ancient Wine: The Search for the Origins of Viticulture* (Princeton, NJ: Princeton University Press, 2003), 246, 267–68 is surprisingly skittish whenever the subject turns to the Eleusinian Mysteries and characterizes them as "still shrouded in mystery."

125. Walter Burkert, *Ancient Mystery Cults* (Cambridge, MA: Harvard University Press, 1987), 90–91.

126. Farrell, *Plato's Use of Eleusinian Mystery Motifs*, 1–64 contains a fine summation of the ritual and the scholarly debates surrounding the various initiatory minutiae.

127. Carl Kerényi, *Eleusis—Archetypal Image of Mother and Daughter* (New York: Pantheon Books, 1967), 23 indicates that the word "Eleusis" is "differentiated by accent and inflection from *eleusis*, 'arrival', but, like it, is related, according to the rules of Greek vowel gradation, to Elysion, the realm of the blessed."

128. Bérard, "Festivals and Mysteries," 109.

129. "As for what the ordinary initiate could expect . . . we have only the traditions of the Purifications. The rite is difficult to separate from the other aspects of the Anthesteria, which was a three-day wine festival (open to all and not restricted to the candidates for initiation) to which the ghosts of departed family members were invited." See Carl A. P. Ruck, "Mixing the *Kykeon*—Part 3," *Eleusis: The Journal of Psychoactive Plants* 4 (2000): 24.

130. The rites of the Lesser Mysteries appear to have been held in the spring, during the month of Anthesterion, on the banks of the Ilissos. The Greater Mysteries were held during the fall, during the month of Böedromion.

131. Carl A. P. Ruck, "Mushrooms and Mysteries: On Aristophanes and the Necromancy of Socrates," *Helios* 8, no. 2 (1981): 13.

132. Erika Simon, *Festivals of Attika: An Archeological Commentary* (Madison, WI: The University of Wisconsin Press, 1983), 33.

133. Ruck, "The Wild and the Cultivated," 186 and Evans, *The God of Ecstasy*, 67–68.

134. Naddaf, *The Greek Concept of Nature*, 170–71 n. 19.

135. Wasson et al., *The Road to Eleusis*, 97. "Eurydice, Creusa, and Helen were all picking flowers when they experienced the sacred marriage with death. Such ecstatic rituals associated with flowers formed a very ancient tradition in Greek religion and can be traced to precedents in the Minoan period."

136. See chapter 6, below.

137. McKenna, *Food of the Gods*, 132. For a general introduction to the mutable nature of the Eleusinian and Dionysiac Mysteries see Mylonas, *Eleusis and the Eleusinian Mysteries*, Martin P. Nilsson, *The Dionysiac Mysteries of the Hellenistic and Roman Era* (New York: Arno Press, 1975). Robert F. Healy, *Eleusinian Sacrifices in the Athenian Law Code* (New York and London: Garland Publishing, 1990) provides an interesting discussion of some stone fragments that suggest the upper classes of Athens were adjust-

ing the city's legal codes governing Eleusinian related practices, in part to further tame them, during Plato's lifetime.

138. The total cost for an individual to have been initiated would have been a little more than a month's wages, plus the cost of lodging in Athens if they had traveled from elsewhere. See Wasson et al., *The Road to Eleusis*, 46.

139. Farrell, *Plato's Use of Eleusinian Mystery Motifs*, 12–14. See also Kerényi, *Eleusis*, 177. On *aischrologia* see Rosen, "Hipponax fr. 48 Dg. and the Eleusinian *Kykeon*," 419–20. The fast was not necessarily for the entire nine days as there is some indication the sacrificial pigs were part of a ritual feast after their slaying. It is also possible the initiates fasted only during the day.

140. There is also no evidence in any surviving account books of "expenditures on theatrical equipment or actors at Eleusis. Nor is it likely that the Greeks, who were so sophisticated about drama, would have fallen for some kind of stagecraft." See Wasson et al., *The Road to Eleusis*, 88, and cf. Kerényi, *Eleusis*, 26–7. Maureen B. Cavanaugh, *Eleusis and Athens—Documents in Finance, Religion, and Politics in the Fifth Century B.C.* (Oxford: Oxford University Press, 2000) presents a new text with detailed commentary concerning Eleusinian financial account-inventories.

141. See Kerényi, *Eleusis*, 84, Pedro Lain Entralgo, *The Therapy of the Word in the Ancient World* (New Haven, CT: Yale University Press, 1970), 58–9, Marvin W. Meyer, ed., *The Ancient Mysteries: A Sourcebook* (New York: Harper and Row, 1987), 10–13, and Farrell, *Plato's Use of Eleusinian Mystery Motifs*, 41–61. Our sources for these portions of the initiatory rites are early Christian writers whose motivations were less than honest.

142. Also spelled *epopts*.

143. William R. Halliday, *The Pagan Background of Early Christianity* (New York: Cooper Square Publishers, 1970), 255 n.1.

144. Walter F. Otto, "The Meaning of the Eleusinian Mysteries," in *The Mysteries— Papers from the Eranos Yearbooks*, ed. Joseph Campbell (Princeton, NJ: Princeton University Press, 1955), 23–27, Kerényi, *Eleusis*, 98–9, Richard Seaford, "Dionysiac Drama and the Dionysiac Mysteries," *Classical Quarterly* 31, no. 2 (1981), 256, 259–60, Rosen, "Hipponax fr. 48 Dg. and the Eleusinian *Kykeon*," 424, Christopher Brown, "Empousa, Dionysus, and the Mysteries: Aristophanes *Frogs* 285ff.," *Classical Quarterly* 41, no. 1 (1991): 42–3, 47, Wasson et al., *The Road to Eleusis*, 47, and Farrell, *Plato's Use of Eleusinian Mystery Motifs*, 59. Brown argues that the initiates at Eleusis were "terrified by the appearance of a specter" similar to the one that terrorizes Dionysus and Xanthias in the *Frogs*. The first half of the play "contains a number of details that would cause the audience to assume that the chorus is composed of initiates into the Eleusinian Mysteries."

145. Nietzsche was no stranger to Greek literature: was he thinking of the *kykeon* Demeter drinks in the *Homeric Hymn to Demeter*?

146. Nietzsche was also no stranger to drug-induced visions and hallucinations. See Allison, *Reading the New Nietzsche*, 56 n. 12.

147. Nietzsche describes this joyful Greek "frenzy"—being in a state of ecstasy— using the German word *rausch*, which roughly means "intoxication." In *The Twilight of the Idols*, written in 1888 and published in 1889 shortly after his collapse, Nietzsche again includes the use of drugs as part of the frenzy of artistic creation.

148. Including Kerényi, Graves, Wasson, Ruck, Rosen, and Webster on the one hand and Burkert, Salleres, and Valencic on the other.

149. Walter Burkert, *Ancient Mystery Cults*, 108–109 makes this argument as part of a two-page polemic against Wasson et al. in *The Road to Eleusis*.

150. Rosen, "Hipponax fr. 48 Dg. and the Eleusinian *Kykeon*," 418.

151. McGovern, *Ancient Wine*, 268.

152. Rosen, "Hipponax fr. 48 Dg. and the Eleusinian *Kykeon*," 422 writes that, at least by classical times, while it was true "the *kykeon* could be a simple, secular food/drink" there is evidence that the Homeric references to the *kykeon*, even *Iliad* 11.754–58, "reflect an inherited pre-Greek religious ritual."

153. Rosen, "Hipponax fr. 48 Dg. and the Eleusinian *Kykeon*," 422.

154. McGovern, *Ancient Wine*, 268.

155. In the original Greek: *Iliad* 11.624, *Odyssey* 10.290 and 10.316.

156. See chapter 7, below, for the importance of regimen in the Greek conception of health.

157. Rosen, "Hipponax fr. 48 Dg. and the Eleusinian *Kykeon*," 417 n. 9.

158. For example, "the diction of the fragment is distinctly Homeric" and while we do not know the contents of Hipponax' *kykeon* "its original ritual and psychotropic properties are nevertheless confirmed by its Homeric background." The *pharmakon* the fragment refers to, then, "really is a drug" and not simply a metaphor for physical relief. See Rosen, "Hipponax fr. 48 Dg. and the Eleusinian *Kykeon*," 423.

159. Barley groats, if soaked in water long enough, will begin to ferment, creating a weak beer. The thesis is easy to put aside, since the *kykeon* does not appear to have been mixed until the last moment. See Ruck, "Mixing the *Kykeon*—Part 3," 21. In the *Homeric Hymn to Demeter* the goddess refuses to drink wine offered to her, and given that "every act in this narrative had mythic meaning, it seems that drinking the alcoholic beverage did not go with the drinking of the *kykeon*. The two kinds of inebriation were incompatible." See Wasson et al., *The Road to Eleusis*, 64.

160. The origins of the Greek word for mystery, *mysterion*, remain disputed. Graves, *Difficult Questions, Easy Answers*, 84 suggested that since the Lesser Mysteries occurred during the spring festival of *anthesterion* or "flower springing," the Greater Mysteries that occurred in the early fall hint at the possibility that *mysterion* may well derive from *myko-sterion*, or "mushroom springing." October is the season for a number of mushrooms and, so Graves' argument goes, the source of the *epopteia* was a hallucinogenic mushroom. Graves ignores the *kykeon*, which he characterizes as innocuous "mint-water" and focuses instead on sacrificial cakes shaped like piglings or *phalloi*, contending a hallucinogenic mushroom might have been ground up and baked within the cakes, either a *stropharia* or *panaeolus*. His arguments owed much to discussions, dating back to 1949, with his longtime friend the enthnomycologist Gordon Wasson, who had himself suggested the same possibility since the 1950s. See for example R. Gordon Wasson, "The Divine Mushroom: Primitive Religion and Hallucinatory Agents," *Proceedings of the American Philosophical Society* 103 no. 3 (1958): 221–23. Wasson's published position in the late 1970s, however, argued that it was indeed the *kykeon* and not the cakes that contained a powerful drug. Peter Webster, "Mixing the Kykeon," *Eleusis: Journal of Psychoactive Plants and Compounds* 4 (2000), 5–6 gives numerous reasons for ruling out any *Psilocybe* species.

161. The poppy figures prominently in Eleusinian iconography. We know from clay tablets dating from the Minoan-Mycenaean period that poppy harvests were truly immense, so great the amounts were for a long period of time assumed to have been grain, not the source of an intoxicating drug. In Cretan cult practice poppies were used to produce opium; quite possibly the poppy followed Demeter from Crete to Eleusis in some fashion. The use of opium in the large cake, the *pelanos*, broken into pieces and shared among the initiates at Eleusis, is at least possible. Kerényi nominated opium as the active ingredient of the Eleusinian *kykeon*. See Kerényi, *Dionysus*, 23–4. See also "The Prepara-

tion and Effect of the *Kykeon*" in Kerényi, *Eleusis*. Burkert, *Ancient Mystery Cults*, 108–9 rejects the use of opium at Eleusis given "the problem of how opium could have been procured for thousands of initiates who did not even smoke." Kritikos and Papadaki, "The History of the Poppy and of Opium and their Expansion in Antiquity in the Eastern Mediterranean Area," 7–9 in their study of the poppy and opium in antiquity show more sophistication noting "the method of smoking opium in a pipe as practiced in modern times is not necessarily the one practiced in antiquity." As noted above, ingestion of opium in antiquity was done in a variety of ways, none of which involve smoking it in the manner of a nineteenth-century opium den. The Greeks were by no means shy about their use of the poppy nor about listing the other ingredients in the *kykeon* and, most importantly, the mind-altering effects of opium do not match the symptomology of the *epopteia*, so it is doubtful that opium was an ingredient in the sacred potion.

162. The *kykeon*'s other ingredient, mint (*menthe pulegium*), may have very mild intoxicating properties, but only if boiled and the sources are clear that what was added was fresh mint. In any event it is doubtful that mint alone could have been the cause of visual disturbances. Mint appears to have played a symbolic role in Eleusinian myth; being Hades' concubine, Mint was "dismembered by the jealous wife Persephone." See Wasson et al., *The Road to Eleusis*, 111. Mint did have a number of medicinal uses in antiquity. See chapter 7, below. It is mentioned as a contraceptive and abortifacient in the Hippocratic *Nature of Women* (32). It was also an effective remedy to calm nausea. See Ruck, "Mixing the *Kykeon*—Part 3," 22–23.

163. Garnsey, *Food and Society in Classical Antiquity*, 39.

164. The ingenious if not definitive argument concerning ergot, first put forward in the late 1970s by Wasson et al. in *The Road to Eleusis*, gathered evidence from textual, archeological and ethnobotanical sources, and combined it with an investigative open-mindedness sadly lacking in most of classical scholarship. See chapter 6, below, for a summary of more recent research. Surprisingly McGovern, *Ancient Wine*, 268 does not acknowledge *The Road to Eleusis* nor does he list the ingredients of the *kykeon* drunk at Eleusis. He writes instead that "a range of ancient texts, extending down to Plato and the Eleusinian Mysteries, suggest that many ingredients (herbs, spices, wine, milk, honey, oil and water) were tossed into the brew." While he apparently agrees that the *kykeon* of Eleusis was "psychoactive" like other such mixtures, he appears to conflate the Eleusinian *kykeon* with the *kykeon* of Homer, which he characterizes as another example of what he calls "Greek grog." The Eleusinian *kykeon* was certainly not a grog.

165. Robert Sallares, *The Ecology of the Ancient Greek World* (Ithaca, NY: Cornell University Press, 1991), 364 takes issue with equating *erysibe* with ergot, writing that it is "preferable to retain the equation of *erysibe* with cereal rust . . . which is by no means synonymous with ergot." He concedes however that identifying what *erysibe* truly refers to is "difficult" because in the classical sources "the descriptions are devoid of detail" (Sallares, *The Ecology of the Ancient Greek World*, 291). His insistence on a strict association between *erysibe* and cereal rust, in other words, is just as speculative, and rather more shrill. Albert Hofmann's argument was quite modest: "we have no way to tell what the chemistry was of the ergot of barley or wheat raised on the Rarian plain in the 2nd millennium [BCE]. But it is certainly not pulling a long bow to assume that the barley grown there was host to an ergot containing, perhaps among others, the soluble hallucinogenic alkaloids." Quoted in Wasson et al. *The Road to Eleusis*, 42.

166. Wasson et al., *The Road to Eleusis*, 126. The *Etymologicum Genuinum* is an anonymously authored lexical encyclopedia dating to Constantinople circa 950 CE.

167. Carl A. P. Ruck, "The Offering from the Hyperboreans," in *Persephone's Quest: Entheogens and the Origins of Religion*, ed. R. Gordon Wasson (New Haven, CT: Yale University Press, 1986), 251.

168. E. D. Phillips, *Greek Medicine* (London: Thames and Hudson, 1973), 214–15 n. 309.

169. Wasson et al., *The Road to Eleusis*, 126. This awareness has persisted in European herbalist folklore. See Wasson et al., *The Road to Eleusis*, 36 and Schultes and Hofmann, *Plants of the Gods*, 102–3. The French word for darnel is *ivraie*, from *ivre*, "drunk." See Garnsey, *Food and Society in Classical Antiquity*, 39.

170. Wasson et al., *The Road to Eleusis*, 126.

171. See my argument in chapter 6, below.

172. Wasson et al., *The Road to Eleusis*, 93, citing scholium to Nicander, *Alexipharmaka* 217.

173. Wasson et al., *The Road to Eleusis*, 93, emphasis mine. See also Ruck, *Sacred Mushrooms of the Goddess and the Secrets of Eleusis*, 64–65.

174. Bloom's translation notes mention the language of the *Republic* takes on a religious solemnity when alluding to Eumolpus and Eleusis but at the same time he indicates Adeimantus appears to be at least implicitly "criticizing . . . official Athenian [religious] understanding." In this passage of the *Republic* Plato mixes images of the *symposion* with Eleusinian themes; lacking knowledge of the *kykeon* Bloom unsurprisingly translates the phrase in a manner invoking alcohol. To describe the teaching of the son of Musaeus as an "eternal drunk" is awkward and, given that wine was not permitted at Eleusis, it is highly unlikely that alcohol would have been the intoxicant provided by Eumolpus. Waterfield's translation of the *Republic*, which has "eternal intoxication," should be regarded as superior here.

Chapter Five

Socrates Accused

Why was Socrates put on trial by the *demos*, eventually being executed? Much of what appears to have taken place both prior to and at his actual trial, as depicted in Plato's *Apology*, must be viewed with some caution as a carefully screened refashioning of the historical events.[1] Any answer to this oft-asked question, then, must range well beyond the text of the *Apology*, and even beyond the dialogues altogether.[2] To arrive at something approaching a satisfactory answer we need to start by looking at what Socrates was on a formal level accused of doing, who made the accusation(s), the historical background—in particular the events of 415 BCE—and the popular image of Socrates, which may reveal the presence of informal charges present but unaccounted for in the surviving documentation of the actual trial.

The Formal Charges

Plato tells us, in the probably genuine Seventh Letter, that the charge was one of impiety, *asebeia* (325c). The wording of the formal indictment varies slightly depending on the source: Plato's *Apology*, Xenophon's *Memorabilia*, or Diongenes Laertius' *Lives of the Eminent Philosophers*. The differences are relatively minor: in the *Apology* the order of the charges are the reverse of the *Memorabilia* and the *Lives*, and whereas the *Apology* has Socrates accused of not believing in the gods of the *polis*, in the *Memorabilia* there is mention of "carrying in" new divinities. In the *Lives* (2.40), widely regarded by scholars as the best source, "carrying in" is replaced by "introducing":

> This is a charge drawn up and confirmed by Meletus, son of Meletus, of the deme Pitthus, against Socrates, son of Sophroniscus, of the deme Alopece. Soc-

rates is accused of not believing in the gods in whom the city believes and of introducing new divinities; he is also guilty of corrupting the young. Penalty: death.

Officially, at least, Socrates would appear to have been accused of introducing new gods and corrupting the young. Oddly, however, commentators have concluded, based on what Plato has to say about the standard charge against *philosophers generally*—for example *Apology* 23c–d and *Laws* 966d–967d—that Socrates *in particular* was brought to trial on charges of atheism.[3] The charge of corrupting the young is similarly reduced to teaching them to be atheists—for example *Apology* 26a–b and *Euthyphro* 2b–3b. Socrates was not, strictly speaking however, charged with being an atheist. Socratic impiety was thought to consist of a belief in other gods, and there was quite possibly a general belief that he, like other philosophers and some of his associates, profaned religious ritual, in particular the Eleusinian Mysteries.[4]

The Accusers

Among other deficiencies, the *Apology* of Plato does not present the speeches of Socrates' accusers, nor does the dialogue discuss the fact that a number of other philosophers, both in Athens and elsewhere, were prosecuted on the basis of nearly identical charges.[5] Let us for the moment examine the first deficiency and ask: who were the men who formally accused Socrates? The men who governed Athens at the time of Socrates' trial contrasted sharply with the aristocrats with long family lineages who dominated politics a half-century earlier. They were prosperous farmers, slave proprietors, and owners of commerce and manufacturing.[6] These men were Anytus, Lycon, and Meletus.

Anytus was the son of a wealthy tanner. He held several high-ranking political offices during his career and was a leading participant in the revolt against the Thirty Tyrants in 403 BCE that restored democratic rule. Xenophon's Socrates exhibits a typical aristocratic condescension towards this new governing class, whose occupations were frequently the target of slanderous political jokes, tanners especially so "because of the use of urine in the tanning process."[7] In the *Meno* Plato depicts Anytus as hostile to sophists and sophistry, and as holding a degree of animosity towards Socrates personally (90a–95a). In Diogenes' *Lives* it is said Anytus "could not endure the ridicule of Socrates" so he first "stirred up against him Aristophanes and his friends" and later "helped to persuade Meletus to indict him" (2.38). Plutarch records that Anytus was reputed to have been a frequent but spurned suitor of Alcibiades—if true it is relevant considering the well-known feelings of Alcibiades for Socrates, for example in Plato's *Symposium*.

Anytus' son was evidently a youth with intellectual potential. He apparently studied with Socrates for a brief time, against his father's wish that he ply the family trade. In Xenophon's *Apology*, as Socrates is being taken away to prison, the philosopher points to a "swaggering" Anytus and says he is being put to death "because when I saw that he was under consideration by the State for the most important offices, I suggested he ought not to educate his son in a tannery" (29). This might be the ridicule Diongenes' mentions. Xenophon also reports that Socrates predicted Anytus' son would refuse the sort of life his father had envisioned for him, but without prudent guidance he would "succumb to some base motivation and make considerable progress as a degenerate" (*Apology* 30). At least according to Xenophon Socrates was proven correct: the young man "spent his days as well as nights drinking," became a drunkard, and finally "became worthless to his country, his friends, and himself" (31). In Plato's *Apology* there must be an element of cutting irony then as Socrates suggests that Anytus apparently has told the jury that everyone's sons would be "utterly ruined" if he were acquitted and allowed to continue his teaching (29c, and cf. *Meno* 91c). Anytus' son was not corrupted by Socrates, but by the *pharmakon* of wine (most likely at symposia), and this only became possible because he was *deprived* of Socrates' teaching.

Nothing is said of Lycon in Plato's *Apology* other than that he made his charges "on behalf of the rhetoricians" (23e). Diongenes' *Lives* refers to him as a demagogue and notes he helped prepare the prosecution's case (2.38). In Xenophon's *Symposium* there is mention of a Lycon whose son, Autolycus, defended him when Callibus, in charge of the Spartan garrison in Athens, tried to strike Lycon with his staff. A talented wrestler, Autolycus seized Callibus by the legs and threw him to the ground. Socrates' former pupils Critias and Charmides, the leaders of the Thirty Tyrants, had Autolycus put to death in order to mollify the Spartan Callibus. It is not surprising that Plato's *Apology* would be entirely silent on the subject, or the many other executions carried out by the Thirty.[8] Instead of responding directly, Plato merely has Socrates say (*Apology* 33a) that he "was never anyone's teacher" and argue on a number of other occasions that virtue cannot be taught. This position, as well as Plato's silence, "is certainly peculiar, not to say provocative."[9] Anytus and Lycon were plaintiffs for whom the charge of corrupting the youth may have had poignant meaning. For deeply personal reasons, rather than simply identification with the occupations Plato associates them with, these men would have had reason to want Socrates punished, and the Athenian court system as it existed at the beginning of the fourth century was a vehicle for them to achieve that end.

Meletus, who according to Plato supposedly made his charges on behalf of the aggrieved poets, may have had different motivations. The *Speech Against Andocides*, purportedly written at the time of Andocides' trial in 400 BCE for religious offenses connected to the Eleusinian Mysteries, zealously emphasizes the case's moral and religious aspects.[10] Meletus, Epichares, or Agyrrhios would have delivered it, though the latter two do not appear to have been the sort of "blind bigot" the speech "was written for, if not by."[11] The author of the *Speech Against Andocides* in fact claims his grandfather was a *hierophant*, indicative of his family belonging to "the Eumolpidae, the hereditary priesthood of the [Eleusinian] Mysteries."[12] There is then, if one accepts this account, compelling reason "to accept the identification: prosecutor of Andocides = speaker of Lysias 6 = prosecutor of Socrates."[13] The presence of Meletus, who was said to have drawn up the formal charges, would be in keeping with the seriousness of the religious motivations behind Socrates' trial.

In another defense speech that has survived, one written several years before Socrates' trial and titled *On the Mysteries*, Andocides contends that during the reign of the Thirty, Meletus had been responsible for the arrest of Leon of Salamis, who was then executed without trial (94). Socrates, as we know from Plato, had gained a certain notoriety for refusing to have Leon arrested (*Apology* 32c–d). Rather than order the arrest Socrates simply went home. It is at the very least odd that Socrates, while mentioning the Leon affair, would "have ignored the golden opportunity afforded him of mentioning the fact that his principal accuser had himself executed the very orders" Socrates himself had refused.[14] At the same time there is no evidence that Socrates took any action to warn Leon of his impending arrest, and by dwelling excessively on the matter the detail could have presented itself to the jury. A quick reference to the incident during the trial was an effective way for Socrates to highlight his refusal to *obey* the Thirty without drawing attention to his apparent failure to actively *oppose* it.[15]

Alcohol and the Mutilation of the *Hermai*

Whatever the motivations driving those named as his accusers, it can be argued that Socrates' trial was yet another echo of the highly charged scandal of 415 BCE, a series of events where offensive public behavior brought on by the use of drugs appears to have played both a direct and indirect role. The events of that summer "affected the lives of many individuals for the next twenty years."[16] Acts of sacrilege prior to its departure poisoned the massive Athenian expedition to Sicily, precipitating a devastating military disaster two years later and ultimately spelling Athens' defeat in the Peloponnesian War.[17] Equally if not more damaging, the incident resulted in the opening of "a fatal breach of mistrust in Athenian political life, between the demos and its traditional aristocratic leaders," leading to the oligarchic coup of 411 BCE and in the longer run the decline and fall of the Athenian empire.[18]

The Sicilian expedition had been approved in an atmosphere Thucydides' *History of the Peloponnesian War* describes as an "excessive enthusiasm" that had apparently overcome nearly everyone.[19] Few dared to oppose the venture, for fear of being labeled unpatriotic. Socrates was an apparent exception, voicing his unease to a number of people, at least according to Plutarch's *Lives* (*Nicias* 13.9, *Alcibiades* 17.5). Shortly before the great armada was launched a mass mutilation of the city's Hermai occurred. The *hermai* were essentially a rectangular stone pillar with the head of the god Hermes atop it, the pillar itself usually being adorned with male genitals. They stood guard before both private temples and homes, and were used to mark boundaries and at crossroads. Hermes was a god of margins and boundaries, "mediating between *oikos* and *polis* ... men and gods, life and death, adolescence and maturity and so on."[20]

The public reaction to the mutilation of the Hermai has often been depicted as a mob-like frenzy, blind, or at the very least marked by a "sense of urgency, almost of panic."[21] This is not completely accurate. Thucydides' *History* indicates the incidents were regarded as an *ill omen* (6.27.3). Most citizens trusted in divination, even Socrates.[22] Athens' seers, *chresmologoi* and *manteis*, or the vast majority of them in any case, had predicted the expedition's success (8.1.1).[23] A sacrilegious act by a single individual or small group was viewed as putting the entire community at risk.[24] No less an authority than Hesiod had warned that the "just penalty" for the "fool schemes" concocted by "those who live for violence and vice," even "one bad man," would consist of divine retribution, even for an entire city: "[Zeus] might lay low their army, or tumble down their city walls, or sink all their ships at sea" (*Works and Days* 276–285). A public response within such an interpretive framework might be non-rational when viewed from an external perspective, but this does not mean it was entirely irrational.

It appears both the faces and phalloi of the *hermai* were damaged, and the incidents of mutilation were so widespread—not to mention suspicious in their timing—that they suggested more than a malicious prank by drunken revelers, a common enough occurrence.[25] It belonged to a "recognized style of aristocratic behavior."[26] The initial dispositions in the Hermai case, as recorded in Thucydides' *History*, mention earlier cases of damage to other statues committed "by young men who were enjoying themselves after having too much to drink" (6.28.2). One of the words used, *agalmata*, implies that these earlier statues were also religious in nature.[27] The mutilation of the *hermai*, however, seemed too well organized, deliberate, and purposeful to be the product of just another violently intoxicated *komos*.

Alcibiades, the brilliant and controversial general who was one of the triumvirate leading the expedition to Syracuse as well as one of its most vocal proponents, desired an immediate investigation since his participation was strongly suspected. He was outmaneuvered by his enemies, who feared his popularity.[28] The fleet sailed as planned, with almost the entire population of Athens journeying down to Piraeus to watch its departure.[29] With Alcibiades out of the picture, an investigation council, the Boule, was formed and given the responsibility of uncovering the truth about the mutilation of the *hermai*. Peisander, later to become one of the most prominent of the four hundred responsible for overthrowing the Athenian democracy in 411 BCE, was among those heading the commission.

Thucydides' *History* indicates the mutilations were regarded as "an omen for the expedition and to have been done as part of a *synomosia* [collaboration] for revolution and the overthrow of the *demos*" (6.27.3). According to Andocides' *On the Mysteries* (36), it was Peisander and his colleague Charicles who were responsible for coming to this conclusion. A decree was also passed "guaranteeing immunity to anyone, citizen, alien, or slave, who knew of any *other* sacrilegious act that that had taken place and would come forward with information about it" (*History* 6.27, emphasis mine). It was this much broader investigative mandate that eventually led to the discovery of numerous profanations of the Eleusinian Mysteries and, as I shall argue, indirectly contributed to Socrates' trial and conviction.

Since the individuals who had perpetrated the mutilation of the *hermai* had acted out of public view, under cover of darkness, the Boule was faced with the problem of securing evidence. The testimony of slaves would also be essential, yet a slave's testimony could not be admitted as evidence unless it was taken under torture, and not without first going through a "cumbersome process of challenge known as the *proklesis*."[30] The situation demanded an alternative; one that was found by invoking a probably ancient rule requiring that in cases of *treason* slaves might be encouraged to denounce their masters.[31] The Athenian concept of treason was rather elastic in comparison to contemporary definitions. In addition to conspiring with foreign powers to betray one's *polis*, or what might be called external treason, in Athens there was furthermore a notion of deceiving the *demos*, or internal treason.[32]

The Boule utilized one of these forms of internal treason, the crime of *katalysis tou demou*—essentially "to deprive the people of their sovereign rights"—to situate the mutilation of the *hermai* as sacrilegious acts indicative of a conspiratorial plot to overthrow the democracy.[33] Until the events of 415 BCE the crime known as *asebeia* was not part of the secular legal code. Charges of this sort, according to Demosthenes, were heard before the Eumolpidae, one of the hereditary Eleusinian priesthoods (601).[34] The *legal* basis of the charges against Alcibiades, then, arose out of *Eleusinian* laws and institutions, not the city's laws. The difference—and a crucial one at that—was that while in the past a religious jurisdiction had judged those accused of profanation of the Mysteries, now "for the first time the prescriptions of the religious authorities were given a secular sanction."[35]

An individual named Diocleides was the first to come forward. He claimed to have seen, in the orchestra of the theater of Dionysus by the light of the moon, three hundred or so men standing in groups ranging in size from five to twenty. After an unsuccessful attempt at blackmailing Andocides' family for profit he came forward with a list of forty-two individuals, thirteen of whom were Andocides' *anchisteia* (close relatives). The character of this account by Diocleides, what amounted to "a *group* of *hetaireiai*, a wider *synomosia*," reinforced preexisting expectations about responsibility for the mutilations.[36] While drinking symposia were most likely practiced by other social classes, they were primarily an activity of leisure, of the aristocracy, and while their primary function was, naturally enough, wine drinking and other recreational activities, the political group, the *hetaireai*, would arise from the drinking group, as would any larger oligarchic *synomosia*.[37] Peisander would use this very same tactic in 411 BCE to overthrow the democracy and install the Oligarchy of the Four Hundred.[38]

While Diocleides' account bears a surface plausibility, it bears the marks of being "a story composed by an outsider," an external description by someone who was himself manifestly "not . . . a member of sympotic circles" trying to ingratiate himself with members of a higher social class.[39] For example he misconstrues *hetaireia* as being largely synonymous with *anchisteia*. The *hetaireia* was, in addition to simple kinship, definable according to "age, community of interest, social status and wealth."[40] Moreover, it was a moonless sky the night the mutilations occurred. If the Boule became aware of such discrepancies, a reasonable enough assumption, the accusation would quickly have become suspect. It has been suggested that "by making allegations against several prominent members of important and influential families," it was hoped that Diocleides' testimony would force the Boule "to sit on its finding and eventually allow the whole affair quietly to drop."[41]

The strategy backfired when Andocides, reputed to have been one of the guiltiest and currently imprisoned, was convinced to turn state's informer.[42] He and many of his relatives had been imprisoned as a result of Diocleides' accusations (*On the Mysteries* 1.47–68). He admitted that the drinking group he belonged to had been responsible for the mutilations, although he himself had not participated and had in fact argued against the act. Andocides' testimony was filled with holes: how a mere twenty-two individuals perpetrated damage originally attributed to roughly three hundred; how they did so in a single moonless evening; how they operated under a *pistis* (pledge of trust) whose nature is never elaborated on—are all left unexplained. It was also a bit of amazing good fortune that of the twenty-two individuals named by Andocides eighteen had already been named by another informant named Teukros and were all either dead or in exile, while the four remaining individuals would also escape into exile. Yet the Boule accepted his story as substantially true, and was so pleased that Andocides and all whom he did not name were released.[43]

Diocleides later admitted his story was a fabrication and claimed he had been put up to it by Alcibiades' friends.[44] He was referred to a court, tried, found guilty and executed. While his punishment seems harsh, "Diocleides 'perjury' (which is strictly all it was) was regarded as a capital offense" because it was seen as having such widespread public effects.[45] Many of the other individuals who had been arrested were put on trial. It is estimated fifty to one hundred individuals were executed, while a number of others fled into exile to avoid a similar fate. Others received sentences of exile, including two prominent individuals in Plato's *Symposium*, Phaedrus and Eryximachus.[46] Andocides incurred the hate of many for his testimony and spend the next twenty years either in exile or defending himself (*On His Return*) from additional charges of a similar nature. Finally it appears that because of Andocides' decision to turn informer and Diocleides recanting his testimony, Alcibiades found he had made enemies he could scarcely afford to have.[47]

Drugs and the Profanation of the Mysteries

While being at least equally important as a catalyst for "the most massive series of trials in Athenian history," the other half of the scandal of 415 BCE, the alleged profanations of the Eleusinian Mysteries, has scarcely been examined for the depths of its connection to the trial of Socrates. [48] This is surprising given that investigation and accusations concerning this matter continued long after "the Hermae case was regarded as closed."[49] There is reason to suspect the hunt for the sacrilegious took on a life of its own, got out of hand, and began netting not anti-democratic conspirators but rather "many who simply were discovered, like Alcibiades, to have treated the forbidden Mystery ceremony as a private social event for the entertainment" of banquet guests.[50] Drinking the *kykeon* in private symposia, "like Alcibiades and his set" were believed to have done, was "considered a profanation and desecration."[51] In a religious context the magical drug was tolerated—in fact, was indispensable—but outside of that context it was condemned."[52] It was this discovery that resonates in the trial of Socrates, and it was this discovery that Plato again and again attempts to dissociate Socrates from in his dialogues.

We have evidence that participants at symposia frequently engaged in parody of religious *thiasoi* and *orgeones*, "private or semi-public associations for the worship of individual gods."[53] Groups calling themselves the *Kakodaimonistai* (bad spirits), for example, would feast on days of ill omen in a deliberate affront to the pious *Noumeniastai*, who "worshipped the *agathos daimon* [good spirit] at their *symposia*."[54] Plato's contemporary Lysias, in a trial speech against Kinesias, a poet and head of the *Kakodaimonistai*, accuses this group of laughing "at the gods and our laws" and points out a chronic disease Kinesias was suffering from as proof he was as guilty as his godless companions, who had previously come to ruin.[55]

The profanations of the Eleusinian Mysteries took place on a number of different occasions, and were conducted by more than one group, in several different prominent households.[56] There were five sets of accusations. First, Andromachos, Alcibiades' slave, testified that at the house of the metic Poulytion, Alcibiades and nine others had celebrated the Mysteries in front of non-initiates.[57] Second, Teukros, another metic, obtained immunity in exchange for the names of twelve individuals, none of whom were mentioned by Andromachos. Third, Agariste, wife of Alkmeonides, previously the wife of Damon the Music Philosopher, "made a denunciation that in the house of Charmides besides the Olympieion Alcibiades, Axiochos, and Adeimantus celebrated mysteries" (Andocides, *On the Mysteries* 1.16).[58] Fourth, Lydos, a slave, provided information about a celebration in his master's house, again without any overlap in names. These four incidents are listed by Andocides, who claims it to be complete, but Plutarch (*Alcibiades* 22.3) mentions yet another incident, quoting from the formal charges against Alcibiades:

Thessalus, son of Cimon, of the deme Laciadae, indicts Alcibiades, son of Cleinias, of the deme Scambonidae, for committing crime against the goddesses of Eleusis, Demeter and [Persephone], in that he did mimic the mysteries and show them to his companions in his own house, wearing a robe as the hierophant wears when he shows the scared objects, and calling himself Hierophant, Poulytion Torch-Bearer, and Theodorus, of the deme Phegeae, Herald and hailing the rest of the company as Mystae and Epoptae, contrary to the laws and institutions of the Eumolpidae, Kerykes and Priests of Eleusis.[59]

Of all the names in these five sets of accusations Alcibiades is the only one to appear on more than one, being named in the testimony of three different individuals (Poulytion is not named in the testimony of Andromachos, who only says the incident occurred in his home). Androcles, a democratic demagogue, is not named among the accusers but appears to have coordinated the attack from behind the scenes, providing slaves and metics to testify that Alcibiades and his friends "in a drunken revel" had mutilated other sacred images and profaned the Eleusinian Mysteries (Plutarch, *Alcibiades* 19.1, and cf. Andocides *On the Mysteries* 1.27). Androcles would be assassinated by a group of young oligarchs but a few years later in 411 BCE, in part for his conspiring against Alcibiades (Thucydides, *History* 8.65.2).

While these charges were being levied Alcibiades was far away in Syracuse leading the massive Athenian force that had invaded the island now known as Sicily.[60] Recalled to face the charges he escaped his escort and defected to Sparta. He was tried and sentenced to death *in abstentia* and, like the other accused profaners of the Eleusinian Mysteries who fled prosecution, his property was confiscated and sold by the state.[61] His name was also placed under curse by all priests and priestesses.[62] His departure from the campaign in Sicily occurred just as he was beginning to make progress in forging an anti-Syracuse alliance among the other cities on the island.[63] With his talent removed from the stage the strategy came to naught, in the long run guaranteeing a tragic outcome. The expedition would end "in complete disaster after two years of operations, largely through ineptitude on the part of the divided Athenian command and stout resistance by the Syracusans. Some two hundred warships were captured or destroyed, and perhaps as many as forty thousand of the invaders—Athenians and allies—were killed or sold into slavery."[64] Athens would never fully recover.

The nature of the profanation of the Eleusinian Mysteries was not simply parody, or some act of lampooning them. It was "intentional deliberate sacrilege, which involved an accurate portrayal of the Mysteries themselves."[65] There is some disagreement on this point. The opposing view finds it at least odd that a drinking party showing contempt for sacred rites would simultaneously be concerned with (re)performing them faithfully.[66] Whether the profanation of the Mysteries consisted of parody or faithful (re)performance is not of great importance, and it is difficult to see why elements of both couldn't have existed side by side, occurring in conjunction. It is enough to say that the charge of profaning the Eleusinian Mysteries was an extremely *serious* one. A scared ritual had been

performed in the wrong place, at the wrong time, by the wrong people, and had
revealed to non-initiates secrets reserved for those who had undergone the genuine experience. This constituted a capital offense.

There is reason to believe "the house of Charmides" mentioned in Andocides was the home of Charmides the son of Glaucon, Critias' cousin, and
Plato's uncle (brother of his mother, Perictione). This same Charmides "was
well known not only as an associate of the sophists (and of Socrates), but also a
friend of the three men mentioned in [*On the Mysteries*] 1.16."[67] Namely: Alcibiades, Axiochos and Adeimantus. In Xenophon's *Symposium* (4.25) Charmides
is described as a lover of Cleinias, the son of Axiochos, and he is said to have
been persuaded by Socrates to enter politics (3.7, and cf. Diogenes Laertius
Lives 2.29). Andocides' *On the Mysteries* names Charmides as the fellow prisoner who convinced him to become an informant for the Boule (1.49–50, but cf.
Plutarch who names Timaeus as the prisoner who did the persuading).

In the opening scene of Plato's *Protagoras*, a dialogue which as we have
seen contains distinct sympotic overtones, the audience includes Charmides,
Alcibiades, Adeimantus, and Phaedrus of Myrrhine (314e–316a). In the *Protagoras* alone then we find engaged in conversation with Socrates *four* individuals
who would later be accused of profaning the Eleusinian Mysteries. Before discussion of the dialogue's main theme—tellingly whether virtue can be taught—
Protagoras engages in a revealing digression when he acknowledges Socrates'
caution with regard to inducing a city's "most promising young men to forsake
the company of others, relatives or acquaintances, that the conversation may
improve them," because doing so "arouses no small resentment and various
forms of hostility and intrigue" (316c–d). The basis of the charges against Socrates stretched beyond any simple notion of having "corrupted" these young
men; it arose from a profanation scandal that was at its heart a series of drinking
symposia where aristocratic vice went too far, became hubristic.

The Dark Magic of Socrates

If one looks at Aristophanes' comedic depiction of Socrates there is strong reason to believe that the philosopher, too, was widely regarded as a profaner of the
Mysteries, and as a practitioner of sorcery, a *goes, epodos, magos* or *pharmakeus*.[68] At a superficial level this is well-known, there being more or less universal agreement that the "comic poet" of *Apology* 18d, described as being one
of those responsible for creating a climate of public suspicion culminating in the
arrest and trial of Socrates, was in fact Aristophanes.[69] What was the Aristophan-
tic portrait of Socrates, that it could prove so damning in the popular imagination, including the jurors who sat in judgment during his trial? Plato has Socrates
claim in the *Apology* that it amounted to slander (*diabole*), a misrepresentation,
in the sense of being false, of such things as philosophy "making the weaker

speech the stronger" (18b–c, 23d–e). Discussion of the matter frequently ends at this point. It should actually *begin* here.

The first question that ought to be asked is *how* Aristophanes' portrait of Socrates was, for Plato, slanderous. The answer, it may be demonstrated, is that he rhetorically implicates Socrates as being a sacrilegious profaner of the same religious rites as many of his pro-Spartan oligarchic associates, patrons, and friends, namely the Eleusinian Mysteries. The *Clouds* was first produced in 423 BCE, finished third and last at the city Dionysia; a later revision has survived.[70] At the time of its first production Socrates would have been in his early forties while Plato would have been about six.[71] The primary topic of the *Clouds* is the introduction of new and untraditional forms of education into the *polis*, especially rhetoric, the art of winning arguments in court, the assembly and so on by, as we learn in the play itself, "making the worse argument appear the better" (112–15).

Strepsiades is in financial straights because of his son Pheidippides' love of racing horses. After much consideration he believes he has found a way out: send his son to a place of learning, a *phrontisterion*, a "think shop" or "house of thinkers," a word patterned after such terms as *dikasterion* (lawcourt), *bouleuterion* (council chamber), and *telesterion* (initiation hall, as found at Eleusis).[72] While Strepsiades, apparently a country man, believes the men of the *phrontisterion* are fine, upstanding, reflective men his son, more familiar with urban life, replies that the people his father is speaking of are a "rotten lot" made up of frauds with sickly complexions, "men with no shoes, such as that god-forsaken Socrates and Chaerephon" (*Clouds* 100–104). Pheidippides refuses his father's urgent request, so Strepsiades determines to educate himself in these new verbal techniques. Banging on the door of the *phrontisterion* he is met by an abusive student, who informs him that the knowledge within may not be lawfully divulged except to fellow students, calling the school's secrets "holy secrets" or more literally "mysteries" (143). Even early in the play the motif of initiation into the Mysteries is being emphasized.[73] The secrets of knowledge found within the *phrontisterion* may be imparted only to initiates—Eleusis being the basis of the parody.[74]

The Clouds themselves refer to "awe-inspiring rites that none may speak of, where to receive the initiates the temple is opened at the Mystic festival" (302–3). Most commentators recognize that the rites spoken of are those of the Eleusinian Mysteries and the temple is the *telesterion*; the similarity with the name of Socrates' school, the *phrontisterion*, is just as commonly acknowledged.[75] What lies behind the Clouds saying such a thing? Is it poetical, meant to invoke "an aesthetic response," or is it "an encomium of Athens, to which a patriotic response might be expected," or might it be "a catalogue of the Attic religious observances, prominently including the—presumably Eleusinian—mysteries," and intended to elicit "the deepest religious awe"? Or is it something else altogether, namely an *indictment*?

For an audience "believing in Olympians and mystery-cults, already darkly suspicious of the New Learning in all its manifestations," witnessing "Socrates holding bogus mysteries and worshipping false deities" would have evoked "a response not merely of hostility, not merely of disapproval [but rather] a response of pious fear, detestation and execration of Socrates and all his works, along with those of all the other representatives of the New Thought whom Aristophanes bundles together for blanket denunciation."[76] By the late fifth century the Greeks had begun to articulate an understanding of magic as a distinct activity.[77] The magician, whether he was called a *goes*, *epodos*, *magos*, or *pharmakeus* was a figure often associated with, and suspected of, adopting and mimicking "the ceremonies of mystery-cults for impious purposes."[78]

At line 831 of the *Clouds* there is mention of "Socrates of Melos," apparently an allusion to another reputed mystery profaner Diagoras of Melos. Diagoras, "a lyric poet, progressive constitutionalist, and philosopher of the same age as Socrates," allegedly mocked the Eleusinian Mysteries (Lysias 6.17), and may have been the author of the document known as the Derveni papyrus, whose author "castigates the gullibility of initiates into the mysteries—not just state-sponsored ceremonies 'in the cities' like those of Demeter at Eleusis, but especially privates ones, into which one could be admitted on payment of a fee."[79] He was indicted on the charge of *asebeia*, fled to Pellene, and was tried and sentenced to death *in abstentia*.[80] The Athenians demanded his extradition, to no avail, most likely inspiring the line in another of Aristophanes' plays, *The Birds*: "whomever kills Diagoras, the Melian miscreant, shall be paid" (1072–73). There can be read then a clear suggestion of impiety in *Clouds* 831 and at least implicitly Aristophanes may be read as suggesting, *in toto*, "whomever kills Socrates, the Melian miscreant, shall be paid." If Socrates could be accused of profaning Eleusinian ritual as early as 423 BCE, the charges made against so many of his close associates in 415 BCE would certainly have "implicated [their] unconventional and pro-Spartan teacher as well."[81]

When the doors of the *phrontisterion* are finally thrown open for Strepsiades he is astonished to see a group of students digging in the earth. He exclaims "Oh, I see, they're looking for bulbs to eat! Well, you don't need to give that another thought because I know where there are some lovely big ones" (*Clouds* 189–90). Are these bulbs food, or has Strepsiades perhaps merely mistaken them for food? Strepsiades comes from a rural background. Earlier in the *Clouds* (45) he recalls his youth as "overflowing with bees [honey], sheep [cheese], and olive cakes."[82] He would have been familiar with plants of all sorts. It should be pointed out that "numerous but unstated folkloristic and magicoreligious customs . . . hover in the shadows" of ancient textual accounts of plants, herbs and roots.[83] The Greek magical papyri, for example, "show quite vividly the ordinary and sophisticated command of drug compounding by the common people, a command not surprising in view of their usual rural upbringing. They would know the plants from childhood, and they would also know the appropriate magicoreligious connotations and their proper interpretations. Drugs were indeed 'the hands of the gods.'"[84] The Greeks of the Classical Period, as we saw above in chapter 4, believed that mushrooms arose spontaneously from the earth after they had been struck by a cloud's lightning. The importance of the clouds in the *Clouds*, and the digging for "bulbs" by the students of the *phrontisterion*, suggest these may have been understood by the audience as mushrooms in the *Clouds* as well.[85]

The Lesser Mysteries, at which one became a *mystes* in preparation to becoming an *epoptes* in the Greater Mysteries, took place during the winter, during the Greek month of Anthesterion (the Flower Month), roughly our February. The initiates appear to have reenacted Persephone's abduction by Hades at a place called Nysa, an abduction brought on, at least according to the *Homeric Hymn to Demeter*, by the maiden being "charmed" by the *narkissos* "flower."[86] At least one ancient source equates *bulbos* with *narkissos* (Pseudo-Dioscorides *Materia Medica* 4.158). In the *Clouds* one finds mystery initiation parodied as a search for bulbs. That this early scene is intended as a parody of mystery initiation can be further confirmed in lines 250–62. Socrates asks Strepsiades if he genuinely desires knowledge "of the true nature of things," and after the latter responds in the affirmative he is placed on a "sacred bed" with his head crowned with a wreath, while the "sieved meal of subtlety" is sprinkled over him.[87] "We do this to everyone when they're being initiated," Socrates explains. Persons known as *goetes* and *epodoi*, especially, were said to offer "initiation into ecstatic mystery-rites (*teletai*)."[88]

Additional clues may be found in Aristophanes' *Birds*, a work produced in 414 BCE, after the expedition to Syracuse had been launched but before it had met with disaster. Near the end of the play at lines 1553–64 is a curious scene. Socrates is described as performing a rite of necromantic magic, known as *psychagogia*, for a cowardly Peisander, who is hoping to find the courage that has deserted him. A distinct specialty, *psychagogia* involved the drawing up of the spirits of the dead from the Underworld.[89] The passage reads:

> Amidst the Shade-foots, there is a certain swamp where Socrates, unwashed, summons up souls. Amongst his clients came Peisander, who begged to see a spirit that had forsaken him while he remained alive. He had carried a lamb as victim for sacrifice and, like Odysseus of old, he slit its throat, whereupon to him from the depths there came up towards the camel's trench a spirit, Chaerephon, the "bat."

This too has the character of a "veiled accusation."[90] The practice of *psychagogia* had "a degree of contempt attached to it."[91] A detailed examination of the context of this complex scene shows it to be "a sustained reference to the profanation of the Eleusinian Mysteries."[92]

The swamp setting has been mistaken by some as being located far from Athens.[93] It can however be identified as being none other than the sacred swamp at the base of Athens's Acropolis, the temple of Dionysus.[94] This temple was opened once per year, for twenty-four hours, as part of the Anthesteria festival of the new wine. The spirits of the dead were thought to be resurrected from their subterranean burial, joining together with the living to celebrate the unearthing of the wine-filled *pithoi*. Special tables, complete with their own liq-

uid spirits, were set out for the dead "so that the ghosts . . . could be welcomed
but kept at an appropriate distance."[95] There are indications this wine could produce visions: Plutarch's *Questiones Symposia* refers to it as a *pharmakon* (3.7.1)
while Aristophanes' *Acharnians* appears to make reference to hallucinations
(1166–67). A ceremony predating the secularization of Athens's politics and
having some relation to the Lesser Mysteries was held in the temple. Being the
Athenian entrance to Hades, because it evoked the grave's putrification, this
swamp was the sort of place where "one could expect to summon up spirits, as
in fact, another comedian, the poet Eupolis, appears to have done in a play produced about this same time, the *Demes*."[96] Grave markers in the shape of mushrooms, long mistaken for *phalloi*, were a common practice in ancient Greece.[97]

   This is the same swamp Dionysus rows across before encountering the
spectral Empousa and the happy initiates of Eleusis in yet another play by Aristophanes, the *Frogs*. Rowing through the swamp to find the recently deceased
Euripides, Dionysus reunites with his slave Xanthias (who had walked around
the swamp). The two of them are then confronted by a shape-changing apparition, namely Empousa, and scramble about in comedic terror, commenting on
her continually morphing form. The encounter between Dionysus, Xanthias, and
Empousa plays on "a specific feature of the Eleusinian Mysteries. We hear a
good deal of [*phasmata*] appearing during the celebrations of the Greater Mysteries."[98] Empousa was in some manner associated with Hecate, a divinity associated with darkness and magic and who was believed to control apparitions,
phasmata.[99] She played a mediating role in Eleusinian myth, accompanying Persephone on her seasonal journey to and from Hades.[100]

   The Shade-foots, or *Sciapodes*, are perhaps the most important element of
all, for it is among them that Socrates is portrayed as communing with the dead.
The *Sciapodes* were a fantastic race of people with a single leg and a broad foot
resembling that found on some species of water fowl. They would at times rest
lazily on their backs and shade themselves from the sun's heat with their up-
raised foot, while at other times they would leap about with incredible vigor.
This race also bore the name *Monocoli* (Pliny, *Natural History* 7.2.23 and Aulus
Gellius, *Attic Nights* 9.4.9), an epithet that was also used by Theophrastus to
refer to single stemmed plants (*How Plants Grow* 2.25, *History of Plants*
9.18.8). The earliest accounts in Greek, from the sixth and fifth centuries BCE,
place the Sciapodes' homeland in India, in the Indus Valley. In the *Rg Veda*, a
collection of hymns preserving the oral traditions of the Aryan peoples prior to
their migration to both Greece and the Hindus Valley, there are six references to
Aja Ekapad, apparently an archaic name for the mushroom God Soma, meaning
the "Not-Born-Single-Foot." The *Sciapodes* would appear to have been "a Hellenic version of the deity Soma with the epithet Aja Ekapad."[101] The black magic
conducted by Socrates that Aristophanes is parodying in the *Birds* is, like the
search for "bulbs" within the *phrontisterion* in the *Clouds*, an indication that
fungi may have played a role within the Lesser Eleusinian Mystery.[102]

   The strophe which starts amongst the Sciapodes is matched antistrophically
by a later scene (lines 1694–1705):

Amongst the Revealers by the Hidden Water is a naughty race of Tongues-in-bellies, who harvest and sow, gather fruit with their tongues and pick figs. Babbling like foreigners is this race, students of Gorgias and Philippus—and because of them, those Tongues-in-bellies, these Philippuses, everywhere in Attica the tongue is a sacrificial victim cut apart.

This equally complex passage is related to the earlier one both structurally, since "it is danced to the same choreographed rhythms and melody," and thematically, with fantastical peoples, the element of water, and sacrificed flesh.[103]

The Tongues-in-bellies, or *Englottogastores*, are lawyers who imitate foreigners like Gorgias and Philippus, well-known teachers of rhetoric. Philippus is parodied as a son of Gorgias in Aristophanes' *Wasps* (421). Like Peisander, the prosecutor of the Mystery investigation, Aristophanes depicts these lawyers as being hypocrites, again in ways that would have evoked the subject of Mystery profanations. Oratorical talent consists of cultivating bribe money, for to pick figs "indicates people who give evidence in court against others for bounty," while lawyers are greedy men resembling Baubo, a diminutive female creature with a mouth on her belly, who amused the grieving Demeter after the abduction of Persephone. The goddess then ended her refusal to eat or drink and asked to be served the *kykeon*.[104]

The Revealers, or *Phanai*, are those who give evidence in court, again evoking the case of the Mystery Profanations because *Phanai* is verbally indistinguishable from *phanai* (torch processions), such as those that took place during the initiate's journey from Athens to Eleusis and in Dionysiac cult generally; it is just such a torch procession of Eleusinian initiates that greets Dionysus in the *Frogs* after he crosses over into Hades. The comical element consists of these paid witnesses implicating their accusers in the very crime they prosecute, "since the official charge against the guilty was that they had 'revealed' the mystery."[105] The hidden water, or *klepshydra*, simultaneously refers to the water clock used to time speeches in court and the fountain of the same name beneath the Acropolis where "Queen Creussa conceived and bore her son Ion while gathering flowers."[106] The sacrificed tongue cut in two recalls the camel-lamb offered by Peisander to Socrates, while intimating that lawyers and orators butcher speech, quibbling with words like their teachers do, making the worse argument the better, as it is said of Socrates in the *Clouds*. The cutting apart of discourse taught by Socrates in the *Clouds* calls to mind "the prohibition of secrecy imposed upon the central events of Eleusinian initiation."[107]

It is possible the act of profaning the Eleusinian Mysteries may have included the drinking of the *kykeon* as a substitute drug for the *symposion*'s wine.[108] In Aristophanes' *Lysistrata*, produced in 411 BCE, Peisander, the chief investigator of the profanations, is himself parodied. Like Alcibiades, Peisander aligned himself with the *demos* until it no longer suited his ambitions, whereupon he began plotting its overthrow, prosecuting the former chief witness for the prosecution, Andocides, and making arrangements, ultimately successful, for

Alcibiades' recall from Sicily. Essentially Aristophanes was claiming that Peisander's allegiance was for sale, an accusation he had first made in the *Babylo-
nians* fifteen years earlier. In the *Lysistrata* (489–491) the hypocritical Peisander
is described as part of a city whose entire politics have become a mix up (*pant
ekykethe*) with conspirators "mixing up some rumbling tumult" (*aei tina kor-
korygen ekykon*) or stomach upset (*korkorymous*). This accusation clearly puns
upon the word for the Eleusinian "mixed potion," the *kykeon*. Here again Aristophanes alludes to the scandal of 415 BCE, in a rhetorical move attempting to
associate Peisander with the hubristic sympotic behavior of many aristocrats,
first and foremost Alcibiades.

In a surviving fragment of a comedy by Eupolis, the *Demes*, an informant
tells a judge that he has observed a foreigner wrongfully drink the Eleusinian
kykeon, his certainty arising from the fact that he saw barley groats (*krimnon*) in
the man's moustache. This man had tried to bribe the informant into testifying
that what he had seen was simply porridge, not the sacred mixture. The foreigner is described as walking through Athens "overtaken by a hallucinatory
fever (*epialos*, like a nightmare)."[109] This passage gives another indication that
performing the Mysteries for the enjoyment of banquet guests by the members
of the Athenian oligarchic class may have included unsanctioned use of the
Eleusinian sacramental *pharmakon*, yet another aristocratic affront to democracy's ordinary social norms in the manner of the drunken violence of the *komos*.

A wide variety of deviant behaviors, "be they pharmaceutical, philosophical, pious, or political," could on occasion "fall under *asebeia*."[110] Unlike the
mutilation of the *hermai*, the profanations of the Eleusinian Mysteries were not
meant to be discovered. The purpose of this *asebeia*, as Thucydides tells us, was
to express "an undemocratic contempt for the laws," and the gods and goddesses
of the *demos* (*History* 6.28.2, and cf. 6.27.2). Many of Socrates' associates, or at
least the associates Plato depicts him as interacting with in dialogue after dialogue, were themselves accused of these politically charged impious acts, apparently with some good cause. The ecstatic use of one or more intoxicants, at a
minimum the frequently drugged wine of antiquity and possibly even the Eleusinian *kykeon* itself, appears to have been a part of that expression of contempt,
practiced by groups influenced by Sophistic teachings. It is not surprising then
that Plato exhibits such an interest in criticizing, reforming, recasting and rede-
fining the *symposion* in so many of his writings.[111]

And Socrates himself? There is enough evidence on hand to believe he
would have been widely regarded as holding political and religious attitudes
similar to those implicated in the scandal of 415 BCE, and that like other philosophers he was believed to have engaged in similarly impious acts, even *the
same* acts, and profaning the Eleusinian Mysteries was one of the worst offenses
there was. Having been found guilty, Socrates was allowed to propose his own
punishment. His suggestion to the jury as recorded in Plato's *Apology* (36d–e)—
free dinners for life in the *prytaneion*, "the highest honor that the democratic city
can bestow"—certainly has an insulting irony to it.[112] The existence of this tradi-

tion, in its origins aristocratic, may have "grated with the democrats, because it involved *ad hominem* privileges."[113] One of the few individuals who would have enjoyed this right was a priest of Eleusis.[114] Regardless of his actual guilt or innocence, Socrates' unorthodox political and religious views would have made him an easy target for public suspicion in the even more volatile climate that existed in Athens at the very end of the fifth century.

It would appear, furthermore, "that the common suspicion about people like Socrates was that they were apt to have derived ideas about other realities from drug induced visions."[115] While this may sound fantastic to both those who defend the Socratic mission and those who are critical of it, the fact remains that the social deviance associated with the practice of magic, and encompassed under the charge of *asebeia*, clearly "included . . . the making or using of *pharmaka*."[116] A feeling of "guilt by association" may well have saturated the atmosphere of Socrates' trial for impiety. Association *with whom*, and guilty *of what*, are things we will never be able to answer to our complete satisfaction. Two things seem fairly certain however. The philosopher appears to exhibit *all* of the deviance *asebeia* can include, not merely this or that aspect of it, and Socrates, in his own way, was executed for profaning the Mysteries and for practicing an intoxicating variety of verbal sorcery as much as for anything else.[117]

Notes

1. Bruce Lincoln, "Socrates' Persecutors, Philosopher's Rivals, and the Politics of Discursive Forms," *Arethusa* 26, no. 3 (1993): 233.

2. For a concurring view see Peter J. Ahrensdorf, "The Question of Historical Context and the Study of Plato," *Polity* 27, no. 1 (1994): 118.

3. The reduction of *asebeia* to atheism is frequently made even by those who believe in the necessity of studying "the appropriate historical context of Plato's defense of the philosophical life." See Ahrensdorf, "The Question of Historical Context and the Study of Plato," 135.

4. Another commonly held view is that the official charges were merely a pretext for a political agenda, i.e. a settling of scores following the restoration of democracy after the defeat of the Thirty Tyrants. John Burnet, *Greek Philosophy: Thales to Plato* (London: Macmillan and Company, 1962), 182–3, 186 argues that since ancient Greece lacked a "conception of religious orthodoxy" we must "at once set aside that [Socrates' trial] was for not believing the stories about the gods," concluding that "Plato indicates in the clearest possible manner that Socrates really owed his death to his political attitude." I. F. Stone, *The Trial of Socrates* (New York: Little, Brown, and Company, 1988), 138–9, and cf. 237–47 contends "it was the political, not the philosophical or theological, views of Socrates which finally got him into trouble. The discussion of his religious views distracts from the real issues." This viewpoint is not universal and the religious element of Socrates' trial has come under scrutiny as serious in its own right, for example in Thomas C. Brickhouse and Nicholas D. Smith, *Socrates on Trial* (Princeton, NJ: Princeton University Press, 1989), 69–87, and 1994: 173–5 and Ahrensdorf, "The Question of Historical Context and the Study of Plato," 119–27.

5. See Ahrensdorf, "The Question of Historical Context and the Study of Plato," 118–120.

6. See Barry S. Strauss, *Athens after the Peloponnesian War: Class, Faction, and Policy 403–386 BC* (Ithaca, NY: Cornell University Press, 1986), 11–12, and cf. Plato's *Symposium* (221e).

7. Strauss, *Athens after the Peloponnesian War*, 12.

8. It is believed that as many as 1,500 citizens were killed during the short reign of the Thirty. See Joseph M. Bryant, *Moral Codes and Social Structure in Ancient Greece: A Sociology of Greek Ethics from Homer to the Epicureans and Stoics* (Albany, NY: State University of New York Press, 1996), 226.

9. Joseph M. Bryant, "Enlightenment Psychology and Political Reaction in Plato's Social Philosophy: And Ideological Contradiction?" *History of Political Thought* 11, no. 3 (1990): 394 n. 55.

10. The work may also have been a pamphlet written after the fact and circulated by Andocides' enemies.

11. J. L. Marr, "Andocides' Part in the Mysteries and the Hermae Affairs of 415 B.C.," *Classical Quarterly* 21, no. 2 (1971): 334 n. 1.

12. Marr, "Andocides' Part in the Mysteries and the Hermae Affairs of 415 B.C.," 334 n. 1.

13. Marr, "Andocides' Part in the Mysteries and the Hermae Affairs of 415 B.C.," 334 n. 1.

14. Marr, "Andocides' Part in the Mysteries and the Hermae Affairs of 415 B.C.," 334 n. 1.

15. In contrast to Socrates' close associate Chaerephon, who went into exile. In the same manner Socrates' reference to certain comedic poets would have easily been comprehended as a jibe at Aristophanes' portrait of Socrates in the *Birds* and *Clouds*, without the necessity of dwelling upon the veracity of what may have been genuinely incriminating elements of him in either of those works.

16. Oswyn Murray, "The Affair of the Mysteries: Democracy and the Drinking Group," in *Sympotica—A Symposium on the* Symposion, ed. Oswyn Murray (Oxford: Clarendon Press, 1990), 149.

17. The armada that sailed for Sicily comprised some 207 warships (*triremes*) and some 50,000 to 60,000 men. See Michael Attyah Flower, *The Seer in Ancient Greece* (Berkeley, CA: University of California Press, 2008), 114.

18. Murray, "The Affair of the Mysteries: Democracy and the Drinking Group," 149, and cf. C. A. Powell, "Religion and the Sicilian Expedition," *Historia* 28, no. 1 (1979): 15.

19. Hereafter in this chapter simply *History*.

20. A. M. Bowie, *Aristophanes—Myth, Ritual, and Comedy* (Cambridge, UK: Cambridge University Press, 1993): 139.

21. Richard A. Bauman, *Political Trials in Ancient Greece* (New York: Routledge, 1990), 64.

22. Plato *Apology* 31c–d. On Socrates' own divinatory powers see Mark L. McPherran, "Socratic Reason and Socratic Revelation," *Journal of the History of Philosophy* 29 (1991): 345–73.

23. Powell, "Religion and the Sicilian Expedition," 15–20. Ancient Greek sorcery, including the use of books of oracles when deliberating *polis* policy, is discussed in chapter 8, below. See for example Mathew W. Dickie, *Magic and Magicians in the Greco-Roman World* (New York: Routledge, 2001), 69.

24. Powell, "Religion and the Sicilian Expedition," 21, and cf. Ahrensdorf, "The Question of Historical Context and the Study of Plato," 122, 126–27.

25. Oswyn Murray, "Forms of Sociality," in *The Greeks*, ed. Jean-Pierre Vernant (Chicago: University of Chicago Press, 1995), 240. See also chapter 2, above.

26. Murray, "The Affair of the Mysteries: Democracy and the Drinking Group," 157.

27. Murray, "The Affair of the Mysteries: Democracy and the Drinking Group," 151.

28. William N. Ellis, *Alcibiades* (New York: Routledge, 1989), 59.

29. Ellis, *Alcibiades*, 62.

30. Bauman, *Political Trials in Ancient Greece*, 64.

31. *Asebeia*, too, "since it might draw down the wrath of the gods on the state as a whole," was an offense "for which denunciation (*menysis*) on the part of slaves was encouraged." See Dickie, *Magic and Magicians in the Greco-Roman World*, 51.

32. Marr, "Andocides' Part in the Mysteries and the Hermae Affairs of 415 B.C.," 335.

33. Bauman, *Political Trials in Ancient Greece*, 6, 64–65.

34. Bauman, *Political Trials in Ancient Greece*, 106-118.

35. Bauman, *Political Trials in Ancient Greece*, 65–66.

36. Murray, "The Affair of the Mysteries: Democracy and the Drinking Group," 151, emphasis Murray's.

37. Murray, "The Affair of the Mysteries: Democracy and the Drinking Group," 150 argues that the *hetaireia*'s line of descent can be traced "perhaps from the Homeric poems, and certainly from the activities of the *synomotai* of Alcaeus and the aristocratic factions of sixth-century Athens, through to the late fifth-century political and aristocratic groups which, somewhat ineffectually under normal circumstances, tried to maintain an influence in the world of mass democracy."

38. Thucydides' *History* records that Peisander "went around the *synomosiai* already existing in the city for lawsuits and elections, urging them to come together and plan to overthrow the *demos*" (8.54.4).

39. Murray, "The Affair of the Mysteries: Democracy and the Drinking Group," 152.

40. Murray, "The Affair of the Mysteries: Democracy and the Drinking Group," 151.

41. Marr, "Andocides' Part in the Mysteries and the Hermae Affairs of 415 B.C.," 328.

42. Bauman, *Political Trials in Ancient Greece*, 63 writes that based on Andocides' account, "the fellow-prisoner who persuaded him was his cousin, Charmides." As Murray, "The Affair of the Mysteries: Democracy and the Drinking Group," 152 notes, he must also have been "under pressure from his relatives," who may have feared being dragged down with him.

43. Marr, "Andocides' Part in the Mysteries and the Hermae Affairs of 415 B.C.," 326.

44. Marr, "Andocides' Part in the Mysteries and the Hermae Affairs of 415 B.C.," 328.

45. Marr, "Andocides' Part in the Mysteries and the Hermae Affairs of 415 B.C.," 335 n. 1.

46. Peter H. Von Blackenhagen, "Stage and Actors in Plato's *Symposium*," *Greek, Roman and Bzyantine Studies* 33, no. 1 (1992): 54.

47. On the exile of Alcibiades see Sara Forsdyke, *Exile, Ostracism, and Democracy: The Politics of Expulsion in Ancient Greece* (Princeton, NJ: Princeton University Press, 2005): 170–75, 181–203, 267–71.

48. Bauman, *Political Trials in Ancient Greece*, 66.

49. Marr, "Andocides' Part in the Mysteries and the Hermae Affairs of 415 B.C.," 326.

50. Carl A. P. Ruck, "Mushrooms and Philosophers," in *Persephone's Quest: Entheogens and the Origins of Religion*, ed. R. Gordon Wasson (New Haven, CT: Yale University Press, 1986), 155 and cf. Murray, "Forms of Sociality," 240, who concurs.

51. Georg Luck, *Arcana Mundi—Magic and the Occult in the Greek and Roman Worlds. A Collection of Ancient Texts* (Baltimore, MD: The Johns Hopkins University Press, 2006: 38.

52. Luck, *Arcana Mundi*, 38.

53. Murray, "Forms of Sociality," 240.

54. Murray, "The Affair of the Mysteries: Democracy and the Drinking Group," 157.

55. Fridolf Kudlien, "Early Greek Primative Medicine," *Clio Medica* 3 (1968): 318. Kudlien describes Kinesias' group as being "influenced by the sophistic movement."

56. Murray, "The Affair of the Mysteries: Democracy and the Drinking Group," 154, and Marr "Andocides' Part in the Mysteries and the Hermae Affairs of 415 B.C.," 328–29.

57. The profanations in the house of Poulytion are spoofed in Pherecrates' comedy *The Kitchen or All Night Dinner Party.*

58. Damon is mentioned in Plato's *Republic* (400b–c).

59. Anne Mary Farrell, *Plato's Use of Eleusinian Mystery Motifs* (Ph. D. Diss., University of Texas at Austin, 1999), 47 indicates that Plutarch was known to have had access to documents from the fifth and fourth centuries BCE but we cannot know for certain how accurately or faithfully he quotes from them.

60. A number of authors mistakenly indicate that because of the profanation scandal Alcibiades was *prevented* from embarking with the invasion fleet, and/or that he was *immediately* exiled by his countrymen. See for example Robin A. Waterfield, *Plato—Symposium* (New York: Oxford University Press, 1994), 97–98. Neither of these was the case: he sailed with the fleet and led the campaign until his recall to face the charges months later.

61. Robert W. Wallace, "Charmides, Agariste, and Damon: Andokides 1.16," *Classical Quarterly* 42, no. 2 (1992): 332.

62. Bauman, *Political Trials in Ancient Greece*, 65.

63. Walter M. Ellis, *Alcibiades* (New York: Routledge, 1989), 63–64.

64. Bryant, *Moral Codes and Social Structure in Ancient Greece*, 224. See also Simon Hornblower, "The Religious Dimensions of the Peloponnesian War," *Harvard Studies in Classical Philology* 94 (1992): 169–97.

65. Murray, "The Affair of the Mysteries: Democracy and the Drinking Group," 156.

66. Wallace, "Charmides, Agariste, and Damon: Andokides 1.16," 328–29 n. 2.

67. Wallace, "Charmides, Agariste, and Damon: Andokides 1.16," 331.

68. The terms were largely interchangeable. The lack of a single word for magician "points to the absorbing and homogenizing of quite separate forms of expertise." See Dickie, *Magic and Magicians in the Greco-Roman World*, 28. I will return to the subject of ancient Greek magic in chapter 8, below.

69. Thomas G. West, trans., *Plato's Apology of Socrates* (Ithaca, NY: Cornell University Press, 1979), 52 n. 19, for example.

70. The full context is summed up by Sansone: "*The Clouds* was produced at a time when the Athenians were involved in a major war and only a few years after their city had been ravaged by a devastating epidemic, which some contemporaries undoubtedly attributed to divine disfavor. It is likely, therefore, that Aristophanes was simply reflecting a popular view, that the advanced thinkers like Socrates and Euripides, were engaged in a program of probing and questioning that was in danger of overturning traditional believes and values." See David Sansone, *Ancient Greek Civilization* (Malden, MA: Blackwell Publishing, 2003), 156.

71. Eric A. Havelock, "The Socratic Self as it is Parodied in Aristophanes' *Clouds*," *Yale Classical Studies* 22 (1972): 9.

72. Alan H. Sommerstein, *The Comedies of Aristophanes. Vol. 4—Wasps* (Warminster, Wilts, UK: Aris and Phillips, 1982), 164 n. 94 and Brickhouse and Smith, *Socrates on Trial*, 181.

73. A. W. H. Adkins, "Clouds, Mysteries, Socrates and Plato," *Antichthon* 4 (1970): 13.

74. Richard Seaford, "Dionysiac Drama and the Dionysiac Mysteries," *Classical Quarterly* 32, no. 2 (1981): 253.

75. Adkins, "Clouds, Mysteries, Socrates and Plato," 14, for example.

76. Adkins, "Clouds, Mysteries, Socrates and Plato," 15–17. I agree with Adkins that in the minds of the majority of the original audience the scenes "would have been regarded not as amusing but as blasphemous."

77. See Dickie, *Magic and Magicians in the Greco-Roman World*, 18–46 on this complex and fascinating subject.

78. Dickie, *Magic and Magicians in the Greco-Roman World*, 29.

79. "The priests at Eleusis . . . would have been angered by the mockery of public initiation in column 20 and the revelations about the initiates' sacrifices to the Eumenides, specially Athenian deities, in column 6." See Richard Janko, "Socrates the Free Thinker," in *A Companion to Socrates*, ed. Sara Ahbel-Rappe and Rachana Kametkar (Malden, MA: Blackwell Publishing, 2006), 54–57.

80. Sommerstein, *The Comedies of Aristophanes. Vol. 2—Clouds*, 1982, 201 n. 830. See also Walter Burkert, *Greek Religion: Archaic and Classical* (Malden, MA: Blackwell Publishing, 1985), 316.

81. Ruck, "Mushrooms and Philosophers," 160.

82. Elizabeth Craik, "Diet, *Diaita*, and Dietetics," in *The Greek World*, ed. Anton Powell (New York: Routledge, 1995), 391 points out that olive groves were "emblematic of the Attic countryside."

83. John Scarborough, "The Pharmacology of Sacred Plants, Herbs, and Roots," in *Magika Hiera—Ancient Greek Magic and Religion*, ed. Christopher A. Faraone and Dirk Obbink (New York: Oxford University Press, 1991), 149.

84. Scarborough, "The Pharmacology of Sacred Plants, Herbs, and Roots," 163.

85. "Mushrooms are similar to bulbs in their fantastic appearance." See Raimo Anttila, *Greek and Indo-European Etymology in Action* (Philadelphia, PA: John Benjamins, 2000), 106.

86. See chapter 4, above.

87. Craik, "Diet, *Diaita*, and Dietetics," 391 observes that barley groats or *ouali* "had a common ritual significance, the sacrificial animal being sprinkled with, or in some cases made to eat, this fodder."

88. Dickie, *Magic and Magicians in the Greco-Roman World*, 33.

89. Dickie, *Magic and Magicians in the Greco-Roman World*, 30–31. In Homer's *Odyssey* Odysseus summons up the spirit of the dead seer Teiresias, while a play by Aeschylus called *Psychagogia* was, according to the grammarian Phrynichus of Bithynia (fl. second century CE) in his *Sophistic Preparations*, reportedly about this practice.

90 Ruck, "Mushrooms and Philosophers," 153.

91. Dickie, *Magic and Magicians in the Greco-Roman World*, 326 n. 47. In Euripides *Alcestis* (1127–28) Hercules takes offense to king Admetus thinking the woman Hercules has wrestled from the grip of Hades is not his wife, Alcestis, but merely an apparition, saying the king is making a *psychagogos* out of someone who is his *xenos*, a guest-friend. Dickie observes that the point of the remark "would seem to be either that it is a little strange for Admetus, a king, to admit to enjoying a relationship of guest-friendship with anything so lowly as a professional summoner up of the souls of the dead or more likely that it is insulting of him to call his friend a *psychagogos* and to suggest that he can do no better than bring back a ghost."

92. Carl A. P. Ruck, "Mushrooms and Mysteries: On Aristophanes and the Necromancy of Socrates," *Helios* 8, no. 2 (1981): 1. A very different interpretation may be found in Daniel Ogden, *Magic, Witchcraft, and Ghosts in the Greek and Roman Worlds—A Sourcebook* (New York: Oxford University Press, 2002), 27 who reads the same passage as a comic reworking of moments in works like the *Odyssey* and Aeschylus' *Psuchagogoi*. Ruck's reading, in the context of evidence presented in the rest of this chapter, seems the more persuasive but the passage is, unquestionably, a difficult one.

93. Leo Strauss, *Socrates and Aristophanes* (Chicago: University of Chicago Press, 1996), 160, for example.

94. Erika Simon, *Festivals of Attika: An Archeological Commentary* (Madison, WI: University of Wisconsin Press, 1983), and cf. Ruck, "Mushrooms and Philosophers," 156.

95. R. Gordon Wasson, Albert Hofmann, and Carl A. P. Ruck, *The Road to Eleusis: Unveiling the Secrets of the Mysteries* [Twentieth Anniversary Edition] (Los Angeles: William Dailey Rare Books, 1998), 92.

96. Ruck, "Mushrooms and Philosophers," 156.

97. D. C. Kurtz and J. Boardman, *Greek Burial Customs* (London: Thames and Hudson, 1971), 242–44.

98. Christopher Brown, "Empousa, Dionysus, and the Mysteries: Aristophanes *Frogs* 285ff," *Classical Quarterly* 41, no. 1 (1991): 42. Johnston writes that "Lucian's humorous *katabasis* includes the appearance of the Erinys Tisiphone out of the dark, which one of the characters says reminds him of what happens during the Eleusinian initiations." See Sarah I. Johnston, *Restless Dead: Encounters between the Living and the Dead in Ancient Greece* (Berkeley, CA: University of California Press, 1999), 132, referring to Lucian *Cataplus* 22.

99. Johnston, *Restless Dead*, 133. "*Empousai* are associated with Hecate in classical sources and are described by late sources specifically as *phasmata* that Hecate can send forth, which virtually identifies them as one type of angry ghosts whom Hecate controlled."

100. Brown, "Empousa, Dionysus, and the Mysteries," 42–43 draws the conclusion that the swamp scene in the *Frogs*, where Dionysus and Xanthias are frightened by an apparition, ultimately derives from "a visual experience," most likely Eleusis, given that the initiates clearly "saw the rites" but he does not make a connection between this experience of an apparition and the drinking of the *kykeon*. As we saw in chapter 4, above, the *kykeon* appears to have contained some sort of *pharmakon*, most likely one derived from ergot.

101. Ruck, "Mushrooms and Philosophers," 166–67.

102. Ruck, "Mushrooms and Philosophers," 176.

103. Ruck, "Mushrooms and Philosophers," 158, and cf. Ruck "Mushrooms and Mysteries," 6–7, and Dickie, *Magic and Magicians in the Greco-Roman World*, 31.

104. Ruck, "Mushrooms and Philosophers," 158, and cf. *Homeric Hymn to Demeter* 204–12.

105. Ruck, "Mushrooms and Philosophers," 158.

106. Ruck, "Mushrooms and Mysteries," 7, and on Ion see Carl A. P. Ruck, "On the Sacred Name of Iamos and Ion: Ethnobotanical Referents in the Hero's Parentage," *The Classical Journal* 71, no. 3, (1976): 235–52.

107. Ruck, "Mushrooms and Philosophers," 158.

108. Peter Webster, "Mixing the *Kykeon*," *Eleusis: Journal of Psychoactive Plants and Compounds* 4 (2000): 2.

109. Carl A. P. Ruck, "Mixing the *Kykeon*—Part 3," *Eleusis: Journal of Psychoactive Plants and Compounds* 4 (2000): 21. There may even be a pun indicating that "the incriminating 'crumbs' of barley" were "purples of barley," highly relevant since ergot of barley is in fact dark purple. See Wasson et al., *The Road to Eleusis*, 58. I discuss the symptoms of ergot intoxication in greater detail in both chapter 4, above, and chapter 6, below.

110. Phillips 1991: 262. Dickie, *Magic and Magicians in the Greco-Roman World*, although he acknowledges the use of drugs in magic on several occasions (usually in the form of love-potions and poisons, and rarely mentioning any specific drug), and notes the strong link between magic and the sacrilegious mystery-initiation, oddly he hesitates to say that the charge of *asebeia* would have been used to prosecute someone accused of practicing magic.

111. See chapter 3, above.

112. Murray, "Forms of Sociality," 235.

113. Peter Garnsey, *Food and Society in Classical Antiquity* (Cambridge: Cambridge University Press, 1999), 133–34.

114. According to Murray, "Forms of Sociality," 235–36, in addition to the priests of Eleusis, the right of permanent dining was limited to "the two closest descendants of the trannicides Harmodius and Aristogeiton, those 'chosen by Apollo,' those who have won a major contest at the four great international games and (probably) the generals (*Inscriptiones Graecae* 13. 131); the archons would also have been present."

115. Ruck, "Mushrooms and Mysteries," 24.

116. C. R. Phillips, "*Nullum Crimen sine Lege*: Socioreligious Sanctions on Magic," in *Magika Hiera—Ancient Greek Magic and Religion*, ed. Christopher A. Farrone and Dirk Obbink (New York: Oxford University Press, 1991), 271 n. 10. See also chapter 8, below.

117. It is worth noting that after the appearance of a now lost pamphlet titled *Accucation Against Socrates* "published in 393/2 BCE [by] the rhetorician Polycrates," Libanius (312–392 CE), in his rebuttal *Apology of Socrates*, tells the Athenians: "Anaxagoras was justly imprisoned for his impiety regarding the sun and moon; you banished Protagoras fairly and appropriately for asking whether the gods exist or not; you were wise to promise a reward for the person who would kill Diagoras, since he mocked Eleusis and the ineffable mysteries; but who can say there is a book or an argument about the gods by Socrates that is contrary to law? As you cannot show us one, Anytus . . . you still do not convict Socrates" (154–5). Quoted in Janko, "Socrates the Freethinker," 57. Janko believes this "shows that Polycrates, and most probably Socrates' real prosecutors, did accuse him on these grounds." Socrates was said to have been born on the sixth day

of the Thargelia, the day when "the Athenians would purify their city" (Diogenes Laertius, *Lives* 2.44). He was, in a way, a *pharmakos* for the Athenians' *hubris*. Cf. Michael Morgan, *Platonic Piety: Philosophy and Ritual in Fourth Century Athens* (New Haven, CT: Yale University Press, 1990), 204 n. 119 who suspects the same.

Chapter Six

Socrates Rehabilitated

The *Phaedrus* is a dialogue saturated with religion, the ecstatic and drugs.[1] It begins with Socrates being lured out of the city by the sight of a scroll under Phaedrus' cloak, which he calls a *pharmakon* (230d).[2] There is no remedy or poison here; the *pharmakon* is a potent magic, a charm, intoxicating.[3] The dialogue's first two speeches—one read by Phaedrus (purported to have been written by the rhetorician Lysias), the other by Socrates—denounce in familiar Platonic fashion the madness of *eros*, contrasting it with sound-minded *sophrosyne*,[4] which is praised.[5] The term Plato uses, *mania*, "is often translated as 'madness'" but the term "was closer to 'possession', a state causing unusual behavior, though not necessarily frenzy or madness as such; *mania* affects normal behavior."[6] Insights achieved while in this state are "not reached by the measuring, counting, and reckoning of the *logistikon*, but by non-discursive processes less perfectly transparent to the agent's awareness and possibly more difficult to control."[7] While in such a state of mind one acts less on the basis of pure intellect and more on the basis of "feeling and response, by complex receptivity," of which it is virtually impossible to give a systematic and well-defined account of afterwards.[8]

Having finished his speech Socrates is about to depart across the waters of the Illissos but he is recalled by his *daimonion* (242b–d). Whereas in the *Symposium* Diotima's exposition on *eros*, as retold by Socrates, situated it as an intermediary between the sensible world of the forms—i.e. denied *eros'* divinity—in the *Phaedrus* Socrates speaks of his need to be purified, implying that he, like the poet Stesichorus, "needs to recover his sight."[9] Homer was reputed to have been blind; Stesichorus doubted Homer's account of Helen and was stricken blind for his blasphemy, until he retracted his account. Socrates proposes to deliver a third speech, a "palinode to Love," that will cleanse their ears of the earlier proposition that non-rational insights are useless (if pleasurable) evils, because "in fact madness, provided it comes as a gift from heaven, is the channel by which we receive the greatest blessing" (244a).[10] The third speech, the palinode, is itself "the perfect *pharmakon*, both remedial of the blindness of his previous speech, and preventative of error in the discussion to follow."[11]

States of Mania in Plato's *Phaedrus*

Socrates gives four examples of this divinely inspired possession.[12] The first, consisting of divination, prophecy, and the like, is the product of individuals in a "state of frenzy" whose usefulness to other individuals and the community, if returned to their "sober senses," would amount to "little or nothing" (244b–c). Although abstract, owing to the philosophical nature of the discussion, this passage appears to confirm "that the most famous seer in Greece, the Pythia at Delphi, used to prophesy in a state of ecstasy."[13] Next, madness can be a valuable guilty conscience of sorts, leading one to discover "in rites of purification and initiation ways to make the sufferer well and keep him well thereafter" (244d–e).[14] The anger of the dead, thought capable of producing ill-health in the living, was called *menima*. In the case of the *Phaedrus* this passage explicitly refers to the "great sufferings" that "ancient *menimata*" have caused "particular families."[15] Wandering holy men who combined "initiations into mysteries" with "the practice of magic" in order to "cure men of the effects of their and their ancestors' wrongdoing" were a common feature of the religious landscape of fifth-century Greece.[16] Third, there is the "possession and madness of the poet in the grip of the muses" (245a). The "self-possessed" (*sophronountos*) poetic techniques are "utterly eclipsed" by "the performance of the divinely inspired madman" (245a).[17] Lastly, the lover truly "transported" (*kekinemenos*) by *eros* is preferable to the disinterested sort held up for admiration in the earlier speeches (245b–c).

There can be little doubt that what we find here, in the *Phaedrus*, is an attitude toward states of ecstatic displacement, especially the "possessed" variety, considerably more nuanced than that exhibited in some of the other middle dialogues, where there are frequent attempts to problematize manifestations of ecstasy arising from either internal-psychological sources or external-physical sources.[18] Plato appears to be reconsidering the extensive discussion that had occurred in the fifth century concerning <u>techne</u>, "an orderly systemization of practice in some area that would yield increased control over ungoverned aspects of behavior," a debate that had turned to mathematics for its answers and in the guise of Pythagorean epistemology had influenced him deeply.[19] What the *Phaedrus* expresses in contrast to the traditional notions of *techne* is that

[c]ertain states of madness or possession are . . . both helpful and honorable, even necessary sources of the "greatest goods." The thoroughly self-possessed person, who subdues emotion and feeling to *techne*, will neither aid his or her city much through prophecy, nor achieve honor and fame as a poetical teacher,

nor be the best lover. The ethical thinker cannot, it seems, afford to make sharp and simplistic distinctions between bad madness and good *sophrosyne* as the first two speeches did, as the *Republic* and *Symposium* did.[20]

— Nussbaum

Additionally, in the discussion of the tripartite soul and the myth of the charioteer that immediately follow the four forms of madness, Plato attempts to demonstrate that (1) the emotions and appetites are a necessary *motivational* source, (2) these same elements play an important role in *guiding* us toward rational understanding, and (3) frenzy and the actions it inspires have a *valuable* place in the best human life. This is a departure from the positions laid out in works such as the *Phaedo, Republic,* and *Symposium* which argued by way of contrast that (1) the "appetites are blind animal forces reaching out for their objects without discrimination or selectively," (2) "appetites tend naturally to excess when not suppressed," (3) the "passions cannot function cognitively . . . invariably [they are] sources of distortion," and (4) the "intellectual element is both necessary and sufficient for the apprehension of truth and for correct choice."[21]

Plato's opinion of pharmakon wavers!

An Intoxicating Setting

The conversation of the *Phaedrus* takes place in a locale unique among Plato's writings. It is the only time in the dialogues that Socrates leaves his "urban haunts" in favor of a "green place outside the city walls . . . by the banks of a flowing stream"; here, according to legend, "a pure young girl was carried off by an impassioned wind god."[22] Superficially this is exactly what happens but there is more to the dialogue's setting than its sexually charged rural charms. The settings of the *Phaedrus* are never or nearly never accidental. The pairing of a theme of the dialogue with a "significant site" recurs continually, a "theatrical geography" exhibiting "an infallible calculation or necessity."[23] If this is so then it may be equally if not more important to point out that the conversation of the *Phaedrus* takes place not far from Agrai, "the scene of the Lesser Mysteries."[24]

The temple of Agrai,[25] the site of the Lesser Mysteries, is described as being "two or three stades [one-quarter of a mile]" further downstream (229c).[26] Located on the banks of the Ilissos, the name Agrai "recalls the lygos blossoms and the plane trees immortalized by Plato in his dialogue between Socrates and Phaedrus."[27] The spot where one crosses over to the temple is where Socrates believes Oreitheyia was carried off. To cross the Ilissos might also suggest a trip to the central sanctuary of the Anthesteria (festival of flowers), the Limnaion, the temple of Dionysus in the Marshes. The Anthesteria was a "vegetation festival" with roots dating back to at least the Late Bronze Age.[28] The worship of "the Cretan Dionysus and the Eleusinian goddesses Demeter and Persephone, with whom he was intimately associated, [have] been traced back to a pre-Indo-European horizon, beyond which their ancestries are lost in time."[29] The religions that emerged in Greece "under the demand of individualism in the first millennium [BCE]" may have been only a "renewal," a latest cycle, of "eons of collective agricultural rituals" and "ancient shamanic traditions."[30]

Plato is being carefully subtle, merely alluding to a religious background through the settings and tone of his dialogue. The tone would have been far more apparent to his contemporaries—many of whom would have either experienced or at least had some secondhand knowledge of the rites alluded to—than to the modern interpreter. The *Phaedrus*, which includes a discussion of the mysteries of spiritual life "which must begin on the level of physical love and which lead to the great vision of the Ideas," parallels the Lesser Mysteries and the Greater Mysteries in a manner that would have been perfectly clear to Plato's contemporaries: at Agrai the tone of the *myesis* was more "physical" while at Eleusis the *epopteia*—the state of "having seen"—was more "spiritual."[31]

Oreithyia was reputed to have met her demise because she was *playing with Pharmaceia* not, as the literature routinely contends, simply because Boreas, made irrational by his sexual desire, carried her off. Oreithyia may be rendered "she who rages in the mountains" or "mountain ecstatic female" and *pharmaceia* "the use of drugs." The sophist rationalization mocked by Socrates consists of an unfortunate demise owing to ecstatic rapture brought on by drug intoxication. The reduction of Boreas to a libidinal figure is equally unconvincing. Being abducted—breathed upon by the wind[32]—"is a rather transparent metaphor for 'inspiration' and chthonic possession" and Boreas, the cold north wind, was "an apt figure for a deadly ravisher of vegetation," in this case a daughter of Hyakinthos, "a vegetative deity who changed upon his death into the hyakinthos, another pre-Indo-European plant name assimilated into Greek."[33] Oreithyia's grandson was reputed to be Eumolpus, the first hierophant of Eleusis. In Book II of the *Republic* Eumolpus is implicitly criticized as being associated with a pedagogy emphasizing that "the best possible reward for goodness" is an "eternal intoxication" (363d).[34] This is especially telling given the metaphors depicting Eleusinian initiation that occur later in key passages of the *Phaedrus*.

In his first speech Socrates takes on the persona "of Phaedrus a Murrhinousian man," while the second, he announces, will be in the guise of "Stesichorus, son of Euphemus, from Himera" (244a). The names are significant. Murrhinous was the deme name of the historical Phaedrus.[35] Just as was the case with the earlier reference to Oreithyia, "Murrhinousian man" appears to have connotations of religion and the ecstatic, not simply sexual passion.[36] Once we allow these concerns to enter the discussion, plant-derived *pharmaka* are likely to follow. Myrrh was a plant with prominent associations with Dionysian cult mentioned in, for example, Euripides' *Bacchae*. Socrates could thus be read as linking Phaedrus to the telesitic madness of Dionysus which is mentioned shortly thereafter. Myrrh was, furthermore, among the many substances the ancient Greeks added to wine during the mixing ceremony which accompanied the *symposion*, reputedly with their own intoxicating effects.[37]

The reference to Stesichorus is even more direct. Euphemus means "reverent in speech," while Stesichorus (ca. 640 BCE–555 BCE) was a lyric poet who reversed his opinion on Helen's abduction so as to recover his own sight; Himera (from *himeros*), his home city located in Sicily, "might as well be called Desire Town or Passionville."[38] Sexual pleasures, the *aphrodisia*, are unquestionably an important ethical theme in Plato's middle dialogues, but they are not the primary issue. Ecstasy is the problem, because through it one had access to *the truth*. Like the poet, Socrates announces prior to his second speech that he must purge himself of his original offense by using an ancient method of purification (*katharmos*) so as to recover his vision (243a–c). Given the Eleusinian language and imagery that follow shortly thereafter, we may even say that the remedy which figuratively restores Socrates' sight is a sort of philosophic potion, one that produces a philosophic epiphany of essential beauty, an *epopteia* not unlike that of the Greater Mysteries described shortly thereafter at *Phaedrus* 251a–e.[39]

The Eleusinian Mysteries in the *Phaedrus*

It has long been recognized that the central myth of the *Phaedrus* found between 246a and 256e—the culmination of the struggle for "the perception of Being"—is depicted as "a religious procession which culminates in the ceremony of mystic initiation."[40] At 250b–c in particular Plato obliquely disparages the beautiful vision of the Eleusinian Mysteries as inferior to the variety accessible to the philosopher.[41] The passage begins by saying there are few individuals who are capable of envisioning, with their "feeble faculties," the original forms in their earthly "counterfeits" (250b). There was a time, however, prior to our descent into mortal form, that we were permitted to see beauty in its full radiance, some doing so in the company of Zeus, others in the company of other gods, "and were initiated into what is right to call most blessed of mysteries" (250c). Socrates recounts that, because these initiates are still whole and pure (*kathoroi*) and untouched by the evils that await us in mortal life, they are permitted, as part of their "final initiation," to gaze upon "complete and onefold and still and happy (*eudaimonia*)" apparitions, who are revealed to them (*epopeuontes*) "in pure light (*augai katharai*)" (250c).[42] These apparitions he speaks of are "*phasmata* (singular *phasma*) in apparent distinction to ordinary mental images, or *phantasmata* (singular *phatasma*)."[43] The entire passage, in other words, is "replete with terms that either directly or indirectly evoke the mysteries."[44] Plato uses the term for initiation, *telete*, and specifically uses the words for the two levels of Eleusinian initiation, *myesis* and *epopteia*. On top of which he mentions sublime apparitions even if he found them unsatisfactory, owing to their being insufficiently perfect, simple and still.[45]

Another reference to the moment when the initiate experienced the *epopteia* occurs at 251a–e, also during Socrates' second speech. The passage begins ". . . he who is newly initiated (*arititeles*), who at that time beheld many of these things, when he sees a god-like face or something which is a good image of beauty, first he shudders (*ephriksen*), and then something of the fear (*deimaton*) he experiences at that famous time (*tote*) comes over him, and then reverence as at the sight of a god" (251a).[46] Plato is "explicitly referring here to those who were newly initiated, the referent *tote* appears to be the time of initiation."[47] The passage continues:

> Next, with the passing of the shudder, a strange sweating and fever seizes him . . . [while his soul] throbs with ferment in every part [experiencing, like the pains of growth] ferment and a painful irritation . . . [but soon he] is filled with joy . . . [Though] the whole soul is round about stung and goaded into anguish . . . [it soon has] refreshment and respite from [these] stings and sufferings, and at that moment tastes a pleasure that is sweet beyond compare.[48]

Unlike the previous speeches which were characterized by clinical detachment, the second speech by Socrates enters into the subject matter, "capturing through imagery and emotive language the feeling of being in a state of *mania*."[49] This point or something like it is made frequently in the literature on Plato and is largely uncontroversial.[50] At the same time the literature on the *Phaedrus* typically claims that the soul's "receptivity and growth" rests on the use of "unmistakably sexual metaphors," but this sort of explanation too easily dismisses the botanic nature of much of ancient Greek religion.[51] This literature even ignores its own evidence, for example, that "plant imagery is used to characterize the receptivity and growth of the entire soul."[52]

A Case of Ergot Intoxication?

If on the one hand the *Phaedrus* "invokes both the mystery experience of feeling uncomfortable and perplexed as well as the later experiences of awe and reverence at the sight of the divine goddesses revealed to them at the high point of the Eleusinian Mysteries,"[53] and if on the other it is true that *Phaedrus* 251a–e has a double connotation, being an aggregate of both sexual excitement and plant growth, should we break off the discussion, proceed no further, and assert it would be a mistake "to look behind the imagery for a specific bodily state" that would encompass the somatic symptoms Plato describes?[54] Is there nothing the analyst may legitimately do other than "observe the fusion" of two sets of metaphors and "apprehend a development of ideas that obey no law but that of fantasy"?[55] Not only is it *not* a mistake to look for a specific bodily state within the passage, it is both *necessary* and *possible* to do so. Far from being tampering, an analysis of the imagery deployed by Plato is so crucial that without it a fully nuanced reading of the *Phaedrus* is simply impossible.

Plato's descriptive blend of divine inspiration and human infatuation draws *its* inspiration not from fantasy but from a pharmacologically induced bodily experience that occurred at the culmination of initiation into the religious mysteries of Eleusis.[56] This can be demonstrated in two ways. First, it is widely agreed the passage is expressed metaphorically from within the language of mystic initiation. The ocular description contained in *Phaedrus* 251a–e, including an awe (*deina*) inspiring encounter with a divine apparition, is consistent with many of the other veiled descriptions of the Eleusinian *epopteia* written centuries before and after the composition of the dialogue.[57] Second, initiates into the Mysteries, as we saw in chapter 4, above, culminated their experience by drinking the *kykeon*. Meaning "the mixture," the *kykeon* contained barley (*alphi*, or more fully *alphiton*), mint (*glechon/blechon*), and water (*hydron*). The *phasmata* that followed drinking the potion, the essence of the sublime *epopteia* hinted at by Plato and many other ancient writers, strongly suggest that some form of ergot, a potent ecstasy-inducing *pharmakon* found attached to various cereal grasses, was present in the *kykeon* as well.

The physiological discomfort described within Plato's passage—trembling or shuddering (*phrikes*), sweating (*idros*), stinging sensations, and ocular visions—bears a noticeable similarity to the symptoms of darnel intoxication. What medical literature calls *ergotismus convulsivus* is characterized by "nervous convulsions and epileptiform symptoms," as well as occasional delirium.[58] *Ergotismus convulsivus* "begins with pain and itching of the extremities . . . [and] may end in a psychosis."[59] The symptoms of darnel poisoning in man consist of "apathy, giddiness, or a feeling of intoxication, accompanied by ataxia, various abnormal sensations, mydriasis, nausea, vomition, gastric pain, and diarrhea."[60] Bread making in the pre-industrial era "paid little attention to the quality of the mixtures, into which entered grasses with stupefying seeds such as darnel" and this bread "besides disturbing the mind by making people act as if drunk, causes much weariness and nausea."[61] The effects of the contemporary drug LSD (*Lysergic acid diethylamide*), in addition to the to-be-expected visual disturbances, include "gastrointestinal upset, chills, hyperglycemia, hypertension, mydriasis, tachycardia and panic."[62] The mint in the *kykeon* may have helped alleviate the gastric discomfort an ergot-based *pharmakon* would have produced.[63]

The parallels with *Phaedrus* 251a–e are easy enough to discern. Medical descriptions, however, are modern clinical assessments based almost entirely on laboratory experience with the drug's pharmacology. They do not take into account the particular set of individual and cultural expectations an initiate into the Eleusinian Mysteries would have had, nor the unique ritual setting experienced by a drinker of the *kykeon*: thousands of fellow initiates crowded into a torch-lit temple; sonorous religious chanting; a gong being struck; an expectation of Persephone herself appearing along with the new-born Brimos; the promise—extraordinary in the context of the ancient Greco-Roman world's deep pessimism "regarding the fate of the individual after death"[64]—of securing life eternal on the Isles of the Blessed after their passing.[65] All these things would have shaped and influenced the *kykeon* drinker's drug-taking experience.[66]

There is additional evidence knowledge of ergot was widespread in the ancient world.[67] The Hippocratic works *Diseases of Women* and *Sterile Women* both mention a substance called *melanthion* (black flower). This substance, obtained from wheat and used for gynecological and obstetrical purposes, "cannot refer to an ordinary plant, but is more likely . . . the well known fungal parasite ergot, found on various grass-crops and cereals."[68] Psychotropic alkaloids of the genus *Claviceps* may be found on several plants, each of which was present in ancient Greece: barley, wheat, and darnel.[69] "The effects of darnel (the French *ivraie*, from the apparent etymology *ivre* or 'drunk'), blended in excessive quantities with grain, have been known since remote times."[70] Known to the Greeks as *aira*, darnel was also called *thyaros* (the plant of frenzy). Aristotle's *On Sleep* contains a list of plants called *hupnotika* (which produce a heaviness of the head) that mentions the poppy, mandragora, wine, and darnel (456b). Darnel's mind-altering effects are described or alluded to in many ancient sources including Theophrastus (*History of Plants* 8.8.3), Plautus (*Miles Gloriosus* 315–23), Ovid (*Fasti* 1.691) and Pliny (*Historia naturalis* 18.44).

Plato's Knowledge of Ergot

Many scholars have noted "the depiction of coming to know the form of the good in [Book VII of Plato's] *Republic*—ascending out of a cave, moving from darkness into bright light—also includes many elements of the *epopteia* of the Eleusinian Mysteries."[71] Less recognized is a discussion in *Republic* Book X. Between the famous discussion of poetry and the Eleusis-influenced myth of Er that concludes the dialogue, Plato provides a definition of the good and the bad that includes among the latter "blight for grain" which like "rot for wood" or "rust for iron and bronze" attaches itself to the good like "an evil and an illness" (608d–609a). Barley, the Eleusinian grain, was believed to be particularly susceptible to *erysibe*, "rust," and Demeter, the "Barley Mother" of Eleusis, could be referred to as Erysibe (Demeter the Blaster), "as though her gift of grain could exist only through the aversion of the darker persona that was her own and its antithesis."[72] This passage of the *Republic* also compares favorably with the Roman poet Ovid (43 BCE–17 CE), who wrote "Rust, grip not the tender crops but rather grip the hard iron. Forestall the destroyer. Better that you should gnaw at swords and baneful weapons" (*Fasti, Verses* 4.901).[73] In Latin *robigo* means "rust, blight, blast" and Robigus was the god who warded off grain mildew; the festival called the Robigalia was named for her/him.[74]

Plato continues the same passage writing that "just as the badness of a body, which is a disease, melts and destroys a body and brings it to the point where it is not even a body" so the soul can be corrupted and reduced to a condition of vice. Vice, like the "rust" found to be infesting grain, would dissolve and destroy the soul to the point where it is not even a soul, or at least not a human soul. The destruction Plato speaks of in this passage of the *Republic* is not total, a complete annihilation. It is rather a transformation, or more accurately a reversion. Vice, as an alien presence, diseased and corrupting, threatens to revert the subjective to the pre-subjective, the civilized to the pre-civilized (610b). On an

[margin handwritten note:] Plato's cave linked to Mysteries

agricultural level the wild *aira*, the "plant of frenzy," was similarly viewed as an atavistic reversion constantly threatening Attica's cultivated barley. Theophrastus, for example, mentions *aira* as a weed found among food grains in his *History of Plants* (1.5.2).[75] The *Republic*'s association of grain rust with external physical deterioration, which in turn is likened to an internal obliteration of the sober soul, may be seen as harnessing knowledge of the effects of ergot in a metaphorical manner to suit the needs of a philosophical argument.[76]

Preparing the *Kykeon*

That ancient Greece had knowledge of ergot is one thing. Transforming it into a *pharmakon* used annually for centuries by countless initiates in a religious ritual is another. The procedure known to the hierophantic priests at Eleusis would have had to have been *simple* and yet *easy to reproduce* year after year, using *available methods*, and yet their recipe for preparing the *kykeon*, or some key portion of it, must have been just as easily *kept a secret*. The last matter, secrecy, is perhaps the most straightforward to account for: "the easily dried sclerotia of ergot *are* quite capable of being stored, retaining their alkaloids for considerable periods, and certainly *could* have been stored for at least a year without preservatives, in containers of minimal size easily secreted in the confines of the temple. Thus stored ergot might have augmented supplies in lean years."[77]

The first hypothesis about the use of ergot in the preparation of the *kykeon* argued that psychoactive lysergic acid alkaloids such as ergonovine[78] could have been separated from the poisonous ergopeptine alkaloids[79] by soaking the ergot-infected grain in water, as the former are water-soluble while the latter are not.[80] The limited attempts at testing the hypothesis have been disappointing; *Claviceps purpurea* produces at best modest psychoactive effects while at the same time producing "significant discomfort, cramping, and lassitude."[81] More recent research has suggested "the Greek priests must have discovered some way to *transform* naturally-occurring supplies of *C. purpurea*: they must have found a technologically simple process to alter the alkaloidal spectrum of ergot."[82] If ergot, wood ash (pearlash), or the ash of some other plant such as barley, and water are heated for several hours, the resulting partial hydrolysis would convert the toxic ergopeptine alkaloids into psychoactive ergine and isoergine.[83] The resulting liquid would be filtered and then either exposed to the air for a few days, transforming the unpalatable potassium carbonate into potassium bicarbonate, or wine or vinegar added (a "mixture" in the manner of other *kykeon* recipes) to neutralize the ashes. While the ergine and isoergine compounds are about 1/10 the potency of LSD (and closely resemble the Aztec *ololiuqui*), the dosage needed to produce mind-altering effects is still incredibly small: 1 to 5 mg. The amount needed "to provide happy visions for all"[84] has thus been estimated at "5gm total alkaloids, corresponding to 0.5 kg of ergot" per 1,000 initiates.[85] "Modern yields of ergot from cultivation on rye can yield hundreds of kilograms per hectare. Thus it seems reasonable that the Greek priests could easily have harvested enough ergot from the nearby barley fields. Ripe ergots can easily be collected from the grain in the field, as they fall off the grain head even with strong wind."[86]

Philosophy as Supplementation

It has been suggested by more than one interpreter that Plato's discussion of passion in the *Phaedrus* arose out of a particular personal experience. The dialogue, written around 365 BCE, "has the character of a love letter, an expression of passion, wonder, and gratitude," with Socrates and Phaedrus acting as stand-ins for the actual relationship between Plato and Dion of Syracuse.[87] The *Phaedrus*, in this reading, has largely been distilled down to a "moving and extraordinary description of passionate love," wherein the mental aspiration of the philosopher has "an internal structure closely akin to that of the lover's sexual yearnings and fulfillments."[88] Unfortunately what these sorts of analyses are capturing are Plato's literary talents. The surface of the text has mesmerized modern readership to the extent that a number of battles with philosophy's competitors—won through the superimposition of philosophy's metaphysical *epopteia* on top of the original, drug-induced Eleusinian *epopteia*—are being waged in a labyrinth of subterranean caverns. What we find in the philosophical works beginning with Plato is the imagination of the philosopher setting a new, "higher *visio beatifica* above the Eleusinian vision, building on this religious experience, known to almost every Athenian, as on an existing, self-evident foundation," in a manner that simultaneously attests to the existence of various sorts of ecstatic visions, acknowledges their potency, and disparages them as being events of lesser luminescence, lesser perfection.[89]

What Plato may have meant or intended to say is often of secondary importance to what he might have said, but did not, or was even compelled to say "by those constraints which mythical discourse still imposed, even when [such] myths were taken as incredible and their messages censored."[90] One has only to look with a sufficient degree of patience to see, in its use of the language of ecstatic religion, that the *Phaedrus* "functions against its own metaphysical assertions, not just by creating ambiguity, but by inscribing a systematic 'other message' behind or through what is being said."[91] It is remarkable how often visual *phasmata* are referred to in ancient Greek writings and how little serious attention they receive, either being missed, ignored, or misinterpreted, equated with the modern sense of the "illusionary" with its connotations of deceptive falsehood. For Plato, however, the *epopteia* would have clearly been a rival means for accessing *truth*.

In one of Plato's last dialogues, the *Statesman*, the religious terminology has all but fallen away but the message is largely the same as we find in the *Phaedrus* 246a–256e. Plato emphasizes that "the supreme things of all, the things of highest worth," cannot be demonstrated via "sensible analogies"; they exist only in our minds, and cannot be "fitted to a sense imprint in a way to give true satisfaction" (285e–286a). These "incorporeal realities," the "fairest and highest of all realities," according to Plato, "can be certainly displayed by discourse and in no other way" (286a).[92] Thus, to understand them each of us must acquire "the power to give and receive argument on all subjects" (286a). The power Plato refers to here is that of "dialectical proficiency and capacity for reasoned presentation of truth" (287a). Although problematic from the perspective of philosophy, there would seem to have been óther, often non-discursive, ways of beholding celestial truths in ancient Greece, and one of these was probably a *pharmakon*-induced moment of religious ecstasy, the Eleusinian *epopteia.*

The *Phaedrus* adapts from *religious* tradition and utilizes a *religious* vocabulary to depict, in a phenomenological fashion, the nature of philosophical inquiry.[93] Into this decanter of religious terms "which are especially reminiscent of Eleusis," it might be said, Plato "pours the wine of philosophy."[94] But this is to state the situation backwards. It is into his vision of philosophy that Plato injects the symptomatology of Greek religious ecstasy, the experience of the most sacred *pharmakon* of mystic religion, the Eleusinian *kykeon*. Few authors write from one source of motivation, least of all one as complexly intolerant as Plato. Socrates and Phaedrus may well be, on a superficial level, stand-ins for Plato and Dion of Syracuse. But Plato's appropriation of religious dialogue, particularly religious dialogue from rites and cults that so highly valued plants and their *pharmaka*, cannot be glossed over in the name of the interpreter's suppositions. The purpose of Plato's *Phaedrus* is to give the Eleusinian *epopteia* a *khairein* which means, all at once, a send-off, salute, vacation, and dismissal, burying a drug-induced religious epiphany in an outpouring of paroxysmic supplementation. Most of the current literature completely misses the burial and spends its time in seemingly endless musings over the outpouring.

Was Plato himself initiated into the Eleusinian Mysteries? Did he himself drink the *kykeon*? We cannot entirely rule the possibility out; experiencing the mysteries was the most important religious experience of anyone who could speak Greek and lived in the Mediterranean world for close to a thousand years. What we do know is that Plato's Socrates "develops a rational revision of ecstatic ritual based on the conviction that human beings can attain divine status. Such a development has both religious and political dimensions, and it is radical, indeed revolutionary in both regards."[95] Given that he largely opposed religious revelation as, in the last analysis, inferior to philosophic introspection and discourse, I would think it plausible to venture that what we find in the *Phaedrus* is a complex and loosely drawn composite, reflecting testimony Plato might well have surreptitiously received from initiates and his own experiences—direct or indirect—with the drug-infused wines that were common in the ancient world.[96] In the *Laws* the nameless Athenian (Plato?) claims to have a sound knowledge of sympotic custom, based in part on *direct experience* (639d). In the alchemy of his imagination, religious and other forms of ecstatic dissolution, such as the deliberate fracturing of the identity that went on within the *symposion*, were absorbed and neutralized within the rational formula of philosophy.

Even a conclusion as cautious as this, however, requires us to look at the *Pheadrus* and many of Plato's other dialogues from a virtually new perspective. The initiates at Eleusis witnessed the *phasma* of Persephone. Plato's use of a term like *phasmata* "suggests that he regarded the preexistence of the soul as a prenatal initiation into theophanic mystery that the philosopher must spend his earthly days attempting to recollect and comprehend."[97] In contrast to other, more hostile dialogues, the *Phaedrus* is, arguably, a sophisticated qualification of Plato's position vis-á-vis states of psychological *mania*, the drug-induced vision of the Eleusinian Mysteries, the *epopteia*, in particular. But a qualification is all it would be. Like the *Symposium*, the *Phaedrus* is another manifestation of Plato's "contribution to the religious conception of philosophic inquiry as ecstatic rite."[98] The ecstatic can be added to philosophy, as a supplement, but in the act of so doing it is replaced by the philosophic. Philosophy's opposition to the *pharmaka* of its many competitors is consistent, never recanted or retracted, for the simple reason that to do so would undermine, if not call into doubt entirely, the use of philosophy itself.

Notes

1. An early version of this chapter appeared as Michael A. Rinella, "Supplementing the Ecstatic: Plato, the Eleusinian Mysteries, and the *Phaedrus*," *Polis—Journal of the Society of Greek Political Thought* 17, no. 1&2 (2000): 61–78.

2. The line reads "You seem to have discovered a *pharmakon* for getting me out [of the city]." Translating *pharmakon* as "prescription" in this context is misleading; the speech Phaedrus carries may be made of paper like a physician's note one brings to a contemporary pharmacist but Socrates is essentially saying that he's already taken the drug (or been charmed by the talisman) and is feeling its effects. See for example William S. Cobb, trans., *The Symposium and Phaedrus—Plato's Erotic Dialogues* (Albany, NY: State University of New York Press, 1993).

3. See my discussion of Greek magic in chapter 8, below. For now, it is merely worth noting that the same ingredients used to create ink might also be used in incense or spell components. An interesting discussion of these inks and incenses may be found in Flint Dibble, *Magic, Drugs, and Magic Drugs* (Senior Thesis, University of Pennsylvania, 2004), 15–20. On the materials used in the composition of magical amulets, talismans, and the like, see chapter 10, below.

4. As already mentioned in chapter 2, above, the literal meaning of the noun *sophrosyne* was "to keep the mind safe."

5. Arne Melberg, *Theories of Mimesis* (New York: Cambridge University Press, 1995), 33–34 writes that Socrates' first speech is delivered in a manner "that imitates a sophistic *mania* to promote an idea that he does not believe in. . . . Moreover the *mania* . . . is apparently a *pharmakon* that, correctly used, leads us to the loftiest truths, but in a bad dosage leads to reprehensible wrong. Socrates' first speech is such a wrong: he is imitating a sophistic and therefore (in Platonic logic) reprehensible argument."

6. Matthew Dillon, *Girls and Women in Greek Religion* (New York: Routledge, 2003), 180.

7. Martha C. Nussbaum, *The Fragility of Goodness—Luck and Ethics in Greek Tragedy and Philosophy* (New York: Cambridge University Press, 1986), 204.

8. Nussbaum argues that this is the exact position the intoxicated Alcibiades takes contra Socrates' Diotima in the *Symposium*. See Nussbaum, *The Fragility of Goodness*, 165–99.

9. Nussbaum, *The Fragility of Goodness*, 211.

10. The implication here is that *mania* could occur in ways less than divine; who Plato might accuse of doing so is left largely unspecified in the *Phaedrus*.

11. Patricia B. Phillippy, *Love's Remedy: Recantation and Renaissance Lyric Poetry* (London and Toronto: Associated University Press, 1995), 51.

12. Walter Burkert, *Greek Religion: Archaic and Classical* (Malden, MA: Blackwell Publishing, 1985), 111 lists Plato as distinguishing "the prophetic madness of Apollo from the telestic madness of Dionysus, before adding, as other types of madness, the poetic and the erotic or philosophical enthusiasm."

13. Walter Burkert, *The Orientalizing Revolution—Near Eastern Influences on Greek Culture in the Early Archaic Age* (Cambridge, MA: Harvard University Press, 1992), 79. Burkert has generally dismissed any and all discussion of ecstasy manifesting itself along pharmacological lines in the ancient world as a "rationalizing hypothesis" derived from "chemistry." Quoted in Burkert, *The Orientalizing Revolution*, 62, 67. In the case of the Delphic Pythia he writes that "a medium does not need chemistry" or in other words some sort of *pharmakon*. Quoted in Burkert, *The Orientalizing Revolution*, 80. While this may be true in *some* cases of ancient prophecy, the observation is misleading because it certainly does not apply to *all* cases, or even *most* cases, perhaps not even the Delphic Pythia. Burkert is, ironically, guilty of the very "modern prejudice" (i.e. presentism) he chastises others for in the very same work. See, for example Burkert, *The Orientalizing Revolution*, 41. None the less Hugh Bowden writes that the "idea of chemical intoxication [at Delphi] will not go away." See Hugh Bowden, *Classical Athens and the Delphic Oracle: Divination and Democracy* (Cambridge: Cambridge University Press, 2005), 19. See also William J. Broad, *The Oracle: Ancient Delphi and the Science Behind Its Lost Secrets* (New York: Penguin Books, 2007). Both Bowden and Broad should be consulted as an antidote to Burkert here.

14. Whereas Hamilton's translation of the *Phaedrus* translates this passage as "rites of purification and initiation," Rowe translates the same passage as "secret rites of purification." See Walter Hamilton, trans., *Plato—Phaedrus and Seventh and Eighth Letters* (New York: Penguin Books, 1973) and C. J. Rowe, trans., *Plato: Phaedrus* (Wiltshire, UK: Arts and Phillips, 1986). Most mystery religions have secrets, of course, so the passage may or may not be a reference to the Eleusinian Mysteries. It is also important to realize that just as there numerous anachronisms in Plato's dialogues so one finds a great deal of overlap, even within a single work, of Dionysiac, Eleusinian, Orphic and Corybantic practices, among others. On this overlap see Michael L. Morgan, *Platonic Piety: Philosophy and Ritual in Fourth Century Athens* (New Haven, CT: Yale University Press, 1990), 39, 63–64 and Daniel Mendelsohn, "ΣΥΓΚΕΡΑΥΝΟΩ: Dithyrambic Language and Dionysiac Cult," *The Classical Journal* 87, no. 2 (1992): 110. What these four cults have in common is that they provide their believers, to a greater or lesser degree, with the experience of *ekstasis*. I have concentrated on Dionysus and Eleusis in this work due to the evidence that ecstasy was attained by pharmacological means in those sects; the frenzy induced by certain forms of music and dance, for example, has elicited and continues to elicit moral/ethical commentary, and is deserving of separate study. A dis-

cussion of Plato and Corybantic cult, which utilized the frenzy of dance, may be found in Ivan M. Linforth, "The Corybantic Rites in Plato." *The University of California Publications in Classical Philology* 13, no. 5 (1946): 163-72.

15. Burkert, *The Orientalizing Revolution*, 66, and cf. Plato's *Laws* (854b).

16. Matthew W. Dickie, *Magic and Magicians in the Greco-Roman World* (New York: Routledge, 2003), 73. See Euripides' *Bacchae* (233–38), where "Pentheus' decrying the god Dionysus as a foreigner from Lydia and a *goes epodos* who conducts ceremonies of initiation" suggests as much.

17. Nussbaum, *The Fragility of Goodness*, 213.

18. Including instances where the condition is brought on by the intoxication of wine or by some other *pharmakon*.

19. Martha C. Nussbaum, *Love's Knowledge: Essays on Philosophy and Literature* (New York: Oxford University Press, 1990), 107.

20. Nussbaum, *The Fragility of Goodness*, 212.

21. Nussbaum, *The Fragility of Goodness*, 221–22. While an interpretation of the *Phaedrus* along these lines would appear to be essentially accurate, it is all the same rather curious that Plato's second form of divine madness disappears from Nussbaum's discussion. Recapping his argument at 265b Plato is quite explicit, distinguishing between "four kinds of divine madness" and ascribing them to four divinities. The inspiration of the prophet is ascribed to Apollo, the inspiration of the mystic is ascribed to Dionysus, the inspiration of the poet is ascribed to the Muses, and the inspiration of *eros* is ascribed to Aphrodite and Love. Dionysus simply evaporates from Nussbaum's discussion.

22. Nussbaum, *The Fragility of Goodness*, 204; see also 470 n. 4.

23. Jacques Derrida, *Dissemination* (Chicago: University of Chicago Press, 1981), 69.

24. Carl Kerényi, *Eleusis—Archetypal Image of Mother and Daughter* (New York: Pantheon Books, 1967), 45, and Anne Mary Farrell, *Plato's Use of Eleusinian Mystery Motifs* (Ph.D. diss., University of Texas at Austin, 1999), 83–84.

25. Also spelled Agra.

26. Erika Simon, *Festivals of Attika: An Archeological Commentary* (Madison, WI: The University of Wisconsin Press, 1983), 27 writes that the "rites of Agrai were . . . clearly prerequisites for the Eleusinian Mysteries."

27. Kerényi, *Eleusis*, 49.

28. Simon, *Festivals of Attika*, 92–93.

29. Mary Settgast, *Plato—Prehistorian. 10,000 to 5,000 B.C. in Myth and Archeology* (Cambridge, MA: Rotenberg Press, 1986), 88. On the pre-Greek origins of Demeter and Persephone see Raimo Anttila, *Greek and Indo-European Etymology in Action: Proto-Indo-European *ag-* (Philadelphia, PA: John Benjamins, 2000), 164–66.

30. Settgast, *Plato—Prehistorian*, 172. The possible use of drugs in the worship of Dionysus and at the Eleusinian Mysteries is discussed in chapter 4, above.

31. Kerényi, *Eleusis*, 46. According to Kerényi, "*Myesis* can be rendered by the Latin word *initia*, 'beginnings,' or its derivative *initiatio*, or initiation, signifying introduction into the secret. For *myesis* comes from the verb (*myeo*) which denotes the action. The simpler verb *myo*, from which the noun derives, implies the element of the secrecy. It means nothing other than 'to close,' as the eyes do after seeing. The self-evident first object of this verb is the subject itself; he closes himself after the manner of a flower. But a second object is possible, which must be very close to the subject, to his very own possession. Such an object is the secret . . . *The* Mysteries, those that imparted the greatest

secret, were those of Eleusis . . . The *mystai*, 'initiates,' came in ritual procession to this festival of 'vision,' at which the *epopteia*, the state of 'having seen,' was attained."

32. "The wind is traditionally an abductor to the otherworld, for the metaphor 'inspiration,' which in Latin literally implies 'blowing upon' (*inspirare*), existed also in Greek as *empnein*." Carl A. P. Ruck, "The Offerings of the Hyperboreans," in *Persephone's Quest: Entheogens and the Origins of Religion*, ed. R. Gordon Wasson (New Haven, CT: Yale University Press, 1986), 229. Hesiod's *Theogny* speaks of the muses having "breathed song into" him (31).

33. Carl A. P. Ruck, "The Wild and the Cultivated: Wine in Euripides Bacchae," in *Persephone's Quest: Entheogens and the Origins of Religion*, ed. R. Gordon Wasson (New Haven, CT: Yale University Press, 1986), 184. See also Ruck, "The Offerings of the Hyperboreans," 230.

34. Robin Waterfield, trans., *Plato—Republic* (New York: Oxford University Press, 1993). Many writers indicate that Plato is describing doctrines of the Orphic Mysteries in this passage, for example Oswyn Murray, "Forms of Sociality," in *The Greeks*, ed. Jean-Pierre Vernant (Chicago: University of Chicago Press, 1995), 240. The passage appears to mix both traditions, as Murray implicitly concedes on the following page, writing that the primary motivation for being initiated into the *Eleusinian* Mysteries was that "it provided a guarantee of sympotic life after death."

35. W. R. M. Lamb, trans. *Lysias* (Cambridge, MA: Harvard University Press, 1943), 425.

36. In an easily missed footnote Nussbaum, *The Fragility of Goodness*, 427 n. 23 observes that "the myrrh tree (Greek *murrhis*) . . . has ritual associations in Attic culture as an aphrodisiac." This briefest of references to ancient *pharmaka* is a container that, once opened, makes a singularly "erotic" reading such as Nussbaum's unsustainable. Perhaps unsurprisingly the subject of drugs never reappears in her interpretation of the dialogue.

37. Aristotle's *On Drunkenness*, quoted in Atheneaus (11.464c–d), and Dioscorides *On Medical Matters* (1.77) both mention myrrh's addition to wine. As we saw in chapter 1, above, it was common practice in the ancient world to suffuse wine with alcohol-soluble herbs, spices and unguents.

38. Nussbaum, *The Fragility of Goodness*, 211. For additional details regarding Stesichorus see G. O. Hutchinson, *Greek Lyric Poetry: A Commentary on Select Larger Pieces* (New York: Oxford University Press, 2001).

39. Phillippy recognizes that the presence of the *pharmakon* in the *Phaedrus* runs even more deeply than Derrida suspected but *Love's Remedy* makes no connection with Eleusis and the generally religious language present in the dialogue.

40. Anne Lebeck, "The Central Myth of Plato's *Phaedrus*," *Greek, Roman, and Byzantine Studies* 13, no. 3 (1972): 271.

41. Kerényi, *Eleusis*, 95–99.

42. Adapted from Farrell, *Plato's Use of Eleusinian Mystery Motifs*, 36–37.

43. Christopher Collins, *Reading the Written Image: Verbal Play, Interpretation, and the Roots of Iconophobia* (University Park, PA: Penn State Press, 2008), 30.

44. Lebeck, "The Central Myth of Plato's *Phaedrus*," 271.

45. Kerényi, *Eleusis*, 98–99.

46. Translation in Farrell, *Plato's Use of Eleusinian Mystery Motifs*, 75.

47. Farrell, *Plato's Use of Eleusinian Mystery Motifs*, 76.

48. Translation in R. Hackforth, *Phaedrus: Introduction, Translation and Commentary* (New York: Cambridge University Press, 1952).

49. Nussbaum, *The Fragility of Goodness*, 215.

[handwritten margin note: link between sexual eros and spiritual/mystical]

50. Nussbaum, *The Fragility of Goodness*, 214 argues that Plato is "clearly claiming that certain sorts of essential and high insights come to us only through the *guidance* of the passions. Socrates' story of the growth of the soul's wings shows us what lies behind this claim." Similarly Charles Griswold, *Self-knowledge in Plato's* Phaedrus (New Haven, CT: Yale University Press, 1986), 123–24 states that the passage is a "phenomenology of love—or, perhaps ... of the experience of falling in love," a juxtaposition of "someone whose memory of Beauty is still fresh and someone whose memory is dim."

51. Nussbaum, *The Fragility of Goodness*, 217. While conceding the metaphors of the passage are "startling" and "complex," Griswold, *Self-knowledge in Plato's* Phaedrus, 121 interprets the passage in a near identical manner, writing "instead of explaining the desire for philosophy as a modification of sexual desire, Socrates explains sexual desire as a low manifestation of the desire for wisdom." Farrell, *Plato's Use of Eleusinian Mystery Motifs*, 74–75 discusses the passage with better emphasis on initiation into the Mysteries but retains the same view: "Plato draws a parallel between the experiences of the lover and the experiences of the initiate in the *Phaedrus*. Seeing a beautiful boy both stimulates desire for the boy and sets one on the path to recollecting beauty itself."

52. Nussbaum, *The Fragility of Goodness*, 216. Nussbaum's position begs the question: if the ancient Greeks were so preoccupied with *sex*, why the emphasis on *plant* imagery?

53. Farrell, *Plato's Use of Eleusinian Mystery Motifs*, 96.

54. Lebeck, "The Central Myth of Plato's *Phaedrus*," 272–73.

55. Lebeck, "The Central Myth of Plato's *Phaedrus*," 273–74.

56. Additional details may be found in chapter 4, above.

57. See Michael A. Rinella, *Plato, Ecstasy, and Identity* (Ph.D. diss., State University of New York at Albany, 1997), 420–30.

58. R. Gordon Wasson, Albert Hofmann, and Carl A. P. Ruck, *The Road to Eleusis: Unveiling the Secrets of the Mysteries* [Twentieth Anniversary Edition] (Los Angeles: William Dailey Rare Books, 1998), 36, 42–44. See also 93–94.

59. Erwin H. Ackerknecht, *History and Geography of the Most Important Diseases* (New York: Hafner Publishing Company, 1965), 139.

60. John M. Kingsbury, *Poisonous Plants of the United States and Canada* (Englewood Cliffs, NJ: Prentice Hall, 1964), 485–86.

61. Piero Camporesi, *Bread of Dreams—Food and Fantasy in Early Modern Europe* (Chicago: University of Chicago Press, 1989), 121. Kingsbury indicates that as little as one ounce of darnel seed can produce symptoms in man and animals. In addition, toxicity is not confined to the seeds, as analysis has indicated *Claviceps purpurea* in darnel flour. Since cakes were ritually passed and eaten at Eleusis, it is possible they too might have been partially responsible for the *phasmata* experienced by initiates.

62. Paul L. Schiff, "Ergot and its Alkaloids," *American Journal of Pharmaceutical Education* 70, no. 5 (2006): 98.

63. Peter Webster, "Mixing the *Kykeon*," *Eleusis: Journal of Psychoactive Plants and Compounds* 4 (2000): 4 writes "mint is a known remedy for the slight nausea often accompanied with various lysergic acid compounds including the psychedelic ones as well as erotamine taken as a remedy for migraine." See also Carl A. P. Ruck, "Mixing the Kykeon—Part 3," *Eleusis: Journal of Psychoactive Plants and Compounds* 4 (2000): 22–23.

64. Daniel Perrine, "Mixing the *Kykeon*—Part 2," *Eleusis: Journal of Psychoactive Plants and Compounds* 4 (2000): 13.

65. Kerényi, *Eleusis*, 16.

66. Perrine, "Mixing the *Kykeon*—Part 2," 13 writes that "it is clear that when an appropriately intense set and setting are present, nearly every participant who receives [a sacramental drug] experiences an unforgettably transformative theophany."

67. Schiff, "Ergot and its Alkaloids," 98 writes "the earliest authenticated reports of the effects of ergot occurred in Chinese writings in approximately 1100 BC, when the substance was used in obstetrics. A magic spell found in a small temple in Mesopotamia dating to 1900–1700 BC referred to abnormally infested grain as *mehru*, while Sumerian clay tablets of the same period described the reddening of damp grain as *samona*. The Assyrians of this era were sufficiently knowledgeable to differentiate between different diseases affecting grain and by 600 BC writings on an Assyrian tablet alluded to a 'noxious pustule in the ear of grain.' References to grain diseases have also been found in various books of the Bible in the Old Testament (850–550 BC). In 550 BC the Hearst Papyrus of Egypt described a particular preparation in which a mixture of ergot, oil, and honey was recommended as a treatment for hair growth. . . . Around 350 BC the Parsi wrote of 'noxious grasses that cause pregnant women to drop the womb and die in childbed,' while in 322 BC Aristotle postulated that grain rust was caused by warm vapors. Around 286 BC the Greeks concluded that barley was more susceptible than wheat to rust infections, and that windy fields had less rust than damp, shady low-lying ones."

68. E. D. Phillips, *Greek Medicine* (London: Thames and Hudson, 1973), 112, 214–15. Hippocrates noted its use in halting postpartum hemorrhage. The use of ergot by midwives is mentioned in the writings of the German physician Adam Lonitzer in 1582, and by early nineteenth century American physicians John Stearns and David Hosack; the latter specifically recommending that it not be used for accelerating childbirth and only to control postpartum hemorrhage. See Carl A. P. Ruck, *Sacred Mushrooms of the Goddess and the Secrets of Eleusis*, 154.

69. There was also a belief that another species of ergot, *Claviceps paspali*, which grows on the wild grasses such as *Paspalum distichum*, might have been present in ancient Greece but this has recently been the subject of some doubt. See Webster, "Mixing the *Kykeon*," 8 n. 3.

70. Camporesi, *Bread of Dreams*, 123. See also 121–22.

71. Farrell, *Plato's Use of Eleusinian Mystery Motifs*, 120–21.

72. Wasson et al., *The Road to Eleusis*, 126. See also Anttila, *Greek and Indo-European Etymology in Action*, 107, who mentions similar epithets for Apollo the Blighter and Zeus the Blighter.

73. Quoted in Ruck, *Sacred Mushrooms of the Goddess*, 152.

74. Anttila, *Greek and Indo-European Etymology in Action*, 106–7. The term *contere* was used for the process of rusting, and referred to the slow continual action by which rust wears away and consumes the substance of iron.

75. Peter Garnsey, *Food and Society in Classical Antiquity* (Cambridge: Cambridge University Press, 1999), 39 indicates that Galen's *On the Property of Foodstuffs* expresses an interest in darnel. Galen noted these weeds "induced headaches, ulcers and other skin diseases," but he "missed or passed over their 'stupefying' effects." Garnsey lumps Galen with Theophrastus, Ovid and Pliny to argue the latter were equally unaware of ergot intoxication but the evidence presented here and in chapter 4, above, suggests otherwise.

76. "It should be remembered that the appearance of ergot on its host has all through history led to the conclusion that ergot was merely malformed or sun-burned or 'rusted' grains of the cereal host in question. It wasn't until the 20th Century that ergot was generally recognized as another species altogether, a fungal parasite of the grain on which it

appeared. Thus the Greeks very probably also made this error." See Webster, "Mixing the *Kykeon*," 7 n. 2.

77. Webster, "Mixing the *Kykeon*," 6.

78. Also known as ergometrine or ergobasine. Like many natural drugs it has a chemical structure similar to, but less potent than, a man-made synthetic substance like LSD.

79. Such as ergotamine and ergotoxine. These are abortifacient and dangerously vasoconstrictive.

80. Wasson et al., *The Road to Eleusis*, 42–43, 63. Cf. Anthony Preus, "Drugs and Psychic States in Theophrastus' *Historia plantarum* 9.8–20," in *Theophrastean Studies*, ed. William W. Fortenbaugh and Robert W. Sharples (New Brunswick, NJ: Transaction Books, 1988), 83 and Terrence McKenna, *Food of the Gods: The Search for the Original Tree of Knowledge* (New York: Bantam Books, 1992), 134–136. The arguments within *The Road to Eleusis* were simply too extraordinary at the time of their initial publication and the work was almost entirely ignored. Where classicists and political philosophers are even aware of the work today, it is almost entirely secondhand, from sources hostile to the original publication (see note 84, below, for example). Shortly before his death in 1986, Wasson noted *The Road to Eleusis* had had such a minimal impact that he was forced to conclude the "Greek departments both in American and British Universities seemed intellectually inert." Quote in R. Gordon Wasson, *Persephone's Quest: Entheogens and the Origin of Religion* (New Haven, CT: Yale University Press, 1986), 28.

81. Webster, "Mixing the *Kykeon*," 3–4.

82. Webster, "Mixing the *Kykeon*," 6, emphasis in the original.

83. The technical details may be found in Perrine, "Mixing the *Kykeon*—Part 2." Perrine, "Mixing the *Kykeon*—Part 2," 13 notes that in 1932 "ergine, not lysergic acid, was in fact the first characteristic ergot compound to be isolated in pure form."

84. Walter Burkert, *Ancient Mystery Cults* (Cambridge, MA: Harvard University Press, 1987), 108 was being entirely rhetorical when he penned this line. His works consistently refused to address the topic of drugs and antiquity, particularly drugs at Eleusis, seriously. In another work, *Homo Necans*, he dismisses Kerényi's hypothesis that "the *kykeon* might have been a hallucinogen" with the unelaborated comment that the latter's argument "is a dubious borrowing from chemistry." See Walter Burkert, *Homo Necans—The Anthropology of Ancient Greek Sacrificial Ritual and Myth* (Berkeley, CA: University of California Press, 1983), 287. In *Ancient Mystery Cults* he dismisses the ergot hypothesis of Wasson et al. in *The Road to Eleusis* without the benefit of a single page reference, and makes several errors about ancient pharmacology in the space of just two pages. See Burkert, *Ancient Mystery Cults*, 108–109. Rebuttals of the objections made by Burkert may be found in David Fideler, *Alexandria 2: The Journal of Western Cosmological Traditions* (Grand Rapids, MI: Phanes Press, 1993), 80–94 and Charles Stein, *Persephone Unveiled: Seeing the Goddess and Freeing Your Soul* (Berkeley, CA: North Atlantic Books, 2006), 112–118.

85. Webster, "Mixing the *Kykeon*," 8 n. 4.

86. Webster, "Mixing the *Kykeon*," 8 n. 4. Ustinova, relying more on Burkert's hostile polemic rather than the actual text of *The Road to Eleusis*, fails to recognize this, writing "the question remains where the quantities of ergot-infested grain . . . necessary for thousands of initiates, was procured." See Yulia Ustinova, *Caves and the Ancient Greek Mind: Descending Underground in the Search for Ultimate Truth* (New York: Oxford University Press, 2009), 233 n. 73.

87. Nussbaum, *The Fragility of Goodness*, 229–30.

88. Nussbaum, *The Fragility of Goodness*, 215–17. Similar arguments may be found in Cobb, *The Symposium and Phaedrus.*

89. Kerényi, *Eleusis*, 98–99.

90. Adi Ophir, *Plato's Invisible Cities: Discourse and Power in the* Republic (New York: Routledge, 1991), 169–70. While I am in agreement with this observation, Ophir's text says nothing about what impact the initiations at Eleusis may have had on Plato's writings, yet Eleusis may well be *the* mythical discourse overshadowing, at the very least, the middle dialogues.

91. Derrida, *Dissemination*, xiii.

92. See chapter 9, below.

93. Morgan, *Platonic Piety*, 162.

94. Morgan, *Platonic Piety*, 172.

95. Morgan, *Platonic Piety*, 30.

96. The pharmacology of ancient wines is discussed in chapter 1, above.

97. Collins, *Reading the Written Image*, 30.

98. Morgan, *Platonic Piety*, 80. Morgan concludes, correctly I believe, that in the *Symposium* Plato does more than merely utilize words and images drawn from the Eleusinian Mysteries: "he replaces the mysteries with philosophic inquiry." Eleusis "represents the capacity of the polis tradition and Delphic theology to co-opt its ecstatic opponents" within an "institutionalized" framework of worship. "Philosophy, *the new Eleusis*, is the Platonic restatement of that opposition and thereby a Platonic response to the Athenian tradition." Quoted in Morgan, *Platonic Piety*, 99, emphasis mine. What Morgan does not recognize, however, is that as philosophy replaces Eleusis, the *pharmakon* of Eleusis is also replaced by the *pharmakon* of philosophy.

→ individual experience elevated beyond polis' institutionalized experiences

Part Three

Plato through the Prism of the *Pharmakon*

Chapter Seven

Medicine, Drugs, and Somatic Regimen

If, as we have seen, intoxication-as-ecstasy was a domain of action that Plato was attempting to cordon off as questionable, what sort of diverse solutions did he propose to deal with it? Plato mixes together two different responses, one primarily ethical, albeit with implications for politics, and one primarily political, albeit with implications for ethics. Chapter 7, chapter 8, and chapter 9 will concern themselves with the elements of the first remedy, while chapter 10 will be addressed to the elements of the second. What was at stake, particularly after the trial of Socrates with the suspicion that he, too, profaned the sacred Eleusinian Mysteries and thereby expressed contempt for the *demos*, was the potential authority of philosophy, as Plato conceived it, to speak to politics. This authority was in a number of crucial respects founded upon Plato's conception of the optimal relationship between philosophy and _medicine_, here defining "medicine" as an extremely broad range of ancient professions that might have claimed knowledge of some curative or healing or conditioning art.[1]

Medicine, including medicinal drugs, occupies a paramount place in Plato's thought. The art of medicine is intertwined with "the moral quest, philosophical ethics and the art of statesmanship."[2] Plato's borrowing from the field of medicine is conspicuous, and his use of medical language pervasive.[3] This is not surprising, really, since in contrast to philosophy medicine enjoyed a generally if not universally good reputation during Plato's lifetime.[4] In contemporary language a "regimen" is commonly defined in terms of a regulated system of diet, exercise, rest and/or general hygiene, intended to improve health or have some other specific effect upon the body. The word for regimen in ancient Greek, a precursor of the word diet, was *diaita*, meaning a manner of living, a place for living, or a summer house.[5] *Diaita* figures heavily in the set of informal solutions Plato advances to contend with the problem of intoxicated ecstasy.

Disease, Medicine, Cure

Just about every culture has basic assumptions about the body, health, and disease. As was mentioned briefly in chapter 4, above, medical practice was characterized by theurgy, "in its widest sense of supernatural or divine agencies in both diseases and their treatment" until the development of Hippocratic medicine in the fifth century BCE.[6] Diseases were assumed to arise from the actions of an outside agency and not, for example, from the malfunction of an internal organ or dietary/hygienic practice.[7] Typically disease was thought to be due to the displeasure of some divinity or the result of demonic intrusion.[8] In Egyptian and Babylonian aetiology, for example, the physician's task was to augury the source of the illness and appease it, or expel the demon possessing the sick person's body. The established means for accomplishing either task were "prayers, supplications, sacrifices, spells and incantations."[9] Common were noxious remedies whose foul contents, taken internally, were thought to make further residence distasteful to the demonic presence.[10]

Greek medicine and pharmacy of the archaic period combined theurgy with "the practical application of drugs, foreshadowing later . . . Greek medicine."[11] In the *Iliad* Apollo sends a plague upon the Greeks camped outside of Troy after Agamemnon mishandles the god's priest Chryses. A seer named Calchas is consulted, augury is used to divine the cause of Apollo's anger, and the god is mollified through prayer and sacrifice; afterwards the camp is cleansed of "defilements" (1.46–52). Apollo is addressed as Smitheus or "mouser" suggesting the possibility that mice were the source of the plague.[12] In the *Odyssey* sickness is said to originate in an "attack by a hateful demon" (5.396). Meeting his mother in Hades, Odysseus asks whether her death was the result of Artemis' arrows or a less divine "long sickness" (11.171–73). The wounds the hero suffers while on a boar hunt during his youth (19.455–58) are said to be treated by the sons of Autolycus, who stop the bleeding by binding the wounds and chanting *epodai* (incantations). The incantations compel "the deity to perform his healing function."[13] Hesiod in his *Works and Days* (100–104) describes how Zeus, angered at Prometheus' theft of fire, exacts vengeance by sending Pandora to Epimetheus, setting loose countless diseases upon humanity. While they are sent by a divine power, the diseases act spontaneously.[14]

It is only with the writing of Alcmaeon of Cronton (ca. sixth century BCE) that disease conceptualized in ontological terms begins to be rejected in favor of a very different explanation based on "disturbances of the body's natural equilibrium. . . . and, in consequence, subject to the same rules that operate in the world at large."[15] Alcmaeon drew upon the natural philosophy of the Milesian Anaximander, who had argued that the cosmos consisted of "a balance or even a legal contract" between opposed forces, in order to argue that human health was the outcome of an "equilibrium (*isonomia*) of [the] powers composing it, while the supremacy (*monarchia*) of any one of them causes disease."[16] The use of the terms *isonomia* and *monarchia* by Alcmaeon mark "the application of politico-

political-social concept
applied to physics and medicine
Medicine, Drugs, and Somatic Regimen 151

social concepts to the physical sphere," and its extensive "subsequent influence can be traced through the physician Philistion of Locri and thence to Plato."[17]

The ancient Greek word for illness, *nosos*, simultaneously encompassed both the ailments of the body and the suffering of social disturbances. In the aetiology of Greek medical theory right up to and including Plato's lifetime, "social and physio-psychic ills were not clearly differentiated," while the concept of the act of healing and the administration of justice were fused together.[18] The influence of this fusion is evident in the isomorphism of soul and *polis* in Plato's *Republic*.[19] The Greek medical traditions on the island of Cos and the settlement of Cnidus in Asia Minor, along with the Sicilian tradition of medical knowledge, centered on the writings of Empedocles (504–433 BCE), Pausanias and their disciples. Each had an influence on Plato. The foundation of Empedocles' conception of health in such works as *On Nature* and *Purifications* was the four-element theory (earth, air, fire, water). When any one of these elements predominated the result was a deviation "from perfect health or wisdom or even sanity."[20] The importance of this theory can scarcely be exaggerated as it exercised "a dominant role in Western science for over two millennia."[21]

Plato may have rejected the notion that the elements were divine, but he nonetheless followed in the footsteps of his pre-Socratic predecessors, modifying "the original theory to bring it more into accord with empirical phenomena," maintaining that "the elements undergo a continuous process of intermutation."[22] Philistion wrote on medicine in the fourth century BCE, combining Empedoclean four-element theory with the four powers (hot, cold, wet, dry). Plato may have known Philistion personally for he is mentioned as being the medical advisor of Dionysius II in Plato's *Second Letter* (324d). Although the authenticity of the letter is seriously questioned it nonetheless appears to establish Plato's acquaintance with Philistion, or at least its possibility. In addition a well-known fragment by the comic poet Epicrates mentions "a certain doctor from the land of Sicily" while making fun of the Platonic method of *diairesis* (Athenaeus 2.59). We also know from the *Seventh Letter* that Plato visited Italy before continuing on to Sicily (326b).

In any event the influence of Philistion's medical theory on Plato's *Timaeus* appears a near certainty.[23] The *Timaeus* fashions a somatic aetiology that is heavily dependent on Sicilian medicine, particularly Philistion. Plato offers a three-fold classification of disease:

> Disease occurs first through excess or deficiency of one of the elements, earth, air, fire, and water, and through misplacement of these substances in the body. A second class occurs when substances such as marrow, bone, flesh and sinew, formed of the elements in various proportions, become corrupted and the process of their formation is reversed. The products of this decomposition are carried everywhere through the vessels, feuding among themselves and at war with everything in the body that keeps its orderly array and position. These inharmonious humors . . . engender disease whenever the blood is not replenished naturally from meat and drink. A third class of diseases arise from blockage of inspired air [*pneuma*] in the blood vessels and round the sinews and tendons.

which causes convulsions. . . . These morbid humors overcome the fibrine in the blood and eventually dissolve the marrow, the basis of life, thus causing death.[24]

The medical theory of the fifth century BCE had already added the four humors—blood, phlegm, black bile, and yellow bile—which like Empedocles' four elements "play a role in the body analogous to that played by the elements in the world at large."[25] In the Hippocratic *Nature of Man*, for example, the author writes that the humors are found in every man and "constitute the nature of his body, and through these he feels pain or enjoys health. Now he is particularly healthy when these constituents are in due proportion to one another with regard to blending, power, and quantity, and when they are perfectly mixed" (4.1–7). In addition to the belief in the four elements, powers, and humors, each season—spring, summer, fall, winter—was thought to play a role in health and disease.[26]

It was in Italy that Plato formed a close friendship with the Pythagorean statesman, general, and mathematician Archytas. The Pythagoreans held the world was an orderly unit, a *kosmos*, and the key to understanding all nature lay in mathematics.[27] The linkage between "*number and order* . . . pervades the literature form Homer on; it lies at the heart of Pythagorean epistemology, of which Plato was probably a serious student."[28] One sees in Plato, for example *Republic* 560d, a reflection of this Pythagorean worldview, wherein whatever is "measurable or commensurable is graspable, in order, good" while anything "without measure is boundless, elusive, threatening, bad."[29] There can be little doubt that for Plato ecstasy, including the powers and pleasures of drug intoxication, fell in the latter group.

Medicina magica vs. *Medicina scientifica*

It has been argued that little or no connection or continuity existed between Greek *medicina magica* and early *medicina scientifica* as represented by the Hippocratic Cnidian and Coan schools. The aetiology of the latter can be distinguished through its being "for the most part free from magical and religious elements and based upon natural causes."[30] There is, within this viewpoint, a firm boundary between Hippocratic medicine and earlier healing because "in these treatises disease is regarded as a natural process, a disturbance of the equilibrium of the body, and physiology replaces divine nosology."[31] Yet other sources indicate these two realms were "closely connected" and argue in favor of an ongoing "real and deep-rooted communication between the two."[32] Within this viewpoint Greek medicine from at least the seventh century BCE "used procedures that are to our eyes indistinguishable from the techniques used by sorcerers."[33] Recent analysis has gone so far as to reject the very categories "magic," "religion," and "science" as being artifacts of nineteenth-century religion and anthropology, as well as the still pervasive belief in the "supposedly unimpeachable truth" of contemporary science.[34]

The Greek word for seer, *mantis*, comes form *mainein*, connoting a state of frenzy or ecstasy, and *mainesthai*, connoting madness. Magic-wielding seers were a well-known occupational stratum in the ancient Greek world.[35] Divination took such forms as bird augury—in the *Iliad* Agamemnon's seer Calchas is a skilled bird-diviner, "the clearest by far of all the seers who scan the flight of birds" (1.80–81)—and hepatoscopy, divination based on the examination of an animal's liver.[36] Plato makes derogatory remarks about the former in the *Phaedrus* (244c) and the latter in the *Timaeus* (71a–72c). In the *Meno* "prophets and the tellers of oracles" are said to engage in nothing more than "well-aimed conjecture" (95c), while in the *Phaedrus* the life of a seer is assigned a fifth-place ranking among souls that have caught "sight of part of what is true" (248c–e). The considerable influence divination exerted on political affairs is treated as unwarranted in the *Statesmen* (290c–d) and in need of curtailment in the *Laws* (908d, 909d).

Among Greek seers there existed no recognized "orders" in the medieval monastic sense, but a tradition of sorts existed. Greek seers were concentrated into groupings associated with a family name. The demi-god Melampus was one such notable seer, curing the daughters of King Proteus, who had been driven mad and were wandering the countryside under the delusion they were cows. Their cure comes through a prescription of frenzied dancing and a *pharmakon* consisting of black hellebore, a substance recommended in several ancient texts as a cure for madness.[37] In addition to the famous Melampodidae, there were "the Iamidae from Olympia and Klytiadae connected with them [whose] . . . activities lasted for centuries," as well as the "Telmissians in Karia," and finally "the priest families in Eleusis, the Eumolpidae and Kerykes, who officiated for about one millennia until the mysteries were finally outlawed by the Christian emperor."[38]

Elements of Egyptian, Babylonian, and Iranian magic exerted a substantial influence on Greek medicine, including the Hippocratic variety, such as (a) the student as a "son" up for adoption, (b) the transmission of knowledge to this son characterized as an "initiation," with (c) the candidate for knowledge required to take an oath of secrecy.[39] The *Papyri Graecae Magicae* do not distinguish between magic and mystery cult, calling magic a mystery (*mysterion*) and like terms.[40] The family of Asclepiads had the requirement of secrecy, as did the famous Hippocratic Oath; the latter describes the transmission of knowledge as the imparting of secrets akin to initiation into a mystery religion. "Holy things are shown to holy men; such things are not permitted for the profane until they are initiated through the rites of knowledge."[41] Plato, too, likens the acquisition of philosophic knowledge as an act of initiation, in works such as the *Phaedrus* and *Symposium*.

The *Iatromantis*

Greek *medicina magica* can be exemplified in the figure of the *iatromantis* (plural *iatromanteis*), the physician-seer. This shaman-like figure appears to be, as it is in other cultures, a forebear or ancestor of the more rationalistic physician.[42] The profession is mentioned by the tragedian Aeschylus in his *Hicetidae* (5.262). As in other pre-scientific cultures, the *iatromantis* practices more than simply medicine. Like his more strictly magical predecessor, the *mantis* (seer), or the inspired poet, the *iatromantis* was expected to know the past, present, and future. He was a prophet and purifier, one who had the specific trait of soul journeys, of "long ecstasies or 'disappearances.'"[43] In Plato's dialogues Socrates exhibits characteristics that parallel this shamanistic behavior, for example in the *Symposium* (175a–b, 220c–d).

Empedocles combined weather magic and medical skills in a shamanic manner writing, in one surviving fragment, "you will learn *pharmaka* for ailments and for help against old age. . . . You will check the force of tireless winds, which seep over the land destroying fields with their blasts . . . you will bring back restorative breezes . . . you will bring out of Hades the life-force of a dead man."[44] Empedocles introduces himself in his *Purifications* (115.3) as "a seer and healer" and describes himself as "banished from the gods and wandering about." Epimenides of Knossos (Crete), a semilegendary rootcutter living a century before Socrates and Plato, was reputed—according to Aristotle's *Rhetoric* (1418a)—to have "prophesied 'not over that which was to come, but over that which is past.'" Epimenides was also said to have "received a miraculous food from the nymphs which allowed him to get by without ordinary sustenance, a no-hunger drug (*ailmon*). He kept it in a hoof—as if ordinary containers could not hold it."[45]

Five Rivals of the *Iatros*

The Greek physician, the *iatros* (plural *iatroi*), was in competition and dispute with a host of rival individuals and occupational groupings. Medicine was not simply confined to professions that privileged the written word. There were many additional occupational strata practicing medicine in ancient Greece who left no written record of their activities.[46] In other words "useful knowledge" about medicine "circulated in massive quantities along informal channels on the ground, leaving but few traces in the stratosphere of dignified writings" composed by philosophers such as Plato.[47] These traces can be found, however, if one looks carefully enough. In addition to the "rational" schools of medicine there were in ancient Greece at least five other occupational practices that could lay claim to the power of healing knowledge, and would have had expertise in drugs. There were (a) *rhizotomoi* (rootcutters), (b) *pharmakopolai* (drug-sellers),

(c) *maiai* (midwives), (d) itinerant sellers of purifications, charms and the like, and (e) religious medicine, such as the many temples of Asclepius.

The *rhizotomoi* might be described as a semi-professional class whose distinct standards of knowledge concerning roots and herbs mirrored "the deepest traditions of Greek 'inquiry' on several, simultaneously applied levels from pure 'magic' to utter rationalism."[48] Macrobius (fl. 430 CE) in his *Saturnalia* mentions a ritual by which Medea, in Sophocles' lost play *Rhizotomoi* (*Rootcutters*), would gather poisonous herbs. With eyes averted the roots would be cut with a bronze sickle and their "juice" collected in bronze jars. Quoting from *Rhizotomoi* directly, Macrobius describes Medea as performing the act of cutting "naked, shrieking and wild-eyed" (5.19.10). We find the nameless Athenian of Plato's *Laws* lamenting at one juncture (836b) that while orderly education may temper most desires in the case of *eros*, the cause of countless evils for individual cities, "what herbal drug [*pharmakon*] can you cut to liberate these people from such a danger?" Plato's question is rhetorical, but it points to the *techne* of rootcutters and drug-sellers. Theophrastus' *History of Plants* relies heavily on *rhizotomoi* and *pharmakopolai* as sources of information even as it struggles to sift out "useful facts from the merely mythical."[49] The drug-seller Aristophilos from Plataea, Theophrastus records with a healthy dose of skepticism, claimed to posses drugs that could make the user either more or less potent, and he could adjust the effects as he desired: "The impotency from it can be either total or temporally delimited as, for example, two months or three months, so that it can be used on servants when one wants to punish and discipline someone" (9.18.4).[50]

Both the *rhizotomoi* and the *pharmakopolai* would appear to have been commonplace in both the countryside and the *agora*, hawking their drugs for any number of pains and ailments. They were also well-known for having a variety of love potions, aphrodisiacs, and sexual ointments at their disposal. Comic and tragic playwrights, when referring to these drugs, would not have described pharmacological lore incomprehensible to their audiences. These "simultaneously magicolegendary and empirical-practical" references to herbs and drugs would have been made with the presumption of their ready recognition "by the Athenians who sat through their productions, staged in honor of Dionysus," who was—as argued above in chapter 4—the god of *all* drugs.[51] Referring to thorn apple (*Datura stramonium*), one of the two plants known in ancient Greece under the name *strychnos*, Theophrastus in the *History of Plants* hints at the sophistication of these occupations, writing "Of this three twentieths of an ounce of weight is given, if the patient is to become merely sportive and to think for himself a fine fellow; twice this dose if he is to go mad outright and have delusions; thrice the dose, if he is to be permanently insane; . . . four times the dose is given, if the man is to be killed" (9.16.6).[52]

The *maiai*, or midwives, "controlled a well-developed body of information and had skills that were recognized and valued, especially in the community of women."[53] This information extended beyond pregnancy and childbirth and would have included "advice about fertility, abortion, contraception, and even (in imagination if not in reality) sex determination."[54] Euripides' *Hippolytus* (293–96) hints at knowledge reserved to women; Phaedra's nurse "advises her to seek the help of women if her condition is a 'delicate' one, but to resort to doctors if it is something 'that can be told to men.'"[55] The midwife is referred to in a famous passage of Plato's *Theatetus*, where the philosopher describes her maieatic power over the mind of the woman struggling to give birth or desiring an abortion as consisting of the application of drugs (*pharmaka*) and melodic incantations (*epodai*).[56] No Hippocratic work on obstetrics has survived, although it is not clear whether this was by accident or due to a division of labor that kept certain aspects of feminine health in the hands of the *maiai*. The *Epidemics* discuss cases of postpartum complications.[57] Most likely *maiai* handled normal births, with a male physician "called in only if there were complications."[58] There are hints in other Hippocratic texts that women, including midwives, "assisted, or were advised by, Hippocratic doctors in deliveries, both normal and abnormal."[59] Plato mentions women physicians in the *Republic* (452d).

The exact number of drugs known to ancient Greek midwives will never be known, but it must have been extensive and would have extended into all the areas where the midwife was supposed to possess special knowledge. We can get a hint of their number from works by their male rivals who presumably are borrowing from the "competition." Two works of the Hippocratic corpus, *Diseases of Women* and *Sterile Women*, mention a large number of *pharmaka* used for gynecological and obstetrical purposes. These include the opium poppy, henbane, and the root of white mandrake.[60] The use of mint/pennyroyal (*Mentha pulegium*) during antiquity as a contraceptive and abortifacient is mentioned in the Hippocratic *Nature of Women* (32). Aristophanes places pennyroyal potions as the sort of thing one finds among the sellers of eels, reed mats, and the like in his *Acharneneses* (861, 869, 874). References in several other texts of later antiquity, such as Dioscorides' *On Medical Materials* (3.31.1) and Galen's *Properties and Mixtures of Simples* (6.3.7), confirms its popularity. It was effective: along with its extract, the ketone pulegone, *Mentha pulgeium* acts as "a mild irritant to the kidneys and bladder in excretion and reflexively stimulates uterine contractions."[61] Pennyroyal was used in numerous other medicinal recipes (e.g., Pliny *Natural History* 20.54). In the case of the Hippocratic writings it is safe to assume these pharmaceutical details "are extracts gathered from midwives' oral traditions or (perhaps more relevantly) from an ever-present prostitutes lore."[62]

The influence of the practitioners of purifications was considerable. Through promise and persuasion they could, Plato says in the *Laws* (909b), convince not only individuals, not only whole families, but whole cities to pay them wages. In the *Republic* (364b–c) these same individuals come under criticism for going to wealthy households claiming "that the gods have provided them with a power based on sacrifices and incantations" and if the person or one of his ancestors has committed an offense then they can surreptitiously "heal it with pleasures and feasts; and if he wishes to ruin some enemies at small expense, he will injure just and unjust alike with certain evocations and spells."

The cult of Asclepius was introduced in Athens in the final third of the fifth century BCE, during the Peace of Nicias, and quickly spread throughout the ancient Mediterranean. The temples of Asclepius were famous for providing cures through the practice of "incubation," i.e. dream therapy. A person would sleep in the temple, dream, and upon waking describe what had been seen. The "cure" would be based on the priest's interpretation of the dream. So what exactly was Asclepian medicine? Was it "magic, unsanctioned religion, sanctioned religion, or science?" We are inclined to label it as something like "magico-religious but with some cures of real scientific value" but while this may hold explanatory power for us, it says nothing of the value it held for the original practitioners. Persons living in the ancient world might label Asclepian healing according to their social status, and/or the brand of polytheism they adhered to, and/or the philosophical doctrine they subscribed to. In Plato's *Symposium* (186e) the physician Eryximachus refers to Asclepius as "our common ancestor" by which he means he is claiming to be one of the Asclepiadae, a figurative descendent of the legendary founder of Greek medicine, "who were members of a *koinon* or guild."[63] In the *Phaedrus* (270c) Hippocrates is referred to as "the Asclepiad doctor."

In the *Pythian Odes* Pindar (518–438 BCE) tells us what traditional Asclepian medicine consisted of: gentle incantations (*epodai*); soothing liquid remedies (*pharmaka*) to drink; healing amulets (also called *pharmaka*) attached to the limbs of the patient; and surgical incisions (3.47–59). This poem, composed in the 470s, reflects "medicine's venerated and dual methods (drugs and surgery), with the addition of magical herbs that could be hung or worn appropriately."[64] Plato's *Republic*, written a century later, lists incantations and amulets as healing techniques (426b). Both the reputed biological sons and the adoptive "subtle sons of Asclepius" within contemporary Athens are criticized by Plato as, in contrast to their divine forbear, encouraging an idle way of life devoted to pleasure by using euphemisms for diseases easily avoided with a properly restricted dietary regimen, while using "drugs and cutting" to drive out diseases (*Republic* 405c–d, 407c–d, 408a–b). It should be noted, however, that Plato's philosopher-king is himself described as a statesmanlike (*politikon*) Asclepius in the *Republic* (407e), begging the question of what sort of medicine such an individual might practice.[65]

Drug Remedies, Drug Poisonings

Drug therapy was well advanced by the time Plato wrote his dialogues, and needs to be considered in the light of the similarity the Greeks drew between social and physio-psychic ills and the administration of justice. Ancient Greek knowledge of plant-based drugs (*pharmaka*), "even in the earliest times, is astonishing, but they probably took over much of it from other cultures, from the Egyptians, the Scythians, and the Thracians."[66] The various Egyptian medical papyri "consist largely of prescriptions of drugs interspersed with magical spells to impart efficacy."[67] The most frequently cited substances are beer, resin, and wine.[68] Egyptian medicine, especially pharmacology but also elements of gynecology and surgical techniques and practices, appears to have exerted an enormous influence on the Greeks. Both the *Iliad* and the *Odyssey* make "numerous references to the use of pharmaceuticals" used medicinally.[69] In the *Illiad* Zeus orders the treatment of the wounded Ares. The healer covers his wound "with pain-killing drugs" (5.1043). Helen's soothing drug added to everyone's wine in the *Odyssey* (4.244–51) is said to originate in Egypt, while Aristophanes refers to the fame of the drugs of Egypt in his *Peace* (1253). Diocles of Carystus, who lived and worked in fourth-century Athens, wrote the first list of plants that produce effects on the human body, the *Rhizotomika*, a work that is believed to have influenced Theophrastus' *History of Plants* while establishing a tradition that continued until the *On Medical Materials* of Dioscorides, a work that continued to be consulted until the seventeenth century.[70]

Throughout classical antiquity "pharmacy and toxicology remained aspects of medical practice that occasionally purloined venerated superstitions or religious customs or that with leaps of uncertainty adapted and adopted facets of philosophical physical therapy (especially the concepts of elements, qualities and humors) to account for the observed actions of the drugs."[71] While rejecting divine explanations of drugs and their effectiveness, ancient medicine and pharmacology were so emphatic in dismissing the magico-religious and philosophical interpretations of their competition that what was left within their work was "either a jumble of empirical observations or a strange and quixotic denial of the efficacy of any drugs."[72] The ancient notions of "humors and qualities" as a means for explaining how drugs worked within the body dominated western pharmacy until the mid-nineteenth century.

In the Hippocratic Corpus, including such works as *Regimen in Acute Diseases* and *Internal Affections*, drug therapy is largely secondary to or an ancillary part of dietetics.[73] Even so the number of drugs mentioned in the Hippocratic texts are too numerous to list.[74] The following are named as emenogogues or diuretics: anise, cardamom, caraway, cinnamon, chamomile, cassia, coriander, elderberry, ergot (*melanthoin* "obtained from wheat"), fennel, juniper, mint, myrrh, parsley, rue, saffron, and sage.[75] The Hippocratic gynecological works *Diseases of Women* and *Sterile Women* mention more drugs than any other works in the corpus. Opium is frequently recommended in the gynecological treatises, particularly for uterine conditions. Still other substances are recommended as balsams for hardening of the cervix and for puerperal ulcers.

Even the best works on ancient Greek medicine are notably squeamish when it comes to discussing drugs.[76] One such *pharmakon* was black hellebore (*Helleborus niger*) used in conjunction with "shouting and orgiastic dancing" and which was intended to cure madness. Being one of the "black" vegetables, black hellebore was "believed to belong to 'subterranean beings,' serving, therefore, as magic apotropaea," but it also "is a real and effective cathartic which regular medicine took over as a 'rationalized' remedy against madness," particularly the condition known as melancholy.[77] Henbane (*Hyoscyamus niger*) was another such plant, preparations of which "have atropinlike effects and . . . some limited utility in modern therapeutics."[78] Henbane exhibits the many-sided nature and inherent instability of the *pharmakon*; containing scopolamine, ingestion induces "an intoxication followed by narcosis in which hallucinations occur during the transition state between consciousness and sleep."[79]

Dioscorides mentions the addition of a plant called *apsinthion* to wine in his *On Medical Materials* (3.26). *Apsinthion* means "undrinkable" and refers to the extremely bitter taste of the leaves of *Artemisia absinthium*, commonly known as wormwood.[80] The plant is mentioned in the Ebers Papyrus. Medicinally, absinthe soaked in wine was recommended by Pythagoras to aid childbirth, by Hippocrates for jaundice, rheumatism, anemia, and menstrual cramps, and by Galen as an emetic.[81] Hippocrates of Cos in his *Internal Affections* (52) recommends as a treatment for tetanus grinding "wormwood, bay leaves, or henbane seed with frankincense; soak this in white wine, and pour it into a new pot; add an amount of oil equal to the wine, warm and anoint the patient's body copiously . . . also give him a very sweet white wine to drink in large quantities." In modern times an emerald colored liquor containing wormwood, named absinthe, was one of the most popular drinks in Western Europe, particularly France, between 1850 and the First World War.[82] Unlike most other spirits it was bottled at a very high proof but then, in a manner recalling ancient practices, diluted with water before it was consumed.[83]

Ancient pharmacology did not possess minutely delineated and scrupulously policed boundaries between medicines, intoxicants, medicines with intoxicating properties, and intoxicants with medicinal value; quite the opposite. Yet these distinctly modern boundaries continue to color even some of the best discussions of ancient pharmacology. Bitumen (native asphalts found in Asia Minor) was applied to doorways during festivals, in particular the Anthesteria, to prevent the entrance of evil spirits, and is mentioned frequently in the formulae of magical texts.[84] Bitumen when mixed with wine was taken as a medicine; Pliny the Elder in his *Natural History* recommends the mixture for chronic cough, dysentery, and as a means to hasten menstruation (35.180, 182). The same substance was among many used by the ancient Greeks "as a preservative or to improve the taste [of wine], as Pliny claims for resin."[85] Here then we find one substance that might have been called a *pharmakon* in ancient Greece being used, alternately and simultaneously, as a protective ward in a religio-magical ritual, as a medicine-remedy in a physician-patient ritual, and as a mix with alcohol in a presumably convivial host-guest ritual.

Neither did ancient pharmacology always make clear delineations between poisons, toxins with intoxicating properties, or intoxicants with toxic properties. In the *Alexipharmaka* Nicander enumerates animal, vegetable, and mineral poisons, including aconite, white lead, hemlock, henbane, certain mushrooms and opium, together with their symptoms and specific remedies.[86] He divides these into those which kill quickly and those that kill slowly. The cures are almost always herbal and often include olive oil as an emetic to induce vomiting. Even hemlock, the *pharmakon* famous for being the poison that killed Socrates, produces in smaller doses "delirium and excitement" on the one hand and can be a "powerful sedative" on the other.[87] Known to the ancient Greeks as *koneion*, we are told by Theophrastus in his *History of Plants* of a certain Thrasyas of Mantinea who discovered a potion that induced swift and easy death by combining hemlock, the opium poppy, and other substances (9.16.8). Nicander appears to be aware of cases of recreational, or at least nonlethal, use of hemlock, describing it as a "noxious draught [that] assuredly looses disaster upon the head bringing the darkness of night: the eyes roll, and men roam the streets with tottering steps and crawling on their hands; a terrible chocking blocks the passage of the windpipe; the extremities grow cold; and in the limbs the stout arteries are contracted; for a short while the victim draws breath like one swooning, and his sprit beholds Hades" (*Alexipharmaka* 186–94).[88]

Poisons were well-known in antiquity, particularly in the context of warfare.[89] In ancient Greece the bow or *toxon* might be used to deliver an arrow dipped in poison, signified by words such as *toxikon*.[90] Arrow poison itself might be called a *toxikon pharmakon* (literally, "poison to smear arrows with"). In the *Odyssey* (1.261) Athene, speaking of the absent Odysseus to his son Telemachus, describes him as seeking a poison to smear on his bronze arrows, something no decent man would do. These same poisons were evidently either accidentally or deliberately drunk in antiquity, it being the drinker's fate, according to the *Alexipharmaka*, to have "all his wits . . . stunned and overthrown," leaving him making "bleating noises, babbling endlessly in his frenzy; often too in his distress he cries out loud even as one whose head, the body's master, has just been cut off with the sword . . . the man in [this] frenzy of mind bellows and howls incoherently, and as he glances sidelong like a bull, he whets his white teeth and foams at the jaws" (213–22).[91] Aristotle's *History of Animals* refers to aconite as *pardalianches* or "panther killer," while Theophrastus in his *History of Plants* (9.16.4–7) mentions its use by physicians, although only with difficulty, and its use by others as a poison. Both authors appear to have been aware of "the most powerful of aconites, *Aconitum ferox*, or Indian aconite, used in India as an arrow poison to kill large animals."[92] The death of Aristotle was said to have been the result of drinking aconite (Diogenes Laertius *Lives*, 5.6).

Nicander writes that a drinker of the "deadly drink brewed with the chamaeleon-thistle [chamomile, classification *Chamaemelum nobile*], which has a smell like that of basil" will "in his frenzy" gnaw "his tongue with his dog-teeth, for at times his madness overmasters his wits" (*Alexipharmaka*, 279–84). A "hateful brew" mixed with white lead causes the "eyes to behold strange illusions" (85). One should avoid any liquid smelling like pitch and tasting like fresh juniper berries, for "swooning delusions hold in bondage that which is human" in victims of this draught (125–26). A loathsome drink, deadly and hard to remedy, called Coriander, produces madness and causes a person to "utter wild and vulgar words like lunatics, and like crazy Bacchanals bawl shrill songs in the frenzy of the mind unabashed" (157–61).[93]

Philosophy and Medicine

Plato's arguments concerning physical or somatic regimen are quite extensive, and usually hostile to the prevailing traditions. As we have seen in the preceding sections of this chapter, Greek medicine developed from strictly supernatural explanations of disease and their treatment to a conception based on disease as a disequilibrium within the body, with treatment conceived of as a restoration of the disturbed equilibrium. While there were many approaches to curing a disease within this aetiology—everything from "baths, massages, gymnastic exercises, and even changes of climate" to dietetics—drug therapy was certainly among the most important.[94]

In the *Charmides* (156e) we find Socrates recalling what he learned from a Thracian physician, telling those around him "physicians among the Greeks are powerless against the majority of diseases, for they ignore the whole." A good physician, so says the pupil of Zalmoxis, always treats "the maladies of organs by ministering as well, with a suitable regimen, to the whole of the body" (*diaita epi pan to soma*). A physician, in treating the body, cannot treat it in isolation of the soul, yet some physicians erroneously believe it is possible to "produce health of the body apart from the health of the soul" (157b). In the *Republic* as well Socrates criticizes "the current art of medicine" as being overly grounded in an epistemology of individual diseases, with physicians treating only the "body in a body" to the detriment of the "soul within the body" (406a, 408d). The *Charmides* (156e) in contrast argues that it is the soul that is the *source* "both of bodily health and bodily disease" for the whole person. The *Phaedrus* attacks conventional Hippocratic medical doctrine on precisely these grounds. If one is to "place any reliance in Hippocrates the Asclepiad," Plato writes, one cannot treat *just* the health of the body (270b–c). We must go "beyond Hippocrates" (*pros to Hippocrates*) and be assured the patient's mind contains an orderly set of "persuasions" and "convictions" and "virtues" (270b).

In the *Republic* Plato contrasts the treatment of illness in the common artisan and the man of leisure. When the average craftsman finds himself ill he locates a physician, gets a *pharmakon* to "vomit up his disease or purge it out from below," and returns as quickly as possible to his "accustomed regimen," i.e. the business of conducting his particular area of technical-artistic know-how (406d–e). He has no time to be sick. He either recovers his health or he has the good sense to die and in doing so "is rid of his troubles." In contrast is the man of leisure, the sort of man that would be reading a dialogue like the *Republic*. On the one hand there were men like the master gymnast Herodicus, who spend their entire lives treating their illness to the exclusion of anything else, engaging in "an excessive care of the body." Given the value that the Greeks placed on athletics, it is not surprising physical trainers would have had "a good opportunity to develop medical knowledge."[95] Their know-how would have extended to include a number of ointment-drugs. On the other hand there were those whose life of overindulgences left them "full of humors and winds like a marsh" and who acted to corrupt the medical profession with their ability to pay generous sums for so-called cures. They turn physicians into base and greedy men, willing to give subtle euphemisms "like 'flatulences' and 'catarrhs' to diseases" (405c–e). Both sorts of men live in a state of constant anxiety about their somatic health, becoming distressed if they should depart a bit from their accustomed *diaita*.

What we find here is yet another expression of a concern that members of Plato's own social class, the Athenian elite, not use *pharmaka* for other than immediate medical purposes. The question at hand is "whether the rich man must practice [the same regimen as the craftsman]" (407a–b). Drugs, even those used for ostensibly "medical-curative" purposes, are problematic if they merely sustain what is already an essentially diseased lifestyle—the lifestyle of a diseased soul. We should not look favorably on men who are always "needing *pharmaka*, not because [they have] met with wounds or some of the seasonal diseases, but as a result of idleness and a way of life such as we have described" (405c–406b). If we look at these individuals favorably, Plato writes, it would be as if "one fancied that a diseased body which had been subject to medical purgation" by a drug "were at its best in that condition," rather than a body "which has never stood in need of such treatment" in the first place (*Laws* 628d).

The *Timaeus* is "an amalgamation of Pythagorean religion and mathematics and Empedoclean biology."[96] With these Plato hoped to provide a powerful metaphysical base for Socrates' ethical teachings. The universe, as shaped by the Demiurge or Divine Craftsman, exhibits within itself clear evidence of "reason and moral law," and if this is the case men living their own lives in accord with this reason and moral law act not contrary to nature, as the sophists contended, but with nature.[97] Toward the end of the dialogue the focus of the work turns from the macrocosm to the microcosm: the human body and the diseases to which it is prone. The macrocosm was the work of the all-benevolent-Demiurge, while the creation of the human body was entrusted to those whom Plato calls the younger gods. The philosopher goes against Empedocles and sides with Alcmaeon and Diongenes, believing the seat of the intellect, the *logistikon*, lay in the head, not the heart. This part of the soul is the handiwork and gift of the Demiurge, and is immortal (30b). In the thorax the younger gods placed a second, mortal, two-part soul. The upper half, the *thymoeides*, resides in the throat and contains "courage and passion and love of contention" (69e–79a), while the lower half, the appetitive *epithymetikon*, is tethered to the liver "like an untamed beast" (70d–e).

This should all sound familiar, of course, as it is the tripartite psychology of the *Republic* being given a physiological underpinning of sorts. In the *Republic* those people Plato refers to as drones in Books VIII and IX behave as if imprisoned by an *epithymetic compulsion* that is beyond the ability of their soul's spirited and reasoning parts to overcome.[98] They are called the *disease* of an orderly regime, causing trouble in a manner analogous to the way phlegm and bile cause trouble for a body (552c, and cf. 563e–564b). Injustice is characterized as a "meddling, interference, and rebellion of a part of the soul against the whole"

(444b), the troublesome part clearly being the bestial, pleasure-hungry *epithymetikon*. In the *Timaeus* (81e–82b) the analogy is reversed, Socrates giving "a medical analysis of the operations of bile in the human body in terms of *stasis* and images taken from political strife."[99] The body may expel bile "like an exile from a state in which there has been civil war, whence arise darkness and dysenteries, and all such disorders" (85e–86a).[100]

Plato's physiological explanations within the *Timaeus* rest not so much on any scientific study (even by the standards of fourth-century science) than on a desire to keep as much as possible the seat of reason free from the corrupting influences of the body.[101] Physiology is continually subordinated to teleology. ✸ The abdomen or what Plato calls "the lower belly" serves as a receptacle for superfluous food and drink, while the intestines are "convoluted so that the food should be prevented from passing quickly through and compelling the body to require more, thus producing insatiable gluttony and making the whole race hostile to philosophy and culture and rebellious against the most divine part of our nature" (73a). The account of digestion, movement of the blood, and respiration provided by Timaeus is all of "a very low order and is patently not based on human or even animal dissection."[102]

After finishing with the extended discussion of diseases of the body Socrates then announces that there are certain "diseases of the soul" and indicates that such conditions are a product of somatic regimen, what Plato calls "bodily habit" (86b). Illness of the soul can take two forms: madness (*mania*) and stupidity (*amathia*). *Mania*, the general term in the Classical Period for madness or insanity, occurs thirty times in Plato.[103] Both *mania* and *amathia* are conditions far removed from wisdom, being described in the *Timaeus* as *anoia*, folly. To suffer from either of these states of mind, or from "excessive pleasures or pains," is to endure the gravest sort of malady. Under their affliction a man is unable to "see or hear anything aright; he is delirious, and at that moment unable to obey reason" (86b–c). Plato goes on to write that the soul of such an individual is kept in a "state of disease and derangement," soaring and plummeting in helpless response to the whims of the body's demands, until madness becomes the norm (86d). Another late dialogue, the *Sophist*, similarly calls ignorance a *paraphrosune*, a derangement (228c–d), while the *Republic* describes ignorance as a kind of "emptiness" of the soul (585b).

In the *Timaeus* Plato refuses to accept the more commonplace belief that individuals are willingly vicious or wicked (86d). The vice-ridden soul, he believed, was *sick*, owing to "some bad habit of body or unenlightened training" established at an early age (86e). Loss of balance in the mind can be traced to these two causes. Regarding the first, bodily habit, Plato offers a physiological diagnosis, steeped in the medical theory of the day and espoused by "rational" medicine. When the humors that move about in the body become trapped with no outlet for escape they mingle with the movements of the soul, inducing "all kinds of mental diseases, more or less violent and serious: and rushing to the three regions of the soul, in the part which each attacks they multiply manifold forms of moroseness and melancholy [in the *epithymetikon*], of rashness and

timidity [in the *thymoeides*], of forgetfulness and dullness [in the *logistikon*]"
(87b).

Plato assails the "so-called physicians" who repeatedly explain any disease,
even mental diseases, according to strictly physical criteria. In contrast he argues
that illnesses can result from entirely psychological causes, as for example the
result of a strong and passionate mind overtaxing a weak and fragile body, or
when a strong body is misled by a "small and feeble mind" (88b–c). In other
words, madness and stupidity. Echoing the notion of going "beyond Hippocrates" that he articulated in the *Phaedrus*, Plato insists in the *Republic* (408e)
that a good physician must treat the soul even as he cares for the body, for it is
impossible "for a soul to have been, and to be bad, and to care for anything
well."

The single precaution and most sensible "treatment" for unfortunate states
of mind such as madness and stupidity is an integration of the care of the body
and the care of the mind at one and the same time: "neither should the soul be
exercised without the body or the body without the soul, in order that they may
be a match for each other and attain balance and heath" (*Timaeus* 88c). Balance,
symmetry, proper "proportion" as Plato calls it, can be recognized intuitively by
even common men in small relations (like the simple mathematical relationships
Socrates helps the young slave recognize in the *Meno*), but in matters of higher
importance, involving the relationship between the body and the soul, encompassing "health and sickness and virtue and vice," even well-bred and educated
men are heedless (87c–d).

Neither the body nor the mind must allow itself to be passively led by external sources. Both must, if possible, "never be inactive" (88d, and cf. *Republic*
380e–381a). On a physical plane the body's particles should be kept constantly
"astir" and in a state of vibration so as to supply a defense against the forces of
heat and cold and dryness and moisture which were, as we have seen, viewed in
Greek medicine as the sources of aging and illness. If we moderately exercise
our body we bring these particles "into orderly relation with each other" and
thereby "bring about a healthy state" within ourselves (88d–e, and cf. *Theatetus*
153a–b and *Republic* 404b and 404e). The best method is gymnastic exercise, as
it is self-initiated, followed by such motion as that brought about by another
agency, for example the swinging motion resulting from being on a ship at sea.
The Spartan hunt, the *krypteia*, is praised in the *Laws* (633b) as "an admirable
source of suffering, in which [men] are forced to go barefoot in winter, sleep on
the ground, and fend for themselves without any servants, while running all over
the countryside all night long, until dawn."[104]

A distant third form of restoring order to the particles, one that ought to be
resorted to only by "absolute necessity," is "medical purgation effected by drugs
[*pharmakeutikes katharseos*]" (*Timaeus* 89a–c, and cf. *Theatetus* 153c–d and
Laws 789c). Plato objects to drugs because the *pharmakon* "goes against natural
life: not only life unaffected by any illness, but even sick life, or rather the life of
the sickness."[105] In other words the reasonable person turns to drugs only as a
last resort, and only when all other means of restoring order to the physiological

universe have failed.[106] Even then, if the disease involves "imminent danger," the illness may have reached its "fixed span of existence" as determined by its "triangles" and "beyond which its life cannot be prolonged" (89c–d).[107] Drugs should not be used to interfere with a disease that could otherwise run through its "appointed period," as they may increase the number of ailments or render a benign malady malignant. Since diseases are an imbalance of our body's "particles" we ought to "manage them by regimen," and even then only insofar as we "can spare the time," recalling the discussion of the craftsman and the man of leisure in the *Republic*. The body should avoid being provoked by the "troublesome mischief" of medical treatment and by that Plato most assuredly meant, among other things, *drug* treatments, as much as possible.[108]

On a psychological plane the mind becomes ill, loses its balance, because of inadequate education and training: "when, besides these vicious conditions [causing the body to become ill] there are added bad governments and bad principles of public and private speech; when moreover no studies to be an antidote [to *mania* and *amathia*] are pursued from youth up, then it is that all of us who are wicked become so, owing to [these] two causes beyond our control" (87a–b, and cf. *Republic* 492a and 573c). The fault lies not with the individual, for their tendency to commit the sort of evil behavior that disorders their body and soul was imprinted at the level of *thought* and *language* long before the appearance of their wicked actions. The blame for wicked behavior "must lie with those who train [rather] than those who are trained, with the educators [rather] than with the educated," a thinly disguised jab at philosophy's pedagogical competitors, most especially the sophists (87b, and cf. *Republic* 377b–c and 492a).

Plato indicates in one of the more difficult passages of the *Timaeus* that there is "only one proper therapy (*therapeia*)" for disorder arising out of thought and speech, namely "to give each the nourishment and motion which are akin to it. And the motions which are naturally akin to the divine principle within us are the thoughts and revolutions of the universe" (90c–d). By following these divine principles a man may "correct the courses of the head that were corrupted at our birth, and should render the thinking component [i.e. the *logistikon*] like the object of its thought in accordance with its primal nature (*archaia physis*), so that having assimilated them he may attain to that best life which the gods set before mankind" (90d).[109] The *Timaeus* begs off further discussion of this training as such a topic, we are told, belongs more properly to a discussion of *ethics*. In turning to these questions of thought, language, and the formation of ethics we begin to shift into the second and third senses with which Plato utilizes the concept of *diaita*, or regimen.

[margin handwritten note: • contemplation of the heavens as a cure for madness]

Notes

1. Randall B. Clark, *The Law Most Beautiful and Best: Medical Argument and Magical Rhetoric in Plato's* Laws (Lanham, MD: Lexington Books, 2003), 27. Although writing primarily about the *Laws*, Clark is on the mark when he writes that "As Plato

seeks over the course of this lengthy dialogue to suggest both the potentialities of and limitations on the use of rational discourse in political life, we see his protagonist engaging in, making reference to, or analogizing from the practice of *many* therapeutic arts, both rational and subrational."

2. John P. Anton, "Dialectic and Health in Plato's *Gorgias*: Presuppositions and Implications," *Ancient Philosophy* 1, no. 1 (1980): 51.

3. Anton, "Dialectic and Health in Plato's *Gorgias*," 49, and Trevor J. Saunders, *Plato's Penal Code—Tradition, Controversy, and Reform in Greek Penology* (Oxford: Clarendon Press, 1991), 164.

4. D. S. Hutchinson, "Doctrines of the Mean and the Debate Concerning Skills in Fourth Century Medicine, Rhetoric and Ethics," *Apeiron* 21, no. 2 (1988): 18.

5. While it is true the Greek word *diaita* is not identical to "regimen" in its meaning, there is substantial overlap.

6. John Scarborough, "The Pharmacology of Sacred Plants, Herbs, and Roots," in *Magika Hiera: Ancient Greek Magic and Religion*, ed. Christopher A. Fararone and Dirk Obbink (New York: Oxford University Press, 1991), 142.

7. Fridolf Kudlien, "Early Greek Primitive Medicine," *Clio Medica* 3 (1968): 310, Walter Burkert, *The Orientalizing Revolution—Near Eastern Influences on Greek Culture in the Early Archaic Age* (Cambridge, MA: Harvard University Press, 1992), 55–73, 75–79, and James Longrigg, *Greek Rational Medicine: Philosophy and Medicine from Alcmaeon to the Alexandrians* (New York: Routledge, 1993), 6–25.

8. Longrigg, *Greek Rational Medicine*, 6. See also Nancy H. Demand, *Birth, Death and Motherhood in Classical Greece* (Baltimore, MD: The Johns Hopkins University Press, 1994), 87.

9. Longrigg, *Greek Rational Medicine*, 6.

10. The Egyptian *Hearst Papyrus*, for example, mentions the practice of coprotherapy, combining the use of incantation and the consumption of an excremental "remedy."

11. Scarborough, "The Pharmacology of Sacred Plants, Herbs, and Roots," 142. All quotes from Homer's *Iliad* and *Odyssey* in this chapter are from the translations by Robert Fagles and line numbers refer to his translation, not the line numbers of the original Greek text. Robert Fagles, trans., *Homer—The Iliad* (New York: Penguin Press, 1990) and Robert Fagles, trans., *Homer—The Odyssey* (New York: Penguin, 1996).

12. E. D. Phillips, *Greek Medicine* (London: Thames and Hudson, 1973), 16–17.

13. Longrigg, *Greek Rational Medicine*, 15.

14. Longrigg, *Greek Rational Medicine*, 13.

15. Longrigg, *Greek Rational Medicine*, 52

16. Longrigg, *Greek Rational Medicine*, 52, citing Aetius 5.30.1.

17. Longrigg, *Greek Rational Medicine*, 52–53, and cf. 62–63.

18. Burkert, *The Orientalizing Revolution*, 57.

19. Daryl H. Rice, "Plato on Force: The Conflict between his Psychology and Political Sociology and His Definition of Temperance in the *Republic*," *History of Political Thought* 10, no. 4 (1989): 568.

20. Longrigg, *Greek Rational Medicine*, 71.

21. Longrigg, *Greek Rational Medicine*, 113.

22. Longrigg, *Greek Rational Medicine*, 113.

23. Phillips, *Greek Medicine*, 127.

24. Phillips, *Greek Medicine*, 125.

25. Phillips, *Greek Medicine*, 92.

26. See John Scarborough, *Medical Terminologies: Classical Origins* (Norman, OK: University of Oklahoma Press, 1987), 224–27.

27. Longrigg, *Greek Rational Medicine*, 113–14. Longrigg writes that by under-standing the *kosmos* "man himself can become progressively purified until he ultimately escapes the cycle of birth and attains immortality."

28. Martha C. Nussbaum, *Love's Knowledge: Essays on Philosophy and Literature* (New York: Oxford University Press, 1990), 107. Emphasis in the original.

29. Nussbaum, *Love's Knowledge*, 107.

30. Longrigg, *Greek Rational Medicine*, 1.

31. Longrigg, *Greek Rational Medicine*, 14.

32. Kudlien, "Early Greek Primitive Medicine," 305. See also Demand, *Birth, Death and Motherhood in Classical Greece*, 63–70.

33. Mathew W. Dickie, *Magic and Magicians in the Greco-Roman World* (New York: Routledge, 2001), 24.

34. C. R. Phillips, "*Nullum Crimen sine Lege*: Socioreligious Sanctions on Magic," in *Magika Hiera—Ancient Greek Magic and Religion*, ed. Christopher A. Faraone and Dirk Obbink (New York: Oxford University Press, 1991), 260–76. See also Hans Dieter Betz, "Magic and Mystery in the Greek Magical Papyri," in *Magika Hiera: Ancient Greek Magic and Religion*, ed. Christopher A. Fararone and Dirk Obbink (New York: Oxford University Press, 1991), 244–45, and Dickie, *Magic and Magicians in the Greco-Roman World*, 18–19.

35. Dickie, *Magic and Magicians in the Greco-Roman World*, 61 observes that there was "no strict differentiation" between seers and magicians and these occupations, like others that grew out of "the rituals of religion," persisted in one form or another "until the end of pagan antiquity" and continued to be "a problem in an increasingly Christianized Roman Empire."

36. On hepatoscopy see Burkert, *The Orientalizing Revolution*, 46–51.38.

37. Aristophanes *Wasps* 1489, Pliny *Natural History* 25.23 and 25.58, Dioscordides *On Medical Materials* 4.162.4, Hippocratic *On Internal Diseases* 7.284–89. In *On Internal Diseases* black hellebore is prescribed for delirium accompanied by visual hallucinations.

38. Burkert, *The Orientalizing Revolution*, 43, and cf. Kevin Clinton, "The Sacred Officials of the Eleusinian Mysteries," *Transactions of the American Philosophical Society* 64, no. 3 (1974).

39. Burkert, *The Orientalizing Revolution*, 44–46.

40. Betz, "Magic and Mystery in the Greek Magical Papyri," 249.

41. Quoted in Burkert, *The Orientalizing Revolution*, 44.

42. Kudlien, "Early Greek Primitive Medicine," 306.

43. Kudlien, "Early Greek Primitive Medicine," 306–7 and Robert M. Torrance, *The Spiritual Quest—Transcendence in Myth, Religion, and Science* (Berkeley: University of California Press, 1994), 136–40, 155–56, 159–63 both point out the similarities between the *Iatromantis* and shamanism.

44. Quoted in Scarborough, "The Pharmacology of Sacred Plants, Herbs, and Roots," 142. See Diogenes Laertius 8.59 who was relying on the authority of Satyrus, a biographer of the Hellenistic era.

45. Burkert, *The Orientalizing Revolution*, 62. According to Pausanias, when Epimenidies died his body was found to be covered with tattoos. The Greeks regarded this as odd, since tattoos were reserved for slaves. It is possible, however, that Epimenides had an association with the shamanic religions of Central Asia, where tattooing is associated with shamanic initiation.

46. G. E. R. Lloyd, "Methods and Problems in the History of Ancient Science—The Greek Case," *Isis* 83, no. 4 (1992): 569.

47. John J. Winkler, "The Constraints of Eros," in *Magika Hiera: Ancient Greek Magic and Religion*, ed. Christopher A. Faraone and Dirk Obbink (New York: Oxford University Press, 1991), 220.

48. Scarborough, "The Pharmacology of Sacred Plants, Herbs, and Roots," 138. The Greek word *rizoma* meant "the mass of roots of trees."

49. Scarborough, "The Pharmacology of Sacred Plants, Herbs, and Roots," 149–151, and cf. Anthony Preus, "Drugs and Psychic States in Theophrastus' *Historia plantarum* 9.8–20," in Theophrastean Studies, ed. William W. Fortenbaugh and Robert W. Sharples (New York: Routledge, 1988), 78–80. Clark, *The Law Most Beautiful and Best*, shares their views.

50. Quoted in Clark, *The Law Most Beautiful and Best*, 31.

51. Scarborough, "The Pharmacology of Sacred Plants, Herbs, and Roots," 143, see also 144–45.

52. Quoted in Clark, *The Law Most Beautiful and Best*, 32. The other substance named strychnos was deadly nightshade (*Atropa belladonna*). This substance was used to "induce sleep" while the thorn apple, it was believed, "causes madness" (*manikos*).

53. Demand, *Birth, Death and Motherhood in Classical Greece*, xix.

54. Demand, *Birth, Death and Motherhood in Classical Greece*, 63.

55. Demand, *Birth, Death and Motherhood in Classical Greece*, 101.

56. See chapter 10, below, for a longer discussion of this passage.

57. These are listed in Demand, *Birth, Death and Motherhood in Classical Greece*, 168–83.

58. Demand, *Birth, Death and Motherhood in Classical Greece*, 19.

59. Demand, *Birth, Death and Motherhood in Classical Greece*, 67. Some of them may have been literate.

60. Demand, *Birth, Death and Motherhood in Classical Greece*, 20. Demand prefers to downplay the ancient reliance on drugs, making a rather unconvincing argument that the differences between *ponos* (pain of childbirth) and *odyne* (sharp sudden pain) support the idea that "the use of painkillers was probably confined to complicated deliveries."

61. Scarborough, "The Pharmacology of Sacred Plants, Herbs, and Roots," 145.

62. Scarborough, "The Pharmacology of Sacred Plants, Herbs, and Roots," 145.

63. Longrigg, *Greek Rational Medicine*, 24. See also Demand, *Birth, Death and Motherhood in Classical Greece*, 94–95.

64. Scarborough, "The Pharmacology of Sacred Plants, Herbs, and Roots," 143. Cf. Dickie, *Magic and Magicians in the Greco-Roman World*, 25.

65. See Clark, *The Law Most Beautiful and Best*, and my own arguments in chapter 10, below.

66. Georg Luck, *Arcana Mundi—Magic and the Occult in the Greek and Roman Worlds. A Collection of Ancient Texts* (Baltimore, MD: The Johns Hopkins University Press, 2006), 481. Regarding the Egyptian knowledge of drugs see Lise Manniche, *An Ancient Egyptian Herbal* (Austin, TX: University of Texas Press, 1989).

67. Longrigg, *Greek Rational Medicine*, 8–10. The Egyptian Ebers Papyrus, which has been dated to 1,500 BCE, contains some 800 recipes.

68. Patrick E. McGovern, *Ancient Wine: The Search for the Origins of Viniculture* (Princeton, NJ: Princeton University Press, 2003), 133.

69. Clark, *The Law Most Beautiful and Best*, 28. For example the *Iliad* describes *pharmaka* as evil (22.94), soothing (4.218), and pain-killing (5.401, 5.500), and the *Odyssey* describes them as evil (10.213), baneful (4.230, 10.236), accursed (10.394), murderous (1.261), life-destroying (2.329), and good (4.227, 4.230). Adapted from Henry E. Sigerist, *A History of Medicine, Volume II: Early Greek, Hindu, and Persian Medicine*

(New York: Oxford University Press, 1961), 28. Line references are to the text in the original Greek.

70. Phillips, *Greek Medicine*, 132. See also Philip J. Eijk, trans., *Diocles of Carystus —A Collection of Fragments with Translation and Commentary. Volume One: Text and Translation* (Leiden, Netherlands: Brill Academic Publishers, 2000).

71. Scarborough, "The Pharmacology of Sacred Plants, Herbs, and Roots," 152.

72. Scarborough, "The Pharmacology of Sacred Plants, Herbs, and Roots," 152–53.

73. We have evidence a work on pharmacology, the *Pharmakitis*, was part of the Hippocratic corpus, but it is lost.

74. An excellent source in this regard is Lawrence M. V. Totelin, *Hippocratic Recipes: Oral and Written Transmissions of Pharmacological Knowledge in Fifth-and Fourth-century Greece* (Leiden, Netherlands: Brill Academic Publishers, 2009).

75. Phillips, *Greek Medicine*, 112.

76. Longrigg, *Greek Rational Medicine*, mentions drugs only four times in an entire work devoted to Greek medicine. Burkert, *The Orientalizing Revolution* 62, 67 is worse: he manages to mention a text called the *Pharmakeutria* by Theocritis (a work containing black magic spells and love charms), and a pot called a *pharmake* used in certain purification ceremonies, yet never once mentions the use of actual drugs in either magical or divinatory contexts. Totelin, *Hippocratic Recipes*, is a notable exception.

77. Kudlien, "Early Greek Primitive Medicine," 307–8.

78. Scarborough, "The Pharmacology of Sacred Plants, Herbs, and Roots," 149, 158 writes about the "injustice of inserting presentism" yet his description of henbane as "a rather poisonous plant" is at best cryptic and explains very little, while his discussion of ancient pharmacological knowledge, confined solely to drugs possessing *therapeutic utility* sounds suspiciously like presentism. Many drugs can be medicinal remedies at one dosage, recreational intoxicants at another dosage, and lethal poisons at still another. This, however, is a modern viewpoint and ancient discourse about *pharmaka* rarely if ever approaches such a perspective.

79. Richard Evans Schultes and Albert Hofmann, *Plants of the Gods—Their Sacred, Healing, and Hallucinogenic Powers* (Rochester, VT: Healing Arts Press, 1992), 86.

80. Doris Lanier, *Absinthe, The Cocaine of the Nineteenth Century* (Jefferson, NC: McFarland & Company, 2004), 1.

81. See Barnaby Conrad, *Absinthe—History in a Bottle* (San Francisco: Chronicle Books, 1988), 85–86. Pliny the Elder wrote that the champion of a chariot race customarily drank a cup of *apsinthion* leaves soaked in wine, as a reminder that every triumph had a bitter side.

82. In addition to ethanol (70%–80%) and *Artemisia absinthium*, absinthe of the sort enjoyed during the nineteenth century's "green hour" contained several herbs including anise, fennel, melissa, hyssop, juniper, angelica, nutmeg, star anise, and veronica. The rise and fall of this drink and its enormous influence on the poetry, literature and visual arts of the period is the subject of an ever expanding literature. In addition to Conrad, *Absinthe* and Lanier, *Absinthe*, see also F. Clifford Rose, ed. *The Neurobiology of Painting* (San Diego, CA: Academic Press, 2006).

83. Conrad presents laboratory evidence that thujone, found in absinthol, the oil derived from the wormwood plant, has a molecular structure similar to THC (tetrahydrocannabinol) found in the hemp plant (Conrad, *Absinthe*, 152–54). The effects of thujone remain contested, however. See for example A. Dettling, et al., "Absinthe: Attention Performance and Mood under the Influence of Thujone," *Journal of Studies on Alcohol* 65, no. 5 (2004): 573–81.

84. R. J. Forbes, *Studies in Ancient Technology, Vol. 1* (Leiden, Netherlands: Brill Academic Publishers, 1964), 99.

85. Forbes, *Studies in Ancient Technology, Vol. 1*, 102. On the use of resins in wine see chapter 1, above.

86. Nicander's views on opium may be found in Richard Davenport-Hines, *The Pursuit of Oblivion: A Global History of Narcotics* (New York: W. W. Norton, 2004), 30–31.

87. Preus, "Drugs and Psychic States in Theophrastus' *Historia plantarum* 9.8–20," 95. Dickie, *Magic and Magicians in the Greco-Roman World*, 55 writes that "in Late Antiquity hemlock seems to have been one of the principal ingredients in love-philtres."

88. The Christian writer Hippolytus (ca. 170–236 CE), in his *Refutation of All Heresies* (5.8), mentions that the Hierophant at Eleusis consumed hemlock to prevent the sort of nocturnal ejaculations and untimely erections that would offend ritual purity. While his motives are clearly polemical it seems unlikely he would refer to a use of hemlock that would strain the credulity of his readers.

89. See Adrienne Mayor, *Greek Fire, Poison Arrows, and Scorpion Bombs: Biological and Chemical Warfare in the Ancient World* (New York: Overlook Duckworth, 2003).

90. Antoinette Hayes and Steven G. Gilbert, "Historical Milestones and Discoveries that Shaped the Toxicology Sciences," in *Molecular, Clinical and Environmental Toxicology. Volume 1: Molecular Toxicology (Experientia Supplementum)*, ed. Andreas Luch (Basil, Switzerland: Birkhäuser Verla, 2008), 2.

91. This passage recalls a seemingly curious observation (651a) in Aristotle's *Parts of Animals*, where bulls are said to be mentally deranged (*ekstatikoi*) because they are among those animals having "thick and abundant fibers in the blood," making them "of a more earthly nature, and of a choleric temperament, and liable to bursts of passion." Quoted in Preus, "Drugs and Psychic States in Theophrastus' *Historia plantarum* 9.8–20," 97 n. 29. In his *History of Animals* Aristotle indicates that just as human beings do, animals seek out herbal remedies (611b–612b, and cf. Preus, "Drugs and Psychic States in Theophrastus' *Historia plantarum* 9.8–20," 83, who concurs).

92. Preus, "Drugs and Psychic States in Theophrastus' *Historia plantarum* 9.8–20," 84–85.

93. Henbane is also mentioned by Nicander but the text of the *Alexipharmaka* appears to have a gap/lacuna right at the point where one would expect to find the description of the symptoms of henbane consumption. See A. S. F. Gow and A. F. Scholfield, *Nicander—the Poems and Poetical Fragments* (Cambridge: Cambridge University Press, 1953), 196. Henbane contains a high concentration of scopolamine, whose ingestion induces "an intoxication followed by a narcosis in which hallucinations occur during the transition state between consciousness and sleep." Quoted in Schultes and Hofmann, *Plants of the Gods*, 86. Dioscorides indicates that henbane produces "frenzies" (*On Medical Materials* 6.68.2).

94. Longrigg, *Greek Rational Medicine*, 53.

95. Erwin H. Ackerknecht, *History and Geography of the Most Important Diseases* (New York: Hafner Publishing Company, 1965), 45.

96. Longrigg, *Greek Rational Medicine*, 113.

97. Longrigg, *Greek Rational Medicine*, 114–15.

98. See chapter 2, above.

99. Kostas Kalimtzis, *Aristotle on Political Enmity and Disease—An Inquiry into Stasis* (Albany, NY: State University of New York Press, 2000), 195 n. 6.

100. Benjamin E. Jowett, trans., *Plato: Timaeus* (Upper Saddle River, NJ: Prentice Hall, 1959).

101. Longrigg, *Greek Rational Medicine*, 133, 147.

102. Longrigg, *Greek Rational Medicine*, 135.

103. Gerald C. Moss, "Mental Disorders in Antiquity," in *Diseases in Antiquity—A Survey of the Diseases, Injuries, and Surgery of Early Populations*, ed. Don Brothwell and A. T. Sandison (Springfield, IL: Charles C. Thomas, 1967), 714 n. 30. *Paranoia* is also used to denote mental derangement, most notably at *Laws* 929d–e in the discussion of how a son ought to proceed if he believes his father mentally unstable.

104. A similar sort of admiration is expressed by Alcibiades in Plato's *Symposium* (220a–c, 220e–221c). He describes to the other guests at Agathon's *symposion* that in Potidea Socrates walked barefoot over the winter ice, to the annoyance of his well-bundled compatriots, and during the retreat from Delium he retains a remarkable composure and is quite capable of fending for himself even though he is unmounted, a decided disadvantage in ancient warfare when the defender was put to flight.

105. Jacques Derrida, *Dissemination* (Chicago: University of Chicago Press, 1981), 100.

106. Cf. Giovanni Reale, "According to Plato, The Evils of the Body Cannot Be Cured without also Curing the Evils of the Soul," in *Person, Society and Value: Towards a Personalist Concept of Health*, ed. Paulina Taboada, Kateryna F. Cuddeback, and Patricia Donohue-White (Dordrecht, Netherlands: Kluwer Academic Publishing, 2002), 26, who writes "In the *Timaeus* Plato . . . clarifies his thoughts on the use of drugs. In his judgment, one should use drugs with caution and with great moderation since, in certain cases, the harm is greater than the benefit."

107. Plato's explanation of disease is firmly rooted in his geometrical atomism. See Longrigg, *Greek Rational Medicine*, 143.

108. It is "Aetius's streamlining of Galen's pharmacological theories" that becomes "the ultimate origin of the 'drugs by degrees' system, used by pharmacists until the middle of the nineteenth century." Even though we no longer rely on "the senses of smell, touch, taste, and sight to provide medical terminologies, the impact of Greco-Roman concepts of elements, qualities, and humors (as perceived by the senses) is still part of medical English as well as other kinds of English." Quoted in John Scarborough, *Medical Terminologies*, 223–24. In the case of opium Galen largely repeats what had already been put down by Dioscorides (*On Medical Materials* 4.64); Dioscorides' work in turn appears to presume a certain familiarity with Theophrastus' *History of Plants*. See Scarborough "The Pharmacology of Sacred Plants, Herbs, and Roots," 4–8.

109. Quoted in Joseph M. Bryant, "Enlightenment Psychology and Political Reaction in Plato's Social Philosophy: An Ideological Contradiction?" *History of Political Thought* 11, no. 3 (1990).

Chapter Eight

Magic, Drugs, and Noetic Regimen

The soul's participation in health, *euexia*, is asserted, directly and indirectly, again and again by Plato, in such dialogues as the *Phaedo* (89d), *Republic* (408e), *Philebus* (63e) and *Laws* (960d). As early as the *Gorgias* Plato begins to extend the medical term for somatic health, *euexia*, to what may be termed mental or noetic health. Socrates speaks of a healthy soul (479c, 525e, 526d) and of psychic diseases (481b, 512b). Plato deploys the Greek word for regimen, *diaita*, in regard to moderation (*sophrosyne*) being a certain rule of the self.[1] The behavioral domains that are to be brought under the governance of *sophrosyne* are themselves extremely consistent throughout the dialogues: to a large degree they consist of a rejection of the desire for, and pleasures of, food, sex, and intoxication. These desires, as we saw in chapter 7, belong to the lowest part of the soul, the *epithymetikon*. The importance of "being moderate and in control of oneself," the master of what the *Gorgias* (491d–e) describes as certain enslaving "passions and appetites" that in their totality push the mind into unhealthy states of identity-expunged ecstasy, is a near perennial theme of his dialogues. The *Republic* (389d–e), *Phaedrus* (237d–238a), *Philebus* (45d–e) and *Laws* (730e–734e) each emphasize nearly identical threats to noetic order, something that may be characterized as the guardian or the ramparts of identity.

In the *Republic* Socrates and Thrasymachus, while squaring off on the sophist's aggressive definition of justice, do concur that "managing, ruling and deliberating" are peculiar to the soul (353d). This rule is not easy and is fraught with conflict. At the very beginning of the *Laws* we are informed that "humanity is in a condition of public war of every man against every man, and private war of each man with himself" (626d). And soon thereafter, with regard to the soul: "a war against self exists within each of us" (626e). Just as the threat of *stasis* threatens to disrupt the identity of every *polis*, the threat of internal *stasis* or what Plato calls *stasiazonta* lurks within individuals, a sentiment expressed decades earlier in the *Republic* (430e–431d) where we are told the productive classes of society, especially, are driven by these base desires (580e–581a, and cf. 431c). As we saw in chapter 2 the ancient Greeks viewed *stasis* as a form of disease and "came to the conclusion that violent outbreaks were the advanced state of disease in which the normal noetic processes of political life were radically altered for the worse."[2]

psyche / *ortos*

Plato's moral psychology rests on his metaphysical ontology, wherein reality is divided into a higher, immaterial realm of perfect, eternal being (*ousia*) and a lower tangible world of perpetual flux or becoming (*genesis*). Diotima tells Socrates in the *Symposium* that just as the cells in the body are continually changing so are a person's noetic attributes: "habits, dispositions, beliefs, opinions, desires, pleasures, pains and fears are all varying all the time for everyone" (207e–208a). In his epistemology Plato distinguishes between knowledge (*episteme*), the basis of which is to be found in cognition (*noesis*) of the eternal and unchanging Forms, on the one hand, and opinion (*doxa*), the basis of which is to be found in perception (*aisthesis*) of particulars, on the other. *Doxai* usually translates as "opinions" or "beliefs" but in an earlier time, in tragic poetry for example, the term meant "visual hallucinations." Aeschylus (525–456 BCE), for example, in his *The Libation Bearers* (1048–62), contains a scene where Orestes sees terrifying hallucinations (*doxai*) and is described as being in a confused state of mind (*taragmos es phrenas*).

Plato's *Theatetus*, a dialogue whose primary concern is defining knowledge, retains at least a trace of this earlier meaning. Socrates speaks of his art as an arduous one, for above and beyond the practices of an ordinary midwife, with her simple chants and drugs, in his case "the patients are to be delivered of phantoms and sometimes of realities" and the differences between true and false offspring are difficult to distinguish (150a–b). In the *Republic* Socrates describes three ways in which people are deprived unwillingly of the truth: robbery, force and *magic* (413b).[3] Psychologically the appetitive part of the soul is "blind," i.e. the desires felt by this part of the soul are pursued regardless of whether their fulfillment would be good or bad for the whole. In contrast the reasoning part of the soul has the good of the whole in mind, and ought to be in command. The appetitive part of the soul exerts what may be called a relentless epithymetic compulsion that drives a person "like a beast" in pursuit of water when consumed by thirst (439b).

Located far from the head this part of the soul called the *epithymetikon* is incapable of understanding reason, as we learn in the *Timaeus* (71a): "even if it did have some share in the perception of reasons, it would have no natural instinct to pay heed to any of them but would be bewitched for the most part both day and night by images and phantasms (*eidolon kai phantasmaton*)." There is every indication, then, that for Plato a person only enjoyed "full and truly 'human' health . . . in the good order of [a virtuous] set of psychic habits."[4] There is a distinct need for a new discussion of Plato, magic, and noetic harmony. While magic is for most of Plato's contemporaries unproblematic if not wholly above suspicion, to be used "freely and unabashedly"[5] by most social strata, Plato cam-

magic

paigns against it even while appropriating from it, and more importantly for this
work it may be demonstrated that where there is *mageia*, drugs (*pharmaka*) are
not far behind.

The Ancient Greek Concept of Magic

It must be conceded that our picture of magic in ancient Greece is both limited
and skewed.[6] It is skewed because the surviving texts speak primarily about the
activities of magicians who catered to the rich and powerful, the sorts of individuals who possessed the power to influence the politics of the *polis*. Discussing the practices of the ordinary magic-worker was largely "beneath the dignity
of Plato and the tragic poets."[7] It is limited because, while what may be characterized as the practice of "magic" almost surely existed throughout ancient
Greece, nearly everything in the way of documentation that has survived refers
to the activities of magicians within one city-state, Athens. Finally, even in the
case of Athens we have very little reliable knowledge about ordinary magic-
workers, the sort of individual who would have been sought out by folks of
modest means, magicians who circulated in "the world of prostitutes [both male
and female], tavern-keepers and brothel mongers and the assorted ancillaries
associated with them."[8] Both classicists and anthropologists have struggled with
"the nature of magic and of its relationship to on the one hand religion and on
the other to science" while seeking "to provide a definition . . . that will hold for
all cultures and that will at the same time explain what it is that all procedures
thought of as magical have in common."[9] Even so, it is possible to get a sense of
both magic's gradual conceptualization and definition. In Classical Greece the
development of magic as a distinct practice had reached a point where, while not
tightly defined, parameters did exist.

Magic before Magic: Circe, Medea, and Hecate

As we saw in chapter 4, above, drugs are present throughout much of Homer's
Odyssey. Circe prepares a mixture (*kykeon*) containing "baneful drugs" (*pharmaka lugra*) for the members of Odysseus' crew, and later she tries to use her
malignant drugs to unseat the reason of the hero himself. Her behavior is without doubt complex and meant to be viewed as malevolent and terrifying.[10] But is
she "the first extant witch in Greek literature"?[11] The Greek text employed by
Homer gives no evidence of the poet possessing either a concept of magic or
that he viewed the actions of Circe as sorcery.[12] The hallmarks of what would
become the major criticisms of sorcery in the fifth and fourth centuries BCE,
such as its secrecy, impiety and sacrilegious nature, are nowhere to be found.
We are not told how Circe acquired any of the *pharmaka* in her possession, but
the fact that Hermes gives Odysseus the *moly* plant to counteract her drugs at

least suggests the poet viewed Circe as a cutter of roots, a *rhizotomos*. Centuries later Diodorus Siculus (fl. first century BCE) writes (4.45) "Circe . . . devoted herself to understanding drugs of all sorts, and discovered all kinds of qualities and unbelievable powers of roots."[13]

Medea and Hecate, like Circe, were ancient semi-divine experts in *pharmaka*.[14] Unlike Circe, unfortunately, no account of them dating back to Homer has survived. There is reason to believe, however, that the power in their possession arose from either the same or similar traditions, and is based on a knowledge no less pharmaceutical than that possessed by Circe. Dionysius of Miletus (so-called Scytobrachion), a mythographer whose work dates from between 270 and 220 BCE, "consistently rationalizes the inherited tales of myth and magic."[15] In his *Argonautica* "Medea is not a witch but a practicing herbalist who comes to be deeply troubled by her father Aeetes' barbarian ways and helps the Argonauts because she finds them kindred spirits in their unfailingly civilized behavior."[16] In Diodorus, who drew to some extent on Dionysius, Medea's magic "is entirely worked through the medium of drugs."[17] Medea and Circe are the offspring of Hecate, "a keen contriver of many drugs (*pharmaka*)," who discovered aconite, acquired "great experience" slipping drugs into the food of strangers, and "destroyed her father with a drug and so took over his throne" (4.45).

Over time, however, figures such as Circe did come to be identified as sorceresses. By the fourth century BCE Circe, for example, is assumed to be a sorceress in works such as Aristophanes' *Wealth* (303–10). The Corinthian courtesan Lais "is presented as a Circe who mixes *pharmaka* and brings magic to bear on (*manganeuousa*) the comrades of Philonides, an Athenian whom Aristophanes pillories."[18] As the centuries roll on Circe's myth progressively deteriorates until it reaches a stage where the *rhizotomos* of the *Odyssey* evaporates and only the sorcery remains. Plutarch, in his *Moralia* (139a), after complaining that just as "women who devise love potions [*philtra*] and sorceries [*goeteiai*] against their husbands and control them through pleasure share their lives with bewildered, mindless, and ruined men," says that Circe, too, found the men she had enchanted and transformed into animals "were of no benefit to her," in contrast to Odysseus with whom she found love because he "retained his mind."[19] In Pliny's *Natural History* Circe is one of the early investigators of plants (15.10–12). In the aetiological myth of the Roman historian Gnaeus Gellius she is one of three daughters of Aetes who settled in hills south of Rome, practicing magic capable of producing ocular illusions.[20] In Claudius Aelianus' *On the Nature of Animals* she has the power to kill, but instead of using drugs she does so simply by touch (1.54). Finally, in Augustine's *City of God* there is mention of certain women, primarily innkeepers, who like Circe give drugs with cheese to travelers, changing them into beasts of burden (18.18).[21]

Wandering Holy Men, Seers, and Wonder Workers

Magic as a distinct category of thought—a human activity recognized as separate and distinct from religion or medicine—began to emerge, albeit slowly and incrementally, during the fifth and fourth centuries BCE. It was rarely if ever viewed as a fully distinct and unique occupational practice in Athens during the Classical Period: "it is virtually impossible to point to men who were magicians and magicians only. They are almost always found to follow some other calling, but one that is closely related to their magic working."[22] Magicians almost without exception appear to have had a concern with the divine. "Very often the magician is also a soothsayer (*mantis* or *chresmologos*) or an interpreter of prodigies (*teratoskopos*); he may also offer ritual purifications (*katharmoi*); he may provide initiations into mystery-rites [*mysteria*]; and finally he may be a mendicant holy man (*agyrtes*)."[23]

The *agyrtes* or "beggar priest" was someone who moved from city to city, earning a living by begging.[24] Although destitute they were not necessarily completely obscure individuals. They may have been persons down on their luck but with sufficient wits to scratch out a living performing private religious ceremonies. The *chresmologos* or *mantis* were traveling "religious entrepreneurs" who typically possessed a book or books of oracles and "who professed to be able to mediate between the human and divine."[25] They, too, "generally belonged to the class of the dispossessed and rootless."[26] The *thaumatopoios* was, literally, a "wonder-worker."[27] The practice of *thaumatopoiia* covered "not only conjuring-tricks, but also juggling, acrobatics and marionette shows."[28] This is not to say that a "pure" magician couldn't have existed. There is simply not enough evidence to conclude so. Nor is there evidence of the magic practiced by men and women being viewed as entirely separate and distinct activities: "Plato's use of the masculine gender in describing the magic-working of *agyrtai* and *manteis* proves that he believed men practiced black magic, but does not mean that he was not speaking generally and not also thinking about women."[29]

The Sorcerer and Sorceress

Many terms were used to identify the men and women who practiced magic. That there is not a single term but rather many "points to the absorbing and homogenizing of quite separate forms of expertise."[30] The male practitioner of "magic" went by several names. The *goes* (plural *goetes*) practiced *goeteia*.[31] They were believed to possess the power to raise the spirits of the dead, a technique known as *psychagogia*.[32] As we saw in chapter 5, above, this is the technique that Aristophanes portrays Socrates practicing in the *Birds*. The *goetes* were also specialists responsible for binding spells known as *katadesmoi* (also called *katadeseis*), including curses.[33] The *epodos* (plural *epodoi* or *epaoidoi*) was, like the *goes*, thought to offer "initiation into ecstatic mystery rites (*tele-*

tai).[34] The fact that *epodos* means "one who sings over" or "one who directs song at something" also suggests "the *epodos* was not originally a magician, but a man who specialized primarily in singing over persons afflicted with various physical ills to cure them of the ill or at any rate to alleviate their sufferings."[35] The *magos* (plural *magoi*) practiced *mageia* or *mageutike* (*techne*).[36] They were thought to be able to bring about the disappearance of persons, pull the moon out of the sky, cause the sun to disappear, and alter the weather.[37]

The *pharmakeus* (plural *pharmakeis*) practiced *pharmakeia*.[38] Despite their name an individual called a *pharmakeis* did not wholly or simply "confine their activity to the use of drugs or poisons (*pharmaka*), although they too will have had their origins in persons expert in *pharmaka* and in the allied calling of the cutting of roots (*rhizotomia*)."[39] Clearly, however, drugs and magic were heavily intertwined, and a knowledge of drugs would have been possessed by many of the occupations that fell under the heading of "magic" just as they would have been possessed by the many occupations that fell under the heading of "medicine." Whatever the different origins of these many different callings, by the fifth century BCE each of these terms, be it *goes, epodos, magos, pharmakeus*, etc., had become largely interchangeable.[40]

The female practitioner of magic had her own names and areas of expertise. She might be a *pharmakis* (plural *pharmakides*), or *pharmakeutria* (plural *pharmakeutriai*), or a *goetis* (plural *goetides*). Masculine terms such as *goetes* and *magoi* might also be applied to women, though uncommonly. As complex as the kaleidoscope of male practitioners of magic in ancient Greece might appear, the "common ancient assumption was that women were more likely to be expert in magic than men."[41] A sorceress could be described as *polypharmakos*, "knowing many drugs," an indication they frequently used *pharmaka* and magic to achieve "the desired affect."[42] Medea's speech in Euripides' play *Medea* gives some indication "that women were particularly expert in the department of black magic that involves the use of harmful drugs."[43] Plutarch describes the wife of Philip of Macedon and the mother of Alexander, Olympias (ca. 376–316 BCE), as having destroyed the mind of Arrhidaeus, Philip's son by another woman, with drugs (*Alexander* 77).[44] The truth of Plutarch's account is not the important issue, but rather that it possibly reflects an understanding that certain drugs were capable of causing permanent noetic degradation, and that women were believed to possess knowledge of their deployment. The typical sort of women who practiced magic were prostitutes, holy women, and more inconspicuous women such as the wives, daughters, nurses, and female servants sequestered within the female portion of the *oikos* known as the *gynaeceum* or *gynaikonitis*. About this last group, especially, we know very little; the life of ordinary women was only rarely deemed worthy of comment, and most of the written record that has survived to the present was composed by men with little motivation to describe these activities of women accurately and/or without bias.

Spells and Drugs

By Plato's lifetime magic was considered an art, a *techne*.[45] Plato was aware of many forms of magical practice.[46] He mentions the use of spells, incantations, and drugs that can reduce men to inarticulate numbness (*Meno* 80a).[47] He mentions the deliberate summoning of ghosts for haunting others (*Laws* 933d) and the calling up of the dead from the underworld (*Laws* 909b).[48] He describes the creation of the illusions of things that are not there (*Sophist* 234c, 235a, 241b, *Statesman* 303c) and repeatedly alludes to the belief a *goes* was able to miraculously morph himself into several different forms (*Euthydemus* 288b, *Republic* 380d, 381e, 382a).[49] He speaks of spells that draw and attract persons, presumably whether they like it or not (*Philebus* 44c, *Republic* 572e–573a). And he speaks of casting spells over fierce wild animals and reducing them to submission (*Gorgias* 483e). Finally, and most importantly for our purposes, the magician knows what drugs (*pharmaka*) "to put into food to effect alterations in states of mind" (*Laws* 649a).

The sorcerer and sorceress, like the *rhizotomoi*, *pharmakopolai*, and other quasi-medical professions discussed in chapter 7, above, were yet another repository of pharmacological knowledge operating largely "on the ground" and utilizing a large number of drugs, practices largely beneath the lofty musings of the literate aristocracy, particularly philosophy.[50] The sorcerer, however, gained his expertise in drugs not from practical learning but rather from divine assistance. In one spell the purpose of a summoned *daimon* is to provide the magician with knowledge of magic drugs (PGM I 42–195). The spell a sorcerer would use might be called a *pharmakon*, a word "used of poisons, magical substances, spells in which substances and words are used, and perhaps magical formulae."[51] A *philtron* was a term restricted to the practice of erotic magic, but here too the substances—many if not almost all of them mind-altering—were "put into food to induce sexual passion in the person who consumes or imbibes it," or it might be "a substance used as an ointment," or "a substance accompanied by a spoken spell designed to elicit the same result," and finally it might be "a spoken spell intended to provoke sexual desire."[52]

The *Papyri Graecae Magicae* (PGM) were discovered in the Egyptian desert in the early nineteenth century and are written mainly in ancient Greek, with some Demotic Egyptian and Coptic.[53] They consist of several longer scrolls which may comprise a sort of "magician's handbook," as well as over a hundred fragmentary pieces of papyri.[54] The rituals described within them are for the solitary magician, and meant to "take place in secret, oftentimes at night."[55] They contain a mixture of "prayers, remedies, and prophecies, offerings, apotropaic protection, initiation rites, dreams, visions, and especially spells intended to achieve a specific result."[56] Most often the goal of the spell caster was to "invoke and demand/bind the presence and aid of divine beings, *daimones*, for a variety of reasons including prophecy, forcing a victim to fall in love, or victory in a legal issue."[57]

The papyri mention over four hundred fifty "plants, minerals, animal products, herbs and other substances" in the many hundreds of "spells, incantations, formulas and imprecations" found within.[58] Frequently they are mentioned as forming the basis of incense burned (and explicitly or implicitly inhaled) or ointments applied to the body (and absorbed); in addition, although less frequently, there are also those consumed internally—this is "characteristic of many ancient aromatic essences prepared with olive oil or wine."[59] Examples[60] from the *Papyri Graecae Magicae* include manna, styrax, opium, myrrh, frankincense, saffron, bdella, mixed with spurge and fragrant wine (PGM IV.1830–40);[61] frankincense, laurel, myrtle, fruit pit, stavesacre, cinnamon leaf, and costus pounded and blended with Mendesian wine and honey and made into pills (PGM IV.2677–81);[62] water, myrrh, calf's snout plant, laurel branch, with fumigation of myrrh, frankincense, and frog's tongue (PGM V.195–201);[63] styrax, malabathron (probably *Cinnamomum tamala*), costus (*Saussurea lappa*), frankincense, Indian nard (probably *Nardostachys jatamansi*), cassia (*Cinnamomum cassia*), myrrh (PGM XIII.17–20);[64] and malabathron, styrax, nard, costus, cassia, frankincense, myrrh, mixed with wine and burned (PGM XIII.350–57).

Another substance, wormwood (*Artemisia absinthum*), a plant with a bitter taste and strong aroma, is mentioned in twenty-one different spells within the *Papyri Graecae Magicae*.[65] We read of the juice/oil (PGM IV.2140–44), seeds (V.370–446 and VII.593–619), root (XII.397–400), fragments (VII.993–1009), and the heart of the plant (XII.401–44) all being employed. Nearly all these spells "describe results that could be attributed to the intoxicating or hallucinogenic effects of wormwood."[66] The plant was clearly associated with the divine. The Greek name for the plant, *artemisias*, suggests "a religious connection to the deity Artemis."[67] The spell *Solomon's Collapse* indicates that after several days of abstinence the magician and the medium

> go to an open space equipped with the proper accoutrements for a successful and safe possession for divination. While wearing and holding the appropriate plants (signs of the particular deity), the fairly long spell is spoken 7 times, then incense is offered and libations are poured to the divine and it is spoken again 7 times. At this point the medium falls to the ground and the magician sits next to him asking for prophecy. And both should be crowned "with a garland of indigenous wormwood, both him and you for god delights in the plant" [PGM IV. 915–916].[68]

Another spell, *Slander Spell to Selene*, specifies wormwood must be picked at sunrise; this is important because we know thanks to Theophrastus (*History of Plants* 9.8.5–7) of similar rituals that were attached to the gathering of other pharmacologically potent plants like black hellebore and mandrake. On occasions wormwood is burned as incense and intentionally inhaled, although this is rare in the papyri. There are instances such as the *Memory Spell* detailing wormwood being mixed with ink, which is then drunk in water (PGM I.232–247). Although the wormwood in this particular spell is fumigated (leaving it powerless to affect the mind), there are other occasions (PGM VII.222–249 and VIII.64–110) where, although the ink is not drunk, pulverized juice of worm-wood is part of the ink. On other occasions ink of this kind is applied to the skin of the magician, and the thujone within the ink could be absorbed through the skin. Another spell (PGM II.64–184) requires the magician to smear a mixture containing nightshade all over himself. Additional drugs mentioned in the papyri include henbane, darnel, hemlock, and vetch.

Another substance known to ancient magicians and mentioned in the *Papyri Graecae Magicae* was *kyphi*, "a very ancient Egyptian incense, ointment and edible drug, containing up to thirty-six ingredients, all pharmacologically active."[69] These included wine, myrrh, juniper, and camel's thorn oil. Used in the mysteries of Isis as well as in magic, it was probably hallucinogenic.[70] The recipes for *kyphi* show a gradual refinement over time, from dynastic Egypt to the writings of Hippolytus of Rome (ca. 170–236 CE)[71] to the *Medical Compendium* of seventh-century Byzantine physician Paul of Aegina (ca. 625–690 CE). This long history "destroys an accepted mythology of modern medical historians" who either "assume ancient medicine and pharmacy developed to a certain point, then remained utterly static for centuries," or try to deny the same substance "would be part of a magical tradition but also a drug adapted into the pharmacies of learned medicine, suggested by the ten ingredient *kyphi* given by Dioscorides."[72]

Magic, Mystery Initiation, and Impiety

What was problematic about magic, at least in the Greek world of the fifth century BCE, and in particular Athens? Because of its associations, from earliest times, with mystery cults, magic itself came to resemble mysteries to such an extent that "some of its ceremonial became inextricably confused with mysteries."[73] Magic contains the *exclusivity* and *secrecy* characteristic of a mystery cult. The *Papyri Graecae Magicae*, which as we have just seen contain numerous references to *pharmaka*, do not distinguish between magic and mystery cult, calling magic a mystery (*mysterion*) and like terms.[74] Magic is a hidden knowledge, learned only with difficulty, at the hands of an expert, while mystery cults such as Eleusis promised "initiates advantages in this life and the next" but only to those who had been made ritually pure, and what was seen and heard, such as the *epopteia*, the initiate was forbidden to reveal.[75] Without secrecy the attraction of magic "disappears and it becomes just another cult-activity."[76] Magic needs a religious orthodoxy that forbids or at least frowns on it.

Clement of Alexandria (ca. 150–211/216 CE), who developed a brand of Christian Platonism, reports in his anti-pagan tract *Exhortation to the Greeks* (22) that Heraclitus of Ephesus (ca. 535–475 BCE), the pre-Socratic Greek philosopher, had prophesied fire and destruction lay in store for vagabonds who wandered by night (*nyktipoloi*), magicians (*magoi*), followers of Dionysus (*bac-*

choi), maenads (*lanai*), and initiates into the mysteries (*mystai*), because they "are initiated in an unholy manner into the mystery-rites followed by men." It is of course by no means certain that Heraclitus truly ever said such things or that Clement has accurately paraphrased them, but it is still "entirely feasible that the words quoted by Clement represent what Heraclitus wrote."[77] What is important about the practices that Clement describes Heraclitus as commenting on is that "the impiety Heraclitus saw in these ceremonies of initiation lay in part in their being performed *privately* and apart from the cults that the city sanctioned."[78]

Trials for Magical Impiety

While there is no evidence of any specific legislation regarding sorcery during the Greek Classical Period, magicians were, it appears, at least occasionally the subject of legal action. The Areopagus was a court that oversaw cases of homicide, cases involving the use of *pharmaka*, and arson.[79] A *pharmakon* could be used to simply poison a person, of course, either intentionally or accidentally, without any *magical* intention, but "the use of physical substances in combination with verbal spells and rituals as *pharmaka* raise the possibility of prosecutions before the Areopagus of persons accused of bringing the death of another by sorcery on the ground that they had administered *pharmaka*."[80] In the Aristotelian *Magna Moralia* (1188b), for example, we read of a woman who had given a love-philtre to a man who drank it and subsequently died; having administered the drug out of love, rather than with a view to killing him, the Areopagus ruled her motivation was not murder and acquitted her.[81]

The love potion or *philtron* (plural *philtra*), is mentioned many times in Greek literature, for example in Euripides' *Andromache*. Hermione, the daughter of king Menelaus, accuses Andromache of having employed drugs to render her both unattractive in the eyes of her husband, Achilles' son Neoptolemus, as well as destroying her womb and making it barren (155–60).[82] Andromache denies she is using any such "secret drugs [*pharmaka*]" (29–35) and replies to her accuser: "It is not because of my drugs that your husband hates you, but because you are unpleasant to him. I'll tell you a love potion [*philtron*]: it is not beauty but good character that delights one's lover" (205–8). To Menelaus she denies "bewitching [*pharmakeuo*] your daughter [Hermione] and causing her to miscarry her babies" (355–60). Theophrastus, in his *History of Plants*, mentions at least three substances that were mixed with wine and used to enhance the mood or as aphrodisiacs in love potions—oleander, cyclamen, and mandrake (9.19.3). Such potions were a noetic threat to "a philosophical (and therefore minority) model of normatively rational and self-controlled masculinity" for two reasons.[83] First, love potions "threaten the 'natural' superiority of the mind over the body; and when used by social inferiors against men, they jeopardize the superiority and autonomy of the putatively more rational male elites and the social institutions they command."[84]

Athens in the Classical Period had no law against magic *per se*. It would appear that so long as a magician "kept to magic and did not presume to play the part of priests in private religious ceremonies" they could work without the constant threat of a charge of *graphe asebeias* hanging over their head.[85] It was at least possible, however, that the charge of *asebeia* was used to prosecute cases of impiety that arose out of the sort of magic-working that profaned the sanctioned religious mysteries of the *polis*. As we saw in chapter 5, above, the statute concerning impiety, *asebeia*, lacked either theological or ideological consistency and could—though it is by no means certain—encompass a wide variety of behaviors, "be they pharmaceutical, philosophical, pious, or political," either singly or in some mixture.[86] A practitioner of sorcery might, apparently, be tried for impiety (*asebeia*).[87] The motivation, it appears, was "disciplining what could be represented as undesirable religious innovation."[88]

The best example, and even it is admittedly sketchy, is of a woman named Theoris who was accused of being a sorceress in fourth-century Athens. There are three sources that discuss this case: a speech titled *Against Aristogiton* from the corpus of Demosthenes, a fragment that Harpocration, a Greek grammarian of Alexandria (fl. second century CE), attributes to the historian and politician Philochorus of Athens (fl. third century BCE, died ca. 261 BCE), and the *Life of Demosthenes* by Plutarch. In *Against Aristogiton* (25.79–80) we read: "You put to death the accursed Theoris, the Lemnian, the sorceress [*pharmakis*], the woman herself, and all her family. The reason for this was her drugs [*pharmaka*]. This man [the brother of Aristogeiton] got these drugs of hers and her incantations [*epodai*] from her maid [who was the man's mother], the woman who gave all the information about her at her trial."[89] Philochorus is said to have identified her as "a diviner (*mantis*)" who was "executed for impiety *asebeia*." Plutarch's *Life of Demosthenes* (14.5) indicates Theoris was a priestess (*hiereia*) who was, thanks to the efforts of Demosthenes, executed for "being in general detrimental, and in particular for teaching slaves to be deceitful."[90]

Theoris was neither a "local witch" nor some "poor destitute old woman"— she was either someone important enough in her own right or she was someone who possessed important enough connections that a prosecution would prove advantageous.[91] She was "clearly a figure of some renown or notoriety" for the speaker in *Against Aristogeiton* appears to assume her name will draw the recognition of the jury.[92] We know she had a maidservant, possessed knowledge of *pharmaka*, and knew *epodai*. The fact that her maidservant passes the knowledge of those incantations on to her son suggests a book of spells, which in turn implies Theoris was literate.[93] Literacy, given the economic realities of ancient Athens, could not have been common, meaning that anyone who could read and who possessed a book would be endowed with unusual "power, authority, and charisma."[94]

On the one hand, Theoris may have been a *demi-monde*. These women tended to be "slaves in origin but either have their freedom purchased for them or establish a *de facto* freedom for themselves."[95] Unlike other women they were free to move about in public, and would "set up their own establishments with the help of well-to-do male patrons and admirers, have maidservants, and when their days as prostitutes or courtesans are over, the more intelligent and enterprising become madams and live off the earnings of younger women, while the others have to revert to living as common prostitutes."[96] On the other hand, the text of *Against Aristogeiton* describes this person, who is the son of her maid and the brother of Aristogeiton, as being an "evil-eye-er (*baskanos*)" who "plays magical tricks [*manganeuei*] and cheats and claims that he cures epileptics [*epileptoi*], while he himself is caught [*epileptos*] in wickedness of every kind."[97] Her maid was able to take over her practice, which "clearly implies that at one level what she did was perfectly acceptable," and the curing of epileptics certainly suggests the magical "purificatory healing of the kind denounced by the Hippocratic *On the Sacred Disease*."[98]

Another trial was that of Ninos who was executed between 350 and 340 BCE. Demosthenes, mocking the heritage of Aeschines, a political rival, refers to the fact that a woman was executed for doing what his mother Glaucothea, a priestess (*hiereia*), did.[99] That this other woman was Ninos may be gleaned from another source, which mentions "the woman was called Ninos and that she was accused by a certain Menecles of having made love-philters for young men; another explanation of the passage, which appears to belong to an alternative tradition of interpretation, says that Ninos was executed because the ceremonies she performed were felt to have made a mockery of the real mysteries" while Glaucothea had, thanks to an oracle, been allowed to "conduct initiations into the mysteries of Sabazios."[100] Menecles was described as belonging to a group who frequently brought accusations against others, and there is evidence her son later took legal action against him. This suggests, first, "that not everyone thought Ninos deserved to be convicted and executed" and, second, that the woman's family "must have had some standing in Athenian society."[101] If she was executed for having conducted an illicit version of the same initiations carried out by Glaucothea, namely the mysteries of the god Sabazios, the "charge in that event was almost certainly *asebeia*."[102] Arguing that the Jews "were not the only people jealous of their religious tradition," Josephus (37–ca.100 CE) gives a list of individuals accused of impiety in Athens: it "begins with Socrates, who is followed by Anaxagoras, Diagoras, and finally Ninos."[103]

Socrates and Magic

Socrates exhibits knowledge of magic in the works of both Xenophon and Plato. In Xenophon's *Memorabilia* he pays a visit to the home of Theodote, a well-to-do *hetairai* who is having her portrait painted. If the literary evidence linking the practice of magic with that of prostitution is a bit thin, the material record leaves little doubt that prostitutes in Athens "lived in a milieu in which sorcery was, if not endemic, certainly present to a degree that it was not in other sectors of society."[104] Theodote describes herself as making her living through the generosity of male friends (3.11.4), triggering a discussion of friendship and the retention of friends. Socrates then indicates (3.11.16–17) he can't get away from his female friends (*philai*) who have learned the use of both love potions (*philtra*) and incantations (*epoidai*) from him. Theodote immediately inquires as to what he knows of these subjects. Socrates replies the reason his students such as Apollodorus and Antisthenes never leave his side is the result of "many love potions (*philtra*), incantations (*epoidai*), and erotic magic (*inux*) spells."

The *inux* was one form of "violent and invasive erotic magic" almost always used by men "to drive women from the homes of their fathers or husbands," the notable exception being *hetairai* and other prostitutes who appropriated the same spells "to draw men out of their homes and into their own arms."[105] Theodote insists that Socrates lend her his *inux*, so that she may use it on him. Socrates exclaims he wasn't "planning to be drawn to you, but rather I want you to come to me!" The scene is clearly meant to be humorous, but we should not dismiss its importance either. First, Socrates presents himself (however ironically), or is (mis)understood by others, as practicing magic of one form or another on too many occasions. Second, as I have argued in chapter 5, above, there appears to have been a popular perception of Socrates as a practitioner of black magic, something that was considered impious and could have been a component of the charge of impiety he was tried and executed for.

Plato makes widespread use of the language of magic and spells.[106] The "special form of words uttered by the sorcerer to effect his purposes" was *epaoide*, often reduced to *epode*.[107] *Epode* and its various cognates appear no less than fifty times in Plato, encompassing "the dialogues of his youth to those of his extreme old age."[108] These include the *Charmides, Laws, Phaedrus, Republic, Theatetus, Gorgias, Euthydemus, Menexenus, Symposium,* and *Epinomos*.[109] *Epode* is translated from the original Greek only with difficulty. Much like the word for drug, *pharmakon*, the meaning of *epode* shifts restlessly between "conjuration, charm, incantation, or spell."[110] The *epode* is also constantly referred to in order to describe the psychologically effective word.[111] The tradition of using *epode* this way was well established by the time Plato wrote. In Sophocles' *Oedipus at Colonus*, in response to her father's anger, Antigone reminds him "Other men too have terrible sons and a sharp anger (*thumos*) against them, but assuaged by the spells (*epodai*) of friends their angry nature is dispelled (*exepaidontai*)" (1192–94). In the *Phaedo* (77e, and cf. 78a) Socrates tells us we must sing spells to ourselves to ward off the childish fear of death while the belief in judgment after death, too, should be repeated "to oneself like a spell (*epode*)" (114d).

Magical therapy in the case of the Greeks had a chance to "gain public acceptance to a degree that was unthinkable in the sphere of eastern governmental bureaucracy."[112] Lacking "straightforward institutions of monarchic power and law," the wellspring of Greek civilization was freedom.[113] It was undoubtedly true that, just as in the case of medicine, there was no shortage of individuals in ancient Greece "who were willing to make use of the wrath of the spirits of the dead in order to direct it against personal enemies, through black magic."[114]

Plato can be seen as responding to this on numerous occasions. In the *Laws* (932e–933a) he constructs a discussion of unscrupulous physicians and magicians who "do mischief by the practice of spells, charms, incantations or other such sorceries," in the context of the legal penalties to be meted out for "injury inflicted by drugs" (*pharmakois*).[115] Earlier in the same dialogue, during a discussion of a drug to induce fear (*phobou pharmakon*), the Athenian dismisses the likelihood that such a drug exists, either as a gift of the gods or by human invention, leaving aside the claims made by magico-medical quacks (*goetas*) whose concoctions are unworthy of consideration (649a). Clearly, however, some of Plato's audience, or someone his audience must have been familiar with, must have believed it possible to obtain such a *pharmakon* or a similar magic potion, or else he wouldn't have bothered to make reference to *goetas* or prescribe penalties for drugs made available by them.

Plato uses *epode* in two primary senses. The first retains the medico-magical meaning that had been in place for some time. In the *Laws* Plato speaks negatively of "sorceries [*manganeiai*], incantations [*epodai*], and so-called bindings [*katadeseis*]" that persuade "those bold enough to attempt harm with them" with the belief they can do so, and convince their intended victims "they are being harmed by those who have this power" (933a). This includes "the placing of wax figurines at doors or at crossroads or in some cases on the tombs of [the victim's] ancestors" (*Laws* 933b).[116] Other examples of *epoidai* mentioned by Plato are the charms utilized by midwives along with the drugs they give women (*Theatetus* 149c), and the healing words used by physicians along with burning, cutting, and drugs (*Republic* 426b, *Charmides* 156e). In the *Laws* water is said to be exceptionally important in the growth of every kind of garden produce. Considerably more so than soil, sunlight, or wind, water is easily contaminated. In addition to theft or diversion, it may also be spoiled "by means of sorcery (*pharmakeuein*)."[117] The law must come to its rescue

> If one man intentionally tampers with another's supply, whether of spring water or standing water, whether by drugging (*pharmakeiais*), or digging, or of theft, the injured party shall put the amount of damages on record, and proceed at law before the urban commissioners. A party convicted of putting poison (*pharmakeiais*) in the waters shall, over and above the payment of the fine imposed, undertake the purification of the contaminated springs or reservoir in such a fashion as the canon law may direct this purification to be performed in the individual case (845d–e).

In contrast to early modern Europe where theologians and scientists "could pool their knowledge systems to elaborate 'true' tests of whether someone was a witch,"[118] in ancient Greece no such "socially accepted set of knowledge systems" existed; wherever the latter is the case, "a whole host of local and personal standards will reign."[119] Not surprisingly then Plato, despite his general hostility to the charms, enchantments, spells and drugs of magical practice, occasionally throws up his hands in frustration at the entire matter, since the

Greeks drew no firm differentiations "between naturalistic and religious use of *pharmaka*—the religious use providing the possibility of legal action."[120] In the *Laws* (933a–b) he concludes that it is "not easy to know the truth about these and similar practices, and even if one were to find out, it would be difficult to convince others; and it is just not worth the effort to try and persuade people whose heads are full of mutual suspicion." Plato may have never devoted "serious theoretical thought to defining the notion of magic" and the entire subject may always be "a peripheral issue" in his dialogues.[121] But magic is, all the same, part of his general opposition to those occupations who wield the power of the *pharmakon*. His views on the practice of magic must also be situated amidst the bevy of other occupations whose practices disrupt noetic stability and health.[122]

The second sense in which Plato uses the word *epode* utilizes a "new metaphorical or analogical meaning," one that exhibits "an explicit attitude of moral and intellectual reproach."[123] Plato inaugurated a major semantic shift, transforming the *epode* from magical charm or conjuration into "reasoning or a tale against error or against harmful emotions."[124] The *Symposium*, for example, identifies the "lovers of wisdom" as an "intermediate class" like the spirits that venture back and forth between man and the gods, making possible "all prophecy and religion, whether it concerns sacrifice, forms of worship, incantations, or any kind of divination or sorcery" (202e–203a, 204a–b). Both the magic charm-*epode* and the persuasive word-*epode* are, in Plato, verbal expressions seeking "to produce and do in fact produce a real and effective change in the mind on whom they act."[125] Plato condemns the charm-*epode* as superstition and fraud (*Republic* 364b, *Laws* 909a), while making use of the word-*epode* for his own ends.

We know from sources such as Pindar's *Pythian Ode* (3.47–54) and Plato's *Charmides* (155e–156e) and *Euthydemus* (289e, 290a) that incantations and amulets "often accompanied the protective or therapeutic act."[126] In the *Charmides* the character bearing the name of the dialogue asks (155e) if Socrates "knew the cure for [his] headache" (*to tes kephales pharmakon*). Socrates responds that he knows of a certain leaf that when applied with a particular charm is a perfect remedy (*epode de tis epi toi pharmakon*), but that "without the charm there was no efficacy in the leaf." The account gives frustratingly few details since it is meant primarily as an introduction to a discussion of the meaning of what is said to be the best *pharmakon* of all, moderation (*sophrosyne*), but it does preserve a trace of a "folkloristic belief probably contemporary with the dialogue's composition if not indeed personally known to the historical Socrates."[127]

Philosophic *Hygeia*

In the *Republic* Plato distinguishes between the noetic capacities of two groups. Philosophers are men "who are able to grasp what is always the same in all respects," the eternal and unchanging, while those who are not philosophers wander all over the place "among what is many" and variable (484a–b). In the *Sophist* Plato tells us that "the supreme things of all, the things of highest worth," cannot be demonstrated via "sensible analogies"—they exist only in our minds and cannot be "fitted to a sense imprint in a way to give true satisfaction" (285e–286a). These "incorporeal realities," the "fairest and highest of all realities," Plato tells us, can be displayed with certainty "*only by discourse and in no other way*" (286a, emphasis mine). Thus, to understand these highest realities each of us must acquire "the power to give and receive argument on all subjects" (286a). The power Plato refers to here is, specifically, that of "dialectical proficiency and capacity for reasoned presentation of truth" (287a).

Only a very small number of individuals will ever be capable of acquiring such proficiency at any given time. In the *Republic* they are said to be the "fewest of all in number" (428e and 429a). In the *Statesman* their number has dwindled to as few as one or two individuals, or at best a very small group (293a). The philosophical capacities of the many are continually denigrated. The *Republic* states quite plainly that it is "impossible" for a "multitude to be philosophic" (494a). The "mental eye of the vulgar cannot bear the light of the divine" that the philosopher is capable of beholding (*Sophist* 254a–b). Correct political administration is a science only a select few can master; "no large body of persons" can possibly fathom it (*Statesman* 297b–c). The issue becomes one of what the popular role vis-á-vis political administration might be once the capacity for participation in it is precluded.[128]

Herophilus of Chalcedon (335–280 BCE) states that some two hundred years before the Greeks had made health a precondition for other goods such as strength, wealth, intelligence, and wisdom. Socrates and Plato drew from this development when they became the first in a tradition that saw somatic and noetic health as being inseparably linked. *Hygeia*, the art of therapy, "came to encompass a variety of purposes: medical, social, political, artistic, ethical, and religious."[129] Philosophic practice becomes, for Plato, *hygeia* of the soul. Medicine is the model of what a *techne* really and truly should be because it (a) is able to explain its own procedures, (b) possesses knowledge based on understanding of the real nature of its subject, and (c) never deviates from service to the good of its object.[130]

The Spell of *Elenchus* and *Diairesis*

The basic treatment modalities of philosophic *hygeia* consist of *elenchus* and *diairesis* on the one hand, and myth (*muthos*) on the other. The dialectical man (*dialektikos*), we are told, "grasps the reason for the being of each thing" and is able to give a precise account (*Republic* 534b). His method for uncovering truth is what the *Republic* (511b) describes as the power of conversing, what the *Phaedo* (90b) calls the art of discussions (*he peri tous logous techne*), what the *Sophist* calls discussion with a particular procedure (*he methodos ton logon*) and is, according to the *Republic* (553b–c), the only art and science truly awake. *Elenchus* and *diairesis* are serious, both unpleasant and painful for the patient exposed to them. Dialectic *elenchus* often produces a disorienting *aporia* in the recipient, who is rendered "bound" and helpless in a manner reminiscent of magical *katadesmoi* (e.g. *Meno* 80b, *Gorgias* 482e, *Laches* 194b, *Republic* 350d and 358b–c, *Theatetus* 168b). Myth in contrast is playful and pleasant; according to the *Statesman* it allays the pain and tedium of the former two methods (268d).

In the *Lesser Hippias* Socrates says that when he desires to understand the wisdom of what another is saying he proceeds to "question him thoroughly and consider again and compare the things said" until he, that is Socrates, has "benefited in some way" (369d–e). In the *Gorgias* Socrates says that unless one or the other of the discussants consents to adhere to the truth of what the other is saying "nothing worth speaking of will have been accomplished" (472b–c, and cf. 474a–475e). Truth emerges from the consensus of an agonistic struggle between speakers. Yet unlike the art of speaking taught by professional sophists, or the rhetoric utilized by the sophist's student in the assembly or the law courts, philosophic discourse scorns, as useless, the claim that *truth* is reducible to the number of witnesses willing to agree with you, and the ability to make one's own position seem more plausible or probable, tactics that often require that the facts of a case be suppressed to enhance the reasonableness of the argument (*Gorgias* 471e–472a, *Laws* 937d, 859b–c, 861c–d). Enlightenment, happiness, and a virtuous soul exist in consociation within the Platonic scheme. In the *Gorgias* Socrates answers Polus that he would be unable to say whether or not the King of Persia is happy or not unless he could also "know what degree of enlightenment and virtue he had attained" (470d, cf. *Laws* 730b).[131]

The basis of knowledge cannot be sensory experience, so it must be "latent within the psyche, antecedent to all sensory experience."[132] The Platonic process of *anamnesis*, remembrance or recollection, brings to light that which we once experienced while in disembodied communion with the eternal Forms. While in theory anyone can grasp an occasional fragment of that sublime state of understanding (as the slave boy is led to an understanding of simple mathematical relationships in the *Meno*), Plato evidently felt that in practice most human beings were too chained to the shadowy *doxai* of material existence to comprehend the innate vision of true reality. That vision, that sight, is accessible only to an initiated few, in much the same way that particular sorts of knowledge were accessible if one had been initiated into a particular mystery religion, school of magic, or physician's guild.

For those not destined to be philosophers/moral physicians, myth allows for the acquisition of true opinion and emotional-epithymetic self-control, the best that can be expected of the multitude. Socrates does not denigrate myths; they are a source of truth, just inadequate by themselves for men of refined intelligence (*Phaedo* 114d). The position is repeated throughout the dialogues (*Meno* 81a, *Symposium* 199a–b, *Republic* 514a–518d, 614b–621a). In the *Republic* myth functions as a "means of indoctrination," the success of which requires "unquestioning acceptance."[133] In the *Laws* the nameless Athenian is willing to go to extraordinary ends to achieve noetic health/harmony in a *polis*. Any law is permissible to achieve this end: action, speech, pleasures, pain, honor, disgrace, fines, or gifts. "We may use absolutely any means to make [the diseased mind] hate injustice and embrace true justice—or at least not hate it" (*Laws* 862d–e). The man beyond cure (*aniatos*) serves a useful purpose, by dying. It is the best thing for all concerned that "such people cease to live—best even for themselves" (863a). Their death will serve as a warning (*paradeigma*) to others, and the state will benefit from the social hygiene produced by the elimination of such scoundrels.

The Spell of Myth

Verbal devices such as myth are utilized by Plato within the *Laws* to establish noetic regimens within the public's mind.[134] At the earliest stages "education is . . . the drawing and leading of children" to the rule of law (*Laws* 659d–e). Songs and other means act as *epodai* for the soul and are part of the production of mental order (659e). Music, in the *Republic*, is called an "antistrophe" to physical training, its opposite and counterpart (522a). It educates not by imparting knowledge, but by instilling habits of harmony and rhythm. Similar habits are learned by listening to speeches; neither are part of the sort of study that leads the soul to ascend from "becoming to being" (521d). To let the "sweet and dirge-like airs" of music pour into oneself "without remission" entails the risk of leaving one "spellbound" (*kelei*). Eventually the high spirited (*thumoeide*) part of the soul "melts and liquefies" until it "completely dissolves away" (411a–b).[135] This would be disastrous, for as we saw in chapter 7, above, the *Timaeus* states that the *thymoeides* helps to keep the appetitive part of the soul, the *epithymetikon*, in check (69e–79a).

Virtually all harmonic modes and rhythms are to be "purged" from men who act "moderately and in measure" rather than form a condition of "illiberality and insolence or madness and the rest of vice" (*Republic* 398d–400c). Plato evidently came under some criticism for retaining the Phrygian mode, because as Aristotle expresses it in the *Politics*, "the Phrygian mode has exactly the same effect as the pipes among instruments: both are orgiastic and emotional," and "Bacchic frenzy and all similar agitation," such as that resulting from hearing the dithyramb, finds expression in the pipes and *the Phrygian mode above all others* (1342a–b). Plato believed that abandoning oneself to music in *small* quantities could be useful, owing to the fact that the spirited part of the soul is made soft and malleable, like iron (*Republic* 411a). The description of the effect of small amounts of wine upon the soul in the *Laws* is nearly identical (666a–c). Plato indicates how deeply intoxication, music and noetic training are *interrelated* when he writes in the *Laws* that a genuinely sound theory on so inconsiderable a topic as intoxication "cannot be surely and adequately expounded apart from a true theory of music, nor that again, from a theory of education at large" (642a).[136]

Myth, speeches, and songs all act as charms in the *Laws*; each creates noetic habituation, each causes people to "charm themselves unceasingly" (665a). Belief in god, for example, arises in the souls of children through "stories, crooned over them, in sport and in earnest, like spells [*epodai*]" (887d). What began as "a conjuration or magical charm" turns, in the *Phaedo*, into "reasoning or a tale against error or against harmful emotions."[137] The spell consists of the long myth of the judgment of the soul after death (*Phaedo* 113d–114c), something Socrates does not claim to have perfect knowledge of, but since it is reasonable to conclude the soul is immortal, the myth should be continually repeated "to oneself like a spell [*epode*]" (114d). To cure the fear of death that resides in the childlike part of ourselves, Socrates tells Cebes, we must "sing spells to him everyday" until the fear has been charmed away (77e). No expense should be spared to find a good charmer (*agathon epodon*) to dispel the fear of death, and in the best circumstances the charm will be found to exist within oneself through mutual exploration with other thoughtful men (78a).

Myth substitutes for argumentation, acting as a charm (*Gorgias* 523a–526d, *Republic* 614b–621b, *Laws* 903a–b). While discussion (*dialegein*) obliges or forces (*biazesthai*) the listener, through the use of argument and reasons (*tois logois*), to confess their errors and recognize the truth, myth "is able to persuade (*peithein*) the favorable acceptance (*apodechoomai*) of that which can and should be believed."[138] Beautiful speeches, as a charm or myth, "elicit a new belief in the mind of the one who listens to it or make more intense the beliefs that already existed deep within the mind."[139] The goal is the modification of the soul of the person to whom the myth is addressed, the production of *sophrosyne*, as is pointed out in the *Charmides* (157a). The good philosopher-cum-magician—and there cannot be any doubt that it is commonly philosopher-cum-*pharmakon*-wielding magician—adapts his captivating arguments to suit the needs of a particular student or a particular audience. The enchanting word places the mind and, to the extent that it is possible, the body, in a state of calm, enlightened, good order. Plato is very far away from the magic or sorcery in the strict sense of impious *goeteia*, the sort of necromancy Aristophanes depicts Socrates as practicing in the *Birds* and Plato himself condemns in the *Laws*.

Socrates' Philosophic Sorcery

The magical power over the mind exerted by the poet, sophist, and others produces false *doxai*. Socratic *elenchus* is aimed at destroying those false *doxai*. What is being dispelled is just as much false hallucinations or phantoms as false opinions. The magic of Socrates is the magic of implacable truth.[140] The *elenchus* is, alternately and simultaneously, counter*magic*, counter*charm* and counter*drug*. It is relatively easy to see how the Socratic version would be misunderstood and lumped together with existing forms of magic. In the *Phaedo*, for example, Simmias asks Socrates "where shall we find a magician (*epodon*) who understands these spells now that you are leaving us?" (77e). Agathon, in the *Symposium*, jests "*Pharmattein boulei me, o Socrates*," kiddingly implying the philosopher is using "a little black magic" to unnerve him before he gives his speech (194a). In the *Meno* (80b) the title character exclaims albeit humorously that Socrates is using his words to bewitch (*goeteuein*), drug (*pharmatteis*), and perform spell-binding incantations (*katepaeidein*) to leave him numb with perplexity. His joking turns on "the belief that sorcery could make a person quite helpless and, in particular, render him totally inarticulate in a court of law."[141] Meno warns Socrates that he had better watch himself: if he were a stranger (*xenos*) behaving like this anywhere but in Athens, it might lead to him being summarily arrested (*apagoge*) as a sorcerer (*goes*).[142]

During the Classical Period Greek magic included a form of binding spell, the *katadesmos*.[143] Inscribed on small, beaten out sheets of lead, the spell would be rolled up and pierced with a nail, and deposited in a location thought best to harm the target of the spell.[144] Much like "the root-cutters' drugs, these tablets could be fabricated to achieve diverse aims: outselling commercial rivals, winning theatrical contests, gaining favorable judgments in court and, of course, bedding the beloved."[145] Perhaps most importantly the text of the spell would often invoke the immobilization of "the enemy's mental and verbal abilities."[146] Plato speaks in a general way about those who make these sorts of binding spells for a price in the *Republic*, writing that if a man "wishes to ruin some enemies at small expense, he will injure just and unjust alike with certain evocations and spells. They, as they say, persuade the gods to serve them" (364b–c).[147]

Plato can be seen as denouncing what he sees as "the 'amoral' aspects of this type of black magic."[148] It is not clear, however, to what extent Plato's denunciations of magic were representative of views held by his contemporaries, or idiosyncratic. What is more clear is that *he* viewed the disruption of noetic stability by the various practitioners of magic as yet another instance of unseating the *logistikon*, and from that perspective it was threatening. The victim of *katadesis* was said to be rendered incapable of speaking, often because they knew a truth harmful to the spell caster.[149] In the case of Plato's text the magically bound Meno's unwillingness to speak arises from his confused realization that he *doesn't* know the truth. The creation of lead *katadesmoi* was routinely denounced in antiquity because acts of black magic, as "unsanctioned" religion, were seen as "threats to social stability and cohesion on account of their harmful intentions and their relationship to the uncanny."[150]

In the *Symposium* Diotima, from Mantinea, does not appear to have been based on any historical person but is, as most scholars have argued, a fictional mouthpiece for Platonic doctrine. Her presence allows Socrates to address what he sees as the superficiality of the speeches delivered by the other guests present at Agathon's *symposion* without violating the celebratory spirit of the occasion or the rule already established by the physician Eryximachus that each person shall give a speech on the subject of Eros. While it may be tempting to view Diotima as an educated courtesan (akin to Aspasia, the common-law wife of Pericles), the primary model for her character is suggested by her place of origin, Mantinea, a name that recalls the profession of *mantis* (seer), though since she claims to possess expertise in a large number of areas besides prophecy, including the art of sacrifice to ward off "the onset of disease," it might be more accurate to view her as an *iatromantis* (healer-seer), an intermediary stage that apparently existed between the *mantis* and the professional physician, the *iatros*.[151] The *mantis*, *iatromantis* and *iatros* would often travel abroad, on temporary sojourns called *epidemia*, hiring out their services.[152] Diotima is said to have come to Athens and given certain instructions that warded off the plague for ten years (*Symposium* 201d–e).

Diotima gives Eros the title of wizard (*pharmakeus*). Eros, however, has the unmistakable features of Socrates, as though Diotima were proposing to Socrates a picture of himself.[153] Eros is a fearsome sorcerer (*deinos goes*), magician (*pharmakeus*) and sophist (*sophistes*). Socrates, like Eros, is a *daimon*, between the divine and the mortal, the medium of all prophecy and religion "whether it concerns sacrifice (*thusias*), initiations (*teletas*), incantations (*epodas*), or any kind of divination or sorcery (*manteian*)" (202e–203a).[154] Socrates' words are said to enchant and possess people like the flute of the satyr Marsyas (215b–c). He produces in the unprincipled Alcibiades an experience of the "madness (*mania*) and Bacchic frenzy (*bakcheia*) of philosophy" (218b). Yet we are told this image of Socrates as a seducing *goes* or *pharmakeus* is only a deceptive "outer casing"—inside are the "divine images of virtue" that the lover of virtue recognizes and follows of his own free will (216e–217a, 222a–b). This is a clear example of "how philosophy opposes a rational love of the good with the enslaving and anti-rational *eros* associated with magic."[155]

Socrates, like Marsyas, can bewitch mankind, only "without any instrument," be it flute, charm, or *pharmakon*. He merely uses a "few simple words (*logois*)" (215c–d). This is not simply a matter of dialectical *elenchus* or *diairesis* dissolving the power of the *epode*, undoing "the charlatanesque confidence of a *pharmakeus* from the vantage point of some obstinate instance of transparent reason or innocent *logos*."[156] Socratic irony "precipitates out one *pharmakon* by bringing it in contact with another *pharmakon*."[157] The *elenchus* is an act of supplementation: it both *adds to* and *replaces* contemporary fourth-century Greek magic. "It is one magic against another, the one taking the former's place, but with opposite aims and means."[158] The *elenchus* allows at least a select few to realize the hallucinatory, phantom–like quality of their false opinions. These *doxai* lead a person to act in ways contrary to the soul's health, into vice, disease of the soul. Once a person realizes they are the cause of their own noetic disorder they feel shame and anger, directed at themselves if the process was successful, with Socrates if the *elenchus* fails. If the disease was recognized it may be cast out, and the soul purified. Socratic *elenchus* bears a strong resemblance to cathartic rites that used spells to cast out fear.[159]

The *Statesman* describes the guardian or sovereign as determining on a case-by-case basis "whether another [discipline] is to be studied" (304c); education, persuasion, and oratory are among the fields to be regulated so that the end result of their practice is the production of "truly sober and right thinking" individuals possessing convictions of honor, right and good in their souls (267b–d, 275a–276e, 295e–296a, 304b–d, 305c–d, 308c–309e). Among the occupations scrambling for a share of the authority to raise mankind in the mass, the *Statesmen* also includes "merchants, farmers and bakers, to say nothing of physical trainers or the medical profession" (267e–268c). A general problem with most if not all of the occupations Plato perceives as being in competition with philosophy is that they provide pleasure over other goods and are not, at least genuinely, concerned with truth, even where they occasionally manage to uncover it, which for the most part they either do accidentally or not at all. The *Statesman* (279a) says they must be eliminated, without exception, from contention.

Noetic order is brought about through the creation of personal mental habits "worthy of honor," what the *Republic* (591b–c) terms a regime or government within the self exercising, ideally, orderly rule of the self, by the self. In the *Statesman* the Visitor explains that those who lack a "disposition that is courageous and moderate, and whatever else belongs to the sphere of virtue," and are instead snared in the psychological grip of an "evil nature," shall be killed, exiled and "punished with the most extreme forms of dishonor" (308e–309a). The remainder, "whose natures are capable of becoming composed and stable in the direction of nobility," the statesman weaves together, the courageous being the warp, the moderate the woof, of the social fabric (309a–b). Weaving is essential. Without it the courageous lose restraint and become mad, while the moderate grow sluggish and become incapacitated (310d–e).

Yet even the practice of weaving (*sumploke*) is simultaneously caught up in the question of the *pharmakon*. Expert knowledge would not try to weave the vicious with the vicious, or the good with the vicious (310e).

> What I propose we should say is that it [i.e. virtue] only takes root through laws, in those dispositions that were both born noble in the first place and have been nurtured [by educators and tutors appointed by the Statesman] in accordance with their nature [i.e. a disposition tending towards either courage or moderation]; and that it is for these [i.e. the warp and woof] that this expert drug by art (*techne pharmakon*) exists (310a).[160]

The wise governor is described in the *Statesman* as "dispensing to the citizens a supreme justice founded on intelligence and science, and so are efficient to preserve them and, so far as may be, to make them better men than they were" (297a–b). The restoration of noetic order in the unbalanced mind is an act of intervention, a remedial, curative counter-magic, often undertaken *in extremis*.

Notes

1. Regimen, above and beyond any definition having to do with dietetics or gymnastic training, can also mean government, authority or administration; along with the words regime and regimentation, its etymological origins can be traced to the Latin *regere*, to rule.

2. Kostas Kalimtzis, *Aristotle on Political Enmity and Disease—An Inquiry into Stasis* (Albany, NY: State University of New York Press, 2000), 5.

3. "Opinions are robbed, Socrates elaborates, by forgetfulness and clever speech, forced away by grief and pain, and exorcised by pleasure or fear." See Randall B. Clark, *The Law Most Beautiful and Best: Medical Argument and Magical Rhetoric in Plato's Laws* (Lanham, MD: Lexington Books, 2003), 106.

4. Pedro Lain Entralgo, *The Therapy of the Word in the Ancient World* (New Haven, CT: Yale University Press, 1970), 125.

5. Mathew W. Dickie, *Magic and Magicians in the Greco-Roman World* (New York: Routledge, 2003), 21.

6. The discussion in this section and those that follow on ancient magic relies heavily on Dickie, *Magic and Magicians in the Greco-Roman World*.

7. Dickie, *Magic and Magicians in the Greco-Roman World*, 49.

8. Dickie, *Magic and Magicians in the Greco-Roman World*, 87.

9. Dickie, *Magic and Magicians in the Greco-Roman World*, 18.

10. To males listening to the poet, at any rate; how the figure of Circe might have been received by girls and women seems more open to debate.

11. Daniel Ogden, *Magic, Witchcraft, and Ghosts in the Greek and Roman Worlds—A Sourcebook* (New York: Oxford University Press, 2002), 98.

12. Dickie, *Magic and Magicians in the Greco-Roman World*, 23.

13. Quoted in Ogden, *Magic, Witchcraft, and Ghosts in the Greek and Roman Worlds—A Sourcebook*, 78.

14. On Medea and Hecate see Ogden, *Magic, Witchcraft, and Ghosts in the Greek and Roman Worlds—A Sourcebook*, 78–93.

15. Susan A. Stephens, *Seeing Double: Intercultural Poetics in Ptolemaic Alexandria* (Berkeley, CA: University of California Press, 2003), 39.

16. Stephens, *Seeing Double*, 40.

17. Ogden, *Magic, Witchcraft, and Ghosts in the Greek and Roman Worlds—A Sourcebook*, 82. On Medea and drugs see also James J. Clauss and Sarah Iles Johnson, eds., *Medea: Essays on Medea in Myth, Literature, Philosophy, and Art* (Princeton, NJ: Princeton University Press, 1997).

18. Dickie, *Magic and Magicians in the Greco-Roman World*, 84.

19. Quoted in Ogden, *Magic, Witchcraft, and Ghosts in the Greek and Roman Worlds—A Sourcebook*, 104. As Ogden points out Plutarch's analogy implies that the motivation for Circe giving drugs to Odysseus' men was to get them to fall in love with

her, making her drugs "failed love potions; this is not something that emerges easily from the Homeric text [Odyssey 10.226–9]."

20. Dickie, *Magic and Magicians in the Greco-Roman World*, 134, and 340 n. 41.

21. Augustine's *Confessions* (4.2) refer to a man whom he calls a *haruspex* (a diviner who inspected the entrails of sacrificed animals who also summoned up spirits for magic). While living in Carthage, where he taught rhetoric, he was offered, for a fee, help in winning a "composition of verse to be held in the theatre. . . . What the *haruspex* proposed to do was to sacrifice living creatures on Augustine's behalf and through the sacrifice win the support of demonic forces that would help Augustine's cause." See Dickie, *Magic and Magicians in the Greco-Roman World*, 285, and on Augustine and magic generally see 307–11.

22. Dickie, *Magic and Magicians in the Greco-Roman World*, 76.

23. Dickie, *Magic and Magicians in the Greco-Roman World*, 61.

24. Dickie, *Magic and Magicians in the Greco-Roman World*, 65–67, and see also 80.

25. Dickie, *Magic and Magicians in the Greco-Roman World*, 67–68.

26. Dickie, *Magic and Magicians in the Greco-Roman World*, 70.

27. Dickie, *Magic and Magicians in the Greco-Roman World*, 74 mentions that a *thauma* is "a wondrous event that can very often only be explained by invoking a supernatural agent. *Thauma* is, in consequence, the word that is used in the New Testament for a miracle."

28. Dickie, *Magic and Magicians in the Greco-Roman World*, 74–5.

29. Dickie, *Magic and Magicians in the Greco-Roman World*, 94.

30. Dickie, *Magic and Magicians in the Greco-Roman World*, 28.

31. Dickie, *Magic and Magicians in the Greco-Roman World*, 30–31. The transitive verb used to refer to the effect of *goeteia* was *goeteuein* or in an intensive form *ek-goeteuein*.

32. Dickie, *Magic and Magicians in the Greco-Roman World*, 30–31.

33. Dickie, *Magic and Magicians in the Greco-Roman World*, 48, and Clark 2003: 35.

34. Dickie, *Magic and Magicians in the Greco-Roman World*, 33.

35. Dickie, *Magic and Magicians in the Greco-Roman World*, 14. Dickie indicates that *epodai* were, originally, most likely always sung "and it is indeed the case that the earliest instances of the genre are in the hexametric verse." See Dickie, *Magic and Magicians in the Greco-Roman World*, 17.

36. The transitive verb used to refer to the effect of *mageia* was *mageuein*.

37. Dickie, *Magic and Magicians in the Greco-Roman World*, 33.

38. The transitive verb used to refer to the effect of *pharmakeia* was *pharmakeuein*.

39. Dickie, *Magic and Magicians in the Greco-Roman World*, 14.

40. Dickie, *Magic and Magicians in the Greco-Roman World*, 14–15.

41. Dickie, *Magic and Magicians in the Greco-Roman World*, 79.

42. Matthew Dillon, *Girls and Women in Classical Greek Religion* (New York: Routledge, 2003), 169.

43. Dickie, *Magic and Magicians in the Greco-Roman World*, 94.

44. An excellent political biography of Olympias is that of Elizabeth Carney, *Olympias—Mother of Alexander the Great* (New York: Routledge, 2006).

45. Dickie, *Magic and Magicians in the Greco-Roman World*, 328 n. 120, referring to *Statesman* 280d–e.

46. The discussion in this section again relies heavily on Dickie, *Magic and Magicians in the Greco-Roman World*. My views differ somewhat, however, as I see the pres-

ence of drugs in ancient magic as more pervasive than Dickie appears willing to concede, at least fully. For the use of drugs in ancient magic I have relied on Ogden, *Magic, Witchcraft, and Ghosts in the Greek and Roman Worlds*, Clark, *The Law Most Beautiful and Best*, Georg Luck, *Aranca Mundi—Magic and the Occult in the Greek and Roman Worlds. A Collection of Ancient Texts* (Baltimore, MD: The Johns Hopkins University Press, 2006), and other sources.

47. Dickie, *Magic and Magicians in the Greco-Roman World*, 57.

48. Dickie, *Magic and Magicians in the Greco-Roman World*, 45.

49. Dickie, *Magic and Magicians in the Greco-Roman World*, 75. Dickie writes that while "Plato repeatedly . . . associates [*goetes*] with *thaumatopoiia*" there is "no reason to suppose that all *thaumatopoioi* were considered *goetes*, nor that all *goetes* practiced *thaumatopoiia*. There was nonetheless an overlap."

50. Until the nineteenth century the drug-using practices of the rural countryside scarcely changed. See for example the study of the pre-industrial European peasantry in Piero Camporesi, *Bread of Dreams—Food and Fantasy in Early Modern Europe* (Chicago: University of Chicago Press, 1989).

51. Dickie, *Magic and Magicians in the Greco-Roman World*, 16.

52. Dickie, *Magic and Magicians in the Greco-Roman World*, 17. John J. Winkler, *The Constraints of Desire: The Anthropology of Sex and Gender in Ancient Greece* (New York: Routledge, 1990), 79, in a section titled "Erotic Pharmacology" writes that the terms "*philtrokatadesmos* and *kharitesion* covered not only prayers and amulets but more directly [aphrodisiac] technologies for stimulating and managing sexual feelings, such as penis ointments."

53. Initially little interest was shown in the documents. They were translated by the end of the nineteenth century but were then largely forgotten.

54. Flint Dibble, "Magic, Drugs, and Magic Drugs: A Survey of Wormwood within the *Papyri Graecae Magicae*" (Unpublished Paper, 2008), 2.

55. Dibble, "Magic, Drugs, and Magic Drugs: A Survey of Wormwood within the *Papyri Graecae Magicae*," 2.

56. Dibble, "Magic, Drugs, and Magic Drugs: A Survey of Wormwood within the *Papyri Graecae Magicae*," 2.

57. Dibble, "Magic, Drugs, and Magic Drugs: A Survey of Wormwood within the *Papyri Graecae Magicae*," 2.

58. John Scarborough, "The Pharmacology of Sacred Plants, Herbs, and Roots," in *Magika Hiera*, ed. Christopher A. Faraone and Dirk Obbink (New York: Oxford University Press, 1991), 156–57.

59. Luck, *Aranca Mundi*, 479.

60. Adapted from Luck, *Aranca Mundi*, 479–80.

61 "Manna seems to be a type of *Boswellia* in a powdered form; styrax or storax is *Styrax officinalis*, opium is the juice of *Papaver somniferum*, myrrh is *Commiphora myrrha*, frankincense is (probably) *Boswellia carteri*, saffron is *Crocus sativus*, bdella is *Balsamodendron mukul*." See Luck, *Aranca Mundi*, 479.

62. "Frankincense is, again, a type of *Boswellia*, laurel would be *Laurus nobilis*, myrtle *Myrtus communis*. The "fruit pit" remains mysterious, while the "wild berry" can be identified as *Delphinion staphisagria*. Cinnamon leaf, also known as malabathrum, is *Cinnamomum tamala*, it seems, and costus is *Saussurea lappa*." See Luck, *Aranca Mundi*, 479.

63. "'Calf's snout' has been identified with *Antirrhinon orontium*. Frog's tongue is not as fantastic as it sounds, for, like the skin glands of Bufo marinus it may yield a hal-

lucinogenic secretion known as bufotenin. Frogs and toads had their well-documented practical use in medieval witchcraft." See Luck, *Aranca Mundi*, 479.

64. "These essences are thought to please the various deities, they are both psychoactive, and they both can affect the practitioner or the client, or both, establishing the presence of the deity. A similar incense ritual is prescribed for the recitation of the Orphic hymns." See Luck, *Aranca Mundi*, 479.

65. According to Flint Dibble, *Magic, Drugs, and Magic Drugs: An Analysis of Artemisias, Wormwood, within the Greek Magical Papyri* (Senior Thesis, University of Pennsylvania, 2004), 57 "the wormwood spells are predominantly found upon a single papyrus, the Great Magical Papyrus of Paris [PGM IV]."

66. Dibble, "Magic, Drugs, and Magic Drugs: A Survey of Wormwood within the *Papyri Graecae Magicae*," 9. Camporesi, *Bread of Dreams*, 20, mentions a tract from 1559 that notes this plant, called *matricaria*, was treasured by women, who placed it in *tortelli*. It was "ritually eaten as a food filled with enigmatic powers," during the feasts for Holy Mary and was even called the herb of Holy Mary.

67. Dibble, "Magic, Drugs, and Magic Drugs: A Survey of Wormwood within the *Papyri Graecae Magicae*," 10.

68. Dibble, "Magic, Drugs, and Magic Drugs: A Survey of Wormwood within the *Papyri Graecae Magicae*," 17. The god may have been Osiris. There is mention of "falconweed" and the falcon was sacred to many deities, including Osiris.

69. Scarborough, "The Pharmacology of Sacred Plants, Herbs, and Roots," 160.

70. Luck, *Aranca Mundi*, 501. One ingredient is juniper, a plant that, like wormwood, contains thujone.

71. Hippolytus in his *Refutation of All Heresies* (9.12) denigrates the supposed faith of well-born and propertied Christian women who have affairs with male servants; not wanting to bear the child of a slave or low-born commoner these women resort to using drugs and other methods to terminate the pregnancy.

72. Scarborough, "The Pharmacology of Sacred Plants, Herbs, and Roots," 160–61.

73. Dickie, *Magic and Magicians in the Greco-Roman World*, 44.

74. Hans Dieter Betz, *The Greek Magical Papyri in Translation including the Demotic Spells* (Chicago: University of Chicago Press, 1992), 249. See also chapter 7, above.

75. Dickie, *Magic and Magicians in the Greco-Roman World*, 39, and see also 73–74 and 116–17.

76. Dickie, *Magic and Magicians in the Greco-Roman World*, 39–40.

77. Dickie, *Magic and Magicians in the Greco-Roman World*, 28 discusses the controversy.

78. Dickie, *Magic and Magicians in the Greco-Roman World*, 29, emphasis mine.

79. Dickie, *Magic and Magicians in the Greco-Roman World*, 55.

80. Dickie, *Magic and Magicians in the Greco-Roman World*, 55. Dickie also points out that even if it was not possible to bring someone before the Areopagus on a specific charge of sorcery, "it would still in theory be possible to bring someone suspected of having encompassed a death by sorcery before the Areopagus charged with deliberate homicide."

81. Christopher A. Faraone, "The Agonistic Content of Early Binding Spells," in *Magika Hiera—Ancient Greek Magic and Religion*, ed. Christopher A. Faraone and Dirk Obbink (New York: Oxford University Press, 1991), 9–10.

82. Dickie, *Magic and Magicians in the Greco-Roman World*, 56 writes that there is "a hint of what might have happened in Athens, if a married woman had been rendered childless by sorcery . . . we might infer that the proper course of action for the husband to

take was for him to bring what in Athenian law was called a *dike blabes*, that is, a private suit for damage."

83. Christopher A. Faraone, *Ancient Greek Love Magic* (Cambridge, MA: Harvard University Press, 1999), 130.

84. Faraone, *Ancient Greek Love Magic*, 130.

85. Dickie, *Magic and Magicians in the Greco-Roman World*, 54.

86. C. R. Phillips, "*Nullum Crimen sine Lege*: Socioreligious Sanctions on Magic," in *Magika Hiera—Ancient Greek Magic and Religion*, ed. Christopher A. Faraone and Dirk Obbink (New York: Oxford University Press, 1991), 262.

87. Dickie, *Magic and Magicians in the Greco-Roman World*, 50.

88. Bengt Ankarloo and Stuart Clark, ed., *Witchcraft and Magic in Europe: Ancient Greece and Rome* (Philadelphia, PA: University of Pennsylvania Press, 1999), 250.

89. Quoted in Ogden, *Magic, Witchcraft, and Ghosts in the Greek and Roman Worlds—A Sourcebook*, 107, but agreeing with Dickie, *Magic and Magicians in the Greco-Roman World*, who reads *pharmakis* as "sorceress" rather than "witch" and inserting "*epodai*" in brackets after "incantations."

90. Quoted in Ankarloo and Clark, *Witchcraft and Magic in Europe*, 250.

91. Dickie, *Magic and Magicians in the Greco-Roman World*, 80. Her trial may have been politically motivated.

92. Dickie, *Magic and Magicians in the Greco-Roman World*, 80.

93. Dickie, *Magic and Magicians in the Greco-Roman World*, 81.

94. Dickie, *Magic and Magicians in the Greco-Roman World*, 73.

95. Dickie, *Magic and Magicians in the Greco-Roman World*, 83.

96. Dickie, *Magic and Magicians in the Greco-Roman World*, 83.

97. Ogden, *Magic, Witchcraft, and Ghosts in the Greek and Roman Worlds—A Sourcebook*, 107.

98. Ankarloo and Clark, *Witchcraft and Magic in Europe*, 250.

99. Dickie, *Magic and Magicians in the Greco-Roman World*, 52.

100. Dickie, *Magic and Magicians in the Greco-Roman World*, 52–53.

101. Dickie, *Magic and Magicians in the Greco-Roman World*, 53.

102. Dickie, *Magic and Magicians in the Greco-Roman World*, 53.

103. Dickie, *Magic and Magicians in the Greco-Roman World*, 53.

104. Dickie, *Magic and Magicians in the Greco-Roman World*, 85. Dickie observes that a "disproportionate number of the spells that seek to impede the success of an enterprise are directed at women who are, to judge by their names, either prostitutes or courtesans or at the persons who live alongside them and with whom they associate, which is to say, pimps, procuresses, brothel-keepers and the keepers of taverns."

105. Christopher A. Fararone, "Priestess and Courtesan: The Ambivalence of Female Leadership in Aristophanes' *Lysistrata*," in *Prostitution and Courtesans in the Ancient World* (Madison, WI: The University of Wisconsin Press, 2006), 217.

106. Christopher Bobonich, "Persuasion, Compulsion, and Freedom in Plato's *Laws*," *Classical Quarterly* 41 (1991): 373–74 suggests that Plato's use of the language of spells (*epodai*) and other magic is largely a playful one, usually lacking seriousness, and one primarily aimed at children, but this is simply not supported by either the context within which he wrote about magic, or the content of his texts about that subject.

107. Dickie, *Magic and Magicians in the Greco-Roman World*, 17.

108. Such as *epado, katepado, exepado* and *epodos*. See Entralgo, *The Therapy of the Word in the Ancient World*, 109.

109. Clark, *The Law Most Beautiful and Best*, 112 and 116, n. 21 lists these as *Charmides* (155e5, 155e6, 155e8, 156b, 156d, 157a4, 157b2, 152b4, 157c, 157d, 158b,

175e, 176a, 176b2, 176b3, 176b6); *Laws* (659e, 664b, 665c, 666c, 671a, 773d, 812c, 837e, 887d, 903b, 906b, 909b, 933a, 933d, and 944b); *Phaedrus* (77e, 78a1, 78a5, 114d, and 267d); *Republic* (364b, 426b, 608a3, and 608a4); *Theatetus* (149d and 157c); *Gorgias* (483e and 484a); *Euthydemus* (289e and 290a); *Menexenus* (80a); *Symposium* (203a); and *Epinomos* (323b).

110. Entralgo, *The Therapy of the Word in the Ancient World*, 110.

111. Entralgo, *The Therapy of the Word in the Ancient World*, 112. See chapter 9, below.

112. Walter Burkert, *The Orientalizing Revolution—Near Eastern Influences on Greek Culture in the Early Archaic Age* (Cambridge, MA: Harvard University Press, 1992), 60.

113. Burkert, *The Orientalizing Revolution*, 60.

114. Burkert, *The Orientalizing Revolution*, 66. Burkert, *The Orientalizing Revolution*, 62 mentions the *Pharmakeutria* (*The Woman Sorcerer*), a work written in the third century BCE by Theocritus, informing the reader the work contains black magic spells but does not elaborate further. Dillon, *Girls and Women in Classical Greek Religion*, 175 writes that in this same work Theocritus "describes how Simaitha, with her assistant Thestuylis, resorts to magic to restore the attentions of Delphis. She had seen him and been smitten with desire; she had sought the aid of old women to get rid of her infatuation, but failed. *Presumably there were drugs or spells to do away with love, as there were ones to cause it; old women, as often elsewhere, are the special repositories of such knowledge*" (emphasis mine). Burkert, *The Orientalizing Revolution*, 67 also mentions that Hesychius refers to a pot called a *pharmake* used in certain ritual ceremonies. Although Burkert's references make clear his awareness of the arguments made by Scarborough, "The Pharmacology of Sacred Plants, Herbs, and Roots," who makes the *pharmacology* of sacred plants, herbs and roots the primary focus of his study of Greek magic, he characteristically chooses to ignore them. The word *pharmakon* does not appear in his index of Greek words, yet one does find entries for frankincense, myrrh, and wine, all substances used as drugs by the ancient Greeks. Nor will one find any entry for drugs in the general index. In a work purporting to deal with the Near Eastern influences on Greek magic this is simply incredible, and should arouse suspicion.

115. Dickie, *Magic and Magicians in the Greco-Roman World*, 44–5, 63–4.

116. This translation from the *Laws* is from Ogden, *Magic, Witchcraft, and Ghosts in the Greek and Roman Worlds—A Sourcebook*, 22. On wax figurines or *kolossoi* see Ogden, *Magic, Witchcraft, and Ghosts in the Greek and Roman Worlds—A Sourcebook*, 245–60.

117. Cf. Thucydides' *History* (2.48.2). Bury's translation of *pharmakeuein* as "sorcery" appears preferable here to those such as Taylor who render the same word "doctoring." The latter seems unsatisfying because it both fails to take into account the existence of the *pharmakeus*, a word usually translated as "sorcerer" or "wizard" as well as the context of Plato's discussion, where soon thereafter we read of poisoning by means of "sorceries, incantations and spells" (*Laws* 933a–e). See R. G. Bury, trans., *Plato—Laws in Two Volumes* (Cambridge, MA: Harvard University Press, 1926) and A. E. Taylor, trans., *Plato—Laws* (New York: E. P. Dutton and Company, 1960).

118. Erwin H. Ackerknecht, *History and Geography of the Most Important Diseases* (New York: Hafner Publishing Company, 1965), 179–80 writes that the manual for witch hunters, the *Malleus Maleficarum*, appeared during the apex of Europe's witch hysteria in the sixteenth and seventeenth centuries. A few physicians of the period, including "Cornelius Agrippa, Weyer, Paracelsus, Cardano, and Della Porta," dared to speak out against the mass exterminations: "the latter two experimented with so-called witch ointments and

proved they could induce hallucinations." These included henbane, belladonna and mandrake, and are discussed in Richard Evans Schultes and Albert Hofmann, *Plants of the Gods—Their Sacred, Healing, and Hallucinogenic Powers* (Rochester, VT: Healing Arts Press, 1992), 86–91.

119. C. R. Phillips, "*Nullum Crimen sine Lege*: Socioreligious Sanctions on Magic," 263. See also Dickie, *Magic and Magicians in the Greco-Roman World*, 49–59.

120. C. R. Phillips "*Nullum Crimen sine Lege*: Socioreligious Sanctions on Magic," 263.

121. Dickie, *Magic and Magicians in the Greco-Roman World*, 45.

122. As even Dickie, *Magic and Magicians in the Greco-Roman World*, 45 appears to concede, it may be "the social disruption that fear of magic causes which prompts him to impose just as severe a penalty on the experts in magic as on those expert in using physical substances to harm others."

123. Entralgo, *The Therapy of the Word in the Ancient World*, 110–11. G. E. R. Lloyd, *Demystifying Mentalities* (Cambridge: Cambridge University Press, 1990), 14–15 points out that the distinction between the metaphorical and the literal was itself coined in ancient Greece. Plato wrote at the very cusp of the appearance of this dichotomy, and while he "has some highly critical remarks to make about the use of images and likenesses . . . he continues nevertheless to employ them very extensively himself, and not just for embellishment. Indeed he does so in some of those critical remarks themselves [*Phaedo* 92c–d, *Sophist* 231a]" (20–1). The distinction becomes much more clearly marked in Aristotle, whose "whole syllogistic depends expressly on terms being used strictly and univocally" (21).

124. Entralgo, *The Therapy of the Word in the Ancient World*, 113.

125. Entralgo, *The Therapy of the Word in the Ancient World*, 120.

126. Roy Kotansky, "Incantations and Prayers for Salvation on Inscribed Greek Amulets," in *Magika Hiera—Ancient Greek Magic and Religion*, ed. Christopher A. Faraone and Dirk Obbink (New York: Oxford University Press, 1991), 103. Kotansky mentions the *Charmides* as the first explicit reference to an amulet applied with an incantation.

127. Kotansky, "Incantations and Prayers for Salvation on Inscribed Greek Amulets," 109, and cf. Jacques Derrida, *Dissemination* (Chicago: University of Chicago Press, 1981), 125. On amulets as a *pharmakon* see chapter 10, below.

128. See the discussion of "pharmacological lying" in chapter 10, below.

129. John P. Anton, "Some Dionysiac References in the Platonic Dialogues," *Classical Journal* 58, no. 2 (1980): 54. Anton describes *hygeia* as becoming a "pervasive value" for Plato.

130. Rhetoric, by way of contrast, is the paradigmatic false *techne*. See chapter 9, below.

131. One is reminded of Nietzsche's *Twilight of the Idols*, especially the section titled "The Problem of Socrates." Nietzsche assaults the equation "Reason=Virtue=Happiness" with an argument that mirrors the incredulity of Polus at 470e ("What? Does happiness consist of that?") as much as it does the sanguine vehemence of Callicles.

132. Joseph Bryant, "Enlightenment Psychology and Political Reaction in Plato's Social Philosophy: An Ideological Contradiction?" *History of Political Thought* 11, no. 3 (1990): 381.

133. Janet E. Smith, "Plato's Use of Myth in the Education of Philosophic Man," *Pheonix* 40 (1986): 22.

134. Smith, "Plato's Use of Myth in the Education of Philosophic Man," 22 argues that the *Laws* are largely an extension of the education program in the *Republic*. This position is not, however, universally agreed to.

135. Socrates describes the effects of listening to long speeches by sophists and politicians in nearly the same terms.

136. Compare this passage of the *Laws* with Strabo, *Geography* 10.3.9–10.

137. Entralgo, *The Therapy of the Word in the Ancient World*, 113.

138. Entralgo, *The Therapy of the Word in the Ancient World*, 119.

139. Entralgo, *The Therapy of the Word in the Ancient World*, 121.

140. Jacqueline de Romilly, *Magic and Rhetoric in Ancient Greece* (Cambridge, MA: Harvard University Press, 1975), 36.

141. Dickie, *Magic and Magicians in the Greco-Roman World*, 57.

142. Dickie, *Magic and Magicians in the Greco-Roman World*, 57. Dickie concludes that the meaning of "Meno's gentle banter is not that there were laws in Athens specifically directed at sorcery, but that someone who had the effect on others that Socrates had was likely to have action taken against him as a sorcerer. What the legal source of the action was must remain obscure."

143. Faraone, *Ancient Greek Love Magic*, 3. Literally a "binding down." Their original intent appears to have been the imposition of temporary constraints but by the fourth century BCE "spells intended to inflict harm on enemies" also went by the name *katadeseis* or *katadesmoi*, and by the middle of the fourth century BCE in "erotic magic to secure the affections of another." See also Dickie, *Magic and Magicians in the Greco-Roman World*, 17.

144. Dickie, *Magic and Magicians in the Greco-Roman World*, 17. The locations were places such as "a recent grave or in the sanctuary of a deity whose sphere of activity was the Underworld. In later times they were placed in wells or in the vicinity of the place in which their intended victims either lived or conducted their activities." See also Clark, *The Law Most Beautiful and Best*, 35.

145. Clark, *The Law Most Beautiful and Best*, 35.

146. Trevor J. Saunders, *Plato's Penal Code—Tradition, Controversy, and Reform in Greek Penology* (Oxford: Clarendon Press, 1991), 62.

147. This passage appears to be translated with some difficulty. In contrast to Bloom, H. S. Versnel, "Beyond Cursing: The Appeal to Justice in Judicial Prayers," in *Magika Hiera—Ancient Greek Magic and Religion*, ed. Christopher A. Faraone and Dirk Obbink (New York: Oxford University Press, 1991), 94 n. 11 translates the passage as "If he wants to hurt an enemy, he will damage both the righteous and unrighteous by means of incantations and spells," while Fritz Graf, "Prayer in Magic and Religious Ritual," in *Magika Hiera—Ancient Greek Magic and Religion*, ed. Christopher A. Faraone and Dirk Obbink (New York: Oxford University Press, 1991), 208 n. 8 translates the very same text as "If someone wishes to harm an enemy, he will with small expense harm him, be he just or unjust, with spells and enchantments, since they persuade, as they claim, the gods to help them."

148. Versnel, "Beyond Cursing," 94 n. 11.

149. Romilly, *Magic and Rhetoric in Ancient Greece*, 133.

150. Versnel, "Beyond Cursing," 62–63.

151. See chapter 7, above.

152. Burkert, *The Orientalizing Revolution*, 42–43. See chapter 7, above.

153. Derrida, *Dissemination*, 117.

154. As Michael Morgan, *Platonic Piety: Philosophy and Ritual in Fourth Century Athens* (New Haven, CT: Yale University Press, 1990), 83 observes, the existence of

daimones was an essential component of traditional Greek piety, which consisted of divination, sacrifices, spells, and magic. Plato identifies love as such a *daimon*, with the significant departure that the *daimon* is present in every individual.

155. Elizabeth Belfiore, "Elenchus, Epode, and Magic: Socrates and Silenus," *Pheonix* 34, no. 2 (1980): 136.

156. Derrida, *Dissemination*, 119.

157. Derrida, *Dissemination*, 119. Alternately, Socratic irony "reverses the *pharmakon*'s powers and turns its surface over—thus taking effect, being recorded and dated, in the act of classing the *pharmakon*, through the fact that the *pharmakon* properly consists in a certain inconsistency, a certain impropriety, this non-identity-with-itself always allowing it to be turned against itself."

158. Romilly, *Magic and Rhetoric in Ancient Greece*, 37.

159. Ivan M. Linforth, "The Corybantic Rites in Plato," *The University of California Publications in Classical Philology* (1946): 140–44.

160. This quote is taken from the translation of Christopher Rowe, *Plato—Statesman* (Indianapolis, IN: Hackett Publishing, 1999) but whereas Rowe has "it is for these that this remedy exists, by virtue of expertise," I have rendered *techne pharmakon* as "drug by art" following Lisa Pace Vetter, *"Women's Work" as Political Art: Weaving and Dialectical Politics in Homer, Aristophanes, and Plato* (Lanham, MD: Lexington Books, 2005), 118. Derrida, interestingly, translates *pharmakon* in this same passage as "talisman." As I have argued throughout this work, Plato uses the term in all its multisided meanings, not simply either as "remedy" or "poison," leaving what he may have intended here—remedy or drug or talisman—difficult to discern with any absolute certainty.

Chapter Nine

Speech, Drugs, and Discursive Regimen

The noetic impact of the spoken word in Plato's time is, unquestionably, a complex subject. It, too, is entwined with the power of magic and *pharmaka*. Homer, in the *Odyssey* (1.337), refers to words as enchantments (*thelkteria*).[1] There is nothing finer in life, Odysseus tells King Alcinous, than the deep joy experienced by a whole people when they listen to a man who sings like a god, "and banqueters up and down the palace sit in ranks, enthralled to hear the bard, and before them all, the tables heaped with breads and meats, and drawing wine from a mixing-bowl the steward makes his rounds and keeps the winecups flowing" (9.1–11).[2] Hesiod in his *Theogny* (27) emphasized the deceptive quality of the word and likens "the effacing power of the poetic *logos* [to] that of a *pharmakon*."[3] In contrast to Homer and Hesiod, who reflected a cosmological view based on myth (*muthos*) wherein human beings were relatively impotent to alter or affect or oppose the actions of often capricious gods, by the sixth and fifth centuries a new view of humanity's role and position in the universe began to emerge. For the sophist Protagoras (ca. 490–420 BCE) the measure of all things was man. "Concerning the gods, I cannot know either that they exist or that they do not exist, or what form they might have, for there is much to prevent one's knowing: the obscurity of the subject and the shortness of man's life."[4] Deference to the gods and the importance of religion certainly remained a force in society, but at the same time—in Athens at least—their authority was joined and supplemented with political and social institutions, most notably the assembly, the courts of law, and the theatre.[5] All three institutions are notable for the emphasis they placed on human discourse (*logos*).[6]

In the case of theatre its importance in ancient Greece is well established. More than simply entertainment, the theatre was regarded as one of the foundational elements of Greek society; to the degree that the Theoric Fund was established to ensure even the poorest citizen could attend.[7] When Plato levels various charges against both tragedy and comedy, it is important to remember that at

205

Athens Dionysus, in the guise of Dionysus Eleuthereus (The One Who Sets Free), was not simply the god who had come to the *polis* to teach Icarius the art of making wine; he "was also patron of dramatic and certain choral productions. At his major festivals there, and only at his festivals, tragedies, comedies, and *dithyrambs* (choral songs and dances celebrating the god's birth and adventures) were produced annually in his sanctuary."[8] A fragment of the poet Pratinas (fl. ca. 500 BCE), preserved in Athenaeus (14.617b), complains that "dithyrambic performance leads to street brawls of young drunkards."[9] Dionysus, god of all *pharmaka*, of which wine was but one of his latter gifts to mankind, is also the god of the theatre, and the setting free is, of course, ecstasy, the break from identity, where "one becomes, as it were, 'different,' 'free' from one's usual self."[10]

Poetry as Verbal Magic

In the world of the ancient Greeks poetry served a more serious and important function than poetry does today.[11] The spoken word, "especially when uttered by notable poets," possessed the authority to "elevate a man among his fellows" if it was laudatory or "destroy him" if it was critical.[12] Socrates attests to this influence in the probably authentic dialogue the *Minos*: "the poets wield great power over opinion . . . either by eulogizing or pronouncing evil" (320e). Prominent among the "first accusers" Plato has Socrates mention in the *Apology* (18a) are the poets. Later in the same dialogue (22a–b) he expresses the dismay he felt when questioning the poets, finding their compositional abilities did not lie with any sort of wisdom, but rather "instinct and inspiration (*phusei tini kai enthousiazontes*) like seers." Far from being trivial, the part of thought with which poetry's imitation keeps company, namely that "part in us that is far from prudence," was a deadly serious matter for Plato (*Republic* 603a–b). The power of tragedy and comedy lies, in part, in their ability to alter human perspective, taking advantage of its perceptive fallibility. Poetry, we read in the *Republic*, acts in a manner similar to "shadow painting, and puppeteering and many other [sleight of hand] tricks [practiced by persons known as *thaumatopoioi*]" (602d).[13]

The power of poetry is nothing short of the miraculous, a *thauma*, and words for magic and charms and the like appear throughout Plato's discussion of poetry in the *Republic*, including Book X with its famous claim of the existence of "an old quarrel between philosophy and poetry" (607b).[14] At the conclusion of this discussion, for example, Socrates says (607e–608b) it might be possible to admit poetry into a well-governed regime, but until its supporters could make that case successfully "we shall chant (*epaidontes*) over ourselves as we listen the reasons we have given [against poetry] as a counter-charm (*epoiden*) to her spell, to preserve us from slipping back into the childish (*paidikon*) loves of the multitude (*ton pollon*)."[15] This echoes the discussion in Book III where we learn the "typical threats to right opinion are the inclinations of the appetitive element

. . . characterized as a kind of 'sorcery' (*goeteuomenoi*) (412e) which deceives and enchants the mind like witchcraft (413a–e)."[16]

The Spell of Tragic Discourse

The poet Theognis ties the enjoyment of weeping with those central pleasures of the *symposion* identified earlier in chapter 1, above, namely drinking and listening to the intoxicating notes of the *aulos*:

You and the flutist, come! We'll laugh and drink
Near the weeper, and enjoy his agonies (1041–1042)

Xenophon's *Symposium* contains a similar moment. When Phillipus the jester fails to make any of the guests laugh, he covers himself and begins to weep (1.14). The weeping itself proves humorous, causing Critoboulus to "burst out laughing at Phillipus' lamentation" (1.16). Later it is remarked that Phillipus prides himself in making others laugh, more justly than the pompous tragic actor Callippides prides himself "because he can make a packed house weep" (3.11). Plato, in contrast, complains that the tragic poets, in presenting heroes who make extended speeches of "lamentation," crying aloud and beating their breasts, create a form of enjoyment that can maim the noetic processes of "even . . . decent men, except for a rare few" (*Republic* 605c–d, cf. 387d). Listening to speeches of grief and sorrow and "giving ourselves over" to the part of the soul which hungers for the satisfaction of "tears (*dakrusai*) and a good cry (*apodurasthai*)" produces moral degeneration in the vast majority; "only a certain few men are capable of calculating that the enjoyment of other people's sufferings has a necessary effect on one's own" (606a–b, and cf. 388d). This opposition to the identity-effacing powers of intense grief is repeated in several dialogues besides the *Republic*, including the *Ion* (535c), *Philebus* (48a), and *Laws* (800d).

Exposure to the suffering of others, Plato explains in the *Republic*, "draws" (*helkon*—a word commonly used in ancient Greek magic spells) men to pain (604b). Reason then "relaxes its guard" (606a). This "plaintive (*threnodous*) part," engorging itself on the "woes (*pathe*) of others," leads the otherwise sound-minded man to abandon himself to excessive grief, behaving in real life in ways more commonly expected of women (605d–e, 606a–b), again recalling the discussion in Book III (395e) where men are cautioned not to imitate the psychological state of women "caught in the grips of misfortune, mourning and wailing." Plato does not allow married women to take part in the funerals of the Euthynai or Examiners who occupy the highest position in the state in his *Laws* (784d).[17] Similarly in the *Phaedo* Socrates sends the women away (116b) before drinking the *pharmakon* and chastises the men when they erupt in tears (117d) at the sight of him willfully drinking it down and thereby carrying out his own death sentence. There is no catharsis to be had in weeping, in contrast to the apparent value Aristotle assigns *katharsis* in both his *Politics* (1341b) and *Poetics* (1449b).[18] Like Plato, however, Aristotle uses terminology "from the register of bodily health to explain literary effect."[19]

The Spell of Comedic Discourse

In Book X of the *Republic* Plato writes that the comic poet evokes the same dangerous wellspring of emotions as the tragic poet (606c). Laughter, like lamentation, is capable of producing uncontrollable tears when strongly experienced. When a man is a lover of laughter, the *Republic* says, he "seeks a mighty change in his condition" (388e). The psychological condition Plato refers to is not the light chuckle or quick guffaw; it is irrepressible, ecstatic laughter.[20] This can be confirmed in the *Philebus*, where comedies are said to produce "a state of mind (*psyche*)" that combines pleasure with distress (48a). When pleasure is mixed with distress it "takes possession of man" and causes him to "leap about in his ecstasy, so that he changes complexion, takes up all kinds of strange positions, pants in strange ways, and is driven completely out of his senses with mad cries and shouts" (47a). In the *Laws*, also, Plato demands that "there must be a restraint of unseasonable laughter and tears and each of us must urge his fellow to consult decorum by utter concealment of all excess joy and grief" (732c).

Uncontrolled laughter and weeping, wherein subjective identity is momentarily submerged or suspended in much the same manner as it is while intoxicated, is the "mighty change" objected to by Plato. The Greek orator Dio Chrysostom (ca. 40–120 CE) was doubtlessly influenced by Plato's views.[21] The *Discourse to the Alexandrians* begins by remarking that Chrysostom's large audience is "practically never at a loss for fun-making and the enjoyment of laughter" (32.1), and criticizes them for making, like the Athenians, "a bad use of the ears" (32.4). After discussing their mindless behavior at other public gatherings such as the assembly and sporting events, he turns to theatre. The people of Alexandria are "moderate enough when they offer sacrifice or stroll by themselves or engage in their other pursuits; but when they enter the theatre or a stadium [they behave] just as if drugs that would madden them are buried there" (32.41). He goes on to compare their shameful behavior at theatrical performances to "certain barbarians" who obtain "a mild intoxication [from] the fumes of a certain incense when burned" (32.56). While the barbarians, after inhaling these fumes, "are joyful and get up to laugh, and behave in all respects like men who have been drinking," the Alexandrians are in Chrysostom's opinion unique in their ability to "reach that state through ears and voice" alone.[22] They leave the theatre "in far worse condition than those who are crazed by wine," staggering "like men suffering the effects of a debauch."

The Spell of Sophistic Discourse

The sophist, in Plato's dialogue bearing that name, is defined as a magician who with "a display of phantoms of arguments on all subjects" deceives the young into believing what they hear is the truth and that the sophist is the wisest speaker on all subjects (*Sophist* 234c). He is "a kind of conjurer, a producer of mimicry of reality" who does not possess *real* knowledge. He is, quite simply, an "imposter or sorcerer" (241b). The *Protagoras* criticizes those sophists who "take the various subjects of knowledge from city to city," peddling their wares while being generally "ignorant of the beneficial or harmful effects on the soul of what they have for sale" (313d–e).[23] Equally ignorant are "those who buy from them, unless one happens to be a physician of the soul" (313e). The philosopher, as we learn in the *Gorgias*, is this moral physician and "cures men of their excesses and makes them better people" (478d). Polus and Callicles, characters within that same dialogue, are essentially paradigmatic case studies of the *Protagoras'* ignorant buyer.

Knowledge of the pandering knack of political rhetoric, as taught by certain sophists whose specialty is instruction in the art of public speaking, is socially bad medicine because like poetry and similar occupations it places both the speaker and his audience in a state of psychological *ekstasis*. What poetry and sophistry share in common is their provision of the pleasure of this displacement of identity, rather than true knowledge. This is made manifest in the *Republic*. The reason philosophy has such a bad reputation and the reason the few truly philosophic minds present in a city are led astray, Socrates explains, is due to the poisonous discourse of the sophists. Sophists, speaking uproariously loud and excessively, praising some and blaming others, sweep up large audiences such as "assemblies, courts, theaters, army camps, or any other common meeting of the multitude" with their linguistic power and carry their audience away in a flood of words—sometimes magnified by the acoustics, such that "the rocks and the very place surrounding them echo and redouble the uproar and blame and praise. Now in such a circumstance, what do you suppose is the state of a young man's heart?" (*Republic* 492b).

The sophist's art, Protagoras admits to Socrates in the *Protagoras*, has been practiced a very long time, only until recently it has been concealed and disguised as poetry, religious initiation, music, or physical training (316d–e). As if to demonstrate this, Protagoras himself claims at one point in the dialogue that he "knows plenty of things—food, drinks, drugs, and many others—which are harmful to men, and others that are beneficial; and others again which, so far as men are concerned, are neither" (334a). Protagoras here alludes to a knowledge of many different drugs—some harmful (poisons, etc.), some beneficial (remedies, etc.), still others neither (intoxicants, aphrodisiacs, etc.). The powers of the sophist and the physician are said to be analogous in the *Theatetus*. Speaking in the guise of Protagoras (who is not actually present in the dialogue), Socrates says "whereas the doctor brings about change by the use of drugs, the professional teacher does it by the use of words" (167b).

The power of the spoken word is itself a drug, a *pharmakon*, that bewitches and intoxicates. At the end of Protagoras' long story in the *Protagoras* (320c–328d), relating to whether virtue can be taught, Socrates concedes that the sophist's eloquent demonstration has left even him "spellbound" and only with effort could he collect himself to deliver a rebuttal. As Protagoras continues to score points against him with the audience, Socrates admits that "at his words and the applause [which followed] things went dark and I felt giddy" (339d–e), phrasing that is distinctly similar to ancient Greek descriptions of intoxication, such as the drinking of wine in the *symposion*.[24] As we saw in chapter 1, above, Plato's uncle Critias was reputed to have described intoxication as a "dark mist" settling upon the eyes, the melting of memory "into oblivion" and the complete lost of reason (Atheneaus 10.432e). Two things are evident here. First, the art of the sophist is another form of harmful, deceitful magic, the practice of which has the capacity to upset even the philosopher's noetic balance.[25] Second, Socrates is clearly implying that the words of the sophist, like a *pharmakon*, have intoxicated the audience, even him.

Dialectic and Rhetoric

The composition of mental health within the soul was, for Plato, in the final determination demonstrated through the confrontation between two forms of discursive engagement: "one rooted in dialectic, the other issuing from rhetoric."[26] Plato's struggle with rhetoric, in particular the relationship between soul/discourse (*logos*) is expressed through the relationship between body/drug (*pharmakon*). That there *is* a relationship to begin with has already been recognized. The "psychotropic character of rhetoric becomes a critical issue in both the *Gorgias*, where Socrates refers to rhetoricians as quacks who are more persuasive than legitimate doctors, and in the *Phaedrus*, where the pharmacological and erotic nature of *technai logon* renders them potential cures as well as dangers, sources of soulful harmony or madness."[27] In Plato the *pharmakon* "is comprehended in the structure of *logos*. This comprehension is an act of both *domination* and *decision*."[28] The domination is more than just some largely abstract literary imposition at the behest of the archmage of metaphysics; with any sort of historical contextualization it is possible to discern in Plato's dialogues a far more earthy polemic being waged against a wide range of rival occupations, many of whom administer, either literally or at least metaphorically, some *pharmakon* and/or some form of identity-effacing ecstasy. We saw in chapter 7, above, that these rivals included many different healing, therapeutic, and purifying arts, from the seller of some potion in the *agora* to the midwife to "rational" medicine practiced by Hippocratic physicians, while in chapter 8 we saw the many magical *technai* that competed with philosophy.

In this chapter we may now add two final examples, perhaps the most important of all—or at least the most *dangerous* of all when viewed from the perspective of the philosopher—sophistic teaching and political *rhetorike*. Carried away—by the rhetorical moment, no doubt—politicians in Plato's *Meno* "are to be considered as acting no less under divine influence, inspired and possessed by divinity" (95d). The *logos* of Plato's moral physician, with its emphasis on the health and well-being of the soul, transplants itself for, grafts itself upon, cross-pollinates itself with, the *pharmaka* of all of philosophy's rivals, and their emphasis on the health and well-being of the body, appropriating their powers and even their pleasures, and with very different ends in mind disposes of the rival experiences themselves. The moral physician, as it turns out, also engages in the practice of preventive medicine, using his orally prescribed *pharmaka* to fashion a verbal consensus. The purpose, as will become clear shortly, is the creation of a stringent *discursive regimen* for every member of the *polis*, political discourse in particular.

The *Gorgias*, like many of Plato's dialogues, contains a thoroughly entangled critique of the undue influence practitioners of medicine, physical training, oratory, and still other occupations exert upon their audience, and their inferiority to philosophy. The physician or gymnastic trainer can, it is true, detect deception in the body of a person who has merely the appearance of true health, but only what Plato calls *the political craft* can diagnose illness where a similar false appearance is found within a man's soul (464a–b). Knowing how to achieve health of the body is an element of knowledge, but only of brute empirical fact. Medicine and physical training, as we saw in chapter 7, above, are faulty owing to their purely somatic orientation, while what Plato calls the "art of government," consisting of legislation and justice (the latter equated with philosophy), is addressed to the health of the soul. Legislation corresponds to physical training, medicine to the administration of justice in the body politic (464b). Legislation is like a regimen of exercise, one that hones and gives "order and proportion to the body" (504a). Philosophy, like a physician dispensing prescriptions, corrects imbalance, restoring order and proportion that is said to comprise the "goodness of a soul" (505b). While Plato may be at odds with the frequent use of drugs by physicians and practitioners of magic, he is not above using the idea of pharmaceutical cleansing or purification to his own advantage. Plato uses the term *euexia*, health or good condition, conspicuously in the *Gorgias*, a term that is directly borrowed from Greek medicine. Plato extends the term from its traditional medical meaning, the somatic sense in which a doctor or physical trainer might use it, and applies it to the health of the soul (464c).

Cooking and oratory are attacked as being only spurious imitations of medicine and philosophy, respectively (463b). We are told shortly thereafter that just as "cosmetics is to gymnastics, so is sophistry to legislation, and as cookery is to medicine, so rhetoric is to justice (465c).[29] Skill in each of the former occupations is merely a habitual "knack" acquired through observation and repetition, having no link with genuine understanding (463b). They cannot be called true arts (*technai*) but are rather intuitive imitations, pandering to their audience with no regard to their welfare, in much the same way as, for example, the *Ion* accuses the epic poetry recited by the rhapsode. All that is provided by these false arts is a certain gratification that "catches fools with the bait of ephemeral pleasures," trickery, leaving "only the appearance of health without the reality" (464a–d). Physical training has its spurious counterfeit in the form of what Plato calls "beauty culture," viewed by him as "a mischievous, base, servile trade," creating "borrowed beauty" to the neglect of true beauty, by use of "artificial adjuncts and make up and depilatories and costume" (465b). Cosmetic—either makeup or perfume—was another meaning of the word *pharmakon*, and cosmetics pose the same dangers as a magic potion or a recreational intoxicant: they "all are part of the festival that subverts the order of the city, its smooth regulation by the dialectician and the science of being."[30]

Only philosophy can grant access to celestial, eternal truths that are the basis of genuine health of the mind. This is not to say that Plato entirely denies that religion, too, permits access to eternal truths. He largely concedes that this may be the case, for example in the *Phaedrus* (250b–c, 251a–e), but visions of the religious sort occur imperfectly and on an irregular basis. If a man is not "fresh from his initiation" Plato tells us, he does not "quickly make the transition" from the relative to the absolute, in the case of the *Phaedrus* absolute beauty (250d–e). A person could not be initiated into the Eleusinian Mysteries and drink the *kykeon* every day, even if they wanted to. The Eleusinian vision, the *epopteia*, however ineffably sublime, would also be inadequate and inferior because it was an experience cordoned off from public discussion by religious restriction, leaving no basis for comparison, measurement, determining veracity, and so on, all of which is required of a reliable *techne* of truth-based noetic stability. While necessary for average men, and all lesser types (women, children, slaves), religion would furthermore be too immersed in pomp, ritual and meeting the largely material needs of the city's clergy to be an adequate route to an *episteme* of eternal truths.

[margin handwritten note: mystery religion not public and so cannot be discussed philosophically]

The Drug of Rhetoric:
Protagoras, Gorgias, Isocrates

The *rhetor* (public orator/politician) is a powerful opponent of philosophy. In the *Theatetus*, during consideration of whether the sense perceptions can be the basis of knowledge, Socrates, speaking as we have just seen in the guise of Protagoras, draws a comparison between sick and healthy perception (170b, and cf. *Protagoras* 320b, 324e–325b). It is not that while in a state of sickness we judge from ignorance, falsely, and while healthy from wisdom, so that we would demand that sickness, and the sick man, be "corrected" to a more true condition. Both states are equally valid, when considered from within their own perceptual criteria. Food, for example, tastes unpleasant when we are ill because while we are in such a state it *is* foul tasting. A change from sickness to health, Socrates-

Protagoras continues, is preferable not because the latter condition is *truer*, but simply because it is *better*. The purpose of education is or at least ought to be the same, namely changing of the soul from a worse to a better state. The critical difference between educating the body and the soul being that "*whereas the physician produces change by means of drugs, the sophist does it by discourse*" (167a, emphasis mine). If he is wise and efficient, the statesman produces a similarly altered state within the public conception of justice: he "makes wholesome things seem just and admirable," replacing "each pernicious convention by a wholesome one, making this both be and seem just" (167c). Sophists, statesmen, poets and philosophers each produce change in men's souls through the pharmaceutical powers of *logos*. The *logos* "can move through the psyche like drugs through the body's interior passages."[31]

The historical Gorgias (ca. 485–380 BCE) makes this same connection in the *Encomium of Helen*. The *Encomium* is "a prototypical example" of the oratorical style the "Athenians loved and philosophers such as Plato scorned."[32] Speech (*logos*) is described as a form of magic (*goeteia*) that has the power (*dynamis*) to compel people to change their opinion by creating/removing pleasure/pain. Gorgias writes that "the effect of speech (*tou logous dunamis*) upon the condition of the soul (*pros ten tes psuches taxin*) is comparable to the power of drugs (*ton pharmakon taxis*) over the nature of bodies (*ten ton somaton phusin*)."[33] The *Encomium* then goes on to say that just as different *drugs* can have a multitude of effects, everything from a complete medical cure to a deliberately induced death, so too in the cases of *speeches*: "some distress, others delight, some cause fear, others make the hearer bold, and some drug and bewitch the mind with a kind of evil persuasion (*ten psuchen epharmakeusan kai exegoeteusan*)" (14).[34]

These lines from the *Encomium* are yet another indication of the complexity of the ancient world's pharmacopeia and explode, among other things, the strangely persistent viewpoint that interprets the term *pharmakon* as a simple dichotomy between medicines and poisons. In ancient Greece nothing could be further from the truth. Neither poisons nor medicine typically embolden or delight and they most certainly do not bewitch the mind. Intoxicants, however, can be said to do *all* these things. While the passage "begins with a clear-cut analogy" of the "different orders of change that may be elicited or produced through drugs and discourse," it concludes "with a set of descriptors for speech that can be just as easily applied to psychotropic drugs, which were widely known to produce pain, enjoyment, fear, and courage."[35] Gorgias "assimilates *logos* to an irresistible drug administered either to heal or to harm at the whim of the practitioner, and assimilates the drug to an occult agent. The same *logos* which as white magic gives pleasure creates pain in the guise of 'bad' persuasion/compulsion, but in either case the defenseless psyche is drugged, not offered a rational invitation to react; and, consistently with Gorgias' irrationalist program, the psychic drugs make their victims feel things, not believe them."[36]

Isocrates (436–338 BCE) was a pupil of Gorgias. Much like his teacher he "employs the positive notion of words as drugs."[37] In his *Peace* (39) he asserts that "there exists no better *pharmakon* for souls when they are ignorant of the truth and filled with base desires than *logos* to boldly rebuke its sins." In his *Busiris* (22) he likens education to medicine, and compares its effects on the soul to that of *pharmaka* on the body. Unlike the more unscrupulous sort of instructor of *rhetoreia* he was willing to assume a moral responsibility for what he taught. The reason: the spoken word does not simply affect the audience—it has a "feedback" effect that affects the *rhetor* himself. Like Plato he exhibits an understanding of a connection between verbal and noetic regimen, advising Nicoles in his *Advice to Nicoles* (38) to speak of noble and honorable topics, so "that your thought may through habit become to be like your words." In his *Antidosis* (283) Isocrates "complains that the Athenians no longer use words in their natural sense, *kata phusin*; instead they 'metamorphize,' or 'transfer' meanings (*metapherousin*), so that words that once described 'the best actions' (*kallista pragmata*) now signify the 'most corrupt activities' (*ta phaulotata*)."[38] Perhaps for this reason Plato, while hardly an admirer of Isocrates, does single him out in the *Phaedrus* (279a–b) as a writer with special potential.[39]

*(margin handwritten note: speech feedback on thought *)*

Rhetorical Malpractice

Gorgias, in the dialogue bearing his name, calls his art rhetoric (*rhetorike*), and under questioning by Socrates defines that art (449e) as an expert knowledge of *logos* (speech/argument) whose concern is the "greatest and best of human concerns" (451d).[40] When pressed to define the latter Gorgias says he can produce "the ability to convince by means of speech a jury in a court of justice, member of the Council in their Chamber, voters at a meeting of the Assembly, and any other gathering of citizens whatever it may be" (452e). With this power the student of rhetoric will have the physician and gymnastic trainer as his slave. The businessman will not make money for himself, but for the speaker who is an expert in the art of persuasion.

In the case of politics the Athenian assembly, the *dikasterion*, was "a large body of jurors empanelled and representing the whole body of citizens. In cases of political importance, this whole body . . . could sit together as court. This was the system which prevailed in the fifth and fourth centuries."[41] Large audiences such as this "obviously encouraged special pleading, playing on the emotions, and exploitation of popular assumptions and personal prejudices," and the Athenian orators "took full advantage of these opportunities."[42] The "mighty man of Chalcedon," probably the Sophist Thrasymachus of Chalcedon (ca. 459–400 BCE), is described in the *Gorgias* as being an expert in "rousing a crowd to fury, and then soothing its fury again by the spell of his words," an expression that is attributed to Thrasymachus in the *Phaedrus* (267c–d). Plato in the *Laws* (937d–938c) condemns rhetoric as something that pollutes and defiles justice, an art that uses pleading to win lawsuits, whether "the things done in each judicial case be just or not."

Gorgias claims that instruction of the sort he provides can all the same create conviction, defined as knowledge of *right* and *wrong*, and insists he can teach it to anyone. Socrates counters by saying there would appear to be two kinds of conviction. One, such as taught by the teacher of oratory, merely produces the belief that one is knowledgeable, without granting knowledge itself, while another, instruction in philosophy, creates the real thing. If this is so, oratory would seem to be of little value. Oratory's primary fault is that it deceptively aims at producing *pleasure*, instead of *goodness*. Gorgias then reiterates his seemingly sensible contention that oratory has considerable power, for it allows men to "dictate policy and get their proposals adopted" (456a). Such a power, a skeptical Socrates retorts, borders on the supernatural.

Gorgias responds to Socrates' incredulity by telling him that he might be surprised if he knew the whole truth of the matter, repeating his larger claim "that oratory embraces and controls almost all spheres of human activity," citing the following anecdote involving his brother, who is a physician, as an illustration:

> It has often happened that I have gone with my brother and other doctors to visit some sick person who refused to drink his medicine or to submit to surgery or cautery, and when the doctors could not persuade him I have succeeded, simply by my use of oratory. I tell you that, if in any city, that you like to name, an orator and a doctor had to compete before an assembly or any other body for the appointment of a medical officer, the man who could speak would be appointed by an overwhelming vote if he wanted the post, and the doctor would be nowhere (456b–c).

Oratory, in other words, charms, beguiles, convinces, overcomes, and intoxicates its recipient just like the *pharmakon* of some magician.[43]

The Gorgias of the Platonic dialogue bearing his name does not wish to imply that the skill he teaches is without ethical standards. On the contrary, he insists there are "limits" to the use of oratory, the orator being as bound "to make a proper use of his oratory as the possessor of the physical superiority" (457a–b). Or, one might easily infer, the possessor of medical training. If the pupil of an orator, and by implication any pupil at all, applied his skill for evil ends, it is he, not the instructor, who is deserving of punishment. Socrates objects to Gorgias' position believing it to be inconsistent. Gorgias, he argues, proposes to teach a skill that can make an ignorant man, in front of a popular audience, more influential than any expert by allowing the ignorant man to appear more knowledgeable than a man actually in the know (459a–c). If Gorgias professes to teach the art of producing conviction, defined as the sort "needed in courts of law and other large assemblies," the subject of which he has described as the ability to discern right and wrong, how can he teach the art of oratory unless the pupil arrives already knowing the truth about "right and wrong, honor and dishonor, good and bad" (459d–e). Gorgias answers that he would have to take it upon himself to train a pupil in such matters. Now he is trapped. How, Socrates asks, if oratory is only concerned with what is right, could it ever produce students who act so wrongly?

Polus now joins the verbal sparring, and his character in the *Gorgias* is a scarcely veiled example of the kind of flawed convictions that a *rhetor* like Gorgias, however well-intentioned, winds up producing. Polus argues that orators, like dictators, have enormous political power since, with their acquired verbal abilities they can "kill or confiscate or imprison at will," citing what would have been a clear-cut example to Plato's audience, a ruler like Archelaus of Macedonia (466c, 468b, 470b–d). It is believed that Archelaus (ruled ca. 413–399 BCE) invited Socrates to his court only to be refused; others including the poet Euripides accepted, at least according to Aristotle's account in his *Rhetoric* (1398a). In the *Crito* Socrates voices his refusal to acquiesce to these despotic individuals even in the face of their magical power to "conjure up fresh hordes of bogeys to terrify our childish minds, by subjecting us to chains and executions and confiscations of our property" (46c).

Socrates makes an extraordinary argument in response to the claim made by Polus, contending orators and dictators are in actuality the *least* powerful men in society, having only the appearance of great power (466b, 479d–e). This claim is further elaborated upon in the *Phaedrus*, where nine ranks of fallen souls are given. To be reincarnated as a sophist or a demagogue is to occupy the eighth rung, while being a tyrant occupies the ninth and lowest rung, short of returning as an actual beast, to which tyrants are often compared (e.g. wolves at *Republic* 566a). Fifth place is reserved for "the life of the soothsayer or an official of the Mysteries," presumably one of the two priesthoods of Eleusis, while fourth place includes physicians. It is the philosopher who occupies the highest rung, "who has seen the most," something that could be read as a swipe at the vision seen by initiates at Eleusis after drinking the *kykeon*, since on experiencing the *epopteia* an initiate became an *epoptes*, literally "one who had seen."

Polus counters Socrates' argument with a typical rhetorical move: he appeals to the common sense of the entire audience, saying that tyrants and orators are clearly admirable because they can avoid punishment for their actions and the end result is that their lives are happy. Socrates continues to press home his counterintuitive opposition, saying these men are in fact not happy, they are in fact among the most wretched and miserable of all men. It is, he argues, far better to suffer wrong, as for example at the hands of these sort of men, than to do wrong oneself. Doing wrong is *aischron*: baser, more ugly, shameful and dishonorable than suffering wrong, hence it is more evil (474c). In contrast what is right is *kalon*: fine, more beautiful, and honorable, hence good. Doing right is more useful and pleasant (474d); in the *Lovers* evil is described as useless in addition to its other defects (136b–e). Doing wrong, Socrates says in the *Gorgias*, may not be more painful than suffering it, but it is more harmful, so on that point it would appear a worse evil than suffering wrong (475b–c). Being punished for wrongdoing, far from being undesirable and something to be avoided, is preferable because, like medical treatment which purifies and restores the body, it purifies and restores the soul (477a, 478a–b).

Punishment (*kolasis*) is beneficial and advantageous from the standpoint of self-interest because it delivers a man from "the worst of all bad things," an unhealthy "state of the soul" (477b–c). To be possessed of a bad soul, i.e. a mentally unbalanced and/or ignorant soul, is not as immediately painful as poverty or somatic disease, but it is "superior in baseness" over these other kinds of badness owing to the tremendous harm and evil it produces (477b–d). Wickedness, excess, indulgence, etc., being the soul's "disease" are the "greatest evil that exists" (477e). Disease of the soul is "the worst of all ailments" (479b–c) and in need of the strongest *pharmakon* as a remedy.[44] To be punished is to be healed from a bad internal state in a way analogous to weakness, disease and deformity (477a–478c). What the Athenian of the *Laws* proposes in order to rectify the criminal's *adikia*, his state of mind, is a psychic cure for a diseased soul: "Now to deal with unjust injuries (and gains too, as when one man's unjust act results in gain for someone). The cases that are curable (*iata*) we must cure (*iasthhai*), on the assumption that the soul has been infected by diseases (*nosoi*)" (862b).

Punishment is an element of noetic regimen, even though the idea is "present in the *Gorgias* only hazily and by implication; indeed the word *diaita* does not even occur."[45] As long as the soul is in a bad state resembling the invalid, the Socrates of the *Gorgias* says, "it must be restrained from satisfying its appetites and prevented from doing anything except what will contribute to its improvement" (505a–b). This habituation of the soul to do good actions at least "suggests some sort of training or regimen."[46] By the time of the composition of the *Republic*, however, regimen is front and center (403c–412b); "only *diaitomenoi*, 'living by regimen,'" may allow a sick person to regain their health.[47] Just as the "drone growing up in a cell is a disease of the hive," the man who does nothing but live an idle life like Homer's dreamingly intoxicated Lotus-Eaters is "a disease of the city" (552c). Health in the *Republic* includes both somatic and noetic health: "just as virtue is the health of the soul, vice, the state of civil war between parts of the soul, is its disease. Just as health is generated in the body by doing healthy actions, so virtue is generated in the soul by following good practices. That is to say, psychic states are induced by the performance of actions of the appropriate kind."[48]

While the ordinary physician may be adept at treating diseases of the body, and hard work may relieve a man plagued with poverty, the cure for vice, excess, wickedness and the like in the *Gorgias* requires *the art of government*, consisting of the power to "rightly employ some kind of justice" (478a). This art is *therapeia* and like a doctor the moral physician who might treat the Athenians must struggle with his patient (521a). Socratic *therapeia* and sophistic oratorical persuasion are easily confused because the "effect of logic and rational analysis on those more accustomed to emotional governance of their minds can feel like a sort of domination and loss of the self, especially when the logic leads to uncomfortable conclusions."[49] Many examples might appear to support this position, but the matter is not quite that simple.

Meno, his lips numbed by the *narke* (stingray) that is Socratic *elenchus*, complains that he can hardly do more than passively concede each point (Meno

80a–b). Meno warns Socrates that in another city he might be arrested and executed as a wizard, a *goes*. Thrasymachus is said to be charmed like a snake (*Republic* 358b) and Alcibiades says that Socrates, like Marsyas, can bewitch mankind, only without any instrument, be it flute, charm, or *pharmakon*: he merely uses a "few simple words (*logois*)" (*Symposium* 215c–d). Drawing, perhaps ironically, on Gorgias' own argument, Socrates fuses magical, oratorical and pharmaceutical power and commands Polus to "be a man and submit to my argument as you would to a doctor" (475d–e). When Socrates enjoins Polus to quiet himself and pay attention *as if Socrates were a doctor*, the submission of Polus, a free man, is not that of a social inferior, yet neither is he Socrates' equal. The closest resemblance would be that of an equal transformed, as though through magical incantation, charm, or some *pharmakon*, into a mute and temporarily inferior position, for whatever time is required for an agreement to be reached on the point in question.[50]

The *Statesman* contains a similar tension/ambiguity. Plato subdivides the art of superintendence into authority that is enforced and that which is voluntarily consented to (276c–d). The despot resorts to force, the true king or statesman enjoys voluntary acceptance. Yet on closer examination the powers of the physician-statesman, his *logos*-based science of herd superintendence, are frequently and suspiciously violent: the enlightened ruler "will permit no training to be given which does not produce a temperament fit to be worked into [the weaving of the social fabric]. . . . Hence those who prove incapable of any share in the brave and modest temper and the other dispositions which tend towards virtue, but are driven by their native evil constitution to irreligion, violence, and crime [the state] expels by the punishment of death or exile, or visits superlative infamy" (308e–309a). The list of offending temperaments is a long one and utilization of death as a corrective mechanism for the incurable increases in frequency, until by the *Laws* "the death penalty is used by Plato rather freely."[51] In this last dialogue the Athenian Stranger remains very much a physician of the soul, characterizing "those wrongdoers who cannot be reformed not as 'unteachable' but rather as 'incurable' and says that they are to be put to death and their corpses expelled from the land (862d–863a). . . . Such punishments are forms of cleansing or purges, but the best ones are violent. 'The best purge is painful, as are all exceptional medicines [*hosa ton pharmakon toioutotropa*].'"[52]

Plato's deontological imperative is that a fine man recognizes any condition of internal mental imbalance and submits himself for noetic rehabilitation, as he tells Polus in the *Gorgias*, "of his own accord . . . as he would to a doctor" (480a). In other words, a genuine administrator of justice, who is clearly the philosopher, is also "a moral physician and cures men of their excesses and makes them better people" (478d). This definition of the philosopher as a moral physician in the *Gorgias* is paralleled in several other dialogues with varying degrees of explicitness. In the *Protagoras* knowledge of what nourishes the soul is said to belong not to the sophist, but to "a physician of the soul" (313e). The *Republic* too describes "an art of medicine for those whose bodies are by nature and regimen in a healthy condition" as being practiced by a "statesmanlike Asclepius" (407c–e). Be it physical or spiritual health, the happiest man is one who was "never . . . ill at all," one who never needed an external cure in the first place (478c). Given, however, that a soul has already become "unhealthy, rotten, wicked, [and] impure," the question then becomes one of determining the man who would rank next in happiness: the one who has undergone "treatment and is cured of his ailment, or the man who has no treatment and continues to suffer?" (479b–c, 478d). The man who is left untreated by some external source is the worst off of the three.

Callicles, who rejects even the veil of scruples Polus cloaks himself in, is the extreme example of the convictions that are likely to result from Gorgias' oratorical training. Social conventions, *nomos*, Callicles argues, are merely "spells and incantations" used as an educational device to tame superior youth into believing that equality is fine and just (483e–484a). The strong man shakes off, smashes, tramples and escapes from these "writings, charms, incantations [and] rules" that are contrary to nature, *physis* (484a). When he does so "there dawns the full light of natural justice," the strong ruling the weak and enjoying the benefits of that rule (484a–b). Strength, as Callicles describes it, consists of wisdom and virility regarding "public affairs and the proper way of conducting them" (491b). Socrates then shifts the conversation from rule over others to rule over oneself. Plato strives to make it clear that rhetoric produces a divorce of power and morality.[53] Rhetoric, as Socrates forces Callicles to demonstrate through his answers, lacks logical precision, is incurably feeble in its advancement towards objective knowledge, and possesses ethics that cannot surpass appeals to hedonistic calculation as regards pleasure and pain.

Callicles' hedonistic position, while not without its appeal, contains a succession of "errors of exaggeration and overstatement."[54] He is made to speak in favor of several seemingly foolish positions. Plato, it could be argued, sets out to sabotage Callicles' position, turning his immoralist stance into "simply a radical—and somewhere simpleminded—hedon[ism]."[55] The position he advocates may be summarized as (a) any restraint of desire is undesirable in the strong man; (b) the strong man should allow his desires to grow as strong as possible; (c) the strong man should allow all his desires to grow; (d) the satisfaction of all desire is pleasant and (e) pleasure is identical with the good. The position is so odd, and easy to modify in Callicles' favor, that it requires explanation. One answer is that the discussion between Callicles and Socrates, largely concerned with the nature of moral life, how one ought to live, also reiterates the other major theme of the dialogue, the nature of rhetoric and its connection with democratic politics. Rhetoric is an art that flatters its audience, giving them what is pleasant rather than what is good; similarly Callicles is attacked as being only concerned with pleasure. A second answer is that the *Gorgias*, like the other middle dialogues, is firmly committed to the view that "ethical hedonism is false," that "pleasure is not the good," and that "a life of physical pleasure cannot be a happy one," because the satisfaction of the desire for pleasure "is by its very nature insatiable."[56]

Like Polus, Socrates believes Callicles will fare poorly until, through self-examination, he discovers the extent of his disease/ignorance, and turns himself over to the moral physician. It is a common theme. In the *Alcibiades I*, having demonstrated that Alcibiades hasn't the least idea of how to advise the city, the young man asks Socrates "How will I care for myself, then, Socrates? Can you explain it? For you really seem like one who's spoken the truth" (124b).[57] Socrates replies in the affirmative adding that, in contrast to Alcibiades' guardian Pericles, who has passed on no wisdom, Socrates has had the benefit of a divine guardian, saying it is "him that I trust in when I say that your glory will come to light through no one else save me" (124c). Socratic *elenchus*, assuming the recipient is willing, provides training in autoscopic techniques that make possible an alternation in the noetic rules of self-governance that are normally too ingrained for anyone to circumvent, allowing a person to recover from "the disease of complex ignorance" (cf. *Republic* 377b, 378d–e). The window for acquiring this technique is rather narrow. The care of the self, the *epimeleia heautou*, must be learned "at the critical age when one leaves the hands of the pedagogues and enters political activity."[58] This *disease*, according to the *Republic*, is the true lie within men's souls, the lie in speeches being merely an imitation, a phantom, "not quite . . . unadulterated" (381e–382d). In the *Lesser Hippias* Socrates asks a favor of Hippias, telling him "be assured you will do me a greater good by giving my soul rest from ignorance than my body from disease" (372e–373a). Socrates, in contrast to Plato's other case studies, is assumed from the start to be a free man who requires only persuasion when his noetic regimen strays from health. The other figures require a slave's physician.

Socrates does not so much converse with Callicles as he lectures at him, as a slave's physician might do to his patient; after some initial, hostile interaction, Callicles contributes less and less to the conversation, until he scarcely says a word. This dialogic pattern is repeated on other occasions, such as the "charming" of the venomous Thrasymachus in Book I of the *Republic*.[59] After his bellicose entry into the conversation (336b–d) and monologue on justice (343b–344c), he is rapidly quieted and after only a short time falls completely silent, the conversation with Socrates taken over by Plato's brothers, Adeimantus and Glaucon. In the remaining nine books he speaks but once (450a) and then only briefly. These encounters point to "one of the paradoxes in which all confrontations with rhetoric, particularly critical ones, become entangled," namely "Plato's disallowance of the tropes of rhetoric from his texts, which self-consciously (even if ironically) identify as anti-rhetorical, belies dialectic's reliance on rhetoric as the contrast by which dialectic defines itself."[60] In Plato's dialogues the power of rhetoric, like the *pharmakon*, "a drug that heals and destroys . . . exerts pressure on the very texts that purport to attack it," and this "distinctive duality" of Plato's rhetoric, existing as both theory and practice simultaneously, "is precisely what Plato finds both fruitful and troublesome and what, by its own nature, he cannot escape."[61]

Rhetoric in Practice

Plato's *Menexenus*, like the *Gorgias*, deals with the power of political rhetoric. Plato walks a fine line in the dialogue, both demonstrating his mastery of the Funeral Oration and yet at the same time engaging in a parody of rhetorical conventions much as he does with the speech of Lysias in the *Phaedrus* and the speech of Agathon in the *Symposium*. Whereas the *Gorgias* deals with rhetoric on a largely theoretical plane, the *Menexenus* is a more practical demonstration, illustrating its arguments "by means of an imaginary funeral oration which parodies the stylistic tricks and the historical falsifications of patriotic oratory."[62] The funeral oration focused "on the interlocking bonds which tie together past, present, and future generations into a single community," the most significant being the association between those gathered (parents, siblings, wives, and children) with those "who died so that the community might have a future."[63]

In the dialogue Socrates delivers a funeral oration he says was previously given by Aspasia, "a teacher of rhetoric not exactly unworthy of consideration" (235e).[64] According to the *Menexenus*, Aspasia, Pericles' foreign-born wife, taught rhetoric to Socrates and "many fine rhetoricians" including the one who excelled all other Greeks, Pericles (235e). The dialogue concludes with Socrates promising to Menexenus[65] that he will continue to inform him of Aspasia's "many fine political speeches" (249e). Aspasia also happened to be a courtesan, wealthy and intelligent in much the same manner as the courtesan Theodote with whom Socrates converses in Xenophon's *Memorabilia*.[66] In that composition, as we saw in chapter 8, above, both philosopher and *hetaira* were able to draw others to themselves through the use of love potions, incantations, and erotic magic spells. In the *Menexenus* those who deliver Funeral Orations are said to "bewitch our souls," and Socrates similarly describes such orators as leaving him "charmed," "drawn beyond myself," and "in a rather uplifted and noble frame of mind" (235a–c, and cf. *Protagoras* 339d–e).

Aspasia's Funeral Oration, along with Diotima's speech on love in the *Symposium*, both utilize terminology drawn from the Eleusinian Mysteries, and are attributed to women by Plato "at least partly because of the probably central role of the priestess of Demeter at Eleusis."[67] Yet while there were priestesses at Eleusis, Demeter's cult was notable for the fact the Hierophant who conducted the ritual for the final grade of initiation was evidently male, as were some of the members of the two hereditary Eleusinian priesthoods, the Eumolpidai and Kerykes. Not only does the Funeral Oration have the power to bewitch and charm, Socrates says that in his case he experiences "pious awe" lasting "for more than three days; the words and the voice of the speaker enter so deeply into my ears that they ring with them and it is only on the fourth or fifth day do I recollect myself and perceive where it is on earth that I am, since until then I had nearly thought I was dwelling on the Islands of the Blessed" (235a–c). The Islands of the Blessed were those that initiates into the Eleusinian Mysteries were hoping to secure an afterlife on. Plato compares the power of oratory to the experience of the pious awe of an Eleusinian *epoptes* because, as we saw in the case of the historical Gorgias, Isocrates and at least Plato's stand-in for the historical Protagoras, speech was viewed as having a power upon the mind like that of intoxicating *pharmaka*, and the evidence suggests the Eleusinian initiation culminated with the drinking of a drugged potion, the *kykeon*, that produced visual *phasmata*.

Philosophic Prescriptions: Fear and Law

The power of *speech*, Socrates says in the *Phaedrus*, "is in fact a leading of the soul" (271d). In the *Phaedrus*, much as he does in the *Gorgias*, Socrates compares rhetoric to the practice of medicine, telling Phaedrus that each examines a "nature," medicine that of the body, rhetoric that of the soul, i.e. noetic disposition. Rhetoric, like medicine, lacks theoretical self-reflection, hence "any attempt to implant health and strength in the body by the use of drugs or diet, or the kind of conviction and excellence you desire in the soul by means of speeches," by either of these occupations will necessarily fail, being merely "empirical knack and not of science" (270b). There is soon thereafter a mention of Gorgias' most famous pupil, Isocrates, and his school of rhetoric (279a–b). Philosophic rhetoric, the *dialektikos* with its "scientific" foundations, has the power to truly understand men's souls, which the genuinely expert speaker adapts, again like a physician, to the needs of each listener-patient (270b–272b, and cf. *Statesman* 293d–e). Here oratory is not as strictly useless as it was in the *Gorgias*; the target here is oratory that is uninformed by a training in dialectic.

What sort of *telos* does the rhetorical discourse of the philosopher push the soul toward? Push toward it? Push on it? The attention of our desires must be, as we are told in the *Laws*, diverted from the "three unwholesome appetites" and "towards the good" (783a). The importance of "being moderate and in control of oneself," the master of these enslaving "passions and appetites" (*Gorgias* 491d–e), which in their totality push the mind into states of ecstasy, is a near perennial theme of the Platonic dialogues. The *Republic* (389d–e), *Phaedrus* (237d–238a), *Philebus* (45d–e) and *Laws* (730e–734e, 839a–b) each define these appetites as consisting of the desire for food, drink, and sex.[68] The method for checking the chaotic "growth and onrush" of these appetites, we are told, consists of the applications of "three supreme sanctions—fear, law, true discourse" (*Laws* 783a).

The first approach, fear, is only efficacious so long as the threat of external punishment is clear, explicit, and immediate. Herein lies the weakness of tyrannical authority, for it relies on fear, the bogies of corporal punishment and/or financial ruination alone, a fact Plato stresses at several points. The second approach, law, is also useless if employed on its own, for it does not address the root cause of social disorder, but only its symptoms. This is the weakness of democratic attempts to legislate morality, for lawmakers "spend their lives setting down many such rules and correcting them . . . ignorant that they are cutting off the heads of a hydra" (*Republic* 425e–426c). The charge is elaborated in greater detail in the *Statesman*, where law is likened to "a self-willed stupid person," incapable of differentiating between individual motivations and particular circumstances, the "all but incessant mutability of human things" (294b–c, and cf. 295e–296a).

The *Statesman* even compares the weakness of the written law to the written prescriptions (*hypomnemata graphein*) left behind by a physician or physical trainer who must be away from his patients or pupils for a time. If one or the other were to return sooner than expected, and observe that a new course of treatment was called for, it would be "utterly ridiculous" to cling to the original written prescription (295b–e). Similarly in the *Laws* Plato writes that the attempt to impose penalties on behaviors that are essentially private, trivial, and commonly engaged in are both "improper and undignified" (788a–b). Where a state is truly "run along excellent lines" and has achieved "every condition favorable to the practice of virtue," the need to write many laws, as the Athenian is about to do, is "a disgrace" (853b–854a). Yet neither can the state remain completely silent, as the authority of *the written law* is undermined if everyone is simply allowed to become habituated within a pattern of petty transgression (788b). *Pathe*, temporary emotional states, have the capacity to become *hexeis*, permanent dispositions.[69] A device is required, above and beyond the law, to make the establishment of a legal code secure (837e–838a).

The *Un*written Law

That solution, the remedy superior to both the tonic of fear and/or the dense foliage of legislation, as discussed in the *Laws*, is discursive regimen. For Plato the remedy for the dangers of the epithymetic drive—the *pharmakon* for the *epithymetikon* so to speak—consists of the production and discursive circulation of social conventions and customs neither "designated laws nor left untouched" (793a–b). In other words, ethics. Ethics set out, on a level less formal than written legislation, *spoken* authoritative standards determining a community's definition of "what is the right way" (733a, cf. 838a–d). These standards secure an "established usage" in our verbal discourse, the overall effect of which is a "voluntary unanimity of language" which a person feels as bound to obey as any written statue (838e). Consisting of various sorts of verbal "commendation and reproach," ethical norms, *the unwritten law* as Plato frequently refers to it, can "educate" men to be "more amenable and well disposed" toward the written law (730b).

Social conventions serve as the preamble to the text of the law, operating as a "sure shield for all the statutes hither to committed to writing" (793c. and cf. *Statesman* 295e–296a). The importance of ethical conventions, Plato insists, can hardly be exaggerated: ethical norms established for behavior in private households, those spaces cordoned off from public scrutiny, are the underpinnings of public law. To the extent that "the right regulation of private households within a society is neglected, it is idle to expect the foundations of public law to be secure," the reason being that "the privacy of home life screens off from the general observation many little incidents [that present] a real danger to the law . . . since the habit of transgression is learned from the repetition of these petty misdeeds" (788b and 790b, and cf. *Republic* 521a). Where the written law is ignored or obsolete, destruction hangs over the community (715d). If *stasis* reigns in private, it is sure to do so in public.

Sound and secure language discipline inures itself at the noetic level or as Plato expresses it, "as a habit of mind" which in turn spurs correct somatic behavior (792d). Where a society's conventions are open to questioning, doubt, and derision, "it is when a builder's supports give way and subside under his edifice; the result is a general collapse of one part upon another, substructure and all that has so admirably been built upon it" (793c). There is in fact no graver danger for any civilized society than "language and such notions" that tamper with longstanding social custom: discourse of this type is a very "serious . . . evil" (797c). Not only do many fall prey to an "uncontrollable urge" to experience pleasure and avoid pain, they "*talk* with a complete lack of inhibition"—and some are so skilled at this sort of chatter that, if left unpunished, their discourse converts others (908b–d, emphasis mine). The problem of democracy is the presence of *parresia*, "unbridled license of the tongue" (*Republic* 557d).

Like an alteration of "bodily regimen, mental habit, or in a word, change of anything," change in a person's *discursive regimen* is always perilous. Discursive habits, as we find them in the *Laws*, are the foundation of healthy somatic and noetic regimens. Because of this, "frequent modifications of moral approbation and disapprobation" by a lawmaker "are of all changes the gravest and need to be most guarded against" (797d–798d). Plato complains that "practically no one takes into account the greatest 'judgment' (*dike*), as it is called, on wrongdoing. This is to grow to resemble men who are evil, and as the resemblance increases to shun good men and their wholesome conversation and cut oneself off from them, while seeking to attach oneself to the other kind and keep their company. The inevitable result of consorting with such people is that what you do and have done to you is exactly what they naturally do and say to each other" (728b).

The atheist is perhaps the most extreme example of a sort of discursively evil individual. The atheist is often "full of cunning and guile [and] is the sort of fellow who will make a diviner and go in for all sorts of legerdemain: sometimes he will turn into a dictator or a demagogue or a general, or a plotter in secret rites; and he is the man who invents the tricks of the so-called 'sophists'" (908d). This discussion recalls the *Republic*, which warned against conversing with a class of people called drones, described as "dread magicians (*magoi*) and tyrant makers" (572e). One should flee from "the company of the wicked" and hope that one's "disease abates (*lophai nosema*)," the *Laws* tells us, otherwise death should be looked upon as the preferable alterative (854c).

A Programmer's Language

Discursive regimen, in the *Laws* at least, has traveled far from the at least nominally interactive—if often enchanting and deceptive—Socratic *elenchus*. The many proposals "for the manufacture and control of discourse" in the *Laws* are "wholly unsocratic."[70] In these proposals we see perhaps a reflection of Plato's final pessimism. Both the law code and its discourse-founding preambles, in seeming contradiction with Plato's earlier works, speak in a monological and tyrannical voice. Conversation "is entirely one way" and even the secondary lawgivers "simply take the system and the principles and apply them as strictly as possible."[71] The Athenian of the *Laws* refers to legislation as a "tyrannical prescription" (722e), one that "orders and threatens like a tyrant or despot who writes his decrees on the wall and is done with it" (859a). The parallel with ancient medicine is noticeable: the slave's physician neither "gives nor receives account" from the patient and merely issues a command and swiftly moves on to the next case (720c). Discursive regimen, as the solution to the danger of *stasis* perceived to be all around, requires that every member of the community "utter one and the same thing, so far as is possible, at all times and through the entirety of their lives, in their songs, their stories, and their discourses" (664a).

After a ten-year period of fine-tuning and modification by the magistrates (772c–d), the lawmaker's code will be declared "incapable of modification" and clothed in this finalized legal texture for all times. The text of the law now transcends history; it remains forever "unchangeable" (798a–b). Equally unchangeable is the daily routine of each individual: "every gentleman must have a timetable prescribing what he is to do every minute of his life, which he should follow at all times from the dawn of one day until the sun comes up at the dawn of the next" (807d–e).[72] Even sleep, that break from rational identity where the darkest desires of the *epithymetikon* can manifest themselves (e.g. *Republic* 571c–d), is to be curbed as much as possible, each person being allowed only so much slumber as their somatic regimen will allow without their health breaking down (807e–808c).

The *Laws* are written in a language meant to become sacrosanct; the aim is to establish a law code with "an almost scriptural status."[73] The text of the legal code becomes the foundation for all discursive regimens. Put another way, the "waywardness of oral discourse will be kept in check by the written text."[74] The text of the law code, its pronouncements on both legal and ethical issues, "*serve to control the citizen's words* as well as their deeds."[75] Discursive regimen is, in a word, "tethered" to the written text of the law code. Written law helps to program the language of every citizen, who is treated as little more than a puppet, a flawed and badly constructed automaton, establishing the ethical priorities that will govern the practice of their discursive regimen throughout their lifetime, and both compliments and sustains the practice of *sophrosyne* within both their noetic and physical regimens.

Plato, on the one hand, treats *stasis* as an epistemological riddle that philosophical metaphysics could solve, and, on the other, he treats it as anarchic political danger. The philosopher, in the manner of a physician, attempts to purge *stasis* from the body of the *polis* by purging it from the body, mind, and speech of each citizen. This purging through regimen is an essential component of the Platonic moral economy.[76] He transforms *stasis* "from existential unease to personal, social and political disease," and in doing so jettisons a "temporal, existential vision of politics."[77] Lost too is the pre-Platonic valuation of moments of identity-blurring *ekstasis*, "the experience of alternation, what derives from and out of *stasis*," the "sensing of the turbulence of life, of being thrown from the past and into the future."[78] The political solution envisioned by Plato is a medical solution; the cure for both *stasis* within the *polis* and *(ek)stasis* within the individual requires a special breed of physician administering a special form of remedial verbal therapy, a philosophic *pharmakon*.[79]

Notes

1. Valerie I. Flint, *Witchcraft and Magic in Europe: Ancient Greece and Rome* (London: The Athlone Press, 1999), 172 has "beguilements." Christopher A. Faraone, *Ancient Greek Love Magic* (Cambridge, MA: Harvard University Press, 1999), 97 has "enchantments."

2. Plato singles out this passage as unfit for young men learning self-mastery to hear in Book IV of the *Republic* (390a–b).

3. Pietro Pucci, *Hesiod and the Language of Poetry* (Baltimore, MD: The Johns Hopkins University Press, 1977), 22.

4. Rosamond Kent Sprague, ed. *The Older Sophists: A Complete Translation by Several Hands of the Fragments in die Fragmente der Vorsokratie* (Indianapolis, IN: Hackett Publishing, 2001), 20. A detailed discussion of this fragment may be found in Edward Schiappa, *Protagoras and Logos: A Study in Greek Philosophy and Rhetoric*, second edition (Columbia, SC: University of South Carolina Press, 2003), 117–33.

5. See Simon Goldhill, "The Audience of Athenian Tragedy," in *The Cambridge Companion to Greek Tragedy*, ed. P. E. Easterling (Cambridge: Cambridge University Press, 1997), 54–68.

6. It should be emphasized that the interpretation here is not based on a belief in a linear movement from *muthos* to *logos*, with the latter replacing the former. Such a view is now recognized as being too simple. When we look at Homer, Hesiod, and the Archaic poets on the one hand, and tragedians such as Aeschylus, Sophocles, and Euripides on the other, it becomes clear that the poets and playwrights reveal a high degree of critical self-awareness and reflection on issues more typically associated with philosophy. It is not so much a matter of there being a movement in ancient Greece from *muthos* TO *logos* as it is a complex and continual interplay of *muthos* AND *logos*. See A. W. H. Adkins "Myth, Philosophy, and Religion in Ancient Greece," in *Myth and Philosophy*, ed. Frank Reynolds and David Tracy (Albany, NY: State University of New York Press, 1990), 95–130 (especially 104–17 on Plato).

7. Paul Cartledge, "'Deep Plays' Theatre as a Process in Greek Civic Life," in *The Cambridge Companion to Greek Tragedy*, ed. P. E. Easterling (Cambridge: Cambridge

University Press, 1997), 9–10, and Goldhill, "The Audience of Athenian Tragedy," 66–67.

8. Jon D. Mikalson, *Ancient Greek Religion*, Second Edition (Malden, MA: Blackwell Publishing, 2010), 85.

9. Daniel Mendelsohn, "Συγκραυνόω: Dithrambic Language and Dionysiac Cult." *The Classical Journal* 87, no. 2 (1992): 107-108, 111. Mendelsohn writes that the "fragments of later dithyramb (after about 450 BCE) . . . bear distinct traces of both diction and action associated with early Dionysiac cult," and argues that what was characteristic of dithyramb by the Classical Period, and so concerned Aristotle (*Politics* 1342a-b), "was in fact tame" compared to the wild drunkenness, riotous music, and violent dance of earlier centuries.

10. Mikalson, *Ancient Greek Religion*, 85. As Mikalson writes on the same page the fact that "wine can create such an effect [i.e. ecstasy] requires no argument, but dance and song can also produce it. It is especially apparent in the theater . . ."

11. Morton W. Bloomfield, "Poetry in Early Societies," *Proceedings of the Philosophical Society* 130, no. 2 (1986): 250. See also Griswold 2007: 2. See also Bruno Gentili, *Poetry and Its Public in Ancient Greece: From Homer to the Fifth Century* (Baltimore, MD: The Johns Hopkins University Press, 1988). Worth consulting is F. T. Griffiths, "Poetry as Pharmakon in Theocritis' *Idyll* 2," in *Arktouros: Hellenic Studies Presented to Bernard M. W. Knox*, ed. Glen W. Bowersock (Berlin and New York: Walter de Gruyter, 1979), 81–90.

12. Bloomfield, "Poetry in Early Socrates," 247–48.

13. Matthew W. Dickie, *Magic and Magicians in the Greco-Roman World* (New York: Routledge, 2001), 74–5.

14. On this quarrel see the discussion in Mihai Spariosu, *God of Many Names: Play, Poetry, and Power in Hellenic Thought from Homer to Aristotle* (Durham, NC: Duke University Press, 1991), 141–62. See also Elizabeth Belfiore, "Plato's Greatest Accusation Against Poetry," *Canadian Journal of Philosophy* 9 (1983): 39–62.

15. Bradley Rubidge, "Tragedy and the Emotions of Warriors: The Moral Psychology Underlying Plato's Attack on Poetry," *Arethusa* 26, no. 3 (1993).

16. Rubidge, "Tragedy and the Emotions of Warriors," 255.

17. An extended discussion of women and mourning in ancient Greece may be found in Matthew Dillon, *Girls and Women in Classical Greek Religion* (New York: Routledge, 2002), 268–92.

18. Walker records that "the standard meanings of *katharsis* in ancient Greek are medical and religious. In the medical sense, *katharsis* is 'purgation' of unhealthful substances from the body, usually through the application of some drug, a *pharmakon*," while in an "older, religious sense (from which the medical meaning seems to have derived), *katharsis* is 'purification,' the removal of pollution, by means of some ritual." In Jeffrey Walker, "Pathos and Katharsis in 'Aristotelian Rhetoric: Some Implications," in *Rereading Aristotle's Rhetoric*, ed. Alan G. Gross and Arthur E. Walzer (Carbondale, IL: Southern Illinois University Press, 2000), 76–77.

19. See Louise M. Bishop, *Words, Stones, and Herbs: The Healing Word in Medieval and Early Modern England* (Syracuse, NY: Syracuse University Press, 2007), 83. Bishop goes on to write "Aristotle's usage combines the literary with the bodily, using the one to figure the other. Aristotle uses the term catharsis to indicate the purgation of pity and fear that drama—in particular tragedy and its recounting of a hero's downfall—accomplishes for an audience."

20. Even today we speak of someone in the grips of a "laughing fit" or of an audience's "hysterical laughter," this sort of mirth being one of the few forms of ecstasy left relatively untouched as unproblematic during the industrial era.

21. Herbert Musurillo, *The Acts of the Pagan Martyrs: Acta Alexandrinorum* (New York: Clarendon Press, 1954), 268 indicates the *Discourse to the Alexandrians* was delivered sometime between 105 and 112 CE. Alexandria at this time was apparently notorious for its lack of self-restraint and vice.

22. This passage befuddled at least one translator who wrote that the practice is recorded "in such vague terms one cannot tell whether he had more exact knowledge or not." See J. W. Cohoon, trans., *Dio Chrysostom*, vols. 2 & 3 (Cambridge, MA: Harvard University Press, 1932), 227 n. 1. There are noticeable parallels to Herodotus' account of the Scythians and their use of hemp in the *Histories*. Chrysostom, after his banishment by the emperor Domitian, wandered through the lands north of the Aegean, a "journey through Scythia to the Getae," including the city of Borysthenes, a Greek colony that had ongoing contact with the Scythians and was for a time lost to these barbarians and then reoccupied. He wrote a history called *On the Gaete* but this work is lost to us. Additional details may be found in Malcolm Schofield, *The Stoic Idea of the City* (New York: Cambridge University Press, 1991), 57–58. One suspects that the author of the *Discourse* was familiar with the drug use of the Scythians or a similar people.

23. The description recalls the many mendicant practitioners of magic such as the *agyrtai, chresmologoi*, and *thaumatopoiia*, who often wandered from city to city, living by their wits. Unlike most sophists these individuals were generally destitute. They "were in all likelihood subject to beatings at the hands of the slaves of the agoranomi and the astynomoi, to summary arrest and imprisonment, and to expulsion from Attica, if their activities were believed to be a threat to public order." See Dickie, *Magic and Magicians in the Greco-Roman World*, 60–77.

24. See Part One, above.

25. In the *Protagoras* Socrates demands a ground rule forbidding long speeches when a response by Protagoras wins yet more applause (334c–d). In the *Gorgias* he similarly complains about Polus' long-winded style (461d–462a, and cf. 448d). In the *Alcibiades I* he assures Alcibiades that the method of persuasion he will use will not consist of the long enticing speeches the young man has been used to hearing prior to Socrates approaching him for the first time (106b).

26. John P. Anton, "Dialectic and Health in Plato's *Gorgias*: Presuppositions and Implications," *Ancient Philosophy* 1, no. 1 (1980): 52.

27. John R. Wallach, *The Platonic Political Art: A Study in Critical Reason and Democracy* (University Park, PA: Penn State University Press, 2001), 184.

28. Jacques Derrida, *Dissemination* (Chicago: University of Chicago Press, 1981), 117, emphasis in the original.

29. Remembering here that a cosmetic, too, might be called a *pharmakon*.

30. Derrida, *Dissemination*, 142.

31. Debra Hawhee, *Bodily Arts: Rhetoric and Athletics in Ancient Greece* (Austin, TX: University of Texas Press, 2004), 79.

32. James Jerome Murphy and Richard A. Katula, *A Synoptic History of Classical Rhetoric* (Mahwah, NJ: Lawrence Erlbaum, 2003), 263. It was also available in the form of a written pamphlet that could be purchased.

33. Quoted in Jonathan D. Culler, *Deconstruction: Critical Concepts in Literary and Cultural Studies, Volume 1* (New York: Routledge, 2003), 201. While I agree with Elizabeth Belfiore, "Elenchus, Epode, and Magic: Socrates and Silenus," *Phoenix* 34, no. 2 (1980): 131 that "Gorgias' account of the magic of *logos* is . . . substantially the same

as Plato's account," it would be wrong to simply treat this reference to *pharmakon* as a subcategory of the spell. Belfiore's analysis, one that claims that Plato frequently uses "the vocabulary of magic . . . spells (*epodai*), and drugs (*pharmaka*)" mentions the latter only three times. Clearly, the power of drugs was for Plato every bit as important as that of magic and spells and moreover in the ancient world all three were frequently indistinguishable.

34. Culler, *Deconstruction*, 201.

35. Hawhee, *Bodily Arts: Rhetoric and Athletics in Ancient Greece*, 79.

36. Robert Wardy, *The Birth of Rhetoric: Gorgias, Plato, and Their Successors* (New York: Routledge, 1996), 46.

37. Erika Rummel, "Isocrates Ideal of Rhetoric: Criteria of Evaluation," in Edward Schiappa, ed. *Landmark Essays on Classical Greek Rhetoric: Volume Three* (Davis, CA: Hermagoras Press, 1994), 152.

38. Joy Connolly, *The State of Speech: Rhetoric and Political Thought in Ancient Rome* (Princeton, NJ: Princeton University Press, 2007), 229. Connolly notices the similarity between this passage of Isocrates and both Plato's *Republic* (560d–e) and Thucydides' *History* (3.82.4–5).

39. There is of course some irony in the singling out since Isocrates was eight years Plato's senior and by the time the *Phaedrus* was composed any "potential" he possessed presumably would have either been already realized or have failed to materialize.

40. See Schiappa, *Protagoras and Logos*, 40–9 on the possibility Plato himself coined the term *rhetorike*.

41. Trevor J. Saunders, *Plato's Penal Code—Tradition, Controversy and Reform in Greek Penology* (Oxford: Clarendon Press, 1991), 92.

42. Saunders, *Plato's Penal Code*, 92.

43. Satyrus claimed Gorgias was a pupil of Empedocles, and "had been present when Empedocles had engaged in sorcery (*goeteuein*)." See Dickie, *Magic and Magicians in the Greco-Roman World*, 32. On Empedocles see chapter 7, above.

44. See the afterword, below.

45. Saunders, *Plato's Penal Code*, 167.

46. Saunders, *Plato's Penal Code*, 167.

47. Saunders, *Plato's Penal Code*, 167 n. 67.

48. Saunders, *Plato's Penal Code*, 167. Saunders, *Plato's Penal Code*, 170 n. 86 also writes that "concerning the ancient controversy about the relative merits of regimen and drugs, Plato consistently favors regimen." This is true yet not wholly accurate—speaking thusly is only possible if one is defining "drugs" along *modern* lines. Plato's relationship with the *pharmakon* is simply too complex to speak of drugs in this way. If the *Republic's* lie in speeches can be used "as a preventative, like a drug" (382c), but only when "assigned to doctors" who appear at the same time rulers are mentioned (389b), a claim of regimen trumping drugs doesn't seem tenable. On the subject of "pharmacological lying" see Carl Page, "The Truth about Lies in Plato's *Republic*," *Ancient Philosophy* 11, no. 1 (1991): 1–33, John Hesk, *Deception and Democracy in Classical Athens* (New York: Cambridge University Press, 2000) and chapter 10, below.

49. James Haden, "Two Types of Power in Plato's *Gorgias*," *The Classical Journal* 87, no. 4 (1992): 323.

50. See Randall B. Clark, *The Law Most Beautiful and Best: Medical Argument and Magical Rhetoric in Plato's* Laws (Lanham, MD: Lexington Books, 2003).

51. Saunders, *Plato's Penal Code*, 154.

52. Danielle S. Allen, *The World of Prometheus: The Politics of Punishing in Democratic Athens* (Princeton, NJ: Princeton University Press, 2000), 279.

53. Anton, "Dialectic and Health in Plato's *Gorgias*," 53–54.

54. George Klosko, "The Refutation of Callicles in Plato's *Gorgias*," *Greece and Rome* 31, no. 2 (1984): 129. It has been pointed out by innumerable scholars that the viewpoints of Callicles anticipate those of Nietzsche. See also George Rudebusch, "Callicles' Hedonism," *Ancient Philosophy* 12, no. 1 (1992): 53–86.

55. Klosko, "The Refutation of Callicles in Plato's *Gorgias*," 130.

56. Klosko, "The Refutation of Callicles in Plato's *Gorgias*," 137.

57. Using the translation of David M. Johnson, trans., *Socrates and Alcibiades* (Newburyport, MA: Focus Publishing, 2003).

58. Michel Foucualt, *The Hermeneutics of the Self—Lectures at the College de France 1981–1982* (New York: Picador, 2005), 37.

59. Cf. *Republic* 358b where Glaucon expresses the opinion that "Thrasymachus, like a snake, has been charmed."

60. Joy Connolly, *The State of Speech: Rhetoric and Political Thought in Ancient Rome* (Princeton, NJ: Princeton University Press, 2007), 124 n. 12.

61. Connolly, *The State of Speech*, 124 n. 12, and see also Christine Oravec and Michael Salvador, "The Duality of Rhetoric: Theory as Discursive Practice," in *Rethinking the History of Rhetoric: Multidisciplinary Essays on the Rhetorical Tradition*, ed. Takis Poulakos (Boulder, CO: Westview Press, 1993), 173.

62. E. R. Dodds, *Plato—Gorgias, A Revised Text with Introduction and Commentary* (Oxford, Clarendon Press, 1959), 23–24.

63. Bruce Rosenstock, "Socrates as Revenant: A Reading of the *Menexenus*," *Phoenix* 48 (1994): 338.

64. Scholars have puzzled over an obvious anachronism in Socrates' Funeral Oration in the *Menexenus*. Beginning with Athenian history in mythic times Socrates continues right up to the King's Peace (387 BCE), an event that post-dates his own death by nearly a decade. The historical narrative is followed by an address to the parents and children of the dead, during which Socrates, according to Rosenstock, "Socrates as Revenant: A Reading of the *Menexenus*," 335 "adopts the rhetorical trope of prosopopeia, speaking in the voice of the dead." While it is unlikely, it is remotely possible that Socrates is speaking as a ghost. On the other hand the anachronistic material could simply have been added by a hand other than Plato's, for example a member of his Academy.

65. This Menexenus—*Menexenus, Lysis, Phaedo* 59b—is probably the cousin of the child of Socrates of the same name (*Apology* 34d, *Phaedo* 116b). See Debra Nails, *Agora, Academy, and the Conduct of Philosophy* (Dordrect, Netherlands: Kluwer, 1995).

66. Christopher A. Faraone and Laura McClure, *Prostitutes and Courtesans in the Ancient World* (Madison, WI: University of Wisconsin Press, 2006), 223 n. 13.

67. Rosenstock, "Socrates as Revenant: A Reading of the *Menexenus*," 342.

68. On the appetites and the *Laws* see the chapter titled "Eat, Drink, Man, Woman" in Clark, *The Law Most Beautiful and Best*, 117–46.

69. Saunders, *Plato's Penal Code*, 174 n. 101.

70. Andrea Nightingale, "Writing/Reading a Sacred Text: A Literary Interpretation of Plato's *Laws*," *Classical Philology* 88, no. 4 (1993): 281 n. 14, and cf. 295.

71. Nightingale, "Writing/Reading a Sacred Text," 297.

72. Quoted in Trevor J. Saunders, trans. *The Laws* (New York: Penguin Books, 1986), 297.

73. Nightingale, "Writing/Reading a Sacred Text," 289–90.

74. Nightingale, "Writing/Reading a Sacred Text," 290.

75. Nightingale, "Writing/Reading a Sacred Text," 290, emphasis mine.

76. The term "moral economy" is taken from William E. Connolly, *The Augustinian Imperative: A Reflection on the Politics of Morality* (London: Sage Publishing, 1993) and is discussed in the Introduction, above.

77. Costas M. Constantinou, *States of Political Discourse: Words, Regimes, Seditions* (New York: Routledge, 2004), 9.

78. Constantinou, *States of Political Discourse*, 9–10.

79. See chapter 10, below.

Chapter Ten

Philosophy's Pharmacy

In the *Theatetus* there are a series of attempts to define knowledge.[1] None of the attempts is ever entirely agreed upon and the conversation ends in *aporia*.[2] Early in the dialogue there is a scene known to virtually every student of Plato wherein Socrates likens himself to a midwife. The midwife is described as a woman who is no longer of childbearing age who has had personal experience with childbirth. She has not always been barren, as women who have been barren their entire lives, having no practical experience, cannot be allowed to practice an art of delivery. She is rather a woman who, having passed a certain climacteric, now performs a different role for the good of the community. The midwife's art, according to Socrates, consists of having "the power to bring on the pains, and also, if they think fit, to relieve them; they do it by use of simple drugs [*pharmakeia*] and by singing incantations [*epodai*]. In difficult cases, too, they can bring about the birth; or if they consider it advisable, they can promote a miscarriage" (149c–d).[3]

Whereas the midwife attends to the bodily labor of women, the philosopher attends to the labor of men's souls. As the midwife is barren, so the philosopher is barren: he merely "delivers," through discursive testing and cross-examination, their progeny, optimally wisdom or at a minimum a conscious awareness within themselves that these men lack wisdom (150c–d). Men come to Socrates in a condition of suffering even worse than childbirth—ignorance—but an ignorance on the threshold of some form of greater enlightenment, and it is "this pain my art is able to bring on, and also to ally" (151b). Socrates, in the *Protagoras,* similarly argues that only "a physician of the soul" is capable of resisting the quack remedies marketed by the sophists (313e–314b), while at the same time indicating that physicians' drugs (*pharmaka*) are among those things that can be both good (*agatha*) and painful (*aniara*) (354a).[4] In the *Alcibiades I,* after explaining (106b) that giving "some long speech" is "not my way," Socra-

233

tes' style of questioning soon has the twenty-year-old Alcibiades—who desires to advise the city about how to conduct its affairs—exclaiming a confession of ignorance: "By the gods, Socrates, I don't know what I'm saying, and I've probably been in a most disgraceful way for a long time without noticing it" (127d).

The most common interpretations of the "midwife" passage in the *Theatetus* draw some kind of an analogy—based on 150b at the expense of ignoring the earlier passage at 149c–d—between Socratic *elenchus* facilitating an often uncomfortable birth of wisdom in men and the midwife facilitating the pain of childbirth in women, with perhaps a reference or note mentioning that Socrates' mother, Phaenarete, was reputed to have been a midwife.[5] This is at least partially understandable as virtually all of them have been written in roughly the last hundred years, after midwives had lost most of their traditional roles in obstetrics.[6] What cannot be as easily forgiven is that the initial portion of Plato's metaphor, especially 149c–d, wherein the philosopher compares his art to that of the midwife, appears to rest on *pharmaceutical force* and on the ability of *verbal charms* to produce discomfort or its opposite, not just the uncomfortable process of birthing *per se.*

Midwifery is a socially indispensable task but not, Socrates tells us, "so important as my own performance," because in the case of philosophy the maieutic task is further complicated by the fact that "the patients are sometimes delivered of phantoms and sometimes of realities, and that the two are sometimes hard to distinguish" (150b, cf. 150c). Equally as important, the initial discussion of the philosopher and the midwife in the *Theatetus* anticipates the later discussion within the same dialogue of the *rhetor*, the "man of the law courts," as having a mind "with no health in it" and a soul so "small and warped" that he fawns over the *demos* like a slave fawning over his master, regularly engaging in the telling of lies and "repaying one wrong for another" (172d–173a).

Much like the art of midwifery, Asclepian medical practice included incantations, drugs, and charms, in addition to surgery. In Pindar, *Pythian Odes* 3.47–54, for example, Asclepius treats illnesses by "tending some with gentle incantations, giving others soothing remedies [*pharmaka*] to drink or attaching charms [*pharmaka*] to their limbs from every side, and still others he cures by incisions." In the *Republic* the art of rulership is described as ideally being practiced by a *statesmanlike Asclepius* (407e), and includes the construction of "models of speech" (379a) for those who will supervise the education of the young.

One is hard-pressed to find in the secondary literature on the *Theatetus*, *Republic* and still other Platonic dialogues any sustained discussion of the centrality of these magical *epodai*, sung incantations, or drugs with multivariate powers, even though Socrates says these things are as integral a part of *his* art as that of the midwife or the Asclepian physician. Furthermore, the discussion of the practice of philosophy as a sort of purification of a soul filled with phantoms and lies raises another question: whether Plato believed a mind purified by philosophy might legitimately engage in deceit, and where and when it might do so. This final chapter will attempt to address these two matters.

Deconstruction's Pharmacy

Many dialogues besides the *Theatetus* make the difficulties of philosophy, drugs, and their frequently parallel administration a central concern. Jacques Derrida's well-known essay, "Plato's Pharmacy," observes that, for Plato, the meaning of the ancient Greek word for drug, *pharmakon*, and related words like *pharmakeia* (drug use or administration), *pharmakeus* (wizard), and *pharmakos* (scapegoat), were caught up in a chain of interlocking but less than identical meanings.[7] The presence of the first three are overt and explicit, the last covert and implicit, in Plato's writings, the *Phaedrus* being, for Derrida, the most conspicuous example of this presence/absence. Possessed of a "malleable unity" the various meanings of *pharmakon* have been "dispersed, masked, obliterated, and rendered almost unreadable," not only because of the "imprudence or empiricism of the translators," though this was certainly true, but "first and foremost by the redoubtable, irreducible difficulty" of texts like the *Phaedrus* which mark the "very passage into philosophy," the transformation-transition-transference from a non-philosopheme to a philosopheme.[8]

Derrida points out that there has been a great deal of misunderstanding without, strictly speaking, mistranslation of *pharmakon*. Translations of Plato are "heirs and depositaries" of the tradition of Western metaphysics Plato himself inaugurated, and as such they "produce on the *pharmakon* an *effect of analysis* that violently destroys it, reduces it to one of its simple elements by interpreting it, paradoxically enough, in the light of the ulterior developments [Western metaphysics] itself has made possible."[9] To complicate the matter further Derrida indicates that we find in the *Phaedrus* the question of writing proposed, presented, and asserted as a *pharmakon*—often in relation to the Egyptian legend of Theuth, the mythical inventor of writing—simultaneously bound up in a question of *morality*. For Plato, Derrida argues, the latter is the fundamental question that is at stake and which is, furthermore, "in no way to be distinguished from the questions of truth, memory, and dialectics."[10]

First published in 1968, and still both influential and frequently cited, "Plato's Pharmacy" has not been particularly well served by either those who are friendly or at least neutral to Derrida's reading, or by those critical of it.[11] The latter group appears more concerned with refuting the deconstructive approach to textual interpretation, as opposed to the evidentiary strengths and weaknesses of the essay itself, while the former groups defend the heuristical value of the interpretive approach but largely accept at face value any historical evidence Derrida provides about *pharmaka* in the ancient world.[12] While "Plato's Pharmacy" purports to place us back in the ancient Greek context, a hasty or indolent reading can easily miss those places where the research that rooted Derrida's discussion has become dated, and where on occasion he substituted rhetoric for research to serve his own purposes.[13]

Derrida begins his essay by arguing that the settings of the *Phaedrus* are never a matter of accident. The staging of every theme of the dialogue is carefully paired with a "significant site" of the ancient world and in this "theatrical geography" each pairing "corresponds to an infallible calculation or necessity."[14] Plato begins the dialogue with a send-off, a *khairein*, to myth, in the name of knowing the truth, or more precisely in the name of true knowledge of the self. Walking together outside the city's walls, Socrates and Phaedrus recall Oreithyia's abduction by Boreas as they catch sight of a stream, the Ilissus. Mocking the sophist rationalization of the myth Socrates relates that while playing with Pharmakeia (*sun Pharmakeiai paizousan*), Oreithyia was caught up by the cold north wind (*pneuma Bereou*), thrown to her death, and swept up by a sexually enraptured Boreas.

It is no accident, this "brief evocation" of Pharmakeia—"the use of drugs"—but a foreshadowing of the pharmaceutical forces that mark off the entire dialogue.[15] Derrida's interpretation of this passage as a playful Pharmakeia dragging "down to death a virginal purity and an unpenetrated interior" would certainly have surprised Plato or any of his contemporaries.[16] Oreithyia, who was one of the *hyacinthea* (women of the flower), means "she who rages in the mountains" or "mountain ecstatic woman" and her abduction is best understood in relation to similar ecstatic "seizures" in Greek myth. The wind is traditionally an abductor, being a "rather transparent metaphor for 'inspiration' and chthonic possession."[17] Boreas, the cold north wind, ravishes a frenzied botanical daughter of Hyakinthos, himself a pre-Indo-European deity who upon his death changed into a plant of the same name.[18]

The discussion of the myth at just this moment—by the Ilissus—is equally important due to the proximity of this location to Agrai (from *agra*, the spoils of the chase), the site of the Lesser Mysteries, which involved "the Dionysian theme of Persephone's illegal abduction while gathering intoxicating flowers."[19] Besides Persephone, Eurydice, Creusa, and Helen were all gathering flowers when, in a state of ecstatic rapture, they "experienced the sacred marriage with death."[20] To cross the Ilissus might also suggest a trip to the central sanctuary of the Anthesteria (festival of flowers), the Limnaion, the temple of Dionysus in the Marshes.[21]

After introducing Pharmakeia, Derrida spends much of the first of the two essays that comprise "Plato's Pharmacy" tracking down the paternity of *logos* and reconstituting "the structural resemblance between Platonic and the other mythological figures of the origin of writing," topics which lie outside the concerns of this work.[22] At one point, however, he briefly argues that Socratic irony "precipitates out one *pharmakon* by bringing it into contact with another *pharmakon*," while the power of dialectical wizardry "petrifies and vilifies, anesthetizes and sensitizes, appeases and anguishes" in the manner of a veritable "bestiary."[23] One finds Socrates' words likened to numbing stingrays (*Meno*), prickly bees (*Phaedo*), gadflies (*Apology*), and venomous snakes (*Symposium*). At the same time this power sounds suspiciously like the comparison of dialectics to the midwife's art in the *Theatetus*, where the power of philosophy is explicitly *pharmaceutical*, not part of some bestiary. While Derrida mentions the class of human beings referred to as drones in Books VIII and IX of the *Republic*, he apparently failed to recognize the association made by Plato between these indi-viduals and Homer's Lotus-Eaters, once more a substance more pharmacologi-cal than zoological.[24]

When Derrida turns to a direct examination of the question of philosophy and the *pharmakon* in the second essay, he prefaces his argument with a number of precautionary remarks. Plato, he argues, on certain occasions steers the varied definitions of *pharmakon* down certain "corridors of meaning" in a "voluntary" manner, but to an equal or greater extent the term manipulates *him*. Oftentimes Plato "can not see the links" between these significations and yet these links "go on working of themselves. In spite of him? Thanks to him? in *his* text? *outside* his text? but then where? between his text and the language? for what reader? at what moment? To answer such questions . . . will seem impossible."[25] He goes on to state, in a crucial and largely overlooked qualifying remark, that he is not "reconstituting the entire chain of significations of the *pharmakon*" but only *some* of their meanings, and *some* of their effects, in the course of what will be a discussion of the Platonic problematic of writing.[26] Such was the spell of decon-struction it has often been assumed he was doing just the opposite.

The Greek word for drug, *pharmakon*, rotates on what Derrida describes as a strange and invisible pivot consisting of one and probably more poles. On the end of one continuum *pharmakon* is commonly translated as beneficent drug, e.g. cure or medicine or, more frequently, remedy. Yet the signification of *pharmakon*, as he points out, often in relation to the legend of Theuth, is both beneficent and maleficent "alternately or simultaneously."[27] Remedy is both technically accurate and wholly inadequate because "the word *pharmakon*, even while it means remedy, cites, re-cites, and makes legible that which in the same word signifies, in another spot and on a different level of the stage, poison (for example, since that is not the only thing *pharmakon* means)."[28]

This parenthetical aside admitting *pharmakon* has more than two meanings, like the admission of more than one polar opposition of significations, was in-sufficiently emphasized in "Plato's Pharmacy." Other than a few brief digres-sions, the hundred or so pages that comprise "Plato's Pharmacy" confine them-selves to an examination of the "composition of these two forces and these two gestures."[29] But it should not be the case that we should read Derrida, or Plato, as thinking these were the *only* forces or the *only* gestures. To evaluate the ar-guments of either writer under the assumption that *pharmakon* could be expli-cated within a remedy/poison bifurcation is much too simple.[30] In addition to using the word to denote medicinal remedy or poison, Plato, like other ancient Greeks, used *pharmakon* to mean a host of other things, such as pictorial color, painter's pigment, cosmetic application, perfume, magical talisman, and recrea-tional intoxicant.[31]

The amulet, too, bore the name *pharmakon*.[32] Magical amulets were in great demand for nearly every conceivable situation, including love, wealth, power, victory and especially medical concerns such as injury, disease and daemonic influences.[33] This is not surprising as the "first Greek amulets were constructed out of the same drugs touted by Theophrastus' root-mongers."[34] Since most of these amulets were made of perishable materials, such as "plants, wood, wax, and leather," or recyclable materials such as "gold, silver, and lead," few have survived.[35] They would be tied to the injured limb or hung about the neck of the patient.[36] Ancient wines, as we saw in chapter 1, above, were frequently laced with drugs, some capable of producing insanity or death. The topaz, worn around the neck, was thought to cure the madness "caused from the drinking of certain wines."[37] Pliny the Elder in his *Natural History* writes magicians "falsely claim that amethysts prevent drunkenness, and that [the gems] are so named because of this" [*amethystos* means "not drunk" in Greek] (37.104). One *pharmakon* might be prescribed as a remedy for another *pharmakon*, in an attempt to restore to its previous state an identity effaced when intoxicant turned toxic.[38]

Derrida does mention, albeit only in passing, that the word *pharmakon* "also designates pictorial color," as it does, for example, in Plato's *Cratylus* (434a–b) and the *Republic* (420c).[39] What is true of writing (*graphema*), Derrida argues, is equally true of painting (*zographema*). In the *Cratylus* one finds "the painter who wants to depict anything sometimes uses purple only or any other color (*allo ton pharmakon*), and sometimes mixes up several colors, as his method to paint flesh color or anything of that kind—he uses a particular color (*pharmakon*) as his figures appear to require it" (424c–d).[40] Reflecting certain innovations in Greek art that had taken place in the fifth century, such as shading by Apollodorus and his pupil Zeuxis (a contemporary of Plato), and scene-painting by Agatharchus,[41] the *Republic* takes a dim view of this shadow painting (*skiagraphia*) and accuses the painter, like the poet, of creating only phantom images of the work of the craftsman, who in turn merely imitates the ideal (601a–b). The painter and poet are both thrice removed from what is true. Reality (*onta*) is in the case of both professions confused with appearances (*phantasmata*).[42]

The pigments used in antiquity often contained the same ingredients used in spell components, cosmetics, medicinal remedies, and recreational intoxicants. Little wonder then that one finds, "in Plato, a cluster of mutually reinforcing prejudices that link colour, drugs, dyeing, and cosmetics."[43] Nicander's *Alexipharmaka*, for example, mentions that a "dreadful brew" mixed with white lead —a substance used by artists for centuries—causes the "eyes to behold strange illusions" (85). For Plato they would have posed a similar threat when arranged in pictorial form by the visual artist: the disruption of a unified identity, return to primordial *ekstasis*, unification of subject and object, experience of the Other.[44] Plato himself refers to the practice of painters mixing their own pigments in the *Republic* (501b) and *Cratylus* (424e).[45] Mortar and pestle would have been as common in the artist's studio as other occupations that made use of *pharmaka*, or at certain religious celebrations, or at the wine-mixing ceremony that preceded the aristocratic *symposion*.[46]

Art, like certain forms of poetry, "emphasizes and dramatizes the use of non-rational mental capacities."[47] Painting, in the *Republic*, is said to appeal to the part of the soul that was "irrational, idle, and a friend of cowardice" (604d). The *Republic* accuses painters of deceiving their audience because they can makes sticks look straight and crooked simultaneously, or make the same object look both convex and concave (602c–d). Art that aims at realistic portrayal is both "captivating and potentially delusory" just like other species of the genus *pharmakon*.[48] The painter, too, is a wizard or magician, a *goes*, a *pharmakeus*. As an abstruse procedure understood only by an inner circle of initiates, it is quite natural that Plato would, as he does in the *Republic*, view *skiagraphia* as full of sorcery (602d), providing the viewer with "mere appearances" of true pleasure (586b), while simultaneously trying to usurp their power, likening the philosopher-lawgiver to a painter who uses a "divine pattern" (500e–501c).[49]

While Book X of the *Republic* equates a mimetic danger with the poet-painter, the *Sophist* equates the same danger with the rhetorician-painter (234b). Both sophist and painter, in this latter dialogue, profess to being capable of making anything with a single art, making the practitioner of one of those professions "a magician and creator of the illusion of reality" (235a).[50] The rhetorician-painter fashions a dwelling "like a human dream for the waking" (266c).[51] It has been suggested, correctly I believe, that there must be "a common mental process" linking the *Republic* with the *Sophist*, the activities of the poet, painter, and sophist.[52] But the common ground is not simply the charming pleasures of imitative *mimesis* but rather the deceptive, abrupt, and often violent abrogation of identity brought about by the power of *pharmaka*. Derrida hints at this when he writes that *pharmakon* "is always caught in the mixture (*summeikton*) mentioned in the *Philebus* (46a) examples of which are *hubris*, that violent, unbounded excess of pleasure that makes the profligate cry out like a madman (45e), and 'relieving an itch by rubbing, and anything that can be treated by such a remedy (*ouk alles deomenta pharmaxeos*).'"[53]

In "Plato's Pharmacy" Derrida also briefly discusses that, in addition to pigment, *pharmakon* was also a word for perfume and cosmetics, observing in a rhetorical flourish that "death, masks, makeup, all are part of the festival that subverts the order of the city, its smooth regulation by the dialectician and the science of being."[54] On one level this is certainly true. Painting, the product of the painter grinding and mixing his multi-colored *pharmaka*, "is a sophistic lie, a form of cosmetics that draws upon the same means as dyeing. For those who love truth (essences), the only painting worth recognition would be colorless, i.e. paintless."[55] Color is for Plato "damned by association" with *pharmaka*, with the physical labor of the painter's craft and "with processes intended to deceive, such as the dyeing of fabric or making up of the face" by, especially, women, since cosmetics is "an essentially feminine art."[56] In Xenophon's *Symposium* Socrates states that perfume, something that typifies femininity, has no place in a gathering of men (2.3), and is problematic in a second sense in that the same perfume would smell the same on a man whether he is a slave or free (2.4).[57] Perfumes, like other *pharmaka*, threaten to destabilize the borders of a moderate identity; even today we speak of a perfume's "intoxicating scent."

At the same time, however, when Plato speaks of the practice of diluting wine "hot with madness" in the *Laws* (773d), he is not describing a further softening of what was already a mild recreational *pharmakon*, as most observers regularly assume. Many ancient wines were dangerous to consume unless diluted with water because of, among other things, the perfumes that were added to them.[58] As we observed in chapter 1, above, passages of Theophrastus' *On Odours* are devoted to the addition of perfumes to wine: "it is thought that not only the smells of the perfume contribute to the pleasant taste [of the wine] but also the qualities of the pungency and heat which are found in them." Aristotle's *Sense and Sensibilia* indicates that perfumes were added to liquid foodstuffs such as soups in addition to wine and other beverages (443b–444a).[59]

Derrida's response to these significations—cosmetic, pigment, perfume—that lie outside a dichotomous understanding of *pharmakon* as meaning either remedy or poison is disappointing, as well as questionable. On the one hand he acknowledges the separate unique nature of each meaning and yet, at the same time and through sheer rhetorical force, he largely subsumes them into the latter category, casting them as a subset of poisons. The mesmerizing power of writing and painting lies in their being "like a cosmetic concealing the dead under the appearance of the living. The *pharmakon* introduces and harbors death. It makes the corpse presentable, masks it up, perfumes it with its essence, as it says in Aeschylus."[60] Derrida does not specify where in Aeschylus, though he may be thinking of *Prometheus Bound* (463–522), a work written around 430 BCE. The chained Titan recalls that, lacking drugs, humanity was helpless to fend off diseases until he demonstrated to them the *technai* of pharmacy."[61]

Although Derrida argues that there can be found frolicking in the word *pharmakon* numerous language ambiguities, reflective of a well-regulated conversation between "diverse strata or regions of culture," this communication is, at best, muffled and only hazily present in "Plato's Pharmacy." On the one hand he is excellent at pointing out that "Plato's desire to restrict meaning to a univocal sense" disintegrates due to the multiplicity of meanings of terms like *pharmakon*.[62] It is at the same time peculiar that in an act of resisting the tendency of Western philosophy to proceed through the opposition of dichotomies or polarities, such as good/evil, truth/error, mind/matter, soul/body, etc., "Plato's Pharmacy" itself for the most part interprets *pharmakon* as meaning either remedy or poison when for Plato it had so many additional meanings. Derrida's argument often appears to reproduce, not suspend, the very charm of Platonic binary metaphysics the deconstructionist approach seeks to evade. In the rest of this chapter I will attempt to put this conversation into better focus and examine how Plato, as one of the participants in the cultural discussion Derrida alludes to, incorporated the word *pharmakon* into both his description of philosophic discourse and his arguments on the necessity of a certain kind of lying in politics.

Philosophy's *Pharmakeia*

In contrast to the many other occupations in the ancient world that made use of incantations, drugs, or both, what was the *pharmakon* of philosophy? In the *Charmides* Socrates speaks of having studied with certain Thracian doctors of

Zalmoxis. These physicians, he relates, taught him the use of both "the *pharma-kon* and the charms" he now proposes to administer to the hangover of the at-tractive Charmides (157b). The soul, too, he says, is cured by "means of certain charms [*epodais tisin*], and these charms consist of beautiful words [*logoi ka-loi*]" (157a). Speech, then, is the *pharmakon* of the philosopher, Plato's moral physician. In this regard Plato is not all that different from the famous teacher of rhetoric, Gorgias, who in his *Encomium of Helen* understood the power of speech (*logos*) as being comparable to magic (*goeteia*), having a power over souls that was "comparable to the power of drugs over the nature of bodies" (14). As we saw in chapter 9, above, Gorgias argues that *logos*, like a drug, could distress, delight, instill fear or courage, or even "bewitch the mind with a kind of evil persuasion," describing its powers as being capable of producing lies and illusions within the mind. Plato is almost certainly drawing on the same tradition.

On a number of occasions in Plato's dialogues the conversation itself acts like a medicinal remedy or cure for a condition of illness, namely ignorance. The *Critias* opens with Timaeus asking the Universe to grant "that most effec-tive medicine (*pharmakon teleotaton*), that best of all medicines (*ariston phar-makon*): knowledge (*epistemen*)." The *Laws* laments that while education may grant the knowledge to temper most desires, in the case of *eros*, said to be the cause of countless evils for individuals and cities, "what herbal *pharmakon* can you cut to liberate these people from so great a danger?" (836b).[63] The *Char-mides* is even more complicated, as Socrates, in order to get the attention of the young and handsome Charmides so as to address his soul on the virtues of mod-eration, is convinced by Critias to deceitfully claim he is a physician with a solu-tion for Charmides' morning headaches (157a–b). Even when persuading, So-cratic *elenchus* has a flavor of deception and enchantment.

Socratic examination can also act like an antidote, an *alexipharmakon*, to neutralize the chemistry of something else. In the *Alcibiades I*, before the young Alcibiades can become a participant in the politics of the city, Socrates says he must know himself, that is to say he must acquire training in moderation. With this training he will, when he "approaches the things of the city ... have an anti-dote and suffer nothing terrible" (132b).[64] In the *Laws* too, though Socrates is not present, the good judge is said to possess the writings of the legislator "within his own soul as antidotes (*alexipharmaka*) against other discourse, and thus he will be the state's preserver as well as his own" (957c–d).[65]

Dialectics can act like a venom that debilitates the listener. In the *Sympo-sium* the venom is painful, as Alcibiades exclaims that the bite of Socrates' method of argument is "sharper than any adder" (218a–b), while in the *Meno* the character the dialogue is named after describes Socrates' arguments as "exactly like the flat sting-ray [since] whenever anyone comes in contact with it, it numbs him" (80a–b). Despite his having spoken on the subject of virtue hundreds of times prior to this encounter with Socrates, Meno, claiming he has been be-witched and drugged (*pharmattein*) (80a), now finds his "mind and lips ... liter-ally numb" and he cannot reply to Socrates' questions. In Meno's case the numbing process is ultimately deemed beneficial: along with perplexity numbness precedes the search for truth (84b–c). Similarly Agathon, in the *Symposium*, jests "*Pharmattein boulei me, o Socrates*," indicating that Socrates is using "a little black magic" (of the sort that would probably drug its victim) to unnerve him before he gives his speech (194a).

Dialectics can act like a poison that produces a destruction of sorts. In the *Republic* it is said that whomever is best at guarding against disease is also the best at creating it and escaping the blame, i.e. a poisoner (333e–334b). This is further hinted at in the *Statesman*, where the Eleatic visitor tells the young man who shares Socrates' name that if physicians see fit, they can "keep one . . . safe and sound" but "if they are minded to deface us by incision or cautery, they do it . . . [and despite this behavior] they actually let themselves be paid by the patients relatives, or it may be, by his enemies, to make an end of him" (298a–b). In the *Phaedo* there is the most famous poison of all, the hemlock. Known to the Greeks as *koneion*, the drug frames the argument, appearing early on at 57a–b, and 63d, and then in the final moments at 115a, 115d, 116c, 117a, and 117e. We have in the case of the hemlock one *pharmakon* acting as another sort of *pharmakon*: the entire matter of the death of Socrates is a matter of deception, as the effects of hemlock poisoning do not appear to be truthfully retold by Plato. It is true that we do not know what dosage of hemlock was present in Socrates' *pharmakon*, nor do we know what it was mixed with, but it is all the same worth noting that spotted hemlock (*Conium maculatum*) poisoning consists of more than simply the ascending motor paralysis described in the passage (117e–118a).[66] Years after the fact Plato may have "doctored the story," keeping, in his literary version of Socrates' death, only those symptoms that were "in harmony with Socrates' philosophical ideas."[67]

Dialectics can, finally, act like an intoxicant, producing a sense of strangeness, disorientation, confusion, or ecstasy. Derrida alludes to this on but one occasion in "Plato's Pharmacy," calling the *aporia* of Meno a kind of *narcosis* that results from his exposure to the Socratic stingray, the *narke*. There is far more to Socratic *narcosis* than simply the numbing perplexity Meno experiences. In the *Phaedrus* conversation with Socrates is said to produce detachment, an exodus from the comfort of one's accustomed environment (230d–e), as well as a beatific vision, an *epopteia*, like that seen by the initiates into the Eleusinian Mysteries (250b–c, 251a–e).[68] In the *Symposium* talking with Socrates is likened to the *enthousiasmos* of particular cults (215b–216c). In the *Statesman*, when trying to envision those who "currently handle the affairs of state," the Eleatic visitor expresses puzzlement at what are a "strange sort" of men, able to "interchange their shape and qualities in an instant"—in response the visitor is told he appears to have assumed the manner of someone in a state of hallucination, i.e. "one who beholds strange sights" (291a–c). In the *Alcibiades I* the young Alcibiades is amazed to find that he no longer knows what he is saying: "By the gods, Socrates, I don't know what I'm saying [anymore], and I seem just like someone in a strange state. As you question me, at one time things seem a certain way, but at another time they seem different" (116e–117a). Socrates, in the *Lysis*, likens his inquiry to intoxication, saying "our argument has made us quite intoxicated (*methuomen*)" (222c).[69]

The Pharmakon *of Lying*

If Plato's philosopher is a moral physician, what, exactly, is the drug of philosophy, how and when should such a drug or drugs be administered, and to what temporary and/or longer-lasting purpose? The type of speech discussed in the previous section may be characterized as a "dialectical prescription." The dialectical method, its "mutual questioning and self-examination," the knowing of the self through "the detour of the language of the other" is the essence of the Socratic undertaking: a counter-spell, exorcism, and antidote all at the same time.[70] Where there was disease of the body "the free man could expect [from his physician] more than the means for a cure in the strict sense of the term; he ought to receive a rational framework for the whole of his existence."[71] Where there was disease of the soul the moral physician/philosopher would adapt the philosophic prescription to the needs of an active listener-patient, varying the argument according to the circumstances (*Statesman* 294a–297b; see also 298d–e, and cf. *Laws* 857d). These individuals are largely the aristocratic men who Socrates talks *to* in the dialogues.

A second type of speech is deemed necessary for instilling adherence to philosophy's moral economy in the masses: lying. The *Republic*'s "noble lie," I shall argue in this section, is yet another *pharmakon*, a deceit that supplements the partially or fully deceitful drugs of philosophy's many competitors. In the *Republic* Socrates, Glaucon, and Adeimantus discuss the component parts of what a "city in speech" (369c) ought to include. Adeimantus outlines a simple provincial existence, summed up by Socrates as consisting of elementary goods and services, largely agricultural and mercantile, with staple foods, wine to drink, and pleasant sex to produce just enough children as the city can support (372a–b, cf. 369d–371e). This is the true city, the healthy city, Socrates tells Glaucon when the latter objects to what appears to him to be a city more fit for pigs than men (372e). This association of *truth* with *health* is scarcely accidental. The "feverish" city Socrates and Glaucon go on to describe is one "gorged" with luxuries, requiring many additional non-essential occupations (372e–373c). Glaucon's city includes the "spirit, imagination and *eros*" lacking in the one constructed by Adeimantus, making it the "more adequate, indeed more serious portrayal of the phenomena of political life."[72]

The fevered city, while more faithful to the nature of cities, is at the same time "an untruthful city, a city willing and perhaps needing to resort to imitations, lies, and illusions in pursuing its more sophisticated ways of life, ways not dominated by human necessity and more open to the forms of human freedom."[73] There will be, Socrates tells us, a "much greater need for doctors" in such a city, and by this he means physicians both physical and moral (373d).

The ruler, as a statesmanlike Asclepius (407e), will supervise the education of the young, psychagogy being of the utmost importance if a city's "laws are going to be well-observed" (380b). Children are, for Plato, impressionable and "thoughtless," and it is vital to "shape their souls" while they are at their most "plastic" and malleable (377b–c, 378a, 378d, and cf. *Theatetus* 173a–b).[74]

Along these lines Socrates argues that a god ought not to be depicted in children's stories told by nurses and mothers as a *pharmakeus*, revealing himself as alternately good and evil, morphing his physical appearance from one thing to another, and using deceit to obtain his ends (380d, cf. *Euthydemus* 288b, *Republic* 381e, 382a). We find the same sort of concern expressed in the *Ion*. Ion's constantly shifting attempts to speak about Homer "by art and knowledge," Socrates complains, are "deceiving." Ion will not tell Socrates what he is clever about, he is "simply like Proteus, assuming all sorts of shapes, twisting this way and that until finally you escape me" (541e–542a). The *rhapsoidoi* are not in their right minds when they speak (535b–c), something that surely must have a negative impact on both noetic and discursive regimen when one recalls that Homer "was not only a source of educational material but had become virtually institutionalized in Greek society."[75] In Xenophon's *Symposium* (3.5–3.6), at Socrates' request, each speaker describes the most valuable knowledge in his possession. Niceratus proudly says that, because he has listened to the *rhapsoidoi* "nearly every day," he can now "repeat the whole of the *Iliad* and *Odyssey* by heart." Plato surely would have witnessed the same behavior. Given his depiction of Ion, it is doubtful he would have regarded the noetic and discursive regimen developed by someone like Niceratus as something positive.

Securing the most stringently grounded identity, be it through the formation of bodily habit, mental processes, or interpersonal speech, is of paramount importance for Plato: without it a regime cannot be healthy, and virtually any sacrifice is justified in the name of bringing it about. If anyone is to be allowed to hear of the gods behaving in a less than ideal manner, Socrates says in the *Republic*, the number should be "as few as possible" and even then only as "unspeakable secrets, after making a sacrifice, not of a pig but of some great offering that's hard to come by, so that it will come to the ears of the smallest possible number" (378a).[76] The pig sacrifice and unspeakable secrets Plato refers to were both essential parts of the cost one paid to be initiated into the Greater Mysteries celebrated at Eleusis, the cost one paid to drink the sacred potion, the *kykeon*, and behold the great vision, the *epopteia*.[77] It would have been abundantly clear to Plato's contemporaries that he was trying to make access to a *pharmakon* of political deceit as difficult, indeed more difficult, than access to the *pharmakon* of Eleusis.[78]

Gods cannot deceive, the *Republic* argues, because they are innately good. In contrast, Socrates says, there are occasions where men not only can tell lies, they *ought to*, "as a preventative, like a *pharmakon*" (382c). Falsehood is justifiable when it benefits "the city in cases involving either enemies or friends" (389b). First, lying to children is useful, since it helps establish orderly noetic habits. Second, lying is often required when in the presence of enemies, in order to mislead and ultimately defeat them. Finally, lying is permissible when one's friends are behaving in a mad or mindless manner. This final form of lying should be juxtaposed with the *Timaeus* where the diseases of the soul, said to include madness, stupidity, and excessive pleasures and pains, are described as causing men to see and hear in a distorted manner, a state of delirium where the soul is "unable to obey reason" (86b–c). The general problem for Plato is ecstasy's capacity for bringing about the dissolution of a moderate, stable, singular identity.

The question, then, is not whether or not a political elite ought to engage in lying to those it rules: the "evidence confounds any expectation that 'the will to truth' entails a blanket ban on the use of lies."[79] In the *Phaedrus* (261a–262c) Socrates concedes that effective rhetoric may require the deployment of deception. In the *Hippias Minor* (370e–373c) Socrates praises the Odysseus of Homer's poem for his conscious deployment of lies, in comparison to Achilles who tells lies, but without a conscious awareness of what he is doing. Both, however, are ignorant of justice. The telling of lies, Socrates says in the *Republic*, is *hos pharmakon chresimon*— "useful like a drug" (382c).[80] It is at this very moment in the *Republic*, when the prescription of lies is conceded to be useful, that the word for rulers appears for the first time. Philosophers may need to become rulers, or rulers philosophers, but they both practice their art, their *techne*, as moral physicians, with a monopoly on the *pharmakon* of lying. The question for Plato is not so much *pharmakon*, but rather *pharmakeia*—when and under whose supervision the *pharmakon* of lying may be legitimately administered, "so as not to deserve hatred" (382c).[81] Further evidence of the association made by Plato between medicine/drugs and political speech may be found in the *Phaedrus*, where Socrates says we ought to regard as madness the idea that just because a man was skilled at lying he ought to be accorded political influence, in the same way we would recoil in incredulity when an ordinary person might claim he "had become a doctor from having stumbled across some common or garden drugs (*pharmakios*), when he had no knowledge of the science (*techne*) itself" (270c).

The practice of lying is not something that any layman may be allowed to dispense to his fellow city-dwellers. Lying, the *Republic* tells us, "must be assigned to doctors" (389b). Socrates, being a private man, makes no claim to having a right to lie. In the *Ion* he says "I speak nothing but the truth, as is fitting for a private human being," begging the question as to whether he, i.e. Plato, felt the same standard ought to apply to public human beings, specifically the statesmanlike Asclepius who practices the *techne* of politics. The *Republic* emphasizes that the same standard does not apply. Rulers/moral physicians keep watch "over enemies from without" while policing the behaviors of "friends from within"—lies ensure that the former "will wish to do no harm" and the latter "will be *unable* to" (414b, italics mine).[82]

Lying presented as a *pharmakon* controlled by a select few, and administered to the many, is not some haphazard metaphor injected into the body of a discussion of the responsibilities of thoughtful rulership. There is "an unmis-

takably direct coordination between the appearance of rulers in the city of
speech and the practice of pharmacological lying."[83] It can hardly be coinciden-
tal that the need for a *pharmakon* of deceit is introduced immediately after Plato
has discussed the need for establishing a regime of moderation overseeing the
appetite for food, sex, and intoxicants that dominate the souls of ordinary men
and women. The "need for political rule and the need for a drug of deceit
emerges at the same time."[84]

The philosophic *pharmakon* of lying deals with "pathology rather than development, with correction rather than guidance."[85] In other words it is the very
opposite of dialectics. For those citizens who can reflexively follow society's
unwritten ethics of moderation, who are in other words "willing to respond to a
prescribed course of life," the *Republic* indicates even "a common doctor" will
do when there is illness, i.e. it is not a matter for a moral physician, or for lying
(459c). The *Lysis* hints at largely the same thing: "if there were nothing to harm
us, we should feel no want of any assistance; and thus we should have to face
the fact that it was because of the evil that we felt such a friendly affection for
the good (*tagathon*), since the good is a medicine (*pharmakon*) for the evil,
while the evil is a disease. But where there is no disease, there is no need of
medicine (*ouden dei pharmakon*)" (220d).

If, however, one has within the city people living a "sick" and "worthless
way of life," it is here, we read in the *Republic*, that there is "need for a most
courageous doctor" (425e, 459c). The immoderate individual refuses to alter
their diseased daily regimen searching instead to find someone who will give
them an easy way out, hoping "that if someone would just give them a *pharmakon*, they will be—thanks to it—healthy" (426a). Permeated by internal *stasis*,
the drone personality that will appear later in books VIII and IX of the *Republic*,
these individuals spurn the advice of those who tell them "the truth—namely,
that unless one gives up drinking, stuffing oneself, sex and idleness, there will
be no help for one in drugs, burning, or cutting, nor in charms, pendants, or anything of the sort" (426a–b). We see here, once again, Plato struggling with the
malleable unity of *pharmakon*, while at the same time trying to deploy philosophy's *pharmakon* in opposition to a wide range of occupational practices claiming therapeutic abilities.

In order to cure the many cases of immoderation one will find in the feverish city, "it will be necessary for [rulers] to use many drugs" (459c). Political
leadership, in the name of saving the immoderate from themselves, "will have to
use a throng of lies and deceptions for the benefit of the ruled. And, of course,
we said that everything of this sort is useful as a *pharmakon*" (459c). The *Republic*'s famous noble lie—a more literal translation of *gennaion pseudos* would
be the aristocratic *well-born* lie[86]—is described as a "Phoenician thing" because
it deals with the money-making, appetitive, pleasure-oriented elements of the
soul (414c), rather than the spirited and honor-loving part of the soul, likened by
Plato to places like Thrace and Sparta, or the reasoning and learning part of the
soul "which one could impute to our region," i.e. Attica (*Republic* 435e–436a).[87]
Money making, for Plato, was analogous to the cares and passions of the body,

and is regularly associated in the *Republic* with the non-guardian classes (434c, 441a, 547d, 581d, 583a).

Left to themselves the average citizens of the city, generally uninterested in politics and the long-term stability of the regime they inhabit, cannot be trusted to behave in a manner consistent with the city's good. The "psychic inertia generated by bodily cares is so great it creates a subversive counterweight to all institutions of political rule"—the details of that subversion being discussed in the *Republic*'s Book VIII.[88] It is, however, more than a matter of psychic inertia, a diminishment of the will. It is a *loss* of rational will, an effacement of a self-contained, stable, and consistent identity; what remains is blind desire, epithymetic compulsion. The purpose of the noble lie is one of restraining what in the *Philebus* Plato calls the "intense" pleasures in favor of the cultivation of what he calls the "just" pleasures. In addition to being mixed and adulterated (46b–47a) the *Philebus* describes the intense pleasures as being "intemperate, unrestrained" and exceeding all boundaries (45b and 45e); as sick, degenerate "forms of illness" (45b–46a); as illusory, false, "not real" (44a, 51a); and as possessed, ecstatic, frenzied and "unbalanced to the point of insanity" (45d–e, 47a–b).

Derrida's reading of Plato in "Plato's Pharmacy" largely neglects "the differences among the philosophical spokesmen, interlocutors and settings of the dialogues."[89] I have argued in this concluding chapter that in order to comprehend the workings of the Platonic pharmacy it is precisely these sorts of differences that we must give our attention to. Understanding the *pharmakon* of philosophy as a drug of deceit helps to explain why there are such seemingly irreconcilable assessments of Plato's political theory. The first course of treatment for establishing moderation in the city, dialectics, correlates with, for example, statements made in the *Republic* that learning cannot be imposed: "the free man ought not to learn anything slavishly," because "no forced study abides in the soul" (536e).

The second course of treatment, using the *pharmakon* of deceit, has the net effect of transforming the listener-patient into a passive receptacle, who is then dictated to as slave/physicians do to slave/patients (*Laws* 792c, cf. 720b–e). These are the individuals of the *polis* Socrates often talks *about*. Here one does *not* find a conversation, one does *not* find interactions between equals (however ironic one of them, Socrates, may be), but only the introduction of identical, preestablished injunctions, consisting of social conventions, traditions, and the rest of what Plato calls the unwritten law. This one-direction communication establishes reflexive, habitual patterns of behavior, guarding, preserving and stabilizing identity, household management, and political order. It is not, then, so much a matter of discerning Plato as a friend or foe of freedom and autonomy, or a matter of determining whether he does or does not equate reason with a modern ideal like self-determination. Operating within a dual-tiered understanding of *medicine*, and a multi-tiered understanding of *drugs*, he is both friend and foe, perhaps neither, both alternately and simultaneously. Given the very essence of ancient Greek society, based as it was on several mechanisms intolerable in most contemporary nation-states, from slavery to patriarchy to pedophilia, the search for an answer to such a question would appear at best quixotic.

The essence of the issue *for Plato* in the context of *his* culture can be summed up in a passage from the *Meno*, where oracular priests, prophets, and statesmen are collectively described as people "who under divine inspiration utter many useful truths, but have no knowledge of what they are saying" (99c–d). To be successful without the aid of reason, something Plato clearly thought *was* possible, requires ecstatic displacement, "a proposition which, though leaving open the possibility of valuable products ... nevertheless undercuts the authority of the practitioners."[90] The trick becomes one of being able to utter useful truths while remaining conscious and of a singular identity while one is doing so, knowing precisely what one is saying. The occupation that does this, or at least does it most consistently and proficiently, is philosophy.

In other words, what is required is a *techne*, *episteme*, and *sophia* without the *ekstasis*, and without the *pharmaka*, that the rest of the ancient world—outside of the literate elite male perspective that has reached us in most of the surviving documents—was readily familiar with, comfortable with, and would have seen as unproblematic. The "*eidos*, truth, law, the *episteme*, dialectics, philosophy—all these are other names for the *pharmakon*" of philosophy that must be opposed to the Sophists and, we may note, any of the other occupations philosophy was arranged against. Plato's "inverted *pharmakon*" is, as Derrida points out, "none other than the origin of the *episteme*."[91] There is another room in the pharmacy, however, that Derrida does not visit: the inverted dialectic, itself a *pharmakon* of lying, is none other than the fundamental foundation of Platonic political order.[92]

Notes

1. An earlier version of this chapter appeared as Michael A. Rinella, "Revisiting the Pharmacy: Plato, Derrida, and the Morality of Political Deceit," *Polis—The Journal of the Society of Greek Political Thought* 24, no. 1 (2007): 134–153.

2. *Aporia*, Farrell writes, "literally means without a way or path" and she argues that the insecurity and fright it produces parallels the intentional shaking up of the initiate in mystery religions such as the Eleusinian Mysteries. See Mary Anne Farrell, *Plato's Use of Eleusinian Mystery Motifs* (Ph.D. diss., University of Texas at Austin, 1999), 77.

3. Ancient midwives knew of a number of effective contraceptives, analgesics, and abortificants, and were among society's foremost repositories of pharmacological knowledge. See John Scarborough, "The Pharmacology of Sacred Plants, Herbs, and Roots," in *Magika Hiera—Ancient Greek Magic and Religion*, ed. Christopher A. Faraone and Dirk Obbink (New York: Oxford University Press, 1991), 145 and chapter 7, above.

4. As we saw in chapter 8, above, Socratic *elenchus* and *diairesis* induce pain, while the use of *muthos* is more pleasant and pain-allaying.

5. *Theatetus* 149a, cf. Diogenes Laertius 2.18.

6. During the late nineteenth century midwives in Western industrialized nations became the subject of a sustained attack by a newly emerging professional medicine, pro-

gressive reformers, and pharmaceutical manufacturing interests. See Harris L. Coulter, *Divided Legacy—A History of the Schism in Medical Thought. Volume 3—Science and Ethics in American Medicine 1800–1914* (Washington, DC: Wehawken Book Company, 1973).

7. All direct quotes from "Plato's Pharmacy" are taken from the translation by Barbara Johnson in Jacques Derrida, *Dissemination* (Chicago: University of Chicago Press, 1981). Plato's views on sorcery and the sorcerer are discussed in chapter 8, above.

8. Derrida, *Dissemination*, 71–72.

9. Derrida, *Dissemination*, 99.

10. It is my intention to focus on the word for drug, *pharmakon,* and questions of morality, truth, and dialectics, rather than the origin of writing, memory, and dialectics, the predominant theme of Derrida's essay. In this sense I am in general agreement with Foucault's criticism of Derrida's reading of Plato. See David Hoy, "Derrida," in *The Return of the Grand Theory of the Human Sciences*, ed. Quentin Skinner (New York: Cambridge University Press, 1990), 58–60. See also Roy Boyne, *Foucault and Derrida: The Other Side of Reason* (New York: Routledge, 1990), 53–89.

11. "Plato's Pharmacy" was first published in 1968 in two parts in *Tel Quel*, numbers 32 and 33, and later published together in *le Dissémination* in 1972. Johnson's English translation appeared in 1981. The influence of "Plato's Pharmacy" can be seen operating in works such as Charles Segal, *Dionysiac Poetics and Euripides'* Bacchae (Princeton, NJ: Princeton University Press, 1982) and Adi Ophir, *Plato's Invisible Cities: Discourse and Power in the* Republic (New York: Routledge, 1992). Readings of Derrida's essay from what may be termed a friendly or neutral stance may be found in Jacqueline de Romilly, *Magic and Rhetoric in Ancient Greece* (Cambridge, MA: Harvard University Press, 1975), Elizabeth Belfiore, "Wine and the Catharsis of the Emotions in Plato's Laws," *Classical Quarterly* 36, no. 2 (1986): 421–37, Catherine Zuckert, *Postmodern Platos—Nietzsche, Heidegger, Gadamer, Strauss, Derrida* (Chicago: University of Chicago Press, 1996), Christopher P. Smith, *The Hermeneutics of Original Argument: Demonstration, Dialectic, Rhetoric* (Evanston, IL: Northwestern University Press, 1998) and Terence J. Martin, *Living Words: Studies in Dialogues about Religion* (New York: Oxford University Press, 1998). More negative readings may be found in Yoav Rinon, "Plato's Pharmacy. The Rhetoric of Jacques Derrida (Part 1 of 2)," *The Review of Metaphysics* 46, no. 2 (1992): 369–86, Jasper Svenbro, *Phrasikleia—An Anthropology of Reading in Ancient Greek* (Cornell, NY: Cornell University Press, 1992), and Stanley Rosen, *Hermeneutics as Politics* (New Haven, CT: Yale University Press, 2003).

12. Smith, *The Hermeneutics of Original Argument*, 134–156, and Eric Alliez, "Ontology and Logography: The Pharmacy, Plato, and the Simulacrum," in *Between Deleuze and Derrida*, ed. Paul Patton and John Protevi (New York: Continuum, 2003), 91–94, for example, take Derrida's understanding of ancient pharmacology simply as a given.

13. Leaving aside the question of the date of their composition, the *Tel Quel* articles are now a generation old. We would be remiss to think that our understanding of ancient pharmacology has stood still since the 1960s. In the case of midwives/obstetrics see for example Joe Zias, Harkley Stark, Jon Seligman, Rina Levy, Ella Werker, and Rapheal Mechoulam, "Early Medical Use of Cannabis," *Nature* 363, no. 6426 (1993): 215. Greek wine, and the drugs it was often mixed with, are discussed in chapter 1, above.

14. Derrida, *Dissemination*, 69.

15. Derrida, *Dissemination*, 70.

16. Derrida, *Dissemination*, 70.

17. Carl A. P. Ruck, "The Offerings of the Hyperboreans," in *Persephone's Quest: Entheogens and the Origins of Religion*, ed. R. Gordon Wasson (New Haven, CT: Yale University Press, 1986), 229.

18. Carl A. P. Ruck, "The Wild and the Cultivated: Wine in Euripides' *Bacchae*," in *Persephone's Quest: Entheogens and the Origins of Religion*, ed. R. Gordon Wasson (New Haven, CT: Yale University Press, 1986), 184.

19. Carl A. P. Ruck, "Mushrooms and Mysteries: On Aristophanes and the Necromancy of Socrates," *Helios* 8, no. 2 (1981): 13. Persephone was charmed by a flower whose name, the *narkissos*, is at least suggestive of powers greater than simply the aromatic. See the *Homeric Hymn to Demeter*, 30–1. A number of ancient sources imply, often strongly so, that Socrates was a profaner of the Lesser Mysteries. See chapter 5, above. The historical Phaedrus was implicated in a series of scandals that included the profanation of the Greater Mysteries and forced into exile between 415 and 404.

20. R. Gordon Wasson, Albert Hofmann, and Carl A. P. Ruck, *The Road to Eleusis: Unveiling the Secrets of the Mysteries* (Los Angeles: William Dailey Rare Books, 1998), 97.

21. Erika Simon, *Festivals of Attika: An Archeological Commentary* (Madison, WI: University of Wisconsin Press, 1983), 92–92.

22. A good summation of this portion of Derrida's essay may be found in David Cohen, "Classical Rhetoric and Modern Theories of Discourse," in *Persuasion: Greek Rhetoric in Action*, ed. Ian Worthington (New York: Routledge, 1994), 79. "The essay," Cohen writes, "begins as an interrogation of Plato's criticism of writing in the *Phaedrus*, and in typical Derridean fashion soon invokes a wide variety of other texts and traditions to investigate the problem of the distinction between the 'good' and the 'bad' *logos*."

23. Derrida, *Dissemination*, 119 n. 52.

24. In what appears an allusion to the encounter with the Lotus-Eaters in the *Odyssey* 9.94–115 (Fagles translation), we read in the *Republic* 559d–560d that the youth of democracy are exposed to conversation with "fiery, clever beasts" such as the sophists, whose "false and boasting speeches" act like "drones' honey," making them susceptible to "manifold and subtle pleasures" of every variety. The youth take up residence among these "Lotus-Eaters" and repudiate their elders. See chapter 2, above.

25. Derrida, *Dissemination*, 96

26. Derrida, *Dissemination*, 96

27. Derrida, *Dissemination*, 75.

28. Derrida, *Dissemination*, 98.

29. Derrida, *Dissemination*, 98.

30. An alarming number of references to, and readings of, "Plato's Pharmacy" fail to distinguish any meanings for *pharmakon* other than "remedy" and "poison." Three examples, and they are by no means unusual or unique, would be Hoy, "Derrida," 58, James Jasinski, *Sourcebook on Rhetoric: Key Concepts in Contemporary Rhetorical Studies* (Thousand Oaks, CA: Sage Publishing, 2001), 351, and Joy Connolly, *The State of Speech: Rhetoric and Political Thought in Ancient Rome* (Princeton, NJ: Princeton University Press, 2007), 124 n. 12.

31. Cohen, "Classical Rhetoric and Modern Theories of Discourse," 79, correctly notes that *pharmakon* "has a variety of meanings encompassing drug, medicine, poison, remedy, charm, spell, cure and antidote."

32. Roy Kotansky, "Incantations and Prayers for Salvation on Inscribed Greek Amulets," in *Magika Hiera—Ancient Greek Magic and Religion*, ed. Christopher A. Faraone and Dirk Obbink (New York: Oxford University Press, 1991), 109.

33. Kotansky, "Incantations and Prayers for Salvation on Inscribed Greek Amulets," 107, and John I. Winkler, "The Constraints of Eros," in *Magika Hiera—Ancient Greek Magic and Religion*, ed. Christopher Faraone and Dirk Obbink (New York, Oxford University Press, 1991), 220–21. Rings inscribed with spells appear to have been common as well. Antiphanes (fragment 177) mentions one worn for indigestion, Aristophanes in his *Wealth* (883–85) describes another used for protection from enemies, and Plato in the *Republic* (359d–360b, 612b) describes the fantastic ring of Gyges, which conferred invisibility. See also Herodotus *History* (1.8–13).

34. Randall B. Clark, *The Law Most Beautiful and Best: Medical Argument and Magical Rhetoric in Plato's Laws* (Lanham, MD: Lexington Books, 2003): 34.

35. Clark, *The Law Most Beautiful and Best*, 35.

36. Matthew W. Dickie, *Magic and Magicians in the Greco-Roman World* (New York: Routledge, 2001), 24–25, and Clark, *The Law Most Beautiful and Best*, 34–35. An amulet could also be called either a *periammon* and *periapton*, which derive from the verb *periapto*, "to tie on."

37. Agnes C. Vaughan, *Madness in Greek Thought and Custom* (Baltimore, MD: J. H. Furst Company, 1919), 51, whose citation includes the *Orphica Lithica*, a didactic poem dating to roughly the first century CE describing the magic properties of different stones.

38. According to Pliny's *Natural History* (37), the Greek name for an island in the Red Sea was Topazin ("to seek" or "to search" as if looking). The name may have been a derivative of *topazos* (a "topaz"; origin unknown). The island was reputed to be shrouded in mist. The topaz gem may have been thought to confer the power to see clearly (or, conversely to make one invisible by invoking the island's mist). As we saw in chapter 1 ancient Greek writers such as Critias described intoxication as a mist settling upon the eyes.

39. Rinon's claim that this meaning "does not take place in the Derridian text" is clearly false. See Rinon, "Plato's Pharmacy," 376. See Charles A. Riley, *Color Codes: Modern Theories of Color in Philosophy, Painting and Architecture* (Lebanon, NH: University of New England Press, 1995), 64–65 who discusses Derrida's interpretation of *pharmakon* in the *Cratylus*.

40. See also *Cratylus* 432b–c, *Republic* 420c, and *Statesman* 277c.

41. Michael L. Morgan, "Plato, Inquiry, and Painting," *Apeiron* 23, no. 22 (1990): 130.

42. See Eva C. Keuls, *Plato and Greek Painting* (Leiden, Netherlands: E. J. Brill, 1978), 40, n. 18. Keuls remarks in passing that *Republic* 420c may be punning on the word *pharmakon*, possibly implying that "painters 'intoxicate' their viewers with an illusion of reality" but doesn't develop the point further. Derrida does not appear to recognize the implication of the pun. I would argue this is yet another example of Plato supplementing the *pharmakon* of philosophy for the many *pharmaka* of philosophy's competitors.

43. Paul Hills, *Venetian Colour—Marble, Mosaic, Painting and Glass, 1250-1550* (New Haven, CT: Yale University Press, 1999), 167. Jacqueline Lichtenstein, "On Platonic Cosmetics," in *Uncontrollable Beauty: Towards a New Aesthetics*, ed. Bill Beckley with David Shapiro (New York: Allworth Press, 1998), 83–100 mentions a similar cluster of prejudices, including color, dyes, and cosmetics while, oddly, largely omitting drugs.

44. Cf. Friedrich Nietzsche, *The Birth of Tragedy*, trans. Michael Tanner (New York: Penguin Books, 1993): 17, 26, 64–75.

45. Lichtenstein, "On Platonic Cosmetics," 97 writes "A painter is first and foremost, as Plato says, 'a grinder and mixer of multi-color drugs'" but provides no source

for the quote. Not that the quote is pure fancy. "When artists in fourteenth-century Italy set up shop (*bottega*) for themselves . . . [they] became members of the *arti* (guild) designated for doctors and pharmacists in 1314 because the production of painting involved grinding of color pigments, just as pharmacists ground their own materials into medicine." Quoted in Tiffany Sutton, *The Classification of Visual Art: A Philosophical Myth and its History* (New York: Cambridge University Press, 2000), 42.

46. The manufacture of paint pigments in the ancient world is discussed in R. J. Forbes, *Studies in Ancient Technology—Volume 3* (Leiden, Netherlands: E. J. Brill, 1965), 210–256. Keuls, in *Plato and Greek Painting*, while acknowledging Forbes' discussion of pigments, ignores his other chapters in the same work dealing with cosmetics, perfume, and fermented beverages. Forbes, however, was certain he had unearthed a connection between ancient alchemy and Greek philosophy, with the principles of the former "latent" in the latter. For evidence of this see Forbes, *Studies in Ancient Technology—Volume 3*, 132–33, citing Plato's *Timaeus* 50c–e.

47. Morgan, "Plato, Inquiry, and Painting," 135.

48. Morgan, "Plato, Inquiry, and Painting," 136.

49. See similar statements in the *Philebus*, 53a–b and 59c.

50. Cf. *Republic* 596c.

51. Cf. *Republic* 476b–c, and Aristotle, *Metaphysics* 1024b.

52. Keuls, *Plato and Greek Painting*, 1978.

53. Derrida, *Dissemination*, 99.

54. Derrida, *Dissemination*, 142.

55. Lichtenstein, "On Platonic Cosmetics," 54.

56. Hills, *Venetian Colour*, 167. A good discussion of Plato and painting, though with no reference to the painter's pigment as a *pharmakon*, is Stephen Halliwell, "Plato and Painting," in *Word and Image in Ancient Greece*, ed. N. Keith Rutter and Brian A. Sparkes (Edinburgh, UK: Edinburgh University Press, 2000), 99–116.

57. Foucault discusses the *Phaedrus* (239c–d) as an early example of an already well-developed problemization of male androgyny in Greco-Roman literature, long before its more emphatic condemnation in early Christian ethics. Michel Foucault, *The Use of Pleasure. The History of Sexuality Volume 2* (New York: Vintage Books, 1984), 18–20, and see also 84–86, 160–162.

58. Myrrh, a plant closely associated with the worship of Dionysus, for example, illustrates how diffused and, from the standpoint of modern pharmacology, confused the ancient Greek understanding of drugs must have been. The plant's aromatic qualities were well-known and highly prized in antiquity. Portions of the plant were used as an ingredient in medicinal cures and for purposes of birth control. Recreationally Dioscorides' *On Medical Materials* 1.77 mentions myrrh being added to wine.

59. The Romans went to even further extremes than the Greeks. Pliny the Elder, for example, complains about the immoderate addition of perfumes to wine in his *Natural History*.

60. Derrida, *Dissemination*, 142.

61. Serafina Cuomo, *Technology and Culture in Greek and Roman Antiquity* (New York: Cambridge University Press, 2007), 203. Nor is this an isolated occurrence: according to Cuomo medical imagery abounds throughout the play.

62. Mark Edmundson, *Literature against Philosophy, Plato to Derrida: A Defense of Poetry* (New York: Cambridge University Press, 1995), 82. Edmundson writes on the same page that Plato's desire to confine terms like *pharmakon* compels "a reaction from language: tied in conceptual knots, it chafes, expands, bursts, devolving in the final moments of [Derrida's] essay to something like linguistic flux. Verbal energy presumably

undoes the cold dream of Western mastery, returning us to the untruth of time and chance."

63. Quoted in John J. Winkler, "The Constraints of Eros," in *Magika Hiera— Ancient Greek Magic and Religion*, ed. Christopher A. Faraone and Dirk Obbink (New York: Oxford University Press, 1991), 239, n. 54. Plato is probably alluding to the *rhizotomoi* (rootcutters) and/or the *pharmakopolai* (drug-sellers), semi-professional classes who would have been commonplace in the countryside and the *agora* hawking medicinal drugs, love potions, aphrodisiacs, and sexual ointments. See Scarborough, "The Pharmacology of Sacred Plants, Herbs and Roots," 149–50, and chapter 7, above.

64. That Plato authored the *Alcibiades I* was not doubted in antiquity. Some nineteenth-century scholarship, primarily German, cast doubt up on the authenticity of the work, but more recent scholarship such as Charles M. Young, "Plato and Computer Dating," *Oxford Studies in Ancient Philosophy* 12 (1994): 238 and Nicolas Denyer, *Alcibiades* (Cambridge: Cambridge University Press, 2001), 1–26 have argued in favor of the work as genuine. Denyer dates the work to the 350s BCE. Foucault observed that "we have a text which is chronologically odd and seems to straddle, as it were, Plato's entire work: the youthful references and style are clearly and undeniably present, and then on the other hand, the presence of themes and forms of established Platonism are also quite apparent." See Michel Foucault, *The Hermeneutics of the Subject—Lectures at the College de France 1981–1982* (New York: Picador, 2005), 72–74.

65. Cf. *Laws* 957e–958a. In the absence of rulers who are philosophers, or philosophers who are rulers, discursive regimen in the *Laws* is guarded by administrative functionaries who have been, in essence, inoculated by the written "leaves" left to them by law-giving moral-physician/philosophers.

66. William B. Ober, "Did Socrates Die of Hemlock Poisoning?" *Ancient Philosophy* 2, no. 2 (1982): 115–121. Ober notes that initially there is salivation, nausea, vomiting and irritation of the pharynx. There follows dryness of mouth and an inability to swallow, then "convulsion, weakening of the lower extremities, and paralysis of the skeletal muscles, those regulating the respiratory movements being the last to be affected. The pupils are nearly always dilated, and the patient may suffer from diplopia and amblyopia and impaired hearing." See also the description of hemlock intoxication in Nicander, *Alexipharmaka* 186–94.

67. Ober "Did Socrates Die of Hemlock Poisoning?" 120.

68. See Michael A. Rinella, "Supplementing the Ecstatic: Plato, the Eleusinian Mysteries, and the *Phaedrus*," *Polis—The Journal of the Society of Greek Political Thought* 17, no. 1 & 2 (2000): 61–78.

69. To render *methoumen* as "tipsy" presupposes alcohol. The Greek *methyein*, meaning "to be drunk," was derived from *methyl*, "intoxicating drink," and had connotations of honey/mead and other intoxicants more ancient than wine. By way of contrast *oinoun*, meaning "to intoxicate with wine," was derived from *oinos*, "wine," and was at first less common, slowly becoming an equally generic term for any recreational drug.

70. Derrida, *Dissemination*, 121. Cf. *Phaedo* 78a–b and *Republic* 582d.

71. See Foucault, *The Use of Pleasure*, 107. Foucault, however, scarcely mentions drugs, even when he discusses Greek medicine.

72. Carl Page, "The Truth about Lies in Plato's *Republic*," *Ancient Philosophy* 11, no. 1 (1991): 7. Alan Bloom, in the essay that accompanies his translation of the *Republic*, reads this "emancipation of desire" as the precondition of virtue. See Alan Bloom, *The Republic of Plato. Translation with Notes and an Interpretive Essay* (New York: Basic Books, 1987), 347. Also worth consulting on this matter is Leo Strauss, "Plato," in *History of Political Philosophy*, ed. Leo Strauss and Joseph Cropsey (Chicago: Univer-

sity of Chicago Press, 1987), 33–89. A critique of Page's interpretation of the Noble Lie in the *Republic* may be found in Daniel A. Dombrowski, "On the Alleged Truth about Lies in Plato's *Republic*," *Polis—Journal of the Society of Greek Political Thought* 21, no. 1 & 2 (2004): 93–106. Dombrowski's position is that, in essence, Page employs an elitist "Straussian" reading of Plato in order to justify lying in contemporary politics. He argues that Page's pessimistic view of human nature has less to do with Plato and more to do with later theorists such as Hobbes and Machiavelli. In addition he takes Page to task for conflating a consequentialist view of ethics with Plato's own virtue ethics and for failing to consider the benefits of a deontological ethics. While there may be some merit in each of these points, Dombrowski scarcely discusses Page's emphasis on the Noble Lie being a *pharmakon*, or the role of the *pharmakon* with its multiplicity of meanings in Plato's dialogues.

73. Page, "The Truth about Lies in Plato's *Republic*," 7.

74. Once a person has assimilated a particular discursive regimen, their opinions, the *Republic* tells us, "become hard and difficult to eradicate" (377b, 378d–e), which explains in part why Plato would prefer to banish everyone over the age of ten from the ideal regime before doing virtually anything else (540e–541a). Beyond this age existing regimens are increasingly too ingrained to be reformulated.

75. John G. Gunnell, *Political Philosophy and Time* (Middletown, CT: Wesleyan University Press, 1987), 129.

76. Cf. *Theatetus* 155e–156a.

77. Pigs were cheap and easy to come by, and anyone who could speak Greek and had not been convicted of murder could become an initiate into the Greater Mysteries.

78. The best single argument regarding the possible pharmacological properties of the *kykeon* may be found in Wasson et al., *The Road to Eleusis*. They are also discussed in Rinella, "Supplementing the Ecstatic," 69–75. See also chapter 6, above.

79. John Hesk, *Deception and Democracy in Classical Athens* (New York: Cambridge University Press, 2000), 150.

80. Cf. *Laws* 663d.

81. The shamelessly self-serving lies told by the sort of politician the *Republic*'s Thrasymachus (or the *Gorgias*' Calicles) would approve of come to mind here and would be, for Plato, contemptible.

82. The internal duties of the guardians include economics and management of the city's wealth (421c–422e); the physical size of the *polis* (422a–c); civil and commercial law (425d–427a), including religious law (427b–c), education and the rearing of children (423e–425a); and finally the ethical norms that comprise the unwritten law (425a–c), the last being the focus here. In sum we have the common good, what Leo Strauss described as "the objectives actually pursued by all societies. These objectives are: freedom from foreign domination, stability or rule of law, prosperity, glory or empire." See Leo Strauss, "What is Political Philosophy," in *What is Political Philosophy and Other Studies* (Chicago: University of Chicago Press, 1959), 42. It is more than simply this, however, as for Plato societal stability requires the strictest mental stability, while rule of law requires a virtually unceasing supervision through *unwritten* ethical codes for the body, thought, and speech.

83. Page, "The Truth about Lies in Plato's *Republic*," 18. The discussion here is heavily informed by Page, "The Truth about Lies in Plato's *Republic*," and Hesk, *Deception and Democracy in Classical Athens*.

84. Page, "The Truth about Lies in Plato's *Republic*," 18.

85. Page, "The Truth about Lies in Plato's *Republic*," 18.

86. This is discussed in greater detail in Kateri Carmola, "Noble Lying: Justice and Intergenerational Tension in Plato's *Republic*," *Political Theory* 31, no. 1 (2003): 39–62.

87. Arendt, for example, insists in her essay "Truth and Politics" that "under no circumstances can [the Noble Lie] be understood as a recommendation of lying as we understand it." She admits that Plato viewed "occasional lies" as useful but only in the case of "the enemy or insane people." She even cites the passage in *Republic* 388 that refers to lying as "useful . . . in the way of medicine . . . to be handled by no one but a physician" but makes no mention of the Noble Lie itself being described as a *pharmakon*. Nor does she discuss the wide spectrum of occupations that possessed access to *pharmaka* and whom Plato repeatedly criticizes. See Hanna Arendt, *Between Past and Future* (New York: Penguin, 2006), 291 n. 5. Arendt rips the term *pseudos* out of all context, be it the text of Plato or Greek culture itself, and makes no mention of it being likened by Plato to a *pharmakon*. Here I have to agree, though for different reasons, with Malcolm Schofield, *Plato: Political Philosophy* (New York: Oxford University Press, 2006), 302–3 that Arendt is "simply wrong" regarding the Noble Lie. It is not a "bold flight of invention" but deliberate falsehood. As Dombrowski observes in his critique of Page, the problem is not that Plato endorses lying in an *in extremis* situation to enemies or the mad, the problem is that Plato also endorses lying by philosophers, who possess superior knowledge, to all non-philosophers, who are judged as foolishly ignorant. See Dombrowski, "On the Alleged Truth about Lies in Plato's *Republic*," 100–104.

88. Page, The Truth about Lies in Plato's *Republic*," 25–26.

89. Catherine Zuckert, *Postmodern Platos*, 224.

90. Penelope Murray, "Inspiration and Mimesis in Plato," *Apeiron* 25, no. 4 (1992): 36. In the *Ion* Socrates will grant that the frantic and possessed state that the *rhapsode* Ion places himself in, when he recites Homer, qualifies him as being "a divine praiser of Homer," but at the price of his renouncing any expertise in *understanding* poetry (542a–b, cf. Xenophon *Symposium* 3.6–7, and *Memorabilia* 4.2.10).

91. Derrida, *Dissemination*, 123.

92. This is not to say that Socrates is never a creature of *ekstasis*. This too is part of his Dionysian, Silenus-like personality. His words produce a state of mind that Alcibiades in the *Symposium* likens to religious hysteria, with racing heart and uncontrollable tears (215c–e). To see this inner, secret Socrates is to view something "utterly godlike and golden and beautiful and wonderful," all of which sounds suspiciously like the Eleusinian Mysteries, their *epopteia* Diotima had hinted at earlier in the same dialogue. One's entire belief system is turned upside down and, although free, a man such as Alcibiades finds himself confronted with the reality of his ignorance and "the disturbing realization that my whole life is that of a slave" (215e–216a). Or, one might say, a lie.

Afterword

Toward a New Ethics of the *Pharmakon*

The philosopher Michel Foucault during his final years saw himself as "writing a genealogy of ethics. The genealogy of the subject as a subject of ethical actions, or the genealogy of desire as an ethical problem."[1] What this work, titled *pharmakon* after the ancient Greek word for "drug," has sought to demonstrate is that the emergence of a concern with controlling the desire for *ecstasy*—and as a result controlling a not inconsiderable number of different forms of drug-related behavior—can be traced to the earliest beginnings of Western culture, especially ancient Greece. The difficulties of the *pharmakon*, in all its multi-faceted ambiguity and complexity, constituted what Foucault called a "domain of action" that ancient Greek thought, especially Plato, perceived as a danger to social cohesion and political order. Genealogy in the Foucauldian sense, however, deals with both *emergence* and *descent*. As criminologist Toby Seddon points out in his *A History of Drugs*, genealogy "involves tracing the complex and multiple lines of development from first emergence to the present, with the critical purpose of rethinking the present."[2] In this afterword I will quickly sketch a history of the descent of the ethics of the *pharmakon*. The observations here are tentative and preliminary but are, given the urgent need to rethink the present, needed.

Drug Ethics: From Plato to the Present

In the *Birth of Tragedy* Nietzsche described "blissful ecstasy" as constituting the essence of "the nature of the *Dionysaic*" while "the maintenance of the boundaries of the individual" was at the innermost core of how the Greeks defined *moderation*, with Socrates the greatest opponent of Dionysus.[3] The problem of ecstasy would, undoubtedly, never be far from the surface of any analysis of the

257

drug ethics between Plato and modernity. The difficulties with the *pharmakon* registered by Plato in his dialogues have persisted in Western thought for nearly twenty-five hundred years. Only the manner of the expression of those difficulties has changed. Similarly the set of solutions proposed to keep intrusions of drug-induced Otherness at bay have changed over time. The social construction of intoxication was expressed differently in pagan Roman thought, early Christian and Medieval Christian thought, Protestant thought, and preindustrial modern thought, than it had been in ancient Greek thought. What follows is merely an outline or sketch of the problems, difficulties, and proposed solutions as they unfolded from their beginnings in ancient Greece to the present. The ethics of the *pharmakon* in each time period are, obviously, each deserving of an entirely separate study.

If we take into account how fragile the self-contained psyche must have been in ancient Greece, its rarity even among those members of the Athenian aristocracy who were, by the standards of the day, well-educated, judicious, and reflective, the problemization of the ecstatic, of *ekstasis*, is understandable and can be viewed sympathetically. Plato, it should come as no surprise, was at the forefront of this intellectual opposition to disruptions and alterations of identity that manifested themselves in many different ways, including through *pharmaka*. For example the distinguished scholar of comparative literature Mihai Spariosu writes that in the *Ion* "Socrates employs the analogy of the lodestone in order to describe the mimetic 'frenzy' that spreads from bard to the audience. The archaic audience totally identifies with the singer of tales through *methexis*, mimetic participation, or an ecstatic trance similar to that caused by Dionysian intoxication."[4] Plato, as Foucault describes it, is "the leaven, the soil, the climate, and the environment" for both "a variety of spiritual movements" in Western history and "the development of what could be called a 'rationality.'"[5] A "rationality" that cannot coexist with either *ekstasis* or the *pharmakon*.

In "Plato's Pharmacy" the philosopher Jacques Derrida observes that in the *Phaedrus* "writing is presented to the king as a way of extending the human capacity to remember events," but this offer is rejected by the monarch "on the grounds that writing will be a 'drug' of sorts, a technological supplement making human memory unnecessary."[6] The king's position, Derrida argues, "projects a fantasy in which 'the perfection of the living being would consist in its having no relation at all to the outside.'"[7] Similarly in the *Republic* Socrates explains to Adeimantus that a "fine nature," such as a god's, "admits least transformation by anything else" (381a–b). Or in other words, as Jasper Neel writes, a god "can have no relationship with the *pharmakon*," this substance "from the outside that penetrates by inscribing itself on the inside."[8] In Plato's thought health and virtue (*hugieia kai arete*), "which are often associated in speaking of the body and, analogously, of the soul (cf. *Gorgias*, 479b), always proceed from within. The *pharmakon* is that which, always springing up from without, acting like the outside itself, will never have any definable virtue of its own."[9]

Plato furthers and hastens an ontological assessment—one that we saw in chapter 4 had begun to manifest itself as far back as Homer—that favored view-

ing ecstatic experiences, including those brought about through drug intoxication, as *false* and *wrong* in virtually every form and in virtually every circumstance.[16] While Socrates himself is sometimes said to experience something
closely resembling ecstasy, and is said to produce it within those to whom he
speaks, there are two important differences. First, while he appears to personally
assume certain ecstatic postures, his mind, insulated by reason often to the point
of impossibility, remains as firmly seated as Odysseus under protection of the
moly. In the *Symposium*, for example, he is twice referred to as being in a trance
that renders him oblivious to his surroundings (175b, 220c–d), yet these trances
are from all appearances both self-initiated and self-terminated, and not the result of any external agency, be it human, divine, or based on some *pharmakon*.
Even Socrates' famous *daimon* voices itself only when it wishes him to refrain
from an action, and while Socrates never fails to heed this voice, it should be
emphasized that the choice is his, based on reasoning that reaches a conclusion
synonymous with the exhortation of the *daimon*, and that he is never possessed
or seized by it, as one who "hears voices." Second, with words alone Socrates
overwhelms and lifts people out of their everyday identity. Unlike the musician,
poet/singer, stage-actor, or someone making a political speech, funeral oration,
etc., this Socratic induced *ekstasis* has much of the form but virtually none of the
content of the traditional ecstatic experience.

It would be absurd to vilify Plato for the arguments the dialogues fashion to
bracket and/or chastise the ecstatic as problematic, or the set of solutions *he*
sometimes naively proposes. At the same time it is worth indicating the price *we*
have paid. In Plato we may recognize, as political theorist William E. Connolly
has put it, "corollary tactics installed in modalities of the present."[11] Literary
theorist Timothy Melley, for example, has carried Derrida's reading of the
Phaedrus into the present, pointing out that this same Platonic fantasy consisting
of "the dream of a self hermetically sealed from the external world" is reflected
in the "contemporary American logic of addiction."[12] Derrida, too, sees a thread
running between Plato and the modern War on Drugs in his "The Rhetoric of
Drugs: An Interview."[13] Derrida's position, in sum, is "that every effort to control and contain drugs inevitably reverts to masculinist, homophobic fantasies of
bodily impermeability, fantasies that foreclose even the merest consideration of
more communitarian forms of political organization and communication."[14] It
should be emphasized that none of these writers simplistically describes this
thread between Plato and modernity as a literal, causal one, nor do they argue
that Plato views drugs as moral agents, or that a philosopher of the fourth century BCE such as Plato speaks of a "drug problem" in the same way modernity
has. In other words Plato, like his contemporaries, "would never have blamed a
person's bad behavior on a substance."[15]

In the philosophy and medicine of the Greek Classical Period, Foucault observes, ethical behavior was "a personal choice" undertaken to construct "a
beautiful existence," i.e. "the way in which people are invited or incited to recognize moral obligations" is largely aesthetic.[16] As we saw in the case of the
symposion this was true of the experience of intoxication or *methe* in the drink-

ing ethics of the Athenian aristocracy. By the time of the late Stoicism of ancient Rome there has been, according to Foucault, a shift: ethical behavior is no longer a question of choice, it is something everyone is "obliged to do" as a "rational human being."[17] This obligation-based ethical behavior, as well as the influence of Plato, is abundantly evident in the writings of Dio Chrysosotom (ca. 40–ca. 120 CE), an orator, writer, philosopher and historian.[18] His *Discourse to the Alexandrians* mentions drug use on multiple occasions, in addition to problematizing the lingering noetic harm of various ecstatic states by means of analogy to drug intoxication, such as:

> For the Alexandrians are moderate enough when they offer sacrifice or stroll by themselves or engage in their other pursuits; but when they enter the theatre or the stadium [i.e. the Alexandrian hippodrome near the Serapeum], just as if drugs that would madden them lay buried there, they lose all consciousness of their former state and are not ashamed to say or do anything that occurs to them. And what is most distressing of all is that, despite their interest in the show, they do not really see, and, though they wish to hear, they do not hear, being evidently out of their senses and deranged—not only men, but even women and children. And when the dreadful exhibition is over and they are dismissed, although the more violent aspect of their disorder has been extinguished, still at street-corners and in alley-ways the malady continues throughout the entire city for several days; just as when a mighty conflagration has died down, you can see for a long time, not only the smoke, but also some portions of the buildings still aflame.[19]

Other examples of the social discussion of alcohol and drug ethics in ancient Rome are Seneca the Younger (ca. 4 BCE–65 CE) who describes the heavy use of alcohol by his contemporaries in his *Epistulae Morales*[20] and his contemporary the physician Scribonius Largus (fl. 48 CE) in his *De Compositiones Medicamentorum* (*Drug Recipes* or *On Remedies*).[21] Galen (129–217 CE), of course, knew quite a bit about drugs.[22] Stoic influences are detectable in his short work *Quod optimus medicus sit quoque philosophus* (*That the Best Physician is Also a Philosopher*).[23] Recreational drugs were as prevalent in ancient Rome as they had been in other ancient cultures.[24]

During the early Christian era the lodestone-like magnetic pull exerted by the *epithymetikon*, the heavy strings of desire that move the human puppet of Plato's *Laws*, gives way to the eternal temptation of sin.[25] The danger becomes not just an ugly, ignoble and slavish existence in this life but also punishment, perhaps eternal, in the next as well. One finds that within Christian asceticism "the question of purity becomes more and more important," gradually covering over the Greco-Roman world's "aesthetics of existence."[26] The reason "why you take control of yourself" is not to lead a beautiful life; it "is to keep yourself pure."[27] Examples of this new emphasis on purity are easily tracked down. Clement of Alexandria (ca. 150–211/216 CE), in the final chapter of his *Exhortation to the Greeks*, disapprovingly quotes King Pentheus in Euripides' *Bacchae* (918–19), where the hallucinating king sees two suns and two Thebes, as the utterance of a "frenzy-stricken" idol worshipper, and says he pities "him in his frantic intoxication" and "would invite him to the sobriety of salvation; for the Lord welcomes a sinner's repentance, and not his death."[28] He pleads for this "madman" to come to his senses and abandon the thyrsus, the crown of ivy, the mitre, and the fawn skin, or in other words all the accoutrements of the god of ecstasy and drugs, Dionysus. In place of the mountain-top mysteries of Dionysus, he will show the "mysteries of the Word" which are the "mountain beloved of God," the "consecrated mysteries of the *truth*, a mount of *sobriety*, shaded with forests of *purity*" (emphasis mine).

Arnobius of Sicca, a Christian apologist who lived during the reign of the emperor Diocletian (284–305 CE), while refuting charges made by pagan critics that the Christians had brought calamities upon mankind in his *Adversus Nationes* or *Case Against the Pagans*, refers to them as *insanire* and *bacchari*, "the full force of which can hardly be rendered into English" but which suggests, among other things, "that in Arnobius' opinion the critics were uttering statements worth no more than the babblings of the mad and intoxicated."[29] St. John Chrysostom (ca. 347–407 CE), in the fifth of his *Baptismal Instructions* titled "Exhortation to the Neophytes to Abstain from Softness, Extravagance, and Drunkenness, and to Esteem Moderation above All Things," warns his reader that "excess in eating and drinking weakens the strength of the body and destroys the health of the soul. Let us, consequently, flee excess and not become careless in what concerns our salvation; since we know that excess is the root of all evil, let us be careful to cut it out." He concludes his exhortation with the words: "I beg you, let us all be sober."

Moderation in Christian asceticism is no longer founded upon an ethics of responsible use as it once had been, for example in discussion of wine-drinking ethics in the poetry of Theognis.[30] Nor is it Platonic in the sense of allowing, at least in theory and by a philosophic few, heavy drinking so long as the *noos* remains in magisterial control of the desires of the body. Instead, as can be gleaned from Clement and Chrysostom, moderation is equated with excision, with a perpetual absence of somatic intoxication. Truth is equated with sober purity, something that requires pure sobriety. With Christianity there is an introduction of a "pastoral" mode of power, one defined by a "shepherd/flock relationship" that was largely absent in ancient Greece.[31] Beginning in roughly the second and third centuries CE and lasting until the eighteenth—and in an increasingly truncated form up to the present, for as Foucault observes "pastoral power in its typology, organization, and mode of functioning, pastoral power exercised as power, is doubtless something from which we have still not freed ourselves"—the Church was an institution that claimed "to govern men in their daily life on the grounds of leading them to [the salvation of] eternal life in the other world, and to do this not only on the scale of a definite group, of a city or a state, but of the whole of humanity."[32]

At the same time it would be a mistake to view this "pastoral power" as "an invariant and fixed structure through fifteen, eighteen or twenty centuries of Christian history."[33] Foucault emphasizes "the importance, vigor, and depth of implantation of this pastoral power can be measured by the intensity and multiplicity of agitations, revolts, discontent, struggles, battles, and bloody wars that have been conducted around, for, and against it."[34] The Italian historian Piero Camporesi points to "sweetly ecstatic substances in the early history of the Christian West," arguing divine-ness "was perceived sensually, it was inhaled in the form of perfume, it was tasted, it was absorbed by the intestine, it was touched, smelled, drunk, eaten, digested. The ritual drugs opened a door to a whole range of comforting intoxications."[35] He portrays the early modern, pre-industrial Western European "social panorama" as being "traversed by profound anxieties and fears, alienating frustrations, devouring and uncontrollable infirmities and dietary chaos," where alcohol, drugs and "adulterated and stupefying grains contributed to delirious hypnotic states and crises, which could explode into episodes of collective possession or sudden furies of dancing."[36]

Between the late sixteenth century and the early eighteenth century new drugs, drugs which were not present in Classical Greece—for example brandy and spirits made from grain, along with tea, coffee, chocolate and tobacco—"were introduced, found acceptance, and spread with remarkable speed around the globe."[37] The origins of distillation are still disputed but what is clearer is that brandy, the miraculous *aqua vitae*, broke away from physicians and pharmacists "very slowly."[38] We can begin to speak of commercial production, distribution and consumption as originating in the sixteenth century, with the seventeenth consolidating it and the eighteenth popularizing it.[39] Similarly the importance of the "the coffee houses in their golden age between 1680 and 1730 and the salons in the period between regency and revolution," can scarcely be overestimated.[40] Coffee houses and salons were a major hub of what the philosopher Jürgen Habermas calls the "structural transformation" of the bourgeois public sphere in early Western European capitalism.[41] Among the luminaries who frequented the fashionable Café Procope in Paris were leading figures of the European Enlightenment such as Diderot, D'Alembert, Rousseau, and Voltaire.[42] Historian Rudi Matthee pushes Habermas' argument further, contending the rise of the nation-state and the expansion of "new urban centres in western Europe," their "new commercial and administrative elites as well as a rudimentary urban proletariat, and redefined boundaries between private and public spheres," was closely tied with the introduction of these "new substances and the ambience in which they were consumed."[43]

Not everyone approved of the "new drugs."[44] Brandy, tea, chocolate and coffee, for example, were all initially hailed as miracle medicinal cure-alls.[45] Later, an explosion of popular use led to various difficulties.[46] As early as 1493, in the case of brandy, a Nuremburg doctor was observing: "In view of the fact that everyone at present has got into the habit of drinking *aqua vitae* it is necessary to remember the quantity that one can permit oneself to drink and learn to drink it according to one's capacities, if one wishes to behave like a gentlemen" and just three years later, historian Fernand Braudel writes that the city of Nuremburg "was obliged to forbid the free sale of alcohol on feast days."[47] Although hardly more than a limited response of dubious effectiveness on the part of local authorities, such action does suggest the existence of an emerging problem whose difficulties would grow more acute in the next three centuries. Braudel himself hints at most of the recreational drugs introduced into Western Europe between the sixteenth and eighteenth centuries being "forbidden and reauthorized at regular intervals."[48] In each case "violent government prohibitions" failed, the disfavor with which some substances were viewed being "only temporary," due in part to an "unprecedented contraband trade" but most importantly because the prohibitions simply "were ignored" at every level.[49] Faced with an "active capitalist sector [with] a financial interest in [the] production, distribution and success" of these substances, the state eventually capitulated, discovering "it too could profit" through taxation of certain national commodities like tea and tobacco—though overtaxation could backfire.[50]

In addition to the emphasis that it placed on purity, there is, according to Foucault, still a form of obligation present in Christian ethics, only now and in contrast to the sort of obligation found in Stoic thought the "institutions by which [rules for behavior] were imposed were religious institutions. But the form of the obligation was a legal form. There was a kind of internal juridification of religious law inside Christianity."[51] Beginning in the eighteenth century, under the withering gaze of the Enlightenment and the demands of ascendant small-scale capitalism, what Foucault calls "the religious framework" supporting ethical behavior began to first erode and then disintegrate; since then a "medical or scientific approach and a juridical framework" have competed with each other, without resolution.[52] In contemporary drug policy this competition can be seen in the split between advocates of "drug treatment" on the one hand, and "law enforcement" on the other.[53]

Religious and pseudo-scientific discourse on intoxication only gradually receded from within nominally "scientific" discourse. In 1762 Olavus R. Alander, a student of the famed Swedish botanist Carl Linnaeus, wrote a doctoral thesis titled *Inebriantia*, a work characterized by ethno-botonist Richard Evans Schultes as a groundbreaking "treatise on inebrients," one that "was a mixture of scientific and pseudo-scientific information."[54] Quaker physician Benjamin Rush published his pamphlet *An Inquiry into the Effect of Ardent Spirits upon the Human Body and Mind* in 1785, describing the "habitual use" of such spirits as an "odious disease," and the Reverend Lyman Beecher in his *Six Sermons on the Nature, Occasions, Signs, Evils, and Remedy of Intemperance*," delivered in 1825, declared "the intemperate are 'addicted to the sin,' [and] referred to intemperance as an 'evil habit' fueled by 'an insatiable desire to drink."[55] Conversely, religious discourse attempted to reconfigure itself by making "scientific" appeals to its audience, for example Reverend Benjamin Parsons in his treatises *Anti-Bacchus* and especially *The Wine Question Settled* published in 1840 and 1841, respectively.

In philosopher Immanuel Kant's *Metaphysics of Morals*, published in 1797, "fermented drinks" and "narcotics, such as opium and other vegetable products" are responsible for producing a "dream euphoria" (i.e. *ekstasis*) and freedom from care that is both "misleading" and a form of human "debasement." The

Kant ↑

drug user, Kant writes, if not beneath an animal is their equivalent, simply like a beast and "not to be treated as a human being."[56] In a manner reminiscent of Plato he does allow for moderate wine use "bordering on intoxication" since it "promotes friendly conversation." Drugs such as opium, however, make their user withdrawn and uncommunicative. Worse, under their influence the user passes "into a state in which he no longer has clear eyes for *measuring*." As a result drugs and spirits stronger than wine are to be "permitted only as medicine."[57] It is clear, however, that Kant like Plato is deeply suspicious of the *pharmakon* in general, "even in the case of drugs used exclusively for therapeutic ends, even when they are wielded with good intentions, and even when they are as such effective. There is no such thing as a harmless remedy. The *pharmakon* can never be simply beneficial."[58]

Early nineteenth-century developments, such as the isolation of morphine from opium and then its easy administration via hypodermic needles a few decades later, arguably mark an important watershed.[59] They are important for two reasons. First, because they signal the beginnings of a break with pharmacological practices as they had existed since ancient times. The mid-nineteenth century essentially marks the final supplanting of "magical pharmacology" with "medico-scientific pharmacology."[60] Examples of this new medico-scientific literature include *Die narkotischen Genussmittel und der Mensch* [*Narcotic Pleasure Drugs and Man*] published in 1855 by botanist Ernst Freiherr von Bibra—a work that influenced Karl Hartwich's *Die Menschlichen Genussmittel*, [*Mankind's Pleasure Drugs*] published in 1911—and the naturalist Mordecai Cooke's *The Seven Sisters of Sleep* published in 1860. Second, because they mark the rise of both new routes of drug administration as well as the availability of increasingly concentrated man-made synthetic drugs.[61] While he does not name morphine specifically, Derrida argues the theory of addiction "requires the 'technical possibility for an individual to reproduce the act' of drug-taking, an 'easy access' only made possible by 'techno-economic transformations of the market-place and other technologies of the last two centuries.'"[62] The set of solutions proposed to deal with the difficulties arising out of morphine use and opium smoking as well as the use of cocaine, heroin, absinthe, and other drugs, begins to crystallize in the nineteenth century's final two decades, in response to the social, economic and political conditions particular to a still emergent mass-production capitalism. Drug use in this era remained, by and large, less a disease and more a distasteful "habit" and the user a "habitué."

addiction + industrial state

The early years of the twentieth century witnessed still another transformation, the reformulation of recreational drug use as "addiction" and the user as "addict."[63] The term "addiction" traces itself to Roman origins, deriving from Roman law where "a person found guilty might be punished by being 'addicted' in bondage to a master."[64] The term was in use as early as 1600, for example in Shakespeare: "Each man to what sport and revels his addiction leads him to" (*Othello* 2.2.6) although references may be found "to persons 'addicted to' various behaviors as early as 1530."[65] The belief that began to emerge in the late nineteenth century that "a person might be 'in bondage' to a drug, and not able to act with freedom of will" was still, in an important sense, "a new one in human history."[66] While addiction "first came into common usage in the professional literature of the mid-1890s," the term "*addict,* or on occasion, *addictee,* emerged around 1910 to replace the earlier term *habitué* used to designate a person suffering from addiction."[67] The "addict," it has been argued, appeared as mass-production consumer capitalism developed, and as increasingly influential medico-legal institutions began defining drug intoxication as pathology.[68]

The introduction of the continuously moving assembly line and other techniques by Henry Ford and his engineers in the Model T plant located in Highland Park, Michigan in late 1913 can be said to mark a significant moment in "the passage from the old economic individualism" characterized by the skilled craft labor of early capitalism "to the planned economy" of mass-production capitalism.[69] The political theorist Antonio Gramsci, in his essay "Americanism and Fordism," recognized the important connection between the new production methods and the politics of intoxication. The history of industrialization, he wrote, "has always been a continuing struggle . . . against the element of 'animality' in man. It has been an uninterrupted, often painful and bloody process of subjugating natural . . . instincts to new, more complex and rigid norms and habits of order, exactitude and precision which can make possible the increasingly complex forms of collective life which are the necessary consequence of industrial development."[70]

"Prohibition," Gramsci wrote, was in the case of the United States "a necessary condition for developing a new type of worker suitable to 'Fordised' industry."[71] Opposition to and repeal of Prohibition—like the relaxation of overly puritanical sexual mores—became possible because denying large segments of society access to alcohol, in particular the industrial working class, produced "an inherent conflict between verbal ideology . . . and the real 'animal' practice which prevents physical bodies from effectively acquiring the new attitudes."[72] In contrast to their earlier blind faith in the principles espoused in 1911 by Frederick Taylor in *The Principles of Scientific Management,* including its infamous assertion that the labor of the assembly line was so "crude and elementary in its nature" that an "intelligent gorilla" could be trained to perform the job better than any man, "American industrialists [by the time of Prohibition's repeal in 1933] understood that 'trained gorilla' is just a phrase, that 'unfortunately' the worker remains a man," and denying him basic pleasures such as intoxication "can lead [the worker] into a train of thought that is far from conformist."[73]

It is not a coincidence nor surprising, then, that the passage of the Harrison Narcotics Act in 1914, and the experiment with government-imposed prohibition of alcohol begun in 1920, followed so closely on the heels of the publication of Taylor's book on scientific management and the building of Ford's assembly line factory, in an industrial nation-state whose politics remains infused with an extreme religious Puritanism. "Religious moralism was the most efficient weapon against those arch-enemies of industrial discipline and high profits: 'drunkenness, spontaneous holidays, and inattention to work.'"[74] Nor is it surprising that the contemporary recreational drug culture arose during the second half of the 1960s, just as those same assembly line methods of manufacturing were on the cusp of becoming obsolete, when social forces that had never spent a day working in a factory and who had read literary works such as Aldous Huxley's *The Doors of Perception* and William S. Burroughs' *Naked Lunch* began posing questions the traditional Left was ill-equipped or unequipped to answer.[75]

The Post-Industrial Moment: Perils and Possibilities

We are currently living through what I prefer to call the Post-Industrial Moment, an ever more crisis-ridden transition from the old, modernist, Fordist, industrial economy Gramsci was familiar with, and which began to break down at the end of the 1960s, to a post-modern, post-Fordist, post-industrial economy. This new economy is founded upon a technological restructuring centered around the production of informational goods (i.e., an "information economy"), and an organizational restructuring that speeds up the circulation of commodities, the spatial reach of capital, and the expansion of the consumer sector.[76] Invoking the work of both Gramsci and Antonio Negri, Marcia Landy describes the social side of this transition thus: "If the term 'mass worker' characterizes productive/political relations until 1968, the term 'socialized worker' becomes most applicable to the economic and political situation prevailing after 1968."[77] The mass worker enjoyed a measure of protection thanks to the state interventions and regulations typical of Keynesian economics but had, by 1968, "set in motion demands relating not only to questions of social mobility but also to wages expectations, to the regulation of both working and nonworking time, and to subjective conditions concerning social values."[78] These demands resulted in "a crisis in relation to capital and its management of labor," triggering the demise of "the planner state" and the rise of a "consistent motif of antagonism and the growing social subjection and subjectivity of the workers, the increasing awareness of the futility of reformism and of accommodation, and the increasing violence on the part of the state."[79]

Tactically, to socialize the worker, the state in the post-1968 time period has employed weapons that include "deregulation, unemployment, the creation of poverty, competition for labor on the world market, new forms of technological control, and literal state terror."[80] It is in this macro-economic climate that contemporary drug war politics must be situated. If we accept the view "that 'drugs' is an 'invented' governmental category, in the sense of one actively constructed by human beings for specific governmental purposes, which has arisen relatively recently in the context of the emergence of modern industrial capitalism," we should expect that drug policy, and the ethics of the *pharmakon*, will be as different in the early decades of the twenty-first century as they had been in the early decades of the twentieth century, or the early decades of the nineteenth century.[81] We are, then, in the midst of a moment fraught with both peril and possibility. While the discussion to follow is built on examples drawn from the United States, it should be pointed out that the American approach to recreational drug questions has for more than a century been powerfully expressed internationally.[82]

The peril consists in a startling deepening, expansion and militarization of the federal government's law-enforcement apparatus in the name of waging a punitive "war" on recreational drug "criminals" on the one hand, operating in loose conjunction with a large constellation of medical, psychiatric, educational, and self-help occupations emphasizing "treatment" of "the addict" on the other. The hegemonic view of ecstasy mandates the recreational drug user not be recognized "as a subject having a right to speak" but is instead abolished "as interlocutor, from any possible dialogue."[83] The defenders of perpetual sobriety advance their thought in the form of monologues "encased in privileges" they alone possess and "will never agree to question."[84] As a matter of principle they possess the right and authority "to wage war" on drug use in what is, in their eyes, unquestionably "a just undertaking."[85] The recreational drug user is "an adversary, an enemy who is wrong, who is harmful and whose very existence constitutes a threat."[86]

Responding to the events of the middle and late 1960s, the contemporary drug war was launched on October 24, 1969, by the Nixon Administration.[87] After a period of indecision and hesitation the "new Federalism" of the 1980s, 1990s and beyond gave increased leeway to individual states to formulate their own drug policy, but the flexibility was only in the sense of how to identify, detain, prosecute, incarcerate and/or detoxify.[88] The pattern since 1969 is simple and easy to identify: repeated failure and continual escalation.[89] The massive growth in incarceration within the United States since 1980, the erosion of individual and property rights and the eviscerating of democracy are each largely attributable to the so-called War on Drugs:

> Despite consistent criticism across the political spectrum . . . the United States is the world's leader in incarceration; over 2 million Americans are currently imprisoned, which represents a 500% increase since the beginning of the war on drugs. Drug-related incarceration accounts for more than half of all federal inmates, and the number of drug offenders in state prisons has increased more than tenfold since 1980.[90]

This immense prison population, in turn, has been harnessed as a source of cheap "rightless" labor.[91] The urban poor in the United States have been left with three equally unpalatable alternatives: the hopelessness of surviving in an increasingly emaciated welfare state, bullet splattered participation in the illegal drug economy, or arrest, prison and disenfranchisement.[92]

The placid facade of suburban middle class tranquility has been increasingly disturbed by ripples produced by the drug war: paramilitary police raids executing violent "no-knock" warrants,[93] the deployment of new technologies of surveillance such as widespread workplace drug testing, students being required to verify they have not had a drug conviction as a condition for receiving federal educational financial aid, as well as the threat of property seizure through asset forfeiture laws.[94] The most significant rhetorical change in most academic and political discourse on drugs at the national level has been a shift from an imagined "drugs-communism" link before the fall of the Berlin Wall in 1989 to a "drugs-security" link in the 1990s and then a "drugs-terrorism" link in the aftermath of the events of September 11, 2001.[95] The "military-industrial complex" has been joined by a "narco-industrial complex"[96] or perhaps more aptly put a "drug-abuse industrial complex."[97]

When individual states have made tentative moves in the direction of adopting a "harm reduction" model, variants of which exist in several European countries, and voters began passing a number of medical marijuana referenda/initiatives, both the Office of National Drug Control Policy (ONDCP) "drug czar" and the federal police bureaucracies with a vested interest in maintaining the drug war status quo like the Drug Enforcement Agency (DEA), Bureau of Alcohol, Tobacco, and Firearms (BATF), Federal Bureau of Investigation (FBI), and the United States Marshals Service (USMS), were quick to oppose, harass, obstruct, and otherwise interfere with their implementation.[98] The "new Federalism," with its rhetoric of "devolving" power from Washington back to the individual states, clearly does not extend to drug policy alternatives. With no legal profits to be made producing recreational drugs the pharmaceutical giants are willing and eager to pour vast sums of money—their own, foundation grants, government contracts—into conjuring new drugs of normalization to "cure" the craving for other drugs, i.e. recreational drugs.[99] Informational bureaucracies such as the National Institute on Drug Abuse (NIDA) have no interest other than maintaining the funding of their respective fiefdoms, while literally thousands of "private-sector treatment organizations" are now "mobilized politically . . . supporting greater law enforcement, more research, more education, or more treatment."[100] The Unites States at the dawn of the new millennium has reached a condition Gramsci described as "totalitarian social hypocrisy," by which he meant an almost surreal situation—much like the Prohibition era—where state rhetoric and the pleasure-seeking behavior of tens of millions were completely out of sync with each other.[101]

The possibilities: the need for Taylor's hypothetical "trained gorilla" is, if not long a thing of the past, fast becoming so thanks to advances in automation, robotics, and the beginnings of artificial intelligence. Today's drug laws are obsolete artifacts of the Fordist incarnation of capitalism where the workplace, whether blue collar or white collar, was characterized by long fixed hours of brute mechanical repetition. Beginning in the early 1980s and accelerating in the 1990s, that everyday reality has been rapidly giving way to flexible work schedules (telecommuting, etc.) and computer-based work tasks requiring adaptability, flexibility, intelligence, self-initiative, and creativity. In addition, a new generation of recreational drugs, even in the absence of a legal, carefully monitored and regulated market for their creation, distribution, and sale, is just

beginning to appear. It is only a matter of time before one or more of these "de-
signer-drugs" are so safe and innocuous to use that they render the objections
regarding the "dangers" of recreational drug use voiced by drug war proponents
entirely moot. A drug like the aptly named (for this work) Ecstasy, also known
as "E," is not the end of a process of recreational drug development, of ever new
"psyche delicacies"; it is merely the *beginning.*[102]

The theory of addiction, which had by the mid-twentieth century succeeded
in reducing the subject of recreational drug (ab)use to a question of epidemiology (the study of the factors affecting the health and illness of populations), has
come under increasing criticism.[103] Addiction "science" and its practitioners,
having simply accepted ethical "stereotypes and inaccurate perceptions of the
helpless junkie" that arose in the early twentieth century, indiscriminately link
each recreational drug "with the capacity to enslave," and construct their research to "seek out evidence" that supports the view of recreational drug use as
an *illness* to the exclusion of "any other [interpretation] and subsequently impose [that view] on their clientele for reasons that have nothing to do with scientific knowledge."[104] The medico-scientific approach to the drug problem is as
vacuous and bankrupt as the juridico-legal approach.

Changes in the material reproduction of society, the rise of the post-
industrial information economy and the disappearance of the traditional industrial workplace are being accompanied by a growing realization that—as was, in
truth, always the case, as far back as the Lotus-Eaters in Homer's *Odyssey*—
"most people who use drugs do so for their own reasons, on purpose, because
they like it, and because they find no adequate reason for not doing so; rather
than because they fall prey to some addictive illness which removes their capacity for voluntary behavior."[105] Indeed, there is reason to believe that seeking out
states of ecstatic intoxication are a "fourth drive" analogous to the drive to eat,
sleep, and reproduce.[106] The continuing democratization of mass communication
through mediums such as websites, blogs, text messaging, cell phones, popular
music, You Tube, etc., and the rise of funded intellectual centers such as the
Drug Policy Foundation and mobilized political oppositions such as the Marijuana Policy Project have shattered the hegemony of mainstream drug ethics,
which remain attached to a rapidly evaporating modernist, industrialist past.[107]
There is, simply put, no going back.

It has taken nearly three millennia but there are growing indications that we
can no longer afford to battle *ekstasis*, including when it is brought about by
recreational *pharmaka*, with the intent of destroying or eradicating it, for the
sake of some impossible ideal of hermetically sealed subjective identity like that
found in the *nostos* of Homer's Odysseus or in the ever pristine sobriety of Socrates at Agathon's *symposion*. Politics and society must eventually come to
terms with various forms of ecstasy, integrate them into our existence, or fail to
do so and continue to suffer the carceral and anti-democratic consequences. De-
claring peace with recreational pharmaceuticals does not imply nor does it mean
a complete or a permanent surrender of individual identity, as is frequently asserted in contemporary anti-drug rhetoric. Identity is far more firmly entrenched

than when Odysseus touched the shores of the Lotus-Eaters. We can afford to take breaks from identity; we are far more willing and able to return.

The suggestion that expanding the legal availability of naturally occurring and/or synthetic recreational drugs would somehow reverse the course of human civilization, thrust it back into some sort of Paleolithic group consciousness, is sheer hyperbole, and simply not tenable. To end this work where it began, with Foucault, the challenge is to recognize that in the case of our relationship with drug use it is not "necessary to relate ethical problems to scientific knowledge."[108] We in the West have spent "centuries . . . convinced . . . our ethics, our personal ethics, our everyday life," and "other social, economic, and political structures are analytically or necessarily linked."[109] We must "get rid of this idea" because until we do we remain trapped within a belief that we are powerless to change those ethics "without ruining our economy, our democracy, and so on."[110] The need for reconsidering the ethics of drugs within Western culture has never been more urgent.[111] The Post-Industrial Moment signals an opportunity for a fundamental change in our relationship with *all* drugs, a set of new ethico-political axioms for a new millennium. This includes not just recreational drugs, those *pharmaka* that ease the burdens of identity—the same reconsideration is desperately needed for a range of other substances, such as drugs used for birth control, abortifacient drugs, drugs that might be used for physician-assisted suicide, and so-called "performance enhancing" drugs taken in various workplaces.[112] The changes will not come easily or quickly but there is reason to believe that whatever any of us may wish, they are coming.[113]

Notes

1. Paul Rabinow, *The Foucault Reader* (New York: Pantheon Books, 1984), 356. Foucault's "genealogical" approach to studying the ancient Greeks is discussed in the Introduction, above.

2. Toby Seddon, *A History of Drugs: Drugs and Freedom in the Liberal Age* (New York: Routledge, 2010), 4.

3. Friedrich Nietzsche, *The Birth of Tragedy* (New York: Penguin Books, 199), 17, 26, 64–75.

4. Mihai Spariosu, *God of Many Names: Play, Poetry, and Power in Hellenic Thought from Homer to Aristotle* (Durham, NC: Duke University Press, 1991), 21.

5. Michel Foucault, *The Hermeneutics of the Subject—Lectures at the College de France 1981–1982* (New York: Picador, 2005), 77.

6. Timothy Melley, *Empire of Conspiracy: The Culture of Paranoia in Postwar America* (Ithaca, NY: Cornell University Press, 2000), 171.

7. Melley, *Empire of Conspiracy*, 171. Melley is quoting from Jacques Derrida, *Dissemination* (Chicago: University of Chicago Press, 1981), 101.

8. Jasper Neel, *Plato, Derrida, and Writing* (Carbondale, IL: University of Illinois Press, 1988), 80.

9. Derrida, *Dissemination*, 101–2.

10. The partial exception in Plato's case, as we saw in chapter 6, was where ecstasy might be harnessed to maintain socially useful behavior equated, as it is for example in the *Phaedrus*, with a rationalized sort of religious piety.

11. William E. Connolly, *The Augustinian Imperative: A Reflection on the Politics of Modernity* (London: Sage, 1993), xviii.

12. Melley, *Empire of Conspiracy*, 171.

13. Jacques Derrida, "The Rhetoric of Drugs," in *High Culture: Reflections on Addiction and Modernity*, ed. Anna Alexander and Mark S. Roberts (Albany, NY: State University of New York Press, 2000), 19–43. See also Melley, *Empire of Conspiracy*, 161–184.

14. Mike Sell, *Avant-Garde Performance and the Limits of Criticism: Approaching the Living Theatre, Happenings/Fluxus, and the Black Arts Movement* (Ann Arbor, MI: University of Michigan Press, 2008), 129.

15. D. C. A. Hillman, *The Chemical Muse: Drug Use and the Roots of Western Civilization* (New York: Thomas Dunne Books, 2008) 194; see also 216.

16. Rabinow, *The Foucault Reader*, 353, 356. Foucault is of course referring to only a small portion of the adult male population. It is important none the less because the ethics of the Greeks were drawn upon by later eras of antiquity, both pagan and Christian.

17. Rabinow, *The Foucault Reader*, 356.

18. After being banished for criticism of the Emperor Domitian in 82 CE, Chrysostom visited the Delphic Oracle, on whose advice he donned the garb of a beggar, journeying with nothing but copies of Plato's *Phaedo* and Demosthenes's *On the Embassy*.

19. Quote from Dio Chrysostom, *Discourses 31–36*, trans. J. W. Cohoon and H. Lamar Crosby (Cambridge, MA: Harvard University Press, 1940), 213. Chrysostom discusses the Alexandrians' love of music in similar terms.

20. Seneca, as well as a number of non-Stoic writers, is discussed in E. M. Jellinek, Carole D. Yawney, and Robert E. Popham, "Drinkers and Alcoholics in Ancient Rome," *Journal of Studies on Alcohol* 37, no. 11 (1976): 1733–1739. See also Arthur P. McKinlay, "The Roman Attitude Toward Women Drinking," in *Drinking and Intoxication: Selected Readings in Social Attitudes and Control*, ed. R. G. McCarthy (Glencoe, IL: The Free Press, 1959), 58–61.

21. Vivian Nutton, *Ancient Medicine* (New York: Routledge, 2004), 171–86.

22. John Scarborough, "The Opium Poppy in Hellenistic and Roman Medicine," in *Drugs and Narcotics in History*, ed. Roy Porter and Mikuláš Teich (New York: Cambridge University Press, 1995), 17–18 discusses Galen and the use(s) of opium by Stoic philosopher and emperor Marcus Aurelius (121 CE–180 CE). Galen's knowledge of medicinal drugs is discussed in Paul T. Keyser, "Science and Magic in Galen's Recipes (Sympathy and Efficacy)," in *Galen on Pharmacology—Philosophy, History and Medicine*, ed. Armelle Debru (Leiden, Netherlands: E. J. Brill, 1997), 186–94. The date of Galen's death is the source of some scholarly disagreement; the date here agrees with the reasoning found in Nutton, *Ancient Medicine*, 226–27.

23. Darrel W. Amundsen and Gary B. Ferngren, "Evolution of the Patient-Physician Relationship," in *The Clinical Encounter: The Moral Fabric of the Patient-Physician Relationship*, ed. Earl E. Shelp (Hingham, MA: Kluwer Academic Publishers, 1983), 27–28.

24. Such a discussion far exceeds the limits of the present work. A general discussion of the prevalence of recreational drugs in ancient Rome may be found in Hillman, *The Chemical Muse*, 56–87.

25. Plato's influence on the Stoics and Galen, among others, and early Christians such as Augustine, is discussed in Richard Sorabji, *Emotion and Peace of Mind: From Stoic Agitation to Christian Temptation* (New York: Oxford University Press, 2000).

26. Rabinow, *The Foucault Reader*, 365–66.

27. Rabinow, *The Foucault Reader*, 365. On the use of wine see Jessica Warner, "Before there was 'Alcoholism': Lessons from the Medieval Experience with Alcohol," *Contemporary Drug Problems* 19, no. 3 (1992): 409–29.

28. Earlier in the play at lines 325–327 Tiresias says to Pentheus "Your words will not turn me against the god, for you are mad, under a cruel delusion. No drug can heal that ailment—in fact, some drug has caused it." Quoted in Ian Johnston, trans., *Euripides—Bacchae* (Arlington, VA: Richer Resources Publications, 2008), 21.

29. Johannes Quasten, *Ancient Christian Writers: The Works of the Fathers in Translation. Arnobius of Sicca: The Case Against the Pagans* (Baltimore, MD: J. H. Furst and Company, 1949), 269, n. 2. Arnobius was apparently a rhetorician before his conversion. *The Case Against the Pagans* was probably written about 304 CE though this dating is by no means certain.

30. See the discussion of Theognis' *Elegies* in chapter 2, above. The views of drunkenness as intemperance in the thought of Augustine, Aquinas, and others is discussed in Christopher H. Cook, *Alcohol, Addiction and Christian Ethics* (New York: Cambridge University Press, 2006), 52–76.

31. Michel Foucault, *Security, Territory, Population—Lectures at the College de France 1977–78*, (New York: Picador, 2007), 139–147.

32. Foucault, *Security, Territory, Population—Lectures at the College de France 1977–78*, 148.

33. Foucault, *Security, Territory, Population—Lectures at the College de France 1977–78*, 148.

34. Foucault, *Security, Territory, Population—Lectures at the College de France 1977–78*, 148.

35. Piero Camporesi, *The Incorruptible Flesh: Bodily Mutation and Mortification in Religion and Folklore* (New York: Cambridge University Press, 1988), 238.

36. Peiro Camporesi, *Bread of Dreams—Food and Fantasy in Early Modern Europe* (Chicago: University of Chicago Press, 1989), 18, 83–84.

37. Rudi Matthee, "Exotic Substances: The Introduction and Global Spread of Tobacco, Coffee, Cocoa, Tea, and Distilled Liquor, Sixteenth to Eighteenth Centuries," in *Drugs and Narcotics in History*, ed. Roy Porter and Mikuláš Teich (New York: Cambridge University Press, 1995), 24. The process is discussed in detail in David T. Courtwright, *Forces of Habit: Drugs and the Making of the Modern World* (Cambridge, MA: Harvard University Press, 2001).

38. Fernand Braudel, *Civilization and Capitalism, 15th–18th Century, Volume I. The Structures of Everyday Life—The Limits of the Possible* (New York: Harper and Row, 1981), 241–43. Braudel writes that neither "the Greeks nor the Romans" could have had "more than a primitive version" of distillation technology. The traditional view dates the discovery of alcohol to around 1,100 CE in southern Italy but it remains possible "there were stills in the West before the twelfth century."

39. See Braudel, *Civilization and Capitalism, 15th–18th Century, Volume I*, 243–47.

40. Jürgen Habermas, *The Structural Transformation of the Public Sphere—An Inquiry into a Category of Bourgeois Society* (Cambridge, MA: MIT Press, 1989), 32. Habermas on the same page also mentions beverages made with tea and chocolate.

41. Habermas, *The Structural Transformation of the Public Sphere*, 32–33.

42. Braudel, *Civilization and Capitalism, 15th–18th Century, Volume I*, 259. On the growing popularity of tea, coffee and chocolate in the diet of the eighteenth-century upper class, see Piero Camporesi, *Exotic Brew: The Art of Living in the Age of Enlightment* (Malden, MA: Blackwell Publishing, 1994).

43. Manthee, "Exotic Substances: The Introduction and Global Spread of Tobacco, Coffee, Cocoa, Tea, and Distilled Liquor, Sixteenth to Eighteenth Centuries," 25.

44. Matthee, "Exotic Substances: The Introduction and Global Spread of Tobacco, Coffee, Cocoa, Tea, and Distilled Liquor, Sixteenth to Eighteenth Centuries," 24–51 contains a good discussion.

45. Medicinal use: brandy was regarded as a virtual panacea, particularly for "plague, gout, and loss of voice," tea was believed to be an excellent remedy for "colds, scurvy, and fevers," chocolate was said to cure difficulties of the spleen, and coffee for a great many ills, in an anonymous tract from 1671 titled *Usage du caphe, du the et du chocolate* listing scabies and impurity of the blood, weakness of heart, stomach ache and loss of appetite, and "extraordinary relief after over-eating or over-drinking." See Braudel, *Civilization and Capitalism, 15th–18th Century, Volume I*, 242, 249, 252, 257.

46. Habermas notes that in 1674, before the popularity of coffee had really taken off, "there appeared a pamphlet, 'The Women's Petition against Coffee, representing to Public Consideration of the Grand Inconveniences according to their Sex from the Excessive use of that Drying, Enfeebling Liquor.'" See Habermas, *The Structural Transformation of the Public Sphere*, 257 n. 11.

47. Braudel, *Civilization and Capitalism, 15th–18th Century, Volume I*, 242.

48. Braudel, *Civilization and Capitalism, 15th–18th Century, Volume I*, 256. The quote is talking specifically about the question of one substance, coffee, in two particular locations, Cairo and Istanbul, but when one examines the entirety of his discussion it is clear that Braudel believes this pattern to be true of many, if not most, of the substances he discusses and accurate for Europe as a whole.

49. Braudel's meandering discussion of the substances he calls the "new luxuries" is uneven and theoretically unfocused. The most detailed case in favor of this process is presented for tobacco but is implicit or explicit, in varying degrees, in his accounts of several other substances. See Braudel, *Civilization and Capitalism, 15th–18th Century, Volume I*, 262–65 for the discussion of tobacco.

50. Braudel, *Civilization and Capitalism, 15th–18th Century, Volume I*, 247, 252, 260. Interestingly in the wake of the collapse of the American economy in 2008, discussion of a taxed and regulated marijuana industry capable of generating billions arose in several states as a potential measure to ease state budget shortfalls.

51. Rabinow, *The Foucault Reader*, 356.

52. Rabinow, *The Foucault Reader*, 357.

53. In contrast to the viewpoint of law enforcement, contemporary medico-scientific discourse, as I will discuss below, treats recreational drug use as a problem of epidemiology, the study of factors affecting the health or illnesses of populations. See Charles Neuhaus, "The Disease Controversy Revisited: An Ontologic Perspective," *The Journal of Drug Issues* 23, no. 3 (1991): 463–78, Glenn D. Walters, *The Addiction Concept: Working Hypothesis or Self-Fulfilling Prophecy?* (Needham Heights, MA: Allyn & Bacon, 1999), and Helen Keane, *What's Wrong with Addiction?* (Melbourne, Australia: Melbourne University Press, 2002).

54. Richard Evans Schultes and Albert Hofmann, *Plants of the Gods—Their Sacred, Healing and Hallucinogenic Powers* (Rochester, VT: Healing Arts Press, 1992), 177.

55. Figures such as Rush, Beecher, and Parsons mark a "bridge between moral and medical conceptions of chronic drunkenness." See William L. White, "The Lessons of

Language: Historical Perspectives on the Rhetoric of Addiction," in *Altering American Consciousness: The History of Alcohol and Drug Use in the United States, 1800–2000*, ed. Sarah W. Tracy and Caroline Jean Acker (Amherst, MA: The University of Massachusetts Press, 2004), 34. See also William L. White, "Addiction as a Disease: Birth of a Concept," *Counselor* 1, no. 1 (2000): 46–51, 73.

56. Mary Gregor, trans. *Immanuel Kant—The Metaphysics of Morals* (New York: Cambridge University Press, 1996), 180-81. See the discussion of Kant's views of drug use in David Richards, *Sex, Drugs, Death and the Law: An Essay on Human Rights and Overcriminalization* (Totowa, NJ: Rowman and Littlefield, 1986), 173.

57. Richards, *Sex, Drugs, Death and the Law*, 173–74.

58. Derrida, *Dissemination*, 99. Kantian views about drugs, it may be argued, inform the pages of medical and public health journals such as the *American Journal of Mental Hygiene*, whose editors and leading contributors, from roughly 1880 onward, were partially responsible for such early American drug legislation as the Pure Food and Drug Act of 1906 and the Harrison Narcotics Act of 1914.

59. The German pharmacist Friedrich Wilhelm Sertürner first isolated morphine in 1804. He published his paper on the isolation of morphine from raw opium in 1817. The hypodermic needle dates to roughly 1853.

60. Although he is discussing the peasantry of pre-industrial Europe, the historian Piero Camporesi's observations are worth quoting here as they apply as much to ancient Greece as they do the time period he examines: "The culinary recipe, the sorcerer's 'compositions', the apothecary's prescription, the herbalist's unguent, and the ointment-sellers remedy all coincided, in practice, in this type of 'magical pharmacology', interpreted as the secret knowledge capable of rendering people healthy, invulnerable, and rich. Likewise, they overlapped in the constant, sleepless search for magical herbs and roots bestowing oblivion and ecstasy, in dreams and nocturnal diversions, witches' philters and necromantic potions." See Camporesi, *Bread of Dreams*, 20.

61. See, for example, David Courtwright, *Dark Paradise: A History of Opiate Addiction in the United States* (Cambridge, MA: Harvard University Press, 1982).

62. Quoted in Deborah Willis, "Doctor Faustus and the Early Modern Language of Addiction," in *Placing the Plays of Christopher Marlowe: Fresh Cultural Contexts*, ed. Sara Munson Deats and Robert A. Logan (Burlington, VT: Ashgate Publishing, 2008), 136 n. 4.

63. For a general introduction see Eva Bertram, Kenneth Sharpe and Peter Andreas, *Drug War Politics: The Price of Denial* (Berkeley, CA: University of California Press, 1996), 61–77. Another useful work is Timothy A. Hickman, *The Secret Leprosy of Modern Days: Narcotic Addiction and the Cultural Crisis of the United States, 1870–1920* (Amherst, MA: University of Massachusetts Press, 2007). I hope to examine this transformation in a future publication.

64. Stephen Lock, John M. Last and George Dunea, *The Oxford Illustrated Companion to Medicine* (New York: Oxford University Press, 2001), 786. White gives a somewhat different explanation, writing that addiction was "derived from the Latin *addicere*, meaning to adore or surrender oneself to a master." See White, "The Lessons of Language: Historical Perspectives on the Rhetoric of Addiction," 41.

65. Deborah Willis, "Doctor Faustus and the Early Modern Language of Addiction," in *Placing the Plays of Christopher Marlowe: Fresh Cultural Contexts*, ed. Sara Munson Deats and Robert A. Logan (Burlington, VT: Ashgate Publishing, 2008), 135.

66. Lock et al., *The Oxford Illustrated Companion to Medicine*, 786.

67. White, "The Lessons of Language: Historical Perspectives on the Rhetoric of Addiction," 41.

68. See, for example, Janet Farrell Brodie and Marc Redfield, *High Anxieties—Cultural Studies in Addiction* (Berkeley, CA: University of California Press, 2002).

69. Antonio Gramsci, *Selections from the Prison Notebooks* (New York: International Publishers, 1971), 279. This should not be mistaken as Gramsci arguing that the struggle between industrial society and the use of recreational drugs appeared out of nowhere in twentieth-century America. Cf. Krishan Kumar, *From Post-Industrial to Post-Modern Society: New Theories of the Contemporary World* (Malden, MA: Blackwell, 1995), 50–1.

70. Gramsci, *Selections from the Prison Notebooks*, 298.

71. Gramsci, *Selections from the Prison Notebooks*, 279.

72. Gramsci, *Selections from the Prison Notebooks*, 300.

73. Gramsci, *Selections from the Prison Notebooks*, 310.

74. Mike Davis, *Prisoners of the American Dream: Politics and Economy in the History of the US Working Class* (London: Verso, 1986), 22. This theme is examined in detail in John J. Rumbarger, *Profits, Power, and Prohibition: Alcohol Reform and the Industrializing of America* (Albany, NY: State University of New York Press, 1989). Taking breaks to drink alcohol were a staple of life in places of work in pre-industrial America.

75. See, for example, Foucault's views on the events of May 1968 in Rabinow, *The Foucault Reader*, 385–6.

76. See, for example, Manuel Castells, *The Rise of the Network Society. The Information Age: Economy, Society, and Culture, Volume I* (Malden, MA: Blackwell Publishing, 2000).

77. Marcia Landy, *Film, Politics, and Gramsci* (Minneapolis, MN: University of Minnesota Press, 1994), 234.

78. Landy, *Film, Politics, and Gramsci*, 234.

79. Landy, *Film, Politics, and Gramsci*, 234–5.

80. Landy, *Film, Politics, and Gramsci*, 234.

81. Seddon, *A History of Drugs*, 5.

82. Through, for example, massive foreign aid to drug-exporting nations (Columbia, etc.), military intervention within drug producing countries (Afghanistan, etc.), diplomacy and a dominant position within various international agencies that formulate or enact international drug strategies (United Nations, etc.).

83. Rabinow, *The Foucault Reader*, 382.

84. Rabinow, *The Foucault Reader*, 382.

85. Rabinow, *The Foucault Reader*, 382.

86. Rabinow, *The Foucault Reader*, 382. See also William E. Connolly, *Identity/Difference: Democratic Negotiations of Political Paradox, Expanded Edition* (Minneapolis, MN: University of Minnesota Press, 2002). The analogues in contemporary anti-drug discourse: "War on Drugs," "Just Say No," "Zero Tolerance," and so on, are obvious.

87. Jefferson Morley and Malcom Byrne, "The Drug War and 'National Security': The Making of a Quagmire, 1969–1973" *Dissent* 36, no. 1 (1989): 39.

88. Or as Richard Lawrence Miller, *Drug Warriors and their Prey: From Police Power to Police State*, (Westport, CT: Greenwood Publishing, 1996) frames the process: identification; ostracism; confiscation; concentration; annihilation.

89. See Bertram, et al., *Drug War Politics*, 4–5. Nixon both consolidated old federal drug bureaucracies and created new ones, like the DEA, and yet a commission chaired by Raymond Shafer, former Republican Governor of Pennsylvania, ultimately recommended decriminalization of possession and non-profit transfer of marijuana in early 1972. With-

out pressure from Nixon himself, the commission would have probably recommended legalization. Carter largely agreed with the findings of the Shafer Commission and toned down Oval Office anti-drug rhetoric but maintained, and even expanded, the anti-drug efforts begun by Nixon, particularly after 1978. The emphasis on punishment and incarceration became the norm and dramatically escalated during the "Just Say 'No'" Republican administrations that followed the Carter years. Marijuana arrests nearly doubled during Democrat Clinton's tenure in the 1990s and continued to increase during the next Republican administration.

90. Gary L. Fisher and Nancy A. Roget, *Encyclopedia of Substance Abuse Prevention, Treatment, and Recovery* (Thousand Oaks, CA: Sage Publications, 2009), 330. These increases have been abetted by hastily enacted legislation requiring "mandatory minimum" sentences for drug convictions, something that has continually drawn fire from some segments of the judiciary.

91. Susan Kang, "Forcing Prison Labor: International Labor Standards, Human Rights and the Privatization of Prison Labor in the Contemporary United States," *New Political Science* 31, no. 2 (2009): 137–61. Kang observes that this is a symptom of neoliberal ideology, one that gives private companies "access to a low-wage, disciplined labor force without the added costs of overseas production."

92. Mike Davis, *City of Quartz—Excavating the Future in Los Angeles* (New York: Vintage Books, 1992), 267–322 discusses the particularly brutal war waged between the Los Angeles police and the minority community over "crack" cocaine in the mid–1980s. In many instances a drug law conviction is a felony, and felons often lose their right to vote. This, as many critics of drug laws have pointed, out has led to *de facto* disenfranchisement, especially of African Americans. For a wider historical and legal perspective see Doris Marie Provine, *Unequal Under the Law: Race in the War on Drugs* (Chicago: University of Chicago Press, 2007).

93. According to Radley Balko, *Overkill: The Rise of Paramilitary Police Raids in America* (Washington, DC: CATO Institute, 2006) the number has risen to approximately 40,000 annually.

94. Asset forfeiture laws turn the traditional legal presumption of innocence on its head. Under these laws, continually upheld by the courts, the state may seize property and hold it without due process, it being the responsibility of the individual to prove the "innocence" of the seizure, i.e. they must mount an expensive legal challenge to prove the acquisitions of the material was not "drug-related." Few can afford to do so. Frequently these items are sold at auction, the earnings often used to finance additional raids and seizures. A brief discussion of this policy, which has outraged civil libertarians, may be found in Fred Leavitt, *The Real Drug Abusers* (Lanham, MD: Rowman and Littlefield, 2003), 151–52. For a detailed discussion of how these laws work see Stefan D. Cassella, *Asset Forfeiture Law in the United States* (Huntington, NY: Juris Net, 2007).

95. Nixon's linking of communism, the counter-culture, and recreational drug use, for example, is blatantly evident in recently declassified Oval Office tapes from 1971 and 1972. Kevin Zeese, "Nixon Tapes Show Roots of Marijuana Prohibition: Misinformation, Culture Wars, and Prejudice," *Common Sense for Drug Policy Research Report* (March 2002): 1–6. (accessed December 31, 2009 at www.csdp.org/research/shafernixon.pdf). Martin H. Levinson, *The Drug Problem: A New View Using the General Semantics Approach* (Westport, CT: Praeger Publishing, 2002), 187 writes that federal antidrug ads began linking drugs with terrorism within months of the attacks of September 11, 2001. A more detailed discussion may be found in Larry N. George "American Insecurities and the Ontopolitics of US Pharmacotic Wars," in *The Geopolitics of Ameri-*

can Insecurity: Terror, Power and Foreign Policy, ed. Francois Debrix and Mark J. Lacy (New York: Routledge, 2009), 34–53.

96. See Mike Gray, ed. *Busted: Cowboys, Narco-Lords, and Washington's War on Drugs* (New York: Nation Books, 2002).

97. The term was apparently coined in 1973 by Michael Sonnenreich, director of Nixon's National Commission of Marijuana Drug Abuse. He noted that the federal anti-drug effort had in the course of four years increased from $66 to $796 million, and was fast approaching the $1 billion mark. "When we do so, we become, for want of a better term, a drug abuse industrial complex." Quoted in James P. Gray, *Why Our Drug Laws Have Failed and What We Can Do About It: A Judicial Indictment of the War on Drugs* (Philadelphia, PA: Temple University Press, 2001), 42. In 2000 the figure was $19.2 billion.

98. Established in 1988 by the Anti-Drug Abuse Act in order to establish priorities, objectives, and policies for what some critics now call the nation's "narco-industrial complex," the budget and staff of the ONDCP—a Cabinet level component of the Executive Office of the President of the United States—have been scaled back in recent years, thanks in part to the efforts of its critics. It has been a politicized agency since its beginning, leaving it more vulnerable than much larger agencies like the DEA or NIDA who have managed to avoid coming under the same scrutiny.

99. In a situation of irony Socrates himself would have appreciated, the Partnership for a Drug Free America for many years received millions of dollars worth of funding from major pharmaceutical, tobacco and alcohol corporations including American Brands (Jim Beam whisky), Philip Morris (Marlboro and Virginia Slims cigarettes, Miller beer), Anheuser Busch (Budweiser, Michelob, Busch beer), R.J. Reynolds (Camel, Salem, Winston cigarettes), as well as the pharmaceutical firms Bristol Meyers-Squibb, Merck & Company and Proctor & Gamble. The tobacco and alcohol contributions finally stopped in 1997; the contributions by corporate pharmaceuticals remain. See William N. Elwood, *Rhetoric in the War on Drugs: The Triumphs and Tragedies of Public Relations* (Westport, CT: Greenwood Publishing, 1994), Miller, *Drug Warriors and their Prey*, and Timothy Lynch, *After Prohibition: An Adult Approach to Drug Policies in the 21st Century* (Washington, DC: CATO Institute, 2000).

100. Kenneth J. Meir, *The Politics of Sin: Drugs, Alcohol and Public Policy* (New York: M. E. Sharpe, 1994), 49. According to the on-line almanac of the National Institute of Health (www.nih.gov/about/almanac/archive/1999/organization/nida/history.html), NIDA was established in 1974 as "the lead Federal agency for conducting basic, clinical, and epidemiological research to improve the understanding, treatment, and prevention of drug abuse and addiction and the health consequences of these behaviors."

101. Gramsci, *Selections from the Prison Notebooks*, 300.

102. On the drug Ecstasy see Jerome Beck and Marsha Rosenbaum, *Pursuit of Ecstasy: The MDMA Experience* (Albany, NY: State University of New York Press, 1994). I have chosen Ecstasy more for its street name than its actual "newness" as MDMA was first synthesized in 1912. As such it more properly belongs to the era that gave us heroin than the increasingly sophisticated recreational drugs that will almost certainly appear in the coming decades. The term "psyche delicacies" is taken from the title of Chris Kilham, *Psyche Delicacies: Coffee, Chocolate, Chiles, Kava, and Cannabis, and Why they are Good for You* (Emmaus, PA: Rodale, 2001).

103. See, for example, Franklin Truan, "Addiction as a Social Construction: A Post-Empirical View," *Journal of Psychology* 127, no. 5 (1993): 489–500.

104. According to John Booth Davies, *The Myth of Addiction* (Langhorne, PA: Harwood Academic Publishers, 1992), xi. See also Neuhaus, "The Disease Controversy Revisited," 463–78 and Walters, *The Addiction Concept*.

105. Davies, *The Myth of Addiction*, xi. See also Peter Cohen, *Cocaine Use in Amsterdam in Non-Deviant Subcultures* (Amsterdam, Netherlands: University of Amsterdam [Institute for Social Geography], 1989).

106. Ronald K. Siegel, *Intoxication: The Universal Drive for Mind-Altering Substances* (Rochester, VT: Park Street Press, 2005). A very early version of roughly the same position was articulated in Andrew Weil, *The Natural Mind: A New Way of Looking at Drugs and Higher Consciousness* (Boston: Houghton Mifflin, 1972).

107. It is "with music rather than words that drugs have found themselves expressed in the cultures of the West. The convergence of digital technologies and the popularity of Ecstasy produced a revolution in dance music which did nothing to directly challenge the discourse on drugs, but did provide a striking and powerful alternative to all attempts to represent the drug experience. Dance music neither argues nor describes. It adopts no position and makes no case, but simply intensifies and extends the effect of the drugs which have inspired it." Quoted in Sadie Plant, "Writing on Drugs," in *Culture and Power: Challenging Discourses*, ed. Maria José Coperías Aguilar (València, Spain: Universitat de València, 2000), 10.

108. Rabinow, *The Foucault Reader*, 349.

109. Rabinow, *The Foucault Reader*, 350.

110. Rabinow, *The Foucault Reader*, 350.

111. David Lenson, *On Drugs* (Minneapolis, MN: University of Minnesota Press, 1995) is a good introduction. For a more theoretical view see Dave Boothroyd, *Culture on Drugs: Narco-Cultural Studies of High Modernity* Manchester, UK: University of Manchester Press, 2007). For the legal perspective see David Richards, *Sex, Drugs, Death and the Law: An Essay on Human Rights and Overcriminalization* (Totowa, NJ: Rowman and Littlefield, 1986): 157–214.

112. Indeed, an entire book could be devoted to the current absurdities and modern-day "witch hunts," media and otherwise, surrounding each of these other drug issues.

113. See, for example, Nick Bromell, "Just Say Think About It: The New Cultural Assent to Drug Use and Abuse," *The Chronicle of Higher Education*, June 15, 2001: B18–19. See also the chapter titled "Waking Dreams—Drugs in the Future," in Siegal, *Intoxication*, 295–313.

Bibliography

Ackerknecht, Erwin H. *History and Geography of the Most Important Diseases*. New York: Hafner Publishing Company, 1965.

Adkins, A. W. H. "Clouds, Mysteries, Socrates and Plato." *Antichthon* 4 (1970): 13–24.

———. "Myth, Philosophy and Religion in Ancient Greece." Pg. 95–130 in *Myth and Philosophy*, eds. Frank Reynolds and David Tracy. Albany, NY: State University of New York Press, 1990.

Adorno, Theodor and Max Horkheimer. *Dialectic of Enlightenment—Philosophical Fragments*. Translated by John Cumming. New York: Continuum, 1972.

———. *Dialectic of Enlightenment—Philosophical Fragments*. Edited by Gunzelin Schmid Noerr. Translated by Edmund Jephcott. Palo Alto, CA: Stanford University Press, 2002.

Aguilar, Maria Jose Coperias, ed. *Culture and Power: Challenging Discourses*. València, Spain: Universitat de València, 2000.

Ahbel-Rappe, Sara, and Rachana Kamtekar, eds. *A Companion to Socrates*. Malden, MA: Blackwell Publishing, 2006.

Ahrensdorf, Peter J. "The Question of the Historical Context and the Study of Plato." *Polity* 27, no. 1 (1994): 113–35.

Alcock, Joan P. *Food in the Ancient World*. Westport, CT: Greenwood Press, 2006.

Alexander, Anna and Mark S. Roberts, eds. *High Culture: Reflections on Addiction and Modernity*. Albany, NY: State University of New York Press, 2003.

Allen, Danielle S. *The World of Prometheus: The Politics of Punishing in Democratic Athens*. Princeton, NJ: Princeton University Press, 2000.

Alliez, Eric. "Ontology and Logography: The Pharmacy, Plato, and the Simulacrum." Pp. 84–97 in *Between Deleuze and Derrida*, edited by Paul Patton and John Protevi. New York and London: Continuum, 2000.

Allison, David. *Reading the New Nietzsche*. Lanham, MD: Rowman and Littlefield, 2001.

———. "Nietzsche's Dionysian High: Morphin' with Endorphins." Pp. 45–58 in *High Culture: Reflections on Addiction and Modernity*, edited by Anne Alexander and Mark S. Roberts. Albany, NY: State University of New York Press, 2003.

Althusser, Louis. *Lenin and Philosophy and Other Essays*. New York: Monthly Review Press, 2001.

Amundsen, Darrel W. and Gary B. Ferngren. "Evolution of the Patient-Physician Relationship: Antiquity Through the Renaissance." Pp. 3–46 in *The Clinical Encounter:*

The Moral Fabric of the Patient-Physician Relationship, edited by Earl E. Shelp. Hingham, MA: Kluwer Academic Publishing, 1983.

Angus, Samual. *Mystery Religions and Christianity*. New Hyde Park, NY: University Books, 1966.

Ankarloo, Bengt and Stuart Clark, eds. *Witchcraft and Magic in Europe: Ancient Greece and Rome*. Philadelphia, PA: University of Pennsylvania Press, 1999.

Anton, John P. "Some Dionysiac References in the Platonic Dialogues." *The Classical Journal* 58, no. 2 (1962): 49–55.

———. "Dialectic and Health in Plato's *Gorgias*: Presuppositions and Implications." *Ancient Philosophy* 1, no. 1 (1980): 49–60.

Anttila, Raimo. *Greek and Indo-European Etymology in Action: Proto-Indo-European *ag-*. Philadelphia: John Benjamins, 2000.

Archer-Hind, R. D., trans. *The Timaeus of Plato*. New York: Arno Press, 1973.

Arendt, Hannah. *Between Past and Future*. New York: Penguin Books, 2006.

Artamanov. M. I. "Frozen Tombs of the Scythians." *Scientific American* 212 (1965): 101–9.

Arthur, Marylin. "Politics and Pomegranates: An Interpretation of the Homeric Hymn to Demeter." *Arethusa* 10, no. 1 (1977): 7–47.

Austin, M. M. and P. Vidal Naquet. *The Economic and Social History of Ancient Greece*. Berkeley, Los Angeles: University of California Press, 1977.

Baker, Herbert G. *Plants and Civilization, Second Edition*. Belmont, CA: Wadsworth Publishing Co., 1970.

Balko, Radley. *Overkill: The Rise of Paramilitary Police Raids in America*. Washington, DC: CATO Institute, 2006.

Barker, Graeme. *The Agricultural Revolution in Prehistory—Why did Foragers become Farmers?* Oxford: Oxford University Press, 2006.

Barnes, Jonathan, ed. *The Complete Works of Aristotle—The Revised Oxford Translation* (Vols. 1 & 2). Princeton, NJ: Princeton University Press, 1984.

Barnhart, Robert K. *The Barnhart Concise Dictionary of Etymology*. New York: Harper Collins, 1995.

Barrett, Michele. *The Politics of Truth: From Marx to Foucault*. Palo Alto, CA: Stanford University Press, 1991.

Bauman, Richard A. *Political Trials in Ancient Greece*. New York and London: Routledge, 1990.

Beck, Jerome and Marsha Rosenbaum. *Pursuit of Ecstasy: The MDMA Experience*. Albany, NY: State University of New York Press, 1994.

Behr, C. A., trans. *Aristides—Panathenaic Oration and In Defense of Oratory*. Cambridge, MA: Harvard University Press, 1928.

Belfiore, Elizabeth. "Elenchus, Epode, and Magic: Socrates and Silenus." *Phoenix* 34, no. 2 (1980): 128–37.

———. "Plato's Greatest Accusation Against Poetry." *Canadian Journal of Philosophy* 9 (1983): 39–62.

———. "A Theory of Imitation in Plato's *Republic*." *Transactions of the American Philological Association* 114 (1983): 121–46.

———. "'Lies Unlike the Truth': Plato on Hesiod, *Theogny* 27." *Transactions of the American Philological Association* 115 (1985): 47–57.

———. "Wine and Catharsis of the Emotions in Plato's *Laws*." *Classical Quarterly* 36, no. 2 (1986): 421–37.

Bell, Jeffrey A. *Philosophy at the Edge of Chaos: Gilles Deleuze and the Philosophy of Difference*. Toronto: University of Toronto Press, 2006.

Benjamin, Andrew E., ed. *Post-Structuralist Classics*. New York and London: Routledge, 1988.

Bérard, Claude, Christiane Bron, Jean-Louis Durand, Francoise Frontisi-Ducroux, François Lissarrgue, Alain Schnapp, and Jean-Paul Vernant, eds. *A City of Images— Iconography and Society in Ancient Greece*. Translated by Deborah Lyons. Princeton, NJ: Princeton University Press, 1989.

Bérard, Claude. "The Order of Women." Pp. 89–108 in *A City of Images—Iconography and Society in Ancient Greece*, edited by Claude Bérard. Princeton, NJ: Princeton University Press, 1989.

———. "Festivals and Mysteries." Pp. 109–120 in *A City of Images—Iconography and Society in Ancient Greece*, edited by Claude Bérard. Princeton, NJ: Princeton University Press, 1989.

Bérard, Claude, and Christiane Bron. "Satyric Revels." Pp. 131–150 in *A City of Images—Iconography and Society in Ancient Greece*, edited by Claude Bérard. Princeton, NJ: Princeton University Press, 1989.

Berman, Scott. "How Polus Was Refuted: Reconsidering Plato's *Gorgias* 474c–475c." *Ancient Philosophy* 11, no. 2 (1991): 265–84.

———. "Socrates and Callicles on Pleasure." *Phronesis* 36 (1991): 117–40.

Bertram, Eva, Kenneth Sharpe and Peter Andreas. *Drug War Politics: The Price of Denial*. Berkeley and Los Angeles: University of California Press, 2006.

Betz, Hans Dieter. "Magic and Mystery in the Greek Magical Papyri." Pp. 244–59 in *Magika Hiera: Ancient Greek Magic and Religion*, edited by Christopher A. Faraone and Dirk Obbink. New York: Oxford University Press, 1991.

———. *The Greek Magical Papyri in Translation, Including the Demotic Spells*. Second Edition. Chicago: University of Chicago Press, 1992.

Bianchi, Ugo. *The Greek Mysteries*. Leiden, Netherlands: E. J. Brill, 1976.

Bishop, Louise M. *Words, Stones, and Herbs: The Healing Word in Medieval and Early Modern England*. Syracuse, NY: Syracuse University Press, 2007.

Bittlestone, Robert. *Odysseus Unbound—The Search for Homer's Ithaca*. Cambridge: Cambridge University Press, 2005.

Blackman, Shane. *Chilling Out: The Cultural Politics of Substance Consumption, Youth and Drug Policy*. Berkshire, England: McGraw Hill/Open University Press, 2004.

Bloom, Alan. *The Republic of Plato. Translation with Notes and an Interpretive Essay*. New York: Basic Books, 1987.

———. "Ion." Pp. 356–70 in *The Roots of Political Philosophy: Ten Forgotten Socratic Dialogues. Translated with Interpretive Studies*, edited by Thomas L. Pangle. Ithaca, NY: Cornell University Press, 1987.

Bloomfield, Morton W. "Poetry in Early Societies." *Proceedings of the American Philosophical Society* 130, no. 2 (1986): 247–50.

Boardman, John, Jasper Griffin, and Oswyn Murray, eds. *Greece and the Hellenistic World*. New York: Oxford University Press, 1988.

Bobonich, Christopher. "Persuasion, Compulsion and Freedom in Plato's *Laws*." *Classical Quarterly* 42, no. 2 (1991): 365–88.

Booth, Martin. *Cannabis: A History*. New York: St. Martin's Press, 2003.

Boothroyd, Dave. *Culture on Drugs: Narco-Cultural Studies of High Modernity*. Manchester, UK: University of Manchester Press, 2007.

Bowden, Hugh. *Classical Athens and the Delphic Oracle: Divination and Democracy*. New York: Cambridge University Press, 2005.

Bowie, A. M. *Aristophanes—Myth, Ritual and Comedy*. New York: Cambridge University Press, 1993.

——. "Thinking with Drinking: Wine and the Symposium in Aristophanes." *Journal of Hellenic Studies* 117 (1997): 1–21.

Bowra, Cecil Maurice. *Pindar*. Oxford: Clarendon Press, 1964.

Boyne, Roy. *Foucault and Derrida: The Other Side of Reason*. New York: Routledge, 1990.

Brandwood, Leonard. *A Word Index to Plato*. Leeds, UK: W. S. Maney and Son, 1976.

Braudel, Fernand. *Civilization and Capitalism, 15th–18th Century, Volume I. The Structures of Everyday Life—The Limits of the Possible*. Translated by Sian Reynolds. New York: Harper and Row, 1981.

Braund, Susanna and Glenn W. Most, eds. *Ancient Anger—Perspectives from Homer to Galen*. New York: Cambridge University Press, 2003.

Bremmer, Jan N. "Scapegoat Rituals in Ancient Greece." *Harvard Studies in Classical Philology* 87 (1983): 299–320.

Brickhouse, Thomas C. and Nicolas D. Smith. *Socrates on Trial*. Princeton, NJ: Princeton University Press, 1989.

——. *Plato's Socrates*. New York: Oxford University Press, 1994.

Brittlestone, Robert, with James Diggle and John Underhill. *Odysseus Unbound: The Search for Homer's Ithaca*. New York: Cambridge University Press, 2005.

Broad, William J. *The Oracle: Ancient Delphi and the Science Behind Its Lost Secrets*. New York: Penguin Books, 2007.

Brodie, Janet Farrell and Marc Redfield, eds. *High Anxieties—Cultural Studies in Addiction*. Berkeley, CA: University of California Press.

Bromell, Nick. "Just Say Think About It: The New Cultural Assent to Drug Use and Abuse." *The Chronicle of Higher Education* June 15 (2001): B18–19.

Brown, A. D. Fitton. "Black Wine." *The Classical Review* 12, no. 3 (1962): 192–95.

Brown, Christopher. "Empousa, Dionysus and the Mysteries: Aristophanes' Frogs 285ff." *Classical Quarterly* 41, no. 1 (1991): 41–50.

Brown, Theodore W. "Descartes, Dualism, and Psychosomatic Medicine." Pp. 29–30 in *The Anatomy of Madness: Essays in the History of Psychiatry. Volume 1: People and Ideas*, edited by W. F. Bynum, Roy Porter, and Michael Shepard. New York: Routledge, 1985.

Brown, William L. *An Address on Inebriety amongst the Ancients and How they 'Cured' It*. London: Aberdeen University Press, 1898.

Browning, G. K. "Ethical Absolutism in Plato and Hegel." *History of Political Thought* 12, no. 3 (1991): 391–404.

Bruell, Christopher. "On Plato's Political Philosophy." *Review of Politics* 56, no. 2 (1994): 261–82.

Bryant, Joseph M. "Intellectuals and Religion in Ancient Greece. Notes on a Weberian Theme." *The British Journal of Sociology* 37, no. 2 (1986): 269–96.

——. "Enlightenment Psychology and Political Reaction in Plato's Social Philosophy: An Ideological Contradiction?" *History of Political Thought* 11, no. 3 (1990): 377–95.

——. *Moral Codes and Social Structures in Ancient Greece: A Sociology of Greek Ethics from Homer to the Epicureans and Stoics*. Albany, NY: State University of New York Press, 1996.

Bundrick, Sheramy D. *Music and Image in Classical Athens*. New York: Cambridge University Press, 2005.

Burkert, Walter. *Orphism and Bacchic Mysteries: New Evidence and Old Problems*. Berkeley, CA: Center for Hermeneutical Studies in Hellenistic and Modern Culture, 1977.

————. *Homo Necans—The Anthropology of Ancient Greek Sacrificial Ritual and Myth.* Translated by Peter Bing. Berkeley, CA: University of California Press, 1983.

————. *Greek Religion: Archaic and Classical.* Malden, MA: Blackwell Publishing, 1985.

————. *Ancient Mystery Cults.* Cambridge, MA: Harvard University Press, 1987.

————. *The Orientalizing Revolution—Near Eastern Influences on Greek Culture in the Early Archaic Age.* Cambridge, MA: Harvard University Press, 1992.

Burnet, John. *Greek Philosophy: Thales to Plato.* London: Macmillan and Company, 1962.

Bury, R. G. *Plato—Laws in Two Volumes.* Cambridge, MA: Harvard University Press, 1926.

Calhoun, George Miller. *Athenian Clubs in Politics and Litigation.* Austin, TX: The University of Texas Bulletin, 1913.

Campbell, Joseph. *The Masks of God: Occidental Mythology.* New York: The Viking Press, 1964.

Camporesi, Piero. *The Incorruptible Flesh: Bodily Mutilation and Mortification in Religion and Folklore.* Translated by Tania Croft-Murray. New York: Cambridge University Press, 1988.

————. *Bread of Dreams—Food and Fantasy in Early Modern Europe.* Translated by David Gentilcore. Chicago: University of Chicago Press, 1989.

————. *Exotic Brew: The Art of Living in the Age of Enlightenment.* Malden, MA: Blackwell Publishing, 1994.

Carmola, Kateri. "Noble Lying: Justice and Intergenerational Tension in Plato's *Republic.*" *Political Theory* 31, no. 1 (2003): 39–62.

Carney, Elizabeth. *Olympias—Mother of Alexander the Great.* New York: Routledge, 2006.

Carrick, Paul. *Medical Ethics in the Ancient World.* Washington, DC: Georgetown University Press, 2001.

Cartledge, Paul. *The Greeks—A Portrait of Self and Others.* New York: Oxford University Press, 1993.

————. "'Deep Plays'—Theatre as a Process in Greek Civil Life." Pp. 3–35 in *The Cambridge Companion to Greek Tragedy,* edited by P. E. Easterling. New York: Cambridge University Press, 1997.

Cartledge, Paul, Paul Millett, and Stephen Todd, eds. *Nomos: Essays in Athenian Law, Politics, and Society.* New York: Cambridge University Press, 1990.

Cassella, Stephan D. *Asset Forfeiture Law in the United States.* Huntington, New York: Juris Net, 2007.

Castells, Manuel. *The Rise of the Network Society. The Information Economy, Society, and Culture, Volume 1.* Malden, MA: Blackwell Publishing, 2000.

Cavanaugh, Maureen B. *Eleusis and Athens—Documents in Finance, Religion, and Politics in the Fifth Century B.C.* New York: Oxford University Press, 2000.

Chadwick, Henry, trans. *Saint Augustine—Confessions.* New York: Oxford University Press, 1991.

Clark, Matthew C. and Eric Csapo. "Deconstruction, Ideology and Goldhill's Oresteia." *Pheonix* 45, no. 2 (1991): 95–125.

Clark, Randall B. *The Law Most Beautiful and Best: Medical Argument and Magical Rhetoric in Plato's Laws.* Lanham, MD: Lexington Books, 2003.

Clauss, James J. and Sarah Iles Johnson, eds. *Medea: Essays on Medea in Myth, Literature, Philosophy, and Art.* Princeton, NJ: Princeton University Press, 1997.

Cline, Eric H. *Sailing the Wine-Dark Sea: International Trade and the Late Bronze Age Aegean.* Oxford, UK: Tempus Reparatum, 1994.

Clinton, Kevin. "The Sacred Officials of the Eleusinian Mysteries." *Transactions of the American Philosophical Society* 64, no. 3 (1974): 1–143.

Cobb, William S., trans. *The Symposium and Phaedrus: Plato's Erotic Dialogues*. Albany, NY: State University of New York Press, 1993.

Cohen, David. "Law, Autonomy, and Political Community in Plato's *Laws*." *Classical Philology* 88, no. 4 (1993): 301–17.

———. "Classical Rhetoric and Modern Theories of Discourse." Pp. 69–82 in *Persuasion: Greek Rhetoric in Action*, edited by Ian Worthington. New York: Routledge, 1994.

Cohen, Peter. *Cocaine Use in Amsterdam in Non-Deviant Subcultures*. Amsterdam, Netherlands: University of Amsterdam, Institute for Social Geography, 1989.

Cohoon, J. W., trans. *Dio Chrysostom (Volumes 2 & 3)*. Cambridge, MA: Harvard University Press, 1932.

Cohoon, J. W., and H. Lamar Crosby, trans. *Dio Chrysostom, Discourses 31–36*. Cambridge, MA: Harvard University Press, 1940.

Cole, Susan Guettel. "New Evidence for the Mysteries of Dionysus." *Greek, Roman and Byzantine Studies* 21, no. 3 (1980): 223–38.

Collins, Christopher. *Reading the Written Image: Verbal Play, Interpretation and the Roots of Iconophobia*. University Park, PA: Penn State Press, 2008.

Conley, Thomas M. *Rhetoric in the European Tradition*. Chicago: University of Chicago Press, 1990.

Connolly, Joy. 2007. *The State of Speech: Rhetoric and Political Thought in Ancient Rome*. Princeton, NJ: Princeton University Press, 2007.

Connolly, William E. "Beyond Good and Evil—The Ethical Sensibility of Michel Foucault." *Political Theory* 21, no. 3 (1993): 365–389.

———. *The Augustinian Imperative: A Reflection on the Politics of Morality*. London: Sage, 1993.

———. *Identity/Difference: Democratic Negotiations of Political Paradox*. Expanded Edition. Minneapolis, MN: University of Minnesota Press, 2002.

Conrad, Barnaby. *Absinthe—History in a Bottle*. San Francisco: Chronicle Books, 1988.

Conrad, Lawrence I., Michael Neve, Vivian Nutton, Roy Porter, and Andrew Wear. *The Western Medical Tradition—800 BC to AD 1800*. New York: Cambridge University Press, 1995.

Constantinou, Costas M. *States of Political Discourse: Words, Regimes, Seditions*. New York: Routledge, 2004.

Cook, Christopher H. *Alcohol, Addiction and Christian Ethics*. New York: Cambridge University Press, 2006.

Cooke, Albert. "Equanimity and Danger: Distribution of Questions and Style of Confrontation in the Four Dialogues Around Socrates' Trial." *Arethusa* 23, no. 2 (1990): 255–79.

Coolidge, Francis P. "The Relation of Philosophy to *Sophrosyne*: Zalmoxian Medicine in Plato's *Charmides*." *Ancient Philosophy* 13, no. 1 (1993): 23–36.

Corrigan, Kevin and Elena Glazov-Corrigan. *Plato's Dialectic at Play: Argument, Structure, and Myth in the Symposium*. University Park, PA: Penn State Press, 2004.

Coulter, Harris L. *Divided Legacy—A History of the Schism in Medical Thought. Volume I—The Pattern Emerges: Hippocrates to Paracelsus*. Washington, DC: Wehawken Book Company, 1973.

———. *Divided Legacy—A History of the Schism in Medical Thought. Volume III—Science and Ethics in American Medicine 1800–1914*. Washington, DC: Wehawken Book Company, 1973.

Couprie, Dirk L., Robert Hahn and Gerard Naddaf. *Anaximander in Context: New Studies on the Origins of Greek Philosophy.* Albany, NY: State University of New York Press, 2003.

Courtwright, David T. *Dark Paradise: A History of Opiate Addiction in America.* Cambridge, MA: Harvard University Press, 1982.

———. *Forces of Habit: Drugs and the Making of the Modern World.* Cambridge, MA: Harvard University Press, 2001.

Coveny, John. *Food, Morals, and Meaning: The Pleasure and Anxiety of Eating.* New York: Routledge, 2000.

Craik, Elizabeth. "Diet, *Diaita* and Dietetics." Pp. 387–402 in *The Greek World*, edited by Anton Powell. New York: Routledge, 1995.

Crane, Eva. *The World History of Beekeeping and Honey Hunting.* New York: Routledge, 1999.

Culler, Jonathan D. 2003. *Deconstruction: Critical Concepts in Literary and Cultural Studies, Volume 1.* New York: Routledge, 2003.

Cuomo, Serafina. *Technology and Culture in Greek and Roman Antiquity.* New York: Cambridge University Press, 2007.

Cushman, Robert E. *Therapeia—Plato's Conception of Philosophy.* Chapel Hill, NC: The University of North Carolina Press, 1958.

Davenport-Hines, Richard. *The Pursuit of Oblivion: A Global History of Narcotics.* New York: W. W. Norton, 2004.

David, Ephraim. "The Spartan *syssitia* and Plato's *Laws*." *American Journal of Philology* 99, no. 4 (1978): 486–95.

———. "Laughter in Spartan Society." Pp. 1–25 in *Classical Sparta—Techniques Behind Her Success*, edited by Anton Powell. New York: Routledge, 1989.

Davidson, Donald. *Plato's Philebus* (Harvard Dissertations in Philosophy). New York: Garland Publishing, 1990.

Davidson, James. *Courtesans and Fishcakes: The Consuming Passions of Classical Athens.* New York: Harper Perennial, 1999.

Davies, John Booth. *The Myth of Addiction.* Langhorne, PA: Harwood Academic Publishers, 1992.

Davies, John Kenyon. *The Athenian Propertied Families 600–300 BC.* New York: Oxford University Press, 1971.

Davies, Mark I. "Sailing, Rowing, and Sporting in One's Cups on the Wine Dark Sea." Pp. 72–92 in *Athens Comes of Age: From Solon to Salamis*, edited by William A. P. Childs. Princeton, NJ: Princeton University Press, 1978.

Davis, Mike. *Prisoners of the American Dream: Politics and Economy in the History of the US Working Class.* London: Verso, 1986.

———. *City of Quartz—Excavating the Future in Los Angeles.* New York: Vintage Books, 1992.

Deleuze, Gilles and Paul Patton. *Difference and Repetition.* New York and London: Continuum International Publishing Group, 1994.

Demand, Nancy H. *Birth, Death, and Motherhood in Classical Greece.* Baltimore, MD: The Johns Hopkins University Press, 1994.

Denyer, Nicholas, ed. *Alcibiades.* New York: Cambridge University Press, 2001.

Derrida, Jacques. *Dissemination.* Translated with an Introduction and Additional Notes by Barbara Johnson. Chicago: University of Chicago Press, 1981.

———. "The Rhetoric of Drugs." Pp. 19–43 in *High Culture: Reflections on Addiction and Modernity*, edited by Anna Alexander and Mark S. Roberts. Albany, NY: State University of New York Press, 2003.

Detienne, Marcel. *Dionysos Slain*. Translated by Mireille and Leonard Muellner. Baltimore, MD: The Johns Hopkins University Press, 1979.

Dettling, A., H. Grass, A. Schuff, G. Skopp, P. Strohbeck-Kuehner, and H. Haffner, "Absinthe: Attention Performance and Mood under the Influence of Thujone." *Journal of Studies on Alcohol* 65, no. 5 (2004): 573–81.

Devereux, George. "Trance and Orgasm in Euripides' *Bacchae*." Pp. 36–51 in *Parapsychology and Anthropology*, edited by A. Angoff and D. Barth. New York: Parapsychology Foundation, 1974.

Dibble, Flint. *Magic, Drugs, and Magic Drugs: An Analysis of Artemisias, Wormwood, within the Greek Magical Papyri*. Senior Thesis, Department of Classics, University of Pennsylvania, 2004.

——. "Mind-Altering Support for Delphic Vapors." Unpublished paper, 2006.

——. "Magic, Drugs, and Magic Drugs: A Survey of Wormwood within the Papyri Graecae Magicae." Unpublished paper, 2008.

Dickie, Matthew W. *Magic and Magicians in the Greco-Roman World*. New York: Routledge, 2003.

Dillon, Matthew. *Girls and Women in Classical Greek Religion*. New York: Routledge, 2003.

Dillon, Matthew and Lynda Garland. *Ancient Greece: Social and Historical Documents from Archaic Times to the Death of Socrates, Second Edition*. New York: Routledge, 2000.

Dodds, E. R. "Plato and the Irrational." *Journal of Hellenic Studies* 65 (1945): 16–25.

——. *Plato—Gorgias*. A Revised Text with Introductions and Commentary. Oxford: Clarendon Press, 1959.

——. *Pagan and Christian in an Age of Anxiety*. New York: Cambridge University Press, 1965.

——. *The Greeks and the Irrational*. Berkeley, CA: University of California Press, 1968.

——. *The Ancient Concept of Progress*. New York: Oxford University Press, 1973.

Dombrowski, Daniel A. "On the Alleged Truth about Lies in Plato's Republic." *Polis—The Journal of the Society for Greek Political Thought* 21, no. 1 & 2 (2004): 93–106.

Dover, Kenneth J. "Portrait-Masks in Aristophanes." Pp. 266–78 in *Greek and the Greeks, Collected Papers, Volume 1: Language, Poetry, Drama*, edited by Kenneth J. Dover. New York: Basil Blackwell, 1987.

——. "Aristophanes' Speech in Plato's Symposium." Pp. 102–114 in *The Greeks and Their Legacy: Collected Papers, Volume II: Prose Literature, History, Society, Transmission, Influence*, edited by Kenneth J. Dover. New York: Basil Blackwell, 1988.

Dubois, Page. "Phallocentrism and Its Subversion in Plato's *Phaedrus*." *Arethusa* 18, no. 1 (1985): 91–103.

——. *Sappho is Burning*. Chicago: University of Chicago Pres, 1995.

Durand, Jean-Louis, Francoise Frontisi-Ducroux, and Francois Lissarrague. "Wine: Human and Divine." Pp. 121–30 in *A City of Images—Iconography and Society in Ancient Greece*, edited by Claude Bérard, Christiane Bron, Jean-Louis Durand, Francoise Frontisi-Ducroux, François Lissarrgue, Alain Schnapp, and Jean-Paul Vernant. Princeton, NJ: Princeton University Press, 1989.

Dyson, M. "Immortality and Procreation in Plato's Symposium." *Antichthon* 22 (1986): 59–72.

Edelstein, Ludwig. *Ancient Medicine: Selected Papers of Ludwig Edelstein*. Baltimore, MD: The Johns Hopkins University Press, 1967.

———. *The Idea of Progress in Classical Antiquity*. Baltimore, MD: The Johns Hopkins University Press, 1967.

Edmundson, Mark. *Literature against Philosophy: Plato to Derrida: A Defense of Poetry*. New York: Cambridge University Press, 1995.

Efron, Daniel, Bo Holmstedt and Nathan S. Kline, eds. *Ethno-Pharmacologic Search for Psychoactive Drugs*. New York: Raven Press, 1979.

Eijk, Philip J., trans. *Diocles of Carystus. A Collection of the Fragments with Translation and Commentary. Volume One: Text and Translation*. Leiden, Netherlands: E. J. Brill, 2000.

Eisler, Raine. *The Chalice and the Blade: Our History, Our Future*. San Francisco: Harper and Row, 1987.

Eliade, Mircea. *Shamanism: Archaic Techniques of Ecstasy*. Princeton, NJ: Princeton University Press, 1964.

Elliot, Lisa Marie. *Gendering the Production and Consumption of Wine and Olive Oil in Ancient Greece*. M. A. thesis, Miami University, 2006.

Ellis, Walter M. *Alcibiades*. New York: Routledge, 1989.

Elwood, William N. *Rhetoric in the War on Drugs: Triumphs and Tragedies of Public Relations*. Westport, CT: Greenwood Publishing, 1994.

Entralgo, Pedro Lain. *The Therapy of the World in the Ancient World*. Edited and translated by L. J. Rather and John M. Sharp. New Haven, CT: Yale University Press, 1970.

Euben, J. Peter. *The Tragedy of Political Theory—The Road Not Taken*. Westport, CT: Greenwood Publishing, 1990.

Evans, Arthur. *The God of Ecstasy—Sex Roles and the Madness of Dionysus*. New York: St. Martin's Press, 1988.

Eyer, Shawn. "Psychedelic Effects and the Eleusinian Mysteries." Pg. 65–94 in *Alexandria 2—The Journal of Western Cosmological Traditions*, edited by David Fideler. Grand Rapids, MI: Phanes Press, 1993.

Fagles, Robert, trans. *Homer—The Iliad*. New York: Penguin Books, 1990.

———. trans. *Homer—The Odyssey*. New York: Penguin Books, 1996.

Faraone, Christopher A. "The Agonistic Content of Early Binding Spells." Pp. 3–32 in *Magika Hiera—Ancient Greek Magic and Religion*, edited by Christopher A. Faraone and Dirk Obbink. New York: Oxford University Press, 1991.

———. *Ancient Greek Love Magic*. Cambridge, MA: Harvard University Press, 1999.

———. "Priestess and Courtesan: The Ambivalence of Female Leadership in Aristophanes' *Lysistrata*." Pp. 207–23 in *Prostitution and Courtesans in the Ancient World*. Madison, WI: The University of Wisconsin Press, 2006.

Faraone, Christopher A. and Laura McClure, eds. *Prostitutes and Courtesans in the Ancient World*. Madison, WI: University of Wisconsin Press, 2006.

Faraone, Christopher A. and Dirk Obbink, eds. *Magika Hiera—Ancient Greek Magic and Religion*. New York: Oxford University Press, 1991.

Farrell, Anne Mary. *Plato's Use of Eleusinian Mystery Motifs*. Ph. D. dissertation, University of Texas at Austin, 1999.

Feemster, Wilhelmina and Frederick G. Meyer. *The Natural History of Pompeii*. New York: Cambridge University Press, 2002.

Fideler, David, ed. *Alexandria 2—The Journal of the Western Cosmological Tradition*. Grand Rapids, MI: Phanes Press, 1993.

Figueira, Thomas and Gregory Nagy, ed. *Theognis of Megara—Poetry and the Polis*. Baltimore, MD: The Johns Hopkins University Press, 1985.

Fineburg, Stephen. "Plato's *Euthyphro* and the Myth of Proteus." *Transactions of the American Philological Association* 112 (1982): 65–70.

Flint, Valerie, I. *Witchcraft and Magic in Europe: Ancient Greece and Rome*. London: The Athlone Press, 1999.

Fisher, Gary L. and Nancy A. Roget. *Encyclopedia of Substance Abuse and Prevention, Treatment, and Recovery*. Thousand Oaks, CA: Sage Publications, 2009.

Fisher, Nick. "Drink, *Hybris* and Promotion of Harmony in Sparta." Pp. 26–50 in *Classical Sparta—Techniques Behind Her Success*, edited by Anton Powell. London: Routledge, 1988.

——. "The Law of *Hubris* in Athens." Pp. 123–38 in *Nomos—Essays in Athenian Law, Politics and Society*, edited by Paul Cartledge, Paul Millet and Stephen Todd. New York: Cambridge University Press, 1990.

——. "*Hybris*, Status, and Slavery." Pp. 44–84 in *The Greek World*, edited by Anton Powell. New York: Routledge, 1995.

Flower, Michael Attyah. *The Seer in Ancient Greece*. Berkeley, CA: University of California Press, 2008.

Fontenrose, Joseph. *The Delphic Oracle—Its Responses and Operations*. Berkeley, CA: University of California Press, 1978.

Forbes, R. J. *A Short History of Distillation*. Leiden, Netherlands: E. J. Brill, 1948.

——. "Chemical, Culinary, and Cosmetic Arts." Pp. 238–98 in *History of Technology, Volume 1—From Early Times to the Fall of Ancient Empires*, edited by Charles Singer and E. J. Holmyard. New York: Oxford University Press, 1954.

——. "Food and Drink." Pp. 106–46 in *A History of Technology, Volume 2—The Mediterranean Civilizations to the Middle Ages c. 700 BC—c. AD 1500*, edited by Charles Singer, E. J. Holmyard, A. R. Hall and Trevor I. Williams. New York: Oxford University Press, 1956.

——. *Studies in Ancient Technology, Volume 1*. Leiden, Netherlands: E. J. Brill, 1964.

——. *Studies in Ancient Technology, Volume 3*. Leiden, Netherlands: E. J. Brill, 1965.

Forsdyke, Sara. *Exile, Ostracism, and Democracy: The Politics of Expulsion in Ancient Greece*. Princeton, NJ: Princeton University Press, 2005.

Fortenbaugh, William W. and Robert W. Sharples, eds. *Theophrastean Studies on Natural Science, Physics and Metaphysics, Ethics, Religion and Rhetoric*. New Brunswick and Oxford: Transaction Books, 1988.

Fortenbaugh, William W., Robert W. Sharples, and Michael G. Sollenberger. *Theophrastus of Eresus. On Sweat, On Dizziness and On Fatigue*. Leiden, Netherlands: E. J. Brill, 2003.

Foucault, Michel. *Discipline and Punish: The Birth of the Prison*. Translated by Alan Sheridan. New York: Vintage Books, 1979.

——. *The Use of Pleasure. The History of Sexuality Volume 2*. Translated by Robert Hurley. New York: Vintage Books, 1986.

——. "About the Beginnings of the Hermeneutics of the Self—Two Lectures at Dartmouth." *Political Theory* 21, no. 2 (1979): 198–227.

——. *The Hermeneutics of the Subject—Lectures at the College de France 1981–1982*. Edited by Frederic Gros. Translated by Graham Burchell. New York: Picador, 2005.

——. *Security, Territory, Population—Lectures at the College de France 1977–1978*. Edited by Michel Senellart. Translated by Graham Burchell. New York: Picador, 2007.

——. *Psychiatric Power—Lectures at the College de France 1973–1974*. Edited by Jacques Lagrange. Translated by Graham Burchell. New York: Picador, 2008.

Frontisi-Ducroux, Francoise. "In the Mirror of the Mask." Pp. 151–66 in *A City of Images: Iconography and Society in Ancient Greece*, edited by Claude Bérard. Princeton, NJ: Princeton University Press, 1989.

Gagarin, M. "The Athenian Law against Hybris." Pp. 229–36 in *Arktouros: Hellenic Studies Presented to Bernard M. W. Knox*, edited by Glen W. Bowersock. Berlin and New York: Walter de Gruyter, 1979.

Gallop, David, trans. *Plato—Phaedo*. Oxford: Clarendon Press, 1975.

Garnsey, Peter. *Food and Society in Classical Antiquity*. New York: Cambridge University Press, 1999.

Gentili, Bruno. *Poetry and Its Public in Ancient Greece: From Homer to the Fifth Century*. Baltimore, MD: The Johns Hopkins University Press, 1988.

George, Larry N. "American Insecurities and the Ontopolitics of US Pharmacotic Wars." Pp. 34–53 in *The Geopolitics of American Insecurity: Terror, Power and Foreign Policy*, edited by François Debrix and Mark J. Lacy. New York: Routledge, 2009.

Gill, Christopher. "The Death of Socrates." *Classical Quarterly* 23 (1973): 25–8.

Godwin, Joscelyn. *Mystery Religions in the Ancient World*. London: Thames and Hudson, 1981.

Goff, Barbara E. *The Noose of Words—Readings of Desire, Violence, and Language in Euripides' Hippolytos*. New York: Cambridge University Press, 1990.

Golden, Leon. *Aristotle's Poetics—A Translation and Commentary for Students of Literature*. Englewood Cliffs, NJ: Prentice Hall, 1982.

Goldhill, Simon. "The Great Dionysia and Civic Ideology." *Journal of Hellenic Studies* 107 (1987): 58–76.

———. "The Audience of Athenian Tragedy." Pp. 54–68 in *The Cambridge Companion to Greek Tragedy*, edited by P. E. Easterling. New York: Cambridge University Press, 1997.

———. "Reading Differences: The *Odyssey* and Juxtaposition." Pp. 396–431 in *Homer: Critical Assessments. Volume 4—Homer's Art*, edited by Irene J. F. de Jong. New York: Routledge, 1999.

Gooch, Paul. "'Vice is Ignorance': The Interpretation of *Sophist* 226a–231b." *Phoenix* 25, no. 2 (1971): 124–33.

———. "Socrates: Devious or Devine?" *Greece and Rome* 32, no. 1 (1985): 32–41.

Gordon, Benjamin Lee. *Medicine throughout Antiquity*. Philadelphia, PA: F. A. Davis Company, 1949.

Gow, A. S. F. and A. F. Scholfied, eds. and trans. *Nicander—The Poems and Poetical Fragments*. New York: Cambridge University Press, 1953.

Graf, Fritz. "Prayer in Magic and Religious Ritual." Pp. 3–32 in *Magika Hiera—Ancient Greek Magic and Religion*, edited by Christopher Faraone and Dirk Obbink. New York: Oxford University Press, 1991.

Gramsci, Antonio. *Selections from the Prison Notebooks*. New York: International Publishers, 1971.

Graves, Robert. *Difficult Questions, Easy Answers*. London: Cassell and Company, 1971.

Gray, James P. *Why Our Drug Laws Have Failed and What We Can Do About It: A Judicial Indictment of the War on Drugs*. Philadelphia, PA: Temple University Press, 2001.

Gray, Mike, ed. *Busted: Cowboys, Narco-Lords and Washington's War on Drugs*. New York: Nation Books, 2002.

Gregor, Mary, trans. *Immanuel Kant—The Metaphysics of Morals*. New York: Cambridge University Press, 1996.

Gregory, Justina. "Some Aspects of Seeing in Euripides' Bacchae." *Greece and Rome* 32, no. 1 (1985): 23–31.

Grene, David and Richard Lattimore, eds. *The Complete Greek Tragedies—Euripides V.* Chicago: University of Chicago Press, 1969.

Griffith, Tom, trans. *Symposium of Plato.* Berkeley, CA: University of California Press, 1989.

Griffiths, F. T. "Poetry as *Pharmakon* in Theocritis' *Idyll* 2." Pp. 81–90 in *Arktouros: Hellenic Studies Presented to Bernard M. W. Knox*, edited by Glen W. Bowersock. Berlin and New York: Walter de Gruyter, 1979.

Griswold, Charles, Jr. *Self-knowledge in Plato's* Phaedrus. New Haven, CT: Yale University Press, 1986.

——. "Plato on Rhetoric and Poetry." *Stanford Encyclopedia of Philosophy.* 2007. http://plato.stanford.edu/entries/plato-rhetoric/ (accessed December 31, 2009).

Gulick, Charles Burton, trans. *Athenaeus—The Deipnosophists* (7 Volumes). New York: Cambridge University Press, 1951.

Gunnell, John G. *Political Philosophy and Time.* Middletown, CT: Wesleyan University Press, 1987.

Gunther, Robert T. *The Greek Herbal of Dioscorides.* New York: Hafner Publishing, 1959.

Guthrie, W. K. C., trans. *Plato—Protagoras and Meno.* New York: Penguin Books, 1956.

Habermas, Jürgen. *The Structural Transformation of the Public Sphere—An Inquiry into a Category of Bourgeois Society.* Translated by Thomas Burger with the assistance of Frederick Lawrence. Cambridge, MA: MIT Press, 1989.

Hackforth, R., trans. *Phaedrus: Introduction, Translation and Commentary.* New York: Cambridge University Press, 1952.

Haden, James. "Two Types of Power in Plato's *Gorgias*." *The Classical Journal* 87, no. 4 (1992): 313–26.

Hahn, Robert. *Anaximander and the Architects—The Contributions of Egyptian and Greek Architectural Technologies to the Origins of Greek Philosophy.* Albany, NY: State University of New York Press, 2001.

Halliday, W. R. *The Pagan Background of Early Christianity.* New York: Cooper Square Publishers, 1970.

Halliwell, Stephen. "Plato and Painting." Pp. 99–116 in *Word and Image in Ancient Greece*, edited by N. Keith Rutter and Brian A. Sparkes. Edinburgh, UK: Edinburgh University Press, 2000.

Halperin, David M. *Saint Foucault: Towards a Gay Hagiography.* New York: Oxford University Press, 1995.

Hamilton, Walter, trans. *Plato—Gorgias.* New York: Penguin Books, 1960.

——, trans. Plato—*Phaedrus and Seventh and Eight Letters.* New York: Penguin, 1973.

Hanson, Ann Ellis. "Papyri of Medical Content." *Yale Classical Studies* 28 (1985): 25–28.

Hanson, J. Arthur, trans. *Apuleius: Metamorphoses.* Volume 2 of 2. Cambridge, MA: Harvard University Press, 1989.

Harkins, Paul W., trans. *St. John Chrysostom: Baptismal Instructions.* New York and Ramsey, NJ: Newman Press, 1963.

Harris, William V. *Restraining Rage: The Ideology of Anger Control in Classical Antiquity.* Cambridge, MA: Harvard University Press, 2001.

Hartman, Margaret. "The Hesiodic Roots of Plato's Myth of the Metals." *Helios* 15, no. 2 (1988): 103–14.

Hartog, Francois. *The Mirror of Herodotus—The Representation of the Other in the Writing of History*. Berkeley, CA: University of California Press, 1988.

Havelock, Eric A. "The Socratic Self as it is Parodied in Aristophanes' *Clouds*." *Yale Classical Studies* 22 (1972): 1–18.

Hawhee, Debra. *Bodily Art: Rhetoric and Athletics in Ancient Greece*. Austin, TX: University of Texas Press, 2004.

Hawtrey, R. S. W. "Plato, Socrates and the Mysteries: A Note." *Anticthon* 10 (1976): 22–24.

Hayes, Antoinette N. and Steven G. Gilbert. "Historical Milestones and Discoveries that Shaped the Toxicology Sciences." Pp. 1–36 in *Molecular, Clinical and Environmental Toxicology. Volume 1: Molecular Toxicology (Experientia Supplementum)*, edited by Andreas Luch. Basel, Switzerland: Birkhäuser Verlag, 2008.

Healy, Robert F. *Eleusinian Sacrifices in the Athenian Law Code*. New York and London: Garland Publishing, 1990.

Heidegger, Martin. *Sojourns—The Journey to Greece*. Translated by John P. Manoussakis. Albany, NY: State University of New York Press, 2005.

Heilmeyer, Marina. *Ancient Herbs*. Los Angeles: J. Paul Getty Museum, 2007.

Heinrichs, Albert. "Changing Dionysiac Identities." Pp. 137–60 in *Jewish and Christian Self-Definition III: Self-Definition in the Graeco-Roman World*, edited by B. G. Meyer and P. Sanders. London: SCM Press, 1982.

——. "Loss of Self, Suffering, Violence: The Modern View of Dionysus from Nietzsche to Girard." *Harvard Studies in Classical Philology* 88: 205–40.

Henderson, Jeffrey. "Older Women in Attic Old Comedy." *Transactions of the American Philological Association* 117 (1987): 105–30.

Hesk, John. *Deception and Democracy in Classical Athens*. New York: Cambridge University Press, 2000.

Hett, Walter S., and H. Rackham, trans. *Aristotle—Problems. In Two Volumes*. Cambridge, MA: Harvard University Press, 1961.

Hickman, Timothy A. *The Secret Leprosy of Modern Days: Narcotic Addiction and the Cultural Crisis of the United States, 1870–1920*. Amherst, MA: University of Massachusetts Press, 2007.

Hicks, R. D., trans. *Diogenes Laertius—Lives of the Eminent Philosophers (Vols. 1 and 2)*. Cambridge, MA: Harvard University Press, 1959.

Hillman, D. C. A. *The Chemical Muse: Drug Use and the Roots of Western Civilization*. New York: Thomas Dunne Books (St. Martin's Press), 2008.

Hills, Paul. *Venetian Colour—Marble, Mosaic, Painting and Glass, 1250–1550*. New Haven, CT: Yale University Press, 1999.

Hogan, James C. "The Temptation of Odysseus." *Transactions of the American Philological Association* 106 (1976): 187–210.

Holland, Leicester B. "The Mantic Mechanism of *Delphi*." *American Journal of Archaeology* 37 (1933): 201–14.

Hornblower, Simon. "The Religious Dimension to the Peloponnesian War." *Harvard Studies in Classical Philology* 94 (1992): 169–97.

Hoy, David. "Derrida." Pp. 41–64 in *The Return of the Grand Theory of the Human Sciences*, edited by Quentin Skinner. New York: Cambridge University Press, 1990.

Hunter, Richard. *Plato's Symposium*. New York: Oxford University Press, 2004.

Hutchinson, D. S. "Doctrines of the Mean and the Debate Concerning Skills in the Fourth Century Medicine, Rhetoric and Ethics." *Apeiron* 21, no 2 (1988): 17–52.

Hutchinson, G. O. *Greek Lyric Poetry: A Commentary of Select Larger Pieces*. New York: Oxford University Press, 2001.

Hyams, Edward. *Dionysus: A Social History of the Wine Vine.* London: Sidgwick and Jackson, 1987.

Irwin, Terence, trans. *Plato—Gorgias.* New York: Oxford University Press, 1979.

Jackson, Ron S. *Wine Science: Principles, Practices, Perception.* San Diego and London: Academic Press, 2000.

Jaeger, Werner W. *The Theology of the Early Greek Philosophers.* Oxford: Clarendon Press, 1947.

———. *Paideia: The Ideals of Greek Culture.* New York: Oxford University Press.

Janko, Richard. "Socrates the Freethinker." Pp. 48–62 in *A Companion to Socrates,* edited by Sara Ahbel-Rappe and Rachana Kamtekar. Malden, MA: Blackwell Publishing, 2006.

Jaynes, Julian. *The Origin of Consciousness in the Breakdown of the Bicameral Mind.* Boston: Houghton Mifflin Company, 1976.

Jashemski, Wilhelmina Mary Feemster and Frederick G. Meyer. *The Natural History of Pompeii.* New York: Cambridge University Press, 2002.

Jasinski, James. *Sourcebook on Rhetoric: Key Concepts in Contemporary Rhetorical Studies.* Thousand Oaks, CA: Sage Publishing, 2001.

Jellinek, E. M., Carole D. Yawney, and Robert E. Popham. "Drinkers and Alcoholics in Ancient Rome." *Journal of Studies on Alcohol* 37, no. 11 (1976): 1718–41.

Johnston, Ian, trans. *Euripides—Bacchae.* Arlington, VA: Richer Resources Publications, 2008.

Johnston, Sarah I. *Restless Dead: Encounters between the Living and the Dead in Ancient Greece.* Berkeley, CA: University of California Press, 1999.

Jones, P. V. *Homer's Odyssey—A Companion to the Translation of Richard Lattimore.* Carbondale, IL: Southern Illinois University Press, 1988.

Jowett, Benjamin, trans. *Timaeus.* Upper Saddle River, NJ: Prentice Hall, 1959.

Kalimtzis, Kostas. *Aristotle on Political Enmity and Disease—An Inquiry into Stasis.* Albany, NY: State University of New York Press, 2000.

Kang, Susan. "Forcing Prison Labor: International Labor Standards, Human Rights and the Privatization of Prison Camp Labor in the Contemporary United States." *New Political Science* 31, no. 2 (2009): 137–61.

Kanowski, Maxwell G. *Containers of Classical Greece—A Handbook of Shapes.* St. Lucia, Australia: University of Queensland Press, 1984.

Kaufman, Kathy K. *Cooking in Ancient Civilizations.* Westport, CT: Greenwood Press, 2006.

Kaufman, Walter. *Nietzsche: Psychologist, Philosopher, Antichrist.* Princeton, NJ: Princeton University Press, 1968.

———. *The Portable Nietzsche.* New York: Viking Press, 1980.

Keane, Helen. *What's Wrong with Addiction?* Melbourne, Australia: Melbourne University Press, 2002.

Kelly, John C. "Virtue and Inwardness in Plato's *Republic.*" *Ancient Philosophy* 9, no. 2 (1989): 189–205.

Kerényi, Carl. *Eleusis—Archetypal Image of Mother and Daughter.* Translated by Ralph Manheim. New York: Pantheon Books, 1967.

———. *Dionysos—Archetypal Image of Indestructible Life.* Translated by Ralph Manheim. Princeton, NJ: Pantheon Books, 1976.

Kerényi, Carl and C. G. Jung. *Essays on a Science of Mythology—The Myth of the Divine Child and the Mysteries of Eleusis.* Translated by R. F. Hull. Princeton, NJ: Princeton University Press, 1963.

Keuls, Eva C. *Plato and Greek Painting.* Leiden, Netherlands: E. J. Brill, 1978.

Keyes, Clinton W., trans. *Cicero in Twenty-Eight Volumes. Volume XVI: De Republica—De Legibus*. Cambridge, MA: Harvard University Press, 1928.

Keyser, Paul T. "Science and Magic in Galen's Recipes (Sympathy and Efficacy)." Pp. 175–98 in *Galen on Pharmacology—Philosophy, History and Medicine*, edited by Armelle Debru. Leiden, Netherlands: E. J. Brill, 1997.

Kilham, Chris. *Psyche Delicacies: Coffee, Chocolate, Chiles, Kava, and Cannabis, and Why They Are Good for You*. Emmaus, PA: Rodale, 2001.

Kingsbury, John M. *Poisonous Plants of the United States and Canada*. Englewood Cliffs, NJ: Prentice-Hall, 1964.

Klonoski, Richard. "The Preservation of the Homeric Tradition: Heroic Re-Performance in the *Republic* and *Odyssey*." *Clio* 22, no. 3 (1993): 251–71.

Klosko, George. "The Insufficiency of Reason in Plato's *Gorgias*." *The Western Political Science Quarterly* 36, December (1983): 579–95.

———. "The Refutation of Callicles in Plato's *Gorgias*." *Greece and Rome* 31, no. 2 (1984): 126–39.

———. *The Development of Plato's Political Theory*. New York: Meuthen, 1986.

———. "Rational Persuasion in Plato's Political Theory." *History of Political Thought* 7, no. 1 (1986): 15–31.

———. "The Nocturnal Council in Plato's *Laws*." *Political Studies* 36, March (1988): 74–88.

Konstan, David with Elizabeth Young-Bruehl. "Eryximachus' Speech in the *Symposium*." *Apeiron* 16 (1982): 40–6.

Kotansky, Roy. "Incantations and Prayers for Salvation on Inscribed Greek Amulets." Pp. 107–37 in *Magika Hiera—Ancient Greek Magic and Religion*, edited by Christopher A. Faraone and Dirk Obbink. New York: Oxford University Press, 1991.

Kremers, Edward and Glenn Sonnedecker. *Kremers and Urdang's History of Pharmacy*. Madison, WI: American Institute of the History of Pharmacy, 1986.

Kritikos, P. G. and S. P. Papadaki. "The History of the Poppy and of Opium and their Expansion in Antiquity in the Eastern Mediterranean Area." *Bulletin on Narcotics* 19, no. 3 (1967): 17–38, and 19, no. 4 (1967): 5–10.

Kudlien, Fridolf. "Early Greek Primitive Medicine." *Clio Medica* 3 (1968): 305–36.

Kumar, Krishan. *From Post-Industrial to Post-Modern Society: New Theories of the Contemporary World*. Malden, MA: Blackwell Publishing, 1995.

Kurke, Leslie. *Coins, Bodies, Games and Gold: The Politics of Meaning in Archaic Greece*. Princeton, NJ: Princeton University Press, 1999.

Kurtz, D. C. and J. Boardman. *Greek Burial Customs*. London: Thames and Hudson, 1971.

La Barre, Weston. *The Peyote Cult, Fifth Edition*. Norman, OK: University of Oklahoma Press, 1989.

Lamb, W. R. M., trans. *Plato—Lysis, Symposium, Gorgias*. Cambridge, MA: Harvard University Press, 1925.

———, trans. *Lysias*. Cambridge, MA: Harvard University Press, 1943.

Landy, Marcia. *Film, Politics and Gramsci*. Minneapolis, MN: University of Minnesota Press, 1994.

Lang, Mabel L. "Illegal Execution in Ancient Athens." *Proceedings of the American Philosophical Association* 134, no. 1 (1990): 24–9.

Langenheim, Jean H. *Plant Resins: Chemistry, Evolution, Ecology, and Ethnobotany*. Portland, OR: Timber Press, 2003.

Lanier, Doris. *Absinthe, The Cocaine of the Nineteenth Century*. Jefferson, NC: McFarland & Company, 2004.

Lattimore, Richard, trans. *The Iliad of Homer*. Chicago: University of Chicago Press, 1964.

——, trans. *The Odyssey of Homer*. New York: Harper and Row, 1967.

Lawson, R. P., trans. *Origen—the Song of Songs, Commentary and Homilies*. Westminster, MD: The Newman Press, 1957.

Leavitt, Fred. *The Real Drug Abusers*. Lanham, MD: Rowman & Littlefield, 2003.

Lebeck, Anne. "The Central Myth of Plato's *Phaedrus*." *Greek, Roman, and Byzantine Studies* 13, no. 3 (1972): 267–90.

Lee, John W. I. *A Greek Army on the March: Soldiers and Survival in Xenophon's Anabasis*. New York: Cambridge University Press, 2008.

Lenson, David. *On Drugs*. Minneapolis, MN: University of Minnesota Press, 1995.

Lesky, Albin. *A History of Greek Literature*. Translated by Cornelis de Heer and James Willis. Indianapolis, IN: Hackett Publishing, 1996.

Levett, M. J., trans. *Plato—Theatetus*. Edited, with an Introduction by Bernard Williams. Revised by Myles Burnyeat. Indianapolis, IN: Hackett Publishing, 1992.

Levine, Daniel B. "Symposium and *Polis*." Pp. 176–96 in *Theognis of Megara—Poetry and the Polis*, edited by Gregory Nagy. Baltimore, MD: The Johns Hopkins University Press, 1985.

Levinson, Martin H. *The Drug Problem: A New View Using the General Semantics Approach*. Westport, CT: Praeger Publishing, 2002.

Lewis, I. M. *Ecstatic Religion—A Study of Shamanism and Spirit Possession*. New York: Routledge, 1971.

——. *Religion in Context—Cults and Charisma*. New York: Cambridge University Press, 1986.

Lichtenstein, Jacqueline. "Making Up Representation: The Risks of Femininity." *Representations* 20 (1987): 77–87.

——. *The Eloquence of Color: Rhetoric and Painting in the French Classical Age*. Berkeley, CA: University of California Press, 1993.

——. "On Platonic Cosmetics." Pp. 83–99 in *Uncontrollable Beauty: Toward a New Aesthetics*, edited by Bill Beckley with David Shapiro. New York: Allworth Press, 1998.

Lincoln, Bruce. "Socrates' Persecutors, Philosophy's Rivals, and the Politics of Discursive Forms." *Arethusa* 26, no. 3 (1993): 233–46.

Linforth, Ivan M. "Telestic Madness in Plato, *Phaedrus* 244DE." *The University of California Publications in Classical Philology* 13, no. 5 (1946): 163–72.

——. "The Corybantic Rites in Plato." *The University of California Publications in Classical Philology* 13, no. 6 (1946): 121–62.

Lintott, Andrew. *Violence, Civil Strife, and Revolution in the Classical City—750–330 B. C.* Baltimore, MD: The Johns Hopkins University Press, 1982.

Lissarrague, Francois. "Around the Krater: An Aspect of Banquet Imagery." Pp. 196–209 in *Sympotica—A Symposium on the Symposion*, edited by Oswyn Murray. Oxford, UK: Clarendon Press, 1990.

——. *The Aesthetics of the Greek Banquet—Images of Wine and Ritual*. Princeton, NJ: Princeton University Press, 1990.

——. *The Greek Vases—The Athenians and their Images*. New York: Riverside Book Company, 2001.

Lloyd, G. E. R. "Aspects of the Interrelations of Medicine, Magic and Philosophy in Ancient Greece." *Aperion* 9, no. 1 (1975): 1–16.

——. *Magic, Reason, and Experience: Studies in the Origin and Development of Greek Science*. New York: Cambridge University Pres, 1979.

———. *Science, Folklore, and Ideology—Studies in the Life Sciences in Ancient Greece.* New York: Cambridge University Press, 1983.

———. *The Revolutions of Wisdom.* Berkeley, CA: University of California Press, 1987.

———. *Demystifying Mentalities.* New York: Cambridge University Press, 1990.

———. "Methods and Problems in the History of Ancient Science—The Greek Case." *Isis* 83, no. 4 (1992): 564–77.

Lock, Stephen, John M. Last and George Dunea. *The Oxford Illustrated Companion to Medicine.* New York: Oxford University Press, 2001.

Lodge, R. C. *Plato's Theory of Ethics.* New York: Harcourt, Brace, and Company, 1928.

Lombardo, Stanley. *Hesiod—Works and Days and Theogny.* Indianapolis, IN: Hackett Publishing Company, 1993.

Longrigg, James. *Greek Rational Medicine: Philosophy and Medicine from Alcmaeon to the Alexandrians.* New York: Routledge, 1993.

Lonsdale, Stephen H. *Dance and Ritual Play in Greek Religion.* Baltimore, MD: The Johns Hopkins University Press, 2000.

Lothane, Zvi. "Schreber's Ecstasies, or Who Ever Listened to Daniel Paul?" Pp. 233–60 in *High Culture: Reflections on Addiction and Modernity,* edited by Anne Alexander and Mark S. Roberts. Albany, NY: State University of New York Press, 2003.

Lowenstam, Steven. "Aristophanes' Hiccups." *Greek, Roman, and Byzantine Studies* 21, no. 1 (1986): 43–56.

Luck, Georg. *Arcana Mundi—Magic and the Occult in the Greek and Roman Worlds. A Collection of Ancient Texts.* Second Edition. Baltimore, MD: The Johns Hopkins University Press, 2006.

Luyster, Robert. "Nietzsche/Dionysus: Ecstasy, Heroism and the Monstrous." *Journal of Nietzsche Studies* 21, spring (2001): 1–26.

Lynch, Timothy. *After Prohibition: An Adult Approach to Drug Policies in the 21st Century.* Washington, DC: CATO Institute, 2000.

MacDowell, Douglas, trans. *Andokides—On the Mysteries.* Oxford, UK: Clarendon Press, 1989.

Manderson, Desmond. "Metamorphoses: Clashing Symbols in the Social Construction of Drugs." *The Journal of Drug Issues* 25, no. 4 (1995): 799–816.

Manniche, Lise. *An Ancient Egyptian Herbal.* Austin, TX: University of Texas Press, 1989.

Mansfeld, Jaap. "Plato and the Method of Hippocrates." *Greek, Roman, and Byzantine Studies* 21, no. 4 (1980): 341–62.

Marback, Richard. *Plato's Dream of Sophistry.* Columbia, SC: University of South Carolina Press, 1999.

Marr, J. L. "Andocides' Part in the Mysteries and Hermae Affairs of 415 B. C." *Classical Quarterly* 21, no. 2 (1971): 326–38.

Martin, Luther H. "Those Elusive Eleusinian Mysteries." *Helios* 13, no. 1 (1986): 17–31.

Martin, Terence J. *Living Words: Studies in Dialogues about Religion.* New York: Oxford University Press, 1998.

Matheson, Susan B. "The Mission of Triptolemus and the Politics of Athens." *Greek, Roman, and Byzantine Studies* 35, no. 4 (1994): 345–72.

Matthee, Rudi. "Exotic Substances: The Introduction and Global Spread of Tobacco, Coffee, Cocoa, Tea, and Distilled Liquor, Sixteenth to Eighteenth Centuries." Pp. 24–51 in *Drugs and Narcotics in History,* edited by Roy Porter and Mikulas Teich. New York: Cambridge University Press, 1995.

Mayor, Adrienne. *Greek Fire, Poison Arrows, and Scorpion Bombs: Biological and Chemical Warfare in the Ancient World.* New York: Overlook Duckworth, 2003.

McClure, Laura. *Courtesans at the Table: Gender and Greek Literary Culture in Athenaeus.* New York: Routledge, 2003.

McCracken, George E., trans. *Arnobius of Sicca—The Case Against the Pagans*, Volumes 1 and 2. Baltimore, MD: J. H. Furst and Company, 1949.

McCrorie, Edward, trans. *Homer—The Odyssey.* Baltimore, MD: The Johns Hopkins University Press, 2004.

McCumber, John. "Discourse and Psyche in Plato's *Phaedrus.*" *Apeiron* 16, no. 1 (1982): 27–39.

McGovern, Patrick E. *Ancient Wine: The Search for the Origins of Viniculture.* Princeton, NJ: Princeton University Press, 2003.

McGovern, Patrick E., Stuart J. Fleming and Solomon H. Katz, eds. *Origins and Ancient History of Wine.* New York: Routledge, 2000.

McKenna, Terrence. *Food of the Gods: The Search for the Original Tree of Knowledge.* New York: Bantam Books, 1992.

McKinlay, Arthur P. "How the Athenians Handled the Drink Problem of their Slaves." *Classical Weekly* 37 (1944): 127–8.

———. "Ancient Experience with Intoxicating Drinks: Non-Classical Peoples." *Quarterly Journal of Studies on Alcohol* 9, no. 3 (1948): 388–414.

———. "Ancient Experience with Intoxicating Drinks: Non-Attic Greek States." *Quarterly Journal of Studies on Alcohol* 10, no. 2 (1949): 289–315.

———. "Bacchus as Health-Giver." *Quarterly Journal of Studies on Alcohol* 11, no. 2 (1950): 230–46.

———. "Attic Temperance." *Quarterly Journal of Studies on Alcohol* 12, no. 1 (1951): 61–102.

———. "New Light on the Question of Homeric Temperance." *Quarterly Journal of Studies on Alcohol* 14, no. 1 (1953): 78–93.

———. "The Roman Attitude Toward Women Drinking." Pp. 58–61 in *Drinking and Intoxication: Selected Readings in Social Attitudes and Controls*, edited by R. G. McCarthy. Glencoe, IL: The Free Press, 1959.

McPherran, Mark L. "Socratic Reason and Socratic Revelation." *Journal of the History of Philosophy* 29 (1991): 346–73.

Meir, Kenneth J. *The Politics of Sin: Drugs, Alcohol, and Public Policy.* New York: M. E. Sharpe, 1994.

Melberg, Arne. *Theories of Mimesis.* New York: Cambridge University Press, 1995.

Melley, Timothy. *Empire of Conspiracy: The Culture of Paranoia in Postwar America.* Ithaca, NY: Cornell University Press, 2000.

Mendelsohn, Daniel. "Συγκραυνόω: Dithrambic Language and Dionysiac Cult." *The Classical Journal* 87, no. 2 (1992): 105–24.

Merkur, Daniel. *The Mystery of Manna: The Psychedelic Sacrament of the Bible.* Rochester, VT: Parker Street Press, 2000.

Meuli, Karl. "Scythica." *Hermes* 70 (1935): 121–76.

Meuli, Karl and Thomas Gelzer. *Gesammelte Schriften.* Basel, Switzerland: Schwabe, 1975.

Meyer, Marvin W., ed. *The Ancient Mysteries—A Source Book.* San Francisco: Harper and Row, 1987.

Mikalson, Jon D. *Ancient Greek Religion.* Second Edition. Malden, MA: Blackwell Publishing, 2010.

Miller, Andrew M. *Greek Lyric: An Anthology in Translation.* Indianapolis, IN: Hackett Publishing, 1996.

Miller, Richard Lawrence. *Drug Warriors and their Prey: From Police Power to Police State*. Westport, CT: Greenwood Publishing, 1996.

Missiou, Anna. *The Subversive Oratory of Andokides—Politics, Ideology, and Decision-making in Democratic Athens*. New York: Cambridge University Press, 1992.

Montiglio, Silvia. *Silence in the Land of Logos*. Princeton, NJ: Princeton University Press, 2000.

Moore, David. "Deconstructing 'dependence': An Ethnographic Critique of an Influential Concept." *Contemporary Drug Problems* 19, no. 3 (1992): 459–90.

Moorton, Richard F. Jr. "Aristophanes and Alcibiades." *Greek, Roman, and Byzantine Studies* 29, no. 4 (1988): 345–60.

Moravesik, Julius and Philip Temko, eds. *Plato on Beauty, Wisdom, and the Arts*. Totowa, NJ: Rowman and Allenheld, 1982.

Morford, Mark and Robert C. Lenardon. *Classical Mythology*. New York: Longman, 1991.

Morgan, Michael L. *Platonic Piety: Philosophy and Ritual in Fourth Century Athens*. New Haven, CT: Yale University Press, 1990.

Morley, Jefferson and Malcom Byrne. "The Drug War and 'National Security': The Making of a Quagmire, 1969–1973." *Dissent* 36, no. 1 (1989): 39–46.

Moss, Gerald C. "Mental Disorders in Antiquity." Pp. 709–22 in *Diseases in Antiquity—A Survey of the Diseases, Injuries and Surgery of Early Populations*, edited by Don Brothwell and A. T. Sandison. Springfield, IL: Charles C. Thomas, 1967.

Moss, Jeremy. *The Later Foucault: Politics and Philosophy*. Thousand Oaks, CA: Sage Publications, 1998.

Murphy, James Jerome and Richard A. Katula. *A Synoptic History of Classical Rhetoric*. Mahwah, NJ: Lawrence Erlbaum, 2003.

Murray, A. T., trans. *Demosthenes. Volume 6. Private Orations L–LVIII*. Cambridge, MA: Harvard University Pres, 1939.

Murray, James S. "Plato on Knowledge, Persuasion, and the Art of Rhetoric: *Gorgias* 452e–455a." *Ancient Philosophy* 8, no. 1 (1988): 1–10.

Murray, Oswyn. *Early Greece*. Palo Alto, CA: Stanford University Press, 1983.

——. "The Affair of the Mysteries: Democracy and the Drinking Group." Pp. 149–61 in *Sympotika—A Symposium on the* Symposion, edited by Oswyn Murray. Oxford, UK: Clarendon Press, 1990.

——. "The Solonian Law of *Hubris*." Pp. 139–46 in *Nomos—Essays on Athenian Law, Politics, and Society*, edited by Paul Cartledge, Paul Millett and Stephen Todd. New York: Cambridge University Press, 1990.

——. *Early Greece*. Second Edition. Cambridge, MA: Harvard University Press, 1993.

——. "Forms of Sociality." Pp 218–53 in *The Greeks*, edited by Jean-Pierre Vernant. Translated by Charles Lambert and Teresa Lavender Fagen. Chicago: University of Chicago Press, 1995.

Murray, Penelope. "Poetic Inspiration in Early Greece." *The Journal of Hellenic Studies* 101 (1981): 87–100.

——. "Inspiration and Mimesis in Plato." *Apeiron* 25, no. 4 (1992): 27–46.

Musurillo, Herbert, ed. *The Acts of the Pagan Martyrs: Acta Alexandrinorum*. Oxford, UK: Clarendon Press, 1954.

——, trans. *St. Methodius: The Symposium: A Treatise on Chastity*. New York: Paulist Press, 1958.

Mylonas, George. *Eleusis and the Eleusinian Mysteries*. Princeton, NJ: Princeton University Press, 1961.

Mynors, Roger A. B. *Collected Works of Erasmus (Volume 34). Adages IIvii1 to IIIiii100.* Toronto: University of Toronto Press, 1992.

Naddaf, Gerrard. *The Greek Concept of Nature.* Albany, NY: State University of New York Press, 2005.

Nagy, Gregory. "Oral Poetry and the Homeric Poems: Broadening and Narrowing of Terms." *Critical Exchange* 16 (1984): 32–54.

Nails, Debra. *Agora, Academy, and the Conduct of Philosophy.* Dordecht, Netherlands: Kluwer Academic Publishers, 1995.

Neel, Jasper P. *Plato, Derrida, and Writing.* Carbondale, IL: Southern Illinois University Press, 1988.

Nehamas, Alexander. "Plato on Imitation and Poetry in *Republic* 10." Pp. 47–78 in *Plato on Beauty, Wisdom, and the Arts,* edited by Julius Moravcsik and Philip Temko. Totowa, NJ: Roman and Allanheld.

Nelson, Max. *A Barbarian's Beverage: A History of Beer in Ancient Europe.* New York: Routledge, 2005.

Neuhaus, Charles, Jr. "The Disease Controversy Revisited: An Ontologic Perspective." *The Journal of Drug Issues* 23, no. 3 (1993): 463–78.

Nichols, Mary. "The *Republic*'s Two Alternatives: Philosopher Kings and Socrates." *Political Theory* 12, no. 2 (1984): 252–74.

Nietzsche, Friedrich. *The Gay Science.* Translated by Walter Kaufmann. New York: Vintage Books, 1974.

——. *The Birth of Tragedy.* Translated by Shaun Whiteside. Edited by Michael Tanner. New York: Penguin Books, 1993.

——. *The Twilight of the Idols and The Anti-Christ: Or how to Philosophize with a Hammer.* Translated by R. J. Hollingdale. Introduction by Michael Tanner. New York: Penguin Books, 2003.

Nightingale, Andrea. "Writing/Reading a Sacred Text: A Literary Interpretation of Plato's Laws." *Classical Philology* 88, no. 4 (1993): 279–300.

Nilsson, Martin P. *The Minoan-Mycenaean Religion and Its Survival in Greek Religion.* New York: Oxford University Press, 1927.

——. *A History of Greek Religion.* Translated by F. J. Fieldon. New York: Oxford University Press, 1949.

——. *The Dionysiac Mysteries of the Hellenistic and Roman Era.* New York: Arno Press, 1975.

Norlin, George, trans. *Isocrates.* Volume 1 of 3. New York: G. P. Putnam and Sons, 1928.

North, H. *Sophrosune: Self-Knowledge and Self-Respect in Greek Literature.* Ithaca, NY: Cornell University Press, 1966.

Nussbaum, Martha C. "The Speech of Alcibiades: A Reading of Plato's *Symposium.*" *Philosophy and Literature* 3, no. 2 (1979): 131–72.

——. "Aristophanes and Socrates on Learning Practical Wisdom." *Yale Classical Studies* 26 (1980): 43–97.

——. Review of Michel Foucault's *The Use of Pleasure. The History of Sexuality Volume 2* ["Affections of the Greeks"]. *New York Times,* November 10, 1985, pp. 13–15.

——. *The Fragility of Goodness. Luck and Ethics in Greek Tragedy and Philosophy.* New York: Cambridge University Press, 1986.

——. *Loves's Knowledge: Essays on Philosophy and Literature.* New York: Oxford University Press, 1990.

———. *The Therapy of Desire: Theory and Practice in Hellenistic Support.* Princeton, NJ: Princeton University Press, 1994.

———. "The Transfiguration of Intoxication: Nietzsche, Shopenhauer, and Dionysus." Pp. 331–59 in *Nietzsche—Critical Assessments,* edited by Daniel W. Conway with Peter S. Groff. New York: Routledge, 2000.

———. "Eros and Ethical Norms: Philosophers Respond to a Cultural Dilemma." Pp. 55–94 in *The Sleep of Reason: Erotic Experience and Sexual Ethics in Ancient Greece,* edited by Martha C. Nussbaum and Juha Siholva. Chicago: University of Chicago Press, 2002.

Nutton, Vivian. *Ancient Medicine.* New York: Routledge, 2004.

Nybakken, Oscar E. *Greek and Latin in Scientific Terminology.* Ames, IA: Blackwell Publishing, 1959.

Ober, William B. "Did Socrates Die of Hemlock Poisoning?" *Ancient Philosophy* 2, no. 2 (1982): 115–21.

O'Flaherty, Wendy Doniger. "Dionysus and Siva: Parallel Patterns in Two Pairs of Myths." *History of Religion* 20, no. 1 (1980): 81–111.

Ogden, Daniel. *Magic, Witchcraft, and Ghosts in the Greek and Roman Worlds—A Sourcebook.* New York: Oxford University Press, 2002.

Okhamafe, E. Imafedia. *The "Politics" of "Pharmakon."* Ph.D. Dissertation, Purdue University, 1984.

Ophir, Adi. *Plato's Invisible Cities: Discourse and Power in the* Republic. New York: Routledge, 1991.

Oravec, Christine, and Michael Salvador, "The Duality of Rhetoric: Theory as Discursive Practice." Pp. 173–92 in *Rethinking the History of Rhetoric: Multidisciplinary Essays on the Rhetorical Tradition,* edited by Takis Poulakos. Boulder, CO: Westview Press, 1993.

Otto, Walter F. "The Meaning of the Eleusinian Mysteries." Pp. 14–31 in *The Mysteries: Papers from the Eranos Yearbooks,* edited by Joseph Campbell. Princeton, NJ: Princeton University Press, 1955.

———. *Dionysus—Myth and Cult.* Translated by Robert B. Palmer. Bloomington, IN: Indiana University Press, 1965.

Page, Carl. "The Truth about Lies in Plato's *Republic.*" *Ancient Philosophy* 11, no. 1 (1991): 1–33.

Palmer, Ruth. "Wine and Viticulture in the Linear A and B Texts of the Bronze Age Aegean." Pp. 269–86 in *Origins and Ancient History of Wine,* edited by Patrick McGovern. New York: Routledge, 2000.

Pangle, Thomas L., trans. 1980. *The Laws of Plato.* Chicago: University of Chicago Press, 1980.

———, ed. *The Roots of Political Philosophy—Ten Forgotten Socratic Dialogues.* Ithaca, NY: Cornell University Press, 1987.

Parke, H. W. and D. E. W. Wormell. *The Delphic Oracle. Volume 1—The History.* Oxford, UK: Basil Blackwell, 1956.

Parker, Douglas, trans. *Aristophanes—The Acharnians.* Ann Arbor, MI: The University of Michigan Press, 1961.

Parsons, Benjamin. *Anti-Bacchus: An Essay on the Crimes, Diseases, and Other Evils Connected with the Use of Intoxicating Drinks.* London: John Snow, 1840.

———. *The Wine Question Settled: In Accordance with the Inductions of Science, and the Facts of History—In Which Particular Reference is Made to the Character of Ancient Drinks, Especially the Wines of Scripture.* London: John Snow, 1841.

Peele, Stanton. "A Values Approach to Addiction: Drug Policy that Is Moral Rather than Moralistic." *The Journal of Drug Issues* 20, no. 4 (1990): 639–46.

Pellizer, Ezio. "Outline of a Morphology of Sympotic Entertainment." Pp. 177–84 in *Sympotica—A Symposium on the* Symposion, edited by Oswyn Murray. Oxford, UK: Clarendon Press, 1990.

Perrine, Daniel. "Mixing the *Kykeon*—Part 2." *Eleusis: Journal of Psychoactive Plants and Compounds* 4 (2000): 9–19.

Peters, James Roberts "Reason and Passion in Plato's *Republic*." *Ancient Philosophy* 9, no. 2 (1989): 265–84.

Phillippy, Patricia B. *Love's Remedy: Recantation and Renaissance Lyric Poetry*. London and Toronto: Associated University Press, 1995.

Phillips, C. R. III. "*Nullum Crimen sine Lege*: Socioreligious Sanctions on Magic." Pp. 260–76 in *Magika Hiera—Ancient Greek Magic and Religion*, edited by Christopher Faraone and Dirk Obbink. New York: Oxford University Press, 1991.

Phillips, E. D. *Greek Medicine*. London: Thames and Hudson, 1973.

Pickard-Cambridge, Sir Arthur. *The Dramatic Festivals of Ancient Athens*. Second Edition. Oxford, UK: Clarendon Press, 1968.

Pickett, Brent. *On the Use and Abuse of Foucault for Politics*. Lanham, MD: Lexington Books, 2005.

Plant, Sadie. "Writing on Drugs." Pp. 3–10 in *Culture and Power: Challenging Discourses*, edited by Maria José Coperías Aguilar. València, Spain: Universitat de València, 2000.

Pomeroy, Sarah B. "Plato and the Female Physician." *American Journal of Psychology* 99, no. 4 (1978): 496–500.

——, trans. *Xenophon—Oeconomicus—A Social and Historical Commentary*. New York: Oxford University Press, 1994.

Popper, Karl R. *The Open Society and its Enemies, Volume I: The Spell of Plato*. Princeton, NJ: Princeton University Press, 1966.

Poulsen, Sarah B. *Delphi*. Washington, DC: McGrath Publishing, 1973.

Powell, Anton. *The Greek World*. New York: Routledge, 1995.

Powell, C. A. "Religion and the Sicilian Expedition." *Historia* 28, no. 1 (1979): 15–31.

Preus, Anthony. "Drugs and Psychic States in Theophrastus' *Historia plantarum* 9.8–20." Pp. 76–99 in *Theophrastean Studies—On Natural Science, Physics, and Metaphysics, Ethics, Religion, and Rhetoric*, edited by William W. Fortenbaugh and Robert W. Sharples. New Brunswick, NJ: Transaction Books, 1988.

Prior, William J. *Virtue and Knowledge—An Introduction to Ancient Greek Ethics*. New York: Routledge, 1991.

Provine, Doris Marie. *Unequal Under the Law: Race in the War on Drugs*. Chicago: University of Chicago Press, 2007.

Pucci, Pietro. *Hesiod and the Language of Poetry*. Baltimore, MD: The Johns Hopkins Univeristy Press, 1977.

Quasten, Johannes. *Ancient Christian Writers: The Works of the Fathers in Translation. Arnobius of Sicca: The Case Against the Pagans*. Baltimore, MD: J. H. Furst and Company, 1949.

Rabinow, Paul, ed. *The Foucault Reader*. New York: Pantheon Books, 1984.

Rahe, Paul A. *Republics Ancient and Modern, Classical Republicanism and the American Revolution*. Chapel Hill, NC: University of North Carolina Press, 1992.

Rahner, Hugo. "The Christian Mystery and the Pagan Mysteries." Pp. 337–401 in *The Mysteries—Papers from the Eranos Yearbooks*, edited by Joseph Campbell. Princeton, NJ: Princeton University Press, 1955.

Rajchman, John. *Truth and Eros—Foucault, Lacan, and the Question of Ethics.* New York: Routledge, 1991.

Rankin, H. D. "Plato and Man the Puppet." *Eranos* 60 (1962): 127–31.

Reale, Giovanni. "According to Plato, The Evils of the Body Cannot be Cured without also Curing the Evils of the Soul." Pp. 19–31 in *Person, Society, and Value: Towards a Personalist Concept of Health,* edited by Paulina Taboada, Kateryna F. Cuddeback, and Patricia Donohue-White. Dordrecht, Netherlands: Kluwer Academic Publishing, 2002.

Rice, Daryl H. "Plato on Force: The Conflict Between his Psychology and Political Sociology and his Definition of Temperance in the *Republic.*" *History of Political Thought* 10, no. 4 (1989): 565–76.

Richards, David. *Sex, Drugs, Death and the Law: An Essay on Human Rights and Overcriminalization.* Totowa, NJ: Rowman and Littlefield, 1986.

Richter, Gisela M. A. and Marjorie J. Milne. *Shapes and Names of the Athenian Vases.* New York: The Metropolitan Museum of Art, 1935.

Riddle, John M., J. Worth Estes, and Josiah C. Russell. "Birth Control in the Ancient World." *Archeology* 47, no. 2 (1994): 29–35.

Riley, Charles A. *Color Codes: Modern Theories of Color in Philosophy, Painting, and Architecture, Literature, Music, and Psychology.* Lebanon, NH: University Press of New England, 1995.

Riley, Mark T. "The Epicurean Criticism of Socrates." *Phoenix* 34, no. 1 (1980): 55–68.

Rinella, Michael A. *Plato, Ecstasy, and Identity.* Ph.D. dissertation, State University of New York at Albany, 1997.

——. "Supplementing the Ecstatic: Plato, the Eleusinian Mysteries, and the Phaedrus." *Polis—The Journal of the Society of Greek Political Thought* 17, nos. 1 & 2 (2000): 61–78.

——. "Revisiting the Pharmacy: Plato, Derrida, and the Morality of Political Deceit." *Polis—The Journal of the Society of Greek Political Thought* 24, no. 1 (2007): 134–53.

Rinon, Yoav. "Plato's Pharmacy. The Rhetoric of Jacques Derrida (Part 1 of 2)." *The Review of Metaphysics* 46, no. 2 (1992): 369–86.

Robbins, Rosemary. "Contributions to the History of Psychology: XLVIII. Ancient Greek Roots of the Assumptions of Modern Clinical Psychology." *Perceptions and Motor Skills* 66, no. 3 (1988): 903–921.

Roberts, Jean. "Plato on the Causes of Wrongdoing in the *Laws.*" *Ancient Philosophy* 7 (1987): 23–37.

Robertson, Noel. "Athens' Festival of the New Wine." *Harvard Studies in Classical Philology* 95 (1993): 197–250.

Robinson, Matthew and Renee G. Scherlen. *Lies, Damned Lies, and Drug War Statistics: A Critical Analysis of Claims Made by the Office of National Drug Control Policy.* Albany, NY: State University of New York Press, 2007.

Rohde, Erwin. *Psyche—The Cult of Souls and the Belief in Immortality among the Greeks.* New York and London: Routledge and Kegan Paul, 1925.

Romilly, Jacqueline de. *Magic and Rhetoric in Ancient Greece.* Cambridge, MA: Harvard University Press, 1975.

Rose, F. Clifford, ed. *The Neurobiology of Painting.* San Diego: Academic Press/Elsevier, 2006.

Rosen, R. M. "Hipponax fr. 48 Dg. and the Eleusinian *Kykeon.*" *American Journal of Philology* 108 (1987): 416–26.

Rosen, Stanley. *Hermeneutics as Politics.* New Haven, CT: Yale University Press, 2003.

Rosenmayer, Thomas G. "The Family of Critias." *American Journal of Philology* 70 (1949): 404–10.

Rosenstock, Bruce. "Socrates as Revenant: A Reading of the *Menexenus*." *Phoenix* 48 (1994): 331-47.

———. "Athena's Cloak—Plato's Critique of Democratic Rule in the *Republic*." *Political Theory* 23, no. 3 (1994): 363–90.

Ross, Sir David, trans. *The Works of Aristotle: Volume XII. Select Fragments*. Oxford: Clarendon Press, 1952.

Rouget, Gilbert. *Music and Trance—A Theory of the Relations between Music and Possession*. Chicago: University of Chicago Press, 1985.

Rowe, Christopher J., trans. *Plato: Phaedrus*. Wiltshire, UK: Aris and Phillips, 1986.

———, trans. *Plato: Statesmen*. Indianapolis, IN: Hackett Publishing, 1999.

Rubidge, Bradley. "Tragedy and the Emotions of Warriors: The Moral Psychology Underlying Plato's Attack on Poetry." *Arethusa* 26, no. 3 (1993): 247–76.

Ruck, Carl A. P. "Duality and the Madness of Herakles." *Arethusa* 9, no. 1 (1976): 53–75.

———. "On the Sacred Name of Iamos and Ion: Ethnobotanical Referents in the Hero's Parentage." *The Classical Journal* 71, no. 3 (1976): 235–52.

———. "Mushrooms and Mysteries: On Aristophanes and the Necromancy of Socrates." *Helios* 8, no. 2 (1981): 1–28.

———. "Mushrooms and Philosophers." Pp. 179–223 in *Persephone's Quest: Entheogens and the Origins of Religion*, edited by R. Gordon Wasson. New Haven, CT: Yale University Press, 1986.

———. "The Wild and the Cultivated: Wine in Euripides' *Bacchae*." Pp. 179–223 in *Persephone's Quest: Entheogens and the Origins of Religion*, edited by R. Gordon Wasson. New Haven, CT: Yale University Press, 1986.

———. "The Offerings from the Hyperboreans." Pp. 225–256 in *Persephone's Quest: Entheogens and the Origins of Religion*, edited by R. Gordon Wasson. New Haven, CT: Yale University Press, 1986.

———. "Mixing the Kykeon—Part 3." *Eleusis: Journal of Psychoactive Plants and Compounds* 4 (2000): 20–25.

———. "Gods and Plants in the Classical World." Pp. 131–43 in *Ethnobotony: Evolution of a Discipline*, edited by Richard Evans Schultes and Siri von Reis. Portland, OR: Dioscorides Press, 2005.

———. *Sacred Mushrooms of the Goddess and the Secrets of Eleusis*. Berkeley, CA: Ronin Publising, 2006.

Rudebusch, George. "Callicles' Hedonism." *Ancient Philosophy* 12, no. 1 (1992): 53–86.

Rudenko, S. I. *Frozen Tombs of Siberia*. Berkeley, CA: University of California Press, 1970.

Rudgley, Richard. *The Alchemy of Culture—Intoxicants in Society*. London: British Museum Press, 1993.

Rumbarger, John J. *Profits, Power, and Prohibition: American Alcohol Reform and the Industrializing of America: 1800–1930*. Albany, NY: State University of New York Press, 1989.

Rummel, Erika. "Isocrates Ideal of Rhetoric: Criteria of Evaluation." Pp. 143–54 in *Landmark Essays on Classical Greek Rhetoric, Volume 3*, edited by Edward Schiappa. Davis, CA: Hermagoras Press, 1994.

Sailor, Cara L. *The Function of Mythology and Religion in Greek Society*. M.A. Thesis, East Tennessee University, 2007.

Sallares, Robert. *The Ecology of the Ancient Greek World*. Ithaca, NY: Cornell University Press, 1991.

Sandys, J. Edwin. *Isocrates—Ad Demonicum et Panegyricus*. New York: Arno Press, 1979.

Sansone, David. *Ancient Greek Civilization*. Malden, MA: Blackwell Publishing, 2004.

Saunders, Trevor J. "The Structure of the Soul and the State in Plato's Laws." *Eranos* 60 (1962): 37–55.

———, trans. *The Laws*. New York: Penguin Books, 1970.

———. *Plato's Penal Code—Tradition, Controversy, and Reform in Greek Penology*. Oxford: Clarendon Press, 1991.

Saxonhouse, Arlene W. *Fear of Diversity: The Birth of Political Science in Ancient Greek Thought*. Chicago: University of Chicago Press, 1995.

Scarborough, John. *Medical Terminologies: Classical Origins*. Norman, OK: University of Oklahoma Press, 1987.

———. "The Pharmacology of Sacred Plants, Herbs, and Roots." Pp. 138–74 in *Magika Hiera—Ancient Greek Magic and Religion*, edited by Christopher A. Faraone and Dirk Obbink. New York: Oxford University Press, 1991.

———. "The Opium Poppy in Hellenistic and Roman Medicine." Pp. 4–23 in *Drugs and Narcotics in History*, edited by Roy Porter and Mikulas Teich. New York: Oxford University Press, 1995.

Schiappa, Edward. *Protagoras and Logos: A Study of Greek Philosophy and Rhetoric, Second Edition*. Columbia, SC: University of South Carolina Press, 2003.

Schiff, Paul L., Jr. "Ergot and Its Alkaloids." *American Journal of Pharmaceutical Education* 70, no. 5 (2006): 98.

Schmid, Walter T. *On Manly Courage: A Study of Plato's* Laches. Carbondale, IL: Southern Illinois University Press, 1992.

Schofield, Malcolm. *The Stoic Ideal of the City*. New York: Cambridge University Press, 1991.

———. *Plato: Political Philosophy*. New York: Oxford University Press, 2006.

Schultes, Richard Evans. "Hallucinogens of Plant Origin." *Science* 163 (1969): 245–54.

Schultes, Richard Evans and Albert Hofmann. *Plants of the Gods—Their Sacred, Healing, and Hallucinogenic Powers*. Rochester, VT: Healing Arts Press, 1992.

Screech, M. A. "Good Madness in Christendom." Pp. 25–39 in *The Anatomy of Madness—Essays in the History of Psychiatry, Volume I: People and Ideas*, edited by William F. Bynum. New York: Routledge, 1985.

———. *Montaigne and Melancholy: The Wisdom of the* Essays. Lanham, MD: Rowman and Littlefield, 2000.

———, trans. *Michel de Montaigne. The Essays: A Selection*. New York: Penguin Books, 1993.

Seaford, Richard. "The 'Hyporchema' of Pratinas." *Maia* 29 (1977): 81–94.

———. "Dionysiac Drama and the Dionysiac Mysteries." *Classical Quarterly* 31, no. 2 (1981): 252–75.

———. *Euripides Cyclops, with Introduction and Commentary*. Oxford: Clarendon Press, 1984.

Seddon, Toby. *A History of Drugs: Drugs and Freedom in the Liberal Age*. New York: Routledge, 2010.

Segal, Charles. "The Menace of Dionysus: Sex Roles in Euripides *Bacchae*." *Arethusa* 11, nos. 1 and 2 (1978): 185–202.

———. *Dionysiac Poetics and Euripides'* Bacchae. Princeton, NJ: Princeton University Press, 1982.

Selincourt, Aubrey de, trans. *Herodotus—The Histories*. New York: Penguin Books, 1972.

Sell, Mike. *Avant-Garde Performance and the Limits of Criticism: Approaching the Living Theatre, Happenings/Fluxus, and the Black Arts Movement*. Ann Arbor, MI: University of Michigan Press, 2008.

Seltman, Charles. *Wine in the Ancient World*. London: Routledge and Kegan Paul, 1957.

Settgast, Mary. *Plato—Prehistorian. 10,000 to 5,000 B. C. in Myth and Archeology*. Cambridge, MA: Rotenberg Press, 1986.

Seymour, Thomas D. *Life in the Homeric Age*. New York: Biblo and Tannen, 1963.

Shapiro, H. A. *Myth into Art—Poet and Painter in Classical Greece*. New York: Routledge, 1994.

Sharples, R. W. "Plato on Democracy and Expertise." *Greece and Rome* 61, no. 1 (1994): 49–56.

Siegel, Ronald K. *Intoxication—The Universal Drive for Mind-Altering Substances*. Rochester, VT: Park Street Press, 2005.

Sigerist, Henry E. *A History of Medicine, Volume II: Early Greek, Hindu, and Persian Medicine*. New York: Oxford University Press, 1961.

Sikka, Sonia. "Nietzsche's Contribution to a Phenomenology of Intoxication." *Journal of Phenomenological Psychology* 31, no. 1 (2000): 19–43.

Simon, Erika. *Festivals of Attika: An Archeological Commentary*. Madison, WI: The University of Wisconsin Press, 1983.

Simons, Jon. *Foucault and the Political*. New York: Routledge, 1995.

Simpson, Michael, trans. *Gods and Heroes of the Greeks: The Library of Apollodorus*. Amherst, MA: University of Massachusetts Press, 1976.

Sissa, Giulia. *Sex and Sexuality in the Ancient World*. New Haven, CT: Yale University Press, 2008.

Skemp, J. B. "Plants in Plato's *Timaeus*." *Classical Quarterly* 41 (1947): 53–60.

———. "The Spirituality of Socrates and Plato." Pp. 102–20 in *Classical Mediterranean Spirituality: Egyptian, Greek, Roman*, edited by A. H. Armstrong. London: Routledge and Kegan Paul, 1986.

Smith, Christopher P. *The Hermeneutics of Original Argument: Demonstration, Dialectic, Rhetoric*. Evanston, IL: Northwestern University Press, 1998.

Smith, Janet E. "Plato's Use of Myth in the Education of Philosophic Man." *Phoenix* 40 (1986): 20–34.

Smyth, Herbert W., trans. *Aeschylus—Agamemnon, Libation-Bearers, Eumenides, Fragments*. Cambridge, MA: Harvard University Press, 1960.

Sommerstein, Alan H., trans. *The Comedies of Aristophanes. Volume 2—Clouds*. Warminster, Wilts, England: Aris and Phillips, 1982.

———. *The Comedies of Aristophanes. Volume 4—Wasps*. Warminster, Wilts, England: Aris and Phillips, 1982.

Sorabji, Richard. *Emotion and Peace of Mind: From Stoic Agitation to Christian Temptation*. New York: Oxford University Press, 2000.

Spariosu, Mihai. *God of Many Names: Play, Poetry, and Power in Hellenic Thought from Homer to Aristotle*. Durham, NC: Duke University Press, 1991.

Sprague, Rosamond Kent, ed. *The Older Sophists*. Columbia, SC: University of South Carolina Press, 1972.

———. *The Older Sophists: A Complete Translation by Several Hands of the Fragments in die Fragmente der Vorsokratie*. Edited by Diels-Kranz with a new Edition of Antiphon and of Euthydemus. Indianapolis, IN: Hackett Publishing, 2001.

Staden, Heinrich von. "Affinities and Elisions—Helen and Hellenocentrism." *Isis* 83, no. 4 (1992): 578–95.

Stanford, W. B. *Greek Tragedy and the Emotions—An Introductory Study.* London: Routledge and Kegan Paul, 1983.

Stannard, Jerry. "The Plant Called Moly." *Ostris* 14 (1962): 254–307.

———. "Squill in Ancient and Medieval Materia Medica, with Special Reference to Its Deployment for Dropsy." *Bulletin of the New York Academy of Medicine* 50 (1974): 684–713.

Starr, Chester G. "An Evening with the Flute Girls." *La Parola del Passato* 33, no. 183 (1978): 401–10.

Stein, Charles. *Persephone Unveiled: Seeing the Goddess and Freeing Your Soul.* Berkeley, CA: North Atlantic Books, 2006.

Stein, Robert. "Wine-Drinking in New Testament Times." *Christianity Today* June 20 (1975): 9–11.

Stephens, Susan A. *Seeing Double: Intercultural Poetics in Ptolemaic Alexandria.* Berkeley, CA: University of California Press, 2003.

Stockhammer, Morris. *Plato Dictionary.* New York: Philosophical Library, 1963.

Stone, I. F. *The Trial of Socrates.* New York: Little, Brown, and Company, 1988.

Strang, C. "Tripartite Souls, Ancient and Modern: Plato and Sheldon." *Apeiron* 16, no. 1 (1982): 1–11.

Strauss, Barry S. *Athens after the Peloponnesian War: Class, Faction, and Policy 403–386 BC.* Ithaca, NY: Cornell University Press, 1986.

Strauss, Leo. "What is Political Philosophy?" Pp. 9–55 in *What is Political Philosophy and Other Studies.* Chicago: University of Chicago Press, 1959.

———. *The Argument and Action of Plato's Laws.* Chicago: University of Chicago Press, 1975.

———. *Socrates and Aristophanes.* Chicago: University of Chicago Press, 1996.

Strauss, Leo, and Joseph Cropsey, eds. *History of Political Philosophy.* Chicago: University of Chicago Press, 1987.

Sussman, Linda S. "Workers and Drones: Labor, Idleness and Gender Definition in Hesiod's Beehive." *Arethusa* 11, nos. 1 & 2 (1978): 27–41.

Sutton, Tiffany. *The Classification of Visual Art: A Philosophical Myth and its History.* New York: Cambridge University Press, 2000.

Svenbro, Jasper. *Phrasikleia—An Anthropology of Reading in Ancient Greek.* Ithaca, NY: Cornell University Press, 1992.

Tarrant, Harold "Wine in Ancient Greece—Some Platonist Ponderings." Pp. 15–29 in *Wine and Philosophy: A Symposium on Thinking and Drinking,* edited by Fritz Allhoff. Malden, MA: Blackwell Publishing, 2008.

Taylor, A. E., trans. *Plato: Timaeus and Critias.* London: Methuen, 1929.

———, trans. *Plato—Laws.* New York: E. P. Dutton and Company, 1960.

Taylor, Brian. *Responding to Men in Crisis: Masculinities, Distress, and the Postmodern Political Landscape.* New York: Routledge, 2006.

Taylor-Perry, Rosemarie. *The God Who Comes—Dionysian Mysteries Revisited.* New York: Algora Publishing, 2003.

Tecusan, Manuela. "Logos Sympotikos: Patterns of the Irrational in Philosophical Drinking—Plato Outside the *Symposium.*" Pp. 238–60 in *Sympotika—A Symposium on the Symposion,* edited by Oswyn Murray. Oxford, UK: Clarendon Press, 1990.

Torrance, Robert M. *The Spiritual Quest—Transcendence in Myth, Religion, and Science.* Berkeley, CA: University of California Press, 1994.

Totelin, Laurence M. V. *Hippocratic Recipes: Oral and Written Transmissions of Pharmacological Knowledge in Fifth- and Fourth-century Greece*. Leiden, Netherlands: Brill Academic Publishers, 2009.

Touraine, Alain. *Critique of Modernity*. Oxford, UK: Basil Blackwell, 1995.

Toussaint-Samat, Maguelonne. *History of Food*. Translated by Anthea Bell. Boston: Wiley-Blackwell, 1994.

Tracy, Sarah W. and Caroline Jean Acker. *Altering American Consciousness: The History of Alcohol and Drug Use in the United States, 1800–2000*. Amherst, MA: University of Massachusetts Press, 2004.

Truan, Franklin. "Addiction as a Social Construction: A Post-Empirical View." *Journal of Psychology* 127, no. 5 (1993): 489–500.

Turner, Byran S. "The Government of the Body: Medical Regimen and the Rationalization of Diet." *The British Journal of Sociology* 33, no. 2 (1983): 254–69.

Unwin, Tim. *Wine and the Vine*. New York: Routledge, 1996.

Ustinova, Yulia. *Caves and the Ancient Greek Mind: Descending Underground in the Search for Ultimate Truth*. New York: Oxford University Pres, 2009.

Vandenberg, Phillip. *The Mystery of the Oracles*. New York: Macmillan Publishing, 1982.

Vaughan, Agnes Carr. *Madness in Greek Thought and Custom*. Baltimore, MD: E. J. Furst Company, 1919.

Vellacott, Philip., trans. *The Bacchae and Other Plays*. New York: Penguin Books, 1973.

Vernant, Jean-Pierre. *Myth and Thought Among the Greeks*. London: Routledge and Kegan Paul, 1983.

———. *Myth and Society in Ancient Greece*. Translated by Janet Lloyd. New York: Zone Books, 1988.

———, ed. *The Greeks*. Translated by Charles Lambert and Teresa Lavender Fagen. Chicago: University of Chicago Press, 1995.

Versnel, H. S. "Beyond Cursing: The Appeal of Justice in Judicial Prayers." Pp. 60–106 in *Magika Hiera—Ancient Greek Magic and Religion*, edited by Christopher A. Faraone and Dirk Obbink. New York: Oxford University Press, 1991.

Vetter, Lisa Pace. *"Women's Work" as Political Art: Weaving and Dialectical Politics in Homer, Aristophanes, and Plato*. Lanham, MD: Lexington Books, 2005.

Vidal-Nanquet, Pierre. "Plato's Myth of the Statesman, the Ambiguities of the Golden Age and of History." *Journal of Hellenic Studies* 98 (1978): 132–41.

———. *The Black Hunter—Forms of Thought in the Ancient Greek World*. Baltimore, MD: The Johns Hopkins University Press, 1986.

Voegelin, Eric. *The Collected Works of Eric Voegelin. Order and History, Volume II: The World of the Polis*. Edited by and with an Introduction by Athanasios Moulakis. Columbia, MO: The University of Missouri Press, 2000.

Von Blanckenhagen, Peter H. "Stage and Actors in Plato's *Symposium*." *Greek, Roman, and Byzantine Studies* 33, no. 1 (1992): 51–68.

Walker, Jeffrey. "*Pathos* and *Katharsis* in 'Aristotelian' Rhetoric: Some Implications." Pp. 74–92 in *Rereading Aristotle's Rhetoric*, edited by Alan G. Gross and Arthur E. Walzer. Carbondale, IL: Southern Illinois University Press, 2000.

Wallace, Robert W. "Charmides, Agariste, and Damon: Andokides 1.16." *Classical Quarterly* 42, no. 2 (1992): 328–35.

Wallach, John R. *The Platonic Political Art: A Study in Critical Reason and Democracy*. University Park, PA: Pennsylvania State University Press, 2001.

Walsh, David. *Distorted Ideals in Greek Vase-Painting: The World of Mythological Burlesque*. New York: Cambridge University Press, 2009.

Walters, Glenn D. *The Addiction Concept: Working Hypothesis or Self-Fulfilling Prophecy?* Needham Heights, MA: Allyn & Bacon, 1999.

Wardy, Robert. *The Birth of Rhetoric: Gorgias, Plato, and Their Successors.* New York: Routledge, 1996.

Warman, M. S. "Plato and Persuasion." *Greece and Rome* 31, no. 1 (1983): 48–54.

Warner, Jessica. "Before there was 'Alcoholism': Lessons from the Medieval Experience with Alcohol." *Contemporary Drug Problems* 19, no. 3 (1992): 409–29.

Warner, Rex, trans. *Thucydides—History of the Peloponnesian War.* New York: Penguin Books, 1972.

Wasson, R. Gordon. "The Divine Mushroom: Primitive Religion and Hallucinatory Agents." *Proceedings of the American Philosophical Society* 103, no. 3 (1958): 221–23.

———. *Soma: Divine Mushroom of Immortality.* New York: Harcourt, Brace and Jovanovich, 1971.

———. "Fly Agaric and Man." Pp. 405–14 in *Ethnopharmacologic Search for Psychoactive Drugs,* edited by Daniel E. Efron, B. Holmstedt, and N. S. Kline. New York: Raven Press, 1979.

———. *The Wondrous Mushroom: Mycolatry in Mesoamerica.* New York: McGraw-Hill, 1980.

———, ed. *Persephone's Quest: Entheogens and the Origins of Religion.* New Haven, CT: Yale University Press, 1986.

Wasson, R. Gordon, Albert Hofmann and Carl A. P. Ruck. *The Road to Eleusis: Unveiling the Secrets of the Mysteries.* Twentieth Anniversary Edition. Los Angeles: William Dailey Rare Books, 1998.

Waterfield, Robin A., trans. *Plato—Philebus.* New York: Penguin Books, 1988.

———, trans. *Plato—Republic.* New York: Oxford University Press, 1993.

———, trans. *Plato—Symposium.* New York: Oxford University Press, 1994.

Waterhouse, Andrew L. and V. Felipe Laurie. "Oxidation of Wine Phenolics: A Critical Evaluation and Hypothesis." *American Journal of Enology and Viticulture* 57, no. 3 (2006): 306–313.

Webster, T. B. L. *Athenian Culture and Society.* Berkeley, CA: University of California Press, 1973.

Webster, Peter. "Mixing the Kykeon." *Eleusis: Journal of Psychoactive Plants and Compounds* 4 (2000): 1–8.

Weil, Andrew. *The Natural Mind: A New Way of Looking at Drugs and the Higher Consciousness.* Boston: Houghton Mifflin, 1972.

Wender, Dorthea, trans. *Hesiod: Theogny, Works and Days. Theognis: Elegies.* New York: Penguin Books, 1973.

Werner, Paul. *Life in Greece in Ancient Times.* Barcelona, Spain: Liber, 1986.

West, M. L. *Hesiod—Theogny and Works and Days.* New York: Oxford University Press, 1988.

West, Thomas G., trans. *Plato's Apology of Socrates.* Ithaca, NY: Cornell University Press, 1979.

White, F. C. "Love and Beauty in Plato's *Symposium.*" *Journal of Hellenic Studies* 109 (1989): 148–57.

White, William L. "Addiction as a Disease: Birth of a Concept." *Counselor* 1, no. 1 (2000): 46–51, 73.

———. "The Lessons of Language: Historical Perspectives on the Rhetoric of Addiction." Pp. 33–60 in *Altering American Consciousness: The History of Alcohol and Drug*

Use in the United States 1800–2000, edited by Sarah W. Tracy and Caroline Jean Acker. Amherst, MA: University of Massachusetts Press, 2004.

Wildenradt, H. L. and V. L. Singleton. "The Production of Aldehydes as a Result of Oxidation of Polyphenolic Compounds and its Relation to Wine Aging." *American Journal of Enology and Viticulture* 25, no. 2 (1974): 119–26.

Wili, Walter. "The Orphic Mysteries and the Greek Spirit." Pp. 64–92 in *The Mysteries—Papers from the Eranos Yearbook*, edited by Joseph Campbell. Princeton, NJ: Princeton University Press, 1955.

Wilkins, John. *The Boastful Chef—The Discourse of Food in Ancient Comedy*. New York: Oxford University Press, 2000.

Willis, Deborah. "Doctor Faustus and the Early Modern Language of Addiction." Pp. 135–148 in *Placing the Plays of Christopher Marlowe: Fresh Cultural Contexts*, edited by Sara Munson Deats and Robert A. Logan. Burlington, VT: Ashgate Publishing, 2008.

Wilson, Hanneke. *Wine and Words in Classical Antiquity and the Middle Ages*. London: Duckworth Publishing, 2003.

Winkler, John J. *The Constraints of Desire: The Anthropology of Sex and Gender in Ancient Greece*. New York: Routledge, 1990.

———. "The Constraints of Eros." Pp. 3–32 in *Magika Hiera—Ancient Greek Magic and Religion*, edited by Christopher A. Faraone and Dirk Obbink. New York: Oxford University Press, 1991.

Winkler, John J. and Froma I. Zeitlin, eds. *Nothing to Do with Dionysus?* Princeton, NJ: Princeton University Press, 1990.

Winnington-Ingram, R. P. *Euripides and Dionysus—An Interpretation of the* Bacchae. Amsterdam: Adolf M. Hakkert, 1969.

Wohlberg, Joseph. "Haoma-Soma in the World of Ancient Greece." *Journal of Psychoactive Drugs* 22, no. 3 (1990): 333–42.

Wood, Ellen and Neal Wood. "Socrates and Democracy—A Reply to George Vlastos." *Political Theory* 14, no. 1 (1986): 55–82.

Woodruff, Paul. "What Could Go Wrong with Inspiration? Why Plato's Poets Fail." Pp. 137–50 in *Plato on Beauty, Wisdom, and the Arts*, edited by Julius Moravcsik and Philip Temko. Totowa, NJ: Rowman and Allanheld, 1982.

Worthington, Ian, ed. *Persuasion: Greek Rhetoric in Action*. New York: Routledge, 1994.

Young, Charles M. "Plato and Computer Dating." *Oxford Studies in Ancient Philosophy* 12 (1994): 227–50.

Zafiropulo, Jean. *Mead and Wine—A History of the Bronze Age in Greece*. London: Sidgwick and Jackson, 1966.

Zeese, Kevin. "Nixon Tapes Show Roots of Marijuana Prohibition: Misinformation, Culture Wars, and Prejudice." Published by *Common Sense for Drug Policy*, 2002. http://www.csdp.org/research/shafernixon.pdf (accessed December 31, 2009).

Zeitlin, Froma I. "Cultic Models of the Female: Rites of Dionysus and Demeter." *Arethusa* 15, nos. 1 & 2 (1982): 129–57.

———. "Figuring Fidelity in Homer's *Odyssey*." Pp. 117–52 in *The Distaff Side: Representing the Female in Homer's Odyssey*, edited by Beth Cohen. New York: Oxford University Press, 1995.

Zias, Joe, Harkley Stark, Jon Seligman, Rina Levy, Ella Werker, and Raphael Mechoulam. "Early Medical Use of Cannabis." *Nature* 363, no. 6426 (1993): 215.

Zielinski, Tadeusz. *The Religion of Ancient Greece: An Outline*. Freeport, NY: Libraries Press, 1970.

Zuckert, Catherine. "Nietzsche's Rereading of Plato." *Political Theory* 13, no. 2 (1985): 213–38.

———. *Postmodern Platos—Nietzsche, Heidegger, Gadamer, Strauss, Derrida.* Chicago: University of Chicago Press, 1996.

Citation Index

Subject Index

About the Author

Michael A. Rinella received his Ph.D. in political science in 1997. His prior work on Plato has been published in the journal *Polis*. After receiving his degree he became an acquiring editor at the State University of New York Press, where he has successfully edited over three hundred works in the humanities and social sciences, more than a dozen of which have won recognitions and awards for excellence. His efforts have been acknowledged in over one hundred published scholarly works. He also teaches political theory and philosophy, is a freelance writer, and designs titles for the conflict simulation gaming industry.